THE JOURNAL OF INDUSTRIAL ECONOMICS

Volume XXVII SEPTEMBER 1978 No. 1

IAN W. McLEAN and DAVID K. ROUND
Research and Product Innovation in Australian Manufacturing Industries.

PETER STEER and JOHN CABLE
Internal Organization and Profit: An Empirical Analysis of Large U.K. Companies.

JOHN NIGHTINGALE
On the Definition of 'Industry' and 'Market'.

PATRICIO MELLER
The Pattern of Industrial Concentration in Latin America.

MICHAEL W. PUSTAY
Industry Inefficiency under Regulatory Surveillance.

RALPH W. PFOUTS
Profit Maximization in Chain Retail Stores.

BARBARA G. KATZ
Territorial Exclusivity in the Soft Drink Industry.

ISSN 0022–1821

BASIL BLACKWELL OXFORD ENGLAND

Price: Single Issues: £3.50 (U.K.), £4.20 (Overseas), $9.50 (U.S.A. and Canada)
Annual Subscription for Institutions: £11.00 (U.K.), £13.20 (Overseas), $30.00 (U.S.A. and Canada)
Annual Subscription for Individuals: £9.00 (U.K.), £10.80 (Overseas), $24.00 (U.S.A. and Canada

THE JOURNAL OF INDUSTRIAL ECONOMICS
Volume XXVII September 1978 No. 1

RESEARCH AND PRODUCT INNOVATION IN AUSTRALIAN MANUFACTURING INDUSTRIES

IAN W. MCLEAN and DAVID K. ROUND*

> ... the economic analysis of inventive activity is seriously handicapped by our present inability to specify the production function for inventive activity with any pretence of precision (Nathan Rosenberg [6, p. 95]).

EMPIRICAL studies of research and development (R & D) activity in manufacturing typically proceed on the assumption (often implicit) that measures of R & D *inputs* are satisfactory proxies for the *output* which results from industrial research. For example, most investigations of the relationship between a firm's innovativeness and either its size or market power employ expenditure on R & D, or R & D employment as surrogates for innovativeness, despite the obvious point that they are measures of resources devoted to R & D activity in the firm and not of the results of that activity.[1] The explanation for this common procedure is straightforward. R & D inputs are easy to measure, and statistics of R & D employment, R & D professional employment and R & D expenditure are now widely collected. By contrast, the very concept of R & D output is both complex and elusive, and hence measurement poses many difficulties.

The few existing studies of the relationship between R & D inputs and R & D output have used either patent statistics or the sales of new products as measures of R & D output. In a study of American patent data and R & D inputs across several industries in the early 1960s, Mueller concluded that 'there appears to be a significant relationship between what goes into the inventive process and what comes out of it' [4, p. 36]. Several studies of technological change have been made of the U.S. pharmaceutical industry for which there exist data on the proportion of sales attributable to new products. Comanor [1] and Vernon and Gusen [7] employ these data in inquiries oriented more to an examination of the R & D : firm size relationship than to an explicit consideration of some aspect of the underlying research production function. Comanor and Scherer [2], however, compute the direct correlation coefficients between alternative measures of research activity in the U.S. pharmaceutical industry, including patent and new product sales as well as R & D inputs. Together, these studies have led to the

* The data on which this study is based were generously made available by the Australian Department of Productivity, Canberra. We are greatly indebted to Terrie Baker and Graeme Lawrie for research assistance, and to Kevin Davis, Richard Nelson, Phil Pardey, Tom Parry and Clem Tisdell for helpful comments on an earlier draft.

[1] A recent survey of this literature is provided by Kamien and Schwartz [3].

impression that 'reliance on [R & D] "input rather than [R & D]" output figures should provide no great cause for concern' (Rosenberg [5, p. 103]).

This paper reports an inquiry into the relation between R & D inputs (conventionally defined and measured) and a partial measure of R & D output for a large sample of firms covering all industries within the Australian manufacturing sector. Specifically, two measures of *product innovation* were constructed, and the nature of their relation to R & D inputs was examined using both correlation analysis and by estimating one dimension of the underlying research production function. Our principal conclusion is that there may be no sound basis for the widely accepted view that R & D input data provide suitable proxies for R & D output.

I. MEASURING PRODUCT INNOVATIVENESS

The data used in this inquiry were drawn from a Government survey of R & D in the Australian manufacturing sector in 1971–72. The survey is believed to cover most enterprises then undertaking R & D. Elimination of the respondents who had not answered all the key questions required for the present study left a basic sample of 980 firms. The total employment by these firms accounted for 33·2% of manufacturing employment in Australia in that year. This survey included questions not only about R & D inputs but also about innovativeness, making possible a direct examination of the relationship between the two at the firm level. There was, however, one serious omission in the survey. Whereas the data collected on R & D inputs covered the usual categories of employment and expenditure, the information sought concerning the *results* of the firm's R & D activity related solely to *product* innovation, with no information having been requested about changes in production methods.

Difficulties were encountered in interpreting the data on product innovation. Firms were asked to classify their annual output according to the following: (1) products completely new to the firm that year; (2) radical redesigns first produced in that year; (3) slight modifications or restylings first produced in that year; (4) products unchanged in that year; and (5) products discontinued in that year. Although categories (4) and (5) are given fairly unambiguous descriptions, the *degree* of product change implied by the first three categories must be somewhat arbitrary. Furthermore, firms were asked to allocate output on the basis of whether products were new, modified, etc., *to that firm.* A lagged adoptor (or imitator) of a new product or modification to a product developed elsewhere cannot be distinguished in the survey data from the 'true' innovator whose change in product composition results from his own research and development efforts.[2]

Bearing in mind these qualifications, the reported composition of output

[2] It should be noted that the measure of R & D inputs excludes any direct contribution by foreign affiliates of Australian firms.

TABLE I

COMPOSITION OF OUTPUT BY INDUSTRY

Industry	Percentage of total output: New products (1)	Radical redesigns (2)	Slight modification (3)	Unchanged (4)	Discontinued (5)	Index (1) + 0·75 (2) + 0·25 (3) (6)
1. Food, beverages and tobacco	4·71	1·80	6·32	86·30	0·87	7·68
2. Textiles	7·24	6·00	21·62	62·62	2·52	17·15
3. Clothing	14·70	8·70	21·63	46·48	8·48	26·64
4. Wood and wood products	14·65	7·26	11·33	63·47	3·29	22·93
5. Paper products and publishing	8·83	3·88	15·83	69·92	1·54	15·70
6. Chemicals and related products	7·60	4·28	10·82	75·62	1·68	13·52
7. Glass, cement, etc.	5·90	4·03	7·00	82·38	0·69	10·67
8. Basic metal products	7·70	6·30	9·46	75·00	1·54	14·80
9. Fabricated metal products	6·35	6·23	11·07	73·95	2·41	13·79
10. Transport equipment	11·24	14·15	19·92	52·09	2·60	26·86
11. Industrial machinery and domestic appliances	12·39	10·78	16·57	57·89	2·38	24·62
12. Leather, rubber and plastic products	7·07	6·05	13·10	71·50	2·29	14·89
13. Other manufacturing	7·11	6·03	14·57	69·67	2·73	15·28
Total	9·24	7·25	13·32	67·87	2·27	18·01

Figures in columns 1 to 5 may not sum to 100·00 due to rounding.

of firms in each of the 13 industry groups is shown in columns (1) to (5) of Table I.[3] The evidence for the industry groups indicates considerable variation. The food industry appears least innovative with the highest proportion of output constituting products unchanged from the previous year (86%). At the other extreme, the clothing industry registers the lowest proportion of unchanged products (46%), and the highest proportions of new, radically redesigned, slightly modified, and discontinued products.[4] Of the other industries, transport equipment, industrial machinery, textiles and wood tend

[3] The description of industries given in the text is necessarily abbreviated. A fuller description of each is as follows:
(1) food, beverages and tobacco;
(2) textiles;
(3) clothing and footwear;
(4) wood, wood products and furniture;
(5) paper and paper products, printing and publishing;
(6) chemical, petroleum and coal products, including pharmaceuticals;
(7) glass, clay, and other non-metallic mineral products;
(8) basic metal products;
(9) fabricated metal products, excluding machinery and equipment;
(10) transport equipment;
(11) other industrial machinery and household appliances;
(12) leather, rubber and plastic products;
(13) other manufacturing industries.

[4] This result was not altogether unexpected, given the fact that innovation in this industry tends to consist largely of style changes. In addition, it might be expected that this industry would exhibit relatively much shorter lags between R & D inputs and output.

to be relatively innovative, while the remaining industries tend to have relatively more unchanged products in their output mix.

It should be emphasized, however, that of the four industry groups which appear to be most innovative, that is where designated new products and radical redesigns together constitute over 20% of industry output, three (clothing; wood and wood products; and, perhaps to a lesser extent, industrial machinery and domestic appliances) are industries which tend to display a high incidence of frequent, small design changes. Thus what may be regarded as significant changes in product by managers in these industries would probably not often be classified as such by a dispassionate, independent observer. That is, what constitutes R & D output in these industries involves a much more subjective judgement than in other industries like chemicals and basic metal products. In addition, industries like clothing and wood tend to be slow growth industries, and firms in them are therefore more likely to try to stimulate sales by changes which they regard as important, but which may be judged as trivial by an objective reviewer of the industry.

In devising a measure of product innovativeness based on our evidence, two approaches were possible. One was to accept the proportion of sales comprising totally new products as the best indicator of product innovation. This procedure would approximate that adopted by Comanor and Scherer [2]. The alternative approach was to give explicit recognition to the likely importance of innovations that resulted in product improvement which stopped short of constituting a completely new product. In this broader index of product innovativeness, a declining set of weights was assigned to the new, radically redesigned, and slightly modified products. After some experimentation with various and necessarily arbitrary weights, the radical redesigns and slight modifications were weighted as 75 and 25% respectively of completely new products. The resulting index is shown by industry averages in column (6) of Table I.

II. CORRELATION BETWEEN R & D INPUT AND OUTPUT MEASURES

The first step in our examination of the relation between R & D inputs and product innovation is to compute the correlation coefficients between the two, in order to establish whether any one of the various measures of either R & D inputs or R & D output provides a satisfactory surrogate for any other measure. This was the aim of the Comanor and Scherer [2] study of the relation between new product sales, patents, R & D employees, and professional R & D employees in the United States pharmaceutical industry between 1955 and 1960. They measured both simple and partial correlation coefficients, where the latter were arrived at after holding constant the effect of variations in firm size. Although principally interested in the use of patent data as a proxy for the other measures, they reported four partial correlation coefficients between two measures of new products and professional and total

R & D personnel. Over their sample of 57 firms, these ranged from 0·335 to 0·510, and all were highly significant (Comanor and Scherer [2, p. 396]).

We have introduced, in the previous section, two measures of product innovation: P_1 will be used to denote the proportion of total sales which comprises completely new products; and P_2 denotes the weighted proportion of total sales which consists of new, radically redesigned and slightly modified products. Our three measures of R & D inputs are those commonly used in empirical studies of research activity in industry: the ratio of the firm's expenditure on R & D to its total sales (denoted by R_e); the proportion of the firm's workforce which consists of R & D employees (R_n); and the proportion of the firm's workforce which consists of *professional* R & D employees (R_p). The partial correlation coefficients[5] between the alternative measures of P and R for the total sample of 712 firms (for which all relevant data were available) and for each of the 13 industry groups, are shown in Table II.

TABLE II

PARTIAL CORRELATION COEFFICIENTS: PRODUCT INNOVATIVENESS (P) AND R & D INPUT INTENSITY (R)

Industry group (number of firms)	P_1 *with*			P_2 *with*		
	R_e	R_n	R_p	R_e	R_n	R_p
1. Food, beverages and tobacco (73)	−0·0374	−0·0798	−0·0786	0·0392	−0·0793	−0·0862
2. Textiles (16)	0·1687	0·8787[a]	0·9197[a]	0·0773	0·7521[a]	0·7676[a]
3. Clothing (11)	−0·0977	−0·2436	−0·2635	−0·1287	−0·0994	−0·1779
4. Wood and wood products (31)	−0·0251	0·0698	−0·0104	0·0797	0·2079	0·1210
5. Paper products and publishing (15)	0·7700[a]	0·5284[b]	0·4544[c]	0·7751	0·5307[b]	0·4440[c]
6. Chemicals and related products (125)	0·2284[a]	0·2077[b]	0·2479[a]	0·2973[a]	0·2883[a]	0·2630[a]
7. Glass, cement, etc. (27)	0·3139[c]	0·3653[b]	0·3133[c]	0·2640[c]	0·2463	0·2303
8. Basic metal products (33)	0·1080	0·0465	−0·0520	0·3233[b]	0·2543[c]	0·1269
9. Fabricated metal products (84)	0·3181[a]	0·3545[a]	0·4230[a]	0·2145[b]	0·2658[a]	0·2865[a]
10. Transport equipment (30)	0·7308[a]	0·7329[a]	0·6503[a]	0·5879[a]	0·5698[a]	0·5236[a]
11. Industrial machinery and domestic appliances (223)	0·0500	0·4256[a]	0·3317[a]	0·0674	0·3845[a]	0·3221[a]
12. Leather, rubber and plastic products (27)	0·0094	0·2288	0·0836	0·3157[c]	0·7050[a]	0·1501
13. Other manufacturing (17)	0·8612[a]	0·7141[a]	0·1237	0·9509[a]	0·7500[a]	0·0727
Total (712)	0·2117[a]	0·3568[a]	0·2805[a]	0·1713[a]	0·3680[a]	0·2670[a]

Note: Symbols used in the column headings are explained in the text. [a] = significant at 1%; [b] = significant at 5%; [c] = significant at 10%, using a one-tail test.

[5] There was little difference between the partial and the simple correlation coefficients. The explanation is that both P and R are ratios in which the denominator is a measure of the size of the firm's activities; hence size was already largely accounted for in the definition of the variables (cf. Comanor and Scherer [2, p. 396] where the variables were not so defined, and hence major differences between the simple and partial correlation coefficients were reported).

For the sample as a whole (last row of Table II) the correlation coefficients are all positive and highly significant, although it is evident that the various measures of P and R are by no means perfect surrogates. It is also evident that, regardless of whether P_1 or P_2 is used as a measure of product innovativeness, R_n is the best proxy, R_p the next best, and R_e the least satisfactory. An explanation of this ordering may be that R & D employment varies less from year to year than R & D expenditure, and hence the relationship between P and R *in any one year* will be closer where R_n or R_p is used than where R_e is used. However, the pooling of observations across all industries is not entirely appropriate, as no common basis exists for classifying types of innovation across industries. More confidence can be placed in coefficients obtained within individual industries.[6]

A more complicated pattern emerges from an inspection of the industry-level correlation coefficients. In 14 out of 78 cases these coefficients were negative, although in no case were these negative coefficients significant. In addition, all but one of these negative values were concentrated in three industries—food, clothing, and wood. Of the remaining industry groups, seven fairly consistently showed positive and significant results, while the remaining three (leather, basic metals and glass) produced less significant results. Despite the broadness of the industry classification, and thus heterogeneity of product lines within each industry, what might loosely be described as the 'producer goods' industries show the closest links between R & D inputs and product innovativeness. The basic metals industry is an exception, which possibly may be explained in terms of R & D activity in this industry being concentrated in process innovation with relatively little scope for product innovation. However, despite the generally satisfactory results in terms of signs and significance of the correlation coefficients, it is obvious that the coefficients are relatively low. Of the 64 positive coefficients, only 13 are over 0·7, and only 19 are higher than 0·5. Nine of the coefficients higher than 0·5 involve R_n. Thus, it must be emphasized that extreme care must be taken before assuming that any of the R & D input measures are satisfactory proxies for R & D output as defined here.

The fact that the R & D employment variables generally are more closely linked with our R & D output indices than is the R & D expenditure variable suggests that 'purchased' R & D may be an important input into the innovation process. Since research workers normally are required to put technology transfers into effect, as well as to perform indigenous R & D, the employment series probably more successfully captures overall expenditures on innovation-generating activities than does the R & D expenditure series. Broadly speaking, it made little difference to the sign or significance of the correlation coefficients whether product innovativeness was measured by completely new products only (P_1) or whether the wider definition (P_2) was

[6] It was not possible to divide the data into more narrowly defined industries, due to the need to preserve confidentiality of the data.

employed. However, there were enough exceptions to caution against the uncritical acceptance of either index of product innovativeness as a completely satisfactory surrogate for the other in all industries. Thus we have confirmed the finding of Comanor and Scherer [2] that a positive and significant correlation can be found between alternative proxy measures of research activity, although in our much larger sample there was considerable interindustry variation which was not revealed by their study of a single industry.

III. THE NATURE OF THE RELATIONSHIP BETWEEN R & D INPUTS AND OUTPUT

It seems unsatisfactory simply to treat R & D employment, R & D expenditure, and product innovativeness as strict alternatives. Unambiguously, R_e, R_p and R_n are *inputs* into research whereas P_1 and P_2 are clearly indices of research *output*. Explicitly recognizing that research and development is an economic activity which transforms inputs into output not only emphasizes the existence of *causal* relations between the alternative measures which previously have been ignored, but also highlights the importance of estimating formally the underlying R & D input–output relationship. Data constraints made possible the examination of only one dimension of this relationship.[7] Before this is attempted two qualifications must be noted regarding the restrictions which the available data have imposed on this part of the inquiry.

In the first place, any study of the relation between R & D inputs and output at the individual firm level ideally should employ time series rather than the cross-section data which were available for this study. In using research output and input data from the same year we are assuming that the set of rules governing the allocation of resources to R & D activity within the firm over the years immediately prior to 1971–72 has not been modified at all substantially so that the 'input' and 'output' data for 1971–72 relate to each other within some consistent dynamic framework. These conditions, or something analogous, are most unlikely to hold in any particular year in all firms in all manufacturing industries. As with attempts to estimate more conventional production functions using cross-section analysis, however, this does not seem a sufficient reason to abandon all efforts to discover the existence and identify the nature of any relationship between R & D inputs and output.

Second, R & D activity may lead to technical change which either takes

[7] It is tempting to call this relationship a research production function. However, the dependent variable, measuring research output, is an index which does not take into account changes in the production techniques. A properly specified research production function should also include as explanatory variables, other specific determinants of innovation such as purchased R & D embodied in new capital equipment or in licences purchased from other firms, the human capital intensities of firms, and especially in the case of Australia, the extent of foreign ownership of the firm. Other factors will also affect a firm's R & D performance, such as growth in demand, the extent of competition, and entry barriers.

the form of product innovations or changes in the methods employed to produce new or existing products. It is difficult to guess the relative importance of these two within total research 'output' so that where product innovations only are measurable and considered as the outcome of R & D activity, an uncertain bias (particularly in interindustry comparisons) may arise.

Choosing the appropriate functional form in attempting to estimate the relationship between R & D inputs and output raises the difficulty noted by Rosenberg [6] in the passage quoted at the beginning of this paper. Economists' understanding of the nature of the technology under which an innovation, research or knowledge is produced is extremely limited in comparison with their understanding of the technical conditions of production of most goods and services for final use. Our initial decision was to test, with ordinary least squares regression, the hypothesis suggested both in the previously cited literature and also in a sense by the results of the partial correlation tests, namely, that a strictly linear relation exists between R & D inputs and innovativeness. Our model may be expressed as

$$P_i = \beta_0 + \beta_1 R_j \qquad i = 1, 2 \qquad j = e, n, p \tag{1}$$

where P is the proportion of total sales comprising innovations and R is the ratio of R & D inputs to the total activity of the firm. We hypothesize that $\beta_1 > 0$ for all firms engaged in R & D.

As there are two alternative measures of P and three measures of R, six relationships were estimated for the total sample and for each of our 13 industries. In all six regressions involving the total sample, and in 47 of the 78 industry-level regressions, the estimated regression coefficient was positive and significant at least at the 10% level, using a one-tail test. As can be seen from the first two rows of Table III, somewhat greater success was achieved when P_2 rather than P_1 was the dependent variable, and when R_n rather than R_e or R_p was used as the independent variable.[8] Generally, the results

TABLE III

NUMBER OF INDUSTRY-LEVEL REGRESSION RESULTS CONSISTENT WITH HYPOTHESIS (maximum possible in any cell = 13)

Equation	*Dependent variable*	*Independent variable* R_n	R_e	R_p
(1)	P_1	8	6	7
	P_2	11	8	7
(2)	P_1	4	5	2
	P_2	3	6	2

[8] These results now refer to the significance of the simple correlation coefficients rather than the partial coefficients referred to in Table II.

which did not support our hypothesis were not evenly spread across industries, but rather were concentrated in the food, clothing and wood industries. Little significant R & D could be expected in these industries, and what constitutes R & D output would probably involve a much more subjective assessment than in the other industries where R & D is more substantive and objectively verifiable. That is, poor quality data could be the reason for the poor estimates.

However, the unexpected results for some industries may result from the simple linear model improperly specifying the relationship between R & D inputs and output. In order to investigate this possibility, we formulate a model which tests explicitly for the existence of a quadratic relationship between product innovativeness and R & D input intensity. An additional assumption of declining marginal productivity in R & D activity seemed justifiable on theoretical grounds, so that equation (1) was reformulated as

$$P_i = \beta_0 + \beta_1 R_j + \beta_2 R_j^2 \tag{2}$$

and it is expected that $\beta_1 > 0$ and that $\beta_2 < 0$.

For the total sample, the expected signs for β_1 and β_2 were once again found on all six versions of equation (2), and the estimated coefficients were all significant at least at the 10% level. It was noticeable, however, that the values of $\bar{R}^2$ improved very little over those obtained in the linear model, suggesting that the respecification of the functional form could not be regarded as an improvement on purely statistical grounds. None the less, the hypothesis that the 'true' relationship is of the form suggested by equation (2) cannot be rejected on this evidence for the sample as a whole.

At first sight the industry-level regressions employing equation (2) appear to have performed less well than those based on equation (1): as indicated by the bottom two rows of Table III, only 22 of the 78 regressions yielded the expected signs on the estimated regression coefficients at our nominated level of significance. The most important finding, however, was that 12 of these 22 'satisfactory' regression results were for industries and combinations of P_i and R_j that had *not* yielded the expected sign at the minimum 10% level of significance when the linear model was employed. These 12 cases, which are shown in Table IV, were not concentrated in any particular combination of P_i and R_j and they occurred in seven different industry groups—two in each of the clothing, wood, basic metals, leather and other manufacturing industries, and one in both the industrial machinery and paper industries. Clearly, in some circumstances, a non-linear rather than the widely assumed linear relationship appears to exist between inputs into and the output resulting from R & D activity in manufacturing enterprises. However, it must be noted that neither the linear nor the quadratic forms generally explain a large proportion of the total intraindustry variation in R & D output. This suggests either that further investigation into the relevant functional form is necessary; or that our measure of R & D output may not

Table IV

REGRESSION OF PRODUCT INNOVATIVENESS (P) ON R & D INPUT INTENSITY (R): SELECTED INDUSTRY-LEVEL RESULTS

Industry	Dep. var.	Ind. var.	Equation (1) $\hat{\beta}_0$	Equation (1) $\hat{\beta}_1$	Equation (1) $\bar{R}^2$	Equation (2) $\hat{\beta}_0$	Equation (2) $\hat{\beta}_1$	Equation (2) $\hat{\beta}_2$	Equation (2) $\bar{R}^2$	No. of firms
Clothing	P_1	R_e	11·405	198·057 (1·10)	0·01	5·388	1064·710 $(2·32)^b$	−8930·451 $(2·03)^b$	0·12	27
Clothing	P_2	R_e	24·462	130·712 (0·71)	−0·02	18·405	1003·111 $(2·12)^b$	−8989·564 $(-1·99)^b$	0·09	27
Wood	P_1	R_n	13·994	9·309 (0·42)	−0·02	6·914	172·954 $(2·46)^a$	−176·037 $(-2·44)^a$	0·08	51
Wood	P_2	R_n	21·816	15·749 (0·63)	−0·01	9·947	290·080 $(4·03)^a$	−295·105 $(-4·00)^a$	0·23	51
Paper	P_2	R_n	12·301	97·111 (0·93)	−0·01	3·443	633·218 $(2·20)^b$	−3079·294 $(-1·98)^b$	0·11	24
Basic metals	P_1	R_e	6·764	52·322 (0·46)	−0·02	1·635	721·454 $(1·83)^b$	−8153·627 $(-1·76)^b$	0·03	44
Basic metals	P_1	R_n	7·720	−0·345 (−0·01)	−0·02	3·036	263·389 $(1·35)^c$	−1632·296 $(-1·41)^c$	−0·00	44
Industrial machinery	P_1	R_e	12·248	1·422 (0·99)	0·00	8·755	66·441 $(9·49)^a$	−5·165 $(-9·45)^a$	0·23	302
Leather	P_1	R_p	6·326	13·559 (0·51)	−0·03	2·202	264·903 $(3·13)^a$	−1051·119 $(-3·09)^a$	0·23	27
Leather	P_2	R_p	14·025	38·881 (0·83)	−0·01	6·602	491·344 $(3·28)^a$	−1892·202 $(-3·14)^a$	0·25	27
Other manufacturing	P_1	R_p	5·936	14·322 (0·69)	−0·03	1·677	182·877 $(2·77)^a$	−351·164 $(-2·64)^a$	0·26	17
Other manufacturing	P_2	R_p	13·179	14·915 (0·43)	−0·05	6·538	277·726 $(2·41)^b$	−547·535 $(-2·37)^b$	0·19	17

Note: Symbols used in the column headings are explained in the text. ^{a}=significant at 1%; ^{b}=significant at 5%; and ^{c}=significant at 10%.

be entirely appropriate, as has been suggested earlier; or that R & D output depends on many factors other than R & D inputs *per se*, such as technological opportunity or the extent of foreign control in an industry.

IV. SUMMARY AND CONCLUSIONS

Empirical studies of the determinants of technological progressiveness in industry have generally used research and development input, rather than output-related measures, and have not attempted to estimate directly the nature of the relationship between the two. In this paper we have utilized a data source containing information on R & D inputs as well as output, although the form in which the information was collected was less than entirely satisfactory in two important aspects: it related to a single year; and the indices of product innovativeness derived from the survey data constituted only a partial measure of research output.

The principal findings of the present inquiry may briefly be summarized. A considerable amount of support emerged for the generally held view that the R & D input intensity of a firm is positively associated with its product innovativeness, although the extent of that association varied considerably between industries and according to the precise measure of R & D input or product innovativeness chosen. The hypothesis that the relationship between R & D inputs and output is strictly linear was supported in the majority of cases. However, the alternative hypothesis that the underlying relationship is non-linear was also supported by the evidence in a smaller number of instances. The coexistence of these competing hypotheses may be attributable to specification errors in either or both models, or to problems arising from the nature or quality of the data. Neither *a priori* nor theoretical reasoning appear to provide clear justification for choosing one model in preference to the other. However, inspection of the statistical results obtained when both functional forms were estimated indicated very clearly that for at least some industries and with certain variants of the dependent and independent variables, a non-linear form of the model yielded the expected signs on the coefficients at a satisfactory level of significance, whereas the linear model did not satisfy the same requirements.

As with many studies in this area, interindustry variation in findings was considerable, strongly suggesting that generalizations are best made at as disaggregated a level as possible. However, the present inquiry was primarily concerned with the narrower problem of the relationship between R & D inputs and output as such. There would appear to be every justification in our findings for economists to reassess the nature of the production function linking inputs into and the results of industrial R & D activity.

UNIVERSITY OF ADELAIDE

REFERENCES

[1] COMANOR, WILLIAM S., 'Research and Technical Change in the Pharmaceutical Industry', *Review of Economics and Statistics*, **47** (May 1965), pp. 182–90.

[2] COMANOR, WILLIAM S. and SCHERER, F. M., 'Patent Statistics as a Measure of Technical Change', *Journal of Political Economy*, **77** (May/June 1969), pp. 392–8.

[3] KAMIEN, MORTON J. and SCHWARTZ, NANCY L., 'Market Structure and Innovation: A Survey', *Journal of Economic Literature*, **13** (March 1975), pp. 1–37.

[4] MUELLER, DENNIS C., 'Patents, Research and Development and the Measurement of Inventive Activity', *Journal of Industrial Economics*, **15** (November 1966), pp. 26–37.

[5] ROSENBERG, JOEL B., 'Research and Market Share: A Reappraisal of the Schumpeter Hypothesis', *Journal of Industrial Economics*, **25** (December 1976), pp. 101–12.

[6] ROSENBERG, NATHAN, 'Science, Invention and Economic Progress', *Economic Journal*, **84** (March 1974), pp. 90–108.

[7] VERNON, JOHN M. and GUSEN, PETER, 'Technical Change and Firm Size: The Pharmaceutical Industry', *Review of Economics and Statistics*, **56** (August 1974), pp. 294–302.

THE JOURNAL OF INDUSTRIAL ECONOMICS
Vol. XXVII September 1978 No. 1

INTERNAL ORGANIZATION AND PROFIT: AN EMPIRICAL ANALYSIS OF LARGE U.K. COMPANIES

PETER STEER AND JOHN CABLE*

I. INTRODUCTION

PREVIOUS empirical studies of firm and industry profitability have examined many causal factors, but almost without exception these have not included organizational form: the type of internal information and control structure employed by the firm.[1] In this respect empirical work has generally run parallel with orthodox theory, in which the specification of a single-valued production function pre-empts discussion of organizational arrangements, along with all other concrete details of production technology.

In practice the internal organization of firms is very likely to affect their efficiency and hence their profitability. Moreover, the type of internal control apparatus employed and its effectiveness are quite likely to be correlated with variables such as size, growth, and degree of owner- or manager-control. Hence the neglect of this influence in previous work may not only have reduced the ability of the models to explain observed variations in profitability, but also given rise to serious specification bias in the estimated parameters.

The present paper attempts to isolate the effects of internal organization on profitability in a cross-sectional analysis of 82 large U.K. companies in the period 1967–71. Internal organization variables are employed which test for efficiency gains from multidivisional (M-form) organization as identified by Williamson [27], [28]. The classification according to type of organizational form is described in section II. A model incorporating organizational form variables is outlined in section III, and the sample, our data sources and the measurement of variables are all described in section IV. Our empirical results are reported in section V, which is followed by a brief conclusion.

II. THE CLASSIFICATION PROCEDURE

Companies listed among the top 250 in *The Times 1000* in the years 1967–71 were classified by Steer [23] according to the six-way scheme put forward by Williamson and Bhargava [29]. The categories are as follows. The Unitary

* The authors wish to thank John Hiller, Dennis Mueller, Otto Poensgen, Oliver Williamson and an anonymous referee for their helpful comments and suggestions, and Jürgen Runge for programming assistance in the final runs of the empirical analysis.

[1] For one exception see Poensgen [16].

(*U-form*) firm is the traditional, functionally organized enterprise. Holding companies (*H-form*) are divisionalized, but lack the requisite internal control apparatus of the multidivisional. Multidivisionals (*M-form*) are not only divisionalized, but exhibit a separation of operating from strategic decision making, and a characteristic control apparatus is systematically employed. This apparatus is based on internal audits and cash flow allocation among divisions. There is control of externalities arising between divisions, and central manipulation of the incentive systems affecting top divisional management. Transitional multidivisionals (*M′-form*) are enterprises in the process of adjustment. The transition to M-form is not always successful. In the corrupted multidivisional ($\bar{M}$*-form*) the M-form control apparatus is present, but central management is over-involved in operating affairs. Hence the necessary distance relation between strategic and operating decisions is absent and M-form performance is not expected. Finally, firms may be mixed (*X-form*), e.g. a combination of one functionally organized activity (perhaps the firm's original interest) and other activities run in essentially an H- or M-form manner.

Firms were classified on the basis of information of the general type illustrated in the appendix to Williamson and Bhargava. The principal sources were company annual reports and independent information contained in stockbroker analyses and the business and financial media. Reliable classifications were arrived at for a total of 120 firms, the ratio of classification successes to failures falling from 72% among the top 50 firms to 36% below the 200th rank due to a reduction in the amount of information available for 'smaller' firms.

Table I summarizes the outcome of the classification exercise. This corroborates the conclusion drawn by Channon [3] from a somewhat similar, but smaller, classification unavailable to Steer at the time of his work. The 1960s was a period of marked internal reorganization among the largest U.K. companies, with a strong trend away from H- and U-form toward M-form. Among multidivisionals there was a reduction in the incidence of the corrupted, $\bar{M}$-form. By the early 1970s the multidivisional organization was

TABLE I

DISTRIBUTION OF LARGE COMPANIES BY ORGANIZATIONAL FORM

Organizational form	1970/72 (%)	1964/66 (%)
M	35 (29·2)	21 (17·5)
M′	40 (33·3)	12 (10·0)
$\bar{M}$	7 (5·8)	17 (14·2)
H	14 (11·7)	37 (30·8)
U	9 (7·5)	14 (11·7)
X	4 (3·3)	6 (5·0)
Uncertain[a]	11 (9·2)	13 (10·8)

[a] i.e. reliable classification available for one but not both periods.

easily the preponderant type, although as Table I shows only just under 30% of the companies classified had achieved *pure* M-form. This reorganization in the U.K. appears to have lagged behind similar developments in the U.S. Thus, according to Williamson and Bhargava [29, p. 142], 1945–50 was the critical period during which the M-form innovation took on quantitative significance in the U.S., many firms adopting it as a defensive measure from 1950–60, and the conglomerate variant of the structure flourishing in the period 1960–70.

As a check on their accuracy Channon's and Steer's lists were compared. Thirty-nine firms appeared on both lists. Twenty-six had identical classifications and a further seven cases were different on account of differences in the two classification schemes.[2] Of the remaining six cases two can be explained by the availability to Steer of data that were unavailable when Channon made his classification, leaving four genuine disagreements. Whether a discrepancy rate of just over 10% is high or low is open to debate. We prefer to sidestep the question, and where discrepancies are known, use alternative specifications of the organizational form variable in our empirical analysis.

III. THE MODEL

Our basic model assumes:

$$\pi_i = f(\boldsymbol{X}_i) + g(\boldsymbol{Z}_i) + u \qquad (1)$$

where $f(\boldsymbol{X}_i)$ denotes the profit-maximizing level of profit for firm i and $\boldsymbol{Z}_i$ is a vector of variables suggested by other, managerial and behavioural theories. In principle the influence of organization form operates through $f(\boldsymbol{X}_i)$, since it is an aspect of firm-level efficiency and hence ought to be captured in the production function. However in practice organizational form effects must be incorporated through zero/one dummy variables whose allegiance to $f(\boldsymbol{X}_i)$ in the final specification is not strong.

The Dependent Variable

As Phillips [15] has recently noted, there are basically two options when specifying profitability as the dependent variable: the price–cost margin (π/R where R is the values of sales) and the rate of return, either on stockholders' equity (π/E); or on stockholders' equity plus long-term debt (RLC); or on assets (π/K). Theoretical arguments can be put for both methods. In a model which focuses on long-run industry equilibrium, with entry and exit and with existing firms expanding or contracting as a result of their investment decisions, a rate of return seems the logical choice, since it is rates of return above or below competitive levels which according to theory prompt such long-run equilibrating responses. π/E has also been favoured by some

[2] Channon does not recognize the $\overline{\text{M}}$-form (six cases) but has one additional 'grid' type for companies with both high product diversity and significant overseas size (one case).

writers on the grounds that this is what firms acting in shareholders interests would maximize (Benishay [2], Comanor and Wilson [4], Hall and Weiss [8]).

On the other hand, where short-run pricing behaviour is of prime interest and there are constant returns, a strong case can be made from orthodox theory in favour of π/R. For then $c = mc = ac$ so that

$$(2) \qquad \frac{\pi}{R} = \frac{pQ - cQ}{pQ} = \frac{p-c}{p} = L$$

where Q is physical output and L is the Lerner index of monopoly (Cowling [5]). In addition we have what Cowling refers to as Stigler [24] equilibrium:

$$(3) \qquad L = \frac{h(H)}{\eta_p}$$

where H is the Herfindhal measure of seller concentration $0 \leq H \leq 1$. Thus, in this case it is π/R which emerges as the appropriate index of profit performance.

In practice empirical models will frequently pick up both short- and long-run effects. Moreover, as Ornstein [14] has noted, the returns to capital and on sales are related by the identity:

$$(4) \qquad \frac{\pi}{E} \equiv \frac{\pi}{R} \cdot \frac{R}{E}.$$

Two implications follow from this. The first is that where, as is often the case, a capital intensity variable (such as R/E) is included in a profit-margin equation to compensate for the fact that π/R is measured gross of capital charges (Benishay [2]), the only difference in practice between a rate-of-return and profit-margin equation is that one element of the variation explained in the former moves to the right-hand side in the latter. Secondly, in view of (4) it is entirely possible that previous studies have in fact explained the variance in π/R even when π/E has actually been used.[3]

In the present study we do not attempt a definitive resolution of these issues. Results are presented with three different dependent variables, π/R, π/E and RLC. As it turns out the comparison of the rate-of-return and profit-margin equations leads to some insights which otherwise might have been missed.

[3] As the reader may confirm by re-estimating Comanor and Wilson's model, replacing the dependent variable with price-cost margins as provided by Sherman and Tollison [21] (and used by the latter as a measure of cost-fixity). Alternatively, the results of this experiment may be obtained on request from Cable. In brief, the performance of Comanor and Wilson's advertising variable is improved, but their 'capital requirements' barrier to entry loses significance. Evidently in their original, π/E equation 'capital requirements' was not explaining profit but was simply correlated with R/E, as one would expect.

Independent Variables

Among the explanatory variables our primary interest is in the organizational form dummies. On Williamson's arguments M-form firms should outperform others in a wide range of cases. The traditional, functionally organized firm may be optimal below some level of size and diversity of the activities it undertakes.[4] But above this level multidivisional firms are expected to enjoy advantages deriving from the mitigation of internal control loss; the separation of strategic decision making from day-to-day control; and the internalization of certain failures in the external capital market. However, advantages from M-form may not obtain in process-oriented industries, such as steel, where technology does not allow divisionalization of production except at great cost. M-form may also not be superior in highly unstable environments, e.g. in industries where there is very rapid introduction of new products. Thus innovations threatening the position of divisions in a firm decentralized on a product basis might be suppressed at divisional level, and a strong case for centralization at least of research and development activities may exist in such cases. We therefore employ two types of dummy structure for organizational form. One applies an optimal/non-optimal dichotomy, according to the firm's organizational form in the context of its operating environment. On this basis U-form firms, for instance, can sometimes be rated as optimal. We also employ organizational form dummies based solely on the firm's classification, enabling coefficients for individual types of organizational form to be estimated, albeit at the cost of disregarding some subtleties in what constitutes optimality.

The process of acquiring optimal organizational form will impose non-trivial transactions costs. A further dummy variable (T) is therefore included to allow a divergence from expected, M-form performance for M-form firms known to be in transition from other organisational forms. The T variable might reflect two counteracting effects. One is a Hawthorne effect: any change produces temporary improvement. The second is a dislocation effect: reorganization involves cost.

Even after full adjustment to organizational optimality, less than maximum profit will be earned by a firm in which there is scope for discretionary behaviour and management behave in a manner predicted by the managerial and behavioural theories of Baumol [1], Cyert and March [6], Marris [12], Monsen and Downs [13], Scitovsky [20], Simon [22] or Williamson [26]. We therefore include an owner-control dummy, valued one for owner-controlled and zero otherwise, along lines previously followed by Kamerschen [10] and Radice [18], together with a continuous 'managerial taste' variable measuring the degree of representation of management at board level as employed by Williamson [26].

[4] The appropriateness of U-form in firms below the critical levels of size and diversification was not thought to be a problem in the present analysis, which is focused on firms in the top 300.

Firm size and growth are also included in our model. Size is included mainly to allow for the possible effects of firm-level scale economies and diseconomies.[5] Since we expect a strong connection between organizational form and size *a priori*, size is one of the variables most likely to have been subject to specification bias in previous studies, if organizational form matters in explaining profit performance. Growth is present on two grounds. First, it serves to allow for windfall gains from unanticipated growth. Secondly, it helps correct for bias in the dependent variable when this is a rate of return, arising from a tendency for relative overstatement of assets by slow growing firms (Whittington [30]).

Interaction terms are also added in some regressions, between organizational form and size on account of the *a priori* relationship mentioned above, and between owner-control and growth because of the putative managerial preference for growth rather than profit. Since owner-control and organizational form are dichotomous variables, we have in effect introduced slope dummies, allowing the size and growth coefficients to diverge for differently organized firms and owner- vs. manager-controlled firms respectively.

The variables so far discussed exhaust our specification of $\boldsymbol{Z}_i$ and encroach somewhat on $f(\boldsymbol{X}_i)$, particularly in the case of the organizational variables and size. Further insight into $f(\boldsymbol{X}_i)$ is afforded by equation (2). However, as Cowling observes, we cannot be too specific about $h(H)$ except that we know it is conditional on buyer concentration and the probability of repeat purchasing. Moreover in the present analysis our unit of observation is the firm whereas H and η_p are market structural characteristics, and our knowledge of the market distribution of the activities of the firms in our sample is limited. For all of these reasons and because market structural factors are not the primary object of concern to us, we resort to industry dummies to wash out any remaining influences.

Our complete model is thus in linear form but omitting interaction terms:

$$\pi/R = \alpha + \beta_1 \mathrm{OF} + \beta_2 T + \beta_3 \mathrm{OC} + \beta_4 \mathrm{MT} + \beta_5 \mathrm{S} + \beta_6 \mathrm{G} + \sum_{j=7}^{j=10} \beta_j \sum_{k=2}^{k=5} D_k + \beta_{11} R/E + u \tag{5}$$

where

OF = organizational form dummy

T = organizational change dummy (1 for companies in transition to M-form, 0 otherwise)

OC = owner control dummy (1 for owner-controlled, 0 otherwise)

MT = managerial taste (proportion of executive to total directors)

S = firm size

G = firm growth

[5] In equilibrium scale economies will not determine profit variation among firms of different size, but the size distribution of firms itself. Thus only if not all firms have adjusted to optimal scale will profit variation be explained by scale effects.

$D_2 \ldots D_5$ = industry dummies
R/E = ratio of sales to stockholders' equity.

When the dependent variable is π/E, R/E is dropped, and when *RLC* the gearing variable L/E (the ratio of long-term debt to equity) is introduced to allow for the extra compensation which may be paid to shareholders for increased risk due to leverage. The industry dummy D_1 (for the brewing industry) is dropped in order to avoid singularity) problems in estimation. Thus the various dummy variable coefficients measure deviations from our basic observation, a non-optimally organized, non-transitional manager-controlled firm in the brewing industry.

The model is subject to the usual limitations of the single equation approach. On theoretical grounds and in the light of findings by Radice [18] and others we suspect a potentially serious simultaneity problem in respect of firm growth, arising from a causal flow from profitability (in part via internal financing) to growth.[6] Otherwise, however, we note that much of the concern over causality and simultaneous equation bias has surrounded market structure variables in industry level estimates (Phillips [15]), and may therefore be attenuated in the present case. Moreover, as Cowling argues, it may be reasonable to view the system of equations in which performance, behaviour and structure are embedded as recursive, with lags sufficiently long to allow us to pull out individual equations for separate treatment [5, p. 1]. In any case there has been recent confirmation that in the industrial organization area as in others, OLS and TSLS estimates can turn out to describe essentially the same picture (Strickland and Weiss [25]).

IV. THE SAMPLE, DATA SOURCES AND MEASUREMENT OF VARIABLES

The sample comprised 82 of the companies for which organizational form classifications were available, drawn from the food, brewing, electrical engineering and mechanical engineering industries and the distributive trades. The period 1967–71 was chosen for a number of reasons.

1. Coming after a number of years of extensive internal reorganization among companies, but with the diffusion of the M-form innovation incomplete, it provided a sample containing considerable variation in organizational form. It should be emphasized that catching the process in transition

[6] Consistent estimates are obtained from a single equation model as long as there is a lag in the feedback from profit to growth. Thus, in the absence of a lag,

$$\pi=\alpha+\beta G+u$$

and

$$G=\alpha'+\beta'\pi+e$$

so that

$$\pi=(\alpha+\beta\alpha')+\beta\beta'\pi+(\beta e+u)$$

But inconsistency is avoided if, as may reasonably be assumed,

$$\pi_t=\alpha+\beta G_t+u$$

and

$$G_t=\alpha'+\beta'\pi_{t-\tau}+e$$

stage is important for the present analysis. Once all firms in an industry have been reorganized along uniform lines, competition among the firms will tend to drive profits down to a common level (efficiency differences apart). And testing for profit differences between an industry with uniformly poorly organized firms and another with uniformly well-organized firms will, of course, be uninstructive.

2. Information on organization structures tends to be released with a certain lag, so that choice of a period a few years prior to that in which the analysis is carried out enables more accurate classifications to be made.

3. The 1967 Companies Act required companies to reveal information such as turnover and directors' shareholdings, which was not always available for previous years.

4. Four years of data were thought to be sufficiently long for short-run influences on profit to be neutralized in the average for the period as a whole, but sufficiently short that most firms would have a stable organizational form over most of the period.

Dependent Variables

π/E was defined as the ratio of profit after interest and depreciation to the value of ordinary and preference shares plus reserves attributable to them. *RLC* was measured as π/E with the addition of long-term loans to the denominator. π/R was the ratio of profits to turnover. All three variables were four-year averages (1967/8–1970/71) measured alternatively with profits before and after tax, and alternative versions of π/E and *RLC* were constructed with equity valued at the beginning and end of each year. The source used for all financial data was *Extel.* Profit excludes extraordinary items, e.g. from sale of assets.

Organizational Form and Organizational Change

Source material of the kind described in the previous section of the paper was taken from official company files held at *Companies House* and from files held at the *London Graduate School of Business* and the *Manchester Business School.* Where companies had more than one organizational form within the 1967–71 period, they were allocated the form held for the majority of the period. The organizational change dummy identified only M-form firms known to be in a transitional phase.

Owner-Control

The procedure adopted followed the lead of earlier studies by Larner [11], Florence [7] and especially Radice [18]. A firm was designated owner-controlled if *either* more than 15% of stock was held by an identifiable, cohesive group *or* more than 3% of stock was held by managers (Marris [12]). Shareholdings of insurance companies and pension funds were ignored. The sources used were *Annual Reports* of companies and their official shareholder registers.

Managerial Taste
Following Williamson [26] the variable was defined as the ratio of executive to all directors, information being taken from the occupational list of directors accompanying the shareholder register and from the *Directory of Directors.*

Firm Size was the total value of long-term capital, measured at the beginning of the period to minimize feedbacks from profit to size.

Firm Growth was the ratio of the difference between opening and closing size to opening size.

Gearing and *Capital Intensity* were simply L/E and R/E respectively (where L is long-term loans).

Industry Dummies
Construction of the industry dummy structure was subject to the usual problems associated with allocating firms to industries on a principal-product basis. The industry definitions were, however, broad. Companies were distributed among the industries as follows: food 15; brewing 8; electrical engineering 12; mechanical engineering 23; distributive trades 19.

V. EMPIRICAL RESULTS

OLS estimates of nine profit equations are reported in Tables II–IV. In all the reported regressions profits were measured before tax, capital stock at the beginning of the period and firm size and growth in terms of assets. Unreported regressions also used after-tax profits, closing capital stock, size and growth in terms of sales and log size. Results were essentially the same as in the reported regressions, except in one instance which is mentioned later. Explanatory power was generally satisfactory, one-third to one-half of the variation in profitability across the sample being explained by the models employed, which also performed acceptably in terms of overall significance. The industry dummy variables were generally insignificant and appeared to contribute little in the estimation process. Although included in all regressions run, the coefficients are not reported in order to save space. A little surprisingly in view of our *a priori* suspicion of specification bias in previous studies, serious problems of multicollinearity were not encountered: only one zero order correlation coefficient amongst the regressors was (barely) larger than 0·6. This was between the OF and T variables.

Equations (1)–(3) (Table II) report results for the three alternative dependent variables. In all cases a very large and highly significant impact of organizational form is revealed. The OF variable here describes a simple

TABLE II

OLS ESTIMATES: ALTERNATIVE DEPENDENT VARIABLES

Equation	Dependent variable	Constant	OF	T	OC	MT	S	G	R/E	L	$\bar{R}^2$	F
(1)	π/E	0·0836	0·0847***	−0·0454*	0·0424**	0·0275	0·00003	0·0177*			0·331	5·02
			(4·065)	(−1·885)	(2·310)	(0·483)	(0·429)	(1·750)				
(2)	RLC	0·0934	0·0626***	−0·0316*	0·0328**	0·0464	0·00003	0·0165**		−0·1519***	0·398	5·87
			(4·019)	(−1·759)	(2·393)	(1·086)	(0·500)	(2·112)		(−3·557)		
(3)	π/R	0·0689	0·0233***	−0·0030	0·0088	0·0091	0·00008***	0·0015	−0·0063***		0·462	7·33
			(2·967)	(−0·326)	(1·254)	(0·424)	(2·667)	(0·393)	(−4·674)			

Industry dummy coefficients are not reported.
***, **, * Denotes significance at 1, 5 and 10%.

TABLE III

OLS ESTIMATES: INTERACTION TERMS

Equation	Dependent variable	Const.	OF	T	OC	MT	S	G	R/E	(OF×S)	(OC×G)	$\bar{R}^2$	F
(4)	π/R	0·0663	0·0313***	−0·0031	0·0149**	−0·0098	0·00023***	0·0065	−0·0062***	−0·00016**	−0·0074*	0·500	7·24
			(3·506)	(−0·348)	(2·029)	(−0·446)	(3·286)	(1·230)	(−4·740)	(−2·286)	(−1·665)		
(5)	π/E	0·0769	0·1047***	−0·0462*	0·0560***	−0·0149	0·00038***	0·0279*		−0·00039*	−0·0154	0·361	4·812
			(4·337)	(−1·949)	(2·859)	(−0·0253)	(2·000)	(1·965)		(−1·950)	(−1·292)		

Industry dummy coefficients are not reported.
***, **, * denotes significance at 1, 5 and 10%.

TABLE IV

OLS ESTIMATES: ALTERNATIVE ORGANIZATIONAL FORM SPECIFICATIONS

Equation	*Constant*	*Organizational form*		*T*	*OC*	*MT*	*S*	*G*	*R/E*	$\bar{R}^2$	*F*
		Dependent variable π/R									
		OF II									
(6)	0·0732	0·0142* (1·892)		0·0042 (0·476)	0·0115 (1·580)	0·0075 (0·338)	0·00009*** (3·000)	0·0019 (0·490)	−0·0065*** (−4·589)	0·424	6·42
		OF III									
(7)	0·0702	0·0175** (2·450)		0·0034 (0·402)	0·0120* (1·677)	0·0101 (0·460)	0·00009*** (3·000)	0·0016 (0·400)	−0·0065*** (−4·725)	0·442	6·84
		OF IV									
(8)	0·0719	0·0187** (2·426)		−0·0003 (0·034)	0·0097 (1·364)	0·0061 (0·277)	0·00009*** (3·000)	0·0022 (0·557)	−0·0063*** (−4·628)	0·441	6·82
		M-form	H-form								
(9)	0·0838	0·0116 (1·135)	−0·0129 (−1·452)	−0·0017 (0·172)	0·0085 (1·180)	0·0048 (0·218)	0·00008*** (2·667)	0·0010 (0·260)	−0·0060*** (−4·338)	0·443	6·36

Industry dummy coefficients are not reported.
***, **, * denotes significance at 1, 5 and 10%.

optimal/non-optimal dichotomy, with M-form firms classified as optimal, H and $\bar{M}$ firms as non-optimal, and U-form firms allocated to one category or the other on the basis of their operating environment. The coefficients indicate a difference between optimally and non-optimally organized firms of 6–9 percentage points in the rate of return and 2–3 percentage points in the profit margin, compared with means across the sample of 16·9 and 6·0% respectively.

The significance levels of most other variables in Table II differ as between the rate-of-return and profit-margin equations. However, in the case of owner control and size the discrepancies are resolved when interaction terms with growth and organizational form respectively are introduced (Table III equations (4) and (5)). The *a priori* case for including the interaction terms seems fully vindicated by the results, in terms of both the performance of the particular variables concerned and also the improvement in overall significance and explanatory power. We therefore base our interpretation of the results primarily on these equations.

With this extension to the model the OF variable attracts a somewhat larger coefficient, significant at a slightly higher level. The dummy variable for firms in transition to M-form T attracts negative coefficients in both equations suggesting that dislocation costs outweigh any possible Hawthorne type effects. The coefficients imply a (temporary) reduction in profitability equal to about one-half of the ultimate gain in the rate-of-return, and a much smaller proportion in the profit margin equation.[7] However, in these, as in other equations run, the T coefficient was at best significant at 10% and this only in rate-of-return equations. While this may be partly explained by multicollinearity, in view of the comparatively high correlation between T and OF mentioned earlier, it is unlikely that this is the whole explanation and, interestingly, all traces of significance were lost when profits were measured after tax. No doubt the change to M-form organization does involve non-trivial costs, and it may be that these can be shifted to the taxpayer to some extent, although the mechanism for achieving this is not obvious. But to these questions our results have not yielded definitive answers.

With the OF.S term included we obtain separate regressions for optimally and non-optimally organized firms in the profitability-size plane. Taking the constant, OF, S and OF.S terms together as appropriate, the results are:

Optimally organized:

$$\pi/R = 0{\cdot}0979 + 0{\cdot}00007S$$
$$\pi/E = 0{\cdot}1816 - 0{\cdot}00001S$$

Non-optimally organized:

$$\pi/R = 0{\cdot}0663 + 0{\cdot}00023S^{***}$$
$$\pi/E = 0{\cdot}0769 + 0{\cdot}00038S^{***}$$

[7] Our results do not, of course, indicate how long the transitional period is and hence the total reorganization cost. In the course of the classification exercise, however, some firms were observed in a transitional phase over several years.

Thus we observe a highly significant, positive relationship between profit and size for non-optimally organized firms and no significant relationship (with even a very small negative coefficient in one case) for optimally organized firms. As will be recalled, our primary reason for including S was to test for the effect on profit of size economies of various kinds. Most empirical studies of cost functions, whether of a statistical or an engineering nature, suggest an *L*-shaped relationship, with initial economies followed by negligible savings beyond the point of minimum optimum size.[8] This being so, we should expect to observe a positive impact of size on profits only if the sample includes firms below minimum optimum size. In the present sample the average firm size in the optimally organized group was twice that of the non-optimally organized subset (£102·9 million as against £49·7 million). We therefore interpret our results in this area as suggesting that firm-size economies do exist; that some firms in the sample were operating in the region of falling costs; but that in general those firms which had adopted optimal internal organization had also achieved minimum optimal size. The extent to which the optimally organized firms outperform others, taking size into account, is striking. Thus, evaluating the above equations at the group size means, we obtain values of π/R and π/E of 0·1051 and 0·1826 respectively for optimally organized firms, compared with only 0·0777 and 0·0958 for non-optimally organized firms.

The remaining explanatory variables in equations (4) and (5)—OC, MT, G and the interaction term OC.G—provide evidence on the exercise of managerial discretion among the firms in our sample. One variable included to test for this type of effect performed very badly. Thus the managerial taste (MT) coefficients were non-significant and of wrong sign in all equations estimated. It could be that the relationship is more complex than our specification—a simple ratio—allows for. In particular, unduly low executive representation may result in some efficiency loss and also the absolute numbers of executive and other directors may matter. In addition there could be interaction effects with organizational form. Whether refinements in this measure warrant the effort or whether alternatives should be explored is not clear.

Clear indications of managerial behaviour do, however, appear in the performance of the owner-control variable, which is significant at 5% or better in both the rate-of-return and the profit-margin equations when the interaction terms are present. Thus owner-control appears to exert a significantly positive influence on profits, in magnitude approximately one-half that of the impact of organizational form. And although the G and OC.G coefficients are not significant within the usual confidence limits, the coefficient values tend to confirm the existence of slack in the non-owner-controlled firm. Thus taking the G and interaction coefficients together, we find that while profit increases with growth for the non-owner-controlled subset, the

[8] See e.g. Johnston [9], Pratten [17] and Scherer [19].

slope of the relationship is much less for owner-controlled firms, and is in fact slightly negative (−0·0009) in the profit-margin case. As we have already stressed the growth coefficient may be prone to (positive) simultaneous equation bias. If so we may suspect that the true G coefficient is less than the estimate reported in Table III. But the markedly different slopes for the owner-controlled vs. non-owner-controlled groups remain of interest.

What we see here is consistent with the result observed by Radice [18], who found that owner-controlled firms outperformed manager-controlled firms in terms of both profitability and growth. This is brought out clearly in Figure 1, which shows the regression lines for the two subsamples of firms together with the means for each group. If the efficiency frontier of profit-growth combinations resembles the curve EE′ (Marris [12]), the owner-controlled group are operating comparatively close to the region of maximum profit, with growth rates that are high, but not sufficiently so to be at the expense of profit. The other group, by contrast, exhibit unambiguous managerial slack, failing to grow as fast as they might at the profitability levels achieved and vice versa, and to match the performance of owner controlled firms in either dimension.[9] However, as Radice noted in interpreting similar results, the apparent superiority of owner-controlled firms' performance in both dimensions may in part be due to a bias in the composition of the sample. Since all firms appeared in the top 300 companies, and since expansion to such size while preserving owner-control may involve foregoing the exercise of certain external–financing options, it may be that the owner-controlled group in the sample are exceptionally efficiently run companies, relative to all owner-controlled firms and to firms in general. At the same time, the very fact that on this argument the 'exceptionally efficient' management is found in owner- rather than manager-controlled firms (of comparable size) could itself be a reflection of the impact on performance of owner diffusion.

The remaining equa'ions (6)–(9) (Table IV) explore the sensitivity of the results to marginal alterations in the way firms are designated as optimal or non-optimal.[10] The equations are identical apart from the differently specified OF variables and compare with equation (3) of Table I. OF II (equation (6)) and OF III (equation (7)) incorporate some minor amendments to the classification of firms, in the light of Channon's results and also of some information acquired after Steer's original classification was completed. OF II, in addition, treats all U-form firms as suboptimal, while OF III categorises two more U-form firms as optimal, as compared with OF. Equation (8) embodies a straightforward division between M-form firms and the rest (OF IV) and equation (9) applies a three-way classification, distinguishing firms with an expectedly optimal degree of centralization (M-form)

[9] The superior performance of the owner controlled firms is exaggerated in Figure 1(b), since E was measured at the beginning of each year and is therefore relatively understated for the faster-growing owner-controlled group.

[10] Very similar results were obtained with each of the three dependent variables.

from both under- (H-form) and over-centralized firms (the residual $\overline{M}+U$ category).

Taken together these results indicate that the organizational form result is robust, and not critically dependent on quirks of the classification and grouping procedure. The somewhat less good performance of the OF IV and OF II specifications as compared with OF tends to confirm that U-form can be optimal even among firms in the size and degree of diversity categories included in our sample. At the same time, the fact that the organizational form effect is not wholly due to the necessarily subjective differentiation among U-form firms according to the nature of their operating environment,

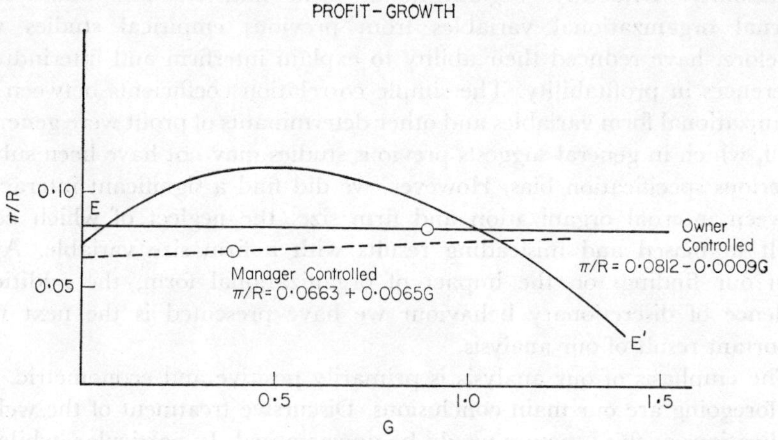

FIGURE 1(a)

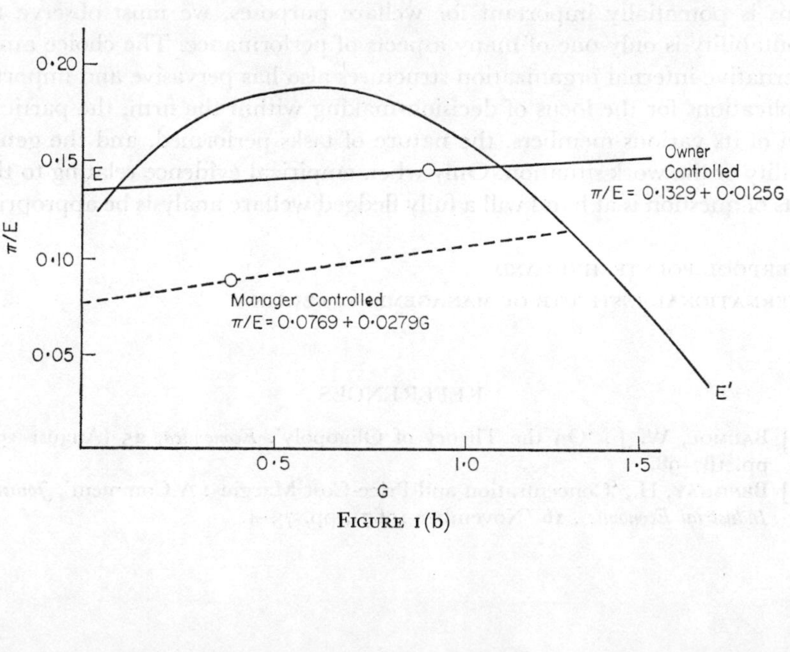

FIGURE 1(b)

and emerges when M-form vs. other firms are considered, is reassuring. In the final equation we see a ranking in which optimally centralized firms are more profitable than above over-centralized firms, as expected, and that under-centralization leads to lowest profit *ceteris paribus*. However, under this more ambitious three-way classification, the differences in performance among the groups are not statistically significant.

VI. CONCLUSIONS

Our results indicate that the internal organization structure of the firms in our sample exerted a statistically significant and large influence on their profitability. Evidently, organizational form matters. The omission of internal organizational variables from previous empirical studies will, therefore, have reduced their ability to explain interfirm and interindustry differences in profitability. The simple correlation coefficients between our organizational form variables and other determinants of profit were generally small, which in general suggests previous studies may not have been subject to serious specification bias. However, we did find a significant interaction between internal organization and firm size, the neglect of which could result in biased and misleading results with a firm size variable. Apart from our findings on the impact of organizational form, the additional evidence of discretionary behaviour we have presented is the next most important result of our analysis.

The emphasis of our analysis is primarily positive and econometric, and the foregoing are our main conclusions. Discursive treatment of the welfare implications at this juncture would be unwarranted. In particular, while the evidence we have presented of the superior profit performance of M-form firms is potentially important for welfare purposes, we must observe that profitability is only one of many aspects of performance. The choice among alternative internal organization structures also has pervasive and important implications for the locus of decision-making within the firm, the participation of its various members, the nature of tasks performed, and the general quality of the work situation. Only when empirical evidence relating to these sorts of question is at hand will a fully fledged welfare analysis be appropriate.

LIVERPOOL POLYTECHNIC AND
INTERNATIONAL INSTITUTE OF MANAGEMENT, BERLIN

REFERENCES

[1] Baumol, W. J., 'On the Theory of Oligopoly', *Economica*, **25** (August 1958), pp. 187–98.

[2] Benishay, H., 'Concentration and Price-Cost Margins: A Comment', *Journal of Industrial Economics*, **16** (November 1967), pp. 73–4.

[3] CHANNON, D. F., *The Strategy and Structure of British Enterprise* (Macmillan, New York, 1973).

[4] COMANOR, W. S. and WILSON, T. A., 'Advertising, Market Structure and Performance', *Review of Economics and Statistics*, **49** (November 1967), pp. 423–40.

[5] COWLING, K. G., 'On the Theoretical Specification of Structure-Performance Relationships', *European Economic Review*, **8** (October 1976), pp. 1–14.

[6] CYERT, R. M. and MARCH, J. G., *A Behavioural Theory of the Firm* (Prentice Hall, Englewood Cliffs, N.J., 1963).

[7] FLORENCE, P. SARGENT, *Ownership Control and Success of Large Companies* (Sweet & Maxwell, London, 1961).

[8] HALL, M. and WEISS, L. W., 'Firm Size and Profitability', *Review of Economics and Statistics*, **49** (August 1967), pp. 319–31.

[9] JOHNSTON, J., *Statistical Cost Analysis* (McGraw-Hill, New York, 1960).

[10] KAMERSCHEN, D. R., 'The Influence of Ownership and Control on Profit Rates', *American Economic Review*, **58** (June 1968), pp. 432–47.

[11] LARNER, R. J., *Management Control and the Large Corporation* (Dunellan, New York, 1970).

[12] MARRIS, R., *The Economic Theory of Managerial Capitalism* (Macmillan, London, 1964).

[13] MONSEN, R. J. and DOWNS, A., 'A Theory of Large Managerial Firms', *Journal of Political Economy*, **73** (June 1965), pp. 221–36.

[14] ORNSTEIN, S. I., 'Empirical Uses of the Price-Cost Margin', *Journal of Industrial Economics*, **24** (December 1975), pp. 105–17.

[15] PHILLIPS, A., 'A Critique of Empirical Studies of Relations Between Market Structure and Profitability', *Journal of Industrial Economics*, **24** (June 1976), pp. 241–9.

[16] POENSGEN, O. H., 'Organizational Structure Context and Performance', *Working Paper* 74–49 (European Institute for Advanced Studies in Management, Brussels).

[17] PRATTEN, C., *Economies of Scale in Manufacturing Industry* (Cambridge University Press, Cambridge, 1971).

[18] RADICE, H. K., 'Control Type, Profitability and Growth in Large Firms: An Empirical Study', *Economic Journal*, **81** (September 1971), pp. 547–62.

[19] SCHERER, F. M., 'Economies of Scale at the Plant and Multi-plant Levels: Detailed Evidence' (mimeo) (1975).

[20] SCITOVSKY, T., 'A Note on Profit Maximization and Its Implications', *Review of Economic Studies*, **11** (1943), pp. 57–60.

[21] SHERMAN, R. and TOLLISON, R., 'Advertising and Profitability', *Review of Economics and Statistics*, **53** (November 1971), pp. 397–407.

[22] SIMON, H. A., 'A Behavioural Model of Rational Choice', *Quarterly Journal of Economics*, **69** (February 1955), pp. 99–118.

[23] STEER, P. S., 'An Investigation into the Managerial Organization of Firms' (mimeo) (1973).

[24] STIGLER, G. J., 'A Theory of Oligopoly', *Journal of Political Economy*, **13** (February 1964), pp. 44–61.

[25] STRICKLAND, A. D. and WEISS, L. W., 'Advertising, Concentration and Price-Cost Margins', *Journal of Political Economy*, **84** (October 1976), pp. 1109–21.

[26] WILLIAMSON, O. E., *The Economics of Discretionary Behaviour* (Prentice Hall, Englewood Cliffs, N.J., 1964).

[27] ——, *Corporate Control and Business Behaviour* (Prentice Hall, Englewood Cliffs, N.J., 1970).

[28] ——, *Markets and Hierarchies* (Macmillan, New York, 1975).

[29] WILLIAMSON, O. E. and BHARGAVA, N., 'Assessing and Classifying the Internal Structure and Control Apparatus of the Modern Corporation', in K. G. Cowling (ed.) *Market Structure and Corporate Behaviour* (Gray-Mills, London, 1972).

[30] WHITTINGTON, G., *The Prediction of Profitability* (Cambridge University Press, Cambridge, 1972).

THE JOURNAL OF INDUSTRIAL ECONOMICS
Vol. XXVII September 1978 No. 1

ON THE DEFINITION OF 'INDUSTRY' AND 'MARKET'

JOHN NIGHTINGALE*

I

THE terms 'industry' and 'market' have been in a state of confusion ever since the 1930s, when Chamberlin and Robinson tried to solve the Sraffa problem of decreasing costs in the short run. Contemporary microeconomic theory assigns an unambiguous meaning to 'industry' only in the cases of perfect competition and perfect monopoly. Outside these theoretical extremes there is no theoretical concept to which the term 'industry' can usefully be applied. The term 'market' is in a not much better situation, with the logic of the theory forcing each product of each producer outside of perfect competition to be assigned its own 'market'.

Despite these theoretical problems the terms 'industry' and 'market' continue to be widely used by economists, not only in applied work but also in all but the most highly refined textbooks and treatises. For example, in the chapter dealing with equilibrium of the firm in J. R. Hicks's *Value and Capital* the concept 'industry' is used without quotation marks in beginning discussion of less than perfectly competitive situations [7, p. 82]. This is precisely the area in which the concept is not clear. Another example is Cohen and Cyert, *Theory of the Firm* [4]. This is a sound 'intermediate' textbook, but the concept of industry is used unselfconsciously throughout, particularly in the monopolistic competition and oligopoly chapters. The very existence of industry economics demonstrates the usefulness and intuitive appeal of the industry as a concept, but even the practitioners in this field fail to deal effectively with the definitional problem, as Brunner points out [2, pp. 165–6].

The loose use of both terms, but more especially 'industry', pervades North American writing. 'Industry' is often used as a synonym for 'market'.[1] Recently a new term, 'line of business', seemingly synonymous with 'sellers in a market' has been used to separate out what will be argued below to be 'market' considerations from misuse of Standard Industrial Classification industry data [5].

As one of the very few who have attempted to create a theoretical basis for industrial economics, P. W. S. Andrews has suggested ways in which both

* I would like to thank Ray Bantow and an anonymous referee for their helpful comments and suggestions.

[1] For example [9, p. 90]: 'Some of this association was due to census classification biases which cause large industries to be large because they are defined too broadly, covering several economically meaningful markets'.

terms could be used by industrial economists. Brunner has recently published a reformulation of these suggestions which, while perhaps embodying Andrews's practice, and the practice of many of those directly or indirectly in the same traditions,[2] in fact changes his explicit definition [2, pp. 36–8]. The question is whether the revision could clarify the practice of industry economics, removing confusion over terminology if it is generally accepted, and lead to better analysis in the field.

Andrews defined an industry as 'any grouping of individual . . . businesses which is relevant when we study the behaviour of any one such business' [12, p. 168]. Having thus defined an industry he went on to describe the 'chief characteristic of an industry' as

> largely a matter of technique and processes; an individual business must be conceived as operating within an 'industry' which consists of all businesses which operate processes of a sufficiently similar kind (which implies the possession of substantially similar technical resources) and possessing sufficiently similar backgrounds of experience and knowledge so that each of them could produce the particular commodity under consideration, and would do so if it were sufficiently attractive.

He pointed out that narrower and wider groupings of businesses would be appropriate to shorter and longer run analyses. But this 'chief characteristic' cannot be a defining characteristic unless his explicit definition is abandoned.

Andrews's definition of industry, contrary to his 'chief characteristic', does not exclude the possibility that, on occasion, a grouping of firms will be required to include firms of differing technical and resource bases. If the behaviour of any one firm is sufficiently affected by some one or more others who may be technically different, then his definition would necessarily include them in the analysis, *and* in the industry.

II

Before proceeding to analyse some implications of the definition of industry it is necessary to explore briefly Andrews's use of the term 'market'. Andrews's understanding of 'market' begins with the group of customers for a product of a firm [1, p. 146]. Thus 'the sales market of an individual business consists of all the people who are sufficiently aware of its product to consider buying it' [1, p. 135]. In explaining one aspect of the behaviour of customers Andrews writes

> The general situation, then, is that, so long as its price is right, an established business will have a more or less clearly defined market, and will be protected from the efforts of would-be competing businesses to

[2] Robinson [9] and Wolfe [13] both followed this practice, as obviously does Brunner.

cut into that market. It will extend its market by offering better service at its price. . . . Its market will, equally, contract if the business fails to offer as good a service as competitors at the given price [1, p. 153].

The 'market' has, therefore, no direct reference to sellers of products at all, but only to buyers of a particular item. But 'market' is also applied to a wider group. For example, 'a businessman will, all the time, be forming impressions of what is happening to the market . . . or, strictly, group of markets—for the kind of product that he sells . . .' [1, p. 155], and again 'if . . . the gross profit margin on any particular market is thought to be unduly generous, it is a comparatively easy matter for other businesses, which have the right equipment and organization already, to "try their arm" in that particular market' [1, p. 167]. Two more quotations show that 'market' as more than a firm's set of customers derives from common usage in economics and the business world, and can be defined away only at risk of the confusion of readers: of businesses which tender for contracts 'A large single contract may be very worthwhile, and may form a substantial part of the total market demand' [1, p. 182], and of advertising in trade newspapers, 'The irregular customer will quite possibly not always be up to date in his knowledge of the state of the market' [1, p. 190].

This last quotation is also the only one cited in which it is not possible meaningfully to substitute 'customers' for 'market'. Here the 'market place' connotation is appropriate. From the point of view of buyers, sellers offer their wares for sale in 'the market'.

When Andrews considers the manufacturer buying his inputs of labour, raw materials and finance, this market place concept again dominates, as it is seen from the customer's viewpoint. Markets for primary raw materials and finance are seen as the institutions which facilitate changes of ownership. These markets are competitive, and trade in goods that are not identified by suppliers. In fact, Andrews slips into conventional (economists') usage in calling customers 'consumers' in discussing primary materials markets [1, p. 209], strong enough evidence of a conventional Marshallian view of these markets. In contrast, Andrews found no need to use the term 'market' in discussing the manufacturing business hiring labour, except in referring to the aggregate 'labour market' [1, pp. 216, 218] and the 'market-rate' [1, p. 221] for unskilled (general skilled) labour. Again, it is not adequate to use 'labour market' to mean 'buyers of labour', a transactions institution would seem more appropriate.

Is it possible to develop a consistent view of the word 'market' for all these contexts, in which the definition also follows common usage? In the context of sales of the output of business, 'market' refers primarily to buyers, usually firms, engaging in the acquisition of goods and services. In the context of primary commodities, reference is to the institutionalized activity of transacting changes of ownership. For finance and labour, similarly, it is the institutional structure within which intending buyers and sellers act that is called 'the market'.

If a definition in terms of 'transactional institution' is adopted it can fit all these cases, as well as common usage. But this does not abolish or solve the original problem for Andrews of defining the limits of the market in any particular case, nor the problem of this note, of distinguishing the concept 'market' from 'industry'.

III

The boundaries of an Andrews 'explicit definition' industry are found by including any business which can affect the behaviour of some one business. Taking first a short-run view, in which most resource inputs are not variable, the industry will consist of all firms which can contest a market in which the business is operating. Some of these firms will be selling in this market, some will be capable of doing so merely by mobilizing fixed resources and hiring variable ones. There would seem to be no need to restrict these businesses to the same techniques of production. A business selling prefabricated steel roof trusses would clearly be affected by the behaviour of one selling prefabricated timber trusses—the same group of buyers would purchase from both sellers—even though the steel fabricator would be quite unable in the short run, to produce timber trusses. But a great many industries defined in the short run would consist wholly of businesses using the same techniques, conforming with Andrews's view of the chief characteristic of an industry [12, p. 168].

As the planning horizon is lengthened, the set of potential competitors expands. In some medium term, the roof truss manufacturers are constrained by the fact that existing carpenters and joiners can rearrange their works and invest in a limited number of specialized machines in order to make timber trusses, and existing structural engineers and steel fabricators can do the same to produce steel trusses. No new firms may be set up but the threat of entry by existing firms into a particular market they do not currently contest (Andrews's cross entry) constrains firms actually selling in a market. Thus the industry consists of more than the firms actually selling in a market [12, p. 168].

When the horizon lengthens to consideration of new businesses being formed and existing businesses engaging in activities in which they have no prior experience or expertise, the Andrews concept of industry is swallowed by the need for a more general analysis.

The implication of this analysis is that on Andrews's explicit definition the industry as a conceptual device is limited to less than the longest of runs, that membership of an industry is not usually clearly bounded in any particular case, but that the analysis of the behaviour of a firm is meaningless outside the context of an industry, or, in the long run, in the context of the economic system which constrains the behaviour of the firm.

It is tempting to conclude that the analysis of competition has swallowed up monopoly. This is not really the case, for power is wielded in many ways by firms and groups of firms—resource ownership, statutory monopoly and in consumer goods markets, more particularly retail markets, product differentiation. These at least partly insulate fortunate businesses from their potential competitors. However, maintaining a clear view of the constraints on the behaviour of a business entails distinguishing various horizons within which different levels of constraint apply.

Where does this leave the distinction between 'industry' and 'market'? The sellers that together sell to buyers in a market would necessarily appear to come from an industry. This follows from the effect the group could have on the behaviour of any individual firm. But the industry can also include many other businesses which separately or together can affect the behaviour of a particular firm selling in the first mentioned market. Not only that, but different firms selling in this market may be significantly affected by different groups of other firms not selling in this market. For example, the timber truss builder may be significantly constrained by a rise in the demand for joiners occasioned by furniture makers coping with an export boom. The steel truss fabricator would be affected by this only to the extent that his timbet truss competitors had to raise quotes to cope with higher costs, thus leaving the truss market more open for the steel fabricators. Should furniture makers be put into the same short-run industry as the truss firms? This line of reasoning simply leads away from industry analysis towards general equilibrium analysis.

Consider as well two important characteristics of present technology. The first is that items intended for the same use are being produced in many materials (the timber/steel truss example) by a number of disparate techniques. The second is the converse, that any given technology is generating new products and creating new uses for old products. Again, Andrews's 'industry' is becoming much more difficult to define, while market analyses are needing to include more disparate sellers than was the case 50 years ago.

The suggestion made by Brunner is that Andrews's 'chief characteristic' [12, p. 168] be taken as the definition of 'industry' [2, p. 37]. This means that each firm in the industry must be able to operate the same processes and produce a technically similar product within the planning horizon in question. Under this definition the timber truss manufacturer would be in a different industry from the steel truss fabricator. Clearly, the behaviour of a firm in one industry, thus defined, could affect that of firms in another industry. Andrews's definition of industry cannot be used, even, or especially, in the short run.

But Brunner's suggestion does offer a means whereby usefully distinct meanings can be attached to 'industry' and 'market': an 'industry' is any grouping of firms which operate similar processes and could produce technically identical products within a given planning horizon. These groupings by no means exhaust the constraints on the behaviour of any particular firm. They encompass constraints on the input side as each firm would be using very similar inputs of labour, raw material and machinery. A market, by contrast, is the institution within which a firm attempts to sell his output or buy an input. A firm's behaviour is constrained by other firms selling in that market and by the behaviour of buyers in the market.

IV

The conclusion is that while Andrews's definition of industry was adequate when his 'chief characteristic' could be relied on almost as a synonym for the definition, Brunner's revision is a useful way in which groups of influences or constraints can be segregated in the analysis of market behaviour or the behaviour of a firm.

Under either definition, the membership of an industry is fundamentally dependent on the planning horizon within which analysis is carried on (loosely, the time scale or length or shortness of 'run').

Under either definition of industry, 'market' is not simply another word for industry, or an alternative frame of analysis, but a distinctive concept dealing with relationships between sellers and buyers. But under the Brunner definition, at least, the sellers in a market are not automatically consigned to one industry.

If the Brunner 'industry' definition, and the transactional institution 'market' definition[3] are adopted much purely semantic confusion could be avoided, and those who practice industrial analysis in economics should more directly see the issues at hand in building models of markets and industries.

One important consequence is that each investigation will necessarily require its own frame of analysis, in some of which the market will be crucial, in others the industry, and in some, both. Robinson [9] suggested this 20 years ago, but was ignored, particularly by econometrical investigators, who seem more concerned with statistical measures of success than with adequate economic theory. More recently Phillips advocated more attention to careful model building in the context of 'industrial econometrics' [8, p. 248].

It would seem impossible to devise an empirically tractable set of classes, even without insisting on mutual exclusion, that would satisfy the demands of analysis of markets and industries. This implies that the International Standard Industrial Classification, or any national version of it, is unable to provide a valid statistical basis for the range of analyses presently worked on it.

SICs are based on the notion of 'activities of establishments', what is carried on at a location by a controlling ownership. Taking the example of the Australian SIC[3], 'Classes' are formed by the statistician observing common patterns of activities. These Classes are aggregated such that secondary activities of establishments in the constituent classes find themselves

[3] This last is, I believe, entirely uncontentious and conforming with common usage.

in the same 'Group' as Classes to which those activities are primary. Only at this second level of aggregation does the statistician judge it worth classifying enterprises (business firms), because very many enterprises own establishments classified to a number of Classes within the same Group [3, p. 13]. Groups, in turn, are aggregated into 'Sub-Divisions' which in their turn, are aggregated into 'Divisions'. Continuity of statistical publications was of some importance in ASIC choices here [3, pp. 17–18]. However, the ISIC 'division' level to which the ASIC Sub-Divisions roughly correspond are formed under criteria of

(a) physical composition and stage of fabrication,
(b) uses, and
(c) process, technology and organization of production [3, p. 8].

While this may seem vague and allowing for considerable argument, an unwritten criterion bound up with the 'continuity of publication' criterion, important to national SICs, is that enterprises should be relatively specialised, i.e. as at Group level, aggregation should diminish the proportion of an activity carried on outside the category within which it is primary.[4]

Can these be seen as Andrews/Brunner (technique defined) industries, with the most detailed level referring to the immediate short run and the more aggregated levels referring to longer planning horizons? The firm which owns an establishment in one Class is likely to be able to mobilize its technical skills on an activity primary to an adjacent Class within the same Group by a rearrangement of resources of a limited kind. Given a longer planning horizon a firm operating establishments within a particular Sub-Division (e.g. fabricating structural steel products, an activity of a Class within the Sub-Division, Fabricated Metal Products), may well be a potential producer in any other Class in that Sub-Division, because it has a basic set of technical, managerial and marketing skills which can be adapted to the fabrication of other metal products.

It may be possible to use such SIC classifications to analyse industry models, where market considerations are unimportant (i.e. where the problem exemplified by the metal truss/timber truss situation is not an issue). But there are many practical problems. One is the geographical problem, that for some activities a small area is appropriate, for others a larger, even global, area is relevant. Another is the homogeneity problem: establishments and enterprises are classified to a single cell, therefore in establishment statistics a proportion of establishment activity will be outside activities primary to the Class to which each establishment is classified, and in enterprise statistics,

[4] Hannah and Kay [6, p. 44], are not the first industrial economists to accuse SIC compilers of mere 'common sense' (their quotation marks) in defining SIC classes. As the above paragraph shows, however briefly, SIC compilers do use a theory, one whose requirements are well defined and within which the scope for arbitrary judgement is severely limited. The problem is that it is not the market definition, cross elasticities of demand significantly positive, which would satisfy the desire of Hannah and Kay for market concentration statistics.

many enterprises will own establishments classified to Groups other than the Group to which the enterprise is classified: in simple terms, firms do not fall neatly into the statistician's classes, no matter how carefully these classes are constructed.[5] A third is the problem that the 'activity' approach itself cuts across technical boundaries in such a way as to define industries which in fact have technical compatibility with one or more other industries and not with others of the same Group. This occurs most often in the catch-all 'other activities' cells. One striking, though not perhaps important, example is in the Sub-Division 'Transport Equipment', where the Group 'Other Transport Equipment' includes the Class 'Boat Building and Repair': establishments mainly engaged in building, converting, fitting or repairing boats or yachts under 50 tons displacement. This class appears to be a market rather than an industry related class.[6] The techniques of production encompass joinery and cabinet work involved in sheetplywood, moulded veneer and planked timber construction, structural steel and aluminium fabrication, fibre-reinforced plastic and ferrocement, to name but a few. This may be a case in which technological change has outstripped the classification, for most establishments specialize in a particular set of techniques and many are owned by enterprises of a diversified form which are classified elsewhere. Needless to say, enterprises engaged in these activities are unlikely to be fitted to enter the building of larger scale ships, railway locomotive and rolling stock manufacture and repair, aircraft building and repair, or transport equipment n.e.c., the other Classes within the Group. This would suggest that any user of industry classifications wishing to establish hypotheses about industry behaviour must discriminate carefully in choosing the set of industries which fufil the requirements of the study. And this, of course, opens the possibility of manipulating samples to suit hypotheses.

But most of the hypotheses subjected to test by the use of SIC data relate as closely to market behaviour as to industry behaviour. The standard example is the attempt to relate profitability of SIC industries to so-called 'seller concentration'. Assume first that there is a model in which seller concentration is an important determinant of profitability.[7] The immediate problem then becomes how to use SIC industry data to elucidate market structure, for *seller* concentration is fundamentally a market concept as the Hannah and Kay example [6, pp. 10–18] makes particularly clear. This problem has been fudged by studies using SIC data. What has, in fact, been done is to relate profitability and size concentration, both measured in various ways, for SIC industries. Phillips's [8] attack on these need not be amplified. It may be worth suggesting that there is room for using SIC data

[5] In the case of the Australian SIC a 'specialization ratio' of 80% and a 'coverage ratio' of 70% are minimum 'general rules' for recognition of Classes [3, p. 50].

[6] Even so the class must encompass many markets for both commercial and pleasure craft, not to mention naval establishments, between which cross-elasticity of demand would be negligible.

[7] [6, pp. 10–18] is a nice example.

selectively if an adequate theoretical basis can be devised, linking aspects of industry performance with aspects of industry structure, such as sales or employment concentration. Interest by economists in such statistics as the share of national or manufacturing output contributed by the largest 100 or 500 corporations or manufacturers suggests that, at least implicitly, some theory exists.[8] A model which included relationships between firms in an industry, rather than between firms in a market, would seem to be quite feasible, though incomplete.

To take the roof truss example once more, seller concentration in the roof truss market cannot be calculated from SIC data, any more than seller concentration in almost every other well-defined market. Enterprises selling roof trusses are, in the Australian SIC, assigned either to 'Wood and Wood Products (except furniture)' or to 'Fabricated Structural Metal Products'. A small part of the market may well be supplied by enterprises outside these two industries, because these enterprises' major activities are not activities primary to either of these industries. But, if we know the market share of wooden to metal roof trusses it could be of some value to know the industrial concentration of the industries within which roof trusses were manufactured. But this is the data of case studies, not of econometrics.

UNIVERSITY OF NEW ENGLAND

REFERENCES

[1] ANDREWS, P. W. S., *Manufacturing Business* (Macmillan, London, 1949).

[2] ANDREWS, P. W. S. and BRUNNER, E., *Studies in Pricing* (Macmillan, London, 1975).

[3] AUSTRALIAN BUREAU OF STATISTICS, *Australian Standard Industrial Classification*, Volume 1, Preliminary Edition (Canberra, 1969) (reprinted 1975).

[4] COHEN, K. J. and CYERT, R. M., *Theory of the Firm* (Prentice-Hall, Englewood Cliffs, 1975).

[5] COX, S. R. and PENN, D. W., 'Industrial Organization Research and the Academic Economist', *Industrial Organization Review*, **IV** (2) (1976), pp. 83–7.

[6] HANNAH, L. and KAY, J. A., *Concentration in Modern Industry* (Macmillan, London, 1977).

[7] HICKS, J. R., *Value and Capital* (Oxford University Press, London, 1939).

[8] PHILLIPS, A., 'A Critique of Empirical Studies of Relations Between Market Structure and Profitability', *Journal of Industrial Economics*, **XXIV** (4) (June 1976), pp. 241–9.

[9] ROBINSON, J., 'The Industry and the Market', *Economic Journal*, **LXVI** (June 1956), pp. 360–1.

[10] SCHERER, F. M., *Industrial Market Structure and Economic Performance* (Chicago, Rand McNally, 1970).

[11] UTTON, M. A., 'Aggregate Versus Market Concentration: A Note', *Economic Journal*, **LXXXIV** (March 1974), pp. 150–3.

[8] Utton [11] argues that aggregate concentration is important because it is related to market concentration. I would argue that he has shown aggregate concentration to be related to industrial concentration.

[12] Wilson, T. and Andrews, P. W. S., *Oxford Studies in the Price Mechanism* (Clarendon Press, Oxford, 1951).

[13] Wolfe, J. N., 'The Representative Firm', *Economic Journal*, **LXIV** (June 1954), pp. 337–49.

THE JOURNAL OF INDUSTRIAL ECONOMICS
Volume XXVII September 1978 No. 1

THE PATTERN OF INDUSTRIAL CONCENTRATION IN LATIN AMERICA

PATRICIO MELLER*

THE purpose of this study is to provide an empirical description of the structure of industrial concentration in the Latin American manufacturing sector.[1] Eighteen two-digit ISIC (Industrial Standard International Classification) industries of ten Latin American countries constitute the sample of this study, and their employment entropy measurements are utilized as indicators of industrial concentration. Given the wide spectrum and large number of Latin American countries used, it is assumed that the results obtained are valid for Latin America as a whole.

There are quite a large number of different indices of industrial concentration; also there are several variables that could be used for measuring concentration.[2] In this study, employment entropy indicators are used. The reasons for this choice are as follows: (i) entropy indicators have properties that make them good proxies for measuring the degree of competition of an industry;[3] (ii) the use of the employment variables facilitates international comparisons, and, in some countries, it is the only variable for which data are available. Entropy figures reflect two facts: (i) the number of firms of an industry, and (ii) the distribution of employment among those firms. Conceptually, entropy is inversely related to concentration (see footnote 3).

Published data of the Census of Manufactures for ten Latin American

* The author is indebted to Terry Echaniz and Lisa Horowitz of the National Bureau for their helpful assistance in data manipulation and computer programming. Financial support for this article was provided by the Rockefeller Foundation within its fellowship grant for the author's stay at the National Bureau of Economic Research. The views expressed in this paper are those of the author and do not reflect those of CIEPLAN or of the National Bureau of Economic Research. I am grateful to H. Michael Mann for editorial help and advice.

[1] Industrial concentration is being used to mean horizontal concentration. As Phlips [5] has pointed out, financial concentration, interlocking directorates, vertical integration, etc., might be more important than horizontal concentration as measures of monopoly or oligopoly power; however, empirical limitations allow only for the computation of horizontal concentration.

[2] See Meller and Swinburn [3] where 20 indexes of concentration are described and compared, and where each index is computed for four variables: employment, capital, value added, and gross value of production.

[3] Theil [9] provides a thorough development of the entropy concept and its use in economics. Horowitz [2] provides a good summary and application of the entropy concept to the measure of concentration. Entropy is a concept of information theory that can be used to measure the degree of uncertainty as to the likelihood that a particular firm of an industry would secure the patronage of a consumer chosen at random.

Entropy measures the inverse of concentration, i.e. as entropy increases, the degree of concentration of an industry will decrease. Entropy increases when: (i) the number of firms of an industry increases, (ii) the relative participation of the firms within the industry tends to be more equal. Entropy has a minimum value of 0 for a monopoly situation, and it has the maximum value when all the firms of the industry have the same relative participation.

countries are used for the computation of entropy. Census years of the different countries do not coincide, but all are in the 1963–68 period. The type of data used corresponds to grouped data at the two-digit ISIC level; firms are grouped according to number of persons employed. For each size class of firms, the total number of firms and total number of people employed is provided. (This is all the information required for the computation of the employment entropy indicators.) One of the problems with this type of data is that different national censuses have different criteria for determining the number and the breakdown of class size of firms (see Appendix).

Table I provides the entropy estimates for 18 two-digit ISIC industries (industries 20 through 38, skipping industry 32, petroleum) for ten Latin American countries. The appendix provides the formulas used in these computations. For an intuitive interpretation of the order of magnitude of these figures, see Horowitz [2].

This study is mainly concerned with the ranking of industries within and across countries. Therefore, the ranking of the 18 manufacturing industries within each country is obtained, and then, the simple average rank ordering across countries is computed; the concordance coefficient[4] of this average rank ordering provides a test of the degree to which the industry rankings of the ten Latin American countries are similar. Table II provides the average ranking of industries for the ten Latin American countries. The concordance coefficient of such ranking is 0·733, which is significant at the 0·01 level. These results indicate that there is a similar structure of concentration in Latin America, i.e. the industries which have high (low) concentration levels in one country, have high (low) concentration levels in another country. Moreover, pair-wise comparison of countries provide Spearman rank correlation coefficients that in all cases (45 cases) are significant at 5%.

From Table II it is possible to observe that the four most concentrated industries in Latin America are:[5] tobacco, basic metals, rubber products, and paper. The four least concentrated industries are: clothing and footwear, food manufacturing, metal products, and furniture. The presence of the metal products among the least concentrated industries produces some surprise. The latter result may be explained by the fact that metal products includes the manufacture, repair, and servicing of hand tools, locks and other hardware, and cutlery for the general public.

To establish the ranking of the ten Latin American countries according to their level of concentration, the average rank ordering of the ten countries with respect to the 18 ISIC industries has been computed. This has been

[4] The concordance coefficients measures the degree of association among different sets of rankings. For computation procedure see S. Siegel [7].

[5] The use of the Herfindahl index as a measure of concentration provides similar types of results. Furthermore, the structure of concentration changes slightly when value added is used instead of employment. See Meller, Léniz and Swinburn [4].

TABLE I

ENTROPY CONCENTRATION INDEXES FOR LATIN AMERICAN MANUFACTURING INDUSTRIES BY COUNTRY

ISIC Code	Type of industry	Countries									
		Argentina	Chile	Colombia	Costa Rica	Ecuador	Mexico	Paraguay	Peru	Uruguay	Venezuela
20	Food manufacturing	8·086	6·904	6·631	6·033	5·572	8·064	6·090	5·741	4·118	6·164
21	Beverages	7·601	6·022	3·987	2·815	4·398	5·527	3·707	4·014	2·809	4·107
22	Tobacco	3·107	0·929	3·634	0·537	0·776	1·840	1·332	0·915	2·083	2·845
23	Textiles	7·008	5·395	3·682	2·944	4·713	6·857	2·190	5·099	3·827	3·229
24	Clothing and footwear	8·187	5·995	6·248	5·104	8·973	7·597	6·276	4·273	4·608	6·847
25	Wood and wood products	8·265	7·154	4·983	4·411	5·843	5·738	5·236	3·920	3·868	5·479
26	Furniture and fixtures	8·295	5·715	5·116	4·694	7·320	5·965	5·332	4·278	3·443	6·569
27	Paper and paper products	5·775	3·173	3·627	2·299	1·633	4·966	1·270	2·757	2·995	3·350
28	Printing and publishing	6·661	5·050	4·781	3·240	4·749	6·647	3·210	4·380	3·302	5·607
29	Leather and leather products	5·910	5·473	4·130	3·770	5·122	5·697	4·578	3·417	3·003	4·145
30	Rubber products	5·551	2·826	2·346	1·280	3·499	5·221	2·597	2·192	1·950	3·033
31	Chemicals	6·443	3·568	5·135	3·636	3·910	6·549	5·670	4·819	4·408	4·970
33	Non-metallic mineral products	7·900	4·354	5·308	3·697	5·399	6·444	6·309	4·193	3·420	4·364
34	Basic metals	5·182	2·335	2·674	1·031	2·183	3·945	2·340	1·803	2·812	0·916
35	Metal products	8·124	5·728	5·711	3·547	6·581	6·796	3·846	4·539	4·171	5·574
36	Machinery except electrical	7·144	4·742	4·586	3·443	4·264	6·067	3·824	3·739	3·586	5·049
37	Electrical machinery and appliances	6·669	3·914	4·401	3·699	5·439	5·832	3·583	3·667	3·066	5·400
38	Transportation equipment	7·579	3·948	4·814	4·860	6·698	6·680	5·030	4·340	4·154	6·894

TABLE II

AVERAGE RANK ORDERING OF INDUSTRIAL CONCENTRATION IN LATIN AMERICA
(lower numbers correspond to the more concentrated industries)

ISIC Code	*Type of industry*	*Rank*
20	Food manufacturing	17
21	Beverages	5
22	Tobacco	1
23	Textiles	9
24	Clothing and footwear	18
25	Wood and wood products	13
26	Furniture and fixtures	15
27	Paper and paper products	4
28	Printing and publishing	10
29	Leather and leather products	6
30	Rubber products	3
31	Chemicals	11
33	Non-metallic mineral products	12
34	Basic metals	2
35	Metal products	16
36	Machinery except electrical	8
37	Electrical machinery and appliances	7
38	Transportation equipment	14
Concordance coefficient		0·733
Number of countries in sample		10

done on Table III. The concordance coefficient of this ranking is 0·617 which is significant at 1%.

In Table III it is observed that Costa Rica and Uruguay are the countries with the highest levels of concentration, while Argentina and Mexico are the countries with the lowest levels of concentration. The overall conclusion would be what seems to be an obvious one: smaller countries have higher levels of concentration while larger countries have smaller levels of concentration. This proposition can be justified by stating that in Latin America, since manufactured exports have had a small importance in the 60s, the size

TABLE III

AVERAGE RANK ORDERING OF LATIN AMERICAN COUNTRIES WITH RESPECT TO INDUSTRIAL CONCENTRATION
(lower numbers imply higher levels of concentration)

Country	*Rank*
Argentina	10
Chile	6
Colombia	5
Costa Rica	1
Ecuador	7
Mexico	9
Paraguay	4
Peru	3
Uruguay	2
Venezuela	8
Concordance coefficient	0·617
Number of industries in sample	18

of the domestic market becomes the main factor in the level of concentration of the manufacturing industries.[6]

CONCLUSIONS

1. There exists a similar pattern of industrial concentration among Latin American countries, i.e. industries having high (low) concentration levels in one country coincide with those having high (low) concentration levels in another country.

The general similarity pattern of concentration suggests that, independent of the degree of development, politics, and the like, there seem to be common economic forces contributing to the presence of, or absence of, market dominance, a finding made elsewhere (Caves [1]). Furthermore, since different countries have, over time, enforced antitrust legislation to varying degrees, the effectiveness of such antitrust legislation to alter existing patterns of concentration has been questioned (Stigler [8] and Pryor [6]). The concentration level of a particular industry is of primary importance in implementing antitrust policy. However, countries may have similar patterns of industrial concentration, but at different levels. This is precisely the other finding of this study.

2. Latin American countries that have smaller (larger) market sizes systematically show higher (lower) levels of industrial concentration.

CIEPLAN—CHILE AND NATIONAL BUREAU OF ECONOMIC RESEARCH
SANTIAGO

APPENDIX

A. Data Sources

Argentina: Census of Manufactures of Year 1963: *Censo Nacional Económico, Industria Manufacturera, Resultados Generales*. Instituto Nacional de Estadísticas y Censos, Buenos Aires, Argentina. The following breakdown of establishment class size is published: 1–10, 11–25, 26–50, 51–100, 101–300, 301–500, 501–1000, 1001–3000, and 3001 and more persons employed.

Chile: Census of Manufactures of Year 1967: *IV Censo Nacional de Manufacturas*. Instituto Nacional de Estadísticas, Santiago, Chile. The following breakdown of establishment class size is published: 5–9, 10–19, 20–49, 50–99, 100–199, 200–499, 500–999, and 1000 and more persons employed.

Colombia: Census of Manufactures of Year 1968: *La Industria Manufacturera en 1968*, Departamento Administrativo Nacional de Estadísticas, Bogotá, Colombia. The following breakdown of establishment class size is published: 1–4, 5–9, 10–14, 15–19, 20–24, 25–49, 50–74, 75–99, 100–199, and 200 and more persons employed.

[6] However, as Phlips [5] has pointed out, the comparison of concentration levels across countries of different sizes is probably meaningless. The size of the market has an important influence on the level of concentration. In order to state the proposition that one country has a higher level of concentration than another, the countries should be put on the same market size basis.

Costa Rica: Census of Manufactures of Year 1964: *III Censo de Industrias Manufactureras, 1964*, Dirección General de Estadísticas de Censos, San José, Costa Rica. The following breakdown of establishment class size is published: 1–4, 5–9, 10–19, 20–49, 50–59, 60–69, and 70 and more persons employed.

Ecuador: Census of Manufactures of Year 1965: *Segundo Censo de Manufacturas y Minería, 1965*, Junta Nacional de Planificación y Coordinación, Quito, Ecuador. The following breakdown of establishment class size is published: 1–4, 5–9, 10–14, 15–19, 20–49, 50–99, and 100 and more persons employed.

Mexico: Census of Manufactures of Year 1966: *VIII Censo Industrial, 1966*, Dirección General de Estadística, Mexico D.F., Mexico. The following breakdown of establishment class size is published. 1–5, 6–15, 16–25, 26–50, 51–75, 76–100, 101–250, 251–500, and 501 and more persons employed.

Paraguay: Census of Manufactures of Year 1963: *Censo Industrial 1963*, Dirección de Estadísticas y Censos, Asunción, Paraguay. The following breakdown of establishment class size is published: 1–4, 5–9, 10–19, 20–49, 50–99, and 100 and more persons employed.

Perú: Census of Manufactures of Year 1968: *Censo de Manufacturas, 1968*, Dirección Nacional de Estadísticas y Censos, Lima, Perú. The following breakdown of establishment class size is published: 10–14, 15–19, 20–49, 50–99, 100–199, 200–499, and 500 and more persons employed.

Uruguay: Census of Manufactures of Year 1968: *Censo Económico Nacional. Industria Manufacturera*. Dirección General de Estadísticas y Censos, Montevideo Uruguay. The following breakdown of establishment class size is published: 1–9, 10–19, 20–49, 50–99, and 100 and more persons employed.

Venezuela: Census of Manufactures of Year 1963: *III Censo Económico: Manufactura*, Dirección General de Estadísticas y Censos Nacionales, Caracas, Venezuela. The following breakdown of establishment class size is published: 1–4, 5–9, 10–49, 50–99, and 100 and more persons employed.

B. Computation Procedure of the Entropy Indexes

Let T_j be the number of people employed by establishment of class size j; A_k is the total number of people employed in industry k, and m is the number of establishment class sizes. Then x_j the relative share of class j in industry k is:

$$x_j = \frac{T_j}{A_k} \tag{1}$$

where

$$\sum_{j=1}^{m} x_j = 1, \quad \text{and } x_j \geq 0.$$

The entropy of industry k is given by:

$$E_k = -\sum_{j=1}^{m} x_j \log x_j + \sum_{j=1}^{m} x_j E_j. \tag{2}$$

The first term of (2) measures the between classes entropy, and the second term measures the within classes entropy. In order to compute expression (2) it is necessary to compute previously the term E_j. This term E_j is computed assuming the extreme values that the entropy within the establishment class size can reach.

Let s_j be the number of establishments of class j. The maximum entropy within a class is reached when all establishments are equal. Then, the maximum entropy $E_j^{\dagger}$ for each class is given by:

$$E_j^{\dagger} = \log s_j \qquad j = 1, 2, \ldots m. \tag{3}$$

Let L_j and U_j be the lower and upper limits of a bounded class j. The minimum entropy within a class is reached when u_j establishment are located in U_j and the rest of the establishments are located in L_j; this will produce the maximum dispersion. u_j is computed by expressión (4).

$$(4) \qquad u_j = \frac{T_j - s_j L_j}{U_j - L_j}.$$

Then, for each of the $m-1$ bounded class sizes, the minimum entropy $E_{\bar{j}}$ is given by expression (5):

$$(5) \qquad E_{\bar{j}} = -u_j \frac{U_j}{T_j} \log \frac{U_j}{T_j} - (s_j - u_j) \frac{L_j}{T_j} \log \frac{L_j}{T_j} \qquad j = 1, 2, \ldots m-1.$$

The minimum entropy in the last unbounded class m is reached when $(s_m - 1)$ establishments are located in the lower bound L_m, and the remaining establishment employs the rest of the persons of the class.

$$(6) \qquad E_{\bar{m}} = -(s_m - 1) \frac{L_m}{T_m} \log \frac{L_m}{T_m} - \frac{T_m - (s_m - 1)L_m}{T_m} \log \frac{T_m - (s_m - 1)L_m}{T_m}.$$

The introduction of (3), (5) and (6) in expression (2) provides a maximum and minimum value of entropy for industry k. The arithmetic average value of these two extreme situations is the entropy concentration index used in this study.

REFERENCES

[1] Caves, R., *American Industry: Structure, Conduct, Performance* (Prentice-Hall, New Jersey, 1972).

[2] Horowitz, I., 'Employment Concentration in the Common Market: An Entropy Approach', *Journal of The Royal Statistical Society*, Series A (General), **133** (3) (August 1970), pp. 463–79.

[3] Meller, P. and Swinburn, C., '5000 Indicadores de Concentración Industrial: Chile, 1967', *Documentos de Trabajo No. 19* (Universidad Católica de Chile, Diciembre 1973).

[4] Meller, P., Léniz, S. and Swinburn, C., 'Comparaciones Internacionales de Concentración Industrial en América Latina', *Ensayos ECIEL*, No. 3, pp. 27–66 (Rio de Janeiro, Agosto, 1976).

[5] Phlips, L., *Effects of Industrial Concentration: A Cross-section Analysis for the Common Market* (North-Holland, Amsterdam, 1971).

[6] Pryor, F. L., 'An International Comparison of Concentration Ratios', *Review of Economics and Statistics*, **54** (May 1972), pp. 130–40.

[7] Siegel, S., *Nonparametric Statistics for the Behavioral Sciences* (McGraw-Hill, New York, 1956).

[8] Stigler, G., 'The Economic Effects of the Antitrust Laws', *Journal of Law and Economics*, **IX** (October 1966), pp. 225–58.

[9] Theil, H., *Economics and Information Theory* (North-Holland, Amsterdam, 1967).

THE JOURNAL OF INDUSTRIAL ECONOMICS
Volume XXVII September 1978 No. 1

INDUSTRY INEFFICIENCY UNDER REGULATORY SURVEILLANCE

MICHAEL W. PUSTAY*

INTEREST in the effects of regulation on the efficiency of the firm has enjoyed a renaissance since the publication of Averch and Johnson's [2] analysis of this problem in 1962. However, Averch and Johnson's constrained profit-maximization paradigm diverts attention from more general means by which regulation may unfavorably affect the efficiency performance of firms. In particular, the presence of regulation may allow firms wittingly or unwittingly to tolerate substantial x-inefficiency in their operations.[1] Since Peacock and Rowley [13] have shown that the *raison d'être* of regulation is threatened if such inefficiency offsets the allocative gains attributable to regulation, assessing the extent of x-inefficiency in regulated industries is of major policy importance.

It has long been argued that inefficient behavior is not viable in competitive markets. Market forces constrain firms in competitive markets to act efficiently as a necessary condition for survival.[2] Even in non-competitive markets other forces exist to pressure managements to act efficiently—potential entry of new firms, the threat of stockholder revolts, the possibility of corporate takeovers, etc. [9].

However, one well-recognized characteristic of regulation is that it oftentimes insulates firms from many of these forces external to the firm that pressure unregulated firms to act efficiently. Regulation protects existing suppliers from the threat of entry by new firms and incumbent managements from the machinations of acquisition-minded entrepreneurs. Moreover, the evolution of regulatory procedure in the United States has led regulators to enforce essentially cost-plus pricing for regulated firms, which causes well-known problems with regard to the firms' incentives to produce efficiently.[3] Regulators do little monitoring of costs beyond assessing whether they were incurred by 'honest, efficient, and economical management'—a phrase

* Discussions with John Barron and Nancy Burstein were most helpful in the development of this paper. The insightful comments of an anonymous referee are also gratefully acknowledged. Remaining errors are of course the sole responsibility of the author.

[1] We will follow Leibenstein's [11] use of the term (x)-efficiency. In particular, we define efficiency to entail operations on, rather than above, the firm's cost curves.

[2] For various aspects of the debate, see Alchian [1], Machlup [12] and Winter [15].

[3] Firm-by-firm rate of return regulation when firms possess perfect knowledge provides different incentives to firms to produce efficiently than what a true cost-plus contract would produce. However, as knowledge is not perfect in the real world, we believe that firm-by-firm rate of return regulation can be meaningfully classified as cost-plus in nature, especially in comparison to the CAB's industry-wide regulation.

which has more legal than economic significance. It would appear then that x-inefficiency could exist in regulated markets.

The US domestic trunk airlines serve as particularly good subjects for examining the effects of regulation on firm efficiency. This is so for two reasons. First, after one has accounted for differences in the route structures possessed by the carriers, the inputs used and the outputs produced by the trunk airlines are essentially homogeneous. This facilitates efficiency comparisons among the carriers. Second, the US Civil Aeronautics Board (CAB, the Board) establishes market prices and an industry-wide rate of return based upon industry-wide average costs. This mode of regulation provides regulated airlines with the same incentives to maximize profits and to act efficiently as unregulated firms face, since from an individual airline's perspective the regulatory 'contract' is no longer cost-plus in nature. Any cost reductions produced by a carrier's management will be reflected dollar for dollar in increased profits except to the trivial extent that such cost reductions lower industry average costs.

While existing CAB regulation grants the trunk airlines the same carrot to produce efficiently as that presented unregulated firms, it insulates if not spares the trunk airlines from the stick (threat of entry, bankruptcy, takeover) that disciplines unregulated firms to produce efficiently. This allows one to assess the importance of the two potential causes of x-inefficiency, inadequate internal incentives and inadequate external pressures.[4] If little x-inefficiency were observed among the trunk airlines, one could conclude that properly structured internal incentives are sufficient to ensure x-efficiency regardless of the extent of external pressures. If much x-inefficiency were observed among these airlines, then it would appear that properly structured internal incentives are insufficient to guarantee x-efficiency. But if the latter were observed, the role of external pressures in promoting x-efficiency would be elevated in importance. As regulation *per se* generally weakens these external pressures faced by firms, one would conclude that x-inefficiency could be a major problem in the regulated sector if much x-inefficiency were observed among the trunk airlines.[5]

The extent of x-inefficiency in the trunk airline industry from 1965 to 1974 will be examined in the remainder of this paper. In section I indices of efficiency are developed for the domestic trunk airlines for these years. The

[4] The distinction between these two factors is useful though perhaps artificial. The desire to profit maximize creates an incentive within (internal to) the firm to produce efficiently. The threat of entry, bankruptcy, or takeover imposes an external constraint on the firm's efficiency performance if the firm wishes to survive. Internal incentives should be sufficient to ensure efficiency given the naive textbook model of the firm; external pressures are needed to ensure efficiency if firms' decisions are reached by 'muddling through' processes or by Friedman's 'habitual reaction, random chance, or whatnot' [7, p. 22].

[5] For example, suppose that the 'innovating remnant' [16] is important in promoting x-efficiency among firms in an industry. If regulation of an industry reduces the population of firms from which this innovating remnant can be drawn, x-inefficiency might be expected to be of greater importance or of longer duration in regulated industries than in unregulated industries.

validity of these indices is tested in section II. Section III explores whether there are systematic and sustained differences in the measured efficiency performances of the trunk airlines. Our conclusions are offered in section IV.

I. MEASUREMENT OF AIRLINE EFFICIENCY

Two basic approaches have been used to measure firm efficiency in the airline industry. The first entails cross-sectionally regressing carrier costs against relevant independent variables. The estimated regression line is then judged to provide 'expected' costs for airline operations. Substituting the values of the independent variables for a carrier into the fitted regression equation yields the expected costs of that carrier. The deviation of each carrier's actual costs from its expected costs is labelled the measure of the carrier's efficiency performance. Gordon [8] used this approach to estimate the efficiency of the trunk carriers in the third quarter of 1961. Straszheim [14] conducted a similar analysis for 32 international airlines using 1962 data. However, measurement over a period as short as a quarter or year may yield misleading measures of true carrier efficiency owing to the potential presence of transitory factors that might affect observed costs.

Douglas and Miller's study [5] of domestic trunk efficiency over a nine-year time span avoided this problem. They regressed costs per ton-mile for the 11 trunk carriers for the years 1962–70 against available ton-miles, average stage length, market density, and a set of yearly time dummies. However, their approach suffers from a peculiarity in the data which becomes apparent when yearly carrier costs per ton-mile are graphed against yearly available ton-miles and when yearly carrier costs per ton-mile are graphed against yearly average stage length. When this is done, the graphed values of the independent variables for most of the carriers occupy a narrow range of the abscissa. However, the values of the independent variables for American, TWA, and United generally are substantially larger than those of the remaining carriers and are distinctly separated from the observations for remaining carriers. Now we shall find below that there is reason to believe that these three carriers are less efficient than the other trunk carriers. But if these three carriers perform less efficiently than the remaining carriers, the fitted regression line will be biased towards overestimating the three carriers' true expected costs because of this data alignment. The efficiency performance of these three carriers will then also be overestimated. Because of this possible bias, the regression approach is not suitable for our purposes.

The second approach is to compare each airline's costs with the costs that the average carrier in the industry would incur if the average carrier in the industry flew the same type of routes as the airline in question. This is the methodology adopted by Boske [3] to study efficiency among the trunk airlines in 1968. This approach is used in this paper to measure airline efficiency performance from 1965 to 1974.[6]

To measure efficiency, airline costs are first divided into three categories—flight costs, capital costs, and passenger costs. Costs in the three categories are assumed to be a function of aircraft block hours and fleet mix, aircraft daily utilization and fleet mix, and revenue passenger miles, respectively. An industry average cost is estimated for each cost category for each year. Efficiency indices for each cost category for each carrier for each year are then developed by comparing each carrier's performance in each cost category relative to the industry average for that year. Each carrier's overall efficiency for the year is then measured by weighting its indices for each cost category by the importance of the cost category in airline operations.

Flight Costs

Flight costs equal the sum of expenditures for flying operations (less rentals), direct maintenance, and insurance as defined in the CAB's accounting system. CAB-sponsored costing studies suggest that for each plane type these costs are a linear homogeneous function of aircraft block hours—i.e.

(1) $$\text{Cost} = \alpha \text{ block hours.}$$ [7]

Fortunately, α is similar for numerous aircraft types. Accordingly, rather than calculate an industry average cost for each aircraft type, we can calculate an industry average cost for groups of aircraft with similar cost characteristics. Following CAB methodology, aircraft were divided into five groups: (1) twin-engined jet and four-engined propeller aircraft, (2) three-engined narrow-bodied jet aircraft, (3) four-engined narrow-bodied jet aircraft, (4) four-engined wide-bodied aircraft, and (5) three-engined wide-bodied aircraft. Note this classification scheme concomitantly groups aircraft with similar 'missions'—respectively, provision of short-haul, medium-haul, and long-haul services for the first three groups and heavy density long-haul services for the last two groups.[8]

Determination of the flight efficiency index for each aircraft in each carrier's fleet is straightforward. Yearly industry average costs per block hour for each of the five aircraft groups are calculated. Division of the appropriate industry aircraft group average by the *i*th carrier's costs per

[6] To use this approach, we must assume that the industry is typified by a constant returns to scale production function—an assumption consistent with empirical findings of Eads *et al.* [6] and Straszheim [14]—and that the inputs used by carriers and the outputs produced by carriers are homogeneous. (As will become apparent, the level of homogeneity assumed is at the aircraft group level—e.g. the inputs used and the output produced are assumed equal for all three-hour flights using four-engined narrow-bodied jets.)

[7] See CAB Docket 21886-9, Exhibits BC-2100 to BC-4023 (especially Exhibit BC-2999A), and Docket 21866-7, Exhibit 3999.

[8] Creating two groups for aircraft whose mission is the performance of heavy density long-haul service is necessary because of the widely divergent costs per block hour of 747s relative to L-1011s and DC-10s.

block hour for the mth aircraft in its fleet yields the ith carrier's flight efficiency index for its mth aircraft. Summing the efficiency indices developed for the $(1, \ldots, k)$ aircraft in the ith carrier's fleet weighted by the importance of the aircraft in the ith carrier's operations yields the ith carrier's flight efficiency index (E_f) for the year. The flight efficiency index for the ith carrier in a given year is thus represented by

$$E_f^i = \frac{\sum_{m=1}^{k} \bar{C}_m^i \times H_m^i}{\sum_{m=1}^{k} C_m^i \times H_m^i} \qquad (2)$$

where C_m^i is the flight costs per block hour incurred by the ith carrier in a given year utilizing the mth aircraft in its fleet,

$\bar{C}_m^i$ is the industry average flight cost per block hour in a given year for the aircraft group of which the mth aircraft in the ith carrier's fleet is a member, and

H_m^i is the number of block hours produced by the mth aircraft in the ith carrier's fleet in a given year.

The calculated values of E_f^i are reported in Table I. Note that values of E_f greater than one represent performances better than the industry average.

The benefit of this approach is that it explicitly accounts for the fact that different groups of aircraft are designed for different missions and have different cost characteristics. Thus the index captures more than how efficiently a carrier uses aircraft m; the index measures how efficiently the carrier has provided the mission aircraft m was designed to attain.[9] The index also explicitly accounts for differences among the carrier's unit flight costs occurring solely because of differences in their route structures, at least to the extent that a carrier's choice of aircraft reflects its route structure.[10]

Capital Costs

The capital efficiency index measures how efficiently each carrier uses its capital stock. As 85–90% of the capital employed by airlines is in the form of aircraft, average daily utilization of aircraft is used to capture this facet of efficiency. Average daily utilization of aircraft also differs among the five aircraft groups, primarily because the ratio of ground time to flight time decreases as stage length increases. To adjust for this factor, separate industry average daily utilization statistics for each year for each of the five aircraft groups are developed. Each carrier's utilization of each of its $(1, \ldots, k)$

[9] This approach captures, for example, the impact of poor equipment selection on carrier performance.

[10] Some of the variations in this index, the capital efficiency index, and the passenger efficiency index may be due to route structure differences among the carriers not captured by the carriers' choice of their aircraft fleets. See the Appendix for a detailed discussion of this problem.

TABLE I

FLIGHT EFFICIENCY INDICES DOMESTIC TRUNK CARRIERS, 1965–74

	1965	1966	1967	1968	1969	1970	1971	1972	1973	1974
American	0·907	0·951	0·967	0·960	1·003	1·003	0·968	0·983	0·961	1·032
Eastern	0·942	0·954	0·980	0·955	0·962	0·998	0·947	0·935	0·927	0·939
TWA	0·972	0·988	0·928	0·965	0·951	0·945	1·016	1·022	0·979	0·941
United	1·003	0·956	0·976	0·971	0·968	0·964	0·984	0·982	1·002	0·981
Braniff	1·148	1·120	1·062	1·048	1·100	1·124	1·079	1·087	1·111	1·241
Continental[c]	1·178	1·214	0·956	1·004	0·984	0·997	0·982	0·983	0·938	1·014
Delta	1·085	1·041	1·044	1·048	1·065	1·078	1·048	1·038	1·054	0·998
National	1·019	1·057	1·011	1·076	1·021	0·902[a]	1·026	0·986	0·992	1·010[a]
Northeast[b]	1·104	1·120	1·005	1·068	0·914	1·006	0·923	0·934	—	—
Northwest	1·247	1·259	1·306	1·233	1·213	1·147[a]	1·164	1·137[a]	1·133	1·086
Western	1·060	1·054	1·150	1·090	1·020	1·074	0·994	1·044	1·090	0·998

[a] Carrier struck for longer than 90 days in the year.

[b] Northeast merged with Delta in 1972.

[c] Continental's Boeing 707 operations were excluded from the calculation of its flight efficiency index and of the industry's average cost per block hour for four-engined jet operations from 1965 to 1969 because of the aircraft's use in Continental's extensive transpacific charter operations.

Sources of cost and output data: US Civil Aeronautics Board, *Aircraft Operating Cost and Performance Report* and *Handbook of Airline Statistics*, various issues.

aircraft in a given year is then compared to the appropriate industry average daily utilization statistic. The indices developed for the aircraft in the carrier's fleet are then aggregated using market values as weights to construct the yearly capital efficiency index for the carrier. The capital efficiency index (E_c) of the ith carrier is

$$E_c^i = \frac{\sum_{m=1}^{k} \text{ADU}_m^i \text{MV}_m^i}{\sum_{m=1}^{k} \overline{\text{ADU}}_m \text{MV}_m^i} \tag{3}$$

where MV_m^i equals the market value of the mth aircraft in the ith carrier's fleet,

ADU_m^i equals the ith carrier's average daily utilization[11] of its mth aircraft in a given year, and

$\overline{\text{ADU}}_m$ equals the industry average daily utilization in a given year of aircraft in the aircraft group of which the mth aircraft is a member.

These indices are reported in Table II. Note that values of E_c greater than one represent performances better than the industry average.

Passenger Costs

The passenger efficiency index (E_p) is constructed by comparing general services and administration expenses (GSA) per revenue passenger mile (RPM) for the ith firm to the industry average general services and administration expenses per revenue passenger mile for the year. The former can be found by dividing the ith carrier's domestic general services and administration expenses by the ith carrier's domestic revenue passenger miles. The latter term is found by first summing the individual carrier statistics over all (1, . . ., n) domestic trunk carriers and then performing the division. The ratio of the latter term to the former yields E_p for the ith carrier:

$$E_p^i = \frac{\dfrac{\sum_{j=1}^{n} \text{GSA}^j}{\sum_{j=1}^{n} \text{RPM}^j}}{\dfrac{\text{GSA}^i}{\text{RPM}^i}} \tag{4}$$

The calculated values of E_p are reported in Table III. Note that values of E_p^i greater than one represent performances better than the industry average.

[11] For reasons explained in the Appendix, average daily utilization of an aircraft has been defined as the sum of the block hours per day performed by the aircraft plus the product of the number of departures per day performed by the aircraft and 30 minutes.

Table II

CAPITAL EFFICIENCY INDICES DOMESTIC TRUNK CARRIERS, 1965–74

	1965	1966	1967	1968	1969	1970	1971	1972	1973	1974
American	0·899	0·993	0·968	0·963	0·982	1·035	1·032	0·996	0·966	0·959
Eastern	1·086	0·988	1·019	0·959	0·999	1·083	1·079	1·118	1·055	1·034
TWA	0·951	1·031	0·990	0·990	0·986	0·998	0·957	0·964	0·919	0·898
United	1·022	0·920	0·949	0·959	0·927	0·946	0·893	0·932	0·906	0·925
Braniff	1·120	1·391	1·162	1·109	1·144	1·172	1·202	1·146	1·155	1·225
Continental[c]	1·351	1·645	1·422	1·186	1·209	1·161	1·179	1·212	1·165	1·280
Delta	1·126	1·232	1·215	1·242	1·234	1·318	1·274	1·244	1·201	1·202
National	1·178	1·114	1·159	1·122	1·139	0·906[a]	1·117	1·094	1·141	0·855[a]
Northeast[b]	0·931	1·016	0·967	1·063	0·981	1·047	0·964	0·987	—	—
Northwest	1·163	1·017	1·047	1·071	1·033	0·590[a]	0·836	0·698[a]	0·964	1·023
Western	0·994	1·087	1·084	1·042	0·954	1·009	1·048	1·053	1·034	1·071

[a] Carrier struck for longer than 90 days in the year.
[b] Northeast merged with Delta in 1972.
[c] Continental's Boeing 707 operations were excluded from the calculation of its capital efficiency index and of the industry's average daily utilization of four-engined jet aircraft from 1965 to 1969 because of the aircraft's use in Continental's extensive transpacific charter operations.

Sources of cost and output data: US Civil Aeronautics Board, *Aircraft Operating Cost and Performance Report* and *Handbook of Airline Statistics*, various issues.

TABLE III

PASSENGER EFFICIENCY INDICES DOMESTIC TRUNK CARRIERS, 1965–74

	1965	1966	1967	1968	1969	1970	1971	1972	1973	1974
American	0·944	0·991	0·924	0·954	0·931	0·915	0·930	0·926	0·920	0·895
Eastern	0·905	0·833	0·881	0·849	0·897	0·960	0·927	0·896	0·853	0·875
TWA	0·984	0·917	0·970	0·941	0·975	0·917	0·976	1·000	0·953	0·982
United	0·961	0·931	0·985	1·014	1·036	1·074	1·058	1·086	1·140	1·123
Braniff	0·896	0·904	0·783	0·855	0·889	0·925	0·942	0·934	0·937	0·880
Continental[c]	1·443	1·709	1·969	1·661	1·549	1·356	1·225	1·147	1·081	1·023
Delta	1·107	1·189	1·066	1·082	1·075	1·064	1·016	1·015	0·972	1·020
National	1·150	1·131	1·090	1·082	1·006	0·789[a]	0·960	1·017	1·003	0·879[a]
Northeast[b]	0·790	0·778	0·746	0·830	0·745	0·892	0·880	0·921	—	—
Northwest	1·296	1·316	1·296	1·289	1·222	1·111[a]	1·192	1·084[a]	1·235	1·293
Western	1·103	1·094	1·017	1·006	0·895	1·030	0·987	0·986	1·033	1·084

[a] Carrier struck for longer than 90 days in the year.

[b] Northeast merged with Delta in 1972.

[c] Continental's indices before 1970 are not strictly comparable to the indices of the other carriers because its extensive transpacific charter operations were included in the accounting data on which these figures were based.

Sources of cost and output data: US Civil Aeronautics Board, *Aircraft Operating Cost and Performance Report* and *Handbook of Airline Statistics*, various issues.

The Aggregate Efficiency Index

Each carrier's yearly aggregate efficiency index is then constructed by weighting the carrier's three component indices for the year by their relative importance in airline operations. The weights selected represent the average importance of the cost category for the industry over the period 1965–74.[12,13] The yearly aggregate efficiency indices calculated for the carriers are reported in Table IV.

Measurement of trunk airline efficiency in this manner has several major benefits. First, it avoids the peculiar data problem that plagues the regression approach. Second, it explicitly accounts for the important effects of route structure on carrier costs by recognizing the different cost characteristics of the different aircraft groups. Third, measured efficiency is independent of the load factor achieved by the airline: allocation of costs in the manner described above also divides airline expenditures into those costs that do vary and those costs that do not vary as the number of passengers carried on a flight increases, *ceteris paribus*.[14] Lastly, by comparing firm performance in each year to the industry performance in the year, industry-wide cyclical and secular trends are accounted for.

Concomitantly, this approach suffers from an arbitrariness in the selection of the cost categories and in the choice of the divisors and weights. The approach also assumes that the efficiency indices reflect only those differences in carrier costs due to efficiency differences. As noted in the Appendix, we are concerned that we may not have fully accounted for non-efficiency related cost differences among the carriers. In particular, the indices may reflect residual influences of congestion delay and route structure-related input price differences among the carriers. A more refined analysis would certainly wish to explore these potential problems. The aggregate efficiency index is of course an imperfect measure of true carrier efficiency as long as the index measures cost differences not related to efficiency differences in addition to true efficiency differences.[15]

[12] Capital costs were determined using the capital recovery factor technique. The before-tax opportunity cost of capital was assumed to be a 20% rate of return; depreciation was based upon the standards promulgated by the CAB in Regulation PS-45 (1971).

[13] Weighting the component indices by their importance in a given year as opposed to their importance over the ten-year period had little effect on the calculated values of the aggregate efficiency indices. Alternatively, one might argue that carrier-specific weights rather than industry-wide weights should be used: conceivably a carrier might reduce its total costs by increasing its costs relative to the industry average in one area while reducing its relative costs in another. However, an overall positive correlation existed among a carrier's flight efficiency, capital efficiency, and passenger efficiency indices in any given year. Moreover, when carrier-specific weights were utilized, the results reported in sections II and III were altered very little. Thus there appears to be little advantage to using carrier-specific weights rather than industry-wide weights.

[14] To the extent that the load factor attained by an airline is a function of carrier competition, rather than a measure of a carrier's efficiency performance, this feature can be deemed a benefit of this approach.

[15] The index could measure at least three other factors. The first is differences in the levels of competition faced by carriers. Differing levels of competition should be manifested primarily in the quantity of flights offered by the carriers, which should be reflected in the carriers' average load factors. Since a firm's load factor does not affect its measured efficiency per-

TABLE IV

AGGREGATE EFFICIENCY INDICES DOMESTIC TRUNK AIRLINES, 1965–74

	1965	1966	1967	1968	1969	1970	1971	1972	1973	1974
American	0·920	0·978	0·950	0·959	0·968	0·975	0·968	0·963	0·946	0·958
Eastern	0·963	0·913	0·950	0·913	0·945	1·004	0·972	0·965	0·928	0·936
TWA	0·972	0·970	0·960	0·961	0·969	0·947	0·985	0·999	0·954	0·947
United	0·991	0·937	0·973	0·986	0·986	1·004	0·992	1·012	1·034	1·025
Braniff	1·038	1·099	0·973	0·984	1·025	1·054	1·053	1·039	1·051	1·089
Continental[c]	1·329	1·523	1·486	1·318	1·271	1·185	1·130	1·107	1·053	1·084
Delta	1·104	1·149	1·095	1·110	1·111	1·132	1·091	1·080	1·057	1·058
National	1·112	1·102	1·080	1·090	1·044	0·857[a]	1·022	1·026	1·033	0·918[a]
Northeast[b]	0·933	0·954	0·890	0·969	0·861	0·970	0·916	0·942	—	—
Northwest	1·246	1·222	1·237	1·216	1·172	0·994[a]	1·094	1·006[a]	1·133	1·155
Western	1·061	1·078	1·079	1·044	0·953	1·039	1·005	1·022	1·053	1·051

[a] Carrier struck for longer than 90 days in the year.
[b] Northeast merged with Delta in 1972.
[c] Continental's indices before 1970 are not strictly comparable to the indices of the other carriers because of its extensive transpacific charter operations from 1965 to 1969.

N.B. Aggregate Efficiency Index $= 0{\cdot}3430\, E_f + 0{\cdot}2483\, E_c + 0{\cdot}4087\, E_p$.

Sources of cost and output data: US Civil Aeronautics Board, *Aircraft Operating Cost and Performance Report* and *Handbook of Airline Statistics*, various issues.

II. TESTING THE EFFICIENCY MEASURES

We would like to assess the validity of the efficiency index. Such an assessment can be made using the well-known analysis of Douglas and Miller [5], who have argued and demonstrated that non-price competition among carriers will cause airlines to earn only normal profits in airline markets regardless of the initial relationships between prices and costs in those markets.

Now by definition profit (π) equals revenue (R) minus cost (C):

$$\pi = R - C. \tag{5}$$

We divide (5) by some measure of output (Q)—e.g. passenger enplanements or revenue passenger miles—to deflate for size effects, thus obtaining

$$\frac{\pi}{Q} = \frac{R}{Q} - \frac{C}{Q}. \tag{6}$$

Douglas and Miller's analysis suggests that there should be no correlation between variables which define a carrier's route structure and π/Q. If Douglas and Miller are correct, rates of return earned by carriers will differ from the fair rate of return only because of differences in the efficiency performances of the carriers. Therefore, if our aggregate efficiency index is a valid measure of efficiency, it should be positively correlated with π/Q, *ceteris paribus*.

We have tested the ability of the aggregate efficiency index and various measures of route structure to explain differences in the profits per unit of output earned by the carriers. Consistent with the Douglas–Miller analysis, none of the route structure variables tested—average stage length, average passenger trip length, average load factor, degree of competition faced, average market density—had a significant rank correlation or product moment correlation with π/Q in more than four of the ten years. However, as Table V indicates, the rank correlation between a carrier's yearly aggregate efficiency index and its profits per unit of output was positive and significant for nine of the ten years.[16] While not shown, the product moment correlation

formance, this form of competition will not distort the firm's efficiency index. Yet the greater the competition a carrier faces, the more likely it may be forced to adjust the timing of its flights so as better to meet the schedule-related demands of passengers in its markets, thus raising its costs. However, as discussed below, measures of the degree of competition faced by a carrier did not explain differences in the carriers' efficiency performances. Second, if the average total cost curve is U-shaped, one may simply be observing those firms operating on the rising portion of the curve paying the penalty for their large size. Existing empirical work ([6], [14]) indicates this objection is not empirically important, however. A third alternative is that certain carriers may be providing a higher quality of service than the industry norm. If travelers value this higher quality service at a level commensurate with the cost of providing the service, then the carrier should be blessed with more traffic and higher profits. But this too does not appear to be empirically important given the results reported in section II.

[16] The year for which the relationship was not significant was 1973. In 1973 the indices of Braniff, Continental, Delta, and Western and of United and National were nearly identical. It is not surprising then that the rank correlation between π/Q and the aggregate efficiency index was low for 1973. However, the product moment correlation between these two variables was significantly positive in 1973, as was the coefficient of the aggregate efficiency index when π/Q was regressed against efficiency.

between π/Q and the aggregate efficiency index was positive and significant for each of the ten years except 1972. In addition, when π/Q was regressed against the aggregate efficiency index and the route structure variables, the coefficient of the aggregate efficiency index was positive and significant for each of the ten years while the coefficients of the route structure variables were generally insignificant.

It is conceivable that this strong correlation between π/Q and measured efficiency might result from some underlying correlation among π/Q, carrier revenue, route structure, and the efficiency index that we had not considered. For example—in contradiction to the Douglas–Miller analysis—suppose carriers who fly in smaller, shorter-haul markets are able to charge higher prices and to provide less costly, lower quality service to their customers than other airlines, *ceteris paribus*. We would then observe a positive correlation between the efficiency index and π/Q which should be attributed to these route structure-related revenue and cost differences rather than to efficiency differences. However, our attempts to find such a relationship among π/Q, route structure, and the aggregate efficiency index using partial correlation methods and regression methods were unsuccessful. The significant positive correlation between π/Q and the aggregate efficiency index is apparently not attributable to the two variables' mutual correlation with some third, route structure-related variable.

TABLE V

RANK CORRELATION (MEASURED BY KENDALL'S TAU) BETWEEN PROFITS PER PASSENGER ENPLANEMENT AND THE AGGREGATE EFFICIENCY INDEX AND BETWEEN PROFITS PER REVENUE PASSENGER MILE AND THE AGGREGATE EFFICIENCY INDEX, 1965–74

	Profits per passenger enplanement	*Profits per revenue passenger mile*
1965	0·60**	0·71**
1966	0·75**	0·71**
1967	0·75**	0·64**
1968	0·56**	0·53**
1969	0·66**	0·60**
1970	0·75**	0·71**
1971	0·45*	0·38*
1972	0·53*	0·49*
1973	0·33	0·27
1974	0·64**	0·60**

** Significant at 0·01 level.
* Significant at 0·05 level.

N.B. Profits defined to be operating profits exclusive of mutual aid payments and receipts plus one half of aircraft rental payments. (One half of aircraft rental payments are added back in order to make the treatment of depreciation and interest expenses for leased aircraft similar to that for non-leased aircraft in calculating operating profits. We assume that depreciation accounts for half of the total aircraft rental payments.)

These findings are consistent with the statement that the aggregate efficiency index is an accurate measure of true efficiency. These findings do not prove that the aggregate efficiency index is an accurate measure of efficiency, however, given the problems discussed at the end of section I. Nonetheless, we are encouraged by these results. The approach developed in section I for measuring efficiency appears to be fruitful: moreover, further refinements in the methodology would allow one to separate more accurately those cost differences among the trunk airlines due to efficiency differences and those cost differences attributable to non-efficiency factors. We conclude that the aggregate efficiency index is a useful though imperfect measure of carrier efficiency.

III. ANALYSIS OF AIRLINE EFFICIENCY

Suppose the deviations of the measured efficiency performances of the carriers from the average industry efficiency performance were simply random. This would suggest that the measured efficiency performances of each of the carriers were similar over time. Any measured deviations could then be attributable to factors like the introduction of a new aircraft type into a carrier's fleet or the phase of the maintenance cycle faced by an airline. Such temporary or cyclical phenomena would be of little interest for our purposes.

However, a significant relationship exists between a firm's measured efficiency performance in one year and its performance in the next year, as Table VI reports.[17] No other variable tested—which included average stage length, average passenger trip length, average load factor, degree of competition faced, average market density, and carrier size (all entered in a variety of different forms in different runs: linearly, lagged, squared, and transformed into natural logarithms)—entered significantly into more than two of the nine yearly regression equations. Though not reported, pooling of data across the ten years yielded a similar relationship between carrier efficiency in year i and carrier efficiency in year $i-1$.

[17] It is interesting to note that the most efficient airlines are those which succeeded in overcoming the greatest external pressures. If we consider the early 1950s, the period in the industry's history when the trunk carriers had just been removed from federal subsidy, we note that the Big Four—American, Eastern, TWA and United—were the major beneficiaries of CAB cross-subsidy programs; the remaining carriers were 'losers' in these programs (see Caves [4, pp. 200–1, 213]). It is true that over time the CAB reduced the inequities created by these cross-subsidy programs by altering the fare structure and by favoring the non-Big Four carriers in the awarding of new routes. But immediately after the trunks went off subsidy, great inequities were present. In order to survive these initially hard times, the non-Big Four were under greater pressure than the Big Four to squeeze the maximum output out of their inputs. Some of the non-Big Four were successful; they survived. Others were not successful; they died (Capital in 1960; Northeast in 1972). We speculate that the management practices that allowed the successful non-Big Four carriers to survive these hard times may have carried over into the period for which we have measured efficiency performance. This may explain the better performance of the surviving non-Big Four carriers.

TABLE VI

RESULTS OF REGRESSING THE AGGREGATE EFFICIENCY INDEX OF A CARRIER IN YEAR i AGAINST ITS AGGREGATE EFFICIENCY INDEX IN YEAR $i-1$, 1966–74

	Coefficient of lagged Aggregate Efficiency Index[a]	R^2
1966	1·26 (0·09)	0·96
1967	0·99 (0·07)	0·96
1968	0·70 (0·06)	0·93
1969	0·85 (0·12)	0·86
1970	0·50 (0·11)	0·88
1971	0·77 (0·17)	0·79
1972	0·80 (0·06)	0·95
1973	0·86 (0·24)	0·83
1974	1·14 (0·29)	0·75

[a] Dummy variables used to exclude observations on struck carriers.
N.B. Standard errors are in parentheses.

Another test of the relationships among the year-to-year efficiency performances of the carriers can be made using the coefficient of concordance [10, pp. 94–100]. This statistic measures the degree of agreement among the rank orderings of different arrays of variables. The coefficient of concordance of the ten rank orderings of the carriers' yearly aggregate efficiency performances reflects a degree of agreement among the ten arrays significant at the 1% level.

Thus the carriers' efficiency performances as measured by the aggregate efficiency indices are not randomly distributed across the ten years. The efficiency indices reflect sustained and systematic differences in the measured efficiency performances of the trunk airlines: some carriers clearly appear to be more efficient than others.

Coupled with the results of section II, this suggests that it would be useful to estimate the cost savings which would have occurred if all carriers had efficiency performances equal to that of the carrier measured as the most efficient in the industry. To do this, we must operationalize the term most efficient. We select as the most efficient airline either the carrier with the highest mean efficiency index over the ten-year period or the carrier with the highest mean efficiency index in each year. Excluding Continental because of comparability problems with its pre-1970 results, Northwest is the most efficient airline over the ten-year span. Using the second criterion, Northwest would be selected as the most efficient airline in every year except 1970, 1971, and 1972, when Continental would be the choice.[18]

To estimate the cost savings that would have occurred if all carriers were as efficient as the most efficient airline using the first selection criterion, each carrier's efficiency index in a given year is first weighted by the carrier's share of the industry's economic costs in that year. These weighted carrier indices are then summed over all carriers. Dividing this sum by Northwest's efficiency index for the year yields a weighted measure of the extent of inefficient resource use in the industry. Using this approach, the ratio of the industry's weighted efficiency index to Northwest's efficiency index ranged from 0·80 (in 1967) to 1·01 (in 1970) with a mean of 0·88 for the ten years.[19] Using the second criterion (i.e. substituting Continental for Northwest in 1970–72) the ratio of the industry's weighted efficiency index to the index of the most efficient carrier ranged from 0·80 (in 1967) to 0·91 (in 1972) with a mean of 0·85.

Two caveats should be offered. First, use of the most efficient carrier over the ten-year span or for each year as the criterion for measuring efficiency yields a relative measure of efficiency, not an absolute measure. It is conceivable that the carriers declared to be most efficient were still performing poorly relative to some absolute measure of efficiency. Second, it would be helpful to compare our observed pattern of airline efficiency performances to that observed for some other industry—preferably unregulated—before one asserted that regulation *per se* induced the differences in efficiency measured among the trunk airlines. It is conceivable that such dispersions of measured efficiency are typical in many competitive industries.

IV. CONCLUSION

It is apparent that there are significant differences in the measured efficiency performances of the domestic trunk airlines. The results of sections II and III indicate that these differences are not temporary phenomena and that these differences significantly explain variations in profitability among the carriers. Furthermore, major cost savings—of the order of 12–15% of total industry costs—would have been obtainable from 1965 to 1974 if all carriers had performed as efficiently as the airline measured as the most efficient in the industry.

It would appear then that Peacock and Rowley's warning—that regulation may induce inefficient resource use which would more than offset any allocative gains attributable to regulation—cannot be dismissed as empirically unimportant on the basis of these results. Furthermore, as CAB regulation creates strong internal incentives for the carriers to act efficiently, any

18 Continental's results are comparable to the rest of the industry's for the period 1970–74. Thus Continental is selected as the most efficient carrier for the years 1970, 1971, and 1972.

19 The calculations for the years 1965–69 were adjusted to exclude Continental.

x-inefficiency induced by CAB regulation must be attributed to the CAB's insulating the carriers from those external pressures that are thought to force unregulated firms to act efficiently—potential entry of new competitors, threat of stockholder revolt, fear of corporate takeover, etc. As other regulatory agencies also insulate the firms they regulate from these external forces, x-inefficiency may be an important problem in other regulated industries as well.

PURDUE UNIVERSITY

APPENDIX

POTENTIAL PROBLEMS WITH THE COMPONENT EFFICIENCY INDICES

Route structure differences among the carriers not accounted for by our methodology may induce some spurious variation among the carriers' flight efficiency indices, capital efficiency indices, and passenger efficiency indices. Problems with these indices will be discussed in turn.

THE FLIGHT EFFICIENCY INDEX

Two problems exist with this index. First, E_f might vary among the carriers solely because of differences in congestion delays faced by the carriers. Congestion delay can be viewed as the sum of three components, congestion delay occurring while the aircraft is at the ramp (which we will call ground congestion), congestion delay occurring while the aircraft is on the taxiway (taxiway congestion), and congestion delay occurring while the aircraft is in the air (inflight congestion). As it is based upon block hours, the flight efficiency index explicitly includes the latter two components of congestion delay. Thus the flight efficiency index will vary spuriously because of congestion differences among the carriers only if (1) the cost per inflight congestion-related block hour differs from the cost per inflight non-congestion block hour, if (2) the cost per block hour on the taxiway is different from the cost per block hour in the air, or if (3) the ratio of ground congestion delays to block hours differs among the carriers.

The cost per inflight block hour flown because of congestion should be less than the cost per normal inflight block hour owing to the reduced fuel and salary costs of the former relative to the latter. For the same reason, the cost per block hour on the taxiway should be less than the cost per block hour in the air. These cost differences *ceteris paribus* should cause congestion delays and E_f to be positively correlated, though the expected effect is small.

On the other hand, ground congestion and E_f should be negatively correlated. The differential impact of these delays on the carriers can be quantified for 1972 using data concerning the average ground delay at 20 large US airports supplied in [18]. Assuming the average ground delay at airports other than these 20 equals the lowest average ground delay reported at any of the 20 airports, the total ground delays imposed on each carrier can be readily calculated. These ground delays can be thought of as block hours that should have been, but were not, considered in totalling each carrier's block hours. By crediting each carrier with these ground delay block hours, each carrier's flight costs per block hour inclusive of ground delays can be calculated.

When we recalculated the carriers' costs per block hour in 1972 to include ground delays, we found that the effect of this adjustment on the carriers' relative flight efficiency indices was generally minor. Moreover, this adjustment overestimates the true differential effect of ground delay costs, as clearly flight costs per block hour accrued because of ground delays are considerably less than flight costs per block hour actually flown.

The two effects on the flight efficiency index of omitting congestion delays thus tend to cancel one another. Both also appear to be small in magnitude. Accordingly, E_f as defined in the text will continue to be used as the flight efficiency index.

The second problem with E_f is that it unfortunately captures some network aspects of the aircraft routing problem. Carriers oftentimes utilize long-haul aircraft in short-haul markets in order to reduce the costs of providing service across their entire route network. We are unable to measure the significance of these network effects. We do believe that these network effects should affect smaller carriers more adversely than larger carriers.

Differences in E_f^i attributable to these network effects should not be labelled x-inefficiency. Nonetheless, such differences do reflect inefficiencies, though they are inefficiencies attributable to CAB regulation: they represent costs borne by the carriers because of their regulation imposed inability to adopt cost-minimizing route networks.

THE CAPITAL EFFICIENCY INDEX

The capital efficiency index may also reflect some unwanted residual influences of differences among the carriers' route structures. Problems could arise in at least two ways.

First, suppose average daily utilization were defined to be aircraft block hours per day. Use of aircraft block hours per day unfortunately ignores differences in the number of flights per day performed by the various carriers. That use of this definition might cause spurious variations in E_c^i can be seen quite easily. Consider two airlines who are able to schedule an aircraft from a given group equally efficiently—e.g. both utilize the aircraft 16 hours per day. Suppose carrier A flies its aircraft on longer flights than carrier B owing to their route structures. The ratio of flight time to ground time would then be higher for carrier A than for carrier B. As ground time is not considered in this definition of ADU_m^i, carrier A would have a higher measured aircraft utilization than carrier B. In fact, using this definition of ADU_m^i, a positive correlation existed between average daily utilization and average stage length for aircraft in a given group in a given year.

To adjust for this problem, ADU^i has been defined to be the sum of aircraft block hours per day plus a proxy for the amount of ground time needed to service the daily flights performed by the mth aircraft in the ith carrier's fleet. This proxy is the product of the departures per day performed by aircraft m in carrier i's fleet times 30 minutes. (This assumed value of the necessary ground time per departure, 30 minutes, was based upon inspection of a sample of ground times scheduled by carriers on intermediate stops of multi-segment flights as reported in the *Official Airline Guide*.) Using this definition of ADU_m^i, there was no significant overall product moment or rank correlation between ADU_m^i so defined and average stage length for aircraft in a given group in a given year. Accordingly, this measure of ADU_m^i, and thus E_c^i, appears to be free of unwanted residual influences of aircraft average stage length.

Differences in the congestion delays faced by carriers might also cause spurious variations in the capital efficiency indices. Note that our definition of ADU_m^i includes block hours flown because of inflight and taxiway congestion. Thus congestion differences could cause the capital efficiency index to vary spuriously only because of differences in the average ground delays imposed upon carriers. But the difference between the average ground delay imposed upon the carrier most affected by ground congestion and the carrier least affected by ground congestion was only three minutes per departure in the year for which good data were available, 1972. As the industry averaged 5·6 departures per aircraft per day and utilized its aircraft 11·4 hours per day in 1972, the effect of ignoring differences in ground congestion suffered by carriers on the measured ADUs is small. (Multiplying three minutes by 5·6 and dividing by 11·4 yields 2·5% as the maximum bias attributable to ignoring ground delays. However, airlines who are most hurt by ground delays tend to enjoy longer hauls than the remaining airlines. Use of industry averages thus overstates the importance of ignoring ground congestion on the measured capital efficiency indices—i.e. the maximum bias is something less than 2·5%.)

THE PASSENGER EFFICIENCY INDEX

Route structure differences among the carriers may also induce spurious variations in the passenger efficiency index. The primary problem with the passenger efficiency index is that it, like the other indices, is predicated on the assumption that the prices of inputs and the substitutability among inputs are similar for all the trunk carriers. But prices of certain inputs—food, telephone service, office space, etc.—do vary by section of the country. To the extent that certain carriers are bound by route requirements to serve high cost sections of the country, the passenger efficiency indices may not truly measure efficiency. However, it is not obvious that such considerations have biased the measured passenger efficiency indices to any significant extent. For example, being a Southern-based airline, Delta might be expected to enjoy some input price advantages over other carriers; Delta does enjoy a high E_p index. But Eastern's routes parallel those of Delta; yet Eastern has a low E_p index. One might expect that carriers flying in cold regions of the country would have higher costs due to climate-related operational difficulties and to interregional differences in input prices; yet Northwest, the northernmost of the trunks, has a high E_p index for the years 1965–74. We must also recognize that carriers are able to adjust the locations of their operations within the confines of their route structures, as exemplified by the transfers of corporate headquarters functions by Eastern from New York to Miami and by Continental from Denver to Los Angeles.

In summary, the component indices may be contaminated by influences of route structure differences among the carriers not accounted for by our methodology. To the extent that such contamination exists, our efficiency indices are imperfect measures of true carrier efficiency.

REFERENCES

[1] Alchian, Armen A., 'Uncertainty, Evolution, and Economic Theory', *Journal of Political Economy*, **58** (June 1950), pp. 211–21.

[2] Averch, Harvey and Johnson, Leland L., 'Behaviour of the Firm Under Regulatory Constraint', *American Economic Review*, **52** (December 1962), pp. 1052–69.

[3] Boske, Leigh B., 'Cost Efficiency in the Domestic Trunk Airline Industry', *Journal of Economics and Business*, **28** (1976), pp. 128–37.

[4] Caves, Richard E., *Air Transport and its Regulators* (Harvard University Press, Cambridge, 1962).

[5] Douglas, George W. and Miller, James C., III, *Economic Regulation of Domestic Air Transport* (Brookings Institution, Washington, DC, 1974).

[6] Eads, George, Nerlove, Marc and Raduchel, William, 'A Long-Run Cost Function for the Local Service Airline Industry: An Experiment in Non-

Linear Estimation', *Review of Economics and Statistics*, **51** (August 1969), pp. 258–70.

[7] FRIEDMAN, MILTON, 'The Methodology of Positive Economics' in *Essays in Positive Economics* (University of Chicago Press, Chicago, 1953).

[8] GORDON, ROBERT, 'Airline Costs and Managerial Efficiency' in *Transportation Economics* (National Bureau of Economic Research, New York, 1965).

[9] HINDLEY, BRIAN, 'Separation of Ownership and Control in the Modern Corporation', *Journal of Law and Economics*, **13** (April 1970), pp. 185–221.

[10] KENDALL, MAURICE G., *Rank Correlation Methods* (Charles Griffin and Company Limited, London, 1955).

[11] LEIBENSTEIN, H., 'Allocative Efficiency vs. X-Efficiency', *American Economic Review*, **56** (June 1966), pp. 392–415.

[12] MACHLUP, FRITZ, 'Theories of the Firm: Marginalist, Behavioral, Managerial', *American Economic Review*, **57** (March 1967), pp. 1–33.

[13] PEACOCK, ALAN T. and ROWLEY, CHARLES K., 'Welfare Economics and the Public Regulation of Natural Monopoly', *Journal of Public Economics*, **1** (1972), pp. 227–49.

[14] STRASZHEIM, MAHLON, *The International Airline Industry* (Brookings Institution, Washington, DC, 1969).

[15] WINTER, SIDNEY G., JR., 'Economic "Natural Selection" and the Theory of the Firm', *Yale Economic Essays*, **4** (Spring 1964), pp. 225–72.

[16] ——, 'Satisficing, Selection, and the Innovating Remnant', *Quarterly Journal of Economics*, **85** (May 1971), pp. 237–61.

[17] US CIVIL AERONAUTICS BOARD, *Aircraft Operating Cost and Performance Report* (Washington, DC, various issues).

[18] US FEDERAL AVIATION ADMINISTRATION, *Airline Delay Trends, 1972–1973* (Washington, DC, 1975).

THE JOURNAL OF INDUSTRIAL ECONOMICS
Volume XXVII September 1978 No. 1

PROFIT MAXIMIZATION IN CHAIN RETAIL STORES

RALPH W. PFOUTS*

BECAUSE they handle a large number of products and because of the multi-plant nature of their operations, chain retail organizations face special problems in pricing and in profit maximization. The primary purpose of this paper is to offer a model based on the actual policies and practices of such organizations. Such a model offers insights into how profit maximization is approximated in such establishments. The model also makes it possible to make some comments on the social welfare effects of chain retailing. For the economist the model raises a matter of methodological interest because it presents a variant of the orthodox model of the profit maximizing firm which represents the actual organization and practices of an important segment of the economy. In particular it presents methods of approximating profit maximization when knowledge of demand is severely limited.

In view of the availability of two notable monographs, those of Holdren [5] and Preston [9], on the economics of retailing, one might wonder if any additional discussion is needed. However, the emphasis of the present paper is different from those of the monographs. Holdren's primary concern is with the market structure of the food retailing industry, especially with the correspondence between the theoretical categories and market actuality. Preston is more concerned with pricing policies and decisions within the individual store and reconciles economic theory with data on prices to explain individual store decisions. The present paper is close in spirit to Preston's work, but places more emphasis on the unusual nature of the profit maximizing problems of the chain store manager and on the role of incomplete information and search and information costs in the pricing decision in a chain's central office. Thus this paper attempts a contribution on a subject somewhat different from those of Holdren or Preston.

PRICING POLICIES AND PRACTICES IN A RETAIL CHAIN ORGANIZATION

Retail chains generally follow the policy of establishing prices at their headquarters and, with some exceptions to be noted below, permitting the managers of individual stores to decide the particular goods and the amount

* I am indebted to Professor James E. Littlefield of the Graduate School of Business Administration, University of North Carolina, Chapel Hill, for guidance in retailing literature and practices and for criticizing earlier drafts. Dr Willard R. Bishop, Jr., Vice-President, Research and Operations of The Super Market Institute, criticized an earlier draft. I also had the benefit of a lengthy interview with a former executive in a chain drugstore company regarding policies and practices in that industry. Finally I am indebted to an unknown referee for very helpful suggestions.

of each good that they will stock [5, p. 100]. This practice is followed by supermarket chains, drug chains and certain types of department store chains. If the chain is sufficiently large, regional offices will be responsible for operations in a number of market areas and will make the price decisions for each market area with the prices varying from one market area to another.

A retail chain may offer upwards of 9000 different products. Consequently it is clear that a carefully detailed study of the demand for each product within each market cannot be undertaken. The costs of such complete information would be greater than the gains that could be obtained.

As a result the establishment of prices by a central office is necessarily a somewhat rough process involving the judgements of the executive making the decision. Usually the pricing process is viewed as that of choosing a markup to be added to the unit cost which will cover overhead and provide a profit while keeping the final price sufficiently low for the product to 'sell'. It might be added that the unit cost to the chains depends on whether the product is purchased in carload or less than carload lots or, if this designation is not appropriate for particular goods, whether the goods are purchased in large lots. Ordinarily a chain establishment will require a product in sufficient amount to purchase in large lots. The point of immediate interest is that the chain can purchase at the lowest available price and that unit cost to the chain is constant [4, p. 182].

As was noted above, the choice of a markup and thus a price is in some part a matter of judgement. Past price and sales data offer guidance, but ordinarily little detailed analysis of such data is undertaken. In addition it is a common practice to use fixed percentage markups for particular kinds of goods [5, p. 100] and [4, pp. 173–5]. Thus canned vegetables might have a fixed percentage markup while dairy products would have a different percentage markup. As a consequence the price of a good can be shown as

$$p_i = c_i + a_i c_i, \qquad i = 1, \ldots, n \tag{1}$$

where p_i, c_i and a_i are the price, unit cost and markup for good i.

It may appear that demand is not taken into account in the pricing process but this is not completely true [8, pp. 85–9]. If the sales of a product are disappointing, the central office will reduce the price although usually only after some delay. Presumably a parallel course of action with prices being raised will be followed if sales are larger than anticipated, although it is sometimes claimed that unless the unit cost increases the chain will retain the same fixed markup and be satisfied with selling a large quantity.

Except for 'loss leader' items and a very small number of specially advertised items it is not clear that there is much direct price competition. It is very likely that the markups for particular goods are very similar if not identical from one chain to another. Thus with identical unit costs and similar or identical markups the prices in competing chains will be similar or identical.

PROFIT MAXIMIZATION WITHIN THE STORE

Even though prices are established on a markup basis by the central office of the chain, some demand function for each product will face any store. In considering the demand for a particular good we take note of the fact that while prices among competing stores are sometimes identical for the same good, they are not always so. In addition we note that the demand for a particular good may depend on the prices of other goods. Consequently we write a demand equation for each good sold by the store as

$$(2) \qquad x_{ti}^D = f_{ti}(\boldsymbol{p}_i, \ldots, \boldsymbol{p}_n, M), \qquad i = 1, \ldots, n$$

where $\boldsymbol{p}_i$ is the vector of prices for the good which are charged by the stores competing in the market and M represents consumers' income within the market area. In (2) x_{ti}^D indicates the quantity of good i demanded per unit of time. The subscript t indicates the type of space within the store that is required by good i; this is a matter which will be developed below. Once the prices have been established the values of x_{ti}^D are also established and thus both the price and quantity demanded are parameters from the standpoint of the store manager.

Suppose that the store manager is instructed to operate his store as profitably as possible. In doing this he faces a constraint in the form of the limitation of space available. That is, he must choose the goods that will return the greatest profit but the total quantity of goods that can be stocked is limited by the storage and display space available in the store. In point of fact the space constraint is more complicated than this because there usually is more than one type of space in a store. For example in a supermarket there will be refrigerator space, freezer space, ordinary shelf space and aisle-end space. In chain drugstores and in department stores there are also different kinds of specialized spaces. Thus within a particular store the manager must maximize profits for each type of space.

There is an additional complication in allocating space among different products. Typically a store manager is required by the central office to stock certain items even though it might be more profitable to use the space for other products. Thus, for example, a chain drugstore is required to stock items such as hydrogen peroxide and epsom salts while a supermarket must carry salt and baking powder. As a consequence, a certain amount of each type of space will be pre-empted by these required goods.

Hence if we let b_{ti} represent the amount of space of type t occupied by a unit of good i we can use $\sum_i b_{ti} x_{ti}^{*D}$ to show the total amount of space of this type occupied by required goods, the asterisk being used to indicate a required good. Of course there will be similar expressions for each type of space, and it is assumed that each good will be assigned to only one type of space.

The gross profit obtained from the required goods may be indicated after introducing the total costs of obtaining and handling the goods. This total can be broken down into two categories, procurement costs and carrying costs. Procurement costs, which include the cost of processing orders, shipping costs and the costs of putting goods into stock, decline as the size of the order increases. On the other hand carrying costs such as taxes, costs of financing, spoilage and insurance increase with order size. Using inventory theoretic methods, an optimum order size can be obtained which minimizes the sum of procurement and carrying costs [10, pp. 32–3] and [4, pp. 301–4]. If a policy of using optimum order sizes for each type of good is followed, the sum of procurement costs and carrying costs may be viewed as a constant for each good because the same quantity would be ordered each time. We assume this to be the case and use h_{ti} to indicate the procurement and carrying costs for each unit of x_{ti}. Then the gross profit from required goods may be shown as

$$\sum_{t=1}^{q} \sum_{i \in t} (p - c_{ti} - h_{ti}) x_{ti}^{*D},$$

where the index $i \in t$ indicates the goods i using space of type t, there being q types of spaces. If a substitution is made from equation (1) to the last expression, we obtain

$$\sum_{t=1}^{q} \sum_{i \in t} (a_{ti} c_{ti} - h_{ti}) x_{ti}^{*D}.$$

It is evident that these profits are not a part of the profit maximizing process because they represent goods that must be stocked in sufficient amount to meet demand regardless of their effects on profit. Of course it may be true that required goods are a necessary prerequisite to profit maximization because a store that did not carry traditional goods might not be patronized as readily by customers as one which did.

In considering the goods that can be used in profit maximizing, that is non-required goods, the manager faces space constraints in which the total amount of space of each type is diminished by the amount taken by required goods. Thus if we use S_t to indicate the total amount of space of type t available and s_t to indicate the amount available after required goods are accommodated, we have constraints of the type

$$(3) \qquad \sum_{k \in t} b_{tk} x_{tk} \leqq S_t - \sum_{r \in t} b_{tr} x_{tr}^{*} = s_t, \qquad t = 1, \ldots, q.$$

In addition the manager faces demand constraints. As was observed above, when the price of a good is fixed, the quantity of the good that the store can sell is also fixed. The manager will presumably not want to overstock the good because the costs of carrying excess inventories, including the space used unnecessarily, would be large. Consequently he faces constraints in the form of

$$(4) \qquad x_{tk} - x_{tk}^{D} \leqq 0, \qquad k \in t;\ t = 1, \ldots, q.$$

The profits from goods occupying space of type t may be shown as

$$\sum_{k\in t} (a_{tk}c_{tk}-h_{tk})x_{tk}, \qquad t=1, \ldots, q. \tag{5}$$

Thus the manager's problem is to maximize profit expressions of the type shown in (5) subject to constraints of the types shown in (3) and (4). Hence we can write the Lagrangian as

$$\begin{aligned} L = & \sum_{t=1}^{q} \sum_{i\in t} (a_{ti}c_{ti}-h_{ti})\, x_{ti} - F \\ & - \sum_{t=1}^{q} \lambda_t \left(\sum_{i\in t} b_{ti}x_{ti} - s_t \right) \\ & - \sum_{t=1}^{q} \sum_{i\in t} \mu_{ti}\,(x_{ti}-x_{ti}^{D}). \end{aligned} \tag{6}$$

Here F represents fixed costs. Since all of the functions involved are linear in the x's, the concavity conditions of the Kuhn–Tucker theorem are satisfied [7]. Consequently we can write the maximizing conditions as

$$\frac{\partial L}{\partial x_{tk}} = a_{tk}c_{tk} - h_{tk} - \lambda_t b_{tk} - \mu_{tk} \leqq 0, \tag{7}$$

$$x_{tk}(a_{tk}c_{tk} - h_{tk} - \lambda_t b_{tk} - \mu_{tk}) = 0, \tag{8}$$

$$\frac{\partial L}{\partial \lambda_t} = \sum_{k\in t} b_{tk}x_{tk} - s_t \leqq 0, \tag{9}$$

$$\lambda_t\Big(\sum_{k\in t} b_{tk}x_{tk} - s_t\Big) = 0, \tag{10}$$

$$\frac{\partial L}{\partial \mu_{tk}} = x_{tk} - x_{tk}^{D} \leqq 0, \tag{11}$$

$$\mu_{tk}(x_{tk} - x_{tk}^{D}) = 0, \tag{12}$$

where $k \in t$ and $t=1, \ldots, q$ for (7) through (12).

For purposes of subsequent discussion we note the economic meanings of the dual variables. In the present context, λ_t is the shadow price of space of type t. Thus $\lambda_t b_{tk}$ is the value of space occupied by a unit of x_{tk}. From (7) it is evident that μ_{tk} may be interpreted as the per unit profit of good k with the shadow value of space taken into account. It may also be interpreted as the increment to profit of a small increase of demand [1]. As a consequence of this interpretation it may be viewed as the value to the firm of being able to sell good k rather than some less profitable good.

Turning now to a direct interpretation of the maximizing conditions, one may note that if the inequality holds in (7), then (8) requires that x_{tk} equal zero. In this event, the inequality holds in (11) and $\mu_{tk}=0$, according to (12). Hence (7) reduces to

$$a_{tk}c_{tk} - h_{tk} < \lambda_t b_{tk}.$$

This last shows that profit per unit is less than the shadow value of the space required by a unit of x_{tk}. Hence the good would not be stocked.

For profit to be at a maximum, it is necessary that the equalities hold in (7), (9) and (11). The first of these assures that the most profitable set of goods is stocked, while (9) assures that space of all types is fully utilized and (11) requires that demands be fully met. Under these conditions (7) may be written as

$$a_{tk}c_{tk}-h_{tk}=\lambda_t b_{tk}+\mu_{tk}. \tag{13}$$

Thus it may be said that profit maximization requires that the gross profit per unit of a good equal the shadow value of space occupied by a unit of the good plus the value to the firm of the good over alternative goods. The condition shown in (13) has a clear intuitive appeal because it shows that the gross profit per unit of a good must be adjusted in accordance with both the space constraints and the demand constraints.

AN ALTERNATIVE APPROACH

The method used in the preceding section provides a formal solution to the profit maximization problem facing the store manager, but it is an indirect method which makes use of dual variables. While this has a theoretical advantage in that it offers a rather complete solution to the problem, it lacks direct intuitive appeal and it makes use of concepts whose actual numerical values might be difficult to ascertain. To offset these difficulties an alternative method which has direct intuitive appeal, indeed it is so intuitively evident that it is likely that it is used by efficient store managers, will be developed.

Since the different types of space are independent of each other so far as sales and profit are concerned, we can apply the method to one type of space, the applications to other types being similar. We assume that there are m goods available to the store which can be handled in the specified type of space. In a practical sense m is so large that virtually no store could handle all of these goods although it could carry $n<m$ of them. The problem may be phrased as

$$\max \Pi_t=\sum_{i=1}^{n-1}(a_{ti}c_{ti}-h_{ti})\,x_{ti}^D+(a_{tn}c_n-h_{tn})\,x_{tn} \tag{14}$$

subject to

$$\sum_i b_{ti}x_{ti}^D+b_{tn}x_{tn}\leqq s_t \tag{15}$$

$$x_{tj}-x_{tj}^D\leqq 0, \qquad j=1,\ldots,n. \tag{16}$$

In stating the problem x_{tn} has been used instead of x_{tn}^D because, as will be seen, when the 'last' good is added there may not be enough space left to accommodate the entire amount of the good that could be sold.

The necessary and sufficient conditions for a solution to the problem posed in (14), (15) and (16 are

(17) $$\frac{a_{t1}c_{t1}-h_{t1}}{b_{t1}} \geqq \ldots \geqq \frac{a_{tn}c_{tn}-h_{tn}}{b_{tn}}, \quad n<m$$

where

$$\frac{a_{tn}c_{tn}-h_{tn}}{b_{tn}} \geqq \frac{a_{t\theta}c_{t\theta}-h_{t\theta}}{b_{t\theta}}, \quad \theta=n+1, \ldots, m.$$

(18) $$\sum_i b_{ti}x_{ti}^D + b_{tn}x_{tn} = s_t,$$

(19) $$x_{ti}-x_{ti}^D=0, \quad i=1, \ldots, n-1$$

$$x_{tn}-x_{tn}^D \leqq 0.$$

The solution clearly has strong intuitive appeal. The relations in (17) state that the goods showing the largest gross profit per unit of space should be stocked. This process should be continued until all space is in use as indicated by (18). The most profitable goods should be offered in sufficient amount to satisfy the demands for them as indicated by (19). In this way the most profitable use is made of the space. It may be noted that (18) and (19) allow for the possibility that the least profitable of the goods may reach the limit of the available space before its demand is satisfied.

That (17), (18) and (19) are both necessary and sufficient for profit maximization can be proved rigorously, but it is probably unnecessary to do so because the nature of the proof is rather obvious. Consequently the proof will be sketched verbally. If (14) is to be maximal, the space must be used in the most profitable way hence (17) must hold. Further the space must be fully utilized hence (18) must hold. Finally the most profitable goods must be offered in sufficient amount to satisfy the demand for them since they contribute more to profitability than other goods. Consequently (19) must hold. Thus (17), (18) and (19) are necessary conditions for profit maximization.

To show sufficiency, we note that if (17) holds, no other goods can replace goods 1, . . . , n without reducing profit and consequently (14) is at a maximum. Further if (18) holds no greater amounts of the most profitable goods can be stocked. Finally if (19) holds, no greater amounts of the most profitable goods can be sold. Thus (17), (18) and (19) are sufficient for profit maximization.

Although the alternative method lacks the completeness of statement of the Kuhn–Tucker approach, it has the advantage of directness and simplicity.

The conditions of the alternative approach can easily be undestood and can be carried out without undue difficulty if the demands for the various goods are stable. This depends not only on consumer preferences remaining stable or changing only slowly but also on competitors' prices and the prices emanating from the central office remaining stable.

Indeed it is clear that, in a practical sense, estimating the demand for a good is the store manager's most difficult problem. Obviously, if he overstocks a good he will be aware of this and will have some idea of how badly he overestimated demand. If, on the other hand, he underestimates demand, he will also be aware of this, although it may be more difficult to determine the degree of underestimation. In either case, he can learn from experience and adjust his ordering accordingly. This, however, may not be as simple as it sounds because, in addition to the possibility of price changes emanating either from within or without the firm, seasonal influences will be present in the case of some goods. No doubt other possible complications, such as growth or contraction of the community or neighborhood or changes of income within the community would sometimes make it difficult to estimate demand accurately. All in all demand estimation would often be a continuous process.

A NOTE ON SOCIAL WELFARE EFFECTS

In view of the fixed prices, can anything be said about the social welfare effects of the store manager's decisions? Clearly the only question is whether in the presence of the fixed prices, the optimum quantities are offered, and this question is easily answered. If $x_{ti} = x_{ti}^D$ for all goods, that is, if at the fixed prices demands are fully met for all goods, then Marshallian consumers' surplus is maximized given the parametric prices. Earlier argument shows that profit maximization requires that all demands be fully satisfied. Of course, this says nothing about optimal prices.

It will be argued in a later section that the prices fixed by the central office are established with a view to maintaining sales and hence profits at acceptable levels. If this is true, then prices are not established in accordance with the marginal cost pricing principle or to take account of optimal deviations from marginal cost pricing [6, p.2]. Consequently prices might move toward optimal values only if competitive forces operating on sales forced them toward optimum values. Clearly freedom of entry is of central importance in this regard.

An additional point relating to welfare can be made. If c_{tk} is added and subtracted in (7) and use is made of (1), we get

$$p_k - c_{tk} - h_{tk} = \lambda_t b_{tk} + \mu_{tk}. \tag{20}$$

The left side of (20) is the gross profit per unit and the right side is the sum of the shadow value of space and the shadow value of stocking the good correctly. Hence the imputed value of the store manager performing these two functions correctly with regard to a particular good is equal to the gross profit per unit of the good.

There is no assurance, as was noted above, that the price in (20) will be optimal. If through the operation of competitive forces the price is optimal, then profit maximization within the store assures that space is used optimally and the good is supplied optimally and, as (20) shows, this will be consistent with optimal pricing.

ESTABLISHING PRICES IN THE CENTRAL OFFICE

The processes involved in establishing prices in a retail chain organization are different from those envisaged in the conventional theory of the firm. In large part this is true because, while a chain has information on costs, it has very limited information about demand and certainly does not have knowledge of a complete demand function for each good. In place of this knowledge it has information on past prices and quantites, the judgement of the price-making executives and the possibility of gaining information by experimenting with different prices. The purpose of the present discussion is to develop a rationale and a model of how prices are established using the means available in a chain.

It was noted earlier that pricing in a chain is usually thought of as a process of marking-up a product, often by a conventional percentage markup, in the expectation that at that price the product will 'sell'. This suggests that one draw the inference that the pricing official has some anticipation as to what the volume of sales for the good in question will be and that this volume will be sufficiently large to be of interest to the company [4, pp. 173–84]. It seems very likely that the executive does not have in mind a single, precise amount of the good that will be sold, but rather some range of volume. In other words he has an 'interval anticipation' rather than a 'point anticipation'. Certainly he must anticipate that sales will be large enough to warrant purchase in large lots or presumably they would be too trifling for the chain to consider. On the other hand he cannot expect that they will be indefinitely large. He would very likely have some anticipation of a maximum quantity that could be sold.

We assume that if actual sales fall between the low and high anticipations, the price-maker will believe that the price he established is satisfactory. After all he has established a price and a range within which he expects the quantity to fall and his anticipations have been realized. The good will show an adequate return. He has, in his view, been justified by the market, and will let the price stand. He has of course found a point on the demand curve for the particular market but, while the good will show a profit at this point, there is no assurance that this point is the profit maximizing point. Before we label this irrational behavior, we should recall that the demand function is not known to the price-maker. He must instead rely on the best substitutes available which are information on past sales and his own judgement. Of course it could be contended that further experimentation with prices might lead to higher profits. But experimentation is costly in terms of executive time and administrative routine, and the results are uncertain. Consequently without some special reason to believe that it would lead to enhanced profits, presumably experimentation will not be undertaken.

A special reason for experimenting with prices would seem to arise if the anticipation of sales prove to be incorrect, that is, if sales are either above the maximum anticipation or below the minimum anticipation. In either of these eventualities, it is clear that the price-maker has misjudged the market. Thus one might infer that some price experimentation would take place to gain further information about the market. Specifically, one would expect that if sales exceeded the anticipated range, the markup would be increased, while the markup would be diminished if sales fell below the minimum anticipation [9, pp. 34–6].

These processes may be described more succinctly by assuming that the price-maker receives and acts on sales information at discrete time intervals (weekly, monthly or quarterly). We use ξ_k^l and ξ_k^u to indicate the smallest and largest values of anticipated sales of k per unit of time. Since we are concerned with market areas rather than individual stores we drop the space subscript and use x_{k1}^D to indicate the quantity of good k sold in the market area in time period 1. Using this notation we may summarize the decision rules by writing

$$\delta a_{k1} \gtreqless 0 \begin{cases} x_{k1}^D > \xi_k^u \\ \xi_k^l \leqq x_{k1}^D \leqq \xi_k^u \\ x_{k1}^D < \xi_k^l \end{cases} \tag{21}$$

where δa_{k1} represents the change in markup at the end of the first time period.

Suppose that $x_{k1}^D > \xi_k^u$, then, according to (21), $\delta a_{k1} > 0$ and the price of good k will be raised when the information on sales becomes available at the end of the first time period. One would expect that at the end of the second time period, the price-maker would investigate to determine whether the price increase had enhanced profit. In doing this he would presumably take into account the effect of the price change on any known substitutes or complements of good k [9], [9–17]. It may be emphasized that knowledge of related goods would have to be known or suspected from sources external to the immediate data because the price-maker does not have a demand equation which could be used to determine such relationships. This also means that relationships of substitution or complementarity may exist which he does not know about. It may be noted parenthetically that many goods would have substitutes; one brand of soup, for example, is a substitute for another.

Then at the end of the second time period, the price-maker would check the profits from good k and the profits from related goods to see if they have increased. A satisfactory outcome may be shown symbolically as

$$(a_{k2}c_k - h_k)\,x_{k2}^D - (a_{k1}c_k - h_k)\,x_{k1}^D + \sum_{\tau} (a_{\tau 2}c_\tau - h_\tau)\,x_{\tau 2}^D - (a_{\tau 1}c_\tau - h_\tau)\,x_{\tau 1}^D > 0. \tag{22}$$

In (22) τ indicates related goods. Making use of $a_{k2}=a_{k1}+\delta a_{k1}$ and $x_{k2}^D=x_{k1}^D+\delta x_{k1}$ with similar relations for the related goods enables us to rewrite (22) as

$$(23)\quad c_k x_{k2}^D \delta a_{k1}+(a_{k1}c_k-h_k)\delta x_{k1}>-\sum_{\tau} c_\tau x_{\tau 2}^D \delta a_{\tau 1}-\sum_{\tau}(a_{\tau 1}c_\tau-h_\tau)\delta x_{\tau 1}.$$

The first term in (23) shows the increment to revenue from the increased markup and the second term shows the decrement of gross profit due to the decline in quantity sold with similar interpretations for the related goods in the righthand member. For the moment we assume that $\delta x_{k1}<0$, in the face of an increase in the markup. The possibility of $\delta x_{k1}\geqq 0$ will be discussed below.

Inspection of (23) shows that if there are no related goods, the left side must be positive if the price change is to be successful. In other words the increment to revenue arising from the increased markup must be greater than the loss of gross profit due to the loss of volume.

If there are related goods and they are predominantly substitutes for good k, the right member of (23) may be negative and will be negative if $\delta a_{\tau 1}=0$, i.e. if the prices of the related goods are unchanged. Then the left member could be negative and the price change judged to be successful if it is larger than the right member. In other words even though the markup increase caused a fall in the gross profit of good k, it may be judged successful if the increased sales of substitutes offset this loss. On the other hand, if the related goods are predominantly complementary the right member of (23) will be positive if $\delta a_{\tau 1}=0$ and may be positive in any case. Then the left must be positive and greater than the right if the price change is to be judged to be successful.

If the markup were lowered because $x_{k1}^D<\xi_k^l$ in (21), then δa_{k1} and δx_{k1} would, of course, have reversed signs and the interpretation of (26) would be changed accordingly.

If a price change is successful according to (23), one is tempted to suggest that further experimentation would be undertaken to attempt to maximize profit but this is a dubious inference. If the quantity sold after the price change is in accordance with the anticipations of the price-maker, he will very likely believe that the price adjustment was sufficiently accurate and further attempts would not be worthwhile. On the side of this view is the fact that price adjustments are costly in terms in executive time and in terms of administrative routine which is necessary to make the new price known to store managers, others in the company and customers. Thus search costs would be appreciable.

Another reason for not undertaking further price adjustments, at least not immediately, is that the price-maker cannot be sure as to why the changes in quantities sold actually took place. Although he would have the information shown in (23) he cannot be certain that the changes in quantities for the primary and related goods were caused by the price change and not by some force extraneous to the calculation. For example a change of income, a change of consumers' preferences or a change in a competitor's price for the same or a related good in the market area could be the cause. Consequently, an atmosphere of uncertainty is generated which may serve to inhibit further experimentation.

In any case it is unlikely that the price-maker will push on in an attempt to extract the last dollar of profit from the market. If a good shows an acceptable gross profit in comparison with other goods and if the quantity sold lies within the anticipations of the price-maker, in his view equilibrium will have been attained. In view of the costs involved in a price change and of the uncertainty of its outcome, it is difficult to say that such a policy is unreasonable.

Suppose that the price increase is not successful, i.e. the inequality in (23) is reversed. This means, of course, that profit was lowered by the price increase. In this event, the price-maker would always have available the possibility of returning to the original price in anticipation of restoring profit, although because of the possibility of the change of profit being due to forces other than the price change this reversal might not be undertaken immediately.

The possibility also exists that if the price increase was unsuccessful, the price-maker might be encouraged not only to remove the price increase but to lower the price below its original level. In other words, the price-maker may decide that his original anticipation of sales were wide of the mark and the elasticity of demand might be sufficient to warrant a lower price. His original price increases having been incorrect he may decide that it is worthwhile to experiment with lower prices.

In this attempt to construct a rationale of how the price-makers in a retail chain organization might behave, it is evident that judgement, 'feel for the market' and other subjective elements are prominent. But in the absence of full knowledge of demand, this must inevitably be the case. Thus it seems important to visualize how the price-maker would act in the face of incomplete information. This is what has been attempted in this section.

SIMULTANEOUS QUANTITY AND PRICE INCREASES

It is possible for the sale of a product to increase when its markup and hence its price is increased. That is, it is possible that $\delta x_{k1} \geqq 0$ when $\delta a_{k1} > 0$. This might occur for several reasons.

First it may be that the good is a Giffen good in the existing price range. That is, enough consumers may regard the good as a Giffen good for it to appear as one in the market. This would presumably be true in a very small proportion of cases. A second reason is that the tastes of buyers may be changing in favor of the good, i.e. the demand equation may be changing.

A third possibility is that the incomes of consumers in the market area may be increasing, thus enabling them to buy a larger quantity of the good in spite of the price increase. Fourthly, it is also possible that competitors have increased their prices for the product even more thus inducing a larger sale. Finally, it may be the case that prices of related goods have been changed either within the firm or by competitors in sufficient amount to permit a larger sale.

If the quantity sold increases when the price of a good is increased, it would seem to be a clear signal that the price should be increased further, but this is not necessarily the case. If the increase is due to price effects either by competitors or within the firm (the fourth and fifth reasons of the preceding paragraph) the pricing executive will have or can get information on the relevant price changes and presumably will infer the reason for the simultaneous sales and price increases. In this event he will be encouraged to experiment with further price increases since he understands the reasons for the market situation.

Similarly, if the sales increase were due to an income increase (the third reason given above), the executive might know or strongly suspect the reason. He might suspect the reason from general information and observation of economic tendencies within the market area. More specifically, an income increase will make itself felt in increased sales of all or most goods sold, thus giving the pricing executive reason to believe that incomes have increased. In this event the executive will be motivated to experiment with price increases not only for the good in question but for other goods.

If the sales increase is due to a change in the functional form of the demand equation or to a Giffen good situation, it is more difficult for the executive to know or infer the reason. Thus he would be inclined to delay price experimentation in an effort to determine whether the increased sale is a peak of the market or a permanent feature. Presumably if sales remained up in a few subsequent periods the increase would be viewed as a change of demand and price experimentation would be undertaken.

EFFECTS OF SUPPLIER PRICE CHANGES ON CHAIN RETAIL PRICES

If the price of a product is changed by suppliers, the general practice among chain retailers is to raise price immediately following supplier increases and to lower following decreases, sometimes with a time lag to permit liquidation of existing stocks at the higher price [3, pp. 178–81]. These practices may not be universally followed, but experience during the past few years suggests very strongly that prices are marked up immediately. Almost everyone who has entered a supermarket or a chain drug store in recent times must have noticed a higher price label on top of a lower one.

If we adopt as a working hypothesis that prices are changed immediately or soon after supplier prices change, there still remains a question of how greatly they will be changed. That is, will the same markup be used after the price change? The general answer is yes, sometimes with minor adjustments to establish 'charm' prices e.g. 79¢ per unit or three for $1 [2, pp. 180–1].

Presumably the rationale for using the same markup includes the argument that experience has shown this markup produces an acceptable sales volume. It is of course clear that this is not necessarily a valid argument because price elasticity may be different at the new price. Another argument for using the same markup is that it provides an adequate return if the good sells. Finally it may be believed that competitors will use the same or approximately the same markup.

In any event, when the retail price is changed in response to a supplier price change, the price-maker must hold some anticipation of what the quantity that can be sold at the new price will be. If the volume lies between his upper and lower anticipation, he will be satisfied with the outcome, otherwise he will adjust his markup in accordance with (21). In other words we are back with our original analysis of price changes and need not pursue the present discussion as a separate subject.

If the arguments of this and the previous sections are valid, an asymmetry between chains' responses to demand and to cost changes arises. We have noted that the response to a cost change in the form of a supplier's price change, will take place immediately or quite soon. On the other hand, demand changes will go unheeded so long as the quantity sold remains between the price-maker's upper and lower anticipations, i.e. if $\xi_k^l \leqq x_{k1}^D \leqq \xi_k^u$, markup and price will remain unchanged even though x_{k1}^D changes from time to time. Thus the firm's prices are more sensitive to cost changes than to demand changes. Basically this difference arises from the fact that while the firm has a good deal of information on costs, it has little information on demand. Thus there is a caution about responding to moderate variations in demand since the cause of the change often would not be known. There would be a fear that demand changes were transitory and irregular and should not be viewed as a basis for action.

UNIVERSITY OF NORTH CAROLINA AT CHAPEL HILL

REFERENCES

[1] Afriat, S. N., 'Theory of Maxima and the Method of Lagrange', *SIAM J. Appl. Math.*, **20** (May 1971), pp. 343–57.

[2] Baumol, W. J. and Bradford, D. F., 'Optimal Departures from Marginal Cost Pricing', *American Economic Review*, **60** (June 1970), pp. 265–83.

[3] Cassady, R., Jr., *Competition and Price Making in Food Retailing* (Ronald Press, New York, 1962).

[4] Dalrymple, D. J. and Thompson, D. L., *Retailing: An Economic View* (Free Press, New York, 1969).

[5] Holdren, B. R., *The Structure of a Retail Market and the Market Behavior of Retail Units* (Prentice-Hall, Englewood Cliffs, N.J., 1960).
[6] Hotelling, H., 'The General Welfare in Relation to Problems of Taxation and of Railway and Utility Rate', *Econometrica*, **6** (July 1938), pp. 242–69.
[7] Kuhn, H. W. and Tucker, A., 'Nonlinear Programming', *Proceedings of the Second Berkeley Symposium on Mathematical Statistics and Probability*, J. Neyman (ed.), pp. 481–92 (University of California Press, Berkeley and Los Angeles, 1951).
[8] Markin, R. J., *The Supermarket: An Analysis of Growth, Development and Change*, rev. edn. (Washington State University Press, Pullman, Washington, 1968).
[9] Preston, L. E., *Profits, Competition and Rules of Thumb in Retail Food Pricing* (Institute of Business and Economic Research, University of California, Berkeley, 1963).
[10] Whitin, T. M., *The Theory of Inventory Management* (Princeton Press, Princeton, 1957).

THE JOURNAL OF INDUSTRIAL ECONOMICS
Vol. XXVII September 1978 No. 7

TERRITORIAL EXCLUSIVITY IN THE SOFT DRINK INDUSTRY*

BARBARA G. KATZ

BETWEEN 1950 and 1970 soft drinks in the United States more than doubled their share of the commercial beverage market, constituting about one-fifth of the latter in 1972, and by 1969 ranked second only to coffee in commercial beverage popularity. By 1970 soft drinks were available in more than 1 million domestic retail sales outlets and yearly per capita consumption reached 388·1 8 oz containers. The wholesale value of soft drink sales in that year was $5·3 billion.[1]

Part one of this paper provides a background description of the market structure of the soft drink industry. Part two examines reasons why syrup manufacturers find territorial exclusivity desirable and evaluates the implication of these exclusive arrangements for market performance.

I. BACKGROUND

The soft drink industry is a two-tiered market structure in which local bottlers are granted exclusive geographic territories in which to distribute products trademarked by a small oligopoly of nationwide syrup producers. The first to partition the entire United States into exclusive sales territories was The Coca-Cola Company, in the years 1900 to 1920. As rivals entered the market, they pursued an identical strategy.

Syrup Manufacturers

The concentrates and syrups (concentrates plus sweeteners) utilized in the manufacture of soft drinks are produced primarily by a small group of companies predominantly for resale to local bottlers whose franchise agreements stipulate they may produce and distribute the trademarked sodas only in specific geographic territories.[2] These agreements also provide that the syrup manufacturers supply technical assistance relating to production, sales

* I am indebted to Art Havenner, Stan Katz, Linda McLaughlin, Almarin Phillips, Larry White and an anonymous referee for their helpful comments. Any mistakes, of course, are mine. Bert Finn-Fernandes provided ample research assistance for this study which was funded in part by a New York University faculty summer grant. This paper is an abridgement of a longer New York University faculty working paper (No. 76–85) of the same name.

[1] For these and other background data see Initial Decision [9].

[2] Some syrups manufacturers also engage in bottling but their overall share of bottling sales is small, and in 1974 was less than 4%, based on data which exclude from total bottling sales the sales of independent private label and contract bottling companies. See U.S. Department of Commerce [15].

and quality control to the bottlers as well as participate with the local bottlers in the advertising and promotion of the trademarked soft drinks.

In 1972, the four largest firms producing flavorings, extracts and syrups (SIC category 2087) accounted for 70% of the value added in that industry grouping.[3] The largest syrup manufacturer, The Coca-Cola Company, had 41·3% of the market sales, while the second largest syrup manufacturer, Pepsico, had 16·9% of the market sales in 1969.[4]

Besides the nationally franchised brands, local and regional manufacturers of soft drinks also distribute their own brands. In most cases these manufacturers do not utilize a franchising system for distribution even when they expand their area of sales, but rather ship their sodas over long distances or build additional manufacturing plants in other locations. In some cases contract bottlers are also used.

Private label sodas constitute another segment of the soft drink market. These private label brands have proliferated greatly since 1960 and are manufactured either by the retailers themselves or by contract bottlers, and are sold under the retailer's name.

Bottlers

Since the 1950s the number of soft drink bottling plants has persistently declined: in 1950 there were more than 6000 operating soft drink plants; in 1960 fewer than 4600; in 1970 slightly over 3100 and in 1974 about 2200.[5] Analysis of the data demonstrates that there has been a steady downward trend in the number of plants with annual sales of under $0·5 million, as well as a decline in the volume of sales for which they are responsible, 16·9% in 1972. Plants with sales of over $2 million have grown significantly, accounting for 71·8% of all soft drink sales in 1973. Within the category of plants selling over $2 million in soft drinks, 41% of those sales came from units selling over $10 million.[6]

The modal plant has increased since 1967 from an annual sales level in the range of $100,000–$300,000 to greater than $2 million in 1973. This increase cannot fully be explained by the rate of inflation over that time period. Clearly, economies of scale in bottling, transportation and financing have combined to increase the size of the economically viable operating plant since the early 1900s. In many instances the historically assigned

[3] See U.S. Bureau of the Census [14]. Due to the vertically integrated nature of the soft drink industry, the concentration ratios based on value of shipments cannot be construed in the usual manner and may be misleading depending on the extent of ignored intrafirm transactions as well as double counting in the transition from syrup manufacturing to bottling; while theoretically preferable, the concentration ratios based on value added are also problematic due in part to their sensitivity to profit rate differentials among firms.

[4] See *Business Week* [1].

[5] The 1950, 1960 and 1974 data are found in Hearings before the Subcommittee on Consumer Protection and Finance of the Committee on Interstate and Foreign Commerce [8]. The 1970 data are found in Hearings before the Subcommittee on Commerce and Finance of the Committee on Interstate and Foreign Commerce [7].

[6] See *Softdrinks* [13].

TABLE I

DATA: SOFT DRINK BOTTLING PLANTS

Plant size by annual sales ($)	1967 Number of plants	1967 Percentage of total sales	1971 Number of plants	1971 Percentage of total sales	1973 Number of plants	1973 Percentage of total sales
Over $2,000,000	161	52·1	463	68·9	617	71·8
1,000,000–2,000,000	289	16·0	230	8·8	372	12·4
500,000–1,000,000	537	15·0	563	10·8	540	9·0
300,000–500,000	549	9·4	496	4·8	372	3·1
100,000–300,000	1252	5·4	767	4·4	536	2·6
Under 100,000	763	2·1	396	0·8	290	0·4
Unclassified	99		75		58	
Total	3650	100·0	2990	100·0	2785	100·0

Sources: *Softdrinks*, January 1968, p. 24; January 1972, p. 23; January 1974, p. 30.

territories are just unable to support even the minimum-sized efficient plant. This has led to the disappearance through merger of the smallest plants[7] and a concomitant increase in large multiplant operations. In 1967, 62·5% of total soda sales were accounted for by large, multiplant bottlers, subsidiaries of large conglomerate corporations and wholly owned subsidiaries of the syrup manufacturers.[8] These same ownership categories were responsible for only 43·3% of total sales in 1958.[9]

Since bottlers, as distinct from syrup producers, do not operate nationwide,[10] concentration ratios for SIC category 2086, bottled and canned soft drinks, understate the relevant market share of the large bottlers. An attempt to assess market share in meaningful markets was conducted in 1963; the four largest bottlers in nine metropolitan areas were found to share, on average, 68% of total soft drink sales.[11]

Bottlers select the equipment employed in the manufacturing process and have full discretion in pricing, although there is insistence from the syrup manufacturer that, given the price, market penetration be maximized. Current delivery practices of bottlers involve a store-door system and bottlers are proscribed from selling soft drinks to retailers if the known intent of the retailer is to trans-ship the product outside of the bottler's geographic territory. This precludes deliveries to chain store warehouses, although sales to chain stores typically account for somewhat more than one-fifth of bottler

[7] The bottling plant attrition rate was 10% in 1967–68, 7% in 1968–69, 5% in 1969–70, 4% in 1970–71 and 2% in 1971–72. See, *Softdrinks* [13].

[8] See Hearings before the Subcommittee on Consumer Protection and Finance of the Committee on Interstate and Foreign Commerce [8, p. 30].

[9] *Ibid.*

[10] There are some exceptions. For example, Shasta which began as a West Coast canned product is now distributed nationwide.

[11] See Hearings before the Subcommittee on Consumer Protection and Finance of the Committee on Interstate and Foreign Commerce [8], in which is cited Part II of a 1963 report on Concentration Ratios in Manufacturing Industry prepared by the U.S. Bureau of the Census for the Subcommittee on Antitrust and Monopoly of the Committee on the Judiciary, U.S. Senate, 90th Congress, 1st Session, 1967.

sales.[12] Bottlers also are restricted from bottling competitive cola products, but may bottle other trademarked sodas. For example, The Coca-Cola Bottling Company of New York bottles Dr. Pepper and Welch's; in Baltimore, Dr. Pepper is bottled by the local Pepsi bottler. This practice, known as 'piggybacking', has increased in frequency in recent years: in 1971, 60% of the licensed Coca-Cola bottlers also bottled sodas trademarked by other companies.[13]

II. TERRITORIAL EXCLUSIVITY: THEORY AND IMPLICATIONS

Vertically imposed territorial exclusivity in the soft drink industry eliminates direct intrabrand competition and creates regional bottlers with monopoly power in the manufacture and distribution of trademarked sodas. Syrup manufacturers had several motives for creating geographical franchises and continue to find these restrictions advantageous for a variety of reasons.

Historical Considerations

Before 1850 soft drinks were sold almost exclusively at fountains for consumption there, but by the late 1800s a growing number of syrup producers entered the business as techniques developed sufficiently to permit bottling. High transportation costs of both filled bottles and returned empties, however, made long distance shipping impractical, limiting bottling to localized areas. Profitably able to produce increased amounts of syrup, but restrained from market expansion by high transportation and distribution costs, the small turn-of-the-century syrup producers began to rely on franchising to increase their sales. By 1904 The Coca-Cola Company, formed in 1892, had already entered into agreements which allowed 123 plants to bottle and sell Coca-Cola. In an effort to induce the authorized bottlers to make the necessary initial as well as continuing capital and promotional investments, the syrup company conferred on them exclusive territories in which they could be assured that no other bottler of the same soda would be able to compete. This was allegedly necessary both to elicit the desired amount of capital equipment (thereby also maintaining some quality control on the final product) and to induce advertising, the gains from which would not be subject to problems of appropriability.[14] In effect, the costless granting of territorial exclusivity by the syrup manufacturers to the bottlers lowered the risk attached to investments in fixed plant and equipment, thereby shifting the marginal efficiency of investment curve outward to the right. Assuming the induced level of bottler investment provided for improved production (i.e. lower average costs) and distribution, the syrup manufacturers would benefit through increased quantity of soda demanded and hence increased

[12] See Transcript [4, p. 660] (Smith). See also Initial Decision [9, p. 33].
[13] See Transcript [4, p. 689].
[14] See Proposed Findings of Fact [12, p. 15].

syrup sales. Increased advertising would shift demand for soda outward and again increase syrup sales. Thus, by entering into these contractual arrangements, the syrup manufacturers gained access to additional markets and assured themselves of wide product availability (with its associated externality: increased sales due to product familiarity), all without the costs associated with distribution of the final product.

Contemporary Advantages

Exclusive geographic territories benefit syrup producers both by increasing bottler profits and by facilitating the recovery of these larger profits by the syrup manufacturers. Some of the profit recovery methods operate by fostering increased syrup sales.

1. *Increased Bottler Profits*

(1) Assuming differential price elasticities of demand for soda in different areas of the country due to variations in income, tastes and preferences, prices of substitutes, and temperature, market-separating price discrimination by the bottlers would seem advantageous to the syrup producers. In the usual case intraband price competition will thwart successful price discrimination; however, by granting the independent franchised bottlers territorial exclusivity, the syrup manufacturers can effectively suppress this intrabrand price competition and foster price discrimination. The existence of a set of wholesale prices of soda implies greater nationwide bottler profits than would have been generated had a uniform price prevailed.[15]

(2) Exclusive territories also lead to a higher volume of advertising than would otherwise be forthcoming from the bottlers. In fact, only seven of the 133 major domestic industries have higher advertising to sales ratios than those in the total soft drink industry, and the ratio for bottlers is more than four times that for syrup producers.[16] In the absence of exclusive territorial arrangements a problem of appropriability would develop where each bottler would hold back on advertising, hoping to reap the benefits of his competitors' expenditures. The higher total volume of advertising associated with territorial exclusivity can be expected to shift demand for soda outward to the right, also making it more inelastic; *ceteris paribus*, bottler profits will increase, as will syrup sales.

(3) Bottlers unable to achieve sufficient economies of scale due to territorial size or managerial considerations are systematically forced from the bottling business. Syrup manufacturers apparently formulate long-run plans for the elimination of small bottlers so that the size distribution of bottlers will change in an orderly manner, minimizing the risk of destructive price com-

[15] See Oi [10].

[16] Cited in statement of J. Halverson in Exclusive Territorial and Customer Restrictions Hearings before the Subcommittee on Monopolies and Commercial Law of the Committee on the Judiciary [5, 319.] Also see Ornstein [11, pp. 81, 82].

petition while providing increased opportunities for large bottlers to maximize profits due to superior technology as well as increased price setting ability. The targeting of bottlers to be eliminated is aided by the existence of territorial exclusivity. For example, in 1967, prior to the FTC complaint, The Coca-Cola Company created a Bottler Consolidation Department for the sole purpose of encouraging mergers between bottlers.[17] Many of the territories are so small that they cannot support full-time operation of an even minimally efficient bottling line; when these franchises are merged into larger bottlers in many cases the small acquired plant is turned into a distribution facility.[18] Taking some liberties in the approach used by Comanor and Wilson[19] to estimate the minimum efficient plant size, and using the information that plants with sales of $2 million and over account for roughly 70% of total sales, the market share of a plant selling $2 million in 1971 is about 0·04% of total market sales. This is approximately seven times the market sales that the modal plant was selling in 1971, indicating that many bottling plants are below the minimum efficient size. Thus, it would seem to be in the interest of The Coca-Cola Company to encourage mergers among its franchised bottlers, and in this way attempt to increase the overall sum of bottler profits.

2. *Recovery by Syrup Manufacturers of Bottler Profits*

Since the demand for syrup is derived from the demand for soft drinks, long-run profits of syrup manufacturers depend on extracting as much of the profits generated by the bottlers as possible, consistent with the long-run viability of the bottlers. Charging different syrup prices to different bottlers would be a way of obtaining the monopoly rents, but would be an illegal use of price discrimination.[20] Instead, alternative methods of profit recoupment are employed.

(1) Bottlers are forced to undertake a major portion of product advertising. In 1963 and 1967, the two years for which these data are available, the advertising to sales ratios (as a percentage) for SIC category 2086 (bottled and canned soft drinks) were 5·02 and 4·83, respectively, and for category 2087 (flavorings, extracts and syrups) 1·28 and 1·10, respectively.[21] Since syrup producers have no need to advertise to their franchised bottlers, it can be assumed that their advertising is aimed at the promotion of soft drink sales. The mean advertising to sales ratio (as a percentage) for 133 major domestic industries over the period 1966–68 was 0·90.[22] Without territorial

[17] See Proposed Findings of Fact [12, pp. 215, 216]. Also Transcript [4, pp. 627, 859, 965].

[18] See Proposed Findings of Fact [12, p. 105].

[19] Comanor and Wilson [3].

[20] For example, see *FTC v. Morton Salt Co.* [6] where quantity discounts to chain stores were declared injurious to independent grocers and disallowed.

[21] See Ornstein [11, pp. 77, 78, 81, 82]. Of course SIC category 2087 encompasses production other than that of syrups for soft drinks, but data were lacking on advertising expenditures in the more narrowly defined category.

[22] See Exclusive Territorial and Customer Restrictions Hearings before the Subcommittee on Monopolies and Commercial Law of the Committee on the Judiciary [5, p. 319].

exclusivity it seems unlikely that the syrup manufacturers, who benefit from the relatively high advertising intensity of the bottlers via increased syrup sales, could have induced such advertising intensity and its accompanying shift of costs onto the bottlers.

(2) Bottlers are forced to exceed profit maximizing output levels. According to the terms of the franchise agreements, bottlers are obliged to serve all would-be customers within the designated market area,[23] and all accounts, regardless of size, are served at an identical price. Territorial exclusivity allows the syrup manufacturer to deal continuously over time with one bottler per area and thereby more easily assess whether or not an individual bottler is indeed serving all potential customers, and redress the situation if it is found to be unsatisfactory.[24] Fear of termination of the franchise acts as a stimulant to increase market coverage. While it is true that even an unregulated monopolist serves all would-be customers at its self-selected price, the threat of franchise termination coupled with the visibility of a single bottler per territory (who for lack of intrabrand competitors cannot claim capricious changes in market share, and who can easily be singled out as the unserving supplier if retail outlets complain to the parent syrup company about failure to obtain service), allows the syrup manufacturer to push the bottlers beyond a profit maximizing output and toward a (constrained) maximization of sales revenue. Claims by bottlers that they service many unprofitable accounts tend to support the sales forcing hypothesis.[25] Given positive marginal costs, the (constrained) revenue maximizing position is consistent with a higher level of output than is the profit maximizing position, generating increased demand for syrup, as well as an externality: increased availability can be expected to shift the demand curve outward, also making it more inelastic, in much the same way as advertising. The stress on pushing sales beyond the profit maximizing point has two effects: overall bottler profits available for 'repatriation' to the syrup manufacturers shrink, but the increased soda availability increases demand for soda and hence syrup sales. It may simply be too difficult to design mechanisms to recoup all the excess profits generated by profit maximizing bottlers, leaving the syrup manufacturers to trade off higher bottler profits for more recoverable profits by forcing bottlers to exceed their desired level of soda sales, thereby profiting from the resulting higher syrup sales.

It is also possible that if the appropriate number of bottlers exists (implying minimized average costs of production throughout the country), and

[23] See, for example, Transcript [4, p. 751].

[24] In the case of The Coca-Cola Bottling Company of Taft, California, large increases in syrup orders were flagged by The Coca-Cola Company which then refused to sell in such extraordinary amounts to Taft.

[25] See Transcript [4, p. 660], and also Initial Decision [9, p. 33]. Of course, it may be that market coverage can be viewed as another form of advertising to which there are marketing externalities: that is, expanded availability may lead to increased purchases in the so-called profitable accounts, in which case there is a problem of jointness. Or perhaps the claim of serving unprofitable units is mainly a response to antitrust attack: witness a similar argument in the securities business concerning the small investor.

if the syrup manufacturers can successfully force the bottlers down the demand curve past the profit maximizing sales point, instead of the familiar left-handed tangency of the demand and average cost curves resulting from free entry into the bottling business, *ceteris paribus*, the entry restrictions and serving requirements together may lower the average costs of bottling the quantity offered for sale.[26] Other things equal, the lower the average cost of production of the final bottled product, the more bottled soda will be sold, and hence the more syrup will be bought by the bottlers.

(3) Bottlers are forced to maintain quality standards established by the syrup manufacturers. Territorial exclusivity makes monitoring quality standards less costly for two reasons: (1) fewer bottlers to monitor, and (2) less likelihood of quality cutting as a response to an intrabrand competitor's attempt to serve the same highly desired accounts. Syrup manufacturers uniformly assert that quality control on an item that depends on flavor uniqueness is imperative, and they are aware of the incentives for quality degradation as well as of the potential for profit recovery by forcing the costs of quality maintenance onto the bottlers. It is in the interest of an individual franchisee to degrade quality as he will benefit nonetheless from the advertising expenditures of the syrup manufacturer as well as the bottlers in adjacent territories. Of course, if all bottlers cut quality, syrup sales will be negatively affected in the long run; therefore, syrup manufacturers attempt to enforce quality standards. To the extent that the costs of quality compliance are thrust onto the bottlers, this absorbs some of their monopoly profits.

(4) Establishing franchise fees and/or royalty payments, as well as setting the syrup price, provide other alternatives for capturing bottler profits. Since the input price must be the same for all bottlers, this cannot be relied upon to recoup more profits from the more successful bottlers, and since many early soft drink franchises were freely granted to desiring entrants, these alternatives are of little practical import to syrup manufacturers.

Implications for Market Performance

The advantages of territorial exclusivity discussed above are interrelated in varying degrees. Consequently their effects are not fully separable either.

It has been argued by Comanor [2, p. 1428] and others that, assuming adequate mobility in capital markets, if opportunities for investment will generate an expected rate of return greater than that which can be anticipated elsewhere, these opportunities will be seized. Territorial exclusivity is not a sufficient condition for such an outcome, although it may be necessary. In fact, it is cases in which it is necessary that represent the distortions created by the absence of competition. If by creating exclusive territories the risk, and hence the cost, associated with capital investment is lowered, other things being equal, this will likely result in over-investment in the restricted industry. Such an investment pattern resulting from risk reduction may be

[26] I am indebted to Larry White for discussion on this point.

efficient from a societal viewpoint, as well as desirable to the syrup producers, but the social gains from this risk reduction may be more than offset by the costs to society from the lack of competition.

Regarding advertising volume and the 'free rider' problem, the existence of territorial exclusivity causes more resources to be channeled into advertising by the bottlers than presumably would be bought in its absence. The resulting impact on resource allocation, however, is unclear as the relationship between the amount of advertising that would in fact be done if there were no territorial restrictions and the socially optimal level of advertising remains unknown, as does a proper definition of the socially optimal level of advertising in the soft drink industry. The usual assumption concerning appropriability is that its absence is indicative of a market imperfection which causes output to be less than the optimal amount. Following this reasoning an argument could be made that advertising, given no territorial restrictions, would be less than optimal, suggesting that the existence of exclusive territoriality, by remedying the inappropriability of benefits to advertising, might indeed generate an optimal amount of advertising. Of course, if in the absence of territorial restrictions more than the socially optimal level of advertising would have been generated due to the existence of other market imperfections (for example, market power), the encouragement to further advertising expenditures that territorial exclusivity provides would only worsen an already existing misallocation of resources. As to the vertical shifting of advertising costs, it is also not clear that it is advantageous from the societal point of view to have substantial advertising shifted to bottlers who, given territorial exclusivity, will tend to find the benefits to advertising appropriable and will therefore be led to advertise more than in a competitive situation. In the absence of territorial exclusivity, if the bottlers advertised less than syrup producers desired, the costs of heightened advertising could be borne by the syrup producers. This would occur only if the additional sales revenue generated by each advertising dollar were greater than or equal to the marginal advertising expense. While social costs would still be ignored, at least private costs would be reflected more adequately.

The welfare effects of third degree price discrimination are not clear. Assuming linearity, total output is the same regardless of whether the price established is the simple monopoly price or a system of market separating discriminatory prices; therefore, there is no improvement in resource allocation given the latter condition. Dropping that assumption, it would be possible for a discriminatory price policy to increase output. Both Basil Yamey [17, pp. 377–80] and Oliver Williamson [16, pp. 11–13] discuss the relationship of increased output under discriminatory pricing to improvements in economic welfare and conclude that due to transactions costs involved in identifying, separating, and policing the submarkets, '. . . economic welfare can be reduced when profits and output are increased' [17, p. 12]. Following their arguments, and also owing to the existence of product differentiation in the soft drink industry which affords market participants market or monopoly power but not complete monopoly, no *a priori* conclusion regarding the change in welfare due to systematic price discrimination can be made.

Market coverage is perhaps one of the more debated issues involved in territorial exclusivity. Lee Preston, for example, states that territorial exclusivity should be permitted if the agreements 'make possible, with no direct reduction in the availability of products of other suppliers, a level of market coverage for the supplier's product substantially greater than could be obtained with overlapping distributorships, and . . . do not result in distributor or supplier profit substantially different from "normal" levels for the risk, skill, and capital involved'.[27] The latter point is probably non-operational in general, and impossible to ascertain in the bottling industry where many franchised bottlers are small, family-owned corporations in which the term profit lacks precise meaning. That is, these family-owned businesses may easily alter the profit residual by changing salaries and the number of relatives employed. The former assertion may be flawed economically. Product availability is an inappropriate reason for antitrust policy to be abrogated: indeed, total market coverage at uniform prices leads to higher prices than would prevail without such territorial restrictions in certain outlets and lower prices in others. As argued above, total market coverage is, however, advantageous to the syrup manufacturer as the demand for syrup is derived from the demand for soda. But it is untrue that social efficiency is served by supplying all outlets at a constant cost when the supplying costs differ greatly. For example, supplying supermarkets is much less costly than is supplying low volume outlets. Discarding the underlying cost structures causes prices overall to be higher, again lessening market efficiency: consumers are deprived of the ability to differentiate their purchasing pattern based on prices. Also, given the prohibition on trans-shipping, larger supermarket chains gain no advantages over smaller ones, although theoretically they could be supplied at lower cost. Of course, syrup manufacturers are also cognizant of the advertising externalities associated with increased market coverage. Preston does not discuss this aspect of jointness, but it is clear that its existence increases prices. If for some reasons of public policy universality of a particular product is deemed desirable, it would be less interfering with allocative efficiency to make separate provisions to achieve that end, rather than allow a restrictive practice such as territorial exclusivity to affect such an outcome, along with host of other distortions.

Limiting the total number of bottlers so that they face increased demand, and at the same time forcing them down the demand curve beyond the profit maximizing output may have a desirable social result if the appropriate number of bottlers is attained; bottling costs may be minimized. Yet, even if

[27] See testimony by L. Preston in Hearings before the Subcommittee on Consumer Protection and Finance of the Committee on Interstate and Foreign Commerce [8].

it could be demonstrated that at one hierarchical level minimum costs might be realized, this would still not be a convincing reason to abandon the traditional economic wisdom in favor of non-interference in market relations. It is reasonable to postulate that although minimum points of average cost curves could be attained, these minima might be even higher than the left-handed tangency costs due, for example, to increased advertising costs. It would still be in order to question whether the predisposition to competitive market arrangements ought to be discarded even if a cost-benefit analysis of territorial exclusivity were to demonstrate that the benefits from cost minimization outweighed the other costs of territorial exclusivity, for such entry limiting and service forcing arrangements can only exist when syrup suppliers wield market power. And the presence of market power in a particular industry and at a particular manufacturing level ought not be ignored because it may create lower costs at another stage of production.

While quality control is certainly in the interest of the syrup manufacturers, it is not clear that a non-competitive policy is necessary to achieve it. Forcing bottlers to assume expenditures for quality maintenance is facilitated by territorial exclusivity and no doubt lowers costs to the syrup producers. The syrup manufacturers gain from spinning off costs of quality control as well as from the monopoly position of their bottlers, but the gains to society from lower costs of quality maintenance for the syrup producers may not be offset by the losses to society from the absence of competition.

NEW YORK UNIVERSITY

REFERENCES

[1] *Business Week* (April 25th, 1970), p. 10.

[2] Comanor, William, 'Vertical Territorial and Customer Restrictions: White Motor and its Aftermath', *Harvard Law Review*, **81** (1968), p. 1428.

[3] Comanor, William and Wilson, Thomas, 'Advertising, Market Structure and Performance', *Review of Economics and Statistics*, **XLIX** (November 1967), pp. 423–40.

[4] Transcript, In the Matter of The Coca-Cola Company, Coca-Cola Bottling Company (Thomas), Inc., Coca-Cola Bottling Works (Thomas), Inc., and Coca-Coca Bottling Works 3rd, Inc., Docket 8855.

[5] Exclusive Territorial and Customer Restrictions Hearings before the Subcommittee on Monopolies and Commercial Law of the Committee on the Judiciary, House of Representatives, 94th Congress, 2nd Session on H.R. 6684, June 24th and July 1st, 1976, Serial no. 41.

[6] *FTC v. Morton Salt*, 334 U.S. 37 (1948).

[7] Hearings before the Subcommittee on Commerce and Finance of the Committee on Interstate and Foreign Commerce, House of Representatives, 93rd Congress, 2nd Session, Serial 93–103.

[8] Hearings before the Subcommittee on Consumer Protection and Finance of the Committee on Interstate and Foreign Commerce, House of Representatives, 94th Congress, 1st session, Serial No. 94–12.

[9] Initial Decision by Joseph P. Dufresne, Administrative Law Judge, In the Matter of The Coca-Cola Company, Coca-Cola Bottling Company (Thomas), Inc., Coca-Cola Bottling Works (Thomas), Inc. and Coca-Cola Bottling Works 3rd, Inc., Docket 8855.

[10] Oi, Walter, 'A Disneyland Dilemma: Two-Part Tariffs for a Mickey Mouse Monopoly', *Quarterly Journal of Economics*, **LXXXV** (February, 1971), pp. 77–96.

[11] Ornstein, Stanley I., *Industrial Concentration and Advertising Intensity*, (American Enterprise Institute for Public Policy Research, Washington, D.C., 1977).

[12] Proposed Findings of Fact submitted by Complaint Counsel in the matter of The Coca-Cola Company, Coca-Cola Bottling Company (Thomas), Inc., Coca-Cola Bottling Works (Thomas), Inc., and Coca-Cola Bottling Works 3rd, Inc., Docket No. 8855.

[13] *Softdrinks* (January 1974), p. 30.

[14] U.S. Bureau of the Census, *Concentration Ratios in Manufacturing Industry*, **II** (1972), pp. 20H–6, 20H–8, 20H–20.

[15] U.S. Department of Commerce, *Franchising in the Economy: 1974–76* (U.S. Government Printing Office, Washington, 1976).

[16] Williamson, Oliver, *Markets and Hierarchies: Analysis and Antitrust Implications* (Free Press, New York, 1973).

[17] Yamey, Basil, 'Monopolistic Price Discrimination and Economic Welfare', *Journal of Law and Economics*, **XVII** (October 1974), pp. 377–80.

THE JOURNAL OF INDUSTRIAL ECONOMICS

Published first in October 1952, this Journal was founded to develop the analysis of the problems facing modern industry. It is concerned with the individual business and its relation to the economy—e.g. with outputs and prices and their behaviour in the market, and with the business decisions which affect these. It therefore aims to contribute both to economic theory and to practical public and private policies in the industrial field. The journal is naturally meant to interest business men as well as economists.

The Editors welcome contributions covering the fundamental categories in economics (such as prices, costs, investment, finance, location, wages and productivity) as well as the broader 'background' circumstances (such as the changing structure of industry, management policy and public monopoly policy). Preference is given to MSS bearing on these subjects from the standpoint of individual firms or industries. Theoretical discussion is welcome. Abstract theory is not barred, but authors in this case should provide an introduction and conclusion, so that non-specialist readers may see what the article is about. Alongside articles of more normal length, the Editors are willing to publish shorter notes, especially when these give interim results of important research studies. Books are not reviewed, although books received will be listed, sometimes with a short note; but substantial review articles will be considered. No payment is made to authors, but 40 free offprints are provided. Contributors are asked to send an Abstract, not exceeding 100 words, with their article.

Editorial Offices:

Manuscripts from North America should be sent to Professor H. Michael Mann, Department of Economics, Boston College, Chestnut Hill, Massachusetts, 02167, U.S.A.; manuscripts from the European Continent should be sent to Professor Louis Phlips, Center for Operations Research & Econometrics, Université Catholique de Louvain, 34 Voie du Roman Pays, 1348 Louvain-la-Neuve, Belgium; and from the U.K. and other countries to the General Editor, c/o Department of Economics, University of Lancaster, Bailrigg, Lancaster, England.

Subscriptions, advertising, reprint enquiries, etc.

All correspondence other than that dealing with contributions should be addressed to the Publisher, Messrs. Basil Blackwell & Mott Ltd., 108 Cowley Road, Oxford OX4 1LR, England.

The journal is published quarterly, and the annual subscription for Institutions is £11 (U.K.), £13.20 (Overseas), $30 (U.S.A. and Canada) post free; the prices of single issues are £3.50, £4.20 and $9.50 respectively, post free. For individual subscribers the rates are £9.00 (U.K.), £10.80 (Overseas), $24.00 (U.S.A. and Canada) post free. Remittances should be sent to Basil Blackwell & Mott Ltd.

A photographic reprint is now available of Vols. 1–13, 1952–65, bound in cloth or paper; single volumes in paper only.

CONTRIBUTORS TO THIS NUMBER

IAN W. McLEAN: Senior Lecturer in Economics, University of Adelaide.

DAVID K. ROUND: Senior Lecturer in Economics, University of Adelaide.

PETER S. STEER: Lecturer in Business Studies, Liverpool Polytechnic.

JOHN R. CABLE: Senior Lecturer in Economics, University of Warwick, and Research Fellow, IIM, Berlin.

JOHN NIGHTINGALE: Lecturer in Economics, University of New England, Armidale.

PATRICIO MELLER: Research Economist, CIEPLAN (Santiago), and National Bureau of Economic Research.

MICHAEL W. PUSTAY: Assistant Professor of Economics, Purdue University.

RALPH W. PFOUTS: Professor of Economics, University of North Carolina at Chapel Hill.

BARBARA GOODY KATZ: Assistant Professor of Economics, New York University Graduate School of Business Administration.

The Contents of Volume XXVI, No. 4, June 1978, were:

Market Structure, Oligopoly, and Stability of Market Shares, by R. E. Caves and M. E. Porter, respectively Professor of Economics, Harvard University and Associate Editor of this Journal, and Associate Professor of Business Administration, Harvard University.

Wage Rates, Concentration and Unionization in French Manufacturing Industries by Frédéric Jenny, Professor of Economics, ESSEC, France, and Associate Editor of this Journal.

Market Structure and Innovation: A New Perspective, by Ronald E. Shrieves, Associate Professor of Finance, University of Tennessee.

Stockholder Control, Uncertainty and the Allocation of Resources to Research and Development, by William A. McEachern and Anthony A. Romeo, Associate Professors of Economics, University of Connecticut.

Estimates of Demand Elasticities for International Telecommunications Services, by John D. Rea and Gerald M. Lage, respectively Associate Professor of Economics, and Professor of Economics, Oklahoma State University.

Printed in Great Britain by Adlard & Son Ltd., Bartholomew Press, Dorking

THE JOURNAL OF INDUSTRIAL ECONOMICS

Volume XXVII DECEMBER 1978 **No. 2**

SIR CHARLES CARTER
Some Problems of the British Post Office.

G. C. FETHKE and K. A. CURRIE
Growth of Firms, Capital Market Uncertainty and Managerial Tenure.

J. F. PICKERING
The Abandonment of Major Mergers in the UK 1965–75.

FRANKLIN R. EDWARDS and BARBARA J. STEVENS
The Provision of Municipal Sanitation Services by Private Firms: An Empirical Analysis of the Efficiency of Alternative Market Structures and Regulatory Arrangements.

D. J. STOREY
Market Structure and Externalities: The Case of Water Pollution in England and Wales.

MARTIN R. J. KNAPP
Economies of Scale in Sewage Purification and Disposal.

A. ENDRES
Monopoly-power as a Means for Pollution-control.

ISSN 0022–1821

BASIL BLACKWELL OXFORD ENGLAND

Price: Single Issues: £3.50 (U.K.), £4.20 (Overseas), $9.50 (U.S.A. and Canada)
Annual Subscription for Institutions: £11.00 (U.K.), £13.20 (Overseas), $30.00 (U.S.A. and Canada)
Annual Subscription for Individuals: £9.00 (U.K.), £10.80 (Overseas), $24.00 (U.S.A. and Canada

THE JOURNAL OF INDUSTRIAL ECONOMICS
Volume XXVII December 1978 No. 2

SOME PROBLEMS OF THE BRITISH POST OFFICE

CHARLES CARTER

THE purpose of this article is to review, from the point of view of an industrial economist, some issues arising from the Report of the Post Office Review Committee, of which I was Chairman. (Cmnd. 6850, July 1977: appendix volume of evidence, Cmnd. 6954, November 1977.) The British Post Office dates back to about 1509, as an agency of the Crown to convey letters; but for a long time the fee for conveyance depended on distance, and was paid by the recipient. The business was greatly changed by the simple but far-reaching business invention of Rowland Hill in 1837, an invention which was to be adopted throughout the world. He observed that it would be much easier if a standard fee could be collected from the sender in advance, by his purchase of an adhesive postage stamp. This made possible an expansion of the business which would have been held back if it had continued to carry the costs of individual assessment of the distance travelled by each inland letter, and of personal collection from the recipient. A 'letter' is not defined by statute, and presumably always included a small 'packet': the conveyance of parcels, up to certain weight limits, was added to the Post Office functions in 1883.

The conveyance inland of messages by the 'electric telegraph' became a Post Office function in 1868, no doubt being regarded as a natural accompaniment of the post because it required a large network of local offices to receive messages and to arrange for their delivery. Consequently, when the telephone appeared, initially developed by local companies and then (from 1889) by the National Telephone Company, the network had to be licensed by the Post Office under the Telegraph Act of 1869. In 1892 the Post Office itself took over the function of providing the trunk lines, and by 1899 it was thought desirable for the Post Office and local authorities to compete with the private telephone systems directly, so that steps were taken to provide a Post Office system in London. In 1911 the National Telephone Company was purchased by the Post Office, which since then has effectively had a telephone monopoly, now with the single exception of the licensed municipal service in the city of Kingston upon Hull.

A feature of the British system which distinguishes it from that in the United States and some other countries is the use, in addition to the main or 'Crown' post offices, of a large number of local shops as 'sub-offices' or agents for the Post Office. There is normally a sub-office in any considerable village, and at least one every two miles in the towns. The existence of this network has been highly convenient to Government, which uses it for the payment of social security benefits, the transactions of a National Savings Bank (a deposit account system), the sale of Government securities designed for small savers, and the issue of licences: in recent years the system has also provided the offices for a current account banking service (Giro).

Having begun its existence as a direct exercise of Royal power, the Post Office was until 1969 a Government department, with its own Minister, the Postmaster-General (the successor to the King's Master of the Posts). In that year it became a 'nationalized industry', that is to say a Government-owned corporation with its own directing Board, established by Act of Parliament, with a duty to offer certain services and to 'break even' financially (in a sense not very clearly defined) over a period of years. There is a general power of direction, at present vested in the Secretary of State for Industry, but normally this is not expected to be used. The Post Office is given a statutory monopoly of the carriage of letters (not extending to parcels) and of telecommunications other than broadcasting. The definition of the services to be offered is not a rigid one, even in the monopoly area: thus the Post Office is not a 'common carrier', bound to accept any letter offered to it, though by custom it operates as though it had this obligation.

The non-postal services of the post offices, referred to above, are of course important in helping to carry the overheads of the whole business, but the present article is confined to two central functions, the communication of messages or information, and the carriage of goods in small parcels. Even so, only incidental references are made to telecommunications: the problems in that field are distinct, and would require a separate article. It must be made very clear that what follows relates to the position when the Committee reported, in 1977: since then the Post Office, under a new Chairman, has made certain changes in line with the Committee's recommendations.

The communication of a message by writing it on a piece of paper, and physically conveying the paper to the recipient, is a very simple form of technology, but it has inherent advantages. The recipient has a semi-permanent record of the message, and (if a reply is needed) he can give it at a time to suit his own convenience. The sender can also, by a simple process, keep a record of what he has sent. These are evident advantages over a telephone call, which, even if recorded, does not provide a very convenient record unless one undertakes the added expense of transcription. They are not advantages over Telex and its derivatives, and there is no doubt that inter-office communication by a generalized telex service and by transfers between computers will grow. But the Post Office delivers letters to some 21 million inland delivery points, and only at a small minority of these is the volume of traffic sufficient to carry the cost of terminal equipment for 'electronic mail'. Furthermore, the amount of information capable of transmission in a simple envelope is very great: not just words and figures, but diagrams, pictures in black and white or in full colour, and the intangible

Announcement and call for papers for the

SIXTH CONFERENCE OF EARIE

(European Association for Research in Industrial Economics)

September 9–11, 1979, in Paris

After several meetings of a loosely organized group of European industrial organization economists, it was decided to hold regular annual conferences within EARIE, rotating between countries. We are now requesting abstracts from potential contributors for the 1979 meeting in Paris.

The aim of the Paris meeting is to:

(1) Consider the latest research under the heading 'European Industrial Organization'. (Therefore any papers falling under this heading, as well as survey papers on the state of the art in I.O., will be considered.)

and

(2) Permit economists and policy makers, working on the problems of European industrial structure, to interact with one another in a conducive environment and to establish further links for research and data exchange.

We hope you can participate!! From those wishing to present a paper, we need a one-page abstract no later than March 15th, 1979 for preliminary screening. The papers which will be distributed in advance, should be received for a final review by the steering committee by June 1st. (See below.) Partial financial support for lodging and transportation should be available for those giving papers.

Abstracts, depending on the topic, should be sent to one of the following individuals, as well as to Frederick Jenny:—

Antitrust and Public Policy:

J. D. Gribbin, Price Commission, Market Tower, Nine Elms Lane, London, S.W.8, United Kingdom.

I.O. and Trade:

Alex Jacquemin, Institut des Sciences Economique, Université Catholique, Rue des Wallons, B-1348, Louvain La Neuve, Belgium.

Industry Studies:

Bo Carlsson, Industriens Utreningsinstitut, Storgatan 19, Box 5037, S-10241 Stockholm, Sweden.

Socialist Economics:

Zoltan Roman, Hungarian Academy of Sciences, 112 Budapest, Budaorsi UT 45, Hungary.

Structure and Innovation:

Einar Hope, Institute of Industrial Economics, P.O. Box 3437, 5001 Bergen, Norway.

Theory:

Raymond De Bondt, Katheolike Universiteit, Economics, Dekenstrat 2, B-3006 Leuven, Belgium.

Incentive Structure:

John Cable, University of Warwick, School of Economics, Coventry, United Kingdom, CV4 7AL.

Government Intervention and Regulation:

Jürgen Müller, IIM–WZB Berlin, Platz der Luftbrücke 2–5, D-1 Berlin 42, West Germany,

or,

Sussex European Research Centre, University of Sussex, Brighton, United Kingdom, BN1 4RF.

Structure and Performance:

Manfred Neumann, Friedrich Alexander Universität, Erlangen–Nürnberg, Postfach 2604, D-8500 Nürnberg, West Germany.

Other Topics:

Frederick Jenny, Department of Economics, ESSEC, Boite Postale 105, F-95001 Cergy, France.

FREDERICK JENNY	JÜRGEN MÜLLER
Local Arrangement Chairman	for the EARIE Steering Committee

Printed by Adlard & Son Ltd., Dorking, Surrey

assurance of personal contact provided by the recognition of handwriting. Any of this *can* be transmitted by other means, but many of the more complex examples seem unlikely to be able to bear the cost of doing so—for instance, the distribution of a full-colour mail order catalogue to 100,000 people.

The letter post service is therefore likely to remain essential, but to lose some of the business for inter-office transfers of information or for the transfer of funds (sending a cheque through the post may become outmoded). At the same time, the number of delivery points tends to increase with the number of separate homes, and their geographical spread with the outward growth of towns. The Post Office therefore has to maintain an increasingly extensive distribution system for a volume of business which has been falling since 1968 and may fall further. Such a situation evidently calls for most careful attention to pricing policy, to the stimulation of demand, and to the efficiency of operation of the system.

It may be asked, however, whether it is not possible to abandon parts of the system. It is, indeed, obvious that the cost incurred in providing a postal service in a scattered area such as (say) the Highlands of Scotland must greatly exceed any revenue to be obtained (under a system of uniform country-wide postal rates). But, although the point is not very clearly set out in the Post Office Acts, there is no doubt that it is politically essential to provide a universal service. What the Act actually says is that the Post Office must satisfy 'all reasonable demands' for the conveyance of letters or for telephone service: it is silent about the circumstances in which a demand may be unreasonable. In effect, however, the community has decided that a universal postal service is so essential a part of civilization that it should be provided without regard to the cost of its outlying parts. Presumably there is nevertheless *some* cost which would be regarded as intolerably great: but this issue does not arise in a small country in which the system is dominated by easy transits between large centres. This is fortunate, for it is difficult to conceive of any satisfactory way of abandoning part of the network of deliveries without causing other grave difficulties.

A basic feature of postal systems, which was part of Rowland Hill's discovery in 1837, is that a variation of postage rates within a country by distance does not justify the cost of administering it. A uniform postage rate, however, needs the protection of a monopoly, since otherwise the cheaper transits will be lost to firms which specialize in providing them alone. The political buttress of the postal monopoly is the promise to provide a universal service; it would be much harder to protect a partial service against claims to compete by other partial services.

The Post Office is not, therefore, able to do much about the elaboration of its system, except by such devices as 'garden gate boxes' and central delivery to blocks of flats, and the practicable changes of this kind are not very great. But can the nature of the task of the mail service be simplified?

The elements of the service are, in the simplest case,

Collection
Outward sorting
Transport
Inward sorting
Delivery

These functions do not fit well together. The best use of a sorting office would come with an even flow of work over a large number of hours in each day—probably, indeed, over the full 24 hours if mechanization is taken to its limit. Once upon a time the flow was made more even by having half a dozen collections and deliveries in the day (in cities). But sending a postman round his 'walk' is now an expensive business, even on wheels: so there is pressure to have fewer collections and deliveries, each dealing with a large mass of mail. The consequence is either to produce large fluctuations in sorting office load, or, if this avoided by storing the letters, to produce delays in the mail. Similarly, the transport function is best organized by bulking the mail, and this does not fit easily with sorting office requirements.

The reconciliation of the functions which is most convenient to the Post Office is to have fewer deliveries (and presumably also fewer collections), and to tolerate greater delays to the mail. This is the effect of the proposal called 'once over the ground', which is that deliveries in urban areas should occur once a day and be spread over a considerably longer period than the present first delivery, being organized in two or more 'waves' visiting different districts. This, however, raises difficulties due to a divergence between Post Office costs and social costs. The present first delivery in towns takes place between 7 a.m. and 9.30 a.m. (9.15 a.m. in London). If 92% of first-class letters are delivered on the next working day, this creates a chance of about 84·6% that the answer to a letter sent on Monday *can* be received on Wednesday. (This assumes that the minority of letters arriving in the second delivery can be dealt with during the afternoon.) But, under 'once over the ground', the probability of next-day delivery would drop to about 85%, because some letters would miss the first 'wave' and wait to the next day: and the chance of getting a reply by return would drop sharply, perhaps to only 50–60%, because a lot of recipients would get *all* their mail too late in the day to be able to reply to it on the same day.

The Review Committee, with the assistance of the Confederation of British Industry, attempted to discover the size of the consequent economic loss, but found it impossible to obtain usable responses from firms about so novel a situation. But there must *be* a loss, since the efficiency of business cannot be entirely unrelated to the speed of transacting it: and, for the smaller change of abolishing Sunday collections, we did in fact identify some significant business losses. The Post Office expectation of gain from 'once over the ground' is small, mainly because the change is opposed by the unions, and it is assumed that their members would have to be induced to accept it by higher wages. We thought, though we could not prove, that it was very likely that the social loss would greatly exceed the Post Office gain. We put the matter in another way by saying that we did not consider 'that a country in grave economic difficulty, with an evident need to work hard to restore its fortunes, should tolerate any further slowing down of what is still a major means of business communication'.

This conclusion, however, leaves us with the problem of uneven work flows, a problem likely to get worse in the smaller post offices as inward sorting (i.e. sorting down to groups of premises on a particular 'walk') is moved to the 80 mechanized offices. We were not satisfied that the possibilities of using more part-time workers at peak periods had been sufficiently explored, but no rapid change in this direction is possible, given a large existing labour force which is predominantly full-time and which has reasonable expectations of job security. So it is necessary to explore the implications of a pattern of work analogous to rush-hour traffic on the railways.

The obvious implication is that the marginal cost of business which can be collected, sorted and delivered in the middle of the day is very low. Labour costs are predominant: the second delivery in towns involves calls at a large number of addresses with a volume of mail only one eighth of the first delivery (and declining): doubling or trebling the volume of the second delivery would cost little. Sorting offices generally have a slack period in the middle of the day. The addition of a complete round of collections might be costly, but men and vehicles should be readily available to pick up bulk postings from firms. Furthermore, there is business available to be handled at the low-cost periods, it has a relatively high elasticity of demand, and the likelihood of obtaining considerable volumes of new business at rates which would yield a contribution to overheads is high.

This business is not the normal second-class mail. The two-tier system (which is simply an extension of the old privilege of the 'printed paper rate') contributes to a more even flow of work in sorting offices, but second-class mail is mostly collected and delivered at peak periods. In order to use the low-cost periods to the full, it would be necessary to develop bulk contract mail (e.g. promotional material), the condition of the contract being that the mail should be available for collection in the middle of a day, and should have a transit time of up to four days, with an expectation of delivery by second post in urban areas. The reason for believing that such mail has a high elasticity of demand is that there are substitutes for direct mail—for instance, press and television advertising, or the delivery of circulars and bills to houses by agencies other than the Post Office. (Postage accounts for some 60% of the cost of direct mail advertising, so variations of rates have a considerable effect.) The market for unaddressed mail (i.e. circulars delivered to every house) is also very considerable, and the Post Office has only a small part of it.

Having regard to the value to the Post Office of any new business which makes a contribution in excess of marginal cost, it may be wondered why the necessary action was not taken long ago. The number of letters posted has been falling (although several other developed countries have both higher, and in some cases increasing, mail volumes per head): and the productivity of postal staff has also been falling, the rigidities of the system tending to produce a high correlation between volume of work and productivity. The postman still has to go round his 'walk', even if there are fewer letters to deliver: a half empty post box costs as much to clear as one which is full: it is only in the sorting office that manpower requirements are significantly related to volume of work, and even there the relation is not precise. The consequence is that the Post Office finds it difficult to maintain productivity by any means other than cutting the standard of service, and this is liable to produce a public outcry and much political pressure for the restoration of the cuts. The incentive to seek out means of increasing mail volume is therefore strong.

The reason why the Post Office has been slow to make the search is in part that it has been deceived by its own cost accountancy. The system has been one of 'fully allocated cost', that is the division of all overheads between the various classes of business. The word 'overhead' is often used carelessly to cover some costs where accurate allocation to a particular business is in principle quite possible, but it is thought easier (and sufficiently accurate) to make a rule-of-thumb division. But there are also true overheads, for which no good principle of allocation exists: these will tend to get allocated by volume of business, so that each item—first- or second-class or bulk mail letter—bears the same share of overheads.

In contrast, if you run a supermarket (and one of the members of the Review Committee was the Finance Director of Sainsbury's, so the comparison came easily to us) you expect each continuing line of merchandise to cover its direct cost—to be worth its shelf space—but you seek to cover overheads (and make a profit) on the total of the whole business, and certainly not *pro rata* on each item. A flexible pricing policy, recovering different amounts of overheads on different lines, is a major instrument of commercial policy.

It was, we thought, a confusion of thought to suppose it to be somehow indecent for the Post Office to act with similar flexibility. In parts of its business where it has a total monopoly, with no effective alternative—as is true in some parts of telecommunications—the Post Office might lay itself open to a charge of unfair discrimination if it loaded overheads unevenly on to different consumers, in order to increase its profits. But it has no monopoly of methods of advertising, or of delivering circulars: the effect of a 'fully allocated cost' system on this type of business is liable to be that it is extinguished.

Another difficulty about flexibility of rates is the danger of transfer of existing business to a lower rate. The Post Office already has some contract mail rates (though with very small discounts, mostly based on the sender doing some of the Post Office's work, e.g. by pre-sorting), so the problem of defining a separate class has already been faced. Obviously that definition must be made so that it covers as little as possible of the existing mail, while opening the door to substantial new business. Nevertheless, there will be some transfer of existing mail: it is a matter of commercial judgement whether the loss so caused is offset by the contribution of the new business. The data given to the Review Committee about potential business in this country (and business actually obtained in some other countries) strongly supported the view that the loss would be exceeded by the contribution from new business.

It is worth while to digress at this point to observe the confusion of thought which arises from the ambiguity of the word 'monopoly'. A monopoly of *all means of achieving an end result* is rare, though it exists in the field of telecommunications (e.g. in links between computers). More commonly there is a *particular technique* for achieving an end result. The postal monopoly is a powerful one for functions such as the conveyance of business documents, because the alternative of sending them by private courier is much more expensive. (We noted, however, that this alternative was very commonly used between the main cities in Australia.) But it is not powerful at all for functions such as advertising, which can be carried out in many other ways.

To sum up: the essential problems of the letter service are that the requirements of society produce an uneven pattern of work, and that a system of virtually unchanged extent has to be maintained even if the volume of mail falls. These factors together argue strongly for increasing the volume of mail by means which use the slack periods of the day. No significant difference to these problems can be expected from mechanization. Apart from the greater use of motor transport, there is no technological change which can make a great difference to collection and delivery, until the day arrives when facsimile transmission by the telecommunications system becomes a generally available alternative to the physical carriage of pieces of paper. The mechanization of sorting is a very modest affair, because there is no early prospect of developing a machine which can, with sufficient reliability, read postcodes. The British system of postcodes represents a finer subdivision of the letter flow than that of any other country except Canada. In order to achieve this subdivision without making the code too long, it uses letters as well as numerals: and the problem of getting a correct machine reading of all the letters of the alphabet, however they may be written or typed, is a formidable one. Therefore the mechanization system depends on the manual translation of the postcode or address into a pattern of phosphor dots (a routine clerical job which is, eccentrically, carried out by Postmen Higher Grade), after which the letters, or more accurately the letters of reasonably standard size, can be machine sorted. The savings from this partial mechanization are small, and they were predominantly handed out to staff by a wage deal required to obtain co-operation in operating the system (though the Post Office now appears to argue that the wage increase would have had to be granted on other grounds, in any case).

The study of mechanization reveals a state of affairs depressingly familiar to those who examine investment programmes: if you feed today's information into the original decision, that decision would probably not have been taken or would have been greatly altered: but looking forward from the present time, with the mechanization programme well under way, it is probably better to complete it than to abandon it. It turns out to be extremely difficult to determine a rate of return, because of a disagreement about which of the wage increases which obtained union acceptance of the programme should be charged against it. The Post Office makes the confusion somewhat worse by offering alternative calculations, one based on assumed future wage and price levels and the other on constant prices, but applying the same rate of discount in both cases (10%). It was our view that a lower discount rate should be used in a constant price calculation. The attempt to assume wage and price levels 12 or more years ahead must in any case be fanciful. Pehaps the best assessment is to be obtained from the Post Office's constant price calculation shown on p. 332 of the Appendix volume of the Report, adjusted to show a 'lead in' payment[1] of about £5½ million (that is to say, taking *half* of the wage increase accepted in 1975 in addition to the 'lead in payment' of 20p acknowledged by the Post Office: see p. 362, though the adjustment in Table 8 has not been made), and further varied by using a discount rate of 3% (this being an estimate of the long-term rate of interest if prices were constant and expected to remain so). On this basis the cumulative present value becomes positive on taking in years up to 1992 and amounts to some £30 million if one looks forward to 1995–96 (of which, however, nearly half arises from the last year, in which credit is taken for the residual value of buildings and equipment). The Post Office would wish in addition to take credit for an assumption that postmen's wages will rise faster than prices. It is thus possible to demonstrate a positive return, but it is long delayed.

A point in the Report which has attracted disagreement relates to the differential between first- and second-class postage rates. The cost difference between these two streams is very small (less than ½p on a letter) *provided that* the volume of first-class mail does not overload the sorting and night transit arrangements for this class, and therefore require their costly extension. A *price* difference as low as ½p might produce this overload, and most commentators have argued for a much larger differential (such as the present 2p), on the grounds obscurely argued in such terms as 'to provide customers

[1] A 'lead-in payment' is an addition to the wage in consideration of an expected future improvement of productivity, paid in advance of that improvement in order to persuade workers to adopt new methods.

with a real choice'. If most first-class mail *had* to use the service, there would be an evident case for the Post Office to act as a discriminating monopoly, setting a first-class rate purely to maximize its profit; though, as indicated above, there would probably be an outcry at the 'unfairness' of such a policy in a public body. But in fact there is a considerable volume of mail open to switch between the two services. Let us suppose that, with a second class rate at 7p, the following proportions of the total mail volume would bear the indicated differentials in order to obtain first class service (the figures are imaginary, and for illustration only):

p	%
0	36
1	22
2	16
3	11
4	7
5	4
6 or more	4

If the differential falls from 2p to 1p, the first-class proportion rises from 42 to 64%. The previous first-class posters get an additional consumers' surplus of 1p per letter: but this is eroded, because—

(a) the Post Office gets an extra 1p on 22% of the post, but loses 1p on 42%,

(b) the Post Office suffers additional costs of about ½p a letter on the 22% switched from second to first class.

Therefore, if it is assumed that, as a nationalized industry, the business has to 'break even' both before and after the change of rates, postage rates must be raised, by an average of about 0·3p, and this leads to a loss of consumers' surplus for all users of the posts (and presumably a change in both mail volume and cost per letter). It should be possible, for any such change in differential, to estimate a change in consumers' surplus, and it is sensible to seek a maximum for this surplus. This is evidently very difficult when the data come from a world which has suffered violent inflationary changes, but, for what they are worth, the facts favour a differential nearer to 1p than to 2p.

The parcel post problem is simple but intractable, and has some affinity to the problem of contracts for advertising mail. The Post Office makes large losses on parcels because it acts as if it were a monopolist without having a monopoly. Post Office parcels are subject to competition from other nationalized and private carriers, and from the use of their own vehicles by mail order houses (which provide a large part of Post Office business). The private user of the parcels service very often has a choice of *not* sending a parcel—for instance, sending a token or an order on a local firm instead.

The Post Office enters this competitive environment offering a superior service, namely delivery to any address however remote; no other carrier in practice provides this. It also, apart from the service for local parcels, carries at a standard rate unrelated to distance or convenience of transit. The rates offered or costs incurred in other methods of carriage are all distance-related. Not surprisingly, therefore, there has been a large loss of the more easily carried business. If British Rail announced one morning that all single passenger tickets would cost £7, however short or long the journey, it is reasonable to suppose that trains from London to Glasgow would be crowded and trains from London to Guildford empty.

If it were to act competitively, the Post Office would start with considerable advantages. Its nationwide service rides on the back of what is already provided for the letter post—though, perversely, the Post Office seems anxious to create a partially separate distribution system for parcels. The costs incurred in adding a parcels service to a letter service must be much less than those incurred in developing an entirely separate system. But it is not enough to say 'go and compete'. On a free competitive business judgement, the Post Office would not provide for the most difficult transits, or would quote for them rates so high that they could hardly ever be used. But the advantage to the public of having one service which (up to a certain weight or size) is universal—i.e. which will deliver to any address—and one which is easily accessible at the familiar collecting-points of the 23,000 post offices, is very great: it is not politically conceivable that the universality could be abolished. It may be supposed that the disadvantage to the Post Office of providing a universal service is largely offset by the relation to an, already universal, letter service: the postman delivering a parcel to a remote farm in the Hebrides will do so in the course of a normal letter round. But, to the extent that this offset is not complete, the Post Office has some claim for help for its parcel post—a point not made in the Report, probably because of a general dislike for subsidies: we admitted indirectly, however, that there might be an internal subsidy from letters to parcels.

There is another difficulty about adopting a straight competitive policy. There is no official definition of a 'letter', but by tradition small packets are accepted in the letter post, and consequently enjoy the uniformity of rates which derives from the Rowland Hill principle. At some point in the scale of weights, alternative possibilities of carriage become serious, and the Post Office monopoly can no longer be deemed to offer protection. At that point distance-related charges should begin; but there are evident boundary problems in changing from a flat to a distance-related scale, and the right point for a change-over is a matter of conjecture. There seems, however, to be little point in overlapping scales for packets and parcels.

The Post Office's main competitors are the British Rail parcels service, and the private distribution systems used by large firms. In principle, a public system should be capable of operating as cheaply as any private system, and, with appropriate distance-related charges and discounts for quantity, successful competition should not be impossible. There is, however a difficulty about the British Rail service, which competes in the Post Office weight range (up to 10 kg), because of the suspicion that (on a proper costing basis) this may be being offered at a loss. It would be appropriate for Government to ensure fair conditions of competition between the nationalized carriers, lest they should competitively bid down prices, relying on the public purse to make up the deficit. The Review Committee suggested that the Post Office might be the sole public sector carrier for smaller parcels (say, up to 3 kg); this is the business for which it is most likely that British Rail is making a loss, and reserving small parcels to the Post Office would make it easier to deal with the overlap with letter-rate packets. The Post Office could then compete with other carriers in the range 3–10 kg. The other public sector hauliers, and the private hauliers, are mostly interested in parcels beyond the Post Office weight limit, so the competition would mainly be with British Rail and with the use of firms' own transport.

The study of the Post Office should be of interest to industrial economists because, although simple economic principles are relevant (and have sometimes been ignored), the detailed decisions are much affected by the institutional framework, by political expectations and by technological fact. This is, in Marshall's words, 'mankind in the ordinary business of life', working in a large, visible and rather special industry: a useful place to try out one's economic preconceptions on a practical problem.

UNIVERSITY OF LANCASTER

THE JOURNAL OF INDUSTRIAL ECONOMICS
Volume XXVII December 1978 No. 2

GROWTH OF FIRMS, CAPITAL MARKET UNCERTAINTY AND MANAGERIAL TENURE

G. C. FETHKE AND K. A. CURRIE*

I. INTRODUCTION

'Managerial' theories of the firm recognize that such structural–institutional factors as separation of ownership from control, oligopolistic markets, capital market transaction costs and modern corporate organizational forms permit managers considerable discretion in pursuing goals other than the neoclassical objective of wealth maximization; these aspects of large firms have been developed by Baumol [1], O. E. Williamson [16], Marris [8], [9], Penrose [11], Solow [13], J. Williamson [15], Yarrow [18] and Jensen and Meckling [6]. Consequently, the performance of managerial firms with respect to pricing, marketing and investment policies may depart considerably from that of their neoclassical counterpart. The extent and social importance of managerial discretion depends primarily upon the efficacy of alternative social-control institutions for enforcing internal efficiency. More particularly, performance depends on product and capital market constraints on the manager's choice set. While most of the empirial evidence regarding the extent of non-wealth-maximizing behavior consists of casual observation of particular abuses, recent empirical work by Grabowski and Mueller [3], Kuehn [7] and Smiley [12] reveals that the latitude for the exercise of managerial discretion may be considerable.

This paper extends the analysis of managerial models of the growing firm by examining the nature of stochastic capital market controls on the latitude of managerial discretion. Specifically, the formulation depicts management's tenure in office to be a random variable whose probability density function depends on the level of managerial discretion, where discretion is defined as the difference between managerial policy and long-run profit-maximization policy. A management that pursues profit maximization will face relatively little threat of capital market discipline, while a more divergent policy subjects managers to a greater threat of removal from office, either from owners or takeover by other firms.

The approach taken here is similar to that of statistical renewal theory. The hazard function of renewal theory becomes the conditional probability that managers will be replaced in some short interval, given that they have survived to that time. There are apparent advantages to this viewpoint.

* We are indebted to Richard Cyert and, especially, the anonymous referees for encouragement and helpful comments.

First, capital market sanctions directly affect tenure of management. Second, the framework defines the concept of managerial discretion and links this important notion to the stochastic operation of the capital market. Third, the model offers an appealing interpretation of the planning horizon. Finally, while we only examine behavior of managers who receive utility from expanding the size of the firm, the approach can be applied to a broader range of managerial models.

Section II develops a traditional wealth-maximizing model for a management whose behavior corresponds with owner-interest. The purposes of this section are to specify the nature of dynamic constraints on the rate of firm expansion, to determine a wealth-maximizing growth path that is parametric to the managerial formulation and to examine the effects on wealth-maximizing growth of changes in key parameters. Section III contains the managerial model. Section IV offers analytical results based on the assumption that optimum growth is constant. Section V provides a summary and conclusion.

II. A WEALTH-MAXIMIZING MODEL

A 'traditional' management selects an investment policy that maximizes the discounted present-value of future earnings, and retains (distributes) these earnings in a manner consistent with the interest of owners. Of several equivalent ways of representing a wealth-maximizing firm, we depict managers as seeking to maximize the present value of net profits (cash flow):

$$V = \int_0^\infty [\Pi\{M(t)\} - C\{\dot{M}(t), M(t)\}] \exp(-it)\, dt, \tag{1}$$

where $i > 0$ is the interest rate, $\Pi\{M(t)\}$ is gross profit, $M(t)$ is the replacement value of tangible assets, $C\{\dot{M}(t), M(t)\}$ is a cost of expansion function and $\dot{M}(t) = \{dM(t)\}/dt$ is net investment.

Several assumptions are used to provide structure for the following analysis.[1] First, gross profit is defined to be net of replacement investment, and average gross profit is assumed to be independent of scale. Thus, $\Pi\{M(t)\} = \pi_N M(t)$ where π_N is a positive constant. Since depreciation of tangible assets is subtracted from gross operating profit, it is described by a pattern of exponential decay. Second, following Penrose [11] and Uzawa [14], the expansion cost function has the separable form, $C\{g(t);\ \alpha\}M(t)$, where $g(t) = \{\dot{M}(t)\}/\{M(t)\}$ is the growth rate of net assets and α is a shift parameter. Expansion costs are increasing, differen-

[1] A more complete discussion of the implications of these and other restrictions on the optimal growth path of the wealth-maximizing firm is contained in Currie and Fethke [2]. There, the value of corporate assets, $M(t)$, is considered to be an agglomeration of physical capital, demand generating 'goodwill' and managerial skill. Conditions are stated which permit aggregation of these multiple assets, measured in dollars, into a composite asset.

tiable and strictly convex for all $g(t)$; without loss of generality, at $g(t)=0$, $C(0)=0$ and $C'(0)=1$. An increase in the shift parameter, α, will increase both total and marginal cost of expansion. Finally, the growth path is bounded ($g_{\min} \leq g(t) \leq g_{\max} < i$). The upper boundary prevents $g(t)$ from becoming too large and, thereby, causing unstable behavior of the firm's market value as $g(t)$ approaches the interest rate. The lower boundary is interpreted as the fastest rate at which assets can be worked off, or reduced.

Given these structural conditions, the market value of the firm becomes

$$V=\int_0^\infty \left\{\pi_N - C\left(\frac{\dot{M}(t)}{M(t)}\right)\right\} M(t) \exp(-it)\, dt, \tag{2}$$

with $\{\dot{M}(t)\}/\{M(t)\}=g(t)$, $g_{\min} \leq g(t) \leq g_{\max}$, and M_0 given.

This representation implies that market value is homogeneous of degree one in initial assets: combining two small firms will yield a large firm whose present value is twice the average present value of the smaller firms. Furthermore, under this homogeneity condition, expansion is independent of initial scale and depends only on average net profitability of assets, π_N, and the interest rate, i. Since these are assumed to be constant over the infinite planning horizon, the optimal growth path is constant, that is, $g^*(t)=g^*$.[2]

Constant growth implies that assets in period t are represented as $M(t)=M_0 \exp(gt)$, and discounted net profit is expressed as

$$\{\pi_N - C(g)\}M_0 \exp\{-(i-g)t\}.$$

Convergence of the integral (2) occurs when $i > g$, a condition that is assured by the boundary restriction on the growth rate. Specifically, we assume that there exists a growth rate, $\tilde{g}$, such that $\tilde{g} \leq g_{\max} < i$ and $C(\tilde{g})=\pi_N$. Consequently, sufficiently high growth rates are unprofitable due to rapidly rising expansion costs. This assumption is similar to that used by Williamson [15] and Solow [13] who examine, in depth, the relationship between the interest rate and the steady-growth path.

The wealth-maximizing growth rate, g^*, results by maximizing

$$V(g)=\{\pi_N - C(g)\}M_0/(i-g), \tag{3}$$

subject to $g_{\min} \leq g \leq g_{\max} < i$. Here $V(g)$ is the present value of the firm.

[2] A proof of the steady growth property when the value of the firm is a linear homogeneous functional is provided by Uzawa [14, pp. 641–3]. At time zero, optimum growth depends on $M(0)$, π_N and i, that is, $g(0)=F\{M(0), \pi_N, i\}$. If $g(t)$ is the optimum path for the increase in assets starting at $M(0)$, then $g(\lambda)$, $t \leq \lambda < \infty$ is optimal with respect to $M(t)$, and can be written as $g(t)=F\{M(t), \pi_N, i\}$. The functional (2) is homogeneous of degree one and $F(M, \pi_N, i)$ is, thereby, homogeneous of degree zero in M, that is, $g(t)=f(\pi_N, i)$. For given values of π_N and i (assuming static expectations), $g(t)$ is constant. Alternatively, a dynamic programming formulation can be established by assuming that the expansion rate is chosen over a small interval. Since the objective function of management is identical for the first and all subsequent intervals, the principle of optimality assures that the growth rate must be constant.

The expression $1/(i-g)$ is the reciprocal of the net profit (dividend) yield and measures 'the number of years' purchase' applied to dividends growing at rate g.[3] A necessary condition for g^* to be a local, interior solution is

$$C'(g^*) = \{\pi_N - C(g^*)\}/(i-g^*). \tag{4}$$

Since $V''(g^*) = -C''(g^*)M_0/(i-g^*) < 0$, the sufficient condition for a local maximum is satisfied. Thus, a growth rate is selected that equates marginal cost of expansion with the increase in the value of the firm per dollar increase in the net present value of assets. Furthermore, if average net profit is greater than the interest rate plus the rate of depreciation of tangible assets ($\pi_N > i + \delta$), then g^* is positive.[4]

With the optimal path determined from equation (4) as a function of the interest rate, average net profit and the expansion cost parameter, $g^* = g(i, \pi_N, \alpha)$, it develops that

$$\frac{\partial g^*}{\partial \pi_N} = \frac{1}{(i-g)C(''g^*)} > 0, \tag{5}$$

$$\frac{\partial g^*}{\partial i} = -\frac{C'(g^*)}{(i-g^*)C''(g^*)} < 0 \tag{6}$$

and

$$\frac{\partial g^*}{\partial \alpha} = \frac{-\left(\dfrac{\partial C}{\partial \alpha} + \dfrac{\partial^2 C}{\partial \alpha \partial g}(i-g^*)\right)}{(i-g^*)C''(g^*)} < 0. \tag{7}$$

When the goal of management is wealth maximization, an increase in average net profit will increase optimal growth; an increase in the rate of interest will decrease growth; and, finally, an increase in the cost of expansion will reduce the optimal growth of the firm. The wealth-maximizing growth path and its determinants are used in the following analysis of a managerial firm, which derives utility from expanding the size of the enterprise.

III. THE MANAGERIAL MODEL

With separation of ownership from control, as well as the other aforementioned institutional features of large firms, maximization of stockholder wealth may not be the best description of managerial motivation. Rather, managers may select a combination of pecuniary and non-pecuniary rewards

[3] Under the model's structure, the method of financing expansion does not affect market value, nor does a restriction to internal financing limit the firm's expansion [9], [15]. For these reasons, this representation as well as most models of the growing firm assumes internal financing of investment [13], [18].

[4] A positive growth rate is optimal because $V'(g) > 0$ for non-positive growth rates when $\pi_N > i + \delta$, where $V'(g) = \{\pi_N - C(g) - (i-g)C'(g)\}/(i-g)^2$. We are here interpreting $g_{\min} = -\delta$ as the fastest rate at which tangible assets can be worked-off. For sufficiently high growth rates, rapidly rising expansion costs imply that $V'(g_{\max}) < 0$. Since $V'(g)$ is continuous, a positive interior solution exists. The strict convexity of expansion costs assures a unique solution on the interior region of the feasible growth paths.

and adopt investment and expenditure policies that enhance their own salaries, emoluments, status and prestige: the values of these variables need not coincide with wealth maximization. While such behavior is formalized by various hypotheses, we adopt the view that managerial utility is closely associated with the size and growth of the firm. This position is consistent with a significant institutional and theoretical literature that emphasizes growth of the firm as the principal source of managerial utility, and includes the contributions of Penrose [11], Marris [8], [9] and J. Williamson [14]. Interpretation and modifications on this theme are provided by Solow [13], Heal and Silberston [4], Yarrow [17] and Herendeen [5].

Following the common practice in the literature as well as keeping in conformance with the wealth-maximizing model in section II, we are led towards a 'steady state' type of analysis. Essentially, the restriction to examine only constant growth policies is one of convenience [9, pp. 11–15] and [4]. Certainly, firms do not grow at steady rates. Such a restriction, however, does enable analysis and discussion of the forces that may permit managers to pursue goals other than wealth maximization. For these reasons most of the literature on growing firms adopts the steady-growth specification.

In general, managerial utility will depend on both the initial size of the firm and its rate of growth. In the following analysis, we assume that initial size is historically given, and that expansion develops from that point. Given this condition and assuming that optimal growth is constant, it is of no consequence whether managers derive satisfaction from maximizing the utility associated growth or by maximizing the size of the firm at all points in time, the preference functions are equivalent.[5] Consequently, the following analysis presumes that managers possess a utility function with the growth of net assets being its only argument. This view does not ignore wealth considerations. The effect and influence of wealth on managerial behavior is represented by a stochastic capital market limitation on the tenure of management.

III. I CAPITAL MARKET LIMITATIONS ON MANAGERIAL TENURE

The purpose of this section is to suggest how the capital market operates to impose stochastic limitations on the exercise and latitude of managerial discretion. We define managerial discretion as the ability of current management to adopt a growth rate that differs from the long-run profit-maximizing rate, g^*, which is the growth rate determined by equation (4). Specifically,

[5] This is not the case if initial size can be selected along with the steady rate of growth. Indeed, Solow [13] demonstrates that selection of initial scale will introduce troublesome analytical consequences into the Marris and Williamson formulations of the growth-oriented firm. Solow, however, also drops the assumption that initial size can be selected by management; this enables a comparison between profit-maximizing and growth-oriented firms.

discretion, '*s*', is defined as the difference between the selected rate of expansion and the wealth-maximizing rate, that is

$$s=g-g^*. \tag{8}$$

The capital market sets a form of stochastic control over the discretionary behavior of managers. The degree of capital market control is described by the properties of a probability density function that represents the threat of replacement.

Managers assume control at time $t=0$ and remain in office until $t=T_s$, the period at which they are removed. While management cannot determine the exact length of their tenure, they can, presumably, affect the probability density function of removal through their selection of a growth rate. Let $f_s(t)$ be the subjective probability density function of removal for a given level of discretion, s, then the probability that a management will be replaced in the interval $(t, t+\mathrm{d}t)$ is

$$Pr(t \leqq T_s \leqq t+\mathrm{d}t)=\int_t^{t+\mathrm{d}t} f_s(\tau)\,\mathrm{d}\tau.$$

The resulting probability distribution function for T_s is

$$F_s(t)=Pr(T_s \leqq t)=\int_0^t f_s(\tau)\,\mathrm{d}\tau, \tag{9}$$

and describes the probability that a management adopting a given level of discretion will be removed from office in the interval 0 to t.

To develop the relationship between the selection of a growth rate, the level of discretion, and the probability of replacement, we introduce a function, $h(s, t)$, called the 'conditional rate of removal function'. This function, which is also called a hazard or intensity function in the mathematical theory of reliability [10, pp, 168–9], is represented as

$$h(s, t)=\frac{f_s(t)}{1-F_s(t)}. \tag{10}$$

In words, $h(s, t)\mathrm{d}t$ is the conditional probability that management will be replaced between t and $t+\mathrm{d}t$, given that it has survived a time T_s greater than t,

$$h(s, t)\,\mathrm{d}t=Pr(t \leqq T_s \leqq t+\mathrm{d}t \mid T_s \geq t).$$

There are a number of plausible assumptions that can be made regarding the properties of $h(s, t)$. We assume the simplest form, namely, the conditional density is independent of time and depends only on the constant degree of discretion, $h(s, t)=h(s)$. This assumption, known as the constant risk hypothesis, implies that

$$Pr(t \leqq T_s \leqq t+\mathrm{d}t \mid T_s \geq t)=Pr(t_s \leq \mathrm{d}t).$$

Thus, the conditional probability of removal from office is the same for any period of length dt.

While the conditional density is presumed to be independent of time, its level depends on the level of discretion selected by management. We assume that the conditional probability of replacement, $h(s)$, is strictly convex with its minimum value occurring at $s=0$. If $h(s)$ is differentiable for all values of s, then $h'(0)=0$. This is the *discretionary case* and will receive the most attention in the following analysis. In the discretionary case, there is risk of replacement that increases at an increasing rate as the chosen growth path deviates from the wealth-maximizing path, g^*. A management that selects g^* faces minimum threat of removal from office, however, it will not enjoy the satisfaction, prestige and status that accompanies a higher path.

It is also possible, if the capital market restriction is particularly tight, for $h(s)$ to exhibit a sharp kink at $s=0$. If this occurs, the optimum path may coincide with the wealth-maximizing rate, g^*, even though management is subjectively willing to trade risk of replacement for higher growth.

It is now a relatively simple matter to interpret the probability distribution associated with replacement of management and to establish the properties of the expected time of removal. For the discretionary case, integration of equation (10) with $h(s, t)=h(s)$ and $F_s(0)=0$, yields

$$F_s(t)=1-\exp\{-h(s)t\}, \tag{11}$$

which is the familiar exponential distribution.[6] For a particular degree of discretion, expected time to replacement is the reciprocal of the conditional density function of removal, that is

$$E[T_s]=\int_{-\infty}^{\infty} T_s f_s(T_s)\, dT_s=\frac{1}{h(s)}. \tag{12}$$

The effect of an increase in the level of discretion on $E[T_s]$ is

$$\frac{\partial E[T_s]}{\partial s}=\frac{-h'(s)}{h(s)^2}<0 \qquad \text{for } s>0. \tag{13}$$

Thus, an increase in managerial discretion will decrease expected tenure.

III. 2 THE MANAGERIAL PREFERENCE FUNCTION

There are a number of specific preference representation for managers who are willing to sacrifice profit for a higher growth rate. Possibly, the

[6] It is interesting to note that managers governed by the exponential theory of replacement produce a Poisson distribution of number of replacements during equal intervals of time if managements that are removed are instantly replaced.

best known formulations are those of Marris [8], [9] and Williamson [15]. Marris argues that managers maximize a continuous function $u\{g, v(g)\}$, where g is the steady growth rate and $v(g)$ is the valuation ratio included as a proxy variable for security; $v(g)$ is usually defined as the ratio of market value of equity to the book value of assets. The valuation ratio, under this structure, presumably varies inversely with the probability of takeover. This analysis also assumes that the initial scale of the firm is historically determined and that steady growth develops from that point into the future.

The formulation that we adopt, like the Marris and Williamson models, depicts managers as deriving utility from the growth of the firm, with initial size of the firm determined by historical forces. The effect of wealth on managerial behavior is represented by a capital market limitation on the tenure of managers, as expressed by the conditional probability of replacement function.[7] For the multi-period case, discounted utility accumulates, until at period T_s management is removed from office. Since the number of periods in office, T_s, is a random variable, the 'life' of managers who pursue discretionary policies is uncertain. Expected utility is represented as

$$(14)\quad U(g, 0, T_s) = \int_{-\infty}^{\infty} \left\{ \int_0^{T_s} \exp(-rT_s)\, u(g)\, dt - c \exp(-rT_s) \right\} f_s(T_s)\, dT_s$$

$$= \int_0^{\infty} \exp(-rt)\, u(g)\{1 - F_s(t)\}\, dt - c \int_0^{\infty} \exp(-rt) f_s(t)\, dt,$$

with $f_s(t) = h(s)\{1 - F_s(t)\}$,

$$\dot{M}(t) = gM(t),$$

$$M(t) \geq 0,$$

$$0 \leq F_s(t) \leq 1,$$

given $M(0) = M_0 > 0$ and $F_s(0) = 0$. The instantaneous utility function, $u(g)$, is twice differentiable, increasing and strictly concave, r is the rate of time preference and c is a lump-sum penalty (measured in units of disutility) that is levied on management at the point of removal from office. Thus, the objective function is conditional expected utility; constraints describe the conditional probability density function of replacing management, along with the definition of growth in terms of net assets; and boundary

[7] Yarrow [17], whose view is closer to our own, introduces a 'managerial security function' that depends on the selected level of various decision variables. In our formulation, expected tenure in office, $\int_{-\infty}^{\infty} T\, dF(t)$, is simultaneously determined with selection of a growth policy. It is not entirely clear what Yarrow considers to be random, nor is it apparent how managers can select the lengths of their planning horizon when there is a finite probability of being taken over in each period. Another recently discussed *internal* control device is the owner-initiated development of management monitoring mechanisms [6].

conditions presume a given initial scale, along with a zero probability of initial replacement.[8]

IV. THE STEADY-GROWTH FORMULATION

Under a constant-growth policy with constant risk of removal, substituting equation (11) into equation (14) and integrating yields a steady-growth form:

$$W = \frac{u(g) - ch(s)}{r + h(s)}. \tag{15}$$

Here W is the present-value of conditional expected utility. The numerator is *net* instantaneous utility: growth in excess of g^* will increase $u(g)$ but will also increase the expected penalty associated with takeover, $ch(s)$. The denominator is the sum of the time preference rate and the conditional probability of replacement, and can be considered to describe a form of risk discounting. In contrast to the usual *ad hoc* justification for risk discounting, the risk discount term in this formulation develops as a consequence of expected utility maximization.[9] Under this formulation, there are two limitations on the exercise of managerial discretion. First, a high value of $h(s)$ implies an effective and vigilant capital market. Second, a large penalty cost, c, will force greater compliance with owner interest by reducing the present-value of growth. The penalty cost can be viewed as a form of internal check on the exercise of managerial discretion, in contrast to the external monitoring embodied in $h(s)$.

We now specify qualitative conditions for optimum growth, and then analyze changes in this optimum with respect to various parameters. Of particular interest are the effects on managerial discretion of changes in variables that determine g^*. Differentiation of $W(g)$ yields

$$\frac{\partial W}{\partial g} = [\{r + h(s)\}u'(g) - \{u(g) + cr\}h'(s)]/\{r + h(s)\}^2, \tag{16}$$

and

$$\frac{\partial^2 W}{\partial g^2} = [\{r + h(s)\}u''(g) - \{u(g) + cr\}h''(s)]/\{r + h(s)\}^2 - 2h'(s)[\{r + h(s)\}u'(g) - \{u(g) + cr\}h'(s)]/\{r + h(s)\}^3. \tag{17}$$

[8] The expected utility expression is theoretically defensible in its own right, however, it can also be justified as being based on the notion of a statistical loss function. Given this interpretation, $-c\int_{-\infty}^{\infty} \exp(-rT_s) f_s(t_s)\, ds$ can be described as a penalty function that effectively substitutes for an explicit probabilistic constraint on the latitude of managerial discretion. This type of interpretation has been offered in another context by Yaari [17].

[9] In the special case with $r = 0$, equation (15) is

$$W = \frac{u(g)}{h(s)} - c,$$

that is, the present value of managerial utility equals expected tenure in office times instantaneous utility, minus the penalty incurred at the instant of takeover.

Optimum growth, $\hat{g}$, occurs when $\partial\hat{W}/\partial g=0$.[10] After adding and subtracting $\{r+h(s)\}ch'(s)$ from the numerator of equation (16), the condition for optimum growth implies, if $u(\hat{g})-ch(\hat{s})>0$, that

$$\text{(18)} \qquad \frac{u'(\hat{g})-ch'(\hat{s})}{u(\hat{g})-ch(\hat{s})}=\frac{h'(\hat{s})}{r+h(\hat{s})}.$$

Thus, optimum growth is determined by equating the elasticity of net utility with elasticity of the discounting factor. Another way to interpret this condition is to use equation (15) and write equation (18) as

$$\text{(19)} \qquad u'(\hat{g})=\{W(\hat{g})+c\}h'(\hat{s}).$$

Thus optimum growth equates instantaneous marginal utility of growth to the expected increase in utility-loss associated with takeover.

In the discretionary case, where $h(s)$ is strictly convex and differentiable, optimal managerial growth can be shown to exceed the profit-maximizing rate, $\hat{g}>g^*$. Upon substitution of g^* into equations (16) and (17) with $h'(0)=0$, we see that

$$\frac{\partial W^*}{\partial g}=[\{r+h(0)\}u'(g^*)]/\{r+h(0)\}^2>0$$

and

$$\frac{\partial^2 W^*}{\partial g^2}=[\{r+h(0)\}u''(g^*)-\{u(g^*)+cr\}h''(0)]/\{r+h(0)\}^2<0.$$

Together, these conditions imply that $g^*<\hat{g}$. If, on the other hand, the capital market constraint is very tight, viz. there is a sharp kink in the $h(s)$ function at $s=0$, then $\hat{g}$ may coincide with g^*.

The effects on optimum growth, now defined from equation (18) as $\hat{g}=\hat{g}(r, c, g^*)$, of changes in the rate of time preference, r, the lump-sum penalty, c, and the wealth-maximizing rate, g^*, are

$$\text{(20)} \qquad \frac{\partial\hat{g}}{\partial r}=-\{h'(\hat{s})W(\hat{g})\}\div\frac{\partial^2\hat{W}}{\partial g^2}\{r+h(\hat{s})\}^2>0,$$

$$\text{(21)} \qquad \frac{\partial\hat{g}}{\partial c}=\{rh'(\hat{s})\}\div\frac{\partial^2\hat{W}}{\partial g^2}\{r+h(\hat{s})\}^2<0,$$

and

$$\text{(22)} \qquad \frac{\partial\hat{g}}{\partial g^*}=[u'(\hat{g})h'(\hat{s})-h''(\hat{s})\{u(\hat{g})+cr)\}]\div\frac{\partial^2\hat{W}}{\partial g^2}\{r+h(\hat{s})\}^2\lesseqgtr 0.$$

Equation (20) indicates that an increase in time preference leads to an increase in optimum growth and thereby a reduction in the expected time to replacement. This proposition is intuitively plausible: the less-valued is future utility, the less important becomes a distant threat of removal

[10] With $\partial\hat{W}/\partial g=0$, the curvature assumptions made regarding $u(g)$ and $h(s)$ ensure that equation (17) is negative.

from office. Equation (21) shows that an increase in the lump-sum penalty imposed at the time of replacement will encourage managers to reduce optimum growth and thereby extend their expected tenure. Thus, if managers are faced with a higher penalty cost at the time of takeover, their choice of a growth rate will get closer to that selected by the traditional, profit-maximizing firm.[11]

From equation (22), the effect on optimum growth of an increase in the wealth-maximizing rate is ambiguous. It is possible, however, to address a more interesting question regarding the impact on discretion ($\hat{s}=\hat{g}-g^*$) of a change in g^* and its determinants. After setting equation (16) equal to zero and substituting for s, we find that

$$\text{(23)} \qquad \frac{\partial \hat{s}}{\partial g^*}=\frac{\partial \hat{g}}{\partial g^*}-1=[h'(\hat{s})u'(\hat{g})-\{r+h(\hat{s})\}u''(\hat{g})]\div\frac{\partial^2 \hat{W}}{\partial g^2}\{r+h(\hat{s})\}^2<0.$$

This result indicates that an increase in wealth-maximizing growth will reduce the amount of discretion. It is also interesting to examine the effects on $\hat{s}$ of changes in the parameters that determine g^*. Using equations (5)–(7), it develops that

$$\text{(24)} \qquad \frac{\partial \hat{s}}{\partial \pi_N}=\frac{\partial \hat{s}}{\partial g^*}\frac{\partial g^*}{\partial \pi_N}<0,$$

$$\text{(25)} \qquad \frac{\partial \hat{s}}{\partial i}=\frac{\partial \hat{s}}{\partial g^*}\frac{\partial g^*}{\partial i}>0,$$

and

$$\text{(26)} \qquad \frac{\partial \hat{s}}{\partial \alpha}=\frac{\partial \hat{s}}{\partial g^*}\frac{\partial g^*}{\partial \alpha}>0.$$

Thus, an increase in average net profit will reduce the degree of discretion, while an increase in the rate of interest and the cost of expansion parameter will increase discretion. When these results are used in conjunction with the definition of expected time to replacement, equation (12), it develops that an increase in average net profit will lengthen the expected time to replacement, and an increase in either the rate of interest or the cost of expansion parameter will reduce the expected time to replacement.

While we have not considered taxes in developing the net profitability concept, it appears that tax and tax credit policies, which influence the

[11] A shift parameter that reflects the capital market's ability to perceive managerial discretion can be introduced into the conditional rate of removal function. Let $h(s, \beta)$ represent the probability of removal in this case, with $h_s \geq 0$, $h_\beta \geq 0$ and $h_{\beta s} \leq 0$. Given these conditions,

$$\frac{\partial \hat{g}}{\partial \beta}=-[u'(\hat{g})h_\beta-\{u(\hat{g})+ch(\hat{s},\beta)h_{\beta s}\}]\div\frac{\partial^2 W}{\partial g^2}\{(r+h(\hat{s},\beta)\}^2>0.$$

Thus, if managers perceive an increase in the probability of takeover at all levels of discretion, optimum growth increases. The tendency for growth to increase is supported by the 'flattening' of $h(s, \beta)$ as β increases. If, however, an increase in β should increase the marginal probability of takeover, $h_{\beta s}>0$, then the sign of $\partial\hat{g}/\partial\beta$ is ambiguous.

profitability of firms, may also affect the exercise of discretion. Equations (24) and (25) suggest that managers may adopt quite different postures over various stages of general business activity. This conjecture, of course, is based on the constant-growth properties of the model and more detailed analysis must wait development of a richer, dynamic expression.

V. SUMMARY AND CONCLUSION

We are able to derive a number of qualitative results for a managerial firm when it is assumed that the optimum policy implies constant growth. First, a managerial firm will grow at a faster rate then the wealth-maximizing firm. Second, an increase in the rate of time preference increases optimum growth and reduces the expected time to takeover. Third, an increase in the penalty imposed on managers at the time of replacement reduces optimum growth and, thereby, narrows the degree of discretion. Finally, with managerial discretion measured as the distance between optimum growth and wealth-maximizing growth, an increase in the wealth-maximizing rate will reduce the exercise of discretion.

UNIVERSITY OF IOWA AND ILLINOIS INSTITUTE OF TECHNOLOGY

REFERENCES

[1] Baumol, W. J., *Business Behavior, Value and Growth*, rev. edn (Harcourt, Brace, New York, 1976).

[2] Currie, K. A. and Fethke, G. C., 'Growth of Profit-maximizing "Creative" Firms', Working Paper Series No. 75–2 (University of Iowa, February 1975, unpublished).

[3] Grabowski, H. G. and Mueller, D. C., 'Life-cycle Effects of Corporate Returns on Retention', *Review of Economics and Statistics*, **LVII** (4) (November 1975), pp. 400–9.

[4] Heal, G. H. and Silberston, A., 'Alternative Managerial Objectives: An Expository Note', *Oxford Economic Papers, 24* (2) (July 1977), pp. 137–50.

[5] Herendeen, J. B., *The Economics of the Corporate Economy* (Dunellen, distributed by Kennikat Press, New York, 1975).

[6] Jensen, M. C. and Meckling, W. H., 'Theory of the Firm: Managerial Behavior, Agency Costs and Ownership Structure', *Journal of Financial Economics, 3* (4) (October 1976), pp. 305–60.

[7] Kuehn, D., *Takeovers and the Theory of the Firm: An Empirical Analysis for the United Kingdom, 1957–1969* (Macmillan, London, 1975).

[8] Marris, R., *The Economic Theory of 'Managerial' Capitalism* (Free Press of Glencoe, New York, 1964).

[9] Marris, R., 'An Introduction to Theories of Corporate Growth', in *The Corporate Economy: Growth, Competition and Innovator Potential* (Harvard University Press, Cambridge, Mass., 1971).

[10] Parzen, E., *Stochastic Processes* (Holden-Day, San Francisco, 1962).

[11] Penrose, E. T., *The Theory of the Growth of the Firm* (Wiley, New York, 1959).

[12] SMILEY, R. 'Tender Offers, Transactions Costs and the Theory of the Firm', *Review of Economics and Statistics*, **LVIII** (1) (February 1976), pp. 22–32.

[13] SOLOW, R., 'Some Implications of Alternative Criteria for the Firm', in *The Corporate Economy: Growth, Competition and Innovator Potential* (Harvard University Press, Cambridge, Mass., 1971).

[14] UZAWA, H., 'Time Preference and the Penrose Effect in a Two-class Model of Economic Growth'. *Journal of Political Economy*, 77 (4) (July 1969), pp. 628–52.

[15] WILLIAMSON, J. H., 'Profit, Growth and Sales Maximization', *Economica*, **XXXIII** (129) (February 1966), pp. 1–16.

[16] WILLIAMSON, O. E., *The Economics of Discretionary Behavior: Managerial Objectives in a Theory of the Firm* (Prentice-Hall, Englewood Cliffs, NJ, 1964).

[17] YAARI, M. E., 'Uncertain Lifetime, Life Insurance, and the Theory of the Consumer', *Review of Economic Studies*, **XXXII** (2) (April 1965), pp. 137–50.

[18] YARROW, G. K., 'Managerial Utility Maximization Under Uncertainty', *Economica*, **XL** (158) (May 1937), pp. 155–73.

THE JOURNAL OF INDUSTRIAL ECONOMICS
Volume XXVII December 1978 No. 2

THE ABANDONMENT OF MAJOR MERGERS IN THE U.K. 1965–75*

J. F. PICKERING

I. INTRODUCTION

As has been increasingly recognized, mergers represent an important means of growth and diversification for many companies. While considerable research attention has been paid to different aspects of mergers that do occur, very little attention seems to have been paid to those cases where a takeover bid has been announced but a merger has not subsequently taken place.[1] Such cases of what we will term 'abandoned mergers' arise for a number of reasons: the bidder may have second thoughts and withdraw or not take active steps to ensure the success of the bid; the potential victim company may mount a successful defence to the bid; the merger may be prohibited following a Monopolies Commission investigation. It is also possible that a contest may develop between two bidders for the same company. As a result of each of these considerations it is clear that the number of mergers that actually occur falls short of the number of individual takeover bids that are announced. The pupose of this note is to provide information on the incidence of major cases of such abandoned mergers in the United Kingdom over the years 1965–75.

II. THE SOURCE OF THE DATA

Since the passing of the Monopolies and Mergers Act 1965 a proposed, or recent, merger may be referred to the Monopolies Commission if the total gross assets of the company to be acquired amount to £5 million or more or where the market share of the combined companies would constitute a technical monopoly (one-third of the relevant market 1965–73 and one-quarter since the Fair Trading Act 1973). While the decision to refer is the responsibility of the Secretary of State, advice is given by the Director General of Fair Trading. This is based upon an initial appraisal of an individual case undertaken by the Office of Fair Trading (OFT) and the expression of views by an interdepartmental Mergers Panel. All proposed mergers

* Thanks are due to the SSRC for financial assistance in a study of the causes and consequences of abandoned mergers; to the Office of Fair Trading for assistance in making available the data on which this paper is based and to Miss B. A. Lawson for research assistance in the preparation of this paper.

[1] There are also undoubtedly a large number of instances which never become public knowledge where possible acquisitions are appraised by companies but are then not proceeded with. Our concern here is only with proposals that are made public.

that would qualify for reference to the Monopolies Commission are considered in this way.[2]

Records have been kept by OFT and its predecessors on various characteristics of the qualifying proposed mergers including the size of the gross assets to be acquired, the Standard Industrial Classification (SIC) of the company to be acquired (at the Order or 2-digit level), the direction of the proposed merger (whether horizontal, vertical or diversifying). Statistical summaries are compiled from time to time and may be published.[3] Between the introduction of merger policy in 1965 and the end of 1975, 1205 actual or proposed mergers had been considered in this way. This figure relates to bids made or proposed.[4] It is therefore greater than the number of qualifying mergers that actually took place and since two or more bids for the same company are separately counted it is also greater than the number of companies that were actually bid for.

Our interest here is in the mergers that did not take place. In order to assist in identifying such cases OFT kindly made available a listing of the cases considered by the Mergers Panel which were clearly public knowledge. For each of these we attempted to establish from various sources whether or not the merger had actually taken place and identified 171 instances where a merger did not appear to have occurred. It is these cases which form the basis of the analysis in the remainder of this paper.

We should, however, also comment in passing on the importance of what are known as 'confidential guidance' cases as a further source of abandonments. While the majority of cases are public knowledge at the time they are considered by OFT and the Mergers Panel, there is also an important minority of instances where one or both of the parties contemplating a merger will seek confidential guidance as to whether such a merger would be likely to be referred to the Monopolies Commission. Between 1965 and 1975, according to OFT, 264 cases (22% of the total) started off as confidential guidance cases. This indicates a high level of usage of the informal advice network. Apparently, the proportion originating in this way was highest in 1966–69. This may be a reflection of greater uncertainty associated with the early years of a new policy. It may also reflect the greater use of this facility by the Industrial Reorganization Corporation.

Many of these instances undoubtedly culminated in a public takeover bid. However, OFT estimate that there may be some 50 cases where the proposals have never been made public and where we must assume a merger has not taken place. While many companies enter into confidential discussions about

[2] Descriptions of the appraisal procedures and the issues that are taken into account are contained in Board of Trade, *Mergers* (HMSO, 1969) and Office of Fair Trading, *Mergers* (HMSO, 1978).

[3] See for example, J. D. Gribbin 'The Operation of the Mergers Panel Since 1965', *Trade and Industry* (17 January 1974), p. 70.

[4] This does not include details of non-qualifying mergers under the 1965 legislation. Statistics of all mergers that actually take place are published in the *Business Monitor* Series.

possible mergers which then do not come to fruition and are never made known to the public, there may be particular interest in those which involved confidential guidance by the competition policy authorities. Unfortunately we do not have any information about these cases or their characteristics. However, it may be suggested that if the confidential guidance was a material influence on the decision not to proceed, these were likely to have been mergers with major market power implications or perhaps a strong hint of conglomerateness. While we obviously cannot assume that all the 50 or so cases were abandoned because of the possibility of a reference it is relevant to point out that between 1965 and 1975 there were fewer than 40 merger references to the Monopolies Commission. This suggests that advice in confidential guidance cases may have been of quite considerable proportionate significance in deterring major mergers.

III. THE OVERALL SIGNIFICANCE OF ABANDONED MERGERS

Table I sets out the yearly distribution of all proposed mergers, excluding newspaper mergers, considered by the Mergers Panel and the number and size,[5] of such cases that were subsequently abandoned (excluding the 50 or so abandonments in confidential guidance cases). In considering abandoned mergers we have also distinguished between abandonments where there was just one bidder and those where there was a contested bid with two or even three bidders for the same company.

Over the period 1965–75 50 cases were identified where there were contested bids with two or more companies bidding at the same time for a third company. It is not always easy to establish retrospectively whether two bids that come close together in time are, in fact, competitive or whether one company steps in as another is withdrawing. Thus it was necessary to refer to press and other material of the time to clarify this. In the 50 contested bids there were 102 bidders since two of the contests had three bidders. While mergers took place in 45 of the cases, there were five contested bids where no merger ensued.

It will be observed from Table I that the 171 abandoned mergers listed account for about 14% of all proposed mergers considered by the Mergers Panel. This proportion is roughly constant year by year. Abandoned mergers were of larger average size and accounted for 23% of the total value of assets. If we take into account also the 50 or so abandoned confidential guidance cases it would appear that about 18% of all the proposed mergers considered by the Mergers Panel failed to take place. While we do not know the value

[5] It is not easy to establish with precision the size of a merger. OFT data relate to the value of the gross assets to be acquired. There may be particular difficulties in valuing assets where a subsidiary of one company is to be acquired by another and estimates may be required. The size of gross assets in financial institutions is of a much greater order of magnitude than the size of assets in manufacturing industry and emphasizes the importance of caution in using data on size of assets.

TABLE I

MAJOR PROPOSED AND ABANDONED MERGERS 1965–75

	All cases considered by the Mergers Panel		Abandoned mergers: Cases involving one bidder only		Abandoned mergers: Cases involving more than one bidder		Abandoned mergers: Total abandoned mergers	
Year	*No.*	*Value of gross assets (£m)*	*No.*	*Value of gross assets (£m)*	*No.*	*Value of gross assets (£m)*	*No.*	*Value of gross assets (£m)*
1965 (part)	48	1 125	1	5	2	141	3	145
1966	63	998	4	51	4	114	8	165
1967	96	2 273	7	147	5	235	12	382
1968	133	8 499	11	3002	10	677	21	3 678
1969	126	3 714	19	474	8	293	27	767
1970	80	2 598	6	337	4	48	10	385
1971	110	1 687	14	272	5	80	19	351
1972	114	3 588	13	424	5	432	18	856
1973	134	4 878	15	1113	5	72	20	1 185
1974	141	7 621	12	405	4	744	16	1 149
1975	160	5 786	12	933	5	47	17	980
Total	1,205	42 767	114	7161	57	2882	171	10 043
Average value of gross assets to be acquired per proposed merger (£m)		35		63		51		59

Note on source of tables: All tables are based upon information supplied by the Office of Fair Trading supplemented where appropriate by various sources of company data.

of assets to be acquired in the confidential guidance cases, we have suggested that these were likely to have been on average amongst the larger cases. If therefore we adopt a conservative estimate that the average value of such assets to be acquired was £60 million, this would indicate that abandoned mergers perhaps accounted for about 30% by value of the cases considered by the Mergers Panel. This would also suggest that the average value of all mergers that did proceed was not greater than £30 million and consequently we can conclude that abandoned mergers were, on average, twice as large as the mergers that did proceed.

The series in Table I indicates that there was a relatively high level of merger activity in 1968–69 and this applied also to abandonments. There is generally thought also to have been a merger boom in 1972–73, but the figures for 1974 and 1975 indicate a continuing high level of merger activity and abandonments. The high value of assets involved in abandoned mergers in 1968 was partly due to the abandonment, following a Monopolies Commission report, of the proposed merger between Barclays and Lloyds Banks. There were, however, other major cases in 1968 including the abandonment of merger proposals between Unilever and Allied Breweries (despite a favourable report by the Monopolies Commission) and the failure of Plessey to acquire English Electric in a contested bid with GEC.

TABLE II

DISTRIBUTION OF MAJOR ABANDONED MERGERS BY SIZE OF ASSETS TO BE ACQUIRED 1965–75

Size group (£m)	Cases involving one bidder		Cases involving more than one bidder		Total abandoned mergers		
	All cases	*SIC XXIV only*	*All cases*	*SIC XXIV only*	*All cases*	*SIC XXIV only*	*Total excluding SIC XXIV*
0–2·5	8	1	0	0	8	1	7
2·6–4·9	8	0	0	0	8	0	8
5·0–9·9	25	4	23	2	48	6	42
10·0–19·9	33	9	9	1	42	10	32
20·0–49·9	19	4	11	1	30	5	25
50·0–99·9	9	0	3	1	12	1	11
100·0–199·9	6	3	9	6	15	9	6
200+	6	3	2	1	8	4	4
Totals	114	24	57	12	171	36	135
Average value of gross assets to be acquired (£m)	62	169	51	107	59	148	35

The actual distribution of the size of mergers in terms of the value of the gross asssets to be acquired is shown in Table II. It will be observed that there is a small number of cases where the value of the assets to be acquired was less than £5 million. These are presumably cases that would have qualified for reference to the Monopolies Commission on the market share criterion alone.

The median size of all abandoned mergers is approximately £15 million and is much smaller than the mean of £59 million. This indicates the strong influence on the average of a relatively small number of large abandoned mergers. While the size distribution of all mergers considered by the Mergers Panel is not recorded, we do known that 13% of all the cases considered involved the acquisition of companies with gross assets of £50 million and over. By comparison, 20% of all the abandoned mergers concerncd the acquisition of assets of £50 million and over.

The overall average size of assets to be acquired is strongly influenced by the asset values of companies in the insurance, banking and finance sector (SIC XXIV). As Table II shows, the average size of assets to be acquired is much greater in this sector than in other sectors. However, while 21% of all abandoned mergers involved the potential acquisition of a company in SIC XXIV, this sector accounted for 25% of all merger proposals. So it is unlikely that this would account for the greater average size of abandoned mergers.

IV. THE INDUSTRIAL DISTRIBUTION OF ABANDONED MERGERS

Mergers are classified by OFT according to the direction of the merger and the SIC of the acquired firm. Three directions of merger are distinguished—horizontal, vertical and diversifying, although the limitations of this have to be recognized since many mergers between multiproduct organizations will involve elements of all three directions.

From Table III we can see that of all merger proposals, horizontal mergers were preponderant with diversifying mergers also much more frequent than vertical mergers. The proportionate distribution is more or less the same on both a numerical and a value of assets basis. This indicates that horizontal and diversifying mergers were of roughly the same average size. The distribution of abandoned mergers is very similar to that for all merger cases, although diversifying mergers constituted a slightly greater proportion of the number of abandonments and horizontal mergers a slightly smaller proportion than their respective shares of the total number of cases considered. However this is adjusted on a size of assets basis since abandoned horizontal mergers are of larger average size (£68 million) than abandoned diversifying mergers (£45 million). Part of this difference is explained by the size of abandoned mergers in the insurance, banking and finance sector but this does not account for all the difference. Excluding abandoned mergers in that one sector the average

TABLE III

DIRECTION OF MAJOR PROPOSED AND ABANDONED MERGERS 1965–75

	Number			*Value of assets (£m)*		
	Horizontal	*Vertical*	*Diversifying*	*Horizontal*	*Vertical*	*Diversifying*
All merger proposals						
No.	911	59	235	32,718	1274	8775
%	76	5	20	76	3	21
Abandoned mergers						
No.	115	11	45	7,830	197	2017
%	67	6	26	78	2	20
Of the abandoned mergers:						
Cases involving one bidder only						
No.	71	9	34	5,699	182	1281
%	62	8	30	80	3	18
Cases involving more than one bidder						
No.	44	2	11	2,131	15	737
%	77	4	19	74	1	26

TABLE IV

INDUSTRIAL CLASSIFICATION OF MAJOR PROPOSED ABANDONED MERGERS 1965–75

SIC Orders	*Proposed mergers No.*	*Abandoned mergers No.*	*Value of abandoned mergers (£m)*
I and II (primary)	27	6	55
III–XIX (manufacturing)	674	102	3 658
of which:			
III Food, drink and tobacco	84	12	709
V Chemicals and allied industries	80	12	514
VII Mechanical engineering	118	25	342
IX Electrical engineering	67	11	1 185
XX (construction)	26	4	181
XXII–XXVI (services)	478	59	6 150
of which:			
XXIII Distributive trades	106	16	531
XXIV Insurance, banking and finance	300	36	5 329
Totals	1 205	171	10 044

size of abandoned horizontal mergers was £38 million compared with £30 million for abandoned diversifying mergers.

Contested bids were proportionately rather more likely to be a cause of abandonment of a horizontal merger than a diversifying merger. The average size of the abandoned horizontal merger was larger where there was just one bidder but in the case of abandoned diversifying bids the larger mergers tended to be those where there was more than one bidder.

Reference has already been made to the effect of abandoned mergers in the insurance, banking and finance sector (SIC XXIV) in raising the average value of abandoned mergers. In fact this sector accounted for 25% of all proposed mergers considered by the Mergers Panel, 21% of abandoned mergers and 53% of the value of the assets to be acquired in abandoned mergers. There were, however, a number of other sectors where the incidence of both proposed and abandoned mergers was also quite high.[6] Table IV analyses this for each of the main types of sector and for the individual SICs which contributed most to merger activity. Besides the financial sector this includes food, drink and tobacco; chemicals; mechanical engineering; electrical engineering; and the distributive trades. It would appear that abandonments constitute a roughly equal proportion of all proposed mergers in each sector. The average value of assets to be acquired in abandoned mergers does, however, vary from sector to sector. We have already noted that the average size of abandoned mergers was particularly high in the financial sector. Abandoned mergers in the electrical engineering industry also had an average size of over £100 million and other sectors where abandoned

[6] The SIC recorded is that of the company to be acquired. In the majority of cases both firms would have been within the same SIC but this cannot be assumed in every case.

mergers were of substantial average size were food, drink and tobacco; chemicals; and construction.

V. CONCLUSIONS

It is clear that since the passing of the Monopolies and Mergers Act there has been a considerable degree of merger activity recorded by OFT and its predecessors. However, the evidence presented here demonstrates that quite a high proportion of all proposed mergers do not take place. There is no evidence to suggest that abandoned mergers differ from all cases in respect of their direction, their SIC or the year in which the merger was proposed. It does however appear that on average abandoned mergers are likely to be larger than all proposed mergers and hence than the mergers that do proceed. Proposed and abandoned mergers occurred most frequently in the financial sector but were also numerically important and/or of large average size in a number of other sectors, particularly food, drink and tobacco; chemicals; mechanical engineering; electrical engineering; construction; and distribution.

While the majority of abandoned mergers involved a bid from only one potential acquirer, about one third of abandonments arose because, in a contested bid, at least one bidder has to be unsuccessful.

Since OFT is concerned with monitoring *proposed* mergers it should be borne in mind that OFT statistics will therefore overstate the incidence of actual mergers. This paper has not been able to present the full picture on abandoned mergers since there are apparently some 50 confidential guidance cases which have not resulted in a public takeover bid and so also constitute abandonments. These would raise still further the quantitative significance of this phenomenon.

Having established the numerical importance of abandoned mergers it is important to investigate their economic significance. Work is currently in progress to investigate the causes of abandonments, the subsequent responses of the parties concerned and to consider their wider implications.

THE UNIVERSITY OF MANCHESTER INSTITUTE OF SCIENCE AND TECHNOLOGY

THE JOURNAL OF INDUSTRIAL ECONOMICS
Volume XXVII December 1978 No. 2

THE PROVISION OF MUNICIPAL SANITATION SERVICES BY PRIVATE FIRMS: AN EMPIRICAL ANALYSIS OF THE EFFICIENCY OF ALTERNATIVE MARKET STRUCTURES AND REGULATORY ARRANGEMENTS

FRANKLIN R. EDWARDS AND BARBARA J. STEVENS*

I. INTRODUCTION

CONCERN about productivity in local government is encouraging city officials to look closely at private market alternatives to the direct provision of municipal services by local government. One important issue concerns the question of which are the most efficient market structures and regulatory arrangements for the provision of such services. There is presently little hard evidence available to guide city officials.[1] The present study seeks to remedy this deficiency by empirically analyzing the alternative market structures and regulatory arrangements used in 77 cities in the United States for the provision of residential refuse collection service by private firms. Refuse collection services constitute an important municipal expenditure. In the fiscal year 1975–76 all municipal governments in the United States spent $13.85 per person on sanitation services other than sewerage. This expenditure constitutes about 9% of basic municipal service expenditures (police, fire, highways, sewerage, parks and recreation, and sanitation).[2]

II. ALTERNATIVE MARKET STRUCTURES AND REGULATORY SCHEMES

There exist several types of structural and regulatory arrangements for the collection of residential solid waste. At one extreme is public provision of collection services, where municipalities directly provide such services to all households and pay for them out of general tax revenues. At the other end of the spectrum is what we call the 'unregulated' arrangement, in which private refuse collectors have complete freedom to enter and leave the industry and where collectors and households are free to negotiate

* This study was supported by the Advanced Productivity Research and Technology Program, Research Applied to National Needs Division, National Science Foundation. The opinions, findings, conclusions and recommendations herein are those of the authors and do not necessarily reflect the views of the National Science Foundation. We wish to thank Steve Savas, Eileen Berenyi, Daniel Baumol, Linda Edwards and members of the Solid Waste Management Project Advisory Panel, as well as an anonymous referee for this *Journal*.

[1] Earlier studies of refuse collection are Dennis Young [6] and Werner Hirsch [2].
[2] US Bureau of the Census [5, p. 2].

whatever refuse service arrangements they wish. In between there are three general regulatory schemes for private collection: contract, franchise, and license. Since the focus of this study is on private collection systems, a detailed description of these arrangements follows.[3]

In contract arrangements, the city selects and directly pays a collection firm to provide refuse collection services to all residents in a given geographic area. Each collector, therefore, is the sole collector of refuse in a particular area. The typical contract between the city and the collector specifies the level of service to be provided (e.g. frequency of pickup, the point of pickup, and the types of refuse to be collected), the payment for each of the services, and the duration of the agreement. Households are given no choice regarding the level of service they will receive or the price they will pay—whether payment is via a user charge or part of general taxes. This is not true of the other private collection systems. In addition, the contract also frequently specifies rate adjustment procedures in the event of changes in the firm's cost, variations in the population served, or increases in some specified price index, and often contains an option to renew the contract if there is 'acceptable performance'. Among contract cities the most important distinction is whether the city assigns collection contracts by competitive bidding or by simply negotiating directly with would-be collectors. In the empirical work later in this paper we attempt to determine whether this difference is important in practice.

Franchise arrangements are similar but not identical to contract arrangements. The city again gives collection firms an exclusive right to provide service in a specified area for a given period of time, usually sets collection prices, and may or may not utilize competitive bidding (in our sample only three franchise cities made use of competitive bidding). There are, however, two important differences. First, franchised collectors negotiate service levels with households and bill them directly, rather than receiving payment from the city as under the contract arrangement. Thus, franchised collectors bear the costs associated with billing and their collection prices must reflect these additional costs. Second, in some franchise cities it is not mandatory for households to take (and pay for) refuse collection, while in others service is mandatory, as in contract cities. In non-mandatory franchise cities households may self-haul if they are dissatisfied with the collection service being provided, whereas in contract cities self-hauling is not a viable option because all households must pay for collection service whether or not they use it. In our empirical analysis we assess the practical significance of this self-hauling option. Except for billing costs, therefore, mandatory franchise cities are identical to contract cities, while non-mandatory franchise cities differ because of the self-hauling option.

Under all other private collection arrangements there is no legal agreement between the collector and the municipal government, although

[3] For a theoretical analysis of these alternatives schemes, see Edwards and Stevens [1].

some regulation may still exist. In general, these arrangements are characterized by a high degree of competition, easy entry, non-exclusive collection territories, and freedom to set prices and service levels through direct negotiation with service recipients. Two kinds of regulation may exist in these cities. In some cities collection firms are required to obtain a hauling license; and in some there is 'bureau' price regulation. Since it is possible that a licensing requirement may impose an important barrier to entry, in our empirical analysis we distinguish between a 'license' city and all other non-contract, non-franchise cities—which we refer to as simply 'unregulated' cities. Finally, we analyze the effectiveness of price regulation (both by 'bureau' and by contract) in all of the arrangements.

In sum, the efficiency of six distinct schemes for the provision of the residential refuse collection service are analyzed: contract with competitive bidding; contract without competitive bidding; mandatory franchise; non-mandatory franchise; license; and unregulated. In addition, the effectiveness of price regulation is analyzed. Of these schemes, the first four are alternative forms of collective action while the last two are 'free-market' or 'independent market adjustment' schemes.

III. EFFICIENCY OF THE ALTERNATIVE COLLECTION SCHEMES

This section investigates the empirical issue of which structural arrangement for refuse collection is the most efficient in practice. We focus on the prices that households pay for a given refuse collection service under different collection arrangements. The lower the price, the more 'efficient' the regulatory scheme is judged to be. Alternatively, we consider a regulation to be ineffective if it does not affect the price that households pay, or if it does not change 'efficiency'.[4]

1. Prices Under Independent Market Adjustment: the Basic Price Equation

To examine the relative efficiency of the various structural arrangements and the effectiveness of the different regulatory devices, we first develop a basic model of the determination of collection prices under independent market adjustment (or assuming no government intervention). Since prices in competitive markets depend upon supply and demand conditions, we begin by specifying demand and supply equations for collection service and then solve these equations for the equilibrium market price to obtain our basic estimating equation. The city is the unit of observation in our empirical analysis.

Like most commodities, a household's demand for a given refuse collection service (e.g. once-a-week, curbside service) is a function of the price of the

[4] Even when important externalities are present, under certain assumptions the prices that households pay for refuse collection will accurately reflect the social as well as the private costs of this service. See Edwards and Stevens [1, Section D].

service, the price of substitute services, and the household's level of income. Total market demand, therefore, is obtained by aggregating over all households. Similarly, the aggregate supply schedule is a summation of firms' marginal cost curves. In competitive markets, each firm produces up to the point where its marginal cost equals the market price, so that the equilibrium quantity supplied is a function of the variables that determine the position and shape of firms' marginal cost schedules. A firm's marginal cost will be determined by cost factors outside the control of the firm, and, if economies of scale exist, on the level of its output. In particular, marginal cost will be higher when factor prices are high, when population density is low (since travel time between households is greater), and when the climate is warm and rainy (because the refuse pickup is heavier). The basic aggregate demand and supply equations, therefore, are:

$$Q_d = f_d(P, PS, Y) \tag{1}$$

$$Q_s = f_s(S, P, W, r, \text{DEN}, \text{RF}, \text{TEMP}) \tag{2}$$

$$Q_d = Q_s \tag{3}$$

where Q_s, Q_d = quantity of collection service supplied and demanded;
P = price of collection service per year, for once-a-week curbside collection;
S = size of collection firm measured by number of trucks;[5]
Y = total income in the metropolitan area;
PS = price of alternative means of refuse disposal, or implicit price of self-hauling;
RF = average annual rainfall in the metropolitan area (SMSA), in centimeters;
TEMP = mean July temperature in the SMSA, in degrees centigrade;
r = cost of capital;
W = the monthly basic wage (exclusive of overtime and fringe benefits) paid by local collectors, expressed in dollars per month;[6] and,
DEN = household density.

Solving equations (1)–(3) for the equilibrium price yields the following reduced-form equation:

$$P = f_p(\overset{-}{S}, \overset{+}{PS}, \overset{+}{Y}, \overset{+}{W}, \overset{+}{r}, \overset{-}{\text{DEN}}, \overset{+}{\text{RF}}, \overset{+}{\text{TEMP}}) \tag{4}$$

[5] S is measured as the total number of collection vehicles owned by the firm, not the total number of collection vehicles used only for residential refuse collection. This measure will be an unbiased estimate of scale only if scale economies are common to all types of refuse collected (e.g. better maintenance).

[6] We assume that this wage rate is independent of the particular structural arrangement. Use of the (less appropriate) 'manufacturing wage rate' for the SMSA did not change our results, however.

where the hypothesized signs of the coefficients are indicated above the variables.

2. Prices When Government Intervenes

When government intervenes to assure that refuse collection service is provided to all residents in the city (as is the case in 'contract' cities), there are two possible sources of cost reduction: the ability to make collectors' routes more contiguous; and the ability to capture scale economies that are not being fully exploited under independent market adjustment arrangements. Alternatively, if collection firms are able to achieve whatever scale economies exist by operating simultaneously in more than one city, so that they always operate at an efficient scale, government intervention may still lower collectors' costs by enabling them to operate at an efficient scale without having to operate in more than one city. There are, presumably, some transaction costs associated with having to operate in several cities. In general, therefore, we might expect government intervention to reduce costs (and therefore prices) by more in small cities than in large cities. All cities should be subject to savings arising out of economies of contiguity, while only small cities should be subject to economies-of-scale savings. (The available evidence indicates that economies of scale vanish when collectors reach a size where they are servicing about 40,000 people.)[7]

There may also be negative aspects to government involvement: it may result in certain cost inefficiencies, and may bestow (consciously or inadvertently) monopoly power on private collection firms, both of which will cause prices to be higher. Whether the potential cost savings will dominate or be dominated by these potential inefficiencies is an empirical issue.

Thus, in order to obtain an empirical estimate of the net effect of these competing considerations, we add to the reduced-form price equation (4) a set of structural and regulatory variables (Z).

$$P = f(Z, PS, Y, W, r, \text{DEN}, \text{RF}, \text{TE MP}, S) \tag{5}$$

Estimation of equation (5) will provide estimates of the impact that each type of government intervention has on prices in the refuse collection industry, and will provide an estimate of the net benefits (or cost) of collective action. More specifically, by estimating equation (5) we can determine the impact of the various structural and regulatory schemes on collection prices (or $\partial P/\partial Z$), holding all other factors constant, including the size of the firm S. Assuming that S adequately accounts for scale economies, therefore, the coefficient of $\partial P/\partial Z$ indicates the effect of the structural schemes independent of scale effects. Or, it measures the net effect of the economies of contiguity and the possible cost inefficiencies associated with government involvement. Alternatively, to the extent that the size of firm

[7] See, for example, Stevens [4], McFarland [3], and note 25 *infra*.

S is itself a function of the structural scheme Z, the $\partial P/\partial Z$ coefficient will understate the impact of Z.[8]

3. *Sample, Data Characteristics, and Institutional and Regulatory Variables*

We utilize data on private collectors operating in 77 cities using some form of private collection system.[9] These data were compiled for the year 1975. In 37 of the cities a contract collection system is used, in 17 cities a franchise system is used, in eight cities a hauling license is required, and in 16 cities not even a hauling license is necessary, although in one of these cities rates are regulated. Thus, in the sample of 77 cities, private collectors are regulated in all but 15 cities.

The sample is derived from an extensive mail and telephone survey. In specific, 128 contract cities were surveyed, 65 franchise cities, and 125 'non-contract/non-franchise' cities, some of which turned out to be license and some unregulated cities. To qualify for inclusion in the sample two factors were required: collectors in the city must have provided once-a-week, curbside service, and both collectors and cities must have supplied complete data for all the variables requested. This means that both the firm providing service and the city government had to respond to questionnaires. The former requirement was imposed so that we could test our hypotheses in the context of standardized prices (what households pay for a given, homogeneous, service), thereby avoiding the thorny empirical problems associated with analyzing a heterogeneous output. This requirement reduced our sample considerably. Nevertheless, the sample represents the total survey fairly well. For example, 4% of the non-contract and non-franchise cities in the sample regulate rates, whereas 6% of all such cities in the complete survey reported rate regulation.

Lastly, the 77 cities in our sample can be classified into nine structural and regulatory classifications: U, L, CCB, COTH, FMAND, FOTH, RR, RRC, and RRB. These variables are defined below, and the number of cities falling into each is given in Table I.

U = cities in which the collector is unregulated, which takes the value of one where the city is not a contract or franchise city and does not require a hauling license, and zero otherwise;

[8] The omission of S has only a trivial effect on the $\partial P/\partial Z$ coefficients. The issue of separating economies of scale effects from economies of contiguities effects is discussed more fully later.

[9] With the exception of the four mandatory franchise cities, these cities also are fairly evenly dispersed across the northeastern, northern, and western regions of the country. None is located in the south. In particular, for each type of structural arrangement, at least 8% of the observations are present in each of the three regions noted above. However, all four mandatory franchise cities are located in the west. Our estimating equations include variables to capture economic differences among regions relevant to solid waste collection, such as the 'annual rainfall' in each city.

TABLE I

NUMBER OF CITIES IN EACH STRUCTURAL AND REGULATORY CLASSIFICATION

Institutional and regulatory classification	*Price regulation (RR)* Fixed in contract (RRC)	Bureau administered (RRB)	*None*
U (16)	0	1	15
L (8)	0	3	5
CCB (12)	12	0	0
COTH (24)	23	1	0
FMAND (4)	1	3	0
FOTH (13)	9	4	0

L = cities that require collectors to obtain a hauling license, which takes the value of one where the city is not a contract or franchise city but does require a hauling license, and zero otherwise;

CCB = competitive bidding contract city, taking the value of one for all contract cities which reported more than two bidders on each contract, and zero otherwise;[10]

COTH = all contract cities other then CCB cities, taking the value of one for such cities, and zero otherwise;

FMAND = mandatory-collection franchise cities, taking the value of one for all franchise cities in which self-hauling is not permitted, and zero otherwise;

FOTH = all franchise cities in which self-hauling is permitted, taking the value of one for such cities, and zero otherwise;

RR = cities in which collection prices are set either in the collection agreement or by a regulatory bureau, taking the value of one for such cities, and zero otherwise;

RRC = cities in which collection prices are set in the collection agreement, taking the value of one for such cities, and zero otherwise; and,

RRB = cities in which collection prices are set by a regulatory bureau, taking the value of one for such cities, and zero otherwise.

As can be seen from Table I, there are six mutually distinct categories, and three that cut across several categories (RR, RRC, and RRB).

4. The Final Estimating Equation

To obtain the final estimating equation, the foregoing structural and regulatory variables are added to equation (4) as in equation (5) above. Also, variables *PS* and *r* are omitted from the equation. The cost of capital *r* is omitted primarily because it is not measurable, although a reasonable

[10] We also investigated an alternative CCB variable defined as any city that simply claimed to be a competitive bidding city. The empirical results were the same.

argument can be made that it does not vary much by region since its major component—the level of the interest rate—is determined in a national financial market. Variable *PS*, the cost to the household of disposing of their refuse by self-hauling (the only alternative to organized collection service), is omitted because it is unobservable and attempts to proxy it were unsuccessful. In particular, *PS* should arguably be a function of the hauling time required in the city and the household's opportunity cost of time. When we measured the latter by the level of income per capita in the city, and the former by both city size (number of households) and traffic congestion (household density), and included these variables in the estimating equation, none of our estimates changed (nor were these variables significant).

In summary, making the further assumption that the structural demand and supply equations are multiplicative in form,[11] the final estimating equation for equilibrium collection prices under all types of collection arrangements is:

$$\ln P_h = \ln a_1 + a_2 \ln S + a_3 \ln Y + a_4 \ln \mathrm{RF} + a_5 \ln \mathrm{TEMP} + a_6 \ln \mathrm{DEN} + a_7 \ln W + a_8 Z + \alpha \tag{6}$$

where P_h is collection price per household,[12] S is the size of collection firm, Y is aggregate income of all households in the city, *RF* is annual rainfall, TEMP is mean July temperature, DEN is household density, W is wage rate of sanitation workers, Z represents the various structural and regulatory variables, and α is a random error-term.

This procedure, of course, assumes that the parameters a_2, a_3, a_4, a_5, a_6, and a_7 are stable across the alternative structural and regulatory groupings. Although the data were not sufficient to test the validity of this assumption for every case, we did estimate appropriate versions of equation (6) for the four separate groupings of contract, franchise, license, and unregulated cities The. null hypothesis of parameter stability could not be rejected. Thus, the assumption of stability across the structural and regulatory classifications was adopted.

5. *Empirical Results*

With six distinct collection schemes plus the possibility of price regulation it is clear that there are a large number of alternative hypotheses to be tested—15 structural arrangement hypotheses and two price regulation hypotheses.[13]

To present the results for all possible hypotheses, we felt the most illuminating expositional device was to estimate (by least-squares regression

[11] Alternate functional forms were tested. The logarithmic form was selected as providing the best fit.

[12] Precisely, annual price per household, net of all disposal fees and franchise fees. In franchise cities 'revenue-raising fees' are often imposed on collectors by the city.

[13] With six distinct structural arrangements, there are 15 possible pairings of such arrangements.

techniques) alternative versions of equation (6) for the entire sample, omitting a different structural arrangement variable each time. These results are reported in the first seven equations of Table II, which together permit the use of the reported *t*-statistics to test directly any of the 15 structural arrangement hypotheses.[14]

The estimates shown in Table II yield the following conclusions:

(*a*) The structural arrangements fall into two distinct groups: CCB and COTH constitute one group, and FOTH, L, and U constitute the other.[15] Collection prices in the latter cities are significantly higher than in the former group of cities, implying that the contract arrangement is the most efficient collection system.[16]

(b) The structural arrangement FMAND cannot be distinguished from either of the two above distinct groupings at an acceptable level of statistical significance. This result is almost certainly due to the fact that there are only four FMAND cities in the sample.[17]

(c) Competitive bidding does not appear to influence collection prices: there is no significant difference between the coefficients of CCB and COTH,

(d) Making collection service mandatory appears to lower collection prices, although this finding is 'weak'. In specific, there is a difference between the coefficients of FMAND and FOTH only at a 15% level of significance.

(e) Price regulation in general has no effect on collection prices (the coefficient of RR is always insignificantly different from zero). In addition, it makes no difference whether price regulation is done by a regulatory bureau or by contractual agreement (there is no significant difference between the coefficients of RRC and RRB in equation (7)).

(f) The 'other' independent variables, taken either individually or as a group, are not statistically significant. It should be recognized, however, that previous studies, while recognizing the potential importance of these

[14] Alternatively, we could have estimated any one of the first seven equations in Table II and computed the appropriate *t*-statistics for each of the 15 hypotheses. This procedure, however, would have hidden rather than illuminated our classification criteria. See note 16, *infra*.

[15] Since the number of competing sellers may be greater than one in the L and U cities and may therefore differ among these cities, we estimated a separate equation for the L and U cities and included the variable 'number of collectors' in the equation. This variable was not significant. It was also insignificant when entered in equation (5).

[16] Structural arrangements are considered to be in the same group if two criteria are met: the difference in the price level between these structural arrangements is not significant at the 5% level; and each of these arrangements has the same relationship with each of the structural arrangements in another group. For example, CCB and COTH are placed in the same group because their coefficients are not significantly different from one another (*t*-statistic of 0·53 in equation (1)), and because both of them have coefficients which are statistically different from the coefficients of FOTH, L, and U (shown by the appropriate *t*-statistics in equations (1) and (2)). This 'strong' criterion minimizes the chance of incorrectly plasing two arrangements in the same grouping, thereby failing to distinguish between them when we should.

[17] However, when similar structural arrangements are pooled, as in equations (8)–(10) in Table II, FMAND can be distinguished from the FOTH-L-U group at the 5% level of significance.

TABLE II

IMPACT OF ALTERNATIVE STRUCTURAL AND REGULATORY VARIABLES ON COLLECTION PRICES
(t-statistics in parentheses)

	Structural arrangement and regulatory variables										Other variables (in logarithms)						
Equation	*Constant*	*CCB*	*COTH*	*FMAND*	*FOTH*	*L*	*U*	*RR*	*RRC*	*RRB*	*Y*	*RF*	*TEMP*	*DEN*	*W*	S^a	R^2/F
(1)	1·155 (0·68)	—	0·056 (0·53)	0·275 (1·52)	0·633 (4·45)	0·885 (2·63)	0·772 (2·54)	0·209 (0·68)	—	—	0·034 (0·98)	0·941 (1·12)	0·228 (0·59)	−0·052 (−1·42)	−0·022 (−1·09)	0·158 (1·56)	0·55 (12, 62) 6·3
(2)	1·210 (0·73)	−0·056 (−0·53)	—	0·219 (1·29)	0·577 (4·84)	0·829 (2·49)	0·716 (2·40)	0·209 (0·68)	—	—	0·034 (0·98)	0·941 (1·12)	0·228 (0·59)	−0·052 (−1·42)	−0·022 (−1·09)	0·158 (1·56)	0·55 (12, 62) 6·3
(3)	1·430 (0·84)	−0·275 (−1·52)	−0·219 (−1·29)	—	0·357 (1·84)	0·609 (1·76)	0·496 (1·55)	0·209 (0·68)	—	—	0·034 (0·98)	0·941 (1·12)	0·228 (0·59)	−0·052 (−1·42)	−0·022 (−1·09)	0·158 (1·56)	0·55 (12, 62) 6·3
(4)	1·787 (1·11)	−0·632 (−4·45)	−0·577 (−4·84)	−0·357 (−1·84)	—	0·252 (0·73)	0·139 (0·45)	0·209 (0·68)	—	—	0·034 (0·98)	0·941 (1·12)	0·228 (0·59)	−0·052 (−1·42)	−0·022 (−1·09)	0·158 (1·56)	0·55 (12, 62) 6·3
(5)	2·040 (1·20)	−0·885 (−2·63)	−0·829 (−2·49)	−0·609 (−1·76)	−0·252 (−0·729)	—	−0·113 (−0·86)	0·209 (0·68)	—	—	0·034 (0·98)	0·941 (1·12)	0·228 (0·59)	−0·052 (−1·42)	−0·022 (−1·09)	0·158 (1·56)	0·55 (12, 62) 6·3
(6)	1·927 (1·16)	−0·772 (−2·54)	−0·715 (−2·40)	−0·496 (−1·55)	−0·139 (−0·45)	0·113 (0·86)	—	0·209 (0·68)	—	—	0·034 (0·98)	0·941 (1·12)	0·228 (0·59)	−0·052 (−1·42)	−0·022 (−1·09)	0·158 (1·56)	0·55 (12, 62) 6·3
(7)	1·159 (0·68)	—	0·060 (0·57)	0·327 (1·53)	0·661 (4·23)	0·813 (3·71)	0·700 (3·74)	—	0·135 (0·80)	0·065 (0·37)	0·031 (0·87)	0·088 (1·03)	0·269 (0·67)	−0·051 (−1·37)	−0·023 (−1·16)	0·169 (1·62)	0·55 (13, 61) 5·78

	Constant	CCB+COTH	FMAND	FOTH+L+U	RR	RRC	RRB	*Y*	RF	TEMP	DEN	*W*	*S*	R^2/F
(8)	1·054 (0·66)	—	0·218 (1·39)	0·609 (5·57)	0·047 (0·36)	—	—	0·038 (1·16)	0·087 (1·07)	0·293 (0·82)	−0·050 (−1·39)	−0·019 (−0·97)	0·155 (1·56)	0·54 (9, 65) 8·54
(9)	1·273 (0·79)	−0·218 (−1·39)	—	0·391 (2·14)	0·047 (0·36)	—	—	0·038 (1·16)	0·087 (1·07)	0·293 (0·82)	−0·050 (1·39)	−0·019 (−0·97)	0·155 (1·56)	0·54 (9, 65) 8·54
(10)	1·664 (1·08)	−0·609 (−5·57)	−0·391 (−2·14)	—	0·047 (0·36)	—	—	0·038 (1·16)	0·087 (1·07)	0·293 (0·82)	−0·050 (1·39)	−0·019 (−0·97)	0·155 (1·56)	0·54 (9, 65) 8·54

* $S=5$ if $S \geq 5$.

variables, have also obtained poor results for these variables (see Hirsch [1] and McFarland [3]). Possible explanations for our results are the existence of specification errors in the estimating equation and/or measurement errors.[18] An implicit assumption which underlies our results, therefore, is that any possible omitted variables or measurement errors are random with respect to the structural and regulatory variables.

In order to obtain the best estimate of the magnitude of the price difference between the two distinct groups of CCB and COTH versus FOTH, L, and U, we pooled similar arrangements and estimated equations (8)–(10) in Table II. These equations treat FMAND as a distinct variable so that it does not obfuscate the estimate of the price difference between the two distinct groups of cities.[19] The estimates show that collection prices are 75% higher in FOTH, L, and U cities than in contract cities, or 43% lower in contract cities than in FOTH, L, and U cities.[20]

Finally, most of this difference in price level cannot be explained by the fact that contract collectors do not incur billing costs, as do refuse collectors in other cities. Although it is difficult to estimate precisely the additional costs that contract collectors would incur if cities did not assume their billing expenses, a survey of 102 cities in which local government provides collection services indicated that from 3 to 9% of total collection costs are attributable to billing expenses. These figures may understate private billing costs, however, because of government's ability to bill jointly for several services and because of its additional coercive power. Indeed, discussions with collectors in franchise cities suggested that billing costs may be as high as 15% of total collection costs per household (or about 18% of total collection costs per household in contract cities).[21] Such an estimate is also consistent with the results in equation (8) in Table II. In particular, since the essential difference between FMAND and contract cities is that collectors in FMAND incur billing costs while collectors in contract cities do not, the coefficient for FMAND (0·218) should represent the price difference due to billing costs. This estimate indicates that prices in FMAND cities are about 24% higher than in contract cities,[22] which is somewhat higher but still consistent with collectors' estimates of about an 18% cost differential. Taking the upper estimate of 24% and adjusting prices in contract cities upward still leaves a substantial price difference between contract cities and FOTH, L, and U cities: prices in the latter cities remain 41% higher than in contract cities (or than in FMAND cities): or, alterna-

[18] Various tests for multicollinearity do not suggest that this is the cause of these results.

[19] Another procedure is to include FMAND alternately in one group and then the other. This procedure yields similar results.

[20] The percentage difference in price between two structural arrangements is equal to $e^{b_1-b_2}-1$, where b_2 is the coefficient of RR and b_1 is the value of the estimated coefficient of the structural arrangement in question (in this case, $+0\cdot609$).

[21] $\frac{0\cdot 15x}{0\cdot 85x}=0\cdot 18$, where x = total collection costs per household in franchise cities.

[22] The figure of 24% comes from $e^{0.218}-1$.

tively, prices are 29% lower in contract cities than in FOTH, L, and U cities,

Thus, our major empirical finding is that in contract cities households pay collection prices that are substantially lower than in other cities, even after a generous adjustment is made for billing cost differences.[23]

IV. CONCLUSIONS AND IMPLICATIONS

Of the various private structural arrangements now in use to collect solid waste in US cities, the best scheme seems to be the contract system: where cities contract with private collection firms, make collection service mandatory, grant exclusive service rights to designated sections of the city, and set prices and service standards in the contractual agreement. Prices that households pay for collection service in non-contract cities are at least 41% higher than in contract cities. In addition, we find that the use of competitive bidding to let collection contracts is neither superior nor inferior to simply negotiating contracts with collectors; that price regulation, in any form, does not affect collection prices; and that requiring collectors to obtain a hauling license does not affect collection prices.

Can the findings that prices are 41% higher in 'non-contract' cities be generalized to imply that the adoption of the 'contract' system of refuse collection service will always result in such a large cost savings? Perhaps. Previous discussion in this paper argued that the cost savings that come from government intervention derive from two sources: economies of scale and economies of contiguity. In general, cost savings should be greatest in small cities. Studies of economies of scale in refuse collection indicate that scale economies may exist up to a collector size of about 40,000 people. Thus, in cities with populations of less than 40,000, increasing the number of households served by a given collector should lower average collection cost because of economies of scale as well as because of economies of contiguity. In large cities, however, most of the benefits should come from economies of contiguity. Alternatively, if refuse collection firms in small cities operate in more than one city simultaneously in order to attain an efficient size, government intervention may still be beneficial because it may eliminate or reduce the transaction costs associated with a multiple-city operation. Once again, this cost savings should be greater for small cities.

Whether our estimated 41% price differential can be attributed solely to economies of contiguity, therefore, depends upon how successfully we have controlled for scale economies in the estimating equations. All of these equations included 'size of collection firm *S*' as an independent variable,

[23] In an effort to determine whether this result was in any way due to systematic variations in contractual provisions, we also examined the effect of the following contractual provisions on collection prices: the presence of an escalator clause in the contract to adjust collection prices for changes in cost; the value (total and per household) of the performance bond if required; the number of years since the contract was entered into; and the presence of an option to renew the contract. None of these variables was significant and its inclusion did not change any of the above results.

as well as size of city *Y*. In no case is the coefficient of *S* significantly different from zero. Thus, variable *S* may not adequately control for scale economies. As indicated previously, variable *S* may not be an accurate measure of firm size with respect to *residential* refuse collection, and may also fail to capture costs associated with multiple-city operations.[24] Consequently, in order to be sure that we are not over-estimating the cost savings due to economies of contiguity, we also employ the procedure of utilizing the findings of previous studies of economies of scale in refuse collection to arrive at a *minimum* estimate for economies of contiguity.

Two types of information are needed to derive this estimate. First, we need an estimate of the extent to which government involvement results in firm size being larger; and, second, we need an estimate of the firm's average cost curve. Previous studies of economies of scale in refuse collection have generally measured firm size as the 'number of people per firm', which is derived by dividing total city population by the number of firms. This can be a poor measure of firm size because it ignores multiple-city operations by collectors. Nevertheless, for our sample, this procedure yields an average firm size of 10,500 people in non-contract (L, U, and FOTH) cities, which will understate firm size if firms in these cities operate in more than one city. Given this estimate, however, and given the fact that the average population size of non-contract cities in our sample is 22,500, collectivizing these cities could be expected to increase average firm size by about 12,000 people for this reason alone. In addition, in the sample used to estimate the above equations, the average size of contract cities (CCB and COTH) is 41,000 people, so that the observed price differential between contract and non-contract cities is further adjusted by calculating what these prices would be *if* average collector size in L, U, and FOTH cities were 41,000 instead of 10,500 people. This procedure attributes as large a portion of the observed price differential to scale economies as possible. Indeed, it probably overestimates the effects of scale.

Previous studies of economies of scale in cities where a single refuse collector services all households (e.g. municipal service and certain contract cities) suggest that average collection prices will fall by about 13% if collector size is increased from 10,000 to 20,000, and by 22% if collector size is increased from 10,000 to 41,000.[25] Thus, after adjusting prices in FOTH, L and U cities downward by 22% to reflect possible scale economy differences between these cities and contract cities, and re-estimating the remaining price difference between these and contract cities, we find that prices in FOTH, L, and U cities are still 10% higher than in contract cities. (See

[24] See note 5, *supra*.

[25] At a 95% confidence interval the range for these price reductions would be: from 1,000 to 20,000, a price decrease of $13 \pm 9\%$; from 20,000 to 30,000, a further decrease of $7 \pm 5\%$; from 30,000 to 40,000, a further decrease of $4 \pm 3\%$. The overall expected decrease is thus 22·3%. See Stevens [4].

Appendix I.) This, then, is the *minimum* price difference attributable to the economies of contiguity which flow from government acting to collectivize refuse collection services.

In summary, we conclude that:

1. Cities can achieve significant cost savings of from 10 to 41% by adopting what we have called the 'contract' service arrangement.

2. The cost savings due to government intervention can be attributed to two factors: economies of scale and economies of contiguity.

3. As city size (and therefore firm size) increases, the major economic benefit of government involvement derives from economies of contiguity.

4. Realization of economies of contiguity alone should, on average, result in a cost savings of at least 10%, no matter what the size of city is.

5. The regulatory strategies of utilizing competitive bidding or price regulation do not seem important as compared to the decision to adopt the 'contract' service arrangement.

COLUMBIA UNIVERSITY

APPENDIX I

DIFFERENCES IN AVERAGE COLLECTION PRICES, ADJUSTING FOR EFFECTS OF SCALE AND BILLING COSTS

Definitions of groups of cities:

C = CCB + COTH = contract cities
LUF = L + U + FOTH = license, unregulated and non-mandatory franchise cities

Adjustment to mean price	*Annual price* ($)		*Differences in prices*	
	C	*LUF*	*LUF* − *C* ($)	$\frac{LUF-C}{C} \times 100$ (%)
Holding independent variables *Y*, RR, RF, TEMP, DEN, and *W* constant	20·42	35·73	15·31	75
Increase prices in contract cities by 24% for billing costs	25·32	35·73	10·41	41
Size of collector adjustment together with the billing cost adjustment	25·32	27·87	2·55	10

REFERENCES

[1] Edwards, F. and Stevens, B., 'Relative Efficiency of Alternative Institutional Arrangements for Collecting Refuse: Collective Action vs. the Free Market', Columbia University Graduate School of Business, Research Paper No. 151 (1976).

[2] Hirsch, W., 'Cost Functions of an Urgan Government Service: Refuse Collection', *Review of Economics and Statistics*, **47** (1) (February 1965), pp 87–92.

[3] McFarland, J. *et al.*, *Comprehensive Studies of Solid Waste Management*. Sanitary Engineering Laboratory, Report No. 72–3, University of California, Berkeley (May 1972).
[4] Stevens, B., 'Scale, Market Structure and the Cost of Refuse Collection', Columbia University Graduate School of Business, Research Paper No. 107 (1976).
[5] US Bureau of Census, *City Government Finances in 1975–1976* (US Government Printing Office, Washington, DC, 1977).
[6] Young, D., *How Shall We Collect the Garbage?* (The Urban Institute, Washington, DC, 1972).

THE JOURNAL OF INDUSTRIAL ECONOMICS
Volume XXVII December 1978 No. 2

MARKET STRUCTURE AND EXTERNALITIES: THE CASE OF WATER POLLUTION IN ENGLAND AND WALES

D. J. Storey

I. INTRODUCTION

Externality theorists have significantly omitted a number of topics, now within the mainstream of economics, from their study. Where a firm imposes external costs upon others a publicly financed authority is assumed to be established which either imposes effluent taxes or physical controls upon dischargers. Theorists, however, presume that firms only incur abatement costs in pollution control, i.e. firms equate marginal abatement costs to the tax rate or accept unquestioningly the physical limits imposed upon them by the authority. The opportunity for firms in practice to exploit, through appeals, tribunals, etc., the enforcement procedures has demonstrated the naivety of such an assumption.[1] Hence any theory of externalities assuming purely passive roles for both dischargers and enforcement bodies must be inadequate.[2]

A second major criticism of externality theorists is their presumption that all polluters are profit maximizers (cost minimizers) operating in a perfectly competitive selling market. Even in the few cases where the perfect competition assumption is relaxed, profit maximization remains the presumed motivation.[3]

This paper tries to examine the effect of relaxing both these assumptions. It demonstrates it is possible to incorporate within the profit maximizing theory of the firm the opportunity for the use of resources in opposing the authority and shows such theory predicts that firms in non-competitive industries are likely to have an advantage in such conflicts over small competitive companies. However, when the profit maximizing hypothesis is replaced by one suggesting that managers may have similar preferences at work to those which they have as a private citizen, opposite predictions are

[1] Freeman [8] quotes the case of a rendering plant in Maryland which was permanently enjoined in 1956 from releasing 'noxious and offensive gases' although it was not until 1970 that the plant was closed.

[2] There has been some attempt to examine the role of enforcement authorities in their relation with dischargers (Downing and Watson [7], Terbonne [19]) but few testable hypotheses have emerged.

[3] Asch and Seneca [2], Lee [9]. These articles develop the argument presented by Buchannan [5] which suggested that externality control on a monopolist might not be Pareto preferred if the reduction in output consequent upon an externality control has larger welfare losses than externality damage.

derived. Here discretionary expenditure—a manifestation of inefficiency—would be greatest where market imperfections are greatest. Clearly this discussion parallels the debate on whether market power leads to greater profits or higher costs through X-inefficiency.

To test whether either of these hypotheses are valid, data on expenditure on water pollution control by industries are compared with indices of market imperfection. This shows as theory would predict that, *ceteris paribus*, expenditure on pollution control is initially high in the very competitive industries but falls with increasing concentration. It then rises at high levels of concentration where the opportunity exists for management to exercise discretion in favour of environmental expenditure.

II. THE PROFIT MAXIMIZING POLLUTER

In this section we presume that a firm wishes to discharge effluent to a river, which in the UK requires the permission of the Regional Water Authority.[4] The authority if it agrees to such a discharge is likely to impose physical controls upon the discharger of the form that the concentration or total quantity of pollutant i shall not exceed K_i^*. This agreement is incorporated into a document called a consent.

The firm faced with such a constraint in practice will decide whether it is worthwhile utilizing resources in an effort to obtain a less severe restriction K_i' (where $K_i' < K_i^*$). The resources which would be used are those of technical and legal staff who would provide technical data on production processes and on proposed and alternative effluent control procedures. These data would include costs of installation and operation of procedures to meet K_i^* compared with those to achieve K'. Where relevant the effect on the overall viability of the company would also be included. The employment of lawyers, should the matter have to be decided by the Secretary of State for the Environment, would also be necessary. In addition the company may incur costs in the form of delays in starting production where a formal appeal is lodged.

Posner [11] has modelled the case of the individual considering whether to take a case to law. We shall modify his analysis only marginally to examine the case of the firm's decision whether or not to appeal against its consent condition.

Assume the case of a firm faced by a demand from the authority to install abatement equipment at cost $A+F$. The first knows it can contest the issue

[4] In 1974 the water industry was reorganized in England Wales. Prior to 1974, which is the period for which data are provided, 29 river authorities were charged with improving the quality of rivers and estuaries but local authorities operated domestic sewage treatment works (which also took about 26% of all industrial effluent). After 1974 nine Regional Water Authorities were established to combine the functions of the river authorities with the operation of the domestic treatment works. At present there is no evidence that the reorganization has resulted in significant change in the methods by which consents to dischargers are allocated.

by appeals, provision of documentation, procrastination, etc., and that if it wins it will only have to pay abatement costs of A. The outcome, however, is uncertain since it is presumed that success is dependent upon the legal and other costs incurred by the firm C and the costs incurred by the authority C'. Another important factor to be considered is whether the case raises any new issues of law or whether it is routine. Thus the outcome of a routine case will be fairly certain and the firm will be able to gauge whether appeals, procrastination, etc., will be worthwhile. Posner argues that since enforcement agencies are likely to be subject to budget constraints they may be reluctant to undertake protracted negotiations with polluters where the outcome is uncertain, partly because there are normally a large number of 'easy' cases available and partly because when the agency performance is assessed it is the total number of 'successful' allocations that is considered. We denote the uncertainty of outcome of negotiations by e which varies with the *a priori* assessment of verdict on both sides.

Posner assumes the probability of a successful appeal p is of the following form

$$(1) \qquad p=\frac{ce}{c+c'}$$

The total cost function which the firm is assumed to minimize is given in equation (2)

$$(2) \qquad Tc=(1-p)(A+c)+p(A+c+F)$$

First order conditions for a minimum are given by (3)

$$(3) \qquad \frac{\mathrm{d}Tc}{\mathrm{d}c}=\frac{Fc'e}{(c+c')}+1=0$$

Posner notes that since

$$\frac{\mathrm{d}c'}{\mathrm{d}c}=\frac{\sqrt{Fe}}{2\sqrt{c}}+1$$

this demonstrates that if the firm's expenditure is large this will encourage the authority to spend less. If the firm is spending only a little the authority will spend more.

Thus the profit maximizing firm can contest the consent conditions imposed by authority and be better off, but the outcome, *a priori*, is uncertain. We now postulate that firms in the less competitive markets will find such expenditure worthwhile. The arguments presented are similar to those used to 'explain' the R & D funds/patents relationship in less competitive markets.

We have seen that opposing the authority can be expensive and uncertain and that traditionally it has been assumed that only firms of large absolute size are likely to have access to resources to be used in this manner. More importantly it can be argued that in a perfectly competitive industry the production and effluent control techniques will, by definition, be identical.

Hence if one discharger were to undertake appeals and obtain a more lax consent there is no way in which it could exclude its competitors from claiming parity of treatment. Equally the authority knows that if it allows relatively lax conditions for the pure monopolist it will not be inundated by requests for similar treatment since such producers may be treated as special cases.

Hence the hypothesis is presented that the less competitive industries will receive more favourable treatment from the enforcing authority. An example of this is quoted by Ackerman *et al.* [1] in discussions of the allocation of loads discharged to the Delaware River, USA. Ackerman found the two most powerful factors positively determining the eventual consent allocation were the production capacity of the firm and whether the firm challenged the initial allocation of waste load. Thus one of two firms, identical in terms of production processes, could obtain less severe restrictions if it undertook studies to demonstrate its 'unique' problems.[5]

Absence of the survival threat to management of firms operating in imperfectly competitive markets means that objectives other than that of profit maximization may be pursued. Necessary conditions for a manifestation of such objectives are the separation of ownership from control and a divergence of interests between owners and managers. Given such conditions we now examine the effect on likely reaction of imperfectly competitive firms to controls on the discharge of effluent.

III. AN ALTERNATIVE HYPOTHESIS: MANAGERIAL DISCRETION

It is generally recognized that imperfections in both the product and the capital market can lead to management pursuing objectives of their own choosing which may be contrary to the profit maximizing goal. Baumol [3], Williamson [22] and Liebenstein [10] have placed different interpretations upon these goals, but all have recognized that, subject to a minimum profit constraint, any argument in the utility function of an individual, *qua* individual, can be a goal to be pursued at work. In practice emphasis has been

[5] Ackerman *et al.* [1] try to explain the ratio of allocated load to plant capacity for eight oil refineries along the Delaware and they derive the following equation:

$$\frac{\text{DRBC}}{\text{BBL}} = 6{\cdot}87 + \underset{(5\cdot4)^*}{45{\cdot}1\ \text{LUB}} + \underset{(2\cdot99)^*}{25{\cdot}24\ \text{OWN}}$$

$$\bar{R}^2 = 0{\cdot}80 \qquad F = 15{\cdot}57$$

Degrees of freedom = 4

* Significant at 95%.

LUB = 1 if heavy oils are produced
0 if not

OWN = 1 if firms did own waste load study
0 if otherwise

DRBC = Delaware River Basin Compact
i.e. the authority allocated load

BBL = Barrels of crude oil per day (plant capacity).

placed on factors likely to influence the salary of the manager, leading to firm objectives such as sales maximization, empire building, etc., or on factors which increase 'leisure' time, i.e. time spent on the golf course or the quiet life. There is no reason, however, why, the arguments in the utility function of the manager at work should differ from those as a citizen.

Since society as a whole has, over the past decade, shown a greater interest in the environment this might be reflected in a greater consciousness of industrial management of their social responsibilities. Take the case of a company discharging effluent into a river so as substantially to reduce the latter's amenity value. Industrial management is likely to live close to the factory (although probably not as close as workers!) and, since the company may employ managers who are interested in sailing, fishing or walking, such personnel may exert pressure within the firm to reduce discharges where possible. Pressure is likely to be exerted primarily by management since empirical evidence suggests that the environment is a middle-class concern. Since management may have more knowledge of the damage being caused by discharges and possibly of the relatively low cost at which abatement equipment may be installed they may, whilst claiming pollution control is motivated by altruism, be pursuing their own self interests in bringing about a cleaner river.

In practice there may be a number of companies discharging into the river so reductions in effluent of a single company may not significantly affect water quality. Nevertheless it is still possible, given an opportunity for discretion, for management to use at least part of this 'slack' to reduce effluent discharges. For example those engineers, skilled in the operation of treatment works, may recognize that their importance/status within the company depends upon the corporate abatement budget. They may argue that whilst the effect on the river of their company's own effluent is not significant, it should not be seen to act in a socially irresponsible manner. Managers concerned with effluent discharges in the various companies may meet to discuss pressures exerted upon them by the river authority and the reactions of their own company and hence equipment installed by others will be common knowledge. Certainly on one major estuary in the United Kingdom although no legal pressure was brought to bear on companies (or even the threat of it!) an agreement was reached between dischargers to reduce existing effluent loads by 50% over a five year period. There is evidence that virtually all companies responded and that the target figure will be achieved.[6] This concern of management for abatement, irrespective of the consequences for the river, is called managerial preference for abatement.

Removal of the profit maximization assumption thus leads to significantly

[6] This refers to the efforts undertaken by industrialists and the Northumbrian Water Authority on Teesside, in North-East England.

different predictions of firm behaviour when faced with discharge constraints.[7] Assuming profit maximization, industries where environmental control expenditure is lowest will be those where the authority is able to exert the greatest pressure on those industries least able to resist. When imperfections in the output and capital markets are assumed, managers may then choose to exercise discretion in favour of environmental controls. Hence those industries having the greatest opportunity for discretion would be expected to spend more on controls, *ceteris paribus*, than more competitive industries. Expenditure, by industry, may be argued to be, *ceteris paribus*, of the U shape shown in Figure 1. The highly competitive industries will spend heavily on control because the authority can impose severe controls upon them in the knowledge that appeal will not be worthwhile. Expenditure is also likely to be high in the relatively uncompetitive industries which will be prepared to 'accept' severe controls knowing it will not imperil existence and with management knowing that they will derive benefit from environmental improvement. Such industries may claim that clean-up is motivated by social responsibility, altruism, etc., but it is only the low levels of competition within those industries that enable such factors to be manifest. It is the 'middle' industries which will derive most benefit from appeals, negotiations, procrastinations over their expenditure since their existence may be threatened by having high expenditure imposed upon them. Most importantly, however, they can claim special case status and thus the authority is unlikely to devote a high proportion of resources to imposing severe consent conditions. Rather the authority will recognize that it is better advised to orientate enforcement funds towards those firms more 'naturally' compliant.

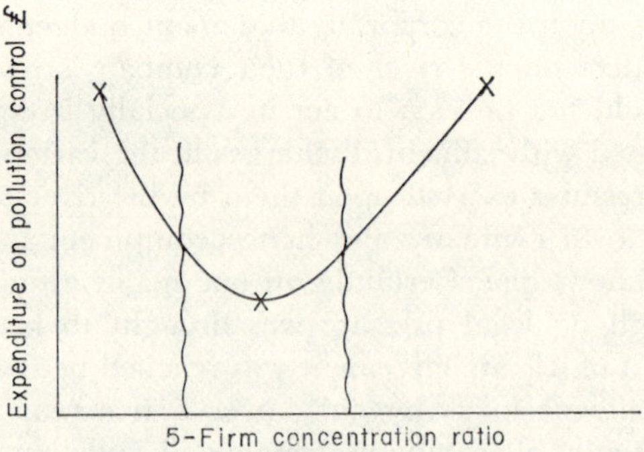

FIGURE 1.

IV. HYPOTHESIS TESTING

To test the existence of a U-shaped relationship between market imperfections and expenditure on pollution control we postulate characterization

[7] The theoretical implications of this are examined in 'Pollution Control and Managerial Discretion' by M. Walker and D. J. Storey (mimeo) [21].

by the form shown in equation (1) rather than equation (2).

(1) $$EXP_i = \alpha_1 + \beta_1 C_i + \beta_2 C_i^2 + \beta_3 \gamma + \epsilon$$

(2) $$EXP_i = \alpha_1 + \beta_1 C_i + \beta_3 \gamma + \epsilon$$

EXP_i = expenditure by industry i on pollution control
C_i = market imperfection index for industry i
γ = variable included for *ceteris paribus* purposes

$\alpha_1, \beta_1, \beta_2, \beta_3$ = coefficients
ϵ = error term

Support for the existence of a U-shaped relationship of the type proposed above will be demonstrated firstly by the total variance explained by factors included in equation (1) exceeding that included in equation (2). In addition the coefficient β_1 should be significantly negative and β_2 significantly positive.

V. WATER POLLUTION CONTROL IN ENGLAND AND WALES: THE VARIABLES

The actual variables used in testing for a U-shaped relationship between market imperfections and pollution control expenditure are shown in Table I whilst derivations are shown in Appendices I and II.

Data on expenditure on water pollution control are taken from the Report of River Pollution Survey of England and Wales 1970, which represents the one and only national survey of costs to industry of controlling effluent discharges to rivers. It was undertaken in 1968 but gives totals for actual

TABLE I
VARIABLES INCLUDED IN REGRESSIONS

A. *EXP_i: Expenditure variables*

1. $CART = \frac{\text{Capital expenditure on water pollution 1960–70}}{\text{Quantity of effluent discharged}}$

2. $HEAP = \frac{\text{Capital expenditure on water pollution 1960–70}}{\text{Total capital expenditure on plant and equipment 1968}}$

B. *C_i: Market imperfection variables*
1. CONCS = Five-firm sales concentration ratio 1972
2. CONCS 2 = $(CONCS)^2$

C. *γ: Ceteris paribus variables*

1.	TOTPRO	Total process water discharged
2.	PROTID	Proportion of total process water discharged to tidal waters
3.	PRONT	Proportion of total process water discharged to non-tidal waters
4.	PROSEW	Proportion of total process water discharged to public sewers
5.	PROPRO	Proportion of total process water discharged into waterways or sewers under the jurisdiction of authorities who brought no prosecutions under the Rivers (Prevention of Pollution) Acts, between 1970 and 1974.
6.	LDIRT	$\text{Log}\left[\frac{\text{Total process water discharged}}{\text{Total sales output 1968}}\right]$

costs incurred 1960–68 and scheduled costs 1969–70. Since the latter represent approximately 50% of all costs it seems likely that most of the 1960–70 costs will have been incurred in the later years of that period thus reducing the problems of non-comparability due to price changes, replacements, etc.

A number of indices of market imperfection suggest themselves. Data on profitability are available but since industries which exercised discretion over pollution control expenditure may also manifest other forms of discretion, it is uncertain whether low profitability is indicative of *X*-inefficiency or perfect competition.

It would have been valuable to have data on internal firm structure within industries since the divorce between ownership and management is fundamental to the managerial preference for the environment thesis. Thus the local manager of a branch plant may be able to justify discretionary expenditure to the main board on ostensibly economic grounds (if we pollute the atmosphere or the river we will get a bad reputation and have difficulty recruiting labour, or local product sale will fall) but in fact he may be presenting his own self interest in not wishing to live in the area and/or find it socially embarrassing to be associated with such anti-social activity. Data on ownership, and firm structure in all industries are not, however, available.

Despite its acknowledged pitfalls, it was decided that five-firm concentration ratio data represented the best indicator available of market imperfections, given that Herfindahl indices did not exist in the form required. Hence it is assumed that a large share of the market taken by the top five firms was at least a necessary condition for managerial discretion and that a low proportion indicated competitive conditions.

The group *Y* variables also require detailed comment since they are unfamiliar to economists. The TOTPRO variable is included to test the effects of scale whilst the PROTID PROSEW and PRONT variable demonstrate whether an industry which discharges most of its effluent to the public sewer, to tidal or to non-tidal waters is required to install more or less abatement equipment. *A priori* it is to be expected that industries which discharge primarily into non-tidal waters will be more tightly controlled since this water is frequently used for abstraction purposes. On the other hand industrial location policy pursued by governments and by companies has been towards locating effluent intensive industries on major estuaries. Tacit support from government has come through the legal framework where consistently less stringent controls have been applied to estuaries.[8]

The PROPRO variable is included to examine the role of the river

[8] The Rivers (Prevention of Pollution) Act 1951, which required all new dischargers to obtain 'consents' specifically excluded estuaries. The Rivers (Prevention of Pollution) Act 1961 required all dischargers, i.e. including those in existence prior to 1951, to obtain consents. Dischargers to estuaries were specifically excluded from the 1951 Act whilst the 1960 Estuaries and Tidal Waters Act ensured that only post-1960, i.e. new dischargers to estuaries, required consents. This remains the legal position today until the Control of Pollution Act 1974 is fully implemented.

authorities in encouraging dischargers to install abatement equipment. There is much debate on the optimal mix of weapons since traditional authorities have claimed that it is unnecessary to take dischargers to court to instigate improvement. Instead they preferred a policy of persuasion but these 'arm-twisting' techniques have been the subject of criticism (see Bugler [6]).

The PROPRO variable tests whether it is advantageous in terms of lower abatement costs to an industry to discharge a high proportion of its total process water into the waterways of authorities that appeared to be lenient with polluters.

Finally the LDIRT index is an attempt to take into account the dirtiness of the industry.[9] The log relationship is chosen partly to offset the effect of extreme values which the index produces and partly because a semi-log relationship looks more appropriate from an examination of the raw data.

VI. RESULTS

Regression equations were derived using all variables apart from the collinear process water variables but many made little contribution to explaining total variation in HEAP or CART. Hence Table II shows the results of the best equations derived as a result of a sequential inclusion/exclusion procedure. Inclusion took place on high values of 't' and contribution to the value of the (adjusted) R^2, in accordance with our *a priori* hypotheses.

Equations (1)–(4) show reasonable grounds for believing the existence of a U-shaped relationship, *ceteris paribus*, between concentration and expenditure on pollution control of the type postulated earlier since the quadratic equations are markedly superior to the linear. In equations (1) and (2) the *ceteris paribus* variable included is PRONT which has a positive sign in accordance with *a priori* theory. In equation (3) the variables included are LDIRT and TOTPRO, the signs of both of which are positive, although at the 5% level only, the former is significant. These results, however, certainly do not suggest the existence of scale economies in pollution control. Rather they indicate that firms which generate the dirtiest effluents per unit of output and those discharging the highest absolute quantities spend more per unit of effluent than the cleaner firms. Whether this is due to diseconomies at the plant level or because of pressure from the authority is unclear, although the latter seems intuitively the most likely. From equation (1) the level of concentration at which expenditure is minimized is approximately 0·47, whereas in equation (3) the value is 0·66. There is, of course, no reason why the two indices of expenditure should have identical minimum values

[9] Some care is needed in interpreting this variable since it examines quantities of effluent discharged in 1968 even after expenditure on abatement 1960–68. It may not fully represent the 'natural' dirtiness of the industry. On the other hand since expenditure 1969–70 was half that of the previous eight years it does give a reasonable indication of the pollution intensity of the industry since the quantity of process water measured is for the year 1968.

Table II

REGRESSION COEFFICIENTS

Dependent	C	LDIRT	CONCS	CONCS 2	PRONT	TOTPRO	R^2	$\bar{R}^2$	
CART	0·6119		− 0·0257	+ 0·00027	+ 0·2483		0·6124	0·5512	(1)
	(2·719)		(3·045)	(3·559)	(2·604)				
CART	−0·1122		+ 0·00364		0·2798		0·3539	0·2893	(2)
	(0·928)		(1·609)		(2·343)				
HEAP	316·88	+25·539	−10·977	+0·0831		+0·7199	0·6329	0·5513	(3)
	(2·52)	(2·311)	(2·324)	(1·97)		(1·999)			
HEAP	104·59	+23·248	−1·958			+ 0·6402	0·5550	0·4748	(4)
	(1·54)	(1·974)	(1·810)			(1·669)			

't' statistics in parentheses
$n=23$

and it is perhaps reassuring that the levels of concentration are approximately between 50 and 70% since studies of advertising expenditure and concentration in the United Kingdom indicate that the inverted U peaks at approximately this level. Sutton [17] for example finds that a peak is reached at 0·64.

Perhaps as interesting as the variables included are those which are excluded. For example there appears to be no significant relationship between discharges into waters controlled by non-fining river authorities and lower control expenditure by companies. This may be regarded as evidence in support of the hypothesis that the non-court weapons of persuasion ('arm-twisting') are no less effective in encouraging industry to abate than extensive use of court proceedings. Equally there does not appear to be any evidence of industries discharging into the public sewers (where in the UK an effluent charge is imposed) installing more abatement, *ceteris paribus*, than those discharging directly into water courses where no fee is paid. It would, however, be unwise to interpret this as indicative of the ineffectiveness of charging since the level of such charges was extremely variable both between and within authorities.

VII. CONCLUSIONS

Given that it can be demonstrated that a U-shaped relationship exists between expenditure on pollution control and at least one index of market imperfections it is important to be clear on the inferences that may be drawn.

First, it demonstrates that neither market structure nor the role of the enforcing authority can be omitted from further developments in externality theory. To do so is to ignore a major influence in determining in practice, expenditure by firms on environmental control.

Secondly, since there is no *a priori* reason why firms in the medium concentrated industries should have significantly higher or lower costs of abatement than other firms this study represents further support for those arguing that water quality improvement has not been achieved in a cost-effective manner. This is because under a system of regulation the 'middle concentration' firms will always have an incentive to challenge the authority rather than install equipment. Given that the first order condition for cost effective achievement of a specified water quality is that the marginal *abatement* costs of all dischargers should be equal (Baumol and Oates [4]) this condition is unlikely to be realised where some firms find it worthwhile to invest funds in challenging the authority rather than in abatement. This may perhaps be cited as support for an effluent tax scheme which its proponents argue reduces the opportunity for appeals, procrastination, etc., since it is applied uniformly to all dischargers. Even this, however, remains a pious hope since in practice it is necessary to weight the tax according to location (Tietenberg [20]) and this as Ackerman *et al.* show can lead to precisely the same types of negotiation as under the present UK regulatory system.

Thirdly, there may be a tendency to assume that the U-shaped curve, and our explanations of the causes of its shape, can be applied to other forms of 'discretionary' expenditure such as health and safety at work. If the data were available it would be an interesting hypothesis to test but unless one can argue that management derive positive pleasure from seeing operatives better protected it is difficult to explain why the expenditure curve should rise in imperfectly competitive industries. This highlights a major inference from the present study, *viz.* the question of whether water pollution generated by imperfectly competitive firms is a true externality since we are arguing that management is affected by its own pollution. The management of imperfectly competitive firms hence act in accordance with economic theory, by internalizing the effects of pollution by the expenditure of funds on abatement.

Finally it should be realized that anti-trust policies, whilst they may increase social welfare by the introduction of greater competition designed to reduce product prices may simultaneously increase social damage from pollution through reducing the opportunity for discretionary expenditure on abatement. This is, of course, a different point from that made by Buchanan who argued, on the basis of a fixed relationship between output and effluent, that increased competition meant increased output and hence increased pollution. Both hypotheses indicate the necessity for a careful analysis to be undertaken prior to the introduction of any policies designed to increase competition.

CENTRE FOR ENVIRONMENTAL STUDIES, LONDON

APPENDIX I

DERIVATION OF VARIABLES USED IN REGRESSION ANALYSIS

1. *CART*

Capital Expenditure on Water Pollution Control 1960–70 is taken from *River Pollution Survey of England and Wales* 1970 [15]. It comprises columns 4+16+26+5+17+27 of Tables 81, 82, and 83. Data on process water are used rather than total effluent because the latter includes the former plus discharge of solely cooling water. The purpose of the distinction is that process water is more polluting than solely cooling water since the only parameter requiring control is temperature. Thus the higher the proportion of solely cooling water to total effluent, *ceteris paribus*, the lower the likely level of expenditure. Data for 28 manufacturing industries are given in the River Pollution Survey but only 23 are used in this analysis. Gas and coke, electricity, coal, iron and steel were excluded because they were primarily within public ownership, whilst ethanol was included with chemical and allied because separate concentration data were not available. The data on costs incurred by industry, as reported in the River Pollution Survey were classified under a CBI code which does not correspond exactly to the SIC. Hence some judgement had to be exercised to derive comparable classifications and this is shown in Appendix II.

2. *HEAP*

Capital Expenditure on Water Pollution 1960–70 is derived from the same source as CART above. This is divided by Total Capital Expenditure on Plant and Machinery (Acquisitions minus Disposals) taken from Census of Production 1968 Summary, Table 2.

3. *CONCS*

Concentration data is taken from the Census of Production 1972, Table 9 (Sales of Goods Produced and Work Done). Weights are applied according to total sales where aggregation of MLHs take place. In some cases, for confidentiality reasons, it is not possible to give a five-firm ratio. Here we follow the procedure outlined by Sutton [17] using the actual value given in the census (for example the ratio given may be for seven firms), taking 5/7 of this value as the lower bound and calculating the arithmetic mean. For further debate on the validity of this procedure see Sutton [18] and Rees [12].

4. *LDIRT*

Data on Process Water Discharged are derived from the Report of the River Pollution Survey 1970, columns 2+14+24 of Tables 86, 87 and 88. Data on output are derived from the Census of Production 1968, Table 1 (Goods Produced and Work Done). The log of these values is taken because although a high effluent/output ratio is likely to result in controls upon the industry this is unlikely to be of a fixed linear relationship.

5. *PRONT*, *TOTPRO*, *PROSEW*, *PROTID*

These variables are all derived directly from the River Pollution Survey 1970. Process water discharged to non-tidal waters is shown in column 2 in Table 86, to tidal waters in column 14 of Table 87 and to sewers column 24 of Table 87. Quantities relate to 1968 discharges.

6. *PROPRO*

This variable is included to define the location of discharge. It examines the proportion of the total load of process water discharged into waterways controlled by 'lax' authorities—defined as those which did not conduct any prosecutions against those breaching the River (Prevention of Pollution) Acts 1951 or 1961. Data on prosecutions are taken from Storey [16].

APPENDIX II

CBI CODE AND MLH

CBI classification	MLH
1. Brewing	231
2. Brickmaking	461
3. Cement making	464
4. Chemical and allied + ethanol	271–279 exc. 274–276 and 279.2 and 279.5
5. Engineering	331–370
6. Food processing	211–219, 221, 229, 232, 239
7. Glass making	463
8. Glue	279 (2)
9. General manufacturing	492–495 and 499
10. Leather tanning	431
11. Metal smelting	321–323
12. Paint making	274
13. Paper and board	481, 482
14. Petroleum refining	262
15. Plastics manufacture	276, 496
16. Plating and metal	390–399
17. Pottery	462
18. Printing ink	279 (5)
19. Mining and quarrying	102, 103 and 109
20. Rubber processing	491
21. Soap and detergent	275
22. Textiles and cotton	411–413
23. Textiles wool	414

REFERENCES

[1] Ackerman, B. R., Ackerman, S. R., Henderson, D. W. and Sawyer, J. W., *The Uncertain Search for Environmental Quality* (Free Press, New York, 1974).

[2] Asch, P. and Seneca, J. J., 'Monopoly and External Costs: An Application of Second-best Theory to the Automobile Industry', *Journal of Environmental Economics and Management*, **4** (1) (1976), pp. 69–79.

[3] Baumol, W. J., 'On the Theory of Oligopoly', *Economica* New Series, **25** (1958), pp. 187–98.

[4] Baumol, W. J. and Oates, W., *The Theory of Environmental Policy* (Prentice Hall Inc., New York, 1975).

[5] Buchannan, J. M., 'External Diseconomies, Corrective Taxes and Market Structure', *American Economic Review*, **64** (March 1969), pp. 174–7.

[6] Bugler, J., *Polluting Britain* (Penguin, London, 1971).

[7] Downing, P. B. and Watson, W. D., 'The Economics of Enforcing Air Pollution Controls', *Journal of Environmental Economics and Management*, **1** (3) (1974), pp. 219–36.

[8] Freeman, A. M., *The Economics of Pollution Control and Environmental Quality* (General Learning Press, New York, 1971).

[9] Lee, D. R., 'Efficiency of Pollution Taxation and Market Structure', *Journal of Environmental Economics and Management*, **2** (1) (1975), pp. 69–72.

[10] LIEBENSTEIN, H., 'Allocative Efficiency versus *X*-Efficiency', *American Economic Review*, **61** (June 1966), pp. 392–415.

[11] POSNER, R. A., 'The Behaviour of Administrative Agencies', *Journal of Legal Studies*, **1** (2) (1972) reprinted in *Essays in the Economics of Crime and Punishment*, G. Becker and W. M. Landes (ed.) (National Bureau of Economic Research, New York, 1974).

[12] REES, R. D., 'Advertising Concentration and Competition: A Comment and Further Results', *Economic Journal*, **85** (March 1975), pp. 165–72.

[13] *Report on Census of Production* 1968, 156 Summary Table, Industry Analysis, Department of Trade and Industry (HMSO, London, 1972).

[14] *Report on Census of Production* 1972, Summary Tables, Department of Industry (HMSO, London, 1977).

[15] *Report of a River Pollution Survey of England and Wales* 1970, Department of the Environment Welsh Office (HMSO, London, 1973).

[16] SUTTON, C. J., 'Advertising Concentration and Competition', *Economic Journal*, **84** (March 1974), pp. 56–69.

[17] ——, 'Advertising and Market Structure: A Reply and Some Further Comments', *Economic Journal*, **85** (1975), pp. 173–6.

[18] STOREY, D. J., 'A Socio-Economic Approach to the Enforcement of Water Pollution Law in England and Wales', *International Journal of Social Economics*, **4** (3) (1977), pp. 207–224.

[19] TERBONNE, R. P., 'Enforcement Costs and the Incentive to Evade Controls on Production', *Journal of Environmental Economics and Management*, **4** (2) (1977), pp. 129–34.

[20] TIETENBERG, T. H., 'Specific Taxes and the Control of Pollution: A General Equilibrium Analysis', *Quarterly Journal of Economics*, **87** (4) (1973), pp. 503–22.

[21] WALKER, M. and STOREY, D. J., 'Pollution Control and Managerial Discretion' (mimeo) (1978).

[22] WILLIAMSON, O. E., *Economics of Discretionary Behaviour: Managerial Objectives in the Theory of the Firm* (Prentice Hall, Englewood Cliffs, NJ, 1964).

THE JOURNAL OF INDUSTRIAL ECONOMICS
Volume XXVII December 1978 No. 2

ECONOMIES OF SCALE IN SEWAGE PURIFICATION AND DISPOSAL

MARTIN R. J. KNAPP*

SUMMARY

Most local public services in Britain are supplied today in a haze of almost total ignorance concerning the economics of production and demand. This paper reports an attempt to clear the haze from one of the oldest and most essential of local public services—the purification and disposal of sewage. A statistical cost function is fitted for a national sample of 172 sewage works using ordinary least squares regression techniques. Strong and pervasive economies of scale in operation and maintenance are observed over much of the relevant output range. The estimated function has implications for long-term planning, for efficiency prescriptions, and for pricing policies.

THE halt in public sector expansion induced by the oil crisis of late 1973 emphasized the need for careful reappraisal of the conditions under which public services are delivered and consumed. Often far removed from the market place, facing no viable close substitutes, many services had been operating in ways which did not always conform with the best principles of business management. The complications of local government reorganization, contemporaneous with the onset of economic recession in the first quarter of 1974, clouded many important policy issues which only reappeared fairly recently. Public service agencies, whether at the national, regional, or local level, have had to come to terms with a reduction in real resources in the face of rising public expectations and needs. The importance of efficiency in the production and allocation of increasingly scarce public services is now clearly recognized. The Layfield Report stressed this very point:

> Taxpayers have the right to expect public services to be provided efficiently: that is, the standard of service desired should be provided at the minimum reasonable cost. People . . . cannot shop around for most of the services provided by public authorities. So public authorities are not under the same pressure as private suppliers to keep their costs down. Special care should therefore be taken to ensure that the financial arrangements promote efficiency [34, p. 51].

Disappointingly, economists, and especially British economists, have been both unwilling and unable to undertake studies of individual public services

* The author is grateful to Dennis Townsend for his encouragement and interest in this study, and to an anonymous referee for constructive comments.

which have the potential for generating useful policy prescriptions. Hirsch's [24] seminal study of economies of scale in local government stimulated few empirical studies and Britain can apparently boast but one concentrated programme of research—that sponsored by the Royal Commission on Local Government in England [42]. There is thus today an embarrassment of almost total ignorance about the economic conditions of the production and supply of many public services, an ignorance that will take much research to dispel.

The present paper reports an attempt to disperse some of the haze surrounding one of the oldest, most essential, and least studied of public services—the purification and disposal of domestic and industrial sewage. Using the techniques of statistical cost analysis it is possible to examine the presence and extent of economies of scale in the operation of individual plants. The problems that have so often dogged the study of publicly provided services, particularly the difficulties of defining and measuring output and the lack of suitably disaggregated data sets, do not arise in this case. It has been possible to exploit the financial and operational data collected by the Chartered Institute of Public Finance and Accountancy for a sample of well over 200 local authority sewage purification and disposal works for the year ending March 31st, 1973. This data collection allows the construction of output indicators which take account of both the quantity and quality dimensions of production and the examination of a number of other potential determinants of operating cost.

After a brief consideration of the historical development of the service, together with an account of the need for treatment and the conventions currently governing it, the cost model is placed in its theoretical context. Optimality in the provision of public services clearly requires due consideration of both the demand and supply sides of the 'market', which in turn requires careful study of the incidence of both externalities and economies of scale. The third section presents the data and the results of the series of cost analyses for a sample of sewage works in England and Wales. Finally, the empirical results are reviewed in a policy context.

SEWAGE PURIFICATION AND DISPOSAL

Urban concentration, a logical consequence of the Industrial Revolution in the early nineteenth century, made imperative the improvement and extension of sewage and sewage disposal systems if public health was not to be seriously damaged. Prior to the Public Health Act of 1948, statutory regulations governing the discharge of domestic and industrial waste were virtually non-existent, and only the serious threat of a cholera outbreak had spurred legislative action. The Act only required the provision of a sewerage system, however, and not of treatment and disposal facilities, and as a result many streams and rivers virtually became open sewers. Bacterial purification of sewage was not adopted until very much later but subsequent developments were rapid and effective.

Until the Water Act of 1973, which took effect on April 1st, 1974, sewerage, sewage purification and disposal, and trade effluent were the responsibility of more than 1300 county borough and county district councils. Under the Public Health Act (1936), each local authority was required to provide public sewers to ensure the necessary drainage of their district, to dispose of the contents of their sewers effectually, and to allow manufacturers to discharge trade effluents into the sewerage system. Local authorities were free to impose charges on trade users of the public sewerage system and could impose conditions on the nature of the trade effluent. Generally speaking it is the strength rather than the volume of trade effluent which calls for these additional impositions. Many local authorities combined together to provide treatment works, especially where the topographical features of the area made it advantageous so to do, or where it was felt economies of scale could be exploited.

In April 1974, responsibility for sewerage and sewage treatment passed to the newly established Regional Water Authorities, who now also had responsibility for water supply, water quality control, river management, and industry planning. The ten Regional Water Authorities are thus independent, multi-purpose bodies, answerable to the Department of the Environment, and responsible for the full hydrological cycle. Although some of the sewerage functions have been delegated to district councils in some areas, on the whole local authorities have little to do with water management today.

Following the classification of Downing [14], it is possible to distinguish between rubbish (generally inorganic, solid wastes), garbage (food wastes of the home or industry), and sewage (organic waste materials and used water).[1] In addition, there is storm sewage—the overland run-off of rainfall and melting snow—which may or may not be transmitted in the domestic sewers. Public responsibility extends over four successive stages: collection from the site of production, transmission from small to larger sewers and then to the treatment site, purification to render the waste harmless or unobjectionable, and finally disposal. It is the final two stages that are the subject of the present study.

The need for careful purification and sensible disposal of domestic and trade sewage should be obvious. The noxious qualities of the effluent are well known and the health hazards of water pollution well documented. Nemerow [36] provides a five-fold classification of the pollutional characteristics, and hence externalities, of this waste which serves both to focus attention on the need for treatment and also to indicate the processes of purification. One of the most common and useful indicators of pollutional strength is the biochemical oxygen demand (BOD) of the waste, defined as the amount

[1] Important studies of the economics of inorganic waste ('refuse') collection and disposal include those of Hirsch [25] and Clark [11].

of oxygen required by bacteria to oxidize the waste into carbon dioxide and water. Because depletion of oxygen in the water will kill fish, damage many micro-organisms, and generally upset the ecological balance, a higher BOD indicates a more dangerous level of pollution.[2] This measure alone is not sufficient, however, for low BOD values may be obtained from effluents which contain heavy metals, for example. Another dimension of water pollution measures the suspended solids found in wastes, particularly industrial wastes. The solids include fine grit and insoluble metal precipitates as well as sewage suspended matter. These solids are measured and removed by fairly simple physical methods but would otherwise cause considerable silting problems. Floating materials and coloured matter, including oil, grease and dyes, form a third characteristic. The pollution in this case is primarily visible, with considerable negative social benefits being conferred on recreational users of rivers and streams. A fourth pollutional dimension is quite simply the volume of effluent. Although domestic sewage is approximately 99·9% water the fact that the total sewage flow per head of the population for the sample of plants used for the present study was 7600 gallons per day gives some indication of the scale of the problem. Finally, Nemerow lists other harmful constituents of sewage, such as feathers, acids and alkalis, inflammables, noxious gases, and detergents. Each of these can cause considerable damage at a number of points in the ecological chain. As we shall see below, each of the five major dimensions will have ramifications for the operation, and hence the operating cost, of sewage purification and disposal works.

THE OPTIMUM PROVISION OF LOCAL PUBLIC SERVICES

Any discussion of the optimum level of provision of a local public service must necessarily take account of both the demand and supply sides of the market, whether that market be notional or real. It is extremely rare, however, to be in a position to provide empirical evidence on *both* sides of the market simultaneously. Rather, empirical studies have been forced to focus on either the production of local public services or on their take-up: only the relatively few cost-benefit studies of isolated services can claim otherwise. Moreover, in the case of British local government services, it is still rare to find a study which combines empirical evidence, whether analytical or descriptive, with an adequate discussion of the underlying theoretical principles. This is disappointing but not altogether surprising, for as Kemper and Quigley [31, p. 3] explain:

> Because local services are heterogeneous, because output is difficult to measure, because spillovers and externalities are important, and because

[2] James [28, p. 168] reports how a measure of BOD is used to classify water as either very clean, fairly clean, doubtful, or bad.

reliable data are difficult to obtain, it is not surprising that the body of existing analysis is rather small. Moreover, because the output of the research is itself a public good, it will be under-supplied if financed at the local level.

In order to determine the optimum provision of a local public service it is helpful to appeal to the familiar calculus of Samuelson [43], as refined by Evans [15]. Pareto optimality (for a social welfare maximum) is thereby adapted to take account of the 'publicness' of the good or service in question. The collection, purification and disposal service is, in the nomenclature of Evans, a local public good with externalities or a semi-public good. Whilst this affords considerable simplification of the Pareto conditions, it is still the case that both demand and supply considerations play their part in the determination of an optimum. Consequently, any discussion of optimal provision must include at least a few comments on the problems of externalities and economies of scale, and the way each of them impinges on the conditions of optimization.

The original rationale for the collection of domestic sewage in British urban areas was to remove the health hazard threatened by a build-up of untreated sewage. The direct benefits to individuals that received the service were thus considerable. However, urban sewage was not treated but merely discharged into streams, rivers, or tidal waters imposing disbenefits on the community at large. Only towards the end of the nineteenth century were these externalities reduced or removed and environmental quality enhanced. Downing [14, p. 13] has succinctly summarized the position thus:

> . . . the benefits and costs of collection and transmission are mostly urban in nature while the benefits of treatment and the costs of release are largely non-urban. The urban complex treats its sewage to reduce the costs of its release to the non-urban society.

The extent and importance of these externalities will depend upon the spatial characteristics of the area. The density of both population and structures, and the physical proximity of communities will obviously determine the importance of the spillover effects (Cowing and Holtmann [12]). What we do know, however, and as British social history so clearly shows, is that a disregard for the positive externalities of sewage treatment and (sensible) disposal will lead to underprovision of the service in urban areas.

On the supply side, the most important elements are the existence and extent of economies of scale and also, possibly, of economies of density. Whilst the existence of local externalities may initially have rationalized public provision of sewage collection facilities, and subsequent regional or national externalities may have inspired public provision of purification services, it is the existence of very considerable economies of scale in the construction and operation of these facilities that keeps the service almost wholly public at the present time.[3]

Economies of scale may be observed in any of four distinct contexts: in the construction and in the operation and maintenance of the sewerage system, and in the construction and in the operation and maintenance of the treatment and disposal works. The sewerage system may further be characterized by economies of density. The costs of constructing a collection and transmission system will be influenced by dwelling density, overall distance, the topography of the land (which may necessitate pumping stations or pressure sewers), the expected volume and quality of the sewerage (some chemicals can damage sewers, although this is rare), and the type of ground in which the sewers are laid. Downing [14] reports evidence from North America to suggest that economies of scale in the construction of sewerage systems are substantial. The costs of operation and maintenance of sewers will be very much smaller than the costs of construction, and probably much less variable.

Turning to the costs of the construction, operation and maintenance of purification and disposal works, North American evidence would once again suggest the existence of significant economies of large scale in both the quantity and quality dimensions.[4] To the best of my knowledge there have been no previous British studies which have addressed the question of economies of scale within a framework which takes adequate account of both the volume of sewage treated and the extent of the treatment itself. The capital intensity of the purification process, the general indivisibility of many of the capital inputs, economies in the use of larger machines (the so-called 'six-tenths rule') and in input specialization, all combine to reduce the average capital cost of treatment and disposal in larger works. As for the costs of operation and maintenance, there are a number of reasons for expecting systematic variation in the average cost of treatment. We shall postpone our discussion of these various influences until after we have introduced the techniques of statistical cost analysis and the data set that we shall use.

THE COST FUNCTION IN PRINCIPLE

The techniques of statistical cost analysis have been widely applied and carefully refined since the pioneering efforts of Dean over 40 years ago (collected and summarized in Dean [13]). In essence, multiple regression analysis is applied to a sample of observations on production units, either in the cross-section or over a period of time or both, taking as the dependent

[3] Many industries discharging noxious effluents do in fact undertake some preliminary treatment themselves, particularly if the pollutional characteristics are marked or of an unusual kind.

[4] See, for example, Downing [14], Frankel [18], Masters [35], and Rowan, Jenkins and Howells [41].

variable the total or average cost of production. Theoretically, the cost function is derived as a reduced-form expression from a production function, a tautological cost equation and an explicit assumption regarding entrepreneurial behaviour. The cost of production is expressed as a function of the level of output and the prices paid for the various inputs, the precise form of the function being dependent upon the underlying assumptions.[5]

Under an assumption of cost minimization by the entrepreneur, the function traces out the stochastic locus of points which indicate the minimum cost of production at each level of output. Whilst it is clear that the purification and disposal services examined in this study are not offered for sale on the open market, there is no reason to believe that cost minimization represents a serious misspecification of entrepreneurial behaviour. Firstly, works managers are under explicit and implicit pressures from their controlling bodies to keep costs as low as possible whilst maintaining a high level of service. As well as the explicit exhortations of successive Ministerial directives and circulars to local authorities, regional water authorities, and works managers to keep the costs of treatment down, there are also known to be pressures from consumers. Consumer feelings, frequently expressed through the ballot box, are sensitive to changes in charging practices and rates, as was amply illustrated in the period following reorganization of the water industry in 1974. With responsibility handed from the local authorities and joint boards to the new regional water authorities, sewage treatment services were no longer assessed for the purposes of allocating the rate support grant. Charges to domestic users in many areas rose quite dramatically and the need for cost minimization was thus further emphasized.

Secondly, there exist a number of private substitutes for the publicly provided treatment and disposal facilities, particularly for industrial users of the sewerage system. Such substitutes include septic tanks, contractual disposal services and, more especially, on-site purification facilities for industrial effluent whose idiosyncratic characteristics often make separate treatment more sensible. The extent to which such substitutes are economically viable obviously depends on the table of charges adopted by the public treatment works. Furthermore, because these charges are calculated as the weighted sum of the unit costs of reception and conveyance, volumetric and primary treatment, biological oxidation of settled sewage, and treatment and disposal costs of primary sludges,[6] there is considerable inducement to keep costs, and hence charges, down.

[5] This is true for both static and dynamic models of production, although the *manner* in which output and prices enter will obviously differ (see Latham and Peel [33]).

[6] Charges and costs are conventionally expressed per cubic metre of trade effluent. Biological oxidation costs and primary sludge costs are weighted by ratios of sewage quality after treatment to quality before treatment, quality being measured in terms of chemical oxygen demand for the former cost element, and suspended solids for the latter. Overhead costs and revenue contributions to capital outlay are included. See Chartered Institute of Public Finance and Accountancy [10, Chap. 6, Appendix B] for details of the recommended guidelines for the control and charging for trade effluent discharges to the sewer.

The theoretical form of the cost function must be modified for use in any practical context. A lack of suitable data frequently forces the researcher to omit input prices from his analysis, whilst a number of additional cost determinants may be suggested in a particular application. Alchian [4], for example, has stressed the need to include variables which capture the many dimensions of output and the majority of empirical cost analyses include product mix and quality, and the state of technology and productivity. Previous studies of local public services have found it necessary to introduce variables which reflect the service conditions affecting variable input requirements such as the age of the fixed capital inputs, and such environmental factors as population density and local situational idiosyncracies. These various cost determinants should be included whenever the necessary data are available and whenever inclusion does not represent a serious misspecification error.

Although the cost function is theoretically the reduced form of a system of equations which includes the production function, it is rare to find a cost analysis which takes explicit advantage of the duality between cost and production functions.[7] Instead, the form of the relationship is dictated by empirical considerations with variables entering and leaving the regression according as they exert significant or insignificant influences upon total or average cost. Given the general climate of ignorance surrounding the supply of most public services it is important to allow sufficient generality of functional form as to capture all possible configurations of association between cost and its various determinants. Within a linear-in-parameters framework one should therefore examine polynomials of up to at least third degree for all major variables and all plausible multiplicative combinations of cost determinants.

THE DATA AND THE REGRESSION VARIABLE

The data for the present study were taken from the last annual collection of sewage purification and disposal statistics published by the Chartered Institute of Public Finance and Accountancy [9] and relate to the financial year 1972/73. For each of 247 individual sewage works in England and Wales information was tabulated on expenditure, income, quantity and quality of average daily flows, and certain features of the works and the service. Missing observations on some of the more important aspects of treatment made it necessary to drop 75 works from the analyses reported in this paper. There were no missing observations on any of the variables for the remaining 172 purification and disposal works.

The dependent variable was selected as average operating cost per million gallons of total daily sewage flow, which includes domestic sewage, storm

7 Exceptions include Nerlove's [37] study of the US electricity supply industry and the more recent study of the Norwegian mechanical pulp industry by Førsund and Jansen [17].

run-off, and trade effluent. The mean value for average operating cost in the sample was £5772.45 per million gallons. Expenditure on employees, repairs and maintenance, power generated and purchased, rent and rates, supplies and services, transport and mobile plant, establishment, and other miscellaneous items was included; debt charges and revenue contributions to capital outlay were not. Expenditure was measured gross of all income from the treatment of trade effluent, the sale of by-products, payments by other local authorities for sewage treatment, and other sources.

There is a long-standing debate regarding the efficacy of estimating an *average* cost function in preference to a *total* cost function. It has been pointed out by Griliches [21] and Casson [8] among others, that there are dangers inherent in correlating and regressing ratio variables as one does in an average cost function. Errors of measurement in the deflating variable can introduce spurious correlation and increase the likelihood of biased and inconsistent parameter estimates. On the other hand, the average cost function is less susceptible to the undesirable influences of multicollinear regressors and heteroscedastic disturbances (Feldstein [16]). Both forms of misspecification reduce the precision of estimation and can lead to the erroneous exclusion of important regressors (see, for example, Johnston [30, sections 5.7 and 7.3]). In the present study the deflating variable is the total daily sewage flow, and we would not expect measurement errors to comprise more than a very small proportion of the total flow. Multicollinearity will still characterize the independent variables of the average cost expression, if only because of the polynomial nature of the functional form, but is unavoidable. We shall test for heteroscedasticity in the estimated equations. However, because the debate does not appear to be any closer to a resolution we shall obtain our estimates by working with an average expression but also report the corresponding total expression for the purposes of comparison.

In contrast to the majority of local public services, the output of the sewage purification and disposal service is readily defined and measured. A set of indicators which between them measure the total volume of sewage and the degree to which harmful constituents are effectively removed will capture the most important dimensions of output. As should be clear from the above, our volume indicator is measured in units of million gallons of total daily sewage flow. The degree of purification can be assessed by comparing the average strength of effluent with the average strength of influent. Three measures of average strength are available in the CIPFA collection of statistics: the biochemical oxygen demand, the permanganate value, and the suspended solids content.[8] The permanganate value of influent and effluent

[8] The biochemical oxygen demand (BOD) is measured as the amount of oxygen required by bacteria to oxidize waste over the first five days, at a temperature of 20°C. The permanganate value (PV) is assessed over four hours at 27°C and gives an indication of the chemically oxidizable matter present in the influent and effluent, particularly in trade effluent. The suspended solids are measured by simple physical methods. See *Methods of Chemical Analysis to Sewage and Effluents* (HMSO, 1956), for further details of the methods of measurement, and Harris [23] for an overview and assessment.

strength is reported for less than half the works included in the sample and is therefore ignored for the purposes of the present analysis. As it happens the results from these tests will overlap to some extent with the parameters being measured by the BOD test (Harris [23]) and indeed a correlation coefficient of 0·62 was found between the percentage of BOD removed and the percentage of PV removed for those works for which data was available. The remaining two measures of average strength effectively capture the most important and noxious dimensions of domestic and industrial sewage.[9]

As well as these measures of the volume and quality of output, there were two other aspects of output which could be assessed with the present data set. One would expect variations in the rate of flow of sewage to the treatment works to have some impact on average operating cost. There is no direct measure of this rate available, but the dry weather flow gives an indication of base flow without the addition of storm sewage. The average daily volume of normal dry weather flow is calculated from the total flow of sewage treatment reaching a works on any working day of the year following seven successive dry days (days during which less than 0·01 inches of rain fell). The ratio of average daily dry weather flow to average daily total sewage flow was thus included as a potential regressor in the cost analysis. Secondly, the ratio of trade effluent to total sewage flow was computed for each works, and included in an attempt to capture some of the variation in influent quality not already measured by the BOD and suspended solids tests. Other things being equal, we would expect average cost of treatment to be positively associated with both ratios.

The type and age of capital equipment employed in the purification and treatment processes may also influence the average operating cost per unit volume of total sewage flow. The characteristics of the capital stock, which will undoubtedly show considerable variation across the sample, will in part determine the amounts that must be spent on certain variable inputs, such as labour and power, in processing a given amount of raw sewage to the required level of purification. Unfortunately, precise details of the capital stock may not be gleaned from the CIPFA data collection, but it *is* possible to identify the methods of purification adopted by each works included in the sample.[10] These methods are not mutually exclusive and where two or

[9] These two dimensions of quality, together with sewage volume, are used by authorities in setting charges for trade effluent discharges to the sewer (see CIPFA [10, section 6, Appendix B]). Dimensions for which no measure was available include toxicity, acidity/alkalinity, temperature, and colouring.

[10] Fourteen methods of purification are distinguished, grouped under five heads: biological filtration (single filtration, double filtration, alternating double filtration, and/or recirculation); activated sludge (diffused air, and/or mechanical); final effluent treatment (land, microstrainers, and/or sand filters); sludge digestion (heated and/or cold); and mechanical dewatering (vacuum filtration, pressing, and/or other methods). The zero-order correlation coefficients were all fairly small, the majority not being significantly different from zero. This would appear to indicate relatively little connection in the use of different purification processes. In warmer climes, and in more sparsely populated areas, oxidation ponds and waste stabilization ponds are often used. The vagaries of the British climate (and the density of population) rule out these 'natural purification' processes.

more of them are designed and used to carry out the same purification process, it is not possible to identify the load handled separately by each. A set of additive and multiplicative dummy variables was included in the regression analysis to indicate the incidence of the various methods of purification, individual variables being included if and when they were statistically significant (see below). We also included a variable which measures the number of years between the date of commencement of operation or any major reconstruction and the date of collection. This crude capital vintage indicator may capture some of the capital stock influence upon operating cost.

Previous authors have mentioned a number of other factors that could be important in explaining variations in average operating cost between treatment works. Downing [14], for example, argues that topography, climate, and soil considerations will all have their effects—either directly through the methods of treatment and disposal that they make possible, or else indirectly through their influence upon the volume, character, and timing of flows to the sewage works. There is no reason to deny the potential importance of these factors, but it is pertinent to note that most of these direct and indirect influences are already modelled by our inclusion of regression variables reflecting the methods of purification and the strength of the influent. Finally, it is sometimes argued that for public services producing pure public goods (locally or nationally) 'there exist either overt or latent institutional constraints requiring that all residents of (the) municipality be served (and therefore) population should be included in any model explaining the average cost of a public service' (Jackson, McDougall, and Wright [27, p. 5]). Given that we have already adequately measured both quantity and quality of output it is not clear how or why a measure of the population served by each works is going to influence operating cost. However, such a measure was available and was examined for statistical significance in our modelling of average cost variations.

A substantial number of regressors was thus assembled for use in the statistical analysis of variations in the average operating cost of sewage purification and disposal works. These variables (detailed in Table I) were then used separately and in multiplicative combination in the regression analysis. The relative scarcity of previous forays into this area of industrial economics made it imperative that all logically possible influences upon average cost be entertained.

THE ESTIMATED COST FUNCTION

The volume of total sewage flow treated annually by each purification and disposal works is largely beyond the control of the works manager or local administrator, particularly in the short run period. It is not unreasonable. therefore, to take the volume or output regressor and its exponents as exo-

TABLE I

VARIABLES USED IN THE REGRESSION ANALYSES

AC	Average operating cost (see text for components) per million gallons of total daily sewage flow
Q	Total sewage flow in million gallons per day
BOD	Proportion of biochemical oxygen demand (five days at 20°C) removed during purification (i.e. degree of purification)
SSI	Average strength of influent (parts per million) as measured by suspended solids content
SSE	Average strength of effluent (parts per million) as measured by suspended solids content
	Biological filtration dummies
BFS	Single filtration = 1; otherwise = 0
BFD	Double filtration = 1; otherwise = 0
BFA	Alternating double filtration = 1; otherwise = 0
BFR	Recirculation = 1; otherwise = 0
	Activated sludge dummies
ASD	Diffused air = 1; otherwise = 0
ASM	Mechanical = 1; otherwise = 0
	Final effluent treatment dummies
FEL	Land treatment = 1; otherwise = 0
FEM	Micro-strainers = 1; otherwise = 0
FES	Sand filters = 1; otherwise = 0
	Sludge digestion dummies
SDH	Heated = 1; otherwise = 0
SDC	Cold = 1; otherwise = 0
	Mechanical de-watering dummies
MDV	Vacuum filtration = 1; otherwise = 0
MDP	Pressing = 1; otherwise = 0
DWF	Ratio of dry weather flow to total sewage flow (million gal/day)
TE	Ratio of trade effluent to total sewage flow (million gal/day)
POP	Total sewage flow per head of the population of the area draining to the works
YR	Number of years since works commenced operation or underwent major reconstruction
Plus a wide variety of additive and multiplicative combinations of the listed variables	

genous variables within the context of the present cost model. Similarly, there is no reason to suppose that the majority of the other potential determinants of average operating cost are not exogenously determined. Each works serves a given population and employs purification processes inherited from previous time periods. The only variables which may have an element of endogeneity are those which measure the degree of purification. The quality of influent is largely beyond the control of the sewage works, except in so far as trade effluent of exceptional strength or character may be refused. The quality or average strength of the effluent from the works was determined in many areas by the standards laid down by the former river boards, although works discharging into the sea were exempt from these regulations. If the degree of purification of a given volume of sewage does have an element of endogeneity, ordinary least squares estimates of the regression coefficients and standard errors will be biased and inconsistent. However, the cause of this so-called simultaneity is probably not particularly important and there will undoubtedly be many other factors which contribute to the residual terms in the cost function. For these reasons, it can be argued (cf. Jackson *et al.* [27], Johnston [29]) that ordinary least squares estimates will suffer very little from bias and inconsistency and may be accepted with confidence.[11]

Simultaneity bias is just one of a number of problems that beset the researcher employing multiple regression techniques. We have already mentioned another two—multicollinearity and heteroscedasticity. Both sources of misspecification will be examined after our presentation of the regression results. One problem of rather more prior significance should however be mentioned at this stage, and this concerns the successive stages of estimation *per se*. In view of the predominantly exploratory nature of the present study it was necessary to estimate a considerable number of alternative functional forms. The criterion used for selection of the final form was to seek the best overall fit of the regression equation (as measured by the R^2 coefficient) that was commensurate with individual regression coefficients of reasonable statistical significance (as measured by the corresponding t-statistics). Bock, Yancey and Judge [7] have warned of the continued use of preliminary testing procedures and a number of authors have pointed out the hazards of 'data mining', particularly the possibility of selecting an incorrect specification of the average cost function. However, the large number of observations relative to the number of independent variables reduces the seriousness of this problem (Bacon [5]).

The stages of analysis eventually led to the estimated average cost function reported on the left-hand side of Table II, where the notation is exactly as given in Table I. The variables SSE, ASM, FES, SDC, DWF, TE and YR did not exert significant influences upon average cost and were thus not included in the final regression. The population variable (POP) was marginally significant but highly collinear with other regressors and thus similarly omitted. The explanatory power of the regression equations was encouragingly high, particularly since the data were originally collected with quite different purposes in mind. The included regressors explained some 60% of the variation in average cost and virtually 90% of the variation in total cost. What is more, multicollinearity was found to be no worse than one would expect from such a set of 'incestuous' regressors, and the Goldfeld and Quandt [20] test as well as a visual scan of the regression residuals, produced no evidence to reject the null hypotheses of homoscedasticity in the average cost equation. (The statistics were equal to 0·468 for the AC expression and 160·9 for the TC expression, both distributed as $F(78, 78)$ on the null hypothesis.) The basic average cost equation was thus sound, whilst Feldstein's [16] contention that a total cost function is more susceptible to the presence of heteroscedasticity is largely borne out. It can be seen that the coefficients sometimes differ when estimated by the direct and indirect

[11] Moreover, from a practical standpoint, the range of exogenous or predetermined variables available and suitable for use as instrumental variables in a two-stage least squares or instrumental variable estimation routine was extremely limited (cf. Johnston [30, section 9·3]).

TABLE II

THE ESTIMATED AVERAGE COST FUNCTION

	Direct estimate†			*Indirect estimate*†		
Regressor	*Coefficient*	*Standard error*	*t-stat.*	*Coefficient*	*Standard error*	*t-stat.*
Constant	−634·38	1659·79	0·38	616·85	1275·16	0·48
Q^{-1}	595·92	61·00	9·77**	−297·84	1707·98	0·17
BOD	4597·48	1756·45	2·62**	1590·11	1422·23	1·12
SSI	2·39	1·59	1·50	6·65	1·06	6·27**
BFS.BOD	−926·36	430·20	2·15*	−1193·60	281·70	4·24**
BFD.BOD	2082·49	867·40	2·40*	−749·72	620·49	1·21
BFA.Q^{-1}	3902·48	1976·25	1·97*	6710·86	3968·61	1·69
BFR.Q^{-1}	977·97	529·16	1·85	−80·44	2292·72	0·04
ASD.Q^{-1}	6294·05	835·40	7·53**	5846·71	3275·18	1·79
FEL	−3091·20	755·72	4·09**	−1020·74	1205·15	0·85
FEL.Q^{-1}	1769·17	573·75	3·08**	−1277·13	5084·63	0·25
FEM.Q^{-1}	2247·41	813·55	2·76**	3698·98	5050·98	0·73
SDH.Q^{-1}	1243·32	464·00	2·68**	3191·00	2309·15	1·38
MDV.Q^{-1}	6377·02	1913·45	3·33**	7982·16	4594·40	1·74
MDP	624·19	528·50	1·18	1398·58	287·51	4·86**
R^2 and F	0·6075	F=17·35**		0·8962	F=96·86**	

† The direct estimates were obtained by regressing average cost on the regressors listed in the first column. The indirect estimates were obtained by regressing total operating cost on the variables corresponding to those listed above (i.e. Q, Constant, BOD.Q, SS.Q, . . .) before dividing throughout the equation by Q.

* Denotes statistical significance at the level $\alpha < 0{\cdot}05$ (95%).

** Denotes statistical significance at the level $\alpha < 0{\cdot}01$ (99%).

methods. However, these differences are nearly all less than two standard errors (of the corresponding estimated coefficient), and thus within the 95% confidence interval. Whilst an 'optimally' estimated total cost function may have revealed a different pattern of appearance for the set of regressors, predictions would have been little different. We therefore continue to work solely with the estimated average cost function.

The main finding of the empirical analysis is that average operating costs trace out an L-shaped curve when plotted against output, implying significant and pervasive economies of scale in the operation of sewage purification and treatment works in the lower region of the observed output range (up to 10 million gallons daily), but few economies thereafter. The basic average cost curve, as illustrated in Figure 1, is a simple hyperbolic function of the daily flow. Attempts to fit more complex functions of Q were singularly unsuccessful in the sense that the inclusion of such variables as Q and Q^2 (and higher powers) had no effect upon the explanation or prediction of AC. What is more, the dummy variables reflecting the purification processing methods used by each works did nothing to alter this basic hyperbolic shape. Our finding of economies of scale is thus in keeping with previous studies of a wide range of both manufacturing industries (Beckenstein [6], Dean [13], Haldi and Whitcomb [22], Pratten [39], Toda [45]) and local public

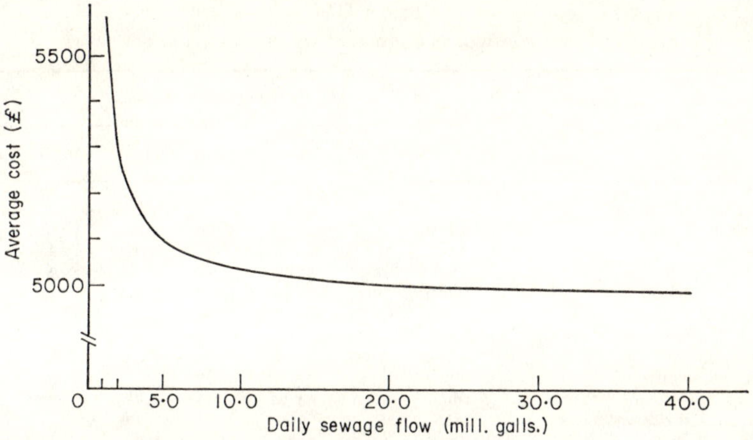

FIGURE 1. The Average Operating Cost Function

services (Ahlbrandt [2], Feldstein [16], Knapp [32], Popp and Sebold [38], Riew [40], Royal Commission on Local Government in England [42]).

The significant method-of-purification dummies were included either in additive form (as with MDP), in multiplicative combination with BOD (as with BFS and BFD), in multiplicative combination with the reciprocal of output (as with BFA, BFR, ASD, FEM, SDH and MDV), or in both additive and multiplicative form (as with FEL). Their importance in the determination of average operating cost can clearly be seen from Table II. However, it is important not to exaggerate their influence, for average costs for the larger works in the sample (with 30 million gallons of daily flow or more) were not greatly different for the various methods of purification. The only methods which appeared to alter average costs markedly in the larger works were the diffused air activated sludge and vacuum mechanical dewatering methods which raised costs, and land treatment of the final effluent which was associated with relatively low average costs.[12] Purification costs for works operating at a much lower level of production are rather more susceptible to the choice of treatment technique.

Two other variables were found to be significant predictors of average operating cost: the proportion of biochemical oxygen demand removed during purification (BOD) and the average strength of influent as measured by the suspended solids content (SSI). The suspended solids content of the effluent (SSE) was found to exert no significant influence upon average cost, and a variable measuring the proportion of suspended solids removed was

[12] This is not the place to describe in any detail the various processes of purification currently in use. The interested reader should instead consult Franklin [19, pp. 98–101], Harris [23, pp. 76–80], James [28, chapter 15], or Masters [35, pp. 154–63] for detailed descriptions, and see the useful classification schema given by the Chartered Institute of Public Finance and Accountancy [10].

TABLE III

EXPECTED COSTS FOR WORKS USING CERTAIN PURIFICATION PROCESSES

	Daily sewage flow (million gal)						
	1·0	2·0	5·0	10·0	20·0	30·0	40·0
Biological filtration							
Single	5216	4918	4739	4679	4650	4640	4635
Double	7361	7063	6884	6824	6795	NA	NA
Alt. double	NA	7137	5787	5338	5113	NA	NA
Recirculation	6389	5602	5130	4972	4894	4867	NA
Activated sludge—diffused air	11518	8073	6006	5318	4973	NA	NA
Final effluent							
Land	4413	3230	2521	2284	NA	NA	NA
Micro-strainers	7746	6324	5471	5187	5045	NA	NA
Sludge digestion—heated	6610	5691	5139	4955	4863	4832	4817
Mechanical de-watering							
Vacuum	11848	8361	6269	5572	5223	NA	NA
Pressing	6080	5782	5503	5543	5514	5504	5499
All other methods	5576	5278	5099	5039	5010	5000	4995

NA indicates that no sewage works using the specified method of purification was operating at or near the specified level of output.

All costs are expected average operating costs, calculated on the assumption that all other variables take their mean values, and are expressed at current (1972/73) prices. (It would of course be possible, although it has not been done in this paper, to compute expected costs for any combination of two or more specific purification processes and tabulate them in the same way.)

similarly unimportant. The influences of BOD and SSI were of the expected signs. For example, Downing [14] argues that additional power per gallon of sewage is required in activated sludge processes if increase removal of biochemical oxygen demand and suspended solids is desired. The general process is succinctly summarized by Nemerow [36, p. 8]: 'An added BOD load, caused by an increase in organic waste, requires more bacterial activity, more oxygen, and more biological-unit capacity for its treatment. This calls for an increase in both capital outlay and daily operating expenses.'

The influence of biochemical oxygen demand removal is captured through the influences of three regressors: BOD, (BFS.BOD), and (BFD.BOD), the last two taking the value of BOD if single or double biological filtration (respectively) is used, and the value zero otherwise. The percentage of biochemical oxygen demand removed ranged from as little as 27·4% in one works, to a sample maximum of 100% in another. The variation of average operating cost with extent and method of purification is best illustrated graphically, as in Figure 2. Only single filtration, double filtration, and 'other' methods are distinguished in Figure 2. It would have been possible to draw similar lines or curves for other methods of purification individually, but each would show the same rate of change of average cost with proportion of BOD removed. In Figure 2, the lines are drawn under the assumption that all regressors other than BOD, BFS and BFD take their sample mean values.

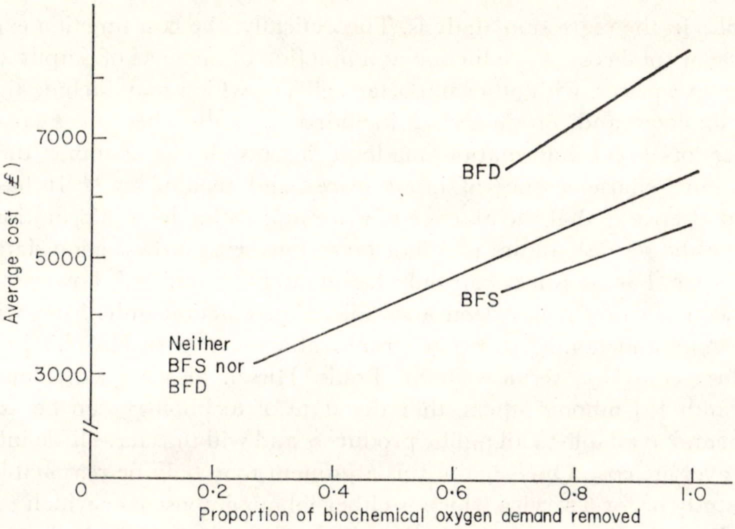

FIGURE 2. The Costs of Purification

The BFD and BFS lines show how average operating costs rise as the proportion of biochemical oxygen demand removed is increased using double and single filtration respectively. These lines are drawn only over the observed ranges of purification.

CONCLUSION

This study has examined the nature of variations in operating cost for 172 local authority and joint board sewage purification and disposal works in England and Wales using data for the financial year 1972/73. The general findings of the study must, however, be tempered by a few conceptual and practical lacunae.

Firstly, all elements of capital cost were omitted from the statistical cost analysis. The capital intensity of the treatment process, and the undoubted presence of substantial indivisibilities in many important capital components, suggest the existence of pervasive economies of scale. There were, however, simply no data available to examine this conjecture. The separation of operating from capital expenditure at all levels of service provision and planning would actually suggest a separate analysis of each, despite the inherent substitutability of capital and other resource inputs. If, as Hirsch [26] argues, the extent of substitution in practice is relatively small, then it would be possible to supplement the present analysis with a later study of capital economies.[13]

Secondly, we were unable to include adequate price and technology

[13] Note that Masters [35, pp. 163–4] roughly apportioned the total costs of sewage purification and disposal in the United States thus: 35% operation and maintenance, 25% capital, and 40% interest payments.

variables in the regression analysis. Theoretically, the cost function expresses average or total cost of production as a function of the level of output and the set of input prices, with other important effects, which may include the state of technology and productivity, included as and when necessary. The absence of direct information made it impossible to examine the cost-influencing characteristics of input prices and technology.[14] It has been argued elsewhere that the absence of price and technology information from local public service studies may not be serious with cross-section data for a single year. Factor prices can only legitimately be omitted, however, if the cross-section study is based on a sample of production units from within a fairly small and homogeneous geographical area, as with Hirsch's [25] look at refuse collection services in St. Louis. Hirsch also argued, along with Ahlbrandt [2] among others, that the state of technology can be assumed known and available to all public producers and will thus have little influence upon average cost. Once again, this argument may only be reasonable for a local study or for a service which is either labour-intensive or which employs capital equipment characterized principally by disembodied technical progress. With a national collection of data for the capital-intensive sewage treatment service (with largely embodied technical progress) it must thus be recognized that the omission of price and technology measures represents a misspecification error.

Thirdly, our estimated average cost function can only be taken as representative of the *short-run* cost-output relationship. This must be the case, not only because we have omitted capital costs, but also because we have chosen not to fit frontier or envelope curves. The function presented here is sufficient for commentary on the operation of the treatment and disposal service and for assessing 'average' scale economies, but an examination of the efficiency of individual production units really requires an estimate of the frontier curve. The simple convex hull of the observations in the plot of average cost against output provides a crude deterministic estimate (Seitz [44]), but it is probably preferable to use either a parametric and/or stochastic estimate (cf. Aigner, Lovell and Schmidt [3]; Førsund and Jansen [17]). Unfortunately the necessary computer routines are complex and as yet unavailable on a wide scale.

Finally, we were unable to take account of weekly, daily and hourly fluctuations in sewage flow. The greater the difference between peak and off-peak flows, and the shorter the period of a 'complete oscillation', the greater will be average operating costs. Periodic fluctuations in the character of the flow will also be important.

These lacunae notwithstanding, one should have a fair amount of confidence in the estimated equation as an approximation to the underlying

[14] Dummy variables reflecting the location of each works within a county borough, London borough, or county council were included as crude proxies for price variation. They were not found to be significant in the regressions. The age of the works is a similarly crude technology indicator.

average operating cost function for public sewage purification and disposal works. The overall goodness of fit is particularly pleasing in view of the fact that the data were not collected with such a cost study specifically in mind.

Our empirically based study of the costs of sewage purification and its subsequent disposal has revealed the existence of strong and pervasive economies of scale over an important range of output values. At all observed levels of production (as measured by the total volume of sewage treated daily to a given degree of purification), and particularly at the lower levels, scale economies may be realized. These can probably be attributed in part to specialization of manpower and equipment, economies of massed resources and of large-scale purchasing, and economies in administration. Sewage purification and disposal is most certainly a 'natural monopoly'. The strength of these scale factors, particularly when coupled with the significant economies one would expect to observe on the capital side, lends support to any attempt by small contiguous local authorities to extend co-operation in public service delivery. The realization of scale economies in practice represents a potentially important social improvement. This support must, however, be tempered by a consideration of the fact that there undoubtedly will be diseconomies of scale in collection and transmission costs (via the sewerage system). The extent of these diseconomies will clearly depend upon population density, local topography, and the location of the works within the area, and could be considerable. Unfortunately, such a consideration must await the publication or collection of a body of statistics of rather more focus than is currently available. The estimated function could also be used to identify individual treatment works whose costs deviate markedly from the level expected of them on the basis of the volume of sewage treated, the average degree of purification, and the processes used. These efficiency indicators are simply obtained as either the regression residuals—the difference between actual and expected average costs—or as the ratio of these two values (cf. Afriat [1]). Finally, the estimated function may allow the Regional Water Authorities to move a little closer to a marginal cost pricing formula which takes account of both the volume and strength of trade effluent discharged to the public sewerage system. At present the system of charges is based on the *average* costs of reception, conveyance, treatment and disposal.

We have been most unusually fortunate in having a national collection of detailed statistics for individual production units from which valid and reliable output and method-of-purification indicators are readily obtained. It remains to supplement the present analysis of operating costs with an examination of the capital costs of purification and disposal, and possibly also with a study of the operating and capital costs of the transmission and collection services.

UNIVERSITY OF KENT AT CANTERBURY

REFERENCES

[1] Afriat, S. N., 'Efficiency Estimation of Production Functions', *International Economic Review*, **13** (October 1972), pp. 568–98.

[2] Ahlbrandt, R. J., 'Efficiency in the Provision of Fire Services', *Public Finance*, **16** (Fall 1973), pp. 1–15.

[3] Aigner, D. J., Lovell, C. A. K. and Schmidt, P , 'Formulation and Estimation of Stochastic Frontier Production Function Models', *Journal of Econometrics*, **6** (July 1977), pp. 21–38.

[4] Alchian, A., 'Costs and Outputs', in *The Allocation of Economic Resources. Essays in Honour of B. F. Haley*, M. Abramovitz *et al.* (eds.) (Stanford University Press, Stanford, 1959).

[5] Bacon, R. W., 'Some Evidence on the Largest Squared Correlation Coefficient from Several Samples', *Econometrica*, **45** (November 1977), pp. 1997–2001.

[6] Beckenstein, A. R., 'Scale Economies in the Multiplant Firm: Theory and Empirical Evidence', *Bell Journal of Economics*, **6** (Fall 1975), pp. 644–57.

[7] Bock, M. E., Yancey, T. A. and Judge, G. G., 'The Statistical Consequences of Preliminary Test Estimators in Regression', *Journal of the American Statistical Association*, **68** (March 1973), pp. 109–16.

[8] Casson, M. C., 'Linear Regression with Error in the Deflating Variable', *Econometrica*, **41** (July 1973), pp. 751–9.

[9] Chartered Institute for Public Finance and Accountancy, *Sewage Purification and Disposal Statistics* 1972–73 (CIPFA, London, September 1974).

[10] Chartered Institute for Public Finance and Accountancy, *Water* (Financial Information Service, volume 28, CIPFA, London, 1977).

[11] Clark, R. M., 'Measures of Efficiency in Solid Waste Collection', *Journal of the Environmental Engineering Division*, ASCE (August 1973).

[12] Cowing, T. F. and Holtmann, A. G., *The Economics of Local Public Service Consolidation* (Lexington Books, Lexington, Massachusetts, 1976).

[13] Dean, J., *Statistical Cost Estimation* (Indiana University Press, Bloomington, 1976).

[14] Downing, P. B., *The Economics of Urban Sewerage Disposal* (Praeger, New York, 1969).

[15] Evans, A. W., 'Private Good, Externality, Public Good', *Scottish Journal of Political Economy* (February 1970).

[16] Feldstein, M. S., *Economic Analysis for Health Service Efficiency* (North-Holland, Amsterdam, 1967).

[17] Førsund, F. R. and Jansen, E. S., 'On Estimating Average and Best Practice Homothetic Production Functions', *International Economic Review*, **18** (June 1977), pp. 463–76.

[18] Frankel, R. J., 'Cost–quality Relationships in an Engineering–Economic Model for Municipal Waste Disposal', paper presented at the American Society of Civil Engineers Water Resources Engineering Conference, Alabama (March 1965).

[19] Franklin, J. S., 'Chemical Treatments', *Industrial Pollution Control: The Practical Implications*, K. A. Tearle (ed.), Chapter 10 (Business Books, London, 1973).

[20] Goldfeld, S. M. and Quandt, R. E., 'Some Tests for Homoscedasticity', *Journal of the American Statistical Association*, **60** (1965), pp. 539–47.

[21] Griliches, Z., 'Cost Allocation in Railroad Regulation', *Bell Journal of Economics and Management Science*, **3** (Spring 1972), pp. 26–41.

[22] Haldi, J. and Whitcomb, S., 'Economies of Scale in Industrial Plants', *Journal of Political Economy*, **75** (August 1967), pp. 373–85.

[23] HARRIS, B. A., 'Biological Treatment', *Industrial Pollution Control: The Practical Implications*, K. A. Tearle (ed.), Chapter 9 (Business Books, London, 1973).

[24] HIRSCH, W. Z., 'Expenditure Implications of Metropolitan Growth and Consolidation', *Review of Economics and Statistics*, **41** (August 1959), pp. 232–41.

[25] ——, 'Cost Functions of an Urban Public Service: Refuse Collection', *Review of Economics and Statistics*, **47** (February 1965), pp. 87–92.

[26] ——, 'The Supply of Urban Public Services', *Issues in Urban Economics*, H. S. Perloff & L. Wingo (eds.) (Johns Hopkins University Press, Baltimore, 1968).

[27] JACKSON, J., MCDOUGALL, G. and WRIGHT, C., 'Economies of Scale and Optimum City Size in the Provision of Local Public Services', Claremont Economic Paper No. 99 (Claremont Graduate School, 1974).

[28] JAMES, G. V., *Water Treatment*, 4th edn (Technical Press, Edinburgh, 1971).

[29] JOHNSTON, J., *Statistical Cost Analysis* (McGraw-Hill, New York, 1960).

[30] ——, *Econometric Methods* (McGraw-Hill, Tokyo, 1972).

[31] KEMPER, P. and QUIGLEY, J. M., *The Economics of Refuse Collecting* (Ballinger, Cambridge, Mass., 1976).

[32] KNAPP, M. R. J., 'Economies of Scale in Public Service Provision: the Case of British Crematoria', Personal Social Services Research Unit Discussion Paper 82 (University of Kent at Canterbury, January 1978).

[33] LATHAM, R. W. and Peel, D. A., 'The Cost Function', *Bulletin of Economic Research*, **28** (1976), pp. 77–84.

[34] LOCAL GOVERNMENT FINANCE: REPORT OF THE COMMITTEE OF INQUIRY (Chairman: Frank Layfield), Cmnd 6453 (HMSO, London, 1976).

[35] MASTERS, G. M., *Introduction to Environmental Science and Technology* (John Wiley, New York, 1974).

[36] NEMEROW, N. L., *Theories and Practices of Industrial Waste Treatment* A ddison-Wesley, Reading, Mass., 1963).

[37] NERLOVE, M., 'Returns to Scale in Electricity Supply', in C. Christ *et al.*, *Measurement in Economics* (Stanford University Press, Stanford, 1963).

[38] POPP, D. O. and SEBOLD, F. D., 'Quasi-returns-to-scale in the Provision of Police Services', *Public Finance*, **28** (January 1972), pp. 46–61.

[39] PRATTEN, C. F., *Economies of Scale in Manufacturing Industry*, University of Cambridge Department of Applied Economics Occasional Paper 28 (Cambridge University Press, Cambridge, 1971).

[40] RIEW, J., 'Economies of Scale in High School Operation', *Review of Economics and Statistics*, **48** (August 1966), pp. 280–7.

[41] ROWAN, P. P., JENKINS, K. L. and HOWELLS, D. H., 'Estimating Sewage Treatment Plant Operation and Maintenance Costs', *Journal of the Water Pollution Control Federation*, **33** (February 1961), pp. 111–21.

[42] ROYAL COMMISSION ON LOCAL GOVERNMENT IN ENGLAND, 1966–69, *Economies of Scale in Local Government Services*, Research Study No. 3, Cmnd 4040 (HMSO, London, 1969).

[43] SAMUELSON, P. A., 'The Pure Theory of Public Expenditure', *Review of Economics and Statistics*, **36** (1954), 387–9.

[44] SEITZ, W. D., 'Productive Efficiency in the Steam-electric Generating Industry', *Journal of Political Economy*, **79** (1971), pp. 878–86.

[45] TODA, Y., 'Estimation of Cost Function When the Cost is Not Minimum: the Case of Soviet Manufacturing Industries, 1958–1971', *Review of Economics and Statistics*, **57** (August 1976), pp. 259–68.

THE JOURNAL OF INDUSTRIAL ECONOMICS
Vol. XXVII December 1978 No. 2

MONOPOLY-POWER AS A MEANS FOR POLLUTION-CONTROL?*

A. ENDRES

SINCE Buchanan's famous essay on externalities and market structure [1], it is a widespread belief that the allocative distortions caused by monopoly-power and external diseconomies can—in principle—compensate each other.[1] The reasoning behind this is as follows:

Compared with the Pareto-optimal situation a polluting monopolist will produce too little as a monopolist and too much as a polluter. These two failures may—in principle—cancel each other and lead to a Pareto-optimal situation.

This note is to point out that a polluting monopolist assumed to produce optimal output will realize the optimal level of pollution only if output-reduction is the sole means to reduce the externality. When other efficient measures are possible, monopoly-power can—even theoretically—never correct the allocative failure of an external diseconomy because the monopolist will not use the efficient input mix.

To obtain the Pareto-condition let us consider a perfectly competitive polluting firm A and a perfectly competitive damaged firm B. x and y are the respective outputs, Q_A and Q_B the respective profits of the two firms. Pareto-optimum is achieved when the joint profit Q^j is maximal. Given output reduction as the sole means of pollution control this leads to

$$(1) \qquad Q^j = Q_A(x) + Q_B(y, x) = p.x - C(x) + Q_B(y, x) = \max!$$

A's Pareto-optimal output and pollution level is determined by[2]

$$(2) \qquad \frac{\partial Q^j}{\partial x} = p - C' + \frac{\partial Q_B}{\partial x} = 0$$

$\partial Q_B/\partial x$ (<0) is the marginal damage induced by A's activity x.

Equation (2) means that the price of x must equal the marginal social costs of x. Thus, if the firms of a perfectly competitive polluting industry are forced (e.g. by a Pigovian tax) to bear the marginal damage they cause, the Pareto-optimal output and pollution level will be produced.

* I would like to thank an anonymous referee for his comments on an earlier draft of this paper.

1 See e.g. Mishan, [3] and Walsh and Tisdell [4]. Similar reasoning was implied already by Wellisz [5].

2 Sufficient conditions are supposed to be fulfilled.

To isolate the effect of market structure on pollution, assume that this competitive polluting industry is taken over by a monopolist. Given *no Pigovian taxes* the decision problem of the monopolist is

$$Q_A = p(x) \,.\, x - C(x) = \max! \tag{3}$$

$$\rightarrow \frac{\partial Q_A}{\partial x} = \frac{\partial p}{\partial x} \,.\, x + p - C' = 0 \tag{4}$$

If we assume the divergency between price and marginal revenue to be equal to the marginal damage, condition (2) is identical to condition(4). In this special case the unregulated monopolist produces the same level of output and pollution as the perfectly competitive industry, regulated by Pigovian taxes.

This result is modified if an additional efficient method for pollution control exists (e.g. installation of filters).

The amount of pollution neutralized by the additional method is called n and the neutralization-costs $N(n)$.[3] The amount of the externality remaining to affect B is $(x-n)$. The new joint profit function for the perfectly competitive firms A and B is $Q^j = p \,.\, x - C(x) - N(n) + Q_B(y, x-n)$.

Maximization of this function yields the result that A's Pareto-optimal *output-level* is determined by equation (2) again. The Pareto-optimal *pollution-level*, however, is determined by equation (2) and

$$\partial Q^j / \partial n = -\frac{\partial N}{\partial n} + \frac{\partial Q_B}{\partial (x-n)} \cdot \underbrace{\frac{\partial (x-n)}{\partial n}}_{=-1} = 0 \tag{5}$$

$$\leftrightarrow \frac{\partial N}{\partial n} = -\frac{\partial Q_B}{\partial (x-n)} \tag{6}$$

This means that neutralization by the additional method has to be carried out until the marginal abatement costs of the method equal B's marginal damage reduction produced by that method.

An unregulated polluting monopolist may—in principle—fulfil condition (2), but will never fulfil condition (6), for there is no incentive for him to employ any resources at all in the additional abatement method. Even if the monopolist produces the optimal output he does not use the additional abatement method and thus misses the optimal input combination.

Thus, monopoly-power as a means for pollution-control is as inefficient as—in a perfectly competitive economy—taxes, on output rather than pollution[4] are.

[3] $N = N(n)$ instead of $N = N(n, x)$ is assumed for simplicity.
[4] See e.g. Meade [2].

REFERENCES

[1] Buchanan, J. M., 'External Diseconomies, Corrective Taxes and Market Structure', *American Economic Review*, **LIX** (1969), pp. 174–7.
[2] Meade, J. E., *The Theory of Economic Externalities*, p. 68 (Genève, 1973).
[3] Mishan, E. J., *The Costs of Economic Growth*, p. 84 (London, 1973).
[4] Walsh, C. and Tisdell, C., 'Non-marginal Externalities: As Relevant and As Not', *Economic Record*, **49** (September 1973), p. 455.
[5] Wellisz, S., 'External Diseconomies and the Government-assisted Invisible Hand', *Economica*, **XXXI** (1964), p. 349, fn. 3.

P. W. S. ANDREWS' MEMORIAL PRIZE

The P. W. S. Andrews' memorial prize is awarded annually for an essay by a young scholar (under the age of 30 or within 8 years of taking his first degree) in the general field of Industrial Economics and the Theory of the Firm, broadly interpreted. The prize is £100, and the winning essay will normally be published in *The Journal of Industrial Economics*. An essay submitted should be a work of original research by the candidate only, not previously published and not previously awarded any other prize. It should not exceed 10,000 words in length.

The next closing date for entries is December 31st, 1979. Intending candidates for the prize should obtain details of the conditions of entry from the Academic Registrar, The University of Lancaster, Bailrigg, Lancaster, England.

THE JOURNAL OF INDUSTRIAL ECONOMICS

Published first in October 1952, this Journal was founded to develop the analysis of the problems facing modern industry. It is concerned with the individual business and its relation to the economy—e.g. with outputs and prices and their behaviour in the market, and with the business decisions which affect these. It therefore aims to contribute both to economic theory and to practical public and private policies in the industrial field. The journal is naturally meant to interest business men as well as economists.

The Editors welcome contributions covering the fundamental categories in economics (such as prices, costs, investment, finance, location, wages and productivity) as well as the broader 'background' circumstances (such as the changing structure of industry, management policy and public monopoly policy). Preference is given to MSS bearing on these subjects from the standpoint of individual firms or industries. Theoretical discussion is welcome. Abstract theory is not barred, but authors in this case should provide an introduction and conclusion, so that non-specialist readers may see what the article is about. Alongside articles of more normal length, the Editors are willing to publish shorter notes, especially when these give interim results of important research studies. Books are not reviewed, although books received will be listed, sometimes with a short note; but substantial review articles will be considered. No payment is made to authors, but 40 free offprints are provided. Contributors are asked to send an Abstract, not exceeding 100 words, with their article.

Editorial Offices:

Manuscripts from North America should be sent to Professor H. Michael Mann, Department of Economics, Boston College, Chestnut Hill, Massachusetts, 02167, U.S.A.; manuscripts from the European Continent should be sent to Professor Louis Phlips, Center for Operations Research & Econometrics, Université Catholique de Louvain, 34 Voie du Roman Pays, 1348 Louvain-la-Neuve, Belgium; and from the U.K. and other countries to the General Editor, c/o Department of Economics, University of Lancaster, Bailrigg, Lancaster, England.

Subscriptions, advertising, reprint enquiries, etc.

All correspondence other than that dealing with contributions should be addressed to the Publisher, Messrs. Basil Blackwell & Mott Ltd., 108 Cowley Road, Oxford OX4 1LR, England.

The journal is published quarterly, and the annual subscription for Institutions is £11 (U.K.), £13.20 (Overseas), $30 (U.S.A. and Canada) post free; the prices of single issues are £3.50, £4.20 and $9.50 respectively, post free. For individual subscribers the rates are £9.00 (U.K.), £10.80 (Overseas), $24.00 (U.S.A. and Canada) post free. Remittances should be sent to Basil Blackwell & Mott Ltd.

A photographic reprint is now available of Vols. 1–13, 1952–65, bound in cloth or paper; single volumes in paper only.

CONTRIBUTORS TO THIS NUMBER

SIR CHARLES CARTER: Vice-Chancellor, University of Lancaster.

GARY C. FETHKE: Associate Professor of Business Administration University of Iowa.

KENT A. CURRIE: Assistant Professor of Economics, Case Western Reserve University, Cleveland, Ohio.

J. F. PICKERING: Professor of Industrial Economics, University of Manchester Institute of Science and Technology.

FRANKLIN R. EDWARDS: Professor, Graduate School of Business, Columbia University, New York.

BARBARA J. STEVENS: President, ECODATA INC.

DAVID J. STOREY: Principal Scientific Officer, Centre for Environmental Studies, London.

MARTIN R. J. KNAPP: Research Fellow, Personal Social Services Research Unit, University of Kent at Canterbury.

ALFRED ENDRES: Wissenschaftlicher Assistant, University of Konstanz.

The Contents of Volume XXVII, No. 1, September 1978, were:

Research and Product Innovation in Australian Manufacturing Industries, by Ian W. McLean and David K. Round, Senior Lecturers in Economics, University of Adelaide.

Internal Organization and Profit: An Empirical Analysis of Large U.K. Companies by Peter S. Steer, Lecturer in Business Studies, Liverpool Polytechnic, and John R. Cable, Senior Lecturer in Economics, University of Warwick, and Research Fellow, IIM. Berlin.

On the Definition of 'Industry' and 'Market' by John Nightingale, Lecturer in Economics, University of New England, Armidale.

The Pattern of Industrial Concentration in Latin America by Patricio Meller, Research Economist, CIEPLAN (Santiago), and National Bureau of Economic Research.

Industry Inefficiency under Regulatory Surveillance by Michael W. Pustay, Assistant Professor of Economics, Purdue University.

Profit Maximization in Chain Retail Stores by Ralph W. Pfouts, Professor of Economics, University of North Carolina at Chapel Hill.

Territorial Exclusivity in the Soft Drink Industry by Barbara G. Katz, Assistant Professor of Economics, New York University Graduate School of Business Administration.

Printed in Great Britain by Adlard & Son Ltd., Bartholomew Press, Dorking

THE JOURNAL OF INDUSTRIAL ECONOMICS

Volume XXVII MARCH 1979 **No. 3**

DENNIS W. CARLTON
Vertical Integration in Competitive Markets Under Uncertainty.

P. E. HART
On Bias and Concentration.

MANFRED NEUMANN, INGO BÖBEL and ALFRED HAID
Profitability, Risk and Market Structure in West German Industries.

DAVID P. BARON and RAYMOND R. DE BONDT
Fuel Adjustment Mechanisms and Economic Efficiency.

ROBERT MICHAELS
Hedonic Prices and the Structure of the Digital Computer Industry.

KEITH MACMILLAN and DAVID FARMER
Redefining the Boundaries of the Firm.

KEVIN HAWKINS
The Price Commission and the Brewing Industry: A Critical Note.

P. J. CURWEN
The Price Commission Report on Books—A Short Critique.

ISSN 0022–1821

BASIL BLACKWELL OXFORD ENGLAND

Price: Single Issues: £3.50 (U.K.), £4.20 (Overseas), $9.50 (U.S.A. and Canada)
Annual Subscription for Institutions: £11.00 (U.K.), £13.20 (Overseas), $30.00 (U.S.A. and Canada)
Annual Subscription for Individuals: £9.00 (U.K.), £10.80 (Overseas), $24.00 (U.S.A. and Canada)

THE JOURNAL OF INDUSTRIAL ECONOMICS
Volume XXVII March 1979 No. 3

VERTICAL INTEGRATION IN COMPETITIVE MARKETS UNDER UNCERTAINTY*

DENNIS W. CARLTON

I. INTRODUCTION

VERTICAL integration has never been a well-understood phenomenon. Although it is possible to postulate conditions such as technological co-ordination where the incentives for vertical integration are obvious, it is still difficult to rationalize the amount of vertical integration that occurs in our economy. The dissatisfaction with the treatment of vertical integration is best expressed by Williamson [11].

> The study of vertical integration has presented difficulties at both the theoretical and policy levels of analysis. That vertical integration has never enjoyed a secure place in value theory is attributable to the fact that, under conventional assumptions, it is an anomaly.

It has always been somewhat of a mystery why businessmen, as well as researchers, so often conclude that the significant force explaining the vertical integration movement has been the desire to obtain a more certain supply of inputs—even though these inputs appear to be sold on what most would call a competitive market. Why are markets not doing their jobs of allocating resources and why should uncertainty create incentives for vertical integration?

Elsewhere (Carlton [2], [3], [4]), I have argued that most markets do not precisely fit the classical requirements that prices can fluctuate instantly to equate supply and demand or that buyers and sellers can always buy and sell all they want of the good. Although it is possible to ignore these complications and still understand certain types of economic behavior, it is the thesis of this paper that only when the question of vertical integration is examined in the context of these more general and realistic competitive conditions (which include the classical conditions as a special case) that the incentives for and consequences of vertical integration can be fully understood. In addition, the analysis provides a justification for the frequently voiced claim of businessmen that they vertically integrated to obtain a more certain source of input supplies.

* This paper was awarded the P. W. S. Andrews Memorial Prize for 1977. It is based on my Ph.D. thesis, 'Market Behaviour Under Uncertainty', MIT, 1975. I wish to thank Professors Franklin M. Fisher, Peter A. Diamond, Robert E. Hall, Paul L. Joskow, Sam Peltzman and Oliver Williamson for helpful comments.

After a discussion of the previous thinking regarding vertical integration, the theory of a single competitive market under uncertainty is presented. Then, the effects of the transmission of uncertainty between different markets are examined. Focusing on this transmission, the analysis shows that vertical integration can be regarded as a means of transferring risk from one sector of the economy to another. Firms have an incentive to integrate to insure a supply of input to satisfy their 'high probability' demand. However, in a market characterized by uncertainty, externalities abound, and it is shown that private incentives for vertical integration can exist even when vertical integration is socially undesirable. The free market cannot be relied upon to achieve the socially desirable allocation of risk and production.

On the other hand, vertical integration does have some desirable attributes. We show that a vertically integrated firm is more likely to introduce socially beneficial technology than is a non-integrated firm. We are thereby led to a Schumpeterian view of the world where static inefficiency in market structure must be tolerated to obtain a type of dynamic efficiency in the introduction of technology.

II. PREVIOUS RESEARCH

The literature in industrial organization is replete with statements to the effect that it is the uncertainty of factor supplies that creates incentives for vertical integration. For example, Chandler [5, p. 37], in his discussion of the reasons for the formation of the largest companies in the United States argues 'the initial motives for expansion or combination and vertical integration had not been specifically to lower unit costs or to assure a large output per worker by efficient administration of the enlarged resources of the enterprise. The strategy of expansion had come . . . from the desire . . . to have a more certain supply of stocks, raw materials and other supplies . . .' In studying Dupont's reasons for integrating General Motors, Chandler [5, p. 84] finds that 'the need for assured supplies demanded increasing vertical integration'. Despite the frequency with which the argument about the need for assured supplies appears in historical studies of vertical integration, usually it is never explained why the factor supply is uncertain, or why an uncertain factor supply should create incentives for vertical integration.

At a more theoretical level, several authors concerned with industrial organization have suggested that uncertainty could provide an incentive for vertical integration. As early as 1937, Coase [6] argued that with constant returns to scale in production the very existence of a firm depends on some sort of market imperfections. The firm organizes when its internal allocative ability is superior to that of a market. Coase claimed that uncertainty about finding sellers of factors of production could provide one justification for the existence of a firm. Applying Coase's reasoning to the question of vertical integration many years later, Malmgrem [9] indicated that the presence of uncertainty could create incentives for vertical integration. 'Activities which tended to fluctuate, causing fluctuations in prices and outputs in the market, could be integrated and balanced against one another.' Malmgrem argued that when prices do not reflect scarcity, vertical integration can occur. More recently, Williamson [11], [12] discussed how uncertainty can make it difficult to deal in a market, and could provide incentives for vertical integration.

Until very recently, there had been no attempt analytically to investigate the claims of the above authors as regards the effect of uncertainty on the incentives for vertical integration. Recently, two economists have sought to bridge this gap in the literature. Arrow [1] investigated the case where vertically integrated firms are able to obtain information about supply conditions earlier than the non-integrated firm. In a paper closely related in topic to this one, Green [7] showed that if rationing is possible in the factor market, then all firms would have an incentive to integrate fully. Green then went on to examine the case where a vertically integrated firm is assumed to have a less efficient technology for producing the input. Prices are exogenous in Green's model so that prices need bear no relation to scarcity or rationing probability. In Green's model, final product firms face no uncertainty in their demand for their product and are able to sell all of their product at the exogenous market price.

In the model of this paper, both output and input firms will face uncertainty in demand. The transmission of uncertainty from the product market to the input market will be an important feature of the model. Prices in each market will be endogenously determined and will be related to rationing frequency. The same input technology will be available to all firms, but firms will differ in their ability to sell the input.

III. MARKET BEHAVIOR WITH DEMAND UNCERTAINTY AND PRICE INFLEXIBILITY

Before developing a model of how markets interact under uncertainty, it is necessary briefly to present a theory of how a single market under uncertainty operates and how the equilibrium price is endogenously determined.[1]

For most markets, prices do not adjust at each instant of the day to keep supply and demand in balance, firms never feel they can sell all they want at the going price, and production cannot occur instantly. More realistic assumptions would be that in order to be an effective 'signal' prices stay fixed for some period of time. An individual firm never knows exactly what demand for its product will be each day, even if total demand for the industry is unchanging. The firm usually will know the probability distribution of demand it faces. Since production is not instantaneous, firms must make production decisions before observing demand, and hence take a risk of either overproducing or underproducing (or, more generally, of having

[1] For a fuller development of the theory, see Carlton [2], [3], [4].

unused or insufficient production capacity). Therefore, in this model, firms must make decisions on price and production before their demand can be observed.

Buyers know the price a firm charges, but do not know whether the firm has any goods left to deliver at any particular time. When he goes to the firm, a buyer knows the probability of being able to purchase the goods at the stated price of that firm (i.e. firms acquire reputations for reliability). A good produced by a particular firm now has two relevant characteristics, its price and the probability that it is available.[2] Consumer preferences can be represented by iso-utility curves in $(1-\lambda, p)$ space, where $1-\lambda$ stands for the probability of obtaining the good, and p is the price. Iso-utility curves slope upward.

The amount of the good with which a firm begins the market period (or more generally the amount of productive capacity available) will affect the probability that a buyer will be able to purchase the good from that firm. Notice that the stochastic structure of demand imposes real costs on the firm. Given the stochastic structure of demand, the expected profits of a firm will depend on the price it charges and on how many customers it is able to satisfy. Equivalently, we can say that expected profit depends on price, p, and the probability of satisfaction, $1-\lambda$. It is possible to draw iso-profit curves in $(1-\lambda, p)$ space. Along the relevant portions, these curves slope upward reflecting the fact that as a firm increases the probability of satisfying a customer by stocking more or having additional capacity, the price must rise to cover the increased risk of having unsold goods, or available, but unused, capacity.

For purposes of this paper, it suffices to consider the case where all firms and all customers are identical. In such markets, firms compete with each other on the utility level [i.e. the $(1-\lambda, p)$ mix] that they offer to consumers. Consumers will choose to frequent only those firms that offer the highest utility levels. Firms have an incentive to bid up the utility level until expected profits are driven to zero. Just as in other competitive markets, in this market equilibrium, no firm offering less than the best deal (i.e. best utility level) in the market will receive any customers.[3] Equilibrium for such markets is depicted in Figure 1 as a tangency between the zero profit curve $(\pi=0)$ and an iso-utility curve $[u(1-\lambda, p)=\bar{u}]$.

[2] For simplicity, we assume no searching on the part of buyers and no inventory holdings on the part of firms. Provided that search and inventory holding are costly, the basic ideas of how markets operate under uncertainty would not be altered by their inclusion. We do not allow firms to trade the good with each other or allow recontracting markets to develop. This last requirement corresponds to the observation that in the real world, we often do not observe such phenomena because of transaction costs.

[3] For any given number of firms, equilibrium involves zero expected profits. The reason is that if the firms were earning positive profits, one firm would have an incentive to offer a slightly better $(1-\lambda, p)$ mix and obtain the other firms' customers. Notice that there is no monopoly power caused by consumer ignorance since customers know firms' reputations. See Carlton [2] for fuller discussions.

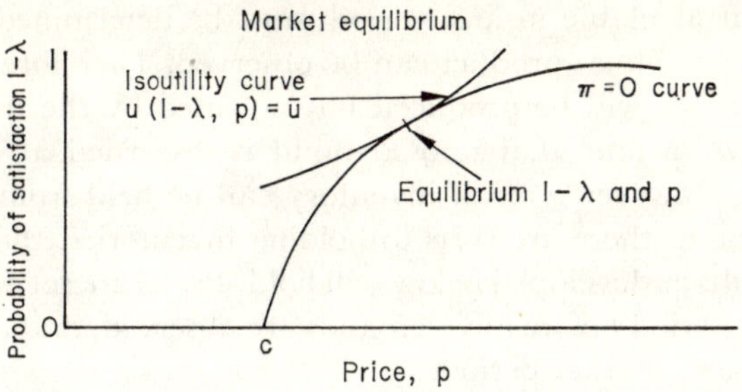

FIGURE 1

We assume for simplicity a constant cost, c, for producing one unit of the good. Notice that if instantaneous production were possible, there would be no risk that a firm need incur. In such a case, the zero profit curve becomes vertical at $p=c$, utility level competition becomes equivalent to price competition, and the equilibrium is identical to the traditional supply and demand equilibrium.

The noteworthy features of competitive equilibrium under uncertainty are that, in general (1) the probability that a customer will be unable to purchase the good definitely exceeds zero, (2) the price will always exceed the constant marginal cost, c, of production, and (3) the total amount supplied and total amount demanded will not in general be equal. In equilibrium, price must exceed the marginal cost of production since the revenue from sold goods must compensate not only for the cost of production of these goods, but also for the cost of production of the unsold goods (or equivalently, compensate for unused but available productive capacity).

With this description of how single markets operate under uncertainty, we can now turn to the study of vertical integration as the transmission of uncertainty between different markets.

IV. THE MODEL

This section presents a simple model of the transmission of uncertainty between a product market and one of its factor markets. The model is intended to elucidate the incentives and consequences of (backward) vertical integration.

There are two types of firms, stage 1 and stage 2 type firms. Stage 1 firms require factor inputs from stage 2 firms to produce the final good. Demand facing an individual stage 1 firm is random during any market period.[4] Therefore, the derived demand of stage 1 firms for factor inputs is random. In the stage 2 factor market, the demand facing any firm is also random. The final good cannot be produced without the factor input, and the amount of

[4] This is the key assumption of the model.

the factor input available in any period must be determined before any of the demands for the final product can be observed. Therefore, there is a risk that a unit of input will be produced but not used by the time the market period ends. We assume that unused input is discarded at the end of the market period. However, even if inventory can be held from one period to the next, as long as there are costs to holding inventories, the same types of qualitative results as developed below will hold. Prices are set at the beginning of each market period before any demands are observed, and are not allowed to vary within any market period.

We allow stage 1 firms the option of producing some of the factor input for itself. We refer to the production and holding of the input by stage 1 firms as vertical integration.[5] If a stage 1 firm produces the factor input for itself, it bears the risk of having unused input at the end of the market period. A stage 1 firm does not sell its inputs in the stage 2 factor market. This last assumption is designed to capture the notion that a vertically integrated firm is trying to produce for its own needs better to assure itself of the supply of the input.[6] Stage 1 firms cannot ship the factor input between themselves, nor can stage 2 firms for the same reasons as discussed in section III. As before, we assume recontracting markets do not develop.

We assume that the production technologies for producing the final product and factor input both involve constant returns to scale. The same technology for producing the factor input is available to both stage 1 and stage 2 firms. It costs c to produce one unit of the factor input. The factor input

[5] In a constant returns to scale world, the firm is indifferent between producing a given quantity of input for itself in advance and purchasing (in advance) that given quantity of input on a long-term contract at the constant production cost. With constant returns to scale and production lags, the only defining characteristic of a vertically integrated firm is that it bear the risk that input will not be sold. The question of whether there are incentives for vertical integration (*either* by long-term contract or in-house production) is the one this paper addresses. The question of which form (long-term contract or in-house production) vertical integration takes is a different question. Transaction costs (Williamson [11], [12]) can explain why in-house production may be the preferred mode of vertical integration.

[6] Let me give one reason to illustrate why this assumption is plausible. There may be transaction costs or other increases in bureaucratic costs as a company expands from being a seller of output to becoming a seller of both outputs and inputs. Complex organizations can increase costs.

This non-sharing of an input supply by output producers is quite common. As an example consider a firm's secretarial pool that is occasionally idle. It is not frequently the case that an employer will try to obtain outside typing in order to keep his secretaries fully busy. Next, consider a firm that keeps stocks of some input for production. This firm will usually not be always willing to sell its input. The firm will usually enter the input market as a seller only if its stock of input starts piling up and the firm becomes convinced that it miscalculated its needs. Only when the firm becomes sure that it has made a sizable miscalculation will it pay for the firm to incur lumpy transaction costs and enter the input market as a seller.

A model with equivalent implications can be constructed by assuming that vertically integrated firms can purchase input from each other, but the input is also demanded by other sectors of the economy, and that vertically integrated firms do not sell to these other sectors.

The idea that it would be fruitful to investigate the case where vertically integrated firms do not sell their input was suggested in Arrow [1]. The assumption of non-selling is discussed further in our conclusions. It does *not* affect the conclusion that vertical integration can be privately desirable but socially undesirable. The assumption is similar in spirit to Green's assumption that a vertically integrated firm has a less efficient production technology than a non-integrated one.

must be produced before its demand can be observed. The final product is produced (instantaneously) by a Leontief technology that requires K units of capital and one unit of the factor input sold in the stage 2 market to produce one unit of the final good. The capital input is always available at a constant price r per unit. Prices of the final product and factor input are set before any demands are observed. Prices will be endogenously determined in accordance with the analysis of section III.

In order to illustrate most simply the effects of uncertainty we adopt the following model to represent stochastic demand to the firm. (The model is intended to be illustrative. Other more complicated and realistic stochastic processes of demand to the individual firm would lead to the same conclusions, but different formulae.) There are L identical customers, N_1 stage 1 firms, and N_2 stage 2 firms with N_2 less than N_1.[7] In each market period, each of the L customers randomly frequents one stage 1 firm where he demands the final product according to his demand curve.[8] Every time a stage 1 firm observes a customer demand for its product, it attempts to obtain the factor input necessary to produce the customer's demand for the final product. The stage 1 firm first tries to use up its own holdings, if any, of the factor input, and then, when its factor holdings are depleted, it enters the stage 2 factor market. Once in the factor market, the stage 1 firm randomly frequents a stage 2 firm to try to obtain the necessary inputs to be able to satisfy its customer. If the stage 1 firm is unable to obtain the input from the stage 2 firm, then the stage 1 firm is unable to satisfy the demand of the customer. This customer returns home dissatisfied. As discussed in section III, customers have preferences, which firms recognize, between the price of the good and the probability of obtaining that good. For any given level of factor holding by the stage 1 firms, we can imagine the stage 1 and stage 2 firms competing in their respective markets on the price and probability of satisfaction until each market reaches the competitive equilibrium described in section III.

The key feature of this market structure is that the amount of the factor input that stage 1 firms decide to hold affects the stochastic nature of the demand that stage 2 firms see. Vertical integration by stage 1 firms affects the risky environment in which stage 2 firms operate. An important question to ask is whether, under competition, firms are forced to take into full

[7] The assumption that $N_2 < N_1$ will ensure that stage 2 firms are more efficient at absorbing risk than stage 1 firms. Despite this comparative disadvantage, we will show that private incentives can encourage stage 1 firms to vertically integrate. We will then show that this vertical integration is socially undesirable. If we assume that $N_2 > N_1$, then stage 1 firms would be the more efficient risk absorbers. The private incentives identified in the subsequent analysis would lead to vertical intergration that would benefit society. One point of the model is to show that private incentives for vertical integration can exist even when vertical integration is socially undesirable.

[8] More precisely, each customer randomly frequents one stage 1 firm from among those firms which he feels are offering the best deals in the market.

account the effect of their operating policies on the transmission of uncertainty to other markets.[9]

V. PRIVATE INCENTIVES FOR VERTICAL INTEGRATION

The way the market of this model operates, there are basically two offsetting considerations involved in the decision of a stage 1 firm to produce a unit of input for itself. First, since it costs only c per unit to produce the input, the stage 1 firm will save $(p_{\text{int}}-c)$ by producing the input itself rather than buying it on the factor market at price p_{int}. (Recall that it is a characteristic of markets that operate under uncertainty that the equilibrium price exceed the cost of production.) In other words, if the stage 1 firm produces the input itself, then the firm assures itself of having the necessary input to make a more profitable sale, if demand should materialize. Offsetting this saving is the potential risk that the input will be produced at cost c, but will not be used because of insufficient demand. By producing the input for itself, the stage 1 firm bears the risk of the unsold input, while when the stage 1 firm relies on the factor market for the input, it is the stage 2 firms who bear this risk.

Let us now consider whether there is any incentive for stage 1 firms to produce the input at all. Suppose that stage 1 firms produce none of the factor input and rely entirely on the stage 2 markets for the input. Imagine that the stage 1 and stage 2 markets have reached equilibrium in the manner described earlier. By the conditions of market equilibrium, expected profits are zero in each market.

There will definitely be an incentive to integrate vertically if the expected profit is positive when a stage 1 firm holds enough input to satisfy one customer when evaluated at the equilibrium associated with no vertical integration. It is straightforward[10] to calculate the profit functions, and to

[9] As mentioned previously, the conclusions developed below depend only on demand being random at the individual firm level. The model with fixed L, N_1, and N_2 is meant to be illustrative. It is one way to generate a simple stochastic demand process for the firm. It is not intended to suggest that having a fixed (non-random) total number of customers is in any way related to the question of vertical integration.

Another possible stochastic process is the Poisson. Demand to stage 1 firms is Poisson with parameter λ_1, and demand to stage 2 firms is Poisson with parameter λ_2, where λ_2 will depend on the amount of vertical integration. With no vertical integration $\lambda_1 < \lambda_2$ has the same content as $N_1 > N_2$ in the model in the text. Because a Poisson and binomial with small probabilities generate indistinguishable random demands to a firm, the model in the text can be reinterpreted as a Poisson one. Note that since the issues of total customer arrival being non-stochastic and the number of firms being discrete are simply not relevant for a Poisson process, they are surely not relevant for the model in the text. The binomial is used only to generate easy-to-use random firm demands. If the reader feels uncomfortable with the assumption in the text of discrete non-stochastic L, N_1, N_2, he can reinterpret all the results in terms of a Poisson process.

Section X discusses more fully the essential features of market operation that are required for the conclusions developed below to apply.

[10] See Appendix. Note that the condition expressing the incentive for vertical integration is derived *without* making any assumptions about the specific probabilistic process generating demand. We now will use the binomial demand process presented earlier to obtain insights into the likelihood of the above inequality being true. The reader who postulates a different stochastic demand process would simply calculate $[1-Pr(0)]$ and use it in the subsequent argument.

derive the condition that there will definitely be an incentive to integrate vertically if

$$[1-Pr(0)]\, p_{\text{int}} > c,$$

where $[1-Pr(0)]$ = probability that at least one customer frequents the stage 1 firm,

p_{int} = price of the intermediate product when purchased in the stage 2 market, and

c = cost of producing the input.

This inequality is intuitively plausible. If a stage 1 firm decides to stock one unit of input, its cost increases, with certainty, by c. Its expected savings from not having to go into the factor market for that one unit of input is $[1-Pr(0)]\, p_{\text{int}}$. When savings exceed costs, the stage 1 firm will hold the factor input.

It is possible to simplify this inequality. Since the random process is binomial with probability $1/N_1$, and size L, we have that

$$[1-Pr(0)] = 1-(1-1/N)^L \doteqdot 1-\exp(-L/N_1).$$

Therefore, we can write that there will definitely be an incentive for vertical integration if

$$\text{(1)} \qquad \left[1-\exp\left(-\frac{L}{N_1}\right)\right] p_{\text{int}} > c.$$

It is clear from the inequality (1), that for fixed L,[11] the inequality is more likely to hold the smaller is the number, N_1, of stage 1 firms. Equivalently, for a fixed number of customers, L, the inequality is more likely to hold as the customer per store ratio L/N_1 becomes larger.

The implications of (1) are disturbing. For *any* value of L/N_1, we know that incentives for vertical integration can exist since it is always possible to choose a set of consumer preferences which yield an equilibrium p_{int} such that the inequality holds. Moreover, for even small values (e.g. 20) for the customer per firm ratio, L/N_1, $1-\exp(-L/N_1) \approx 1$, so that the inequality will hold provided $p_{\text{int}} > c$. But, by the earlier discussion, we know that the equilibrium price in an uncertain market must always exceed its cost, since it is necessary that price not only cover per unit production costs, but also the production cost of unsold goods. Hence, we expect there to be strong incentives for vertical integration.

The incentives for vertical integration come about because the stage 1 firms base their decisions to integrate on the *marginal*, not *average*, probability of using an additional input. The way the markets operate, the price of the

[11] The reader should convince himself that for fixed L and no vertical integration, P_{int} is independent of N_1. It is not possible to determine whether (1) is more likely to hold as the number of customers increases to infinity. As $L \to \infty$, $1-\exp(-L/N_1) \to 1$ so incentives to vertically integrate increase. However, as $L \to \infty$, $p_{\text{int}} \to c$ (Carlton [4]) so disincentives also increase. Which effect will predominate depends on the specific slope of the iso-utility curves that determine market equilibrium.

factor in the stage 2 market reflects not only the cost c of producing the input, but also the average probability of not being able to sell that input. When a stage 1 firm is deciding whether to hold one unit of the input itself, it is not concerned with the average probability of being unable to use any unit of input. Rather, since the stage 1 firm will use its input holdings first, the stage 1 firm is concerned with the probability of being able to use that first unit of input. For even low to moderate values of the customer per firm ratio in stage 1 markets, L/N_1 (e.g. 15–20), this probability is practically 1 (i.e. each stage 1 firm is virtually assured of being able to use up its one unit of input), so that (1) will almost certainly hold since the price of the stage 2 factor, p_{int}, exceeds c. It is precisely because stage 1 firms can use their own input to satisfy their 'high probability' demand and use the stage 2 market to satisfy their 'low probability' demand that incentives for vertical integration occur.[12] The conclusion of this analysis is that it is quite likely that there will exist strong private incentives for vertical integration to occur.

VI. SOCIAL CONSEQUENCES OF VERTICAL INTEGRATION

Having established strong private incentives for at least some vertical integration to occur, we now investigate the welfare consequences of vertical integration. It is useful to keep in mind that there are two distinct welfare issues involved. First, markets under uncertainty are not Pareto-efficient in the absence of insurance markets, and usually lump sum subsidies are required to achieve optimality (Carlton [2], [4]). The second issue is whether a vertically integrated market structure is superior to a non-vertically integrated one, whether or not lump sum subsidies are paid. It is this second issue that we now address.

If all firms within any stage behave identically, then there is always a higher probability that a unit of the factor input will be used if it is held in a stage 2 rather than a stage 1 firm. Stated in another way, since the number of stage 1 firms exceeds the number of stage 2 firms, a unit of the factor will be more frequently used if it is given to a stage 2, and not a stage 1, firm. From this simple observation, we can obtain the following.

Theorem 1

Any market structure involving vertical integration achieves a lower level of expected utility than can a market structure involving no vertical integration.

The reasons why Theorem 1 is true can be explained as follows. The number of final product stage 1 firms exceeds that of factor input stage 2

[12] Again, it is important to stress that these arguments for vertical integration apply for any random per firm demand. The case of binomial demand worked out in the text simply illustrates the strength of the incentives for one particular example.

firms. Therefore, stage 2 firms are more efficient absorbers of risk in the sense that stage 1 firms would have to hold more of the input than stage 2 firms in order to satisfy the same fraction of the population. Although holdings of the input by stage 1 firms reduces the demand seen by stage 2 firms, this reduction in demand is not great enough to offset the inefficient risk absorption by stage 1 firms. Therefore, stage 2 firms must decrease their input holdings by less than the amount that stage 1 firms increase their input holdings, if the same fraction of the population is to be satisfied. So, when stage 1 firms produce any input for themselves, more total input in the system must be produced or the fraction of customers who are satisfied will decline. To satisfy any given fraction of customers, market structures involving vertical integration will have higher total input costs than those involving no vertical integration. Since competition insures that cost savings are passed on to customers, it follows that consumers can always be made better off whenever there is any vertical integration in the system.

VII. THREE POSSIBLE EQUILIBRIUM MARKET STRUCTURES

A market structure is in equilibrium if, at the current level of vertical integration, stage 1 firms have no incentive to alter the amount of input that they produce for themselves, and if the stage 1 and stage 2 markets are equilibrating as discussed in section III. There are three equilibrium market structures. The first one is no vertical integration. The second one is partial vertical integration, in which stage 1 firms are vertically integrated, but still rely on stage 2 markets to provide some inputs. The third one is complete vertical integration, in which each stage 1 firm relies only on itself for its supply of the input and the stage 2 market disappears completely.

With partial vertical integration, the stage 2 market acts like an insurance market for supplying the factor input to the stage 1 market. Whenever a stage 1 firm makes a sale of a final product, it makes a higher per unit profit when it is able to use its own input (produced at cost c) in the manufacture of the final good rather than when it uses an input purchased on the stage 2 market at a price p_{int} (which exceeds c). A stage 1 firm continues to enter the stage 2 market simply because it needs to satisfy its customers. It can be cheaper for a stage 1 firm to satisfy its customer through use of the high price stage 2 market, rather than produce extra input for itself and bear the risk that the unit of input will go unsold.

VIII. THE CONSEQUENCES OF VERTICAL INTEGRATION ON MARKET EQUILIBRIUM

How does the market equilibrium with vertical integration compare to the market equilibrium when vertical integration is not allowed? From Theorem 1, we already know that, compared to the expected level of utility achievable in a competitive equilibrium with no vertical integration, the expected level of utility is lower in any market structure involving vertical integration. Since vertical integration lowers the maximum expected level of utility, it is possible that the level of utility could be driven so low that consumers would prefer not to enter the stage 1 market, causing it to vanish. Having mentioned this possibility, we shall concentrate in the subsequent analysis on the effects of vertical integration when the markets under study remain in existence.

The questions we ask are whether the price, p_f, of the final product, the price, p_{int}, of the factor sold in the stage 2 market, and the probability of satisfaction, $1-\lambda$, are higher or lower in a vertically integrated market structure than in a market structure in which vertical integration is not allowed. This section states the main results and provides explanations for them. (The reader interested in the technical proofs is referred to Carlton [2].)

Suppose that the equilibrium market structure involves complete vertical integration. Under a plausible assumption on preferences,[13] it is possible to establish that the market equilibrium with complete vertical integration involves a higher price and lower probability of satisfaction than does the market equilibrium with no vertical integration. Stage 1 firms are less efficient absorbers of risk than stage 2 firms in the sense that stage 1 firms with complete vertical integration have to produce more inputs than do stage 2 firms, with no vertical integration, to satisfy any given fraction of the population. The final price to the consumer has to rise to cover this increased cost of operation in the case of complete vertical integration. Moreover, because stage 1 firms cannot satisfy customers as efficiently as stage 2 firms, the equilibrium probability of shortage in the case of complete vertical integration rises from its value in the market equilibrium when vertical integration is not allowed. From these two results, it also follows that the total amount of the output that is purchased is lower in the case involving complete vertical integration than in the case involving no vertical integration, provided per capita demand depends negatively on price.

[13] See Carlton [2] for further details. The assumption is analogous to the assumptions of 'normal' goods in economic theory. We assume that if the customer per firm ratio increases so that the consumers are offered a better 'menu' of price-probability of satisfaction combinations, then the consumer will prefer a combination in which he is made better off in both dimensions. (As the customer per store ratio increases, the zero profit curve, used to define equilibrium, shifts up so that consumers are faced with a better set of price-probability of satisfaction choices.) In other words, the consumer will choose a combination with a lower price and higher probability of satisfaction. This assumption appears very reasonable since it is possible to prove (see Carlton [2], [4]) that as the customer per firm ratio increases, the market equilibrium price approaches its minimum possible value of c, and the probability of satisfaction approaches its maximum value of one. Hence the consumer *must* be made better off in terms of both the price and probability of satisfaction for sufficiently large increases in the customer per firm ratio. To see the analogy of the above assumption to consumer theory, note that we usually assume that a consumer in a two good world would increase his consumption of both goods in response to an increase in income (i.e. as his 'menu' between the two goods improves). We also make an assumption that the iso-utility curves are of such a shape that multiple tangencies (i.e. multiple equilibrium) with the zero profit curve do not occur.

Suppose now that equilibrium market structure involves partial vertical integration. The main result is that under appropriate assumptions (see Carlton [2]) the price of the input purchased in the stage 2 market is higher in the case involving partial vertical integration than in the market equilibrium when no vertical integration is allowed. This result follows from the fact that in the case of partial vertical integration, the stage 2 markets become 'riskier'[14] and the stage 2 firms become less efficient absorbers of risk than they were in the case of no vertical integration. This inefficiency results in increased costs to stage 2 firms. To cover their increased costs, the stage 2 firms have to raise their prices to the stage 1 firms. Surprisingly, it does not appear possible to prove that the stage 1 firms pass this increased cost along to the consumer in terms of higher prices for the final good. It seems possible, though I suspect unlikely, that with partial integration, the price of the stage 2 input could rise, but the price of the final good could fall. In this case, we know from Theorem 1 that the probability of satisfaction would have to fall sufficiently so that consumers are worse off in the case of partial vertical integration than in the case of no vertical integration.

In summary then, any market structure involving vertical integration provides a lower level of utility to consumers than can a market structure involving no vertical integration. Any vertical integration causes an inefficiency in the ability of firms to absorb risk, and usually will result in higher prices in the input market. When the equilibrium market structure involves complete vertical integration, we expect that both the probability of shortage and the price of the final good will rise from their equilibrium values in the case when integration is not allowed.

IX. MARKET STRUCTURE AND THE CHOICE OF THE OUTPUT TECHNOLOGY

In this section we examine how market structure and the transmission of uncertainty between firms can influence the choice of technology. So far, we have assumed that there is only one technology to produce the output, namely a Leontief technology which uses K units of capital and one unit of the input, subject to shortages, to produce one unit of output. Now we will assume that there suddenly becomes available a new Leontief technology with input requirements (K_1, l). We examine the incentives for introduction of the new technology in a non-integrated and in an integrated market setting. The main conclusion of this section is that introduction of a new technology that would benefit society is more likely to occur in a market with vertical integration than in one without vertical integration.

In the discussion of market clearing, it is useful to introduce the concept

[14] 'Risk absorbing' efficiency is inversely related to the customer per firm ratio. When stage 1 firms produce some of their own input, the stage 2 firms see less than L customers, so that the customer per firm ratio of stage 2 firms falls from its value in the case of no vertical integration.

of a 'derived' iso-utility curve. A derived iso-utility curve reflects trade-offs between the price of the input and the probability of obtaining the input. These trade-offs translate (through the stage 1 zero profit condition) into trade-offs that the consumer is willing to make between the price of the *final* good and the probability of obtaining the *final* good. A simple example is the best way to illustrate this concept.

Consider the case of no vertical integration. Assuming Leontief technology with coefficients $(K, 1)$, the zero profit condition for stage 1 firms is simply $p_f = rK + p_{\text{int}}$, where p_f is the price of the final good, p_{int} is the price of the input sold on the stage 2 market, and r is the price of capital. Preferences of consumers are represented by $u(1-\lambda, p_f) = \bar{u}$. Substituting in for p_f from the zero profit condition, we find that $u(1-\lambda, rK + p_{\text{int}}) = \bar{u}$ now expresses the consumer trade-offs in $(1-\lambda, p_{\text{int}})$ space.[15] Equilibrium in the stage 2 market is determined by the tangency between this derived iso-utility curve and the stage 2 zero profit curve $(\pi_2 = 0)$.

The important feature about derived iso-utility curves is that their shape will be influenced by the input–output coefficients of the technology. So, for example, if we had a new technology (K_1, l) where $l < 1$, any increase in p_{int} would translate into a smaller price increase in p_f than it would if $l = 1$. In this case, the derived isoutility curves would become flatter than they are in the case of $l = 1$. We will refer to the original $(K, 1)$ technology as the 'original' one, and the (K_1, l) technology as the 'new' one.

First, consider the market equilibrium that would occur if vertical integration is not allowed. Let the equilibrium factor price be p^0_{int}. The stage 1 firms will adopt the new technology *only if* it is more efficient when the price of capital is r and the price of the input is p^0_{int}. But this marginal calculation is not sufficient to guarantee that consumers would not be better off under the new technology. Figure 2 illustrates this point.

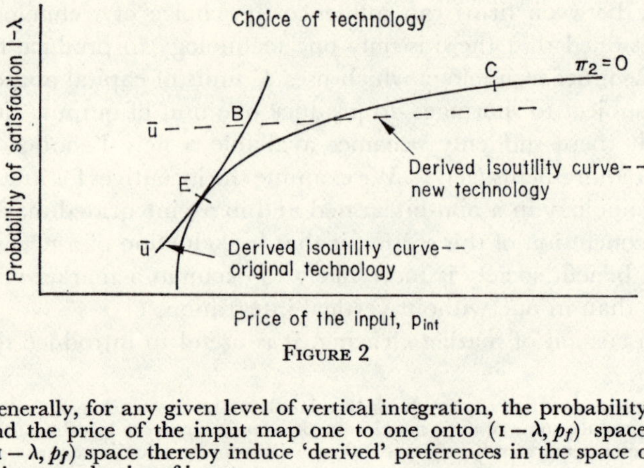

FIGURE 2

[15] More generally, for any given level of vertical integration, the probability of obtaining the input and the price of the input map one to one onto $(1-\lambda, p_f)$ space. Preferences defined in $(1-\lambda, p_f)$ space thereby induce 'derived' preferences in the space of probability of obtaining input and price of input.

Point E is the original market equilibrium. The derived iso-utility curve through point E is drawn using the input–output coefficients of the old technology. The level of utility achieved by consumers along this curve is $\bar{u}$. The derived isoutility curve, corresponding to the same $\bar{u}$ when the input–output coefficients of the new technology are used, is drawn as a dotted line. The fact that the dotted curve passes above point E is equivalent to the statement that the new technology is less efficient than the old technology at the factor price associated with point E. The two derived iso-utility curves cross at point B, where each technology is equally efficient (i.e. $p^{B}_{int}+rK=lp^{B}_{int}+rK_1$). Beyond point B, the new technology is more efficient. Notice that the dotted iso-utility curve crosses the zero profit ($\pi_2=0$) curve. Therefore, there exists some point C (see figure 2) of tangency between the derived iso-utility curve with the new technology and the $\pi_2=0$ curve that represents a level of utility above $\bar{u}$.

Consumers would be better off if all stage 1 firms adopted the new technology so that the market equilibrium would move to point C. Yet, because stage 1 firms have no control over the input market, they will not have any incentive to adopt the new technology, since it is inefficient at the initial market equilibrium E. The existing prices do not provide incentives for stage 1 firms to change technologies, nor for stage 2 firms to alter their behavior.

It is easy to see how vertical integration could remedy this situation. To make the point, it suffices to consider the case of complete vertical integration. Since each stage 1 firm totally controls its production of the input, it can co-ordinate its (p_{int}, $1-\lambda$) mix[16] to its own specifications. Because of this possibility of co-ordination, stage 1 firms will be able (and through competition will be forced) to move immediately to any achievable point that justifies the use of the new technology and makes consumers better off.

It is precisely because vertically integrated firms can exercise control over the characteristics (p_{int}, $1-\lambda$) of the input, that they are able to introduce the new and more desirable technology. With no vertical integration, price signals are not sufficient to convey the benefits of switching to the new technology. Whether consumers would be better off if all stage 1 firms adopted a new technology is a non-marginal change. In this case, marginal incentives at the firm level do not give the correct signals as to whether the non-marginal change is desired. Equivalently, in a competitive market, marginal incentives are not always sufficient to ensure that equilibrium is at a global optimum.[17]

[16] In the case of complete vertical integration, the stage 1 firms effectively act as stage 2 firms since they produce their own input.

[17] That is, if input firms 'experiment' by moving marginally around the initial equilibrium, they are driven back to the initial equilibrium. The reader should notice that there is nothing in this section that uses the fact that there is uncertainty in the market. The conclusion is the general one that vertical integration can be one way of remedying a market failure that occurs when marginal and global incentives differ.

In general, when the choice of technology affects the equilibrium characteristcs (e.g. price, probability of satisfaction) of the input which, in turn, influence the choice of technology, then it is not necessarily true that the individual decisions by firms will lead to the correct technology being adopted. With the ability to co-ordinate its choice of output technology with the characteristics of the input, the vertically integrated firm may introduce the new more desirable technology, while the non-integrated firms, who must take the input characteristics as given in the marketplace, may get locked into the old technology and have no incentive to change production technologies.

In markets characterized by uncertainty, Theorem 1 proves that vertical integration can be socially undesirable. However, socially desirable technologies are more likely to be developed and introduced in a market structure involving vertical integration in which individual firms can co-ordinate input characteristics with their choice of technology, than in a market structure involving no vertical integration in which such individual firm co-ordination does not occur. We are led to the Schumpeterian view of the world that it may be necessary to tolerate some static inefficiency in market structure in order to create an environment in which socially desirable technologies can be developed and introduced.

X. EXTENSIONS, INTERPRETATIONS, EVALUATION

It is easy to extend the model to the situation where the stage 2 input can be sold to demanders who are not stage 1 firms. In the absence of price discrimination among input demanders, the incentives for vertical integration tend to diminish as the stage 2 market expands (since p_{int} approaches c, and $1-\lambda$ approaches 1—Carlton [4]). In general, firms are less likely to integrate when they form a small part of total demand for the input since they would lose the risk pooling economics of large markets as they integrate. However, the incentives can increase if the other demanders of the stage 2 input have very different preferences and/or a riskier demand distribution than stage 1 firms. For example, vertical integration can become attractive when the other input demanders have high variability in their input demand and thereby drive up the input price. In this last situation, vertical integration becomes one mechanism to escape the costs that someone else's variability of demand imposes on the market.

It is straightforward to interpret the 'input' in the model as either capital or labor. The decision to vertically integrate then corresponds to decisions about labor or capital 'hoarding' to ensure that demand, if it materializes, can be met. The assumption that vertically integrated firms do not sell their inputs on the stage 2 market can be thought to reflect the existence of either fixed contracts with no recontracting markets or firms who do not sell their capital or laborers to someone else within a market period because of transaction costs.[18]

A belief in perfect competitive markets leads one to the conclusion that vertical integration does not have any desirable or undesirable features. A belief in competitive markets which possess the demand uncertainty and price inflexibility discussed earlier leads one to very different conclusions, as the simple model just presented illustrates. Which of the two views of competitive markets is appropriate will depend on the particular industry under study.

Sometimes models can be misleading because of the apparent simplicity or form of their assumptions. Let me now restate the four key features of the markets under study in an effort to distinguish the features that are important from those that are merely analytically convenient.

First, firms never feel they can either buy or sell all they want at the going market price. In our model, the corresponding assumption is that firms face demand and supply uncertainty. Not allowing firms at the same stage to trade among themselves or allowing recontracting markets to develop is one simple way to characterize this 'friction' in the market. Clearly, the qualitative features of market operation are unchanged if we allow firms to trade a 'little' among themselves—while if firms trade 'a lot' among themselves (i.e. recontracting markets exist), then we get right back to a perfect competitive market.

The second main feature of the markets under study really follows from the first feature. We require that there be some risk in any period that resources will not be fully utilized. The impact of this statement is that for many markets some unemployment of resources is a *natural* consequence of market operation.

The third feature involves the differential risk that a vertically integrated firm can impose between the use of its own inputs and the inputs of a factor market firm. Because a firm will always choose to use its own inputs first, there is always a higher probability that a firm will use a unit of its own input than a unit of input that factor market firms hold.

The final feature of the markets under study is that a vertically integrated firm be somehow *less* able than a factor market to satisfy input demands of other firms. In the model, we capture this feature by the assumption that $\mathcal{N}_2 < \mathcal{N}_1$ and by the (somewhat extreme) assumption that vertically integrated firms do not provide inputs to other firms. We have already mentioned (p. 195, n.7) that when $\mathcal{N}_1 < \mathcal{N}_2$, the private incentives for vertical integration (see section V) ensure complete vertical integration which for this particular case is socially desirable. As long as $\mathcal{N}_1 > \mathcal{N}_2$, the qualitative results of the model would be unchanged if we let vertically integrated firms do 'some' selling on the input market. We know that for some industries such trading

[18] For a treatment of labor hoarding along these lines, see Hall [8].

does occur, while for others it very rarely occurs, presumably for the transaction cost argument given in section IV. The real question, of course, is how much trading occurs. If there is 'a lot' of trading at flexible prices, then again, we approach a perfect input market and we come back to the classical view of vertical integration.[19] On the other hand, if transaction costs to a vertically integrated firm are high, so that a vertically integrated firm will incur the necessary transaction cost and sell its inputs (or equivalently use its unused capital to produce inputs) to other competitors only if the firm feels that it has sizably miscalculated and has little immediate hope of using that input in satisfying the demand for its final product, then we are driven to the view of vertical integration that this paper presents.

It is important to stress what features of the model are *not* important and are designed only to make the model easy to use. First, the total industry demand need not be fixed. To obtain the conclusions of the model, all that is required is a random per firm demand, which is certainly implied by a random industry demand. Second, the welfare implications of the model derive from the asssumption that vertically integrated firms cannot satisfy demand as efficiently (from a risk sense) as input firms. The assumption that the number of stage 1 firms, N_1, exceeds the number of stage 2 firms, N_2, is a *convenient* way of capturing this feature in the simple model. (Notice that in the simple model if N_1 is less than N_2 then the factor market can never exist, and the simple model becomes uninteresting.) This assumption about the relative magnitudes of N_1 and N_2 is not meant to be an assumption about the relative numbers of establishments in each stage, but rather to be an assumption about the relative ability of each stage to absorb risk. Clearly, an alternative model which can lead to identical welfare conclusions is one which has the factor market able to satisfy input demanders from *other* sectors of the economy while vertically integrated firms cannot. This alternative model could postulate that each output firm obtains some share of total random demand.[20] The input firms then obtain some share of random derived demand. Moreover, there are other sectors of the economy whose demand for input is also random and uncorrelated with the random input demand of the output industry under study. (To avoid complications about externalities, postulate that output firms in all sectors have similar preferences and similar random demands.) Input firms can pool risks, while vertically integrated firms are, by assumption,[21] unable to. With this new model we obtain the

[19] If we maintain the assumption of non-instantaneous price adjustment but allow vertically integrated firms to sell their input, then the first three market features described above guarantee that there will be complete vertical integration for the reasons discussed in section V. Such a market structure *may* or *may not* be socially preferable to the non-integrated one. For N_1 much larger than N_2, the non-integrated market structure will definitely be preferred. For N_1 less than N_2, the integrated market structure will be preferred.

[20] To preserve the competitive environment, we simply require that the share of demand depends on the utility level offered. As in all competitive equilibria, if a firm does not offer the best deal (i.e. highest utility level) its demand goes to zero.

[21] The assumption that vertically integrated firms do not sell their input to other sectors of the economy is based on the same transaction cost type arguments as expressed in section IV.

identical insights into the incentives for and consequences of vertical integration. Notice that in this alternative model there are no incentives for horizontal integration.[22] Incentives for horizontal integration are *not* a necessary consequence of market forces that produce incentives for vertical integration.

The model used in this paper has the advantage that it is simple enough to use analytically and yet maintains the four key features of market operation mentioned above. Given these features of market operation, the strong incentives for vertical integration arise because of the differential risk that a vertically integrated and input market firm face. The undesirable welfare implications of vertical integration result because the vertically integrated firm is a less efficient satisfier of input demand than is an input firm. It is incorrect to interpret the model as saying that all vertical integration is inefficient.[23] Rather the model shows that in a world of uncertainty there can exist very strong private incentives for vertical integration and that these incentives can exist, *even* in cases where such vertical integration may be socially undesirable.[24]

The question then arises as to whether the incentives and consequences that this paper identifies are a significant feature of market operation. The answer to this question will obviously depend on the particular market under study. However, it does seem that the model fits in well with descriptive studies of individual industries.

In an in-depth study of the automobile industry, White [10] examines the reason why auto companies vertically integrate, and, most relevant for this discussion, provides a descriptive explanation of how risks motivate vertical integration. White's descriptive discussion echoes many of the points raised earlier.

We argued that vertical integration was a means of transferring risk between firms. White [10, p. 80] states, '. . . integration is a two-edged sword. Though it reduces the risk of supply failure, it also converts variable costs into fixed costs . . . More money is at stake, . . . the financial penalties of losses (that is, risks) have increased.'

We found that there would exist strong private incentives for vertical integration to occur, and identified the possibility for partial vertical integration. The strong incentives for vertical integration arise because the vertically integrated firm is able to satisfy its high probability demand by itself, and pass on the low probability demand to some other firm. We found that for the case of partial integration, the factor market acted as a type of

[22] I thank Paul Krugman for this observation.

[23] Indeed, if $N_1 < N_2$, vertical integration is socially desirable and will occur for the reasons identified in section V.

[24] It is important to recognize that this statement remains unaffected if we relax the fourth feature and allow vertically integrated firms to sell their input (see footnote 19). The assumption about non-selling of input is made because it is realistic for many markets, and it allows us to develop insights into the possible consequences of partial vertical integration.

insurance market for the final product firm, with the final product firm making less of a profit on any item that used a factor market input than on an item that used an internally supplied input.

On these issues, White [10, p. 80] writes, 'A way of reducing the risks of vertical integration is through partial or tapered integration: a company can produce a portion of its needs of an item and buy the fluctuating remainder. This has the advantage of providing full utilization of its own equipment and allowing the suppliers to absorb the risk of fluctuations in demand. The company has to pay a premium to get someone else to absorb the risks, but the risk transfer is achieved. In the case of a supplier failure, production of the final good does not have to cease . . .' 'Tapered integration plays a large role in the industry' [10, p. 83].

Moreover, as mentioned at the outset of this paper, businessmen frequently say that they vertically integrated to obtain a more certain supply of inputs. Based on such statements and descriptive studies like White's, it does appear that the incentives identified in models of market behavior under uncertainty do exert a significant influence on market outcomes for certain industries.

The results of this research emphasize the importance of distinguishing between market clearing under certainty and under uncertainty. An analyst using a deterministic approach to this problem would be led astray and would be unable to find any desirable or undesirable incentives or disincentives for vertical integration. It is only by explicitly analyzing the effects of uncertainty on market behavior that the incentives and consequences of vertical integration can be fully comprehended.

UNIVERSITY OF CHICAGO

APPENDIX

Let cost $2 = rK + p_{\text{int}}$ and cost $1 = rK + c$. Notice that cost 2 represents the cost of producing one unit of the final good when the factor input is purchased from a stage 2 firm at price p_{int}, while cost 1 is the resource cost when the factor input has been produced by a stage 1 firm at the price c, where c is less than p_{int}. Let $\pi_1(i)$ stand for the profits of a stage 1 firm when it holds sufficient input to satisfy i customers by itself. For the case of no vertical integration (i.e. $i=0$) we have that

$$\pi_1(0) = (p_f - \text{cost } 2) \sum_{0}^{\infty} i\,pr(i)(1-\lambda)x(p_f),$$

where $pr(i)$ = probability a firm obtains i customers, and $x(p)$ = per capita demand.

For the case where the stage 1 firm holds just enough of the input to satisfy one customer, we have

$$\pi_1(1) = \left\{ \sum_{i=1}^{\infty} [(p_f - \text{cost } 1) + (p_f - \text{cost } 2)(i-1)(1-\lambda)]\, pr(i) - pr(0)c \right\} x(p_f).$$

The expression for $\pi_1(0)$ is simply the net revenue per unit times the expected number of goods that are sold. The expression for $\pi_1(1)$ is more complicated, and reflects the fact that if at least one customer appears, then the firm will be able to make a net profit on that customer of ($p_f -$ cost 1), and a net profit of ($p_f -$ cost 2) on each of the remaining customers. The term $pr(0).c$ reflects the risk that the firm will have spent c on production of the input, yet no customers will appear to use that input. Since in equilibrium $\pi_1(0) = 0$, it follows that $p_f =$ cost 2, and that

$$\pi_1(1) = \left\{ \left[\sum_1^\infty pr(i) \right] (p_f - \text{cost } 1) - pr(0)\, c \right\} x(p_f),$$

or

$$\pi_1(1) = \left\{ \left[\sum_1^\infty pr(i) \right] (\text{cost } 2 - \text{cost } 1) - pr(0)\, c \right\} x(p_f),$$

or

$$\pi_1(1) = \left\{ \left[\sum_1 pr(i) \right] (p_{\text{int}} - c) - pr(0)\, c \right\} x(p_f).$$

There will be an incentive for stage 1 firms to hold the input if $\pi_1(1) > \pi_1(0)$, or if $\pi_1(1) > 0$, or if

$$[1 - Pr(0)]\, p_{\text{int}} > c,$$

where $1 - Pr(0) =$ the probability that at least one customer will frequent a stage 1 firm.

REFERENCES

[1] ARROW, K., 'Vertical Integration and Communication', *The Bell Journal of Economics* (Spring 1975), pp. 173–83.

[2] CARLTON, D., 'Market Behavior Under Uncertainty', unpublished Ph.D. thesis, MIT (September 1975).

[3] ——, 'Uncertainty, Production Lags, and Pricing', *American Economic Review*, **67** (February 1977), pp. 244–9.

[4] ——, 'Market Behavior with Demand Uncertainty and Price Inflexibility', *American Economic Review*, **68** (September 1978), pp. 571–584.

[5] CHANDLER, A., JR., *Strategy and Structure: Chapters in the History of American Industrial Experience* (MIT Press, Cambridge, Mass., 1964).

[6] COASE, R., 'The Nature of the Firm', *Economica*, **4** (November 1937), pp. 386–405.

[7] GREEN, J., 'Vertical Integration and Assurance of Markets', Discussion Paper 383 (Harvard Institute of Economic Research, October 1974).

[8] HALL, R., 'An Aspect of the Economic Role of Unemployment', *Proceedings of the International Economics Association* (April 1975).

[9] MALMGREN, H., 'Information, Expectations, and the Theory of the Firm', *Quarterly Journal of Economics*, **75** (November 1961), pp. 399–421.

[10] WHITE, L., *The Automobile Industry Since* 1945 (Harvard University Press, Cambridge, Mass., 1971).

[11] WILLIAMSON, O., 'The Vertical Integration of Production: Market Failure Considerations', *American Economic Review*, **59** (May 1971), pp. 112–23.

[12] ——, *Markets and Hierarchies: Analysis and Antitrust Implications* (Free Press, New York, 1975).

THE JOURNAL OF INDUSTRIAL ECONOMICS
Vol. XXVII March 1979 No. 3

ON BIAS AND CONCENTRATION*

P. E. Hart

I. INTRODUCTION

Has the proportion of total manufacturing activity controlled by the largest enterprises tended to increase in the United Kingdom since 1900? If so, is this increase primarily attributable to waves of mergers? Have the effects of the different internal growth rates of enterprises been important? What has been the role of 'births', in the form of new enterprises, especially those which are subsidiaries of large foreign enterprises? These questions are very important. They raise serious economic, political and sociological issues and attempts to answer them have used some of the techniques of economics, economic history, mathematics, statistics and econometrics. Hart and Prais [8] provided answers to the first three of these questions. More recently Prais [11] has published a deeper analysis of these problems. Briefly, the general level of business concentration has increased since 1900 and, apart from a fall 1939–50, has continued to increase until 1970. Until 1950, the differential internal growth rates of enterprises were more important than mergers in increasing concentration, but mergers became more important in the 1960s.

An alternative view is taken by Hannah [3] and Hannah and Kay [4]. They argue that the Hart–Prais results of 1956 were based on a misleading measure of concentration (the variance of logarithms of enterprises' sizes) and on inappropriate samples of enterprises. When their new measures and new data are used, Hannah and Kay find that concentration increased primarily because of mergers. The present paper compares these two sets of views, denoting Hart and Prais by HP and Hannah and Kay by HK. Although this comparison uses historical data, it is directly relevant to current UK economic policy on mergers. The Government's Green Paper, *A Review of Monopolies and Mergers Policy* [13, p. 99], shows that the HK measure of the contribution of mergers to the growth of concentration in recent years is by far the largest of the available estimates, being no less than 116% in 1957–69 and 95% in 1969–73. The present paper argues that the HK measures have a large upwards bias and hence they should not be used to influence current economic policy nor to interpret the historical importance of mergers.

* I should like to thank L. Hannah, J. A. Kay and S. J. Prais for their helpful comments on an earlier version of this paper. This does not imply that they agree with all the arguments presented here.

The HP data 1885–1955 were the sizes of business units or enterprises (parent companies plus subsidiaries) listed on the London Stock Exchange. Their numbers change over time as new units obtain a Stock Exchange quotation ('births') and as others are taken over or lose their quotation ('deaths'). The total number of units in the whole population in year t, denoted by N, is the sum of quoted plus unquoted enterprises, denoted by $Q_t + U_t$. It is difficult to measure U_t and so we are uncertain about the extent of long period changes in the ratio $Q_t/(Q_t+U_t)$. However, we are confident that the share of Q_t, measured by employment, output, etc., in total manufacturing has increased since 1900.

The size distribution of $Q_t + U_t$ has large positive skewness and to estimate concentration within such a population it would be appropriate to take a stratified sample, starting with a 100% sampling fraction for the largest size stratum and decreasing this fraction for lower size strata. Unfortunately, the absence of sufficient data on U_t made it impossible to adopt such a standard sampling scheme: instead, it was necessary to confine the sample to Q_t, and this was a very rough and ready approximation to a 100% sampling fraction for the largest enterprises and zero for the rest. Many large companies, especially subsidiaries of foreign companies, were in U_t. For example, in 1950 the following companies were not quoted on the London Stock Exchange: Esso Petroleum, General Motors, Philips' Electrical Industries, Shell-Mex and BP, Kodak [10, p. 5]. However, since it was impracticable to draw the type of sample required by statistical theory, it was decided to use the available samples of Q_t to estimate changes in concentration within the population of all firms. To mitigate the effects of changes in Q_t+U_t over time, and in the relative importance of Q_t in the total, it was decided to focus attention on *constant samples* of quoted enterprises in each of six successive subperiods within the whole period 1885–1955.

In the present paper the size of the ith quoted enterprise, measured by its stock market valuation, is denoted by z_i, $z_i > 0$. Its share of the total market valuation of Q_t is y_i. The rth moment of z_i about zero, is given by

$$\gamma_r = \sum_{i=1}^{n} z_i^r/n,$$

so γ_1 is the arithmetic mean of the original distribution of z_i. The geometric mean of z is denoted by α_{0g} and the variance of the natural logarithms of z is given by

$$\sigma^2 = \sum_{i=1}^{n} \{\log_e(z_i/\alpha_{0g})\}^2/n.$$

The number of enterprises in the sample in year t is denoted by n, which must be distinguished from the total number of firms in the population, denoted by N. In the present context, the maximum size of sample in year t is given by $n=Q_t$, but this may be subdivided to allow for 'births' and 'deaths' of quoted enterprises between years t and $t+k$, which are denoted by Q_B and Q_D respectively. Quoted enterprises which survive from year t to year $t+k$ are denoted by Q_S, so $Q_t=Q_S+Q_D$ and $Q_{t+k}=Q_S+Q_B$. With this notation, the HP and HK measures of concentration are compared in section II, while their respective findings on the levels of concentration and on the effect of mergers on concentration are compared in sections III and IV.

II. DIFFERENT MEASURES OF CONCENTRATION

Hannah and Kay [4, Chapter 4], provide an interesting discussion of the desirable properties of concentration measures and propose the following measure denoted by HK(θ),

(1) $$\mathrm{HK}(\theta)=(\Sigma_i y_i^{\theta})^{1/(1-\theta)}, \qquad \theta>0, \qquad \theta\neq 1$$

where y_i is the share of the ith observation in total income, market value, employment, etc. The value of θ is arbitrary and HK provide values between 0 and 2·5. Their measure is in fact the antilogarithm (to the base 2) of R´nyi's [12] general entropy[1] of order θ which is defined as

(2) $$H(y)=\{1/(1-\theta)\}\{\log_2 \Sigma y_i^{\theta}\}.$$

Since $y_i=z_i/\Sigma z_i$ it is possible to relate HK(θ) to γ_r using

(3) $$\begin{aligned}\mathrm{HK}(\theta)&=\{\Sigma(z_i^{\theta})/(\Sigma z_i)^{\theta}\}^{1/(1-\theta)}\\ &=N\{\gamma_{\theta}/\gamma_1^{\theta}\}^{1/(1-\theta)}\end{aligned}$$

where $\theta=r$. For example, with $\theta=2$, (3) becomes

(4) $$\mathrm{HK}(\theta=2)=N\gamma_2^{-1}/\gamma_1^{-2}=1/H_e$$

or the reciprocal of the Hirschman–Herfindahl index.

Hart and Prais [8] used the variance of the logarithms of enterprises' sizes, denoted by σ^2, to measure concentration. If the size distribution of enterprises is lognormal then all the usual measures of concentration can be be calculated from N and σ^2. For example, in a lognormal distribution,

(5) $$\mathrm{HK}(\theta)=N\exp(-\theta\sigma^2/2)$$

and further examples of the relationship between N, and σ^2 and other concentration measures are given by Hart [7]. In particular the following measures may be derived from σ^2: the coefficients of variation, of skewness and kurtosis, the Gini coefficient, the first and second order entropies and

[1] The HK(θ) measure was formulated by John Kay in the mid-1970s independently of Rényi.

their transformation, such as the HK(θ) statistic. Thus for a given lognormal distribution it is wrong to assert that σ^2 measures inequality rather than concentration. It is also wrong to assert that σ^2 violates the principle of transfers, for if a lognormal distribution always holds, a transfer of output from a smaller to a larger enterprise always increases σ^2, as shown in Hart [6]. However, if we reject the assumption of lognormality, possibly on the grounds that its underlying generating model cannot include births and deaths, then such assertions may have some truth in them. Thus part of the actual controversy is really about the justification for the belief that the relevant size distribution is sufficiently close to lognormality. There seems little scope for progress on this part of the controversy. First it is known that the standard statistical tests of significance are not relevant in a distribution generated by a stochastic process,[2] because it is always possible that the equilibrium distribution, or final form, being generated by the stochastic process has not been reached by the time the actual frequency distribution is observed. Secondly, the observed size distributions are usually truncated, so in practice we may be unable to observe a simple two-parameter lognormal distribution. Thirdly, it is not yet known how large the deviations from strict theoretical lognormality have to be before the calculations of measures of concentration and inequality from σ^2 produce misleading results. So for present purposes, let us assume that the observed distributions are not sufficiently close to lognormal to enable us to use σ^2 and N to calculate all the other measures to the level of approximation required.

In the absence of a lognormal model, σ^2 is simply one measure of relative inequality, with properties similar to those of the absolute variance. For example, it can be decomposed very easily, although it must be remembered that the usual F-tests performed in the analysis of variance cannot strictly be applied if lognormality is being rejected. It is not affected by an equiproportionate change in all values of the variable, for in logarithms this is equivalent to adding or subtracting a constant. This is very convenient for it is possible to ignore the effects of price changes when dealing with money values of variables over time. Against these advantages there is the disadvantage that σ^2 does not always increase when output is transferred from a smaller firm, z_i, to a larger firm, z_j.

However, while this 'principle of transfers' type of criticism of σ^2 as a measure of business concentration is usually invalid, it is valid for transfers

[2] See A. Stuart's criticism reported by M. G. Kendall in the discussion of Hart and Prais [8, p. 185]. In the case of the distribution of men's heights, it may be argued that the final form has been reached and so the traditional tests of goodness of fit are appropriate. Even then some mathematical statisticians would claim that statistical tests cannot help us to choose between an approximate generalization and an invalid one, to use the words of Ijiri and Simon [9, p. 114]. Moreover, Savage [14, pp. 254–6], argues that statistical tests should not be applied to extreme null hypotheses (those which would not be readily accepted by anyone as being *exactly* correct). Instead, we should accept them if they are nearly true and if they simplify our task.

in the extreme upper tail of the size distribution. This limitation of σ^2 in the absence of lognormality, can be important in studies of business concentration where transfers within the extreme upper tail are of major interest. Clearly, in such cases other concentration measures, such as the concentration ratio, should be used in addition to σ^2, as of course they usually are.

For the principle of transfers to be violated, both z_i and z_j must be greater than the geometric mean, α_{0g}. In practice α_{0g} is much the same as the median and so, assuming that transfers from z_i to z_j are random, possible violations are confined to about 25% of the bivariate distribution of firms at times t and $t+k$. How likely are such violations within this 25%? Creedy [1] shows that the principle of transfers is more likely to be violated

(a) the smaller the transfer, as a proportion of z_i,
(b) for any given transfer, the larger the ratio z_i/α_{0g},
(c) for any given transfer, the larger the initial ratio z_i/z_j.

He also shows that for values of σ^2 usually found for income distributions, the chance of the principle of transfers being violated in practice is small enough to be ignored.

But we must be careful before applying Creedy's results to problems of business concentration. Values of σ^2 of enterprises' sizes are much larger than for peoples' incomes; the ratio z_i/α_{0g} 1907–50 could reach 2^9 which would satisfy Creedy's conditions (b) and (c). Against this, the major type of transfer in the context of business concentration is a merger, where the whole of z_i is transferred to z_j and this would not satisfy condition (a). The net outcome is uncertain and to make further progress in our assessment of σ^2 we must move from theoretical to empirical analysis, by comparing the results of Hannah and Kay [4] with those of Hart and Prais [8]. The next section compares the estimates of the level of concentration in 1907, 1924, 1939, 1950 and 1955 made by Hannah [3] with the corresponding estimates in Hart and Prais [8] and Hart [5].

III. LEVELS OF CONCENTRATION 1907–55

Table I gives the values of n used by Hart and Prais [8] in block 1. Each row shows the number of firms in the sample, compared between successive dates: for example, the second row shows that HP compared concentration among 516 enterprises in 1924 and in 1939. The use of a constant sample of firms, Q_s, for reasons explained in section II, enabled HP to use the Galton regression model for each subperiod to study the proportionate growth rates of large and small enterprises. Moreover, for each subperiod, apart from 1939–50, concentration increased among the constant samples of firms and 'a preponderating influence is had by the changes in the sizes of those firms that are alive throughout the period' (HP [8, p. 168]). In fact, by confining the analysis to constant samples within each subperiod, it is possible to obtain a plausible chain index of business concentration back to 1885, whether measured by the variance of the logarithms or by any other measure.[3]

The values of n used by Hannah ([3, p. 220], with $HK(\theta=0)=n$) are shown in block 2 of Table I for the years 1907–55. Taking the same subperiod 1924–39, it can be seen that he compared concentration among 726 firms in 1924 with 516 firms in 1939. He included 'deaths' in the initial year of each subperiod, but excluded 'births' in his estimates of $HK(\theta)$ for the years selected by HP.[4] This procedure obviously conflicts with the need to study constant samples. It also exaggerates the estimated proportionate reduction in N, for including 'births', Q_B, would reduce the fall in n. The effects of this bias is the more serious the more the measure of concentration used is affected by n. It is accentuated in Hannah and Kay [4] by the inclusion of some companies not quoted on the London Stock Exchange including some U_{MQ}: for example, they reduce n from 1263 in 1919 to 584 in 1930, and from 1998 in 1930 to 1602 in 1948. The different

TABLE I

ALTERNATIVE ASPECTS OF CONCENTRATION 1907–55

(each row gives comparable figures for years shown)

	1907		1924		1939		1950		1955
1. HP n	456		456						
			516		516				
					1502		1502		
							1981		1981
2. Hannah n	571		456						
			726		516				
					1712		1502		
							2103		1981
3. HP σ^2 (base e)	1·50		2·52						
			2·23		3·13				
					2·43		1·90		
							1·95		2·65
4. HP equivalent H_e	0·0098		0·027						
			0·018		0·044				
					0·0076		0·0045		
							0·0035		0·0071
5. Hannah H_e	0·017		0·033						
			0·021		0·038				
					0·020		0·013		
							0·010		0·018
6. Change $H_e(t+k)/H_e(t)$									
HP		2·75		2·44		0·59		2·02	
Hannah		1·94		1·81		0·65		1·80	

[3] Plausible, because changes in concentration within samples of *surviving* enterprises appeared to dominate the changes in concentration within *all* quoted enterprises in each subperiod. Changes in N over the whole period 1885–1955, which are still unknown, may have affected business concentration, so it is necessary to check changes in σ^2 by using other measures for concentration, such as an absolute concentration ratio, for which a knowledge of N is not required. This is done in Prais [11].

[4] That is, he compared Q_S+Q_D in year t with Q_S in year $t+k$.

definitions of n tend to create differences between the HK(θ) values and the HP σ^2 values.

The latter, in natural logarithms, are shown in block 3 of Table I. They are converted into Hirschman–Herfindahl indices in row 4, using $H_e = \exp(\sigma^2)/N$. The implicit assumption of lognormality is convenient though not strictly justified; the data are distributions which, after logarithmic transformation, are slightly positively skew and leptokurtic. The deviations from strict lognormality tend to produce differences between the HP and the HK estimate of H_e given in row 5 and obtained by taking the reciprocal of Hannah's equivalent number of firms with HK($\theta = 2$).

It can be seen that the HP estimate of H_e at the beginning of a period is always lower than the HK measure; this is presumably attributable to the large differences in n. As a result of this upwards bias in the HK estimate of H_e at the beginning of the period, the proportionate increases in this concentration measure in block 6 are less than those of the HP estimate. But it is important to notice that both sets of estimates show the same direction of change in each period. Even in the exceptional period 1939–50 both estimates indicate a reduction in concentration. In the HP paper it is shown that this fall is the result of small companies growing proportionately more quickly than large companies 1939–50. This average tendency is reduced by the HK inclusion of 210 companies which 'died' 1939–50, so the proportionate fall in this H_e is *less* than that of the HP estimate, in spite of the fact that the HK 1939 estimate of H_e is biased upwards.

Nevertheless, the general agreement between the two sets of estimates is surprisingly good, despite the differences in methods (the assumption of lognormality in block 4 of Table I and the use of σ^2). The differences between the HP and HK results 1907–55 arise because HP used constant samples of firms whereas Hannah did not. The use of σ^2 instead of HK(θ) appears to have had little effect on the results. Hannah and Kay [4, p. 128] agree that the HP measure, σ^2, and the HK(θ) measure, give broadly the same results on changes in the level of concentration, but argue that 'In other respects, however, the use of the variance of logs as an index of concentration can lead to serious errors'. To this assertion, we now turn.

IV. THE EFFECTS OF MERGERS ON CONCENTRATION

Hannah and Kay [4] argue that Hart and Prais [8] underestimated the effect of mergers on concentration over the period 1907–50. First, they claim that the use of σ^2 violated the principle of transfers for it is possible that σ^2 decreased after mergers between large companies in the upper tail of the distribution. Secondly, they argue that the exclusion of mergers involving companies not listed on the London Stock Exchange also had the effect of underestimating the effects of mergers. Let us consider each argument in turn.

Mergers and σ^2

The use of σ^2 to measure the effects of mergers, without assuming log-normality, raises issues which are relevant to many economic size distributions. Indeed, it is instructive to consider the properties of σ^2 and HK(θ) in the context of the formation of household income distributions from the distribution of the incomes of single men and women. Suppose z_i denotes the income of the ith single man and v_i the income of the ith single woman, with $z_i = v_i$, ($i = 1, \ldots, N$) and hence $\delta_z^2 = \sigma_v^2$. If the ith man marries the ith woman (corresponding to what is elsewhere described as perfect assortative mating) they form household i with income $h_i = z_i + v_i$, then $\sigma_h^2 = \sigma_z^2 = \sigma_v^2$. Thus the relative inequality of household incomes is obviously the same as that before the marriage took place in spite of the fact that the absolute variance of household income (in £s squared) is four times that of the income of the single man, or single women, or of the pooling of the two separate income distributions of single people. In addition, we know that the total number of observations has fallen from $2N$ to N. Note that the ratios of moments in the HK(θ) measure in (3) do not change because the product of the subscripts and exponents of moments in the numerator equal those of moments in the denominator. But of course the values of HK(θ) are halved because they are influenced by N. Thus if an entropy changes we should want to decompose the changes into the effects of N and of moment ratios. Similarly if σ^2 changes we may also want to know what has happened to N before reaching any conclusion on inequality or concentration.

The effects of these marriages on the absolute concentration ratio are also interesting. The absolute concentration ratio for the top s units is given by

$$(6) \qquad 1 - F_1(z_s) = \sum_{i=N-s+1}^{N} z_i \Big/ \sum_{i=1}^{N} z_i = 1 - F_1(v_s) = 1 - F_1(h_s)$$

where, for example, $F_1(z_s)$ is the first moment distribution function of z at size z_s and where units are ranked in ascending order $i = 1, \ldots, N$. Thus the concentration of household incomes is the same as that in each of the two separate distributions. This result is consistent with an unchanged σ^2 and with no changes in the ratios of moments in the HK(θ) measures.

Now suppose z_i denotes the output of the ith enterprise in country z, and v_i the output of the ith enterprise in its neighbouring country v. If, following a union of the two countries, the ith enterprise in country z merges with its counterpart in country v then all the previous results hold. Mergers do not affect relative inequality, nor do they affect absolute concentration. However, although the halving of N may have little economic significance for the new union as a whole, it may be extremely important in particular industries; we are less worried about a reduction in the total number of enterprises from 200,000 to 100,000 than with a fall from 10 to 5 in a particular industry. For particular industries, we should require a knowledge of N, γ_1 and γ_2 rather than σ^2 because σ^2 is not affected in the present example when the number of enterprises is halved and the size of each is doubled. This example, similar to that used by Ijuri and Simon [9] to show how the parameter of a Pareto distribution need not be affected by mergers, illustrates some of the hypothetical advantages and disadvantages of σ^2. But in order to reach a conclusion on the use of σ^2 in practice, we must relax all these unrealistic assumptions (such that mergers take place only between enterprises of equal size) and review the comparatively little evidence which is available.

Of course, whether mergers or the differential internal growths are more important in increasing concentration depends on the period being studied. In the short run, say over one year or less, we might expect that there are industries at certain points in time in which mergers are more important than the differential growth of enterprises in increasing business concentration; mergers can take place overnight, while differences in internal rates of growth take much longer to emerge. But in the long run, say over a decade, mergers might be less important. For example, many mergers do not achieve their target market shares. Other mergers are defensive in character, formed to ease the adjustment to declining market shares ('rationalisation'). Some are simply mistakes, possibly fostered by government policy. But all tend to catch the headlines in the press, compared with those enterprises not involved in mergers, and the popular impression is created that even in the long run mergers are the predominant force making for increased business concentration. But did British Leyland, which was developed by mergers, contribute more than Ford to the long run increase in concentration in the motor car industry in the UK? The answer to such questions depends on the time period covered and may also vary with the measure of concentration which is used.

For those enterprises which were quoted in the Stock Exchange, Hart and Prais [8] found that up to 1950 σ^2 was increased by mergers but the amount of this increase was small over a decade compared with the effects of differential internal growth. In the time periods studied between 1907 and 1950, mergers increased the size of the enterprises involved but reduced the variance of their logarithmic sizes. However, the size effect was more powerful and so σ^2 for all quoted enterprises was increased by mergers. It is obvious that in these cases σ^2 did not violate the principle of transfers and was not greatly affected by the reduction in n. The use of a generalized entropy measure such as HK(θ) would have been affected by the reduction in n, and might have given more weight to mergers in the overall increase in concentration. Moreover if such a statistic were used it would clearly be important to decompose it to assess the separate effects of n, γ_1 and γ_2.

To illustrate this last point, let us take the example of mergers in the food industries 1919–39 reported by Hannah and Kay [4, p. 52]. In their sample of quoted companies, and their unquoted subsidiaries, Hannah and Kay show that in this industry n fell from 103 to 45 as the result of mergers and the value of $HK(\theta=2)^{-1}$, or the Hirschman–Herfindahl statistic, rose from 0·0658 to 0·323 over the period 1919–30. They state that σ^2 fell slightly, but do not report the values. This is their only evidence, ignoring their hypothetical arithmetical examples, that σ^2 can in practice violate the principle of transfers. If all the mergers had taken place in 1919, this concentration measure would have been 0·256, or 3·89 times the actual 1919 level. Since the actual level in 1930 was 4·91 times the 1919 level, they claim that mergers were responsible for 79% of the increase in concentration, leaving 21% for differential internal growth. Let us look at this result more closely.

We may decompose the increase in this concentration statistic using (4). The fall in n was responsible for 59% of the increase: the remainder was due to the fall in γ_1^2/γ_2. Though most of the increase is attributable to changes in n, the moment ratio γ_1^2/γ_2, unlike σ^2, also changes substantially. This is simply another example of the relative insensitivity of σ^2, compared with $HK(\theta)$, to changes in n. The major reason for the increase in concentration was the formation of Unilever in 1929 from a merger between Lever Brothers and Van den Bergh and Jurgens. Hannah and Kay [4, p. 52] claim that in the period 1919–30 '58 of the 103 firms in the industry disappear through merger, and the largest firm, Unilever, acquires 19 of them, including seven of its 15 largest competitors, and raises its market share from 22 to 49%'. Obviously, any statistical measurement of changes of level of concentration will depend on the size of this single extreme observation.

What proportion of Unilever's market valuation should be deducted to allow for its activities outside the manufacture of foodstuffs especially for soap, toilet goods and retail distribution? Answers to such questions are inevitably subject to error and the result is that the actual shares of Unilever in the quoted section of the food industries in 1919 and 1930 were probably quite different from 22% and 49% estimated. Whatever percentage is estimated will goven the measure of concentration, for in 1919 Unilever contributed 0·0484 to the H_e index of 0·0658 compared with a contribution of 0·2401 to the 1930 value of 0·3230. Until we know the correct proportion of Unilever's market valuation which should be allocated to the food group of industries in 1919 and 1930, we cannot obtain reliable estimates of the change in concentration in this industry group.[5] We do not even know whether σ^2 violated the principle of transfers, for without a reliable estimate of the share of Unilever we do not have sufficient

[5] The problem of allocating the market valuation of Unilever, or of other giant firms, to individual industries does not arise in studies, such as that made by HP, of business concentration within manufacturing as a whole.

empirical evidence on this question, but merely another hypothetical example of a distribution of firms.

In the case of one section of food manufacture, the margarine industry, Wilson [16] provides the evidence. There were four major firms in 1921: Jurgens, Van den Bergh, Maypole and Lever (through its subsidiary, Planter). Between 1921 and 1927 the sales of Maypole and of Lever declined sharply, while those of Van den Bergh and Jurgens were steady. After 1929 Unilever was the sole private producer of margarine but this monopoly was reached as the result of the relative weakness rather than the relative strength of Lever. The most that can be said to support HK's interpretation of events is that the reduction of N from four to one reduced σ^2! But nobody would use σ^2 to measure concentration among such a small number of firms.

Mergers and n

It is clear that in the assessment of the effects of mergers on concentration we must be very careful when defining n, the number of enterprises in the sample. This is especially true if we use the HK(θ) measure which is likely to be influenced by large changes in n. Thus we have seen the fall in n was responsible for most of the increase in H_e in the HK data. Which definition of n should be adopted? In particular, should we include U_{MQ}, the unquoted firms merged with quoted companies?

If we want to estimate the 'merger rate' for 1919–30 of *all* firms, given that most of our information is restricted to quoted enterprises which are the upper tail of this size distribution, we could use as numerator the number of quoted enterprises which were involved in mergers between 1919 and 1930, say Q_M. The total number of quoted enterprises in 1919, say Q_t could be the denominator. This 'quoted sector merger rate', Q_M/Q_t is an internally consistent estimator for the population merger rate of $(Q_M+U_M)/(Q_t+U)$, where U denotes all unquoted enterprises, of which U_M were involved in mergers. The estimator Q_M/Q_t was used by Hart and Prais [8] to estimate the effect of mergers on aggregate concentration, in accordance with equation (A.1) in the Appendix to this paper, with the before mergers $w_2=Q_M/Q_t$. It was clearly stated in Hart and Prais [8, para. 4.4, p. 168], that Q_M was not used to estimate (Q_M+U_M). Hannah and Kay [4, p. 128] acknowledge this, but argue that Q_M/Q_t underestimates $(Q_M+U_M)/(Q_t+U)$. They claim that many of the quoted firms which would be regarded by HP as growing internally should be properly regarded as growing externally by the acquisition of unquoted firms which may be denoted by U_{MQ}.

This criticism may seem reasonable at first sight, but a moment's reflection will show that it is quite wrong. If U_{MQ} is included in the numerator of an estimator for the full population merger rate $(Q_M+U_M)/(Q_t+U)$, what is the corresponding entry in the denominator? If U_{MQ} is used, the resulting merger rate $(Q_M+U_{MQ})/(Q_t+U_{MQ})$ is clearly very heavily biased upward, since the total number of unquoted firms, U, was of the order of several hundred thousand, if not more, whereas U_{MQ} was in hundreds. The HP ratio Q_M/Q_t is a less misleading estimate of the probability of mergers in the population of all firms.

By including U_{MQ}, which they say HP 'missed', HK in effect used a grossly exaggerated merger rate similar to $(Q_M+U_{MQ})/(Q_t+U_{MQ})$. Their inclusion of such unquoted companies explains why they show a fall in n from 1263 in 1919 to 584 in 1930. It is true that 1919 (unemployment 2·4%) and 1930 (unemployment 14·6%) mark the difference between a post-war boom and a year of slump, and this would exaggerate a downward trend in N, but even so a decline by some 54% in n over 11 years cannot be regarded as a reasonable estimate of the change in the population of firms, N, in this period. This exceptional fall in n is particularly serious when using a general order entropy statistic such as HK(θ) to estimate the effect of mergers on concentration for it is sensitive to large falls in n, as shown in equation (3) and in the example of the food industry 1919–30 above.

The inclusion of unquoted firms by HK also created problems for the measurement of size, for by definition Stock Exchange valuations could not be used. HK used a variety of ingenious expedients to measure the sizes of such firms but inevitably the results are somewhat arbitrary and could also contribute to the differences between HK and HP on the effects of mergers on concentration. But this contribution is probably small compared with the different definitions of n.

As a result of including U_{MQ}, HK obtained higher 'death rates' than in HP. The biased effects of this on the HK merger rate have been discussed above. By including the estimated sizes of 'births' for the initial years of their time periods, HK largely eliminated 'births', Q_B. Thus their near zero 'birth rates' are lower than those of HP. Their 'birth rate' clearly underestimates the population birth rate but it is not yet possible to assess the effects of this on their estimates of the importance of mergers. If the distributions of their omitted births were very highly concentrated, as the result, for example, of the large sizes of the UK branches of multinational companies, then the exclusion of such births would underestimate the effects of internal growth on concentration, and hence overestimate the importance of mergers.

Thus the different definitions of n are important sources of the different estimates of the effects of mergers on concentration made by HP and HK.[6]

[6] These comments on the effects of measurement errors in n call to mind the long discussions on this topic which took place at the time between J. B. Jefferys, S. J. Prais and the present author. Dr. Jefferys directed the business concentration research project of the National Institute of Economic and Social Research from its start in 1954 to 1956 when he was succeeded by I. M. D. Little. Most of the research was concerned with concentration in individual industries and led to the authoritative book by Evely and Little [2]. The HP paper was intended to be an exploratory investigation of aggregate business concentration using new tools and new sources of data. It took less than a year, being ready by the summer of 1955. This supplements the bald statement in Hannah and Kay [4, p. 128], 'Professor Hart tells us that lack of time and resources prevented a fuller treatment of merger in their study . . .'.

It has been shown that the HK overestimated the effects of mergers on concentration. For this reason, it is preferable to use the HP estimate based on Q_M/Q_t. It is not claimed that this ratio is an unbiased estimate of the population merger rate; since Q_t is not a random sample of all firms, it is impossible to make a formal assessment of its bias, or of any other of its statistical properties. It is claimed that it is less misleading than that used by HK. Their upward biased estimates of the population merger rate also exaggerate the effects of mergers on the HK concentration ratios. The different results of HK and HP are due to different estimates of the merger rate, rather than to the use of different measures of concentration. The advantages and disadvantages of the generalized entropy measure, and hence of their transformation such as HK(θ), are well known. In particular, as explained in the Appendix, Theil [15] showed that the Hirschman–Herfindahl index, H_e, and hence HK($\theta = 2$), should not be used to measure the effects of mergers on concentration, and it is surprising that HK ignored his results. However, as also explained in the Appendix, Theil's justified criticism of H_e does not apply to the first order entropy of Shannon, and hence does not apply to HK($\theta = 1$).

V. CONCLUSIONS

There is broad agreement between the HP and the HK estimates of the levels of aggregate business concentration 1907–55. What differences there are between the two sets of estimates arise because HK included in their samples at the beginning of each period many companies which were subsequently merged with quoted companies and which HP classified as 'deaths'. This produced an upward bias in HK's estimate of the decline in N during each period; and since their measure of concentration is substantially affected by n and changes in it, their estimates of changes in concentration are substantially biased.

There is no agreement between the two sets of estimates of the contribution of mergers to the rise in business concentration. The conclusion reached here on mergers and the use of the HP measure, σ^2, is that it is conceivable that a merger between two very large firms may reduce σ^2 (if the size distributions are not lognormal). But in practice there is no evidence that such a result has ever happened for size distributions of manufacturing firms as a whole. Even if it happened, it might not be an altogether perverse result from an economic point of view; for example, if there is a merger between enterprises ranked five and six which intensifies the competition between the top five firms, a reduction in σ^2 might be a good indicator of the change in the economic power of the leading enterprises. That is, the principle of transfers may be a reasonable rule for most of the time, but there are instances when it should be ignored.

However, the effects of the different measures of concentration used by

HP and HK are less important than their different definitions of the relevant sample of enterprises. HK included large numbers of enterprises in the initial years of their time periods which should be excluded if it is desired to avoid using a biased estimate of the effects of mergers on concentration in all manufacturing enterprises. Perhaps the main conclusion to draw on mergers and n is that we need a better estimate of the population merger rate $(Q_M+U_M)/(Q_t+U)$, than provided by either HP or HK. The HP ratio, Q_M/Q_t does not necessarily underestimate it, but the HK rate necessarily overestimates it. Hannah's painstaking research over many years in enumerating and valuing thousands of unlisted companies involved in mergers over the period 1880–1973 is to be welcomed because it has added U_{MQ} to our knowledge of the required numerator, even though $U_{MQ}<U_M$. But we still lack a good estimate of U in the required denominator. Improved estimates of U are linked to the births of firms mentioned in the fourth question in the introduction. There is great scope for modern economic historians to measure the effects of unquoted firms, including those of multinational companies, on industrial structure and performance in the United Kingdom. For example, in the food industries, we might assess the effects of the Co-operative Societies (CWS and SCWS), of the Milk Marketing Board and of foreign companies such as Nestle, Heinz, Quaker Oats, Nabisco and Kellogg. When proper allowance is made for such firms, we may have to revise our present views on the increase in concentration in the food industries 1919–30.

In short, only after the identification and the measurement of the most important unquoted companies 1919–30 not involved in mergers, will it be possible to reach any more definite conclusions on the relative contribution of mergers and internal growth to the rise in concentration.

UNIVERSITY OF READING

APPENDIX

MEASURING THE EFFECT OF MERGERS

1. *Variance of Logarithms*

The HP method of measuring the effects of mergers on concentration was based on

$$\sigma^2 = w_1\sigma_1^2 + w_2\sigma_2^2 + w_1 w_2(\bar{x}_1 - \bar{x}_2)^2 \tag{A.1}$$

where $w_2 = Q_M/Q_t$ and $\bar{x}_2 = \log \alpha_{0g}$ for those firms involved in mergers. The subscript 1 refers to those $Q_t - Q_M$ firms not involved in mergers. The hypothetical value of σ^2 in the initial year, obtained from (A.1) by assuming that all the mergers during the time period took place in the initial year, was compared with the actual value of σ^2. The hypothetical σ^2 exceeded the actual σ^2, but not by very much. Hence mergers appeared to have had less effect than differential internal growth on the observed increases in σ^2. If $(Q_M+U_{MQ})/(Q_t+U_{MQ})$ had been used it is clear that w_1 and $\bar{x}_2$ would have been smaller, and w_2 would have been larger (since $w_1=1-w_2$). It is not possible to say *a priori* how σ_1^2 and σ_2^2 would have changed, but it is likely that the increase in the third term on the RHS of (A.1) would have produced a higher value of the hypothetical σ^2. But $(\bar{x}_1-\bar{x}_2)^2$ would have had a large upward bias.

2. *Hirschman–Herfindahl Statistic*

Theil (1972, pp. 42–5) has shown that the decomposition properties of the Hirschman–Herfindahl statistic, H_e, make it an undesirable measure of the effects of mergers on concentration. The total H_e for quoted companies may be decomposed into the product of a between-group index and an average within-group index as follows

$$H_e=H_{eb}\sum_{j=1}^{2}(Y_j^2/H_{eb})H_{ewj} \tag{A.2}$$

where $j=1$ refers to the Q_t-Q_M firms not involved in mergers.

$$Y_j=\sum_{i\in j} y_i$$

denotes the sum of the shares of firms within each group, $H_{eb}=Y_1^2+Y_2^2$ gives the between-group index, and

$$H_{ew2}=\sum_{i\in 2} y_i^2/Y_2^2$$

gives the within-group index for the Q_M firms involved in mergers. As a result of mergers H_{ew2} and H_{eb} increase, which are desirable results. But although H_{ew1} is constant, because there are no mergers among the Q_t-Q_M firms, the weight on it is drastically reduced by the increase in H_{eb}. Thus the weight attached to the level of concentration within the larger set of Q_t-Q_M firms not involved in mergers varies inversely with increases in concentration among the Q_M firms. Theil's criticism could also be applied to the HP decomposition in (A.1): as the result of mergers w_2 falls and w_1 increases, but the w_i weights refer to relative frequencies and this drawback is less important than in the case of the $1/H_{eb}$ weights which refer to relative shares in total market valuation.

The shortcomings of the H_e statistic in measuring the effect of mergers on concentration also hold for Rényi's second order entropy and for the Hannah–Kay statistic, HK($\theta=2$). Note that the inclusion of U_{MQ} accentuates the shortcomings of H_e by increasing H_{ew2} and H_{eb} and by decreasing the weight on H_{ew1}.

3. *First Order Entropy* (*Shannon's Case*)

Shannon's entropy may be decomposed as follows

$$H(y)=-\Sigma y_i \log y_i \tag{A.3}$$

$$=H(y)_b+\sum_{j=1}^{2} Y_j H(y)_{wj} \tag{A.4}$$

where $H(y)_b=-(Y_1 \log Y_1+Y_2 \log Y_2)$ gives the between-group entropy and

$$H(y)_{w2}=-\sum_{i\in 2}(y_i/Y_2)\log(y_i/Y_2)$$

gives the within group entropy for the Q_M firms involved in mergers. The weight on the Q_t-Q_M firms not involved in mergers is

$$Y_1=\sum_{i\in 1} y_i,$$

or their share in total market valuation, which is invariant with the increase in concentration brought about by mergers among the Q_M firms in group 2. Thus Theil's criticism in paragraph 2 above does not apply to Shannon's entropy, nor to HK($\theta = 1$).

Hannah and Kay estimate y_i by using the share of the ith firm in the total market valuation of $Q_t + U_{MQ}$ firm. The inclusion in the initial year of U_{MQ} relatively small unquoted firms, which subsequently merged with quoted firms, produces lower values of y_i, especially within group 2 containing the firms involved in mergers, than would be the case if the measurement were restricted to the Q firms listed on the Stock Exchange. The HK hypothetical entropy, calculated on the assumption that the mergers between the $Q_M + U_{MQ}$ firms took place in the initial year, decreases because the values of y_i in group 2, and hence $H(y)_{w2}$, decrease. The direction of change in $H(y)$ is correct, but the amount of the increase in concentration implied by this inverse measure is excessive because of the inclusion of U_{MQ} without including the $U - U_{MQ}$ unquoted firms.

REFERENCES

[1] Creedy, J., 'The Principle of Transfers and the Variance of Logarithms', *Oxford Bulletin of Economics and Statistics*, **39** (1977), pp. 152–8.

[2] Evely, R. and Little, I. M. D., *Concentration in British Industry* (CUP, Cambridge, 1960).

[3] Hannah, L., *The Rise of the Corporate Economy* (Methuen, London, 1976).

[4] Hannah, L. and Kay, J. A., *Concentration in Modern Industry* (Macmillan, London, 1977).

[5] Hart, P. E., 'Concentration and its Measurement in the UK', *Die Konzentration in der Wirtschaft*, H. Arndt (ed.), Vol. 1 (Duncker and Humblot, Berlin, 1960).

[6] ——, 'The Variance of the Logarithms and the Principle of Transfers', *University of Reading Discussion Paper in Economics*, Series A, No. 60 (1974).

[7] ——, 'Moment Distributions in Economics: an Exposition', *Journal of the Royal Statistical Society, Series A*, **138** (1975), pp. 423–34.

[8] Hart, P. E. and Prais, S. J., 'The Analysis of Business Concentration: a Statistical Approach', *Journal of the Royal Statistical Society, Series A*, **119** (1956), pp. 150–91.

[9] Ijiri, Y. and Simon, H. A., *Skew Distributions and the Size of Business Firms* (North-Holland, Amsterdam, 1977).

[10] National Institute of Economic and Social Research, *Company Income and Finance 1949–53* (NIESR, London, 1956).

[11] Prais, S. J., *The Evolution of Giant Firms in Britain* (CUP, Cambridge, 1976).

[12] Rényi, A., *Probability Theory* (North-Holland, Amsterdam, 1970).

[13] A Review of Monopolies and Mergers Policy, Cmnd. 7198 (1978).

[14] Savage, L. J., *The Foundations of Statistics* (Wiley, New York, 1954).

[15] Theil, H., *Statistical Decomposition Analysis* (North-Holand, Amsterdam, 1972).

[16] Wilson, C., *The History of Unilever*, Vol. II (Cassell, London, 1954).

THE JOURNAL OF INDUSTRIAL ECONOMICS
Volume XXVII March 1979 No. 3

PROFITABILITY, RISK AND MARKET STRUCTURE IN WEST GERMAN INDUSTRIES*

MANFRED NEUMANN, INGO BÖBEL AND ALFRED HAID

IN a competitive environment rates of return on capital tend to be randomly distributed around some normal rate of opportunity cost of capital that includes a remuneration for risk bearing. Consequently, profits persistently exceeding a normal level can, at least partly, be accounted for by market power of either sellers or buyers or both. Empirical studies of these relationships for West German industries have conspicuously been absent so far. In order to begin filling this gap we shall report the results of a study explaining the mean rates of return of the period from 1965 to 1973 in a large sample of West German joint stock companies by risk and market structure.

Besides risk, explanatory variables are the national degree of three-firm concentration, the export and import ratios, absolute and relative firm size, the rate of growth of sales of the individual firm, and finally the degree of product differentiation. The foreign trade ratios have been included as explanatory variables since in an open economy the relevant market obviously extends the national boundaries.

Unfortunately, there is so far no single comprehensive theory available accounting for the relationships between rates of return, risk and market structure. Various models have been put forward each being concerned with a specific partial relationship. They guided the selection of our explanatory variables. Further inspiration came from empirical studies of industries in the US and other countries (see Weiss [14], Böbel [1]).

I. RATES OF RETURN AND MARKET STRUCTURE: THE DATA

1. *Rate of Return*

The data on individual firms were obtained by utilizing published balance sheets of 334 industrial joint stock companies of West Germany. Of these companies 64 were drawn from the 'Hoppenstedt-Börsenführer' which contains data on the biggest German joint stock companies (subsequently referred to as 'HOPP-sample'). The rest was drawn from the 'Aktienführer der Bayerischen Hypotheken- und Wechselbank' (HYPO-sample). For each

* We gratefully acknowledge helpful comments on an earlier draft from Ernst Heuß, Alexis Jacquemin, Jürgen Müller, Horst Claus Recktenwald, Paul G. Reinhardt, participants of seminars at the University Bonn and the International Institute of Management in Berlin, the European editor of this journal, Louis Philips, and the anonymous referee. We are also indebted to the Hans Frisch-Stiftung in Nürnberg for financial support and to the Deutsches Patentamt in München for data on trade marks held by individual firms.

firm averages of individual data were computed over 1965–73. The selection of firms was guided by the availability of data over the entire period. The selection bias entailed by this procedure could not be avoided.

The rate of return is defined as the ratio of profits to equity capital (including reserves). Four alternative measures of profit and, consequently, four rates of return were employed, i.e. RR 1: net profit after taxation, RR 2: gross profit after taxation (=RR 1+depreciation), RR 3: net profit before taxation (=RR 1+taxes, except taxes on value added), RR 4: gross profit before taxation (=RR 3+depreciation). The usual objections concerning the reliability of published balance sheet data are most serious in the case of net profit after taxation. Actually it turned out that employing RR 1 did not produce sensible results. Employment of the remaining definitions of the rate of return, however, yielded quite similar results.[1] For economic reasons we should prefer gross profit before taxation because it reflects the earnings capacity of the firm. Any market power a firm may enjoy will exert its influence on the gross earnings of the firm.

Admittedly, the information contained in published balance sheet data may be biased. It can, however, be expected to be, on average, always biased in the same direction and so a cross-section analysis will not be impaired. If the bias should be variable over time it will be averaged out by taking means over nine years (1965–73).

The mean values of the alternatively defined rates of return and their coefficient of variation are listed in Table I.

It will be noted that the bigger firms, represented by the HOPP-sample, earn slightly higher rates of return than smaller firms. The coefficient of variation, on the other hand, is much larger in the sample of smaller firms.

TABLE I

MEAN VALUES (M) AND COEFFICIENT OF VARIATION (V) OF RATES OF RETURN IN PERCENTAGE

		HOPP (64)	*HYPO* (270)	*Total* (334)
Net profit after taxation	M	7·34	4·34	4·91
(RR 1)	V	29·48	286·10	229·10
Gross profit after taxation	M	31·86	30·60	30·84
(RR 2)	V	40·93	69·82	64·94
Net profit before taxation	M	37·06	32·51	33·39
(RR 3)	V	73·49	89·13	85·88
Gross profit before taxation	M	61·58	58·78	59·31
(RR 4)	V	59·85	67·97	66·32

[1] The simple correlation coefficients of the rates of return are listed in the following matrix.

RR	2	3	4
1	0·593	0·506	0·384
2		0·689	0·842
3			0·935

2. *Market Structure Variables*

The individual firms were adjoined to the respective three-digit industry where the bulk of the firm's activities is conducted. Averages of various market structure variables employed in the subsequent regression analysis are listed in Table II.

TABLE II

AVERAGES OF MARKET STRUCTURE VARIABLES

	HOPP	*HYPO*
Concentration	27·1316	24·0994
Export ratio	0·1904	0·1803
Import ratio	0·1340	0·1403
Relative size	0·0180	0·0015
Absolute size	0·0056	0·0032
Rate of firm growth	0·1010	0·0642
Trade mark ratio	0·1075	0·1054

II. DETERMINANTS OF THE RATE OF RETURN

1. *Risk*

For risk averters, according to the capital asset pricing model, there is

(i) among portfolios, a trade-off between the expected rate of return of a portfolio and the variance of the portfolio return;

(ii) in an equilibrium, the expected rate of return of a single asset is determined by the risk free rate of return available in the economy and the covariance of the return of this asset with the returns of the market portfolio (Fama and Miller [3]).

In studies concerning the US industry, the variance of the individual rate of return of a firm has been used as an index of risk (Fisher and Hall [4], Hurdle [6]). From a theoretical point of view, this hypothesis is obviously based on the tacit assumption that the single firm is considered by the investors as a portfolio. We do not believe that to be universally true. If the individual firm is viewed by the investors as an asset among others to be held in a portfolio it appears more reasonable to use the covariance as the appropriate measure of risk.

Actually, it turned out that the two samples had to be handled in a different way. For the big firms the covariance either did not significantly contribute to the explanation of the rate of return or it carried a wrong sign. For the smaller firms it was the variance which showed up with the wrong sign. We found it unreasonable to accept the implication that investors are risk lovers. An alternative and more plausible explanation seems to be that the big firms, being widely diversified, are considered as a portfolio by investors and managers. The smaller firms, on the other hand, are viewed as single assets by stockholders.

When it came to measuring the variance and covariance a close look at the data revealed that the mean rate of return of the firm under consideration and also the average rate of return of all West German firms, as published by the Deutsche Bundesbank, which was taken as an approximation for the rate of return of the market portfolio, displayed a downward trend. Therefore, we had to avoid confounding the relationship between the slopes of the trends and the variability of the rate of return over time which we intended to measure. We therefore computed trend free variances and covariances.

In Table III the appropriate risk measure always shows up significantly different from zero and with the theoretically expected sign. The results suggest that investors are risk averters and that risk bearing is, accordingly, compensated by a higher rate of return.

2. *Concentration*

Firm concentration can be considered as a shorthand expression, albeit an incomplete one, for the number and size distribution of suppliers. Theoretically we therefore expect a favourable influence of concentration on the rate of return. Such a relationship can be derived from the well-known Cournot model of oligopoly. According to this model profits are continually decreased if the number of competitors is increased in a comparative static experiment (Ruffin [13]). Fewness can furthermore favour collusion and can thus give rise to higher rates of profit.

In our study concentration is measured by the share in three-digit industries' sales of the three leading firms. We took an average of the degree of concentration of the years 1967, 1968, 1970 and 1972, as published by the Bundeskartellamt. Application of six-firm concentration did not make a significant difference. It is true that the three-digit classification cannot be considered to depict markets in an economically meaningful sense. It can, however, be presumed that a certain degree of three-digit concentration implies a similar degree of concentration in most higher digit industries making up a particular three-digit industry. It must nevertheless be admitted that some degree of inaccuracy is introduced by using the three-digit classification. But, for lack of data, we had no choice.

Actually, we found a distinctly positive relationship between the degree of concentration and profitability. The higher the degree of concentration in an industry the greater the rate of return of firms of this industry.

It will also be observed that concentration seems to exert a more pronounced impact on profitability in the case of the sample of smaller firms.

3. *Foreign Trade and the Relevant Market*

In an open economy the national market to which the degree of concentration pertains cannot be regarded as the relevant market. To account for the influence of foreign trade we first simple added the export and import ratio of the respective industry to the list of explanatory variables.

Table III

PROFITS AS DEPENDENT ON RISK AND MARKET STRUCTURE

	Gross profit before taxation (RR 4)								*Gross profit after taxation (RR 2)*		*Net profit before taxation (RR 3)*	
	HOPP-sample			*HYPO-sample*			*Total*[a]		*Total*		*Total*	
	(1)	(2)	(3)	(4)	(5)	(6)	(7)	(8)	(9)	(10)	(11)	(12)
Constant	0·660* (5·56)	0·347* (7·54)	0·920* (6·40)	0·418* (8·09)	0·201* (7·15)	0·531* (8·37)	0·456* (9·33)	0·554* (10·14)	0·233* (8·73)	0·248* (8·08)	0·234* (6·73)	0·315* (7·94)
Risk												
COV	—	—	—	48·669* (5·09)	47·378* (6·81)	26·496* (2·73)	25·592* (2·83)	24·782* (2·77)	9·449* (1·35)	9·689 (1·39)	25·194* (3·09)	23·815* (2·97)
VAR	3·708* (5·15)	2·354* (4·36)	3·171* (4·41)	—	—	—	3·450* (3·94)	3·641* (4·20)	2·052* (2·17)	2·078* (2·20)	10·606* (4·21)	12·160* (4·82)
Concentration												
Measured	0·005* (2·12)		0·007* (2·78)	0·009* (7·21)		0·009* (7·01)	0·008* (7·17)	0·008* (7·59)	0·002* (3·85)	0·003* (3·87)	0·006* (7·78)	0·007* (8·28)
Modified		0·002 (1·45)			0·003* (3·88)							
Export ratio	−0·776* (2·74)	−0·241* (2·02)	−0·634* (2·29)	−0·538* (4·10)	−0·114 (1·47)	−0·502* (3·71)	−0·591* (5·00)	−0·509* (4·24)	−0·149* (2·22)	−0·141* (2·05)	−0·382* (4·40)	−0·308* (3·48)
Import ratio	−0·405 (1·47)	—	−0·418 (1·60)	−0·318* (1·66)	—	−0·356* (1·81)	−0·342* (2·05)	−0·341* (2·07)	−0·112 (1·18)	−0·113 (1·19)	−0·336* (2·74)	0·336* (2·79)
Firm size												
Relative	−1·459* (1·71)	−0·642* (1·83)		−6·457 (1·09)	1·226 (0·38)		−2·295* (2·20)		−0·798 (1·36)		−1·671* (2·17)	
Absolute			−59·908* (2·95)			−36·348* (2·40)		−37·802* (3·57)		−5·854 (0·97)		−31·465* (3·98)
Growth of firm	−0·547 (0·87)	−0·355 (1·40)	−0·503 (0·83)	0·818* (3·45)	0·552* (4·20)	1·017* (4·22)	0·819* (3·73)	0·922* (4·19)	0·601* (4·83)	0·608* (4·81)	0·527* (3·27)	0·612* (3·81)
Product differentiation	0·266* (2·14)	0·076 (1·48)	0·159 (1·26)	0·068 (0·95)	0·112* (2·86)	0·097 (1·31)	0·144* (2·22)	0·120* (1·86)	0·146* (3·98)	0·144* (3·88)	0·002 (0·05)	−0·019 (0·40)
R^2	0·6683	0·5365	0·6979	0·3953	0·3483	0·3618	0·3923	0·4068	0·2467	0·2446	0·3838	0·4039
$\bar{R}^2$	0·6268	0·4877	0·6601	0·3792	0·334	0·3448	0·3793	0·3903	0·2281	0·2260	0·3686	0·3874

t-ratios in parentheses.
* Significant at least at 5% level (one tailed test).
[a] COV for HYPO-sample. VAR for HOPP-sample.

As can be seen from Table III both the export and the import ratio exert an adverse impact on profitability. Moreover, the unfavourable influence seems to be primarily due to exports. The more common view that imports stimulate competition and thus depress profits receives much less support by the present findings.

On second thought, however, our results are quite plausible and should have been anticipated. First, the effect of imports is comparatively ambiguous. As far as imported products are competing with domestic ones imports give rise to an increase of competition in the respective market. A great part of German imports, however, consists of raw materials and other industrial inputs. Low prices of these imports will have a favourable effect on profits of domestic firms. Second, the impact of foreign competition will primarily be reflected in exports. Since unrestricted international trade favours specialization domestic firms gain new markets abroad and are, at the same time, supplanted from their former domestic markets. A high share of exports in an industry's sales really means that the firms have themselves adjusted to the pressures of international competition. The adverse impact of exports on profitability is supporting evidence for this interpretation.[2]

An alternative hypothesis would assert that firms are able to behave like discriminating monopolists. Domestic and foreign markets should both be expected to contribute to the monopolist's profits. To test this hypothesis we constructed a modified concentration measure

$$\frac{\text{(Sales} - \text{Exports) of the three leading firms}}{\text{(Sales} + \text{Imports} - \text{Exports) of the industry}}$$

representing the ratio of the supply to the domestic market of the three leading firms to the total supply coming forward in the domestic market. The rate of return is then viewed to be determined by the modified concentration ratio reflecting the degree of competition prevailing in the domestic market, and the export ratio, and, additionally, other variables as listed in Table III.

Unfortunately, we were unable to get hold of data of the leading firms' export ratios. Therefore we took the industry's export ratio instead. Since the larger firms usually realize larger export ratios than smaller firms do the modified concentration ratio will be biased upward by our approximation.

The results are reported in Table III (cols. 2 and 5). The overall performance of the model is weak in comparison with the original model. Moreover, the export ratio retains the negative sign. This finding contradicts the hypothesis that exports should have a favourable impact on profitability. So our original interpretation of the export ratio as a measure of competitiveness seems to be more appropriate.

[2] A similar interpretation of the inverse relationship between price-cost margins and export ratios (as well as import ratios) found for a sample of European countries has been put forward by Pagoulatos and Sorensen [12]. It should, however, be noted that exports have been found to enhance profitability in the UK (Khalilzadeh-Shirazi [11]).

It might, however, be objected that the depressing effect of the export ratio on profits is due to the influence of the continuing revaluation of the German mark. This objection can easily be disposed of. Had German firms possessed sufficient market power the worsening of revenues engendered by the revaluations would have been avoided by raising prices. This apparently turned out to be impossible. So it would indeed appear that a high export ratio is indicative of lessened market power. Actually, the adverse impact of exports on profitability can be found to be even more pronounced in the sub-period 1965–69, where the rate of exchange was relatively stable, than in the later period 1969–73 with greater exchange rate instability.

4. *Relative and Absolute Firm Size*

According to a widespread folklore big firms enjoy economies of large scale and are thus able to earn higher profits than smaller firms. Our regression results do not, however, reveal any such superiority of big firms.[3]

Relative firm size is measured by the ratio between individual sales to average sales of all firms in the respective industry. The regression coefficient for this variable is always negative and generally significantly so. Thus, within the range of firm sizes under study smaller German firms tend to be more profitable.

This result is confirmed if, in the regression, relative size is replaced by absolute firm size as measured by the logarithm of a firm's assets. As reported in Table III, absolute size exerts a pronounced adverse influence on profitability.

The reasons for the inverse relationship between size and profitability are not yet clear. One cannot, without further supporting evidence, infer from our findings that big firms are subject to diseconomies of firm size that might be traced to either diseconomies of scale or *X*-inefficiency or both. It can also be argued that bigger firms, being more diversified and thus having a lower covariance with the market portfolio's rate of return, are to a lesser extent exposed to risk than smaller firms and can therefore content themselves with a lower rate of return.

It will first be recollected that the variability of rates of return among firms, as measured by the coefficient of variation, is substantially greater for smaller firms (see Table I, HYPO-sample) than for bigger ones (HOPP-sample). It thus appears that smaller firms are indeed exposed to considerable risk.

Furthermore, Table IV gives some indication that size and risk are inversely related.

Such, however, is only true for the big firms (HOPP-sample). No such relationship could be found for smaller firms where diversification is less probable. Since an inverse association between firms' size and profitability

[3] Similar results were obtained by Jacquemin and Cardon [8] and Jenny and Weber [10]. See also Jacquemin and Phlips [9].

TABLE IV

RISK AS DEPENDENT ON SIZE[a, b]

	Relative size		Absolute size	
	HOPP	*HYPO*	*HOPP*	*HYPO*
VAR	−0·1622 (1·05)	—	−8·7729* (2·77)	—
COV	—	0·0016 (0·04)	—	0·0465 (0·51)

[a] VAR (COV) $= a + b^{*}$ size $+ u$.
[b] t-ratios in parentheses.
* Significant at least at 5% level.

was also found for this group of firms it cannot, in this case, be explained but by diseconomies of firm size. It would thus appear that the inverse relationship between relative firm size and profitability, which was found for all groups of firms, can be accounted for by both the effects of risk and diseconomies of firm size.

There is, however, a seeming contradiction between the adverse impact of size on profitability, as revealed by our regression analysis, and the average rate of return of smaller firms (Table I). In view of the higher average ratio of three-firm concentration within the HOPP-sample we suggest that the higher rate of return of the big firms can be explained by market power. Obviously, the adverse impact of diseconomies of firms size has been overcompensated by the effects of market power enjoyed by large firms.

5. *Growth of Firms*

The average rate of growth of a firm as measured by the slope of the logarithmic time trend of its sales, generally displays a favourable impact on its rate of return except for the sample of bigger firms.[4]

It remains to account for the favourable effect of growth on profits in the case of smaller firms. It might be suggested that smaller firms, being more flexible, tend to take chances more readily than their bigger rivals. It may also be that smaller firms can profitably exploit chances by expanding sales at unreduced prices.

6. *Product Differentiation*

Product differentiation and the marketing goodwill created by past advertising can operate as an effective barrier to entry and can thus give protection from competitive pressure. The rate of return if calculated on the basis of book values of equity capital will be comparatively higher. Should the goodwill capital be included into the base on which the rate of return is computed

[4] This result seems to cast doubt on the validity of the well-known limit pricing model of Gaskins [5] according to which the dominant firms should be favoured by the growth of demand. Our findings support the modified version of the Gaskin model by Ireland [7] which implies that the growth of demand has no effect whatsoever on the profitability of the leading firms.

only a normal rate of profit would be found unless profits are augmented by other factors.

The value of the marketing goodwill of a firm is, of course, not amenable to direct measurement. In West Germany, also, the indirect route of reconstructing the marketing goodwill from past advertising outlays is blocked by the absence of any published data on current advertising expenses. Therefore, we had to find another proxy for marketing goodwill. We noted that effective advertising is usually based on a trade mark that serves as the focus of customers' attention. Furthermore, the greater the variety of products a firm supplies the more trade marks are necessary for effective marketing. This reasoning suggests, first, some weak association between advertising intensity and the implied equilibrium stock of goodwill on the one hand and the number of trade marks of a firm on the other one, and, second, the number of trade marks held by a firm and the degree of heterogeneity of its supply.

It may also happen that some trade marks are only held in order to impede entry for potential competitors.

Guided by these observations we used the number of trade marks registered by the individual firm with the German Patent Office per unit of equity capital as a proxy for the height of barriers to entry created by product differentiation and marketing goodwill.

We expected a positive relationship between this variable and the rate of return. This expectation was fully borne out by our regression results (Table III).

For lack of satisfactory data we were unable to check for the existence of a leverage effect. That was only possible in a somewhat smaller sample. As will be reported elsewhere in more detail, we found a significant leverage effect. It left, however, largely unaffected the explanatory power of the variables examined in the present study. In view of considerable correlation between the debt equity ratio and the other explanatory variables we suggest that the debt equity ratio should be considered as an endogenous variable. Thus the statistical influence of the debt equity ratio on profitability will to a great extent already be captured by the explanatory variables of our model.

7. *Explanatory Power of the Model*

The reliability of the results obtained for gross profits before taxation can be checked by looking at the regression results obtained for alternative concepts of the rate of return. As the last columns of Table III reveal the results are not materially altered by employing net profits before taxation and gross profits after taxation.

The relative importance of the various variables can be assessed by computing elasticities. This is done in the Table V for the total of all firms according to Table III (cols. 7 and 8).

TABLE V

ELASTICITY OF GROSS RATE OF RETURN WITH RESPECT TO EXPLANATORY VARIABLES

	Elasticity col. 7	*Elasticity col. 8*
Risk [a]		
COV	0·0314	0·0304
VAR	0·0468	0·0494
Concentration	0·3287	0·3495
Export ratio	−0·1814	−0·1562
Import ratio	−0·0801	−0·0799
Size		
Absolute	—	−0·2358
Relative	−0·0182	—
Rate of firm growth	0·0983	0·1106
Product differentiation	0·0256	0·0214

[a] Weighted by 64/334 for VAR and by 270/334 for COV.

It is worth noting that the favourable influence of concentration on profitability is not entirely cancelled by the impact of foreign competition.

Since the growth rate of the firm and the risk variables are based on time series estimators there may be errors in these variables. It is known that in this case the slope of the regression is downward biased and the intercept is upward biased. Both estimates are also inconsistent. It is difficult to appraise the amount of the actual bias that is present.

III. CAUSES AND CONSEQUENCES OF CONCENTRATION

1. *Determinants of Concentration*

Thus far the measured degree of concentration was treated as an exogenous variable. That may be incorrect. Concentration may be the consequence of more basic factors. One is tempted to ask whether concentration is an inevitable consequence of technological forces or whether it is the result of efforts of firms to obtain market power. In order to shed some light on these questions we first tried to explain the degree of concentration by a series of economic and technological variables. The result is given in Table VI.

(a) *Barriers to entry*. The most important factor explaining concentration seems to be the minimum efficient firm size. It is measured by that firm size at which 50% of an industry's total sales volume is reached. Although this threshold inside the cumulative frequency distribution is somewhat arbitrary it may nevertheless produce a reliable rank order of industries according to such a firm size that is required for survival. It can safely be assumed that the choice of an alternative threshold would not materially alter that rank order.

If the threshold is comparatively high the existing firms enjoy protection from new competition. The normal process of exit of existing firms will then give rise to a relatively high degree of concentration. Nothing is implied by

TABLE VI

DETERMINANTS OF CONCENTRATION IN 25 INDUSTRIES

Variable	*Regression coefficient (t-ratio)*
Minimum efficient firm size	0·10* (4·42)
Growth of industry demand	−61·34 (1·49)
Capital-output ratio	−4·86 (0·86)
Export ratio	28·10* (1·80)
Import ratio	−2·67 (0·15)
R^2	0·6199

* Significant at least at 5% level (one-tailed test).

this analysis with regard to the underlying causes for the existence of those barriers to entry. They may be technological in nature. But since Minimum Efficient Firm Size, in our study, does not refer to establishments, but to firms, a host of different forces may be at work.

(b) *Growth of industry demand*. The growth of industry demand seems to exert a restraining influence on concentration, probably by favouring entry of newcomers. This results is consonant with our previous finding that profitability of smaller firms is enhanced by growth.

(c) *Foreign trade*. The export ratio displays a favourable influence on concentration. The meaning of this finding is not quite clear.

Possibly, to assert itself in foreign markets a firm must have some minimum size. Consequently, concentrated industries, where the minimum efficient firm size is large, may enjoy comparative advantages as exporters. Such an interpretation may, however, be premature. It certainly cannot be inferred from the mere positive association between the export ratio and the degree of concentration. Taking into consideration all our previous findings an alternative interpretation might have more appeal.

Trade liberalization in the post-war period and especially the realization of the European Common Market engendered an enlargement of markets. It lent impetus to increased international specialization and gave thus rise to higher export ratios in most industries. Consequently, competitive pressures increased and profits tended to be eroded. Recall the negative impact of the export ratio on rates of return. It could have been offset by the post-war concentration movement that gave thus rise to a stabilization of profits. It can therefore be regarded as the natural response by European firms.

If this view is correct increasing concentration should be expected to go along with increasing export ratios. Such is in fact the case. For 25 West

German industries over 1962–72, we obtain a simple correlation coefficient 0·36 (t=1·72) between changes of concentration on the one hand and changes of the export ratio on the other one.

It remains to be seen whether the increasing concentration was the result of anonymous forces or whether it was deliberately created in response to the worsening of profitability.

2. *Whence Concentration?*

If concentration were a policy objective of firms to counteract the eroding impact on profits engendered by foreign trade the measured degree of concentration should be expected to exert an influence on profitability exceeding the effect of concentration as far as it is solely the consequence of anonymous forces. This hypothesis was tested by replacing the degree of measured concentration by its estimated value as determined by the variables enumerated in Table VI. The result is given in Table VII.

In comparison with the regression of Table III, the explanatory power of the model has remarkably increased. For the sample of the bigger firms more than three-quarters, and for the smaller firms two-fifths of the variance of the rate of return can be accounted for by the independent variables.

With regard to the impact of concentration the results reported in Table III and those of Table VII reveal a far reaching similarity. Although the coefficients of regression are not significantly different it may be observed that the estimated value of concentration exerts a more pronounced influence on the rate of return than measured concentration does. Again, since

TABLE VII

BASIC DETERMINANTS OF GROSS PROFIT BEFORE TAXATION

Variable	*HOPP*	*HYPO*	*Total*
Constant	0·7780*	0·4191*	0·4328*
	(6·10)	(6·32)	(7·61)
Risk			
COV		28·2454*	26·9327*
		(3·01)	(3·13)
VAR	2·5966*		3·3279*
	(4·10)		(3·99)
Estimated concentration	0·0097*	0·0097*	0·0096*
	(5·46)	(8·35)	(9·51)
Export ratio	−0·7755*	−0·4943*	−0·5323*
	(3·92)	(3·79)	(4·70)
Import ratio	−0·3605	−0·3060	−0·2834*
	(1·61)	(1·61)	(1·79)
Absolute size	−46·7584*	−27·7441*	−26·8591*
	(2·78)	(1·91)	(2·67)
Rate of firm growth	−0·4635	1·0710*	0·9772*
	(0·92)	(4·61)	(4·66)
Product differentiation	0·0741	0·0596	0·0742
	(0·67)	(0·83)	(1·19)
R^2	0·7756	0·4015	0·4532
$\bar{R}^2$	0·7476	0·3855	0·4397

* Significant at least at 5% level (one-tailed test).

estimated concentration is subject to errors in the variable the estimated slope of the regression for estimated concentration will be biased downward.

We can infer from the present result that the rate of return is significantly affected by concentration only insofar as concentration is determined by the variables listed in Table VI and is thus mainly determined by economies of large scale. Once brought forth, the effect of concentration on profitability may work via the mechanism suggested by the Cournot model or by favouring collusive arrangements. The latter is, however, less probable since the actual degree of concentration exerts not so pronounced an influence on profitability in the case of big firms as it does in the case of smaller firms. If collusion would be dominant it should be expected to be most prevalent among the leading firms of an industry. Such is obviously not the case.

We could not find any evidence that concentration was deliberately created to improve profitability by obtaining monopolistic power. It is more likely that both the increased concentration and dependence on foreign trade was brought about by similar forces.

IV. CONCLUDING REMARKS

We found that risk and market structure on the side of supply account for a considerable part of the rate of return of German joint stock companies. On the other hand, the present study is just a beginning in the area of German industrial organization in which quantitative analysis is badly needed. Without claiming optimality for our specifications, we feel some important insights have been gained.

Many deficiencies remain. One of them is that buyers' market power was not dealt with. Another is that interdependencies between the explanatory variables of our model have not been systematically investigated. It remains to be seen whether additional insights can be obtained by utilizing a simultaneous equations approach.

UNIVERSITÄT ERLANGEN-NÜRNBERG

APPENDIX

AVERAGE THREE-FIRM CONCENTRATION RATIOS

Chemical industry	27·2
Petroleum processing	49·5
Iron-producing industry	32·6
Quarrying	8·8
NE-metal industry	30·9
Rubber and asbestos processing	34·2
Mechanical wood pulp-, chemical wood pulp, paper- and millboard producing industry	29·0

Sawmills and wood processing industry	4·0
Unweighted average concentration ratio for eight producer goods industries	26·6
Steel construction	10·8
Machinery construction	9·9
Electrotechnics	32·1
Vehicle construction	57·9
Iron-, metal-, and tin-ware industry	5·8
Precision mechanics, optics and watches	15·3
Ship construction	61·0
Unweighted average concentration ratio for seven investment goods industries	27·5
Textiles	3·9
Clothing industry	3·8
Plastics processing industry	8·3
Paper- and millboard processing industry	10·8
Glass	27·7
Leather processing and shoe industry	14·3
Leather producing industry	24·0
Ceramics	25·1
Music instruments, toys, jewellery, and sports apparatuses	7·5
Food industry (including tobacco processing industry, average)	42·9
Unweighted average concentration ratio for nine consumer goods industries, plus food industry	18·3

DEFINITION OF VARIABLES

Rate of return: firm's profits divided by equity capital (including reserves)
RR 1: net profit after taxation
RR 2: gross profit after taxation (RR 1 + depreciation)
RR 3: net profit before taxation (RR 1 + taxes, except taxes on value added)
RR 4: gross profit before taxation (RR 3 + depreciation)
(RR 1 – RR 4: average of nine years, 1965–73)

Concentration: share in three-digit industries' sales of the three leading firms; average of four years (1967, 1968, 1970, 1972)

Export ratio: exports of the commodities of an industry divided by the total turnover of the industry; average of four years (1966, 1968, 1970, 1972)

Import ratio: imports of the commodities of an industry divided by the total turnover of the industry; average of four years (1966, 1968, 1970, 1972)

Rate of firm growth: slope of the logarithmic time trend of the firm's sales

Trade mark ratio: number of trade marks registered by the firms divided by equity capital; average of nine years (1965–73)

Capital–output ratio of an industry: average of four years (1966, 1968, 1970, 1972)

Growth of industry demand: slope of the logarithmic time trend of the industry's turnover

Minimum efficient firm size: firm size at which 50% of an industry's total turnover is reached

Relative firm size: sales of the firms divided by the average sales of all firms of an industry; average of nine years (1965–73)

Absolute firm size: logarithm of the firms' assets

Risk (COV): trend-free covariance between the mean rate of return of the firm and the average rate of return of all West German firms

Risk (VAR): trend-free variance of the firms' rate of return.

DATA SOURCES

Bayerische Hypotheken- und Wechselbank (ed.), Wegweiser durch deutsche Aktiengesellschaften, verschiedene Jahrgänge 1969–1975. München, 1970–76.

Verlag Hoppenstedt (ed.), Börsenführer—Stock Guide. Darmstadt, 1976.

Bericht des Bundeskartellamtes über seine Tätigkeit im Jahre 1973 sowie über die Lage und Entwicklung auf seinem Arbeitsgebiet (§50 GWB), BT-Drucksache 7/2250, Bonn, 1974.

Bericht des Bundeskartellamtes über seine Tätigkeit im Jahre 1975 sowie über die Lage und Entwicklung auf seinem Arbeitsgebiet (§50 GWB). BT-Drucksache 7/5390, Bonn, 1976.

Statistisches Bundesamt, Fachserie D—Industrie und Handwerk—Reihe I: Betriebe und Unternehmen der Industrie: I. Betriebe: Beschäftigung und Umsatz. Stuttgart-Mainz, 1962 und 1971.

Statistisches Bundesamt, Fachserie L—Finanzen und Steuern, Reihe 7 (Umsatzsteuern). Stuttgart-Mainz, 1968 und 1972.

Statistisches Bundesamt, Statistisches Jahrbuch für die Bundesrepublik Deutschland, verschiedene Jahrgänge 1965–1974. Stuttgart-Mainz, 1966–75.

R. Krengel/E. Baumgart/A. Boneß/R. Pischner/K. Droege, Produktionsvolumen und -potential, Produktionsfaktoren der Industrie im Gebiet der Bundesrepublik Deutschland, Statistische Kennziffern, 16. Folge, Berlin 1975 bzw. 18. Folge. Berlin, 1976.

Deutsche Bundesbank, Monatsberichte der Deutschen Bundesbank, 27. Jahrgang, Nr. 11. November 1975.

REFERENCES

[1] Böbel, I., Industrial Organization: Eine Übersicht über vorliegende empirische Untersuchungen zur Beziehung zwischen Gewinn und verschiedenen Marktstrukturparametern sowie zur Messung der durch Marktmacht verursachten Wohlfahrtsverluste (Demokrit Verlag, Tübingen, 1978).

[2] Dorfman, R. and Steiner, P. O., 'Optimal Advertising and Optimal Quality', *American Economic Review*, **44** (5) (December 1954), pp. 826–36.

[3] Fama, E. F. and Miller, M. H., *The Theory of Finance* (Holt, Rinehart and Winston Inc., New York, 1972).

[4] Fisher, I. N. and Hall, G. R., 'Risk and Corporate Rates of Return', *Quarterly Journal of Economics*, **83** (1) (February 1969), pp. 79–92.

[5] Gaskins, D. W., 'Dynamic Limit Pricing: Optimal Pricing Under Threat of New Entry', *Journal of Economic Theory*, **3** (3) (September 1971), pp. 306–22.

[6] Hurdle, G. J., 'Leverage, Risk, Market Structure and Profitability', *Review of Economics and Statistics*, **56** (4) (November 1974), pp. 478–85.

[7] Ireland, N. J., 'Concentration and the Growth of Market Demand. A Comment on Gaskins' Limit Pricing Model', *Journal of Economic Theory*, **5** (2) (October 1972), pp. 303–5.

[8] Jacquemin, A. P. and Cardon de Lichtbuer, M., 'Size Structure, Stability and Performance of the Largest British and EEC Firms', *European Economic Review*, **4** (1973), pp. 393–408.

[9] Jacquemin, A. P. and Phlips, L., 'Concentration, Size and Performance in European Firms', in *Markets, Corporate Behaviour and the State*, A. P. Jacquemin and H. W. de Jong (ed.) (Martinus Nijhoff, The Hague, 1976).

[10] Jenny, F. and Weber, A. P., 'Profit Rates and Structural Variables in French Manufacturing Industries', *European Economic Review*, **7** (1976), pp. 187–206.

[11] KHALILZADEH-SHIRAZI, J., 'Market Structure and Price-Cost Margins in United Kingdom Manufacturing Industries', *Review of Economics and Statistics*, **LVI** (1) (February 1974), pp. 67–76.

[12] PAGOULATOS, E. and SORENSEN, R., 'Foreign Trade, Concentration and Profitability in Open Economies', *European Economic Review*, **8** (1976), pp. 255–67.

[13] RUFFIN, R. J., 'Cournot Oligopoly and Competitive Behaviour', *Review of Economic Studies*, **38** (3) (October 1971), pp. 493–502.

[14] WEISS, L. G., 'Quantitative Studies in Industrial Organization', in *Frontiers of Quantitative Economics*, M. D. Intriligator (ed.) (North-Holland Publishing Co., Amsterdam, 1971).

THE JOURNAL OF INDUSTRIAL ECONOMICS
Volume XXVII March 1979 No. 3

FUEL ADJUSTMENT MECHANISMS AND ECONOMIC EFFICIENCY

David P. Baron and Raymond R. De Bondt*

I. INTRODUCTION

Fuel adjustment mechanisms used in electricity and natural gas pricing are formulae that provide for automatic adjustments in output prices in response to changes in the factor prices of boiler fuels and wellhead gas, respectively. Because these adjustments are made automatically, regulatory commissions do not exercise direct review of the appropriateness of the adjustments although they do generally have authority to determine the form of the formulae used.[1] The purpose of this paper is to investigate the implications of these mechanisms for economic efficiency, and the analysis will focus on fuel adjustment clauses for electricity rates, since they have been the subject of the most concern in the US.[2]

Fuel adjustment mechanisms were first utilized in the US during World War I to enable the regulatory process to function in response to the rapid increase in coal prices.[3] 'By 1958, the vast majority of electric utilities had adopted fuel clauses . . . most fuel clauses, however, were limited to commercial and industrial users . . . The percentage of utilities having residential fuel clauses rose from 35% in 1970 to 65% in 1973' [19, p. 5]. As an indication of the pervasiveness of these mechanisms, they are currently allowed in all but five states, Montana, Oregon, Utah, Washington and Wyoming, and in Idaho and Nevada 'FACs are not used or are denied to some categories of utilities' [20, p. VI]. Of the 82 electric utilities responding to an October 3rd, 1974, questionnaire of the Edison Electric Institute, 81 reported that an FAC was included in their tariffs [8]. 'An FPC survey as of January 1st, 1974, showed that 65% of the larger privately owned utilities had fuel adjustment clauses in their residential schedules, 77% had such clauses in their commercial schedules, and 83% in their industrial schedules' [13, p. 315].

* The authors would like to thank Bengt Holmstrom and John Hiller for their helpful comments. The first author's work has been supported in part by a grant from the National Science Foundation, Grant No. SOC 77-07251.

1 A NERA survey indicated that

> In 13 jurisdictions (see Table A) the fuel clause format and/or formula is prescribed by the commission and in 27 others must be approved by the commission. In 33 jurisdictions each change in the adjustment itself is subject to commission review . . . (NERA, 'The Fuel Adjustment Clause: A Survey of Criticisms, Justifications and its Application in the Various Jurisdictions', reprinted as Appendix 1 of [19, p. 51]).

2 After this paper was completed, a report [16] by the Price Commission in the United Kingdom was obtained that discusses a number of similar issues in the UK context.

3 Trigg [17] has provided a study of the origin of these mechanisms.

The House Subcommittee on Oversight and Investigation [19] has estimated the magnitude of the rate increases resulting from fuel adjustments as follows:

> In 1974, following the decision of the Organization of Petroleum Exporting Countries (OPEC) to raise the price of oil, utility fossil fuel costs increased 86·8%, an increase of nearly \$6·2 billion over 1973 (p. 2).'
>
> 'The price of electricity rose \$8 billion in 1974. Automatically two-thirds of that increase was incurred through automatic fuel adjustment clauses (p. 1).'

A study prepared by the Congressional Research Service for the Senate Subcommittee on Intergovernmental Relations and the Subcommittee on Reports, Accounting, and Management indicated that in 1976 electric utilities received rate increases estimated to amount to '\$8·5 billion—\$6 billion through FACs and \$2·5 billion through formal rate cases' [20, p. V].

The magnitude of these cost increases and the fact that they were made without public review has lead to strong criticism of this regulatory instrument. The House Subcommittee on Oversight and Investigations has concluded:

> . . . The Subcommittee finds that fuel adjustment clauses, in any form, are unwise, unnecessary, unworkable, and unfair. Fuel clauses, in the Subcommittee's view, moreover, may be the forerunner of a campaign to undermine utility regulation by means of a full range of automatic adjustment clauses that will render utility commissions virtually powerless while reducing utility management to the not so fine art of adjusting monthly consumer electric bills to reflect the industry's unchecked cost increases [19, p. 1].

The proponents of automatic adjustment mechanisms argue that these mechanisms are necessary to enable utilities to maintain financial viability and to raise capital. The objective of a fuel adjustment clause as stated by the FPC [18] is as follows: '. . . our purpose is protection of the consumers while keeping utilities whole for increases in fuel costs . . . '.[4] Utilities appear to interpret this objective as meaning that fuel adjustment clauses should operate to enhance rates of return rather than simply to match revenues with increases in fuel costs. For example, in response to charges by Silvia M. Siegel that Southern California Edison and Pacific Gas and

[4] The use of automatic adjustment mechanisms may have other benefits. The New Mexico Public Service Commission has stated that:

> In short, this commission and its staff are subject to the tyranny of continuous rate cases, and our other regulatory responsibilities are neglected [14, p. 120].
>
> Lastly, this commission and its staff are also benefited by the new method in that it enables us to concentrate on those neglected areas of regulation and supervision where we may effectively influence events before they develop and, thus, better serve the consumer and public interests [14, p. 138].

Electric Company has overcollected on their FACs, a P.G. and E. spokesman stated

> P.G. and E.'s other cost increases more than offset any 'profits' that it might have gained from short run overcollection under the fuel clause.
>
> A Southern California Edison official, in response to Ms Siegel's allegations, concluded that 'The ultimate test of the fairness of the fuel clause should be the level of rate of return earned by the utility' [19, p. 6].

Whether fuel adjustment clauses are intended to match revenue changes with cost changes or to enhance rates of return, the desire for these automatic adjustment mechanisms results from the processing lag[5] inherent in the rate review process. In approving a comprehensive adjustment mechanism for the Public Service Company of New Mexico, the New Mexico Public Service Commission clearly stated this view.

> In short, the utility has lost all stability and reliability of common stock earnings in the view of investors, and the restoration of his allowed level of earnings, which can be prospective only and not retroactive, must await the outcome of yet another protracted and expensive general rate proceeding, at the conclusion of which the dismal cycle of declining earning begins again [18, p. 129].

The length of the processing period varies among jurisdictions, and according to the Edison Electric Institute

> Recent data, however, suggest that the average time period necessary to complete a rate case from initial filing to the effective date of the new rates, may have stabilized. From just under 9·5 months for cases decided in 1971, the average lag grew to 10 months in 1972 and to nearly 10·5 months in 1973. In 1974, the average case 'life' was also just under 10·5 months [19, p. 112].

Opponents of automatic adjustment mechanisms argue that the adverse effects on a firm's financial strength that result during the processing lag period can be diminished without abdicating regulatory responsibility not only by reducing the processing lag but also by granting interim rate relief and by using future test periods. 'Nearly, 38% of the cases for which final decisions were rendered in 1974 involved interim increases prior to the concluding actions' [19, p. 112]. For cases settled between January 1st, 1976, and March 31st, 1977, 45 of the 166 cases (27%) involved interim rates in effect while the case was in progress.[6] A future test period 'permits

[5] The term 'processing lag' is used by Joskow to refer to the time period between the initiation of a request for a rate change and its final implementation.

[6] The data source is [9].

rates to be established on the basis of estimated costs which will be incurred at the time the rates go into effect as opposed to the more common practice of establishing rates based on costs incurred in the past' [19, p. 113]. There is however little normative theory to guide a commission in determining the amount of an interim rate increase and many commissions are reluctant to grant rates based on forecasts as is necessary with the use of future test periods.[7]

A second criticism of fuel adjustment clauses is that they can be manipulated by utilities to the detriment of consumers. While there are some instances of manipulation cited by the House Subcommittee on Oversight and Investigations [19] and by the Consumers' Union [7], FPC audits, according to W. W. Lindsay, 'do not reveal any widespread effort to "rip off" American consumers of electricity by way of improper administration of fuel clauses' [12, p. 10].

A third argument against fuel adjustment clauses is that they may result in increases in output prices due to higher fuel costs even though average costs are decreasing because of, for example, productivity gains. This, however, appears to be more of a problem of the inability of a commission, and perhaps the unwillingness of the utility, to adjust prices in response to costs that change over time. Even without a fuel adjustment mechanism this problem is likely to be present.[8]

[7] The House Subcommittee on Oversight and Investigations concluded

> With adequate staffing and resources there is no reason why utility commissions cannot significantly reduce the present 10·5 months needed to complete the average electric utility rate case. Should a commission, however, prove incapable of keeping up with its workload, utilities can be granted interim rate relief subject to final commission review and refund. ... The interim rate procedure can be designed, moreover, to provide consumers with safeguards to mitigate against the issuance of arbitrary interim rate increases without detracting from the ability of such proceedings to grant utilities the means to cope with fast rising fuel costs. Such safeguards to include, for example, a public notice and the right to challenge industry subcommissions on the need for interim rate relief and a requirement that commissions grant interim rate relief on the basis of a written decision [18, p. 29].

The primary weakness of this policy alternative is the difficulty in setting an interim rate *before* hearings and staff investigation can take place. W. W. Lindsay of the Federal Power Commission states

> ... interim rate relief is not an acceptable substitute for automatic adjustment. It takes time and money to prepare an application for interim rate relief, and it takes time and effort for a regulatory agency to reach a considered judgment on the extent to which such relief should be granted ... the interim rate tehnique during a period of rapidly rising costs means that the utility will be collecting a large amount of its revenue subject to refund with the attendant uncertainty and adverse impact on capital costs that this entails ... if fuel costs move downward rapidly ... a proceeding to initiate a rate reduction, unless initiated by the utility itself, could only be brought under Section 206 of the Federal Power Act. This means that no rate reduction could be effected by the Commission except after notice and opportunity for hearing and the issuance of a final Commission order all of which could require years [12, p. 12].

[8] Another criticism made by the Congressional Research Service [20] is that the fuel price adjustments are being 'rolled into' basic rates which may retard rate reductions when fuel costs are falling. If the automatic adjustment clause operates symmetrically to pass on fuel cost decreases as well as increases, this argument appears to be an issue of labeling rather than of regulatory efficacity.

A fourth criticism is that the adjustments have been extended to more than just the factor price of fuel and thus represent the automatic pass through of endogenous operating costs rather than exogenous factor price changes. A Congressional Research Service survey indicated that of the 36 commissions that provided information on the costs included in the FACs under their jurisdiction[9]

> . . . in addition to changes in fossil fuel charge, 11 commissions included nuclear fuel costs in the calculation of their FACs; two commissions included hydro-power; one commission included geothermal; 25 included purchased power; 22 included line losses; 18 commissions included transportation charges; 14 had an efficiency factor; six commissions included taxes and fees; six included fuel handling costs; three FACs included fuel-related salaries and labor; one included wheeling charges; one included an allowance for uncollectable expenses; and one included a lag correction factor [20, p. 21].

It is clear that although these costs may be incurred in relation to the usage of fuel, they are endogenous rather than exogenous costs.

A fifth and perhaps most damaging criticism of fuel adjustment mechanisms is that they weaken incentives for efficiency, since if utilities can pass on all fuel cost increases, they may have no incentive to choose the least-cost fuel supply. Critics argue that a solution to this incentive problem is to allow utilities to pass on only a portion of the fuel price increases. With respect to this issue the FPC in Order No. 517 opposed this approach stating

> Other comments suggested that utilities be permitted to recover only a portion of increased fuel costs in order to provide an incentive to bargain for lower cost fuel. It should be noted that to the extent that only a portion of changes in fuel costs are permitted to be reflected in rates, the purposes of the fuel clause (namely to pass on to customers the increases or decreases in the fuel costs actually incurred by the utility) is to that extent defeated [18, p. 40583].

Proponents of FACs argue however that a 'collection lag' provides incentives for the choice of the efficient fuel. The FPC states this view as follows:

> In addition, the lag in collections for fuel expenses inherent in a typical fuel cost adjustment clause provides some incentive for companies to bargain for favorable prices during periods of rising fuel costs [18, p. 40583].

[9] Some of this inclusion is consistent with standard regulatory practice.

> The Uniform System of Accounts expressly permits all costs which are related to the total fossil fuel expenses of utility to be treated as fuel expense. This necessarily includes all items of cost incurred by a company in securing fuel, having it delivered, unloaded, stored and ultimately transferred to the burners to generate electricity. Florida Public Service Commission, Order No. 6557, November 26th, 1974. Cited in [19, p. 64].

The October 3rd, 1974, Questionnaire on Fuel Adjustment Revenue administered by the Edison Electric Institute indicates that of the 81 responding utilities with FACs in operation, three had their fuel adjustment calculated on a 'current month estimated' basis, 16 on the prior month base, 43 on the second preceding month, 15 on an average of prior months, and 12 on other bases. The respondants also indicated that during 1973 or 1974, 26 of the 81 had the lag reduced, presumably at the request of the utilities. Since the length of the collection lag is subject to the jurisdiction of a commission, it can be adjusted to strengthen or weaken the incentive for the choice of the efficient fuel. As will be indicated in section IV, this incentive problem will be shown to be present only when the firm has decreasing returns to scale which is not likely to be the situation for most electric utilities. When this efficiency problem is present, the collection lag will be shown to be a sufficient regulatory instrument to induce the efficient choice among fuel supply sources.

Another potential source of inefficiency involves the substitution of other factor inputs for fuel. An increased factor price should not only lead to the substitution of other fuels for the fuel whose price has increased, but also to the substitution of other factor inputs for fuel. The principal substitution possibility is between capital and fuel, and a substitution of capital for fuel would be anticipated in response to changing relative prices. The limit to this substitution at the generation stage is that 'lead times [are] of from six years for a coal-fired plant to ten years for a nuclear station . . .' [19, p. 144]. While at the *ex ante* or design stage a utility has the opportunity to substitute capital for fuel, for example, by investing in transmission equipment to reduce line losses or by purchasing more efficient generation equipment, once the capital is in place the technology of the plant is largely invariable. *Ex post* substitution is thus limited.[10]

In addition to the issue of the abdication of regulatory responsibility, the principal arguments against the use of automatic adjustment mechanisms center on their impact on economic efficiency. The objective of this study is to investigate the efficiency of both the fuel supply decision and the choice of technology. As will be demonstrated in section III, predicting the direction of this bias is complicated. For example, if a factor price increase is anticipated with probability one, a fuel adjustment clause results in a bias toward the over-utilization of fuel. If, however, the factor price is uncertain but has an expected value equal to the current factor price, the technology chosen by the firm will involve the under-utilization of fuel when, for example, the firm has constant returns to scale. The model utilized to investigate the efficiency issue is introduced in the next section, and the choice of a technology is analyzed in section III. The fuel choice decision is considered in section IV, and conclusions are offered in the final section.

[10] A putty-clay technology will be used to represent the distinction between the *ex ante* choice of technology and the *ex post* operation of that technology.

II. THE MODEL

Prior to developing the model of the firm, the nature of the regulatory environment in which the firm operates will be considered. A central feature of a fuel adjustment clause (FAC) is that it acts directly on the output price without a specific consideration of its effect on the rate of return earned by the firm once the adjustment has been made. While at a later date the earned rate of return may be reviewed and the output price adjusted appropriately, no rate of return constraint is imposed at the time the terms of the fuel adjustment mechanism are exercised. Consequently, a model of regulation of the Averch–Johnson [2] variety with a continually imposed rate of return constraint is not an appropriate description of the regulatory process. A better description of the regulatory process is that a commission sets (or approves) an initial price for a firm's output, with rate of return objectives in mind, but after an adjustment in the price via a fuel adjustment clause, the firm may or may not earn its allowed return. The model will therefore assume that the regulator sets the initial price and changes from the price can occur only through the FAC. To facilitate the analysis, a single factor price change will be considered, and the output price will be adjusted only in response to that change.

Fuel adjustment clauses typically are designed to increase the output price by an amount equal to the increase in average cost. In practice, the formula for the adjustment depends on a variety of factors such as fuel mix and line losses and may be based on the kilowatt hours delivered, the kilowatt hours generated, Btus of fuel consumed, or other bases. The formula to be considered here is based on the fuel cost increase per unit of output at the time that the factor price changes. If initially p_1 is the output price, c_1 the factor price of fuel, f_1 the quantity of fuel used, and $Q(p_1)$ the output, the change in average cost due to a real factor price change to c_2 is $(c_2-c_1)f_1/Q(p_1)$. The adjusted output price p_2 is thus given by

$$p_2=p_1+(c_2-c_1)f_1/Q(p_1).$$

As indicated in section I, opponents of fuel adjustment clauses have argued that the adjustment should be multiplied by a constant $\xi<1$ in order to induce the efficient choice of a fuel, but consideration of such a regulatory instrument will be reserved for section IV.

Both the future factor price c_2 and the time at which the change occurs will be assumed to be uncertain. To represent the timing of the factor price change, let $1-F(t)$ denote the probability that the price has not changed prior to time t. The conditional probability density function for a price change at time t, given that it has not changed prior to t, is thus $k(t)=\dot{F}(t)/\{1-F(t)\}$, which is referred to as the hazard rate.[11] In order to facilitate the analysis, the random variables c_2 and t are assumed to be

[11] Barlow and Proschan [3] provide a treatment of hazard rates.

statistically independent, and the hazard rate will be assumed to be a constant k which implies that $1-F(t)=\exp(-kt)$, so that the time at which the factor price will change is exponentially distributed.[12]

When a factor price change occurs, the firm may not be permitted to collect the adjusted price until after some collection lag τ. As indicated in section I, the average collection lag is likely to be less than two months and varies from a 'current month estimated' basis to a lag of a few months. A 'current month estimated' basis could, for example, be represented by $\tau=0$, while a prior month's base would correspond to $\tau>0$.[13] The length of the lag is assumed to be known, since the lag is typically specified in the tariff. In practice, the collection lag is due to inherent delays in obtaining accounting data, but it may also be used as a regulatory instrument in order to improve efficiency incentives, as considered in section IV.

The time frame of the model can be thought of as consisting of three intervals. During the initial interval $(0, t)$ the output price p_1 is in effect and the factor price is c_1. At time t the factor price changes to c_2, and during the collection lag period $(t, t+\tau)$ the output price remains at p_1. The third interval begins at $t+\tau$ when the output price is adjusted to p_2, and to simplify the analysis, the factor price and the output price are assumed to remain at those levels thereafter. The following Figure 1 illustrates the time intervals and the prices in effect at each time.[14]

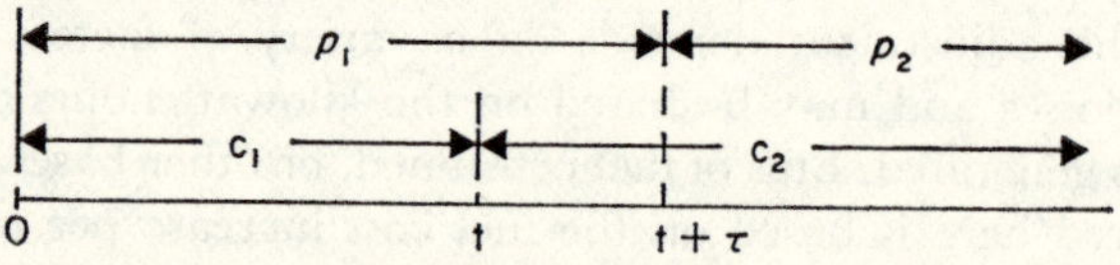

FIGURE 1. Time frame

The production possibilities of the firm will be represented by a simple technology involving two inputs, capital and fuel. An electric utility does not have perfect flexibility with respect to its choice of technology, since, for example, the lead time for the construction of a new plant may range from six years for a coal-fired plant to ten years for a nuclear plant. To represent this situation, the firm will be assumed to have a putty-clay technology so that at time zero the firm can freely choose its fuel–capital ratio, but thereafter the ratio is fixed.

The *ex ante* production function will be specified as homothetic, and

[12] The assumption of a constant hazard rate is made to simplify the exposition and is not necessary for the results obtained.

[13] Models with a lag resulting from delivery of capital equipment have been investigated by Nickell [15].

[14] Output prices are assumed to be constant in time during each of the intervals, since prices established in a tariff remain in effect until a new tariff is posted. An alternative assumption would be to let the prices be functions of time, but with a constant hazard rate and no technological change or demand growth, it can be shown that the optimal prices are constant in t except at t and $t+\tau$.

while homothetic production function specifications have generally been utilized in empirical studies of the electric utility industry, there have been few tests of this assumption. One such test is that of Atkinson and Halvorsen [1] who explicitly tested for homotheticity using a translog specification and concluded that 'the production function is predominately homothetic'. The *ex ante* production function is specified by $Q_i = H\{G(K_i, f_i)\}$, where H is a strictly increasing function and G is a production function that is homogeneous of degree one and i denotes the time interval.[15] The function H thus reflects returns to scale, and taking the inverse and dividing by K_i yields

$$H^{-1}(Q_i)/K_i = G(K_i, f_i)/K_i = G(1, \gamma) = 1/g(\gamma),$$

where γ is the fuel–capital ratio. For notational convenience let $\phi \equiv H^{-1}$, and since H is strictly increasing, so is ϕ. Also g is strictly decreasing in γ, since G is a strictly increasing function.[16] The marginal rate of technical substitution is

$$\text{MRTS} = \frac{\partial Q_i/\partial K_i}{\partial Q_i/\partial f_i} = -\{g(\gamma) + \gamma g'(\gamma)\}/g'(\gamma) > 0,$$

which implies that $g(\gamma) + \gamma g'(\gamma) > 0$.

The firm is assumed to be required to supply any level of demand, and the *ex post* fuel and capital inputs required to produce an output Q_i are determined by the fuel–capital ratio chosen *ex ante*. The inputs are given by

$$K_i(Q_i, \gamma) = g(\gamma)\phi_i, \qquad i = 1, 2$$
$$f_i(Q_i, \gamma) = \gamma K_i\{Q(p_i), \gamma\} = \gamma g(\gamma)\phi_i, \qquad i = 1, 2$$

where $\phi_i \equiv \phi\{Q(p_i)\}$ and $Q_i \equiv Q(p_i)$. Consequently, once the fuel–capital ratio has been determined *ex ante*, the *ex post* inputs are constrained to be on a ray in the (K, f)-plane.[17] The profit π_i, $i = 1, 2, 3$, earned by the firm in each interval is thus

$$\pi_1 = p_1 Q_1 - c_1 f_1 - v K_1 = p_1 Q_1 - \phi_1 M_1$$
$$\pi_2 = p_1 Q_1 - \phi_1 M_2$$
$$\pi_3 = p_2 Q_2 - \phi_2 M_2,$$

[15] This model of technology has also been used in [5] to investigate the optimal design of adjustment mechanisms.

[16] As an example, for a CES function

$$Q_i = A(\alpha K_i^{-z} + \beta f_i^{-z})^{-\eta/z}$$

the functions ϕ and g are given by

$$\phi(Q_i) = Q^{1/\eta}$$
$$g(\gamma_i) = A^{-1/\eta}(\alpha + \beta\gamma^{-z})^{1/z}.$$

[17] Issues associated with the effect of demand growth and technological change will not be considered here in order to focus on the fuel adjustment mechanism itself.

where v is the real cost of capital and $M_i = c_i\gamma g(\gamma) + vg(\gamma)$. The objective of the firm is assumed to be the maximization of the expected discounted profit V which is given by

$$V = \int_0^\infty F(t)\left\{\int_0^t \exp(-rt^0)\pi_1\,dt^0 + \int_t^{t+\tau} \exp(-rt^0)E\pi_2\,dt^0 + \int_{t+\tau}^\infty \exp(-rt^0)E\pi_3\,dt^0\right\} dt,$$

where E denotes the expectation with respect to c_2 and r is the discount rate. Integrating with respect to t^0 and then t yields

$$V = [r\pi_1 + k\{1-\exp(-r\tau)\}E\pi_2 + k\exp(-r\tau)E\pi_3]/\{r(r+k)\},$$

since t and c_2 are statistically independent.

III. TECHNICAL EFFICIENCY WITH A FUEL ADJUSTMENT MECHANISM

For a given initial price p_1 and a specified fuel adjustment clause, the firm maximizes V and hence its optimal γ^* satisfies

$$(1)\quad \frac{\partial V}{\partial \gamma} = -\left[r\phi_1 M_{1\gamma} + k\{1-\exp(-r\tau)\}\phi_1 E M_{2\gamma} + k\exp(-r\tau)\left\{E\left(\phi_2 M_{2\gamma} - \frac{\partial \pi_3}{\partial p_2}\frac{dp_2}{d\gamma}\right)\right\}\right]\Big/\{r(r+k)\} = 0$$

where $M_{i\gamma} = \partial M_i/\partial\gamma$. The second-order condition will be assumed to be satisfied at γ^*. The term $(\partial\pi_3/\partial p_2)/(dp_2/d\gamma)$ represents the price effect of γ on the post-adjustment profit π_3, and the effect of γ on p_2 through the FAC is

$$(2)\quad \frac{dp_2}{d\gamma} = (c_2 - c_1)\phi\{Q(p_1)\}\{g(\gamma) + \gamma g'(\gamma)\}/Q(p_1).$$

The technically efficient fuel–capital ratio depends on the output prices in the three time intervals and hence, technical efficiency must be defined relative to a given price schedule over time. The technically efficient fuel–capital ratio γ^0 corresponding to the prices p_1 and

$$p_2 = p_1 + (c_2 - c_1)\phi\{Q(p_1)\}\gamma^* g(\gamma^*)/Q(p_1),$$

thus satisfies (1) with $\partial\pi_3/\partial p_2 = 0$. The nature of the bias in technology thus depends on the sign of the term

$$(3)\quad E\left(\frac{\partial\pi_3}{\partial p_2}\frac{dp_2}{d\gamma}\right) = \left\{E\left(\frac{\partial\pi_3}{\partial p_2}\right)E(c_2 - c_1) + \operatorname{cov}\left(\frac{\partial\pi_3}{\partial p_2}, c_2\right)\right\}\{g(\gamma^*) + \gamma g'(\gamma^*)\}\,\phi_1/Q_1.$$

Since $g(\gamma^*) + \gamma^* g'(\gamma^*)$ is positive, the direction of the technical bias caused by the fuel adjustment clause is determined by the sign of the term in brackets in (3).

If regulation is effective in maintaining the output price below the price that a firm employing the technology γ^* would set if unregulated, then $\partial\pi_3/\partial p_2 > 0$ and $E(\partial\pi_3/\partial p_2) > 0$. The covariance is negative (positive) if $(\partial\pi_3/\partial p_2)$ is a decreasing (increasing) function of c_2, but in general, monotonicity may not be present. Differentiation yields

$$\text{(4)} \qquad \frac{\partial^2\pi_3}{\partial p_2 \partial c_2} = \frac{\partial^2\pi_3}{\partial p_2^2}\frac{\partial p_2}{\partial c_2} - \phi_2' Q_2' \gamma g(\gamma)$$

$$= \frac{\partial p_2}{\partial c_2}\left(\frac{\partial^2\pi_3}{\partial p_2^2} - \phi_2' Q_2' Q_1/\phi_1\right)$$

$$= \frac{\partial p_2}{\partial c_2}\left(\frac{\partial^2\pi_3}{\partial p_2^2} - \frac{Q_2'\phi_2'\eta_1}{\phi_1'}\right),$$

where $\eta_1 \equiv \phi_1' Q_1/\phi_1$ is the returns to scale measure at the initial output level. By the assumed strict concavity of π_3 at p_2 the first term in brackets is negative, but the second term is positive, so the sign of the covariance in (3) is ambiguous. Consequently, only limited results regarding the nature of the bias can be given. The following results can be established.[18]

Proposition 1

(a) If regulation is effective and a factor price increase (decrease) is anticipated with probability one, that is, $Pr(c_2 \geqslant c_1) = 1$ $(Pr(c_2 \leqslant c_1) = 1)$ with the strict inequality holding with positive probability, then $\gamma^* > (<)\gamma^0$.

(b) If $E(c_2) = c_1$, technical efficiency will result if $\partial\pi_3/\partial p_2$ is constant in c_2, or in general if the case in which the functional form of π_3 is such that cov $(\partial\pi_3/\partial p_2, c_2) = 0$.

Proof

(a) If $Pr(c_2 \geqslant c_1) = 1$, then $dp_2/d\gamma$ in (2) is non-negative for all c_2 and positive for some values of c_2 with positive probability. Since $\partial\pi_3/\partial p_2 > 0$ when regulation is effective, the bias term is the expectation of two non-negative functions which is strictly positive if $Pr(c_2 > c_1) > 0$. An analogous argument holds for an anticipated price decrease.

(b) If $E(c_2) = c_1$, the sign of the bias term given in (3) is the same as that of the term cov $(\partial\pi_3/\partial p_2, c_2)$. This will equal zero only if $\partial\pi_3/\partial p_2$ is constant in c_2 which requires that the term in brackets in (4) be zero for all c_2. This will be zero only for special functions π_3. ■

This characterization of the bias in the choice of technology caused by the fuel adjustment clause is not complete, but several interesting conclusions can be drawn. First, if a fuel such as natural gas or oil is anticipated

[18] These results also hold if demand changes over time.

to rise in price in the future, then the fuel adjustment clause would encourage the overconsumption of that fuel through a technology biased in favour of the employment of that fuel. At a time when the conservation of these fuels is being encouraged, a fuel adjustment clause would hinder the achievement of that goal. This also suggests that an electric utility would have less incentive to convert to alternate fuel sources when that conversion is costly, so the use of legislation requiring conversion from oil to coal might be justified to promote efficiency. Second, if the real price of a fuel is 'expected' to be stable (i.e. $E(c_2)=c_1$), then the fuel-adjustment clause may lead to the use of a fuel–capital ratio that is less than the technically efficient ratio. This reflects the effect of factor price uncertainty, the covariance term, on the marginal profit of the firm which results from the adjustment.

As an example, suppose that the firm has constant returns to scale and that the initial price p_1 was set equal to average cost M_1. The price p_2 is then

$$p_2=p_1+(c_2-c_1)\gamma g(\gamma)=M_2.$$

Evaluating (4) yields

$$\frac{\partial^2\pi_3}{\partial p_2\partial c_2}=\frac{\partial p_2}{\partial c_2}\{Q'_2+(p_2-M_2)Q''_2\}=\frac{\partial p_2}{\partial c_2}Q'_2,$$

which is negative for any demand function. Consequently, if the expected factor price change is zero and the firm has constant returns to scale, the firm will choose a fuel–capital ratio that is lower than the technically efficient level. While this example cannot be extended to a general proposition, it does suggest that the use of a fuel adjustment clause when factor prices are anticipated to be stable 'on average' would lead to the under-utilization of fuel.

The significance of this example lies in the recent empirical results of Christensen and Greene [6] who have concluded using 1970 data that 45% of the electricity generated by the 114 utilities included in their sample was in a region of 'no significant economies or diseconomies' of scale. Since the fuel price changes since the time of the oil boycott have been relatively stable in nominal terms, anticipation of such stability in the future could result in the under-utilization of fuel.

The length τ of the collection lag can be used by a regulator to affect the firm's choice of technology, since an extension of the lag diminishes the time over which the firm receives the adjusted price. To characterize the relationship between γ^* and τ, differentiation of (1) yields

$$\text{(5)}\qquad \frac{d\gamma^*}{d\tau}=-rk\exp(-r\tau)\left[E\{(\phi_2-\phi_1)M_{2\gamma}\}-E\left(\frac{\partial\pi_3}{\partial p_2}\frac{dp_2}{d\gamma}\right)\right]\Big/D,$$

where $D=(\partial^2V/\partial\gamma^2)r(r+k)$ is proportional to the second-order condition

$\partial^2 V/\partial\gamma^2$ which is negative by assumption. The following proposition characterizes the sign of $d\gamma^*/d\tau$ for the case of an anticipated factor price increase.

Proposition 2

If a factor price increase is anticipated, the optimal fuel–capital ratio is a decreasing function of τ.[19]

Proof

First, the sign of $E\{(\phi_2-\phi_1)M_2\}$ will be established. For the case of an anticipated factor price increase assume that $EM_{2\gamma}\leqslant 0$. Then, since $M_{2\gamma}$ is increasing in c_2, $EM_{2\gamma}\geqslant M_{1\gamma}$ because $Pr(c_2\geqslant c_1)=1$. This implies that the first two terms in (1) are non-positive. The term $E(\phi_2 M_{2\gamma})$ may be evaluated as

$$E(\phi_2 M_{2\gamma})=E(\phi_2)E(M_{2\gamma})+\{\gamma^* g'(\gamma^*)+g(\gamma^*)\}\ \mathrm{cov}\ (\phi_2, c_2).$$

The covariance is negative, since ϕ_2 is a decreasing function of c_2, so $E(\phi_2 M_{2\gamma})<0$. Finally, from Proposition 1, $E\{(\partial\pi_3/\partial p_2)(dp_2/d\gamma)>0$ when a factor price increase is anticipated. Hence, $\partial V/\partial\gamma|_{\gamma=\gamma^*}<0$ which contradicts the optimality of γ^*, so $EM_{2\gamma}>0$.

The term $E\{(\phi_2-\phi_1)M_{2\gamma}\}$ may be evaluated as

$$E\{(\phi_2-\phi_1)M_{2\gamma}\}=E(\phi_2-\phi_1)E(M_{2\gamma})+\{\gamma^* g'(\gamma^*)+g(\gamma^*)\}\ \mathrm{cov}\ (\gamma_2, c_2)<0,$$

since $\phi_2\leqslant\phi_1$ for all $c_2\geqslant c_1$, $E(M_{2\gamma})>0$, and cov $(\phi_2, c_2)<0$. Proposition 1 implies that the last term $[-E\{(\partial\pi_3/\partial p_2)(dp_2/d\gamma)\}]$ in (5) is negative, which establishes $d\gamma^*/d\tau<0$.■

The collection lag can thus be utilized to decrease the use of fuel when a factor price increase is anticipated, but this does not imply that the technological bias $(\gamma^*-\gamma^0)$ is a decreasing function of π, since γ^0 is also a decreasing function of τ.

The use of an average cost fuel adjustment formula is based on the presumption that the firm is being regulated under an average cost pricing rule. That is, if the initial price p_1 is equal to average cost,[20] then the adjustment in response to a factor price change is simply equal to the average cost of producing the initial quantity. The output price adjustment however changes the level of output, and unless the firm has constant returns to scale, average cost at the adjusted price will differ from the average cost at the initial output. A firm with increasing returns to scale will thus

[19] The converse of this result cannot be established in general for the case of an anticipated factor price decrease, although $d\gamma^*/d\tau>0$ is likely to result.

[20] The model assumes that the initial price p_1 is not affected by the firm's choice of technology, so the case in which p_1 equals average cost is used here as an illustration. The regulator's optimal choice of p_1 can be made so that p_1 is independent of γ as indicated in the model considered by Leland [11]. The optimal p_1 is considered in [4], when the regulator maximizes consumer surplus subject to the restriction that the firm earn its allowed return.

have an adjusted price below (above) average cost when the factor price increases (decreases), while the opposite relationship will hold for a firm with decreasing returns to scale.

If returns to scale are increasing as has been indicated by many empirical studies of electricity production,[21] an automatic adjustment mechanism that passes on the average cost increase based on the current output level will thus yield an insufficient return when the current regulated price equals average cost including an allowed rate of return. Consequently, if the regulated price was such that the firm was able to earn its allowed return prior to the fuel price increases in the early 1970s, the fuel adjustment clauses that were used to pass on those factor price increases would be insufficient to allow the firm to earn its allowed return after the adjustment. This would then require a rate revision request by the firm and a subsequent formal rate hearing which is the situation that fuel adjustment clauses are intended to avoid. During the 15-month period from January 1st, 1976, to March 31st, 1977, 145 electric utility rate cases were concluded in the US[22] involving firms that had fuel adjustment clauses in effect. While these rate cases were likely to be largely due to factor price increases associated with non-fuel inputs, the effect of average cost fuel adjustment clauses coupled with increasing returns to scale may also have contributed to the deterioration in the firms' earned return, thus requiring rate revision requests.

IV. FUEL ADJUSTMENT CLAUSES AND THE INCENTIVE TO PURCHASE THE EFFICIENT FUEL

One of the principal arguments against fuel adjustment clauses is that they dampen incentives for the choice of the least-cost fuel supply. This section investigates the case in which a long-term fuel supply source is selected at the time at which the technology of the firm is chosen. The choice of technology may, for example, determine the type of fuel to be utilized, so the fuel supply decision involves the choice from among alternative long-term supplies of that fuel. *Ex post* conversion from one type of fuel to another will not be considered here.[23]

To investigate the fuel supply decision, assume that there are two fuels that are perfect substitutes, so that $f_i = f_i^1 + f_i^2$, where f_i^j is the quantity of fuel j consumed in interval i. While perfect substitutes would normally sell at the same price, market imperfections such as those created by government regulations can cause the prices to differ. For example, the price per Btu for interstate natural gas is below the price per Btu for intrastate gas. Similarly, the prices on high- and low-sulphur coal may differ in a

[21] Christensen and Greene find substantial increasing returns to scale for smaller electric utilities.
[22] The source of these data is [9].
[23] *Ex post* conversion is considered in [5].

state because of variations among state pollution control laws and their enforcement. The initial price of each fuel will be assumed to be c_1 and at the same time t their prices will increase to c_2^2 and c_2^1. To facilitate the analysis, the second fuel is assumed to be the more costly after time t in the sense that $Pr(c_2^2 \geqslant c_2^1) = 1$. The second fuel is thus anticipated to be the more costly although the cost difference is uncertain. Letting $\psi \epsilon (0, 1)$ denote the proportion (f_i^1/f_i) of the total fuel supply represented by the first fuel, the amounts of each fuel consumed are

$$f_i^1 = \psi f_i = \psi \gamma g(\gamma) \phi_i$$
$$f_i^2 = (1-\psi) f_i = (1-\psi) \gamma g(\gamma) \phi_i.$$

The fuel cost in the interval (t, ∞) then is $f_2\{c_2^2 + \psi(c_2^1 - c_2^2)\}$, and the adjusted price is

$$p_2 = p_1 + \{\psi(c_2^1 - c_2^2) + c_2^2 - c_1\} f_1/Q_1.$$

The firm determines its optimal fuel mix ψ according to the sign of the term

$$(6) \quad \frac{\partial V}{\partial \psi} = -kE\left\{\{1-\exp(-r\tau)\}(c_2^1 - c_2^2) f_1 + \exp(-r\tau)\left((c_2^1 - c_2^2) f_2 - \frac{\partial \pi_3}{\partial p_2} \cdot (c_2^1 - c_2^2) f_1/Q_1\right)\right\} \Big/ \{r(r+k)\},$$

where E denotes the expectation with respect to the joint distribution of the factor prices. The efficient fuel choice $(\psi = 1)$ will be made if $\partial V/\partial \psi \geqslant 0$ for all $\psi \epsilon [0, 1]$.

To evaluate $\partial V/\partial \psi$, let A denote the term in brackets in (6) and substitute for $\partial \pi_3/\partial p_2$ to obtain

$$EA = E[\![(c_2^1 - c_2^2)[\{1-\exp(-r\tau)\} f_1 Q_1 + Q_1 Q_2 \exp(-r\tau)(f_2/Q_2 - f_1/Q_1) - \exp(-r\tau)(p_2 - \phi_2' M_2) Q'_2 f_1]]\!]/Q_1.$$

Since factor price increases will occur, $Q_2 < Q_1$ for all factor price levels. Then, the term

$$f_2/Q_2 - f_1/Q_1 = (\phi_2/Q_2 - \phi_1/Q_1)\gamma^* g(\gamma^*),$$

is positive (negative) (constant) as returns to scale are increasing (decreasing) (constant). Consequently, if the firm has non-decreasing returns to scale and p_2 is at least as great as marginal cost $(\phi' M_2)$ as seems reasonable, EA is negative and the efficient fuel choice will result for all $\tau \geqslant 0$. If the firm has decreasing returns to scale, the price p_2 is likely to be below marginal cost and EA will be positive for some τ. These results are summarized in the following proposition.

Proposition 3

With non-decreasing returns to scale and a price p_2 at least as great as marginal cost there is no incentive to purchase the inefficient fuel for any $\tau \epsilon [0, \infty]$. With decreasing returns to scale and price no greater than marginal cost, the inefficient fuel supply will result for $\tau \epsilon [0, \tau^*]$ and the efficient choice will result for $\tau \epsilon (\tau^*, \infty)$ where τ^* is such that[24]

$$EA|_{\tau=\tau^*} = 0 \text{ for } \psi = 0. \tag{7}$$

Proof

Only the result pertaining to τ^* remains to be demonstrated. For the case of decreasing returns to scale and $p_2 \leqslant \phi' M_2$, EA is a strictly decreasing function of τ for all $\psi \epsilon [0, 1]$. Defining τ^* as in (7) implies that for $\tau > \tau^*$, EA is negative and hence that $\psi = 0$ is not optimal. The firm will thus choose $\psi = 1$. ■

When a firm's technology is characterized by increasing returns to scale, the regulated price in effect after $t + \tau$ will in all likelihood be at least as great as marginal cost, and the firm will have no incentive to purchase the fuel that is anticipated to have the greater price increase. The regulator then can reduce the collection lag as much as possible without inducing inefficiency. This conclusion would support a policy of making the fuel adjustment on a 'current month estimated' basis ($\tau = 0$). With constant returns to scale a zero collection lag could be utilized with $p_1 = M_1$, and the firm would be indifferent between the two fuel supplies, since $\partial V / \partial \psi = 0$. To insure that the efficient choice will be made, the regulator can set τ so that it is slightly positive.

With decreasing returns to scale the collection lag must be used to overcome the incentive for the choice of the higher cost fuel. Proposition 3 however indicates that the collection lag is a sufficient regulatory instrument to achieve this objective. Modifying the fuel adjustment formula to allow only some fraction of the average cost increase to be passed on, as has been suggested, is not necessary. Furthermore, the use of the collection lag has an important advantage over the use of a pass-through fraction. The use of the collection lag as a regulatory instrument does not affect the adjusted price p_2, for a given p_1, while the pass-through does. It is thus more difficult to predict the effect of the pass-through on the fuel choice.[25]

Proposition 3 pertains to the case in which the regulated output prices are 'appropriate' in the sense that with, for example, non-decreasing returns to scale the price is at least as great as marginal cost. In practice, the regulator may not know if the firm is operating in a region of increasing, constant, or decreasing returns and may have only imprecise information regarding marginal cost. For example, the cost functions estimated by Christensen and Greene indicate a U-shaped cost function, and although they conclude that only one of the 114 firms in their sample had 'significant

[24] The same results obtain if the term can make its fuel supply decision at time t.
[25] An analysis of this point is provided in [4].

scale diseconomies', a substantial number of large firms operated in a region of decreasing, but statistically insignificant, returns in 1970. A regulator thus may prefer to use a positive collection lag in order to be more confident that the firm will select the efficient fuel supply source. In addition, if there are costs associated with the *ex post* conversion from one fuel to another, a positive collection lag provides a greater incentive for conversion.[26] As indicated in Proposition 2, an increase in the collection lag results in the choice of a technology with a lower fuel–capital ratio when fuel factor prices are anticipated to increase. The collection lag can thus be used to induce fuel efficiency and to reduce the amount of fuel consumed although the latter may not be technically efficient. A lengthening of the collection lag, however, reduces the profit of the firm during the $(t, t+\tau)$ period, and hence to provide the firm with a fair-rate of return, a price p_1 higher than average cost may be required. An analysis of the optimal pricing decision by the regulator will not be presented here but can be found in [4] for the case in which c_2 is certain.

V. CONCLUSIONS

Fuel adjustment mechanisms can lead to inefficiency both with respect to a utility's choice of a technology and its selection of fuel supply sources. The fuel supply decision poses an efficiency problem primarily in conjunction with decreasing returns to scale, since a firm with non-decreasing returns to scale and an output price at least as great as marginal cost will choose the fuel supply source that is anticipated to have the smallest factor price increase. When there is an incentive to purchase the inefficient fuel, the collection lag can be extended to induce efficiency. This extension, however, affects the choice of technology by reducing both the technically efficient fuel–capital ratio and the ratio preferred by the firm. The latter ratio will differ from the efficient ratio, but in general the direction of bias cannot be predicted. An anticipated factor price increase will result in a bias toward a technology utilizing a fuel–capital ratio that is greater than the efficient ratio, but an anticipated factor price level with a mean equal to the current factor price can lead to a fuel–capital ratio that is less than the efficient ratio. This results because of the covariation between the factor price level and the marginal profit with respect to the adjusted price. Fuel adjustment clauses thus pose a complex efficiency problem, which can be compensated for but not eliminated by the design of the adjustment formula as indicated in [5]. Whether the use of fuel adjustment

[26] The conclusion of Proposition 3 also may not generalize to other informational contexts. For example, if the firm does not have complete information on the alternative sources of fuel supply and must search for that information, costs associated with search may lead to an incentive problem when the firm has non-decreasing returns to scale. The collection lag could then be used to combat this incentive problem.

mechanisms leads to greater efficiency problems than alternative regulatory processes, such as administrative rate review, remains an open issue.

NORTWESTERN UNIVERSITY AND
KATHOLIEKE UNIVERSITEIT LEUVEN

REFERENCES

[1] Atkinson, S. E. and Halvorsen, R., 'Interfuel Substitution in Steam Electric Power Generation', *Journal of Political Economy*, **84** (October 1976), pp. 959–78.

[2] Averch, H. and Johnson, L., 'Behavior of the Firm Under Regulatory Constraint', *American Economic Review*, **52** (December 1962), pp. 1053–69.

[3] Barlow, R. E. and Proschan, F. *Statistical Theory of Reliability and Life Testing* (Holt, Rinehart and Winston, New York, 1975).

[4] Baron, D. P. and De Bondt, R. R., 'Fuel Adjustment Mechanisms: Efficiency and Regulatory Policy', Onderzoeksrapport Nr. 7802 (Departement voor Toegepaste Economische Wetenschappen, Katholieke Universiteit Leuven, Belgium, 1978).

[5] Baron, D. P. and De Bondt, R. R., 'The Design of Automatic Price Adjustment Mechanisms', Onderzoeksrapport Nr. 7810 (Departement voor Toegepaste Economische Wetenschappen, Katholieke Universiteit Leuven, Belgium, 1978).

[6] Christensen, L. R. and Greene, W. H., 'Economics of Scale in US Electric Power Generation', *Journal of Political Economy*, **84** (August 1976), pp. 655–76.

[7] Consumers' Union, 'The Fuel-Adjustment Caper', *Consumer Reports* (November 1974), pp. 836–9.

[8] Edison Electric Institute, 'October 3, 1974 Questionnaire on Fuel Adjustment Revenue' (New York).

[9] Edison Electric Institute, 'Electric Rate Case Decision Data, January 1, 1976 to March 31, 1977' (New York, 1977).

[10] Joskow, P., 'Inflation and Environmental Concern: Structural Change in the Process of Public Utility Regulation', *Journal of Law and Economics*, **17** (October 1974), pp. 291–327.

[11] Leland, H. E. 'Regulation of Natural Monopolies and the Fair Rate of Return', *Bell Journal of Economics*, **5** (Spring 1974), pp. 3–15.

[12] Lindsay, W. W., 'The Case for Automatic Adjustment Clauses as a Means for Improving Regulation', Eighth Annual Conference of the Institute of Public Utilities, East Lansing, Michigan, November 1976.

[13] NARUC, 'Automatic Adjustment Clauses Revisited', Economic Paper No. 1R, *86th NARUC Annual Convention*, pp. 313–18. Also reprinted in [18], pp. 88–98.

[14] New Mexico Public Service Commission, 'Public Service Company of New Mexico', Case No. 1196, April 22, 1975 (8 PUR 4th, pp. 113–39).

[15] Nickell, S., 'Uncertainty and Lags in the Investment Decisions of Firms', *Review of Economic Studies*, **44** (1977), pp. 249–63.

[16] Price Commission (UK), 'Fuel Cost Adjustment for the Supply of Electricity' (Her Majesty's Stationery Office, London, 1978).

[17] Trigg, R. S. 'Escalator Clauses in Public Utility Rate Schedule', *U. Pennsylvania Law Review*, **106** (1958), pp. 964–97.

[18] US Federal Power Commission, Order No. 517, Docket No. R-479, November 13th, 1974. *Federal Register 39*, No. 224 (Tuesday, November 19th, 1974), pp. 40582–4.

[19] US House of Representatives Subcommittee on Oversight and Investigations, 'Electric Utility Automatic Fuel Adjustment Clauses' (Government Printing Office, Washington, October 1975).

[20] US Senate, 'Electric and Gas Utility Rate and Fuel Adjustment Clause Increases, 1976', prepared by the Congressional Research Service for the Subcommittee on Intergovernmental Relations and the Subcommittee on Reports, Accounting and Management (Government Printing Office, Washington, July 1977).

THE JOURNAL OF INDUSTRIAL ECONOMICS
Volume XXVII March 1979 No. 3

HEDONIC PRICES AND THE STRUCTURE OF THE DIGITAL COMPUTER INDUSTRY

ROBERT MICHAELS*

During the past 20 years, the digital computer industry has grown to an impressive economic stature. UNIVAC I, the first marketed machine, was delivered to its first commercial user in 1954. By 1975, total expenditures on data processing equipment and services in the US had grown to approximately $23 billion [23, p. 48], $5·5 billion of which was spent on rentals and purchase of larger central processing units ('mainframes') produced by a small number of manufacturers. An additional $6·6 billion went for peripheral equipment (tape drives, printers, etc.) made by these firms.[1] In recent years data processing expenditures have grown persistently at approximately 14% per year.[2] Despite its size and growth the industry has received surprisingly little attention from economists, particularly in light of its curious structure.[3] In this paper I will attempt to make some inferences about that structure with the aid of data on technical characteristics of its output. Quality-adjusted ('hedonic') prices for computer systems will be constructed and used to compare pricing policies among manufacturers and to examine the variation of price along some important dimensions of output.

In a recent study of the computer industry, Ratchford and Ford [21, p. 217] found that machines produced by the dominant firm, International Business Machines (IBM), carry a quality-adjusted price premium of 40–50% over those made by its competitors.[4] Their findings have been criticized on several points by Brock [4], whose objections center around errors and inadequacies in their source data. Below I will show that the use of an alternative sample eliminates many of the data problems and yields strikingly different conclusions about price premiums in the industry. After brief introductions to the industry, the analytical technique, and the

* The author wishes to thank Gerald Brock, Lionel Kalish, Sam Peltzman, William Sharpe, Jack Triplett and two anonymous reviewers for their comments on previous drafts of this paper. They are, of course, absolved from responsibility for any errors which remain. He also thanks Elizabeth Girard-DiCarlo of Auerbach Info, Inc. for her valuable aid in supplying some otherwise unavailable data.

[1] These two figures were calculated by the author from estimates in [23, pp. 49–51].
[2] Calculated by the author from [16], unnumbered; and [23, pp. 52–3].
[3] The two standard references are by Sharpe [24] and Brock [5]. The latter covers the events of more recent years, including antitrust developments, in considerable detail.
[4] Several other studies of this type have recently appeared. They include those of Cowling and Cubbin [7] on the UK automobile industry and Cowling and Rayner [8] on the UK tractor market. Boyle and Hogarty [3] concluded, partially on the basis of hedonic prices, that the American auto industry was organized collusively.

data, hedonic price equations are presented for a sample of computer systems. They give little evidence of a general price premium on IBM equipment, and point the way toward some alternative explanations of industry structure.

In addition to IBM, mainframes in the US have been made by Burroughs Corporation, Control Data Corporation (CDC), Digital Equipment Corporation (DEC), General Electric (GE), Honeywell Information Systems (HIS), National Cash Register (NCR), Radio Corporation of America (RCA), Sperry Rand (trade name UNIVAC), and Xerox Data Systems (XDS), formerly Scientific Data Systems. In every year since 1956, IBM has earned about 70% of total industry revenue from rental and sale of central processing units (CPUs) and peripheral equipment [5, pp. 21–23]. Of the other firms named above, none holds over 8% of the market, and three have left the industry after incurring substantial losses.[5] In the size range considered here, computers of foreign origin are virtually non-existent in the United States. IBM itself is the country's seventh largest industrial corporation, with total sales (computer and other divisions) of $18·1 billion in 1977 [10, p. 240].

I. METHOD AND DATA

Consider a firm selecting a computer system. It will choose one whose attributes maximize the computing facility's contribution to profit, other things equal. Since there is no single well-defined measure of computing power, the components chosen for a given installation will in general depend on the tasks to be performed. Thus, following Griliches' [14] and Lancaster's [17] lead in consumption theory, a computer is desired as a generator of profits, and these profits are functionally related to its attributes. Assume that we have an assortment of optimized computer systems (in the sense to be defined below) and a complete set of performance characteristics. Then the price of such a system will be a function of those attributes. This relationship is called a hedonic plane and the residuals from an estimated plane are called hedonic residuals. The hedonic plane is neither a demand nor a supply function,[6] although under perfect competition imputed attribute prices (regression coefficients of the attributes) will be equal across producing firms if their technologies are identical. These prices, however, are partially determined by buyer preferences as well. If the industry

[5] General Electric made its exit from mainframe manufacture in 1970 and RCA did so in 1971. Cumulative losses incurred by GE were between $400 million and $1 billion [20, p. 80], those of RCA were $490 million [11, p. 35]. Their outstanding customer bases were taken over by Honeywell and UNIVAC respectively. In mid-1975, XDS also announced its departure from the industry, citing its initial acquisition of Scientific Data Systems as a 'mistake' [26].

[6] Several recent authors discuss the theoretical significance and empirical applicability of the hedonic method in more rigorous terms. They include Lucas [18] and Muellbauer [19].

produces differentiated outputs, a seller may specialize in products whose attribute prices appeal to only a subset of purchasers.

A correctly estimated hedonic plane provides an *a priori* method of distinguishing 'good' and 'bad' buys. Assume that all attributes relevant to the purchase decision are on the right-hand side of the equation and a hedonic plane is estimated by regression. Of two machines with identical attributes the lower priced model would be expected (eventually) to carry a larger share of the market than the higher priced one. In terms of residuals from such a hedonic plane, customers are more likely to prefer items with negative residuals to similar items (indicated by nearness of attribute vectors) which carry positive residuals. No test, however, has yet been devised to ascertain whether all relevant attributes have been included. In practical cases, residuals can arise because of attributes not included in the estimation, incorrect functional specification, marketing practices unrelated to production costs, discontinuities in demand, and time lags. In the absence of detailed information on the demand and production cost for specific attributes, there is no way of separating these effects by use of the plane alone.[7] Brand name premiums and vintage effects can be easily investigated by adding appropriate dummy variables to the hedonic regression.

In general, the computer user constructs a system which meets his needs by choosing an appropriate set of peripheral equipment to go with his CPU. Most frequently, peripherals made by the producer of the CPU will be used, although 'plug-compatible' devices which substitute for IBM peripherals have made inroads on the market. Because of difficulties in obtaining a satisfactory sample of systems in actual use, a set of standardized configurations assembled by Auerbach Info, Inc. [2], a leading computer information service, will be examined.[8] At the sample date of July 1st, 1971, Auerbach evaluated available machinery over 13 'standard configurations' of CPU and peripherals. These range from simple systems with 8000 bytes (characters) of core storage in which cards are the sole input medium to integrated general purpose systems with 20 tape units and 100 million bytes of random access memory.[9] Peripherals are chosen

[7] Brock [5, p. 30] estimates that the computer industry has 'very high economies of scale relative to other major US industries'. No one investigating hedonic regressions has yet explored the role of differing production costs over suppliers.

[8] Others who have estimated hedonic prices for computers have used different samples. Three unpublished studies cited by Sharpe [24, pp. 350–6] regressed CPU rental on a vector of CPU hardware characteristics. Since their authors were more interested in the existence of a hedonic relation than in industry structure, omission of peripherals (usually about half of system cost) is understandable. Harman [15, pp. 21–3] provides similar estimates, as does Chow [6]. Studies by Ratchford and Ford [21] and Archibald and Reece [1] are discussed below.

[9] [2, 11: 010.102 (January 1971), p. 2] Characteristics of standard systems and a list of sampled systems are available on request from the author. Subscription price for the Auerbach reports is $1000 for the first year and $800 per year thereafter. Relative to systems actually in use, it appears that the very small and the very large are slighted in the Auerbach sample. Neither minicomputers nor large time sharing or distributed processing installations are included in it.

'to result in balanced equipment configurations that will perform effectively in applications of the types indicated by their titles' [2, 030.0000.010 (April 1972), p. 4]. Each machine is only included in those configurations (usually from three to six) for which it is best suited.[10] Computers evaluated by Auerbach accounted for 78% of total computer value installed in the US at the sample date [13]. Most of the remainder consisted of machines then out of production. The price of a system is the sum of the 'basic monthly rental' rates of its components.[11]

Five characteristics are used in the hedonic regressions. They were chosen and constructed after consultation with professionals in attempts to capture both the technology and the economic trade-offs which are faced by a computer user.

1. ADDTIM, fixed point[12] decimal addition time in microseconds, a measure of speed with which a machine can perform arithmetic operations. It would be expected to carry a negative coefficient in hedonic regression.

2. CORPOW, a measure of core memory power. It is defined as the geometric mean of core size (measured in thousands of bytes) and the effective transfer rate of core with itself. The latter is an index of manipulative speed which measures 'the average rate at which data can be transferred from one device or storage location to another over a sustained period of time' [2, 030.0000.010 (April 1972), p. 4]. It is measured in kilobytes per second. Isoquants of core power have a neoclassical shape.

3. CDPOW, an index of punched card input–output capability. Let R be the maximum card reader speed per minute and P be the card punch speed for fully punched cards associated with a given configuration. Then $\text{CDPOW} = \sqrt{R^2+P^2}$. CDPOW isoquants are concave when viewed from the origin, an attempt to capture the complementarity between reading and punching of cards in a card-dominated configuration. It is expected that increases in CDPOW will be associated, *ceteris paribus*, with higher prices, but that the significance of CDPOW as an explanatory variable will be less for larger configurations in which card operations play relatively less important roles.

[10] The entire sample consists of 264 configurations, 55 of which are made by IBM. The only American manufacturers missing from the sample are XDS and DEC, who together accounted for less than 2% of the market.

[11] The actual rental paid by a user is generally computed from a three-part tariff which allows 176 hours of free use per month after the basic monthly rental has been paid. Hours in excess of this amount may be purchased for an additional charge per hour. Since there is no evidence of systematically different use intensity for different brands, we use basic monthly rental as our measure of price throughout what follows. Few users other than government and third-party lessors purchase equipment. No evidence is available on differences between list and transaction prices.

[12] 'Fixed point' denotes a way of representing numbers within the computer. Most medium and large machines also have 'floating point' representations available, which are more useful in scientific computations. Although floating point is probably a more important criterion for larger configurations, we use fixed point in an attempt to maintain some consistency over the entire sample.

4. TAPPOW, an index of magnetic tape power. It is assumed that the number of tape drives in a system and the speed at which they can read or write are substitutes. Then TAPPOW is the geometric mean of the number of drives and their maximum effective read–write speed in kilobytes per second.

5. RACSTR, the amount of random access storage (high speed discs or drums) in a configuration, measured in millions of bytes. In some regressions we include a brand name dummy for each non-IBM manufacturer and a dummy for the two-year period in which a model was introduced. Thus our coefficients give brand name premiums relative to IBM and trend price movements relative to those of machines first installed before 1965.

While some estimates are available on the total outstanding stock of each machine in the sample [13], no such data on the proportions in each configuration are publicly available. Moreover, most actual installations are not duplicates of Auerbach systems but rather extensions and combinations of them. Because of these data limitations all of the reported regressions are unweighted, although experimental tests with a judgmentally weighted sample yielded approximately the same results as are reported in Table I.[13] The semilog form of estimating equation was found to dominate other possible forms in both goodness of overall fit and significance of coefficients in the great majority of cases where alternatives were tried. It is used throughout what follows.

II. RESULTS

Equation (1a) on Table I is a hedonic regression for the entire sample. The technological variables taken as a set do quite well in explaining the observed array of prices for a wide variety of systems. All of their coefficients are significant at the 0·005 level and there appears to be no serious multicollinearity. Equations estimated on the basis of component variables rather than the CORPOW, CDPOW and TAPPOW indexes give both poorer fits and stronger evidence of multicollinearity. Equation 1b includes dummy variables for manufacturer and biennium of first installation. All attribute coefficients are nearly identical between the equations, and

[13] The choice of a weighted or unweighted hedonic regression is not as easy as it might seem, even if we disregard the problem of choosing appropriate weights for a durable. Cowling and Cubbin argue that hedonic planes may be interpreted as 'cost functions derived from a range of models which have survived the competitive environment'. The plane becomes more 'demand oriented' [7, p. 384] when a weighted regression is used. If we wish, however, to estimate market share changes on the basis of hedonic residuals [7], [8], [21], weighting an observation more heavily cuts the size of its residual and renders it a less valuable explainer of the share. An unweighted regression counts mistakes equally with successes, but may be a better indicator of good and bad buys because it avoids the above difficulty. There is generally no reason to assume that all existing models have survived competitively. If the plane is estimated in a short-run or disequilibrium situation, negative residuals might indicate loss-taking in an attempt at market penetration, which may be unsuccessful. Likely instances of this will be encountered below.

TABLE I

REGRESSION ESTIMATES

Variable[b]	Equation[a] 1a	1b	2l	2m	2h	3b	3s
ADDTIM	−0·0017	−0·0019	−0·0004	−0·0004	−0·0070	−0·0015	−0·0094
	(6·48)	(7·47)	(1·24)	(1·89)	(3·87)	(5·19)	(3·39)
CORPOW[c]	0·1295	0·1215	1·3450	0·4184	0·0616	0·1535	0·0722
	(7·85)	(7·52)	(3·69)	(7·54)	(6·04)	(6·19)	(4·14)
CDPOW[c]	0·2258	0·3137	0·4003	0·0722	−0·1970	0·5882	−0·1841
	(2·74)	(3·20)	(4·07)	(0·81)	(1·45)	(4·33)	(0·79)
TAPPOW	0·0306	0·0289	0·0395	0·0028	0·0110	0·0284	0·0185
	(11·87)	(11·97)	(7·96)	(1·35)	(5·02)	(8·85)	(5·11)
RACSTR	0·0034	0·0033	0·0227	0·0013	0·0009	0·0031	0·0026
	(4·33)	(4·56)	(3·02)	(1·40)	(1·97)	(3·40)	(1·44)
I 65–6	—	−0·1883	−0·0741	−0·0257	−0·0316	−0·2542	0·0321
		(2·32)	(0·90)	(0·38)	(0·43)	(2·37)	(0·32)
I 67–8	—	−0·3596	−0·2926	−0·1104	−0·2180	−0·3091	0·0916
		(3·73)	(2·82)	(1·27)	(1·68)	(2·57)	−(0·50)
I 69–70	—	−0·1286	−0·0123	−0·1549	−0·1903	−0·1626	0·0261
		(1·26)	(0·12)	(1·54)	(2·28)	(1·23)	(0·20)
I 71+	—	−0·3952	−0·3488	−0·4538	−0·3086	−0·4168	−0·1769
		(3·58)	(3·26)	(4·22)	(2·73)	(−3·04)	(1·09)
BURR	—	0·1556	0·2423	−0·1177	0·0191	0·0370	0·2217
		(1·18)	(1·68)	(0·96)	(0·15)	(0·23)	(1·18)
CDC	—	0·1263	—[d]	−0·1961	0·0520	0·3445	0·0918
		(1·08)		(2·00)	(0·46)	(1·90)	(0·58)
GE	—	−0·2165	0·1639	−0·0020	0·1142	−0·2711	0·2560
		(2·15)	(2·16)	(0·03)	(0·89)	(2·26)	(1·68)
HONWL	—	−0·0701	0·2120	−0·0125	0·0063	0·0089	0·1211
		(0·76)	(2·67)	(0·17)	(0·05)	(0·08)	(0·82)
NCR	—	−0·3257	−0·0305	−0·2180	−0·0509	−0·2712	−0·3531
		(2·83)	(0·34)	(1·86)	(0·45)	(2·13)	(1·66)
RCA	—	−0·2328	−0·3355	−0·1346	−0·1238	−0·3337	−0·1548
		(2·05)	(2·21)	(1·25)	(0·98)	(2·44)	(0·98)
UNIVAC	—	−0·0457	−0·1722	0·0462	0·0217	−0·1396	0·1901
		(0·45)	(1·78)	(0·44)	(0·23)	(1·09)	(1·44)
Constant	8·571	8·849	7·725	9·223	10·244	8·585	9·705
R^2	0·73	0·78	0·67	0·56	0·74	0·76	0·82
S.E.E.	0·448	0·408	0·252	0·178	0·207	0·405	0·255

Notes: [a] Dependent variable in all equations is natural log of monthly system rental.
[b] Figures below coefficients are *t*-statistics.
[c] $\times 10^{-3}$.
[d] No models by this manufacturer in this size class.

our results show the same type of quality-adjusted price premium for older machines that has been found by others.[14] The coefficients for manufacturers, however, indicate a structure of price premiums which differs somewhat from both Ratchford and Ford's original [21] and adjusted [22]

[14] Some possible explanations for the premium on older machines are given in [21, p. 201]. The premium may also reflect the fact that software for older equipment is better developed and more reliable than for newer equipment. A reviewer has suggested that the prices of older machines are typically held constant when new machines are announced in order to

results. Although they found a consistent and substantial quality-adjusted price premium for IBM CPUs, we find none. If an IBM dummy variable is incorporated in 1b in place of those for other producers its coefficient of 0·11 is insignificant ($t = 1{\cdot}44$) at customary levels. The difference may stem both from the narrow range of characteristics they used (only CPU speed and capacity) and from the fact that we emphasize attributes of an entire system and measure its price more accurately. Brock [4] observed that Ratchford and Ford's measure of the IBM premium resulted in part from memory measurement errors and the use of maximum rather than actual memory sizes. In their reply, however, Ratchord and Ford [22] argued that the only effect of adjusting for this error is to reduce IBM's 1971 price premiums from 40–50% to 30–35%.

Two of the significantly negative brand dummies in 1b belong to RCA and General Electric, who took losses on their computer business from the outset. At the sample date, GE had already left and RCA would soon exit the industry. The quality-adjusted 1971 price of IBM systems was 24% above GE and 26% above RCA. This contrasts with Ratchford and Ford's revised estimates for that year [22] of no significant IBM premium against GE and a 25% premium against RCA. Both our study and the revision of theirs indicate premiums for IBM over NCR, but ours is 38% and theirs is an implausible 145%. We find no significant effects for any other brands although they find IBM premiums of 51% over UNIVAC and 102% over CDC. The current study covers mostly third-generation equipment while theirs includes some earlier machines whose age effects may be only partially captured by the dating variable. The difference in samples may also explain part of the difference in results, since in one unpublished study cited by Sharpe second generation IBM CPUs exhibited a 90% price premium over those of competitors. In a study of third generation CPUs, IBM carried no premium [23, pp. 350–6]. These two regressions, however, used different vectors of attributes as independent variables.

The regressions shown in Table II indicate that estimates of brand premiums for different computer generations are quite sensitive to the choice of a generational breakpoint.[15] Since dates of introduction may differ substantially from dates of high installation volume, they indicate

[15] Because of random delays in first installation dates, it is difficult to identify all machines first installed in a given interval as members of a single technological generation. In addition, cost-effectiveness seems to improve continuously without well-defined breaks which correspond to the usual notion of generation. See Sharpe [24, Ch. 9].

extract rents during the delivery delay period. Although both old and new machines are available at the list prices, virtually no customer chooses the former. One anomalous result persists throughout Table I. The coefficient of the 1969–70 year-of-introduction dummy is often less significant than in surrounding years, and it indicates that equipment introduced in 1969–70 sells for a higher quality-adjusted price than equipment introduced earlier, contrary to the expected pattern. Inspection of the data and residuals indicates that this result stems from the introduction of an abnormal number of cost-ineffective machines in this period, a transitory fluctuation which might be expected occasionally because of randomness in first installation dates.

TABLE II

REGRESSION ESTIMATES BY GENERATION

	Equation[a]			
Variable[b]	1a	1b	2a	2b
ADDTIM	−0·0016	−0·0078	−0·0019	−0·0021
	(6·01)	(7·41)	(5·59)	(4·47)
CORPOW[c]	0·2418	0·0657	0·2371	0·0923
	(8·86)	(3·94)	(7·77)	(5·30)
CDPOW[c]	0·2171	0·1744	0·2117	0·2712
	(2·40)	(1·42)	(1·77)	(2·75)
TAPPOW	0·0275	0·0226	0·0256	0·0330
	(9·51)	(6·24)	(7·54)	(9·68)
RACSTR	0·0023	0·0024	0·0023	0·0029
	(2·53)	(2·44)	(2·15)	(2·94)
I 65–6	−0·1934	—	−0·1817	—
	(2·45)		(2·12)	
I 67–8	−0·3318	—	—	—
	(3·68)			
I 69–70	—	—	—	0·3034
				(3·64)
I 71+	—	−0·4340	—	−0·0255
		(5·33)		(0·27)
IBM	0·1805	0·2384	0·2000	0·0151
	(1·91)	(2·45)	(1·86)	(0·015)
Constant	8·723	9·291	8·765	8·389
R^2	0·77	0·87	0·76	0·81
S.E.E.	0·415	0·315	0·454	0·356

Notes: [a] Dependent variable in all equations is natural log of monthly system rental.
[b] Figures below coefficients are *t*-statistics.
[c] $\times 10^{-3}$.

that assertions about how the price structure has changed with generational changeovers are rather shaky. Equations 1a and 1b in Table II are separate regressions for subsamples of machines first installed before and after January 1st, 1969, respectively.[16] They show significant IBM premiums of 20% over the other manufacturers' average in the earlier period and 27% in the latter. If, on the other hand, the sample is split on January 1st, 1967, equations 2c and 2d in that table indicate that IBM's earlier period premium falls to insignificance in the later sample.[17]

Returning to Table I, we now examine pricing over different segments of the market. Firms attempting to attract a first-time user or induce him to switch suppliers while his computer costs are still small might use high priced models to subsidize lower priced ones. Alternatively, a dominant

[16] Thus the date-of-introduction dummies in 1a are relative to pre-1965 and in 1b are relative to 1969–70. In equation 2b they are relative to 1967–68.

[17] Note that we are evaluating both samples of equipment at 1971 prices, which may introduce a bias. Not all manufacturers would supply us with GSA price lists (See Sharpe [24, pp. 200–1]) for past years, and our source of configuration data lost most of their records in a recent fire.

firm might be taking advantage of high information costs to first-time users and charging premiums on smaller machines on the basis of its reputation. In an attempt to evaluate these possibilities, we split the sample into three equally sized groups by price and run duplicates of equation 1b for low (2l), medium (2m) and high price (2h) configurations.[18] We find no significant premiums for IBM equipment relative to the overall market in any of the size ranges considered.[19] We do, however, find a higher coefficient of variation for quality-adjusted prices at the low end than we do at the high end. (The somewhat unsatisfactory fit of equation 2m stems both from multicollinearity and the narrow range of the dependent variable.) Of the four significant brand differentials in 2l two are positive (GE and Honeywell) and two are negative (RCA and UNIVAC).[20] In 2m, the brands selling at discount are CDC (82% of IBM price) and NCR (81%). In the high price range, all manufacturer premiums vanish.

To an extent, these results are explainable by information cost theory. Buyers at the low end of the scale are more likely to be first-time users and less likely to be CPU switchers than those at the high end. If they have poorer information about computers and their capabilities than do high price users (because the gains from additional search are not worth the cost saving relative to machine size) a higher coefficient of variation of quality-adjusted prices for low price machines would be expected [25]. It would also be more likely that the dominant firm would charge a brand premium in this range than elsewhere, but the evidence that this exists is somewhat weaker. Another potential explanation for the greater dispersion of prices in the low range lies in the user's greater dependence on manufacturer's service and software here than in the high range. It has been suggested that if minicomputers, which generally have little manufacturer software and support available, were included in the low end sample, the dispersion there would be even greater.

The structure of price premiums among IBM's competitors may itself be a source of their difficulty in cracking IBM's market. The two producers whose low-priced machines sell at a discount do not continue their discount policy into higher price ranges. This decreases the gains to a first user who expects to upgrade in the future and wishes to avoid the cost of changing

[18] Breaking the sample by core size of the CPU instead of price generates results similar to those in the table. Of the 73 machines sampled, 31 appear in two different price classes due to different configurations (one model, the NCR 315, appears in all three). Of those machines, however, 22 have only one outlier configuration outside of the dominant price class.

[19] Since our sampled configurations do not include extremely large ones, it is possible that the statement in the text might not hold if we examined them. The sample, however, includes some of the largest CPUs, for which no premiums are found. Since giant configurations usually combine CPUs of various sizes, it is difficult to see why their omission would change the results.

[20] If 2l is run with an IBM dummy instead of those for other manufacturers, its coefficient is 0·13 ($t=1{\cdot}61$), a 14% premium over the market. IBM dummies are insignificant in reruns of 2m ($t=0{\cdot}68$) and 2h ($t=0{\cdot}29$).

suppliers. Of the two manufacturers whose medium-rent machines sell at a discount, one (CDC) provides no configurations in the low-priced range and the other (NCR) sells at the market average for both low and high priced equipment. Given the present amount of computer diffusion, it seems unlikely that many users begin with medium price machines. For those who plan on outgrowing medium price equipment soon, these manufacturers do not offer comparable discounts on high price configurations.

The results of regressions where the sample is split by price can be further checked by dividing the sample into two classes of configurations, business and scientific, and running separate regressions on each. Due to the nature of our sample, these classifications must be quite broad. Business configurations concentrate more heavily on input–output and random access capability relative to the value of the installation than they do on arithmetic processing. Scientific configurations are marked the opposite emphasis.[21] Other things equal, it seems more likely that a user would move among configurations in one of these sets than between the two sets. Scientific users, with more costly installations and more knowledgeable personnel, will probably acquire more information about hardware than business users. Thus we would expect equipment to be more uniformly priced in the scientific than in the business applications. This expectation is borne out in the results of regressions 3b (business) and 3s (scientific). For business systems, three manufacturers (GE, NCR and RCA) rent at discounts relative to IBM ranging from 24 to 29%, while one, CDC, rents at a premium of 41%.[22] For scientific systems, the dispersion of quality-adjusted prices is less, with one discounter (NCR) and one premium pricer (GE), each of whose coefficients is only significant at the 10% level. Computers serving customers with better information show less dispersion of prices, and no notable dependence of price on year of first installation.[23]

Finally we attempt to make some inferences about IBM's attribute pricing policies relative to the rest of the market. Specifically, Ratchford and Ford [21, p. 207] found that they could not reject a null hypothesis of

[21] Regarding possible overlap between the high cost and scientific samples, 52% of the high cost machines were scientific configurations and 65% of the scientific configurations were high cost. The method of splitting out scientific configurations, rather than machines, seems useful because later CPUs are customarily advertised as general purpose machines suitable for either type of application. A virtue of using configuration data is that other components of a system may be priced in such a way as to favor the CPU's use for one type of application. Thus we avoid the difficulty of identifying CPUS as of one class or the other. Of 41 CPUs utilized in the scientific configuration regression, all but five also have configurations in the buiness regression.

[22] Using an IBM dummy yielded an insignificant ($t=1\cdot38$) premium of 13% relative to the market for business systems and an insignificant ($t=0\cdot42$) discount of 4% for scientific systems.

[23] It is uncertain why the vintage effect, strong everywhere else, vanishes here. Possibly changeover to more modern machines is easier for scientific users, and thus older machines cannot rent at a premium. Alternatively, scientific users may place little value on the more reliable software available for older equipment (see n. 14). No evidence is available to test these conjectures.

equality in the slopes of hedonic regressions for IBM and non-IBM equipment.[24] A similar result was found when their sample was broken into price classes. They concluded that this equality was evidence against predatory pricing by IBM. We find, on the other hand, that we must reject a hypothesis of equal attribute prices between IBM and the rest of the market at any reasonable level ($F(12, 243) = 4{\cdot}43$). More to the point, we find it possible to reject null hypotheses of equality at the 5% level between the slope coefficient vectors of all other manufacturers except NCR when they are compared pairwise with IBM. This result holds whether or not an adjustment for vintages is made.[25]

Using the results of this paper to test for predatory pricing by IBM is at best difficult. Brock [4] notes that the US Department of Justice has accused IBM of pricing three specific machines at low levels for differing strategic purposes. Each of the three models is alleged to have been a 'fighting machine' marketed solely to forestall specific competitors in a given application. Brock correctly points out that Ratchford and Ford's test for predatory pricing mentioned above is invalid, since both the complaint and the likely practice of predation involve specific machines or applications rather than entire size or price classes. Only one of the machines at issue, the IBM 360/44, is in our sample. It is alleged that this machine was sold at a discount in order to slow CDC and SDS (later Xerox) penetration of the mid-size scientific market. Relative to the hedonic plane for the entire sample, two of the three 360/44 configurations, both scientific, sold at a slight discount. Relative to the scientific subsample, however, the two scientific 360/44 configurations sold at discounts of 34 and 40% relative to the market. Its nearest neighbors in the IBM line, the 360/40 and 360/50, both sold at slight premiums relative to other scientific configurations. Since a negligible number of 360/44s were actually installed, it is unlikely that the low pricing is evidence of scale economies being passed on to the customer. Thus we cannot reject the possibility of predatory pricing for this machine.

III. CONCLUSIONS

As noted above, our results are at variance with several previous studies, particularly those of Ratchford and Ford [21], [22]. We find that brand premiums on IBM equipment are generally small or non-existent and that the dispersion of quality-adjusted prices is smaller for more costly equip-

24 The revised estimates in [22] do not allow us to make the test on their corrected data.

25 Archibald and Reece [1] used hedonic regressions to test the legitimacy of aggregating different vintages and brands in the construction of quality-adjusted price indexes. They worked with asking prices for used systems and included both peripheral and CPU characteristics among their independent variables. They too were able to reject hypotheses of equal coefficients across manufacturers and vintages, but on the basis of raw attribute variables rather than the performance indicators used here. How they determined the vector of independent variables to use is uncertain. Since Auerbach no longer reports data in a form usable for hedonic regressions, used systems represent a potentially fruitful way to get around the problem of optimizing configurations.

ment. Looking at the implicit prices of hardware attributes, we find no evidence for their equality across manufacturers. Since our sample consists of configurations preselected by experts, we might reasonably infer that manufacturers select vectors of attribute prices which give them an individualized niche in the market rather than attempting head-to-head competition. Given the diversity of uses and users and the likely possibilities for attribute substitution, this might be expected. Although it does not include many of the limited-production machines in the samples used by others, our sample seems superior as an indicator of the factors and equipment which might be investigated by an actual user.

Our incorporation of attributes indicating input–output capabilities is itself sufficient to yield a vanishing price premium for IBM equipment, and IBM's much alleged but little documented superiority in software and support need not be invoked as an explanation of the premium.[26] We have found the pricing of computer systems to be considerably more rivalrous than other authors have found it, and observed price variations to be consistent with economic theory. There is also some evidence for predatory pricing of one of the machines at issue in the US government's ongoing antitrust suit against IBM.[27] We have not yet, however, made any serious headway in explaining IBM's 70% of the mainframe market or its persistent profitability. The analysis of this paper allows us to eliminate some alleged explanations. It does not, however, give us a good candidate with which to replace them.

CALIFORNIA STATE UNIVERSITY, FULLERTON

REFERENCES

[1] ARCHIBALD, ROBERT B. and REECE, WILLIAM S. 'Quality-corrected Price Indexes for Computer Systems: 1970–75', unpublished (US Bureau of Labor Statistics, 1975).

[2] AUERBACH INFO. IND., *Standard EDP Reports*. This source is a series of eight volumes for which the publisher supplies monthly updates which replace some existing sections. Citations give a section number, update month and page number.

[3] BOYLE, STANLEY E. and HOGARTY, THOMAS F. 'Pricing Behavior in the American Automobile Industry, 1957–71', *Journal of Industrial Economics*, **24** (December 1975), pp. 81–95.

[4] BROCK, GERALD W., 'A Study of Prices and Market Shares in the Computer Mainframe Industry: Comment', forthcoming in *Journal of Business*.

[26] Software delivery and implementation for medium and large models of IBM System/360 were sometimes over a year late. 'The initial problems with 360 software did much to damage the company's image with its customers and many manufacturing competitors freely admit that IBM's programming woes helped them to sell users who they formerly could not reach because they were locked into No. 1' [9, p. 39]. For evidence that IBM has produced few software advances, see [12].

[27] U.S.v. IBM, 69 CIV.200 (Southern District, New York).

[5] BROCK, GERALD W., *The U.S. Computer Industry* (Ballinger, Cambridge, Mass., 1975).
[6] CHOW, GREGORY C., 'Technological Change and the Demand for Computers', *American Economic Review*, **57** (December 1967), pp. 117–30.
[7] COWLING, KEITH and CUBBIN, JOHN, 'Price, Quality, and Advertising Competition: An Econometric Investigation of the United Kingdom Car Market', *Economica* N.S., **38** (November 1971), pp. 378–94.
[8] COWLING, KEITH and RAYNER, A. J., 'Price, Quality and Market Share', *Journal of Political Economy*, **78** (November 1970), pp. 1292–1309.
[9] DRATTELL, ALAN, 'And Now a Word From No. 1', *Business Automation*, **16** (November 1967), pp. 34–9, 70.
[10] 'The Fortune Directory of the 500 Largest Industrial Corporations', *Fortune* **97** (May 8th, 1978), pp. 238–63.
[11] GARDINER, W. DAVID, 'Curtain Act at RCA', *Datamation*, **18** (March 1972), pp. 34–41.
[12] GAUDION, E. J., 'Today IBM Announces Yesterday', *Datamation*, **19** (February 1973), pp. 43–5.
[13] 'General Purpose Computer Census', *EDP Industry Report*, **6** (August 31st, 1971), pp. 6–7.
[14] GRILICHES, ZVI, 'Hedonic Price Indexes for Automobiles: An Econometric Analysis of Quality Change', In US Congress, Joint Economic Committee, *Government Price Statistics* (US Government Printing Office, Washington, 1961) pp. 1973–96.
[15] HARMAN, ALVIN J., 'Measurement of Technological Innovation by Firms', RAND Corporation P-5496 (September 1975).
[16] INTERNATIONAL DATA CORPORATION, 'US Computer Hardware Expenditures', unnumbered (May 1972).
[17] LANCASTER, KELVIN, 'A New Approach to Consumer Theory', *Journal of Political Economy*, **74** (April 1966), pp. 132–57.
[18] LUCAS, ROBERT E. B., 'Hedonic Price Functions', *Economic Inquiry*, **13** (June 1975), pp. 157–78.
[19] MUELLBAUER, JOHN, 'Household Production Theory, Quality, and the "Hedonic Technique"', *American Economic Review*, **64** (December 1974), pp. 977–94.
[20] NELSON, W. BARRY, 'Honeywell-GE: Where Will It All End? Or Will It?', *Datamation*, **16** (July 15th, 1970), pp. 80–2.
[21] RATCHFORD, BRIAN T. and FORD, GARY T., 'A Study of Prices and Market Shares in the Computer Mainframe Industry, *Journal of Business*, **49** (April 1976), pp. 194–218.
[22] RATCHFORD, BRIAN T. and FORD, GARY T., 'A Study of Prices and Market Shares in the Computer Mainframe Industry: Reply', forthcoming in *Journal of Business*.
[23] ROETHENBUCHER, OSCAR H., 'The Top 50 Companies in the Data Processing Industry', *Datamation*, **22** (June 1976), pp. 48–59.
[24] SHARPE, WILLIAM F., *The Economics of Computers*. (Columbia University Press, New York, 1969.)
[25] STIGLER, GEORGE J., 'The Economics of Information', *Journal of Political Economy*, **69** (March 1961), pp. 213–25.
[26] 'Xerox to Stop Making, Selling Basic Computers', *Wall Street Journal* (July 22nd, 1975).

THE JOURNAL OF INDUSTRIAL ECONOMICS
Volume XXVII March 1979 No. 3

REDEFINING THE BOUNDARIES OF THE FIRM

KEITH MACMILLAN AND DAVID FARMER

SINCE economists opened up the 'black box' of the firm and found, apparently somewhat to their surprise, that there were people inside, a considerable number of management and behavioural theories have been developed. One of the main criticisms of these theories, however, is that they generally add little to understanding the firm's behaviour in the market place. The great debates that have raged have been over the primacy of particular objectives of the enterprise such as profit maximization or growth maximization, or concerning the constituent elements of managerial utility or organizational slack, rather than on how managers actually behave in the market as buyers or sellers.

The tendency of behavioural or managerial economists has been to rely upon relatively traditional oligopoly theory for an understanding of inter-organizational behaviour in industrial markets. Yet the theory of oligopoly is in no sense unified, being, rather, a collection of insights developed over several decades, deriving from observations of behaviour in very different circumstances. The works of Andrews [1] and Hague [10], for example, are notable in that, although they focus on pricing and marketing behaviour, they mainly concentrate on one side of the market place, that of the seller. There has been hardly any serious research into the behaviour of *buyers* in managerially complex firms. Secondly, most studies tend to take an overall corporate viewpoint, yet we know from writers such as Baumol [3] and Cyert and March [7], not to mention the whole schools of industrial sociology and organization behaviour, that there may be conflicts in the firm between managers in different functions, so that the resulting behaviour may be very different from the original policy. The factors explaining behaviour may not lie entirely in the motivation of top management, but may also depend on how managers in different functions interact, both within the firm and with managers in outside organizations.

Organization theorists such as Cyert and March have suggested that for a managerially complex organization to be viable there must be some kind of 'organizational coalition' across different sub-functions. What the authors wish to suggest in this paper is that viability may be enhanced in industrial markets by the creation of closer vertical relationships between buyers and sellers. It would appear that there are real benefits to be gained on both sides from this 'collaborative dealing', whilst some of the disadvantages of more formal integration seem to be avoided. Indeed, since the first draft of this paper, it is encouraging to note that at least one sector working party of

NEDO has decided to promote such closer collaboration as an integral part of HM Government's industrial strategy.

It is not so much that this is a new phenomenon—indeed, as shall be pointed out, it is much older than the modern joint stock company—but the authors have noted an increasing trend recently towards closer collaboration between buyers and sellers, and have found economic theory wanting in providing a satisfactory explanation. This paper therefore reports an attempt to investigate this trend and to place it in theoretical and historical context.

THE HISTORICAL SIGNIFICANCE OF OWNERSHIP

In the modern business enterprise, the main decision-makers are most likely to be professional managers. The behavioural and managerial theories of the firm have followed from this observation. It should be noted however, that, historically speaking, the importance of professional managers is quite a recent phenomenon. Throughout most of the nineteenth century non-owner managers were not held in high regard in the business world [12]. The preference was to do business between independent entrepreneurs. This is one reason why the joint stock limited liability companies became popular in sectors other than public utilities only towards the end of the ninteenth century. The preferred emphasis was on inter-organizational dealing and sub-contracting. Even within the same factory, as the product moved from process to process, it was not uncommon to find each department under the control of an independent sub-contractor who employed his own workers (13). In essence, therefore, such a form of business organization could be viewed as a confederation of 'firms' in vertical relation to one another. Such an arrangement economized on capital but perhaps, above all, eliminated the need for professional managers, since the entrepreneur managed his own unit of activities.

It is interesting to note that the origins of many of the large firms today are to be found in a similar but wider system of inter-organizational collaboration co-ordinated by an entrepreneurial firm. This was particularly noticeable in the development of the motor industry as we know it today. Both Morris in the UK and Durant in the USA deliberately developed very close relationships with suppliers of components, particularly in so far as co-ordinating plans and facilities were concerned. As a result both suppliers and buyers literally 'grew' together. Both sides flourished as the relationship matured, albeit on a strictly commercial basis [8].

Recent studies of business methods in countries such as West Germany and Japan have stressed the importance of small supplying companies in major industries which have had great success in international markets. Many of the large Japanese manufacturing companies are, in fact, really federations of independent sub-contracting companies together with one major assembly and trading axis. Some writers have suggested that the ability to combine effective co-ordination with decentralized ownership may be a most importance factor in the success of these two economies [6], [11].

INTERNALIZATION AND DEPENDENCE

If there are such considerable benefits to be gained by collaborative relationships between firms, the question must surely be posed as to why there are so many larger, integrated firms in existence today. Most industrial organization texts emphasize the economies to be gained through vertical integration —continuous processes, disproportionate sizes, etc.—but fail to answer why these benefits cannot be obtained by closer relationships stopping short of common ownership. Problems relating to the management of information appear to be the main factors which have led organizational economists to identify the benefits claimed for internalizing, within one organization, vertical market relationships (i.e. those between buyer and seller compared with contractual relationships between independent businesses). Oliver Williamson has discussed this most comprehensively, but his analysis develops the work of several earlier writers. The great advantage which, Williamson argues, internalization or integration brings to the relationship between buyer and seller is 'hierarchy' [14].

Williamson argues that when buyer/seller exchanges are internalized within an organizational hierarchy, the negotiation process is subject to greater controls and is thus likely to render greater efficiency because of the existence of managerial authority. Haggling and extended bargaining between the parties can be resolved by reference to superiors who not only have greater access to information than either party but have greater power to implement the outcomes of these negotiations. A hierarchical system, Williamson argues, is more able to interpret the 'atmosphere' surrounding the negotiation which is the product of the attitudes and experience of the parties, as well as the culture of the organization. In the last resort the matter can be settled by 'fiat' due to the power which superior hierarchical levels have over reward and penalty instruments such as hiring, firing, promotion, salary changes or transfer of personnel. On the other hand, as Williamson has explained, 'inter-organizational disputes can be settled by fiat only rarely, if at all. For one thing it would require the parties to agree on an impartial arbitrator, which agreement itself may be costly to secure. It would also require the rules of evidence and procedure to be established. If, moreover, the occasion for such inter-organizational settlements were common the form of organization converges in effect to vertical integration, with the arbitor becoming a manager in fact if not in name, [15, p. 114]. It is readily admitted, however, by Williamson that economists are not apt to take into account attitudinal influences in understanding the behaviour of individuals or groups. As he puts it, 'scratch an economist and you find a deeply committed rationalist' [14].

Economists are perhaps more familiar with utilizing the notion of market power to explain vertical relationships between organizations. In this respect Blois has argued that where it is exercised by buyer over seller in industrial markets it may achieve many of the same effects which Williamson might suggest can only be gained through internalization. Blois argues that buyers are able to influence suppliers to the extent that, 'many suppliers in a variety of industries are finding it very difficult to maintain their managerial independence from large customers' [4, p. 269]. He argues that this is 'based primarily upon the supplier's dependence for a significant proportion of its total business upon a particular customer' [4, p. 267]. In a later paper he suggests that in many cases legal contracts are not necessary to bind buyer and seller together since this can be achieved by the implicit or explicit exercise of market power. He quotes instances where customers changed either their specifications of scheduling considerably between initial and final orders and concluded that: 'In general the ability of a customer to make special demands upon a supplier will depend upon the importance of the customer to that supplier' [5, p. 38]. This importance, Blois argues, is related to the proportion of the supplier's sales taken by the customer. Where this proportion is high, 'the supplier may well absorb, in the short-term, a considerable proportion of the costs arising from the customer's problems' [5, p. 38].

Whereas it is difficult to deny that the proportionate dependence of sales on a particular customer may be an important determinant of the responsiveness of supplier to that customer's requirement, it does not follow that this kind of dependence is the only factor tending to bind buyer and seller closer together. The historical examples cited earlier also bear testimony to the potential benefits. It does not necessarily follow that increased dependence of supplier on the buyer must lead to exploitation. If closer working relationships can lead to mutual advantages it is understandable, if they are developed further, that this leads to a state of mutual dependence. It may thus be possible through such relationships, both to make economies and to reduce risk and uncertainties in planning and scheduling where market forces may be unable to meet these requirements.

AN INCREASING TREND TOWARDS COLLABORATION?

Recent research by the authors suggests that there may be an increasing trend towards collaboration between buyers and sellers in industrial markets. These indications follow from a recent survey of 65 manufacturing companies selected from the directory of the Institute of Purchasing and Supply. The results from this survey were followed up by arranging a series of conferences involving major purchasing organizations and several hundred of their key supplying companies. The initial survey set out to identify the main ways in which buyers and sellers collaborate; whether this had increased in recent years; the reasons which had stimulated this and the effects which had been experienced. From the research point of view, the conferences were used to clarify and exemplify, in greater detail, the results which had been gained from the survey. Some of these results have been reported elsewhere in more detail by the authors [9].

In outline, the research confirmed what had been thought to be the case for many years by practitioners. The overall impression gained was that buyers tend to retain the same suppliers for very long periods. Buying companies of the kind included in the survey typically deal with several thousand suppliers, but as far as their major suppliers are concerned (that is, those with whom buying companies spend approximately 80% of their annual expenditure), in over two-thirds of the cases respondents retained the same suppliers for over six years. It could be argued that this represented inertia on the part of the procurement managers concerned, but in over 80% of the cases respondents knew of viable alternative sources.

Some 84% of the respondents also indicated that the quality and quantity of information exchanged with suppliers had increased over the last five years. This improvement covered several categories of information relating, for example, to costs, prices, design, production and distribution. There had been many more discussions between buyers and sellers: 71% of respondents reported more discussion with suppliers on quality control, 70% on pricing, 68% on scheduling, 66% on specifications and 65% on forward planning. Almost two-thirds of respondents also said they had developed a much freer exchange of cost data with suppliers. Overall, over 83% of the respondents reported closer and more effective relationships with the source of supply, which meant that the purchasing organization was able to reap considerable benefits in a number of respects. For example, 72% of respondents specifically mentioned closer liaison resulting between purchasing and production deparments in their own firms. On the purchasing side 64% claimed that their purchase price forecasts became more reliable and 56% claimed that their forward buying had become more effective. On the production side, 61% of respondents said that they were able to utilize their own production facilities more effectively and the same proportion also reported more effective use of stores, warehouses and stockyards.

There is evidence here, therefore, that closer relationships have developed between buyers and sellers in industrial markets over recent years. But to what factors can this greater collaboration be attributed? Our investigations would suggest two main groups of factors. The first concerns various raw material shortages which caused problems to buying companies. The most important single problem was the oil crisis in 1973–74 with the resulting disruptions to production, and subsequent rapid escalation of costs. In a less direct way, the miners' strike in 1974 with the resulting three-day week reinforced the importance of energy inputs to the firm's overall viability and survival.

The second group of factors concerned changes in the firm's environment, particularly as a result of Government policies. The effects of price control, for example, may have reduced discretion and flexibility on this particular point which therefore required greater emphasis to be placed on other ways of reducing costs (or increasing profitability). Better co-ordination is clearly one way in which this problem can be approached. And this applies both to the marketing of a company's products (i.e. with their customers) as well as the purchasing of its inputs (its suppliers). It is not surprising, also, that over 60% of the respondents claimed that one of the important reasons for closer collaboration with suppliers was the initiatives of the suppliers themselves. For example, in the fast developing technological field of electronics, the pace of change makes it absolutely essential that such relationships are maintained. All these reasons may be interpreted as the efforts of purchasing and marketing managers in firms which are dealing with each other as buyers and sellers aimed at reducing the effects of uncertainty by close collaboration.

ANTI-TRUST IMPLICATIONS

The closer collaboration between buyers and sellers in industrial markets which has been described above may to some economists seem like an abrogation of orthodox competitive market behaviour. Yet this kind of collaborative dealing is neither necessarily exclusive dealing, nor is it vertical integration. The benefits from collaborative dealing can be realized by both parties without channelling the whole of the supplier's output to one particular buyer, or the buyer taking all of the supply of one particular input from one supplier. Similarly the benefits can accrue without any transfer of legal title to either firm as would be implied under vertical integration. Then really effective collaboration will allow both to be more competitive in their respective markets.

If the benefits from collaborative dealing to both parties are real, it is to be expected that buyer and seller will, over time, draw more closely together (compare, for example, Marks & Spencer and Corah Limited), and may increase the proportion of the product which is exchanged between them relative to the proportion of capacity which is exchanged with other parties. Such a trend which stops short of actual integration of legal title does, it is true, come nearer to exclusive dealing. If this causes increased concentration in the intermediate market, then anti-trust concerns focus on whether this increased market power leads either to discriminatory behaviour or increases the costs of potential entry into the market.

In practice there is little motive for discrimination in favour of either parties to the collaboration unless it truly reflects respective costs. Our initial research suggests, as indicated above, that there are considerable economies to be made by closer collaboration. It should be pointed out, however, that many of these benefits are difficult to quantify other than as an ingredient in overall efficiency in and between both firms. Part of the reason for this is the inadequacy of most accounting systems with respect to the many implications of the flow of materials through manufacturing systems.

As far as the barriers to market entry are concerned it will be apparent that collaborative dealing imposes less permanent barriers to entry than either exclusive dealing or vertical integration. Potential entrants will nevertheless find it difficult to break into a trading relationship between buyer and seller which has been established over a number of years and has proved satisfactory. As Bain [2] has pointed out, in practice the greatest barriers for a potential entrant to overcome are those associated with product differentiation. If collaborative dealing has been successful it is extremely unlikely that buyers will be indifferent to substituting a new and untried supplier for one of long-standing.

ADVANTAGES OVER INTEGRATION

Apart from the anti-trust implications mentioned above there are many other respects in which collaborative dealing has considerable benefits over vertical integration. In the first place the market test is still applicable. No matter how close the relationship between buyers and sellers, no matter how long it has endured, if better trading terms (considering quality, quantity, timing and price) can be obtained elsewhere, there is no permanent tie to stop either party making alternative arrangements. This retained discretion not only helps ensure that mutual benefits endure, but also results in lower fixed costs for the buying organization. The costs of bought-in materials and components appear as direct costs, and benefits will arise in this respect. Moreover, the mutual learning which will most probably have taken place over the years of the relationship may contribute to lower fixed costs within the organization. For example, time taken up in source search, appraisal and selection, in negotiation and in the many aspects of schedule co-ordination could be substantially reduced. Both the buying and selling organizations could also gain benefits derived from smaller size; there being no need to 'invent' management boundaries as in, for example, profit or cost centres in integrated organizations, for they will exist. Separate identities and separate managements will probably result in greater satisfaction and motivation on the part of the managers in each organization who may feel that it is much easier to influence policy in a smaller rather than a larger organization. Finally, there is the possibility of the two separate organizations forming joint ventures to exploit new market or technological opportunities. The mutual trust and confidence which may have developed over several years of successful collaboration could be developed further in this way. Economies would be available in the terms of which the joint venture has access to the finance of both organizations, access to managerial talent would be broader, and perhaps even more importantly the risk would be spread between two organizations rather than confined to one. Even with very large firms an increasing number of new ventures tend to be on a joint or collaborative basis with other businesses.

IMPLICATIONS FOR THE THEORY OF THE FIRM

The kind of closer relationship between organizations which we have denoted above as 'Collaborative Dealing' in intermediate industrial markets suggest an extension of the concept of the firm as a managed economic system. The system is managed in the sense that it is negotiated and co-ordinated by professional managers rather than by owners of buying and selling organizations. The elements which enter the negotiation and co-ordination processes are also of a much greater variety and complexity than is normally assumed in orthodox economic theory. In particular we argue that purchase price can be of less significance than many other factors in the purchasing mix.

The collaborative dealing we have described is the outcome of the self-interest of the partners concerned. These partners tend not to be classical entrepreneurs; in fact in many cases they may not even be senior managers. For them, their performance and motivation is more likely to be related to relationships with peers and superiors within their own organization rather than directly linked either to profits or direct monetary costs which can be attributed to them personally.

It is because there are considerable benefits to be gained from longer term, closer relationships and because there are often high costs associated with opportunism in the market place that closer collaboration is sought. But there are considerable benefits of collaboration over integration, which suggest the need for proactive rather than reactive behaviour. It is too simplistic to believe that the problems of inter-organizational co-ordination can be resolved through integration where the appeal to higher authority inherent in a hierarchical managerial system is the only effective instrument that can be applied. We would argue that in the business world of today, the applicability of a management style which is based entirely on authority derived from hierarchical status is becoming much less effective. Managers have to operate increasingly by gaining the support of subordinates as well as peers (and their counterparts in other organizations) through persuasion and negotiation. It would be going too far to suggest that hierarchical authority is completely outmoded and inapplicable, but we believe that many of the benefits that Williamson would ascribe to internal hierarchical systems, and which Blois would ascribe to the existence of market power, can be gained by both buyer and seller through the development of mutual respect, understanding and trust in a more informal manner. But in addition, it is possible that there are further advantages which accrue to both organizations through remaining unintegrated and thus of smaller size. Clearly our arguments are based merely upon observation, and our research results remain tentative. They nevertheless suggest that economists need to become much more familiar with the circumstances and behaviour of particular management groups in relation to other managers, both within and between organizations, if they are to comprehend fully the factors affecting the allocation of resources within and between modern firms.

BRUNEL UNIVERSITY AND
HENLEY MANAGEMENT DEVELOPMENT AND ADVISORY SERVICE

REFERENCES

[1] ANDREWS, P. W. *Manufacturing Business* (Macmillan & Co. Ltd., London, 1949).
[2] BAIN, J. S., *Barriers to New Competition* (Harvard, University Press 1956).
[3] BAUMOL, W. J., *Business Behaviour, Value and Growth,* 2nd edn (Harcourt Brace & World Inc., New York, 1959).
[4] BLOIS, K. J., 'Vertical Quasi-Integration', *Journal of Industrial Economics,* **20** (3) July 1972, pp. 253–72.
[5] ——, 'Supply Contracts in the Galbraithian Planning System', *Journal of Industrial Economics,* **24** (1) (September 1975), pp. 29–39.
[6] BOSTON CONSULTING GROUP, *Strategy Alternatives for the British Motorcycle Industry* (HMSO, London, 1975).
[7] CYERT, R. M. and MARCH, J. G., *A Behavioural Theory of the Firm* (Prentice-Hall, New Jersey, 1963).
[8] FARMER, D. H. and MACMILLAN, K., 'Effectiveness and Efficiency Between Firms', *Scandinavian Journal of Materials Administration,* **1** (2) (November 1976), pp. 3–12.
[9] ——, 'Voluntary Collaboration vs. Disloyalty', *Journal of Purchasing and Materials Management,* **12** (4) (Winter, 1976), pp. 3–8.
[10] HAGUE, D. C., *Pricing in Business* (Allen & Unwin, London, 1971).
[11] LITTLE, A. D., *New Technology-based Firms in the UK and the Federal Republic of Germany* (Wilton House, London, 1977).
[12] POLLARD, S. ,*The Genesis of Modern Management* (E. Arnold (Publishers) Ltd., London, 1965).
[13] SCHLOSS, D. F., *Methods of Industrial Remuneration* (Williams & Norgate, London, 1892).
[14] WILLIAMSON, O. E., *Markets and Hierarchies: Analysis and Antitrust Implications* (Free Press, New York, 1975).
[15] ——, 'The Vertical Integration of Production: Market Failure Considerations' *American Economic Review* (May 1971), p. 114.

THE JOURNAL OF INDUSTRIAL ECONOMICS
Volume XXVII March 1979 No. 3

THE PRICE COMMISSION AND THE BREWING INDUSTRY: A CRITICAL NOTE

KEVIN HAWKINS

IN its report on beer prices and margins [5], the Price Commission asserted that the ownership of licensed premises (the tied house system) had, by erecting an insuperable barrier to new entrants, given the brewers a protected market within which there was little price competition and thus little incentive to improve efficiency. It will be recalled that the Monopolies Commission (1969) reached broadly the same conclusions, which were criticized by the present writer in an earlier issue of this Journal [2]. The Price Commission, however, broke new ground by seeking to show that much of the investment by the large brewers in improvements to their houses and production facilities since the mid-1960s has been 'inefficient', with no benefits to the consumer in terms of lower prices: 'The simple truth is that the way this trade is organized and run has a profound effect on prices and profits. The question which has to be asked is whether the present situation is contrary to the public interest' [5, pp. 44–5]. The Commission's own answer was plainly in the negative. However, the 'simple truth' on which this answer was based is hardly validated by the Commission's analysis. The salient points of this analysis are briefly discussed below.

I. PRICE COMPETITION

The Monopolies Commission argued that as a result of the brewers' direct involvement in the on-licensed trade through their ownership of public houses, the normal oligopolistic reluctance to engage in price competition had been transmitted from the supply side of the industry to the retail trade. To substantiate its proposition that the tied house system discouraged price competition, the Commission pointed to the apparent strength of such competition in the free trade. The critical distinction which should be made however, is not between the tied and the free trade but between the *on-licensed* and the *take-home* trade. In the latter, the emphasis is clearly on the sale of the product as such and price competition in its pure form is very important. The same can hardly be said, however, of the on-licensed trade where the beer sold is only part of a wider 'package' of amenities. No one can objectively assess the value of all the different amenities provided in the 'package' since the contents will obviously vary from one retail outlet to another and customers will have different views of what constitutes an optimal mix.

The 'package' concept does, however, encourage price *flexibility*, and this attracted the attention of the Price Commission. In its survey of bar prices by type of house, the Commission found that while price differences between managed and tied tenanted houses were 'very small', there were some 'striking' variations in the price of certain types of beer (especially lager) and that average prices in free houses were 'invariably higher' than in brewery-owned outlets. The Commission's survey of gross percentage margins by type of house revealed much wider variations on different beers, but with free houses again enjoying consistently higher margins.[1] The apparent absence of an 'exact relationship between prices and costs' led the Commission to conclude that the brewers' pricing policy (especially on lager) has been geared to what they believe 'the market will stand' and that their managed houses have led prices upward. Yet this analysis begs more questions than it answers. If managed houses are the price leaders, why do free houses charge higher prices and receive higher gross margins than either managed or tenanted houses? The Commission lamely admitted that it had 'not been possible to explore fully' the reasons for the significant price differentials between free and tied houses [5, p. 27]. If the retail margins on the same kind of beers in the same kind of houses are not absolutely identical, does this necessarily imply a lack of competition between them? If, by contrast, margins *were* identical, would this not imply an unacceptable degree of collusion in the industry? By the same token, unless it is assumed that the cost structure of every brewery firm is precisely the same, why should there be an 'exact' relationship between prices and costs? In short, the Commission plainly failed to grasp that the traditional focus of competition in the on-trade, i.e. the competitive provision of amenities, derives essentially from the character of the retailing operation itself and from the continuing role of the public house, whether free or tied, as a *social* institution.[2] To condemn the tied house system simply because it has not reduced retail prices is to misunderstand the real nature of the on-licensed trade.

II. EFFICIENCY AND THE PUBLIC INTEREST

An important theme in the Monopolies Commission's critique of the tied house system was that it had led to a mis-allocation of resources within the industry. It was argued that the closure of high cost production capacity and the development of rational distribution systems had been retarded because both objectives were dependent on the acquisition of national chains of tied

[1] In respect of draught beer the Commission found that free houses consistently charged between 1p and 3p per pint more than the average price in brewers' houses (tenanted and managed). Gross profit margins were, on average, 5% higher in free houses than in tied houses [5, pp. 27–8].

[2] A survey by the OPCS for the Erroll Committee, for example, suggests that the majority of public house customers are more influenced in their choice of house by the opportunities for relaxation, social intercourse and the standard of amentities provided than by the brands of liquor on offer and the prices at which they are sold [6, pp. 59–60].

houses through merger activity. Only when a firm had achieved something approaching national coverage would it be in a position to invest heavily in new, large-scale capacity and produce a relatively small number of standardized brands. This argument was by no means unjustified in the context of the late 1960s, when the industry was only just emerging from a decade of rapid horizontal concentration and the newly formed national groups had barely begun to rationalize their assets. Since 1969, however, all these groups have invested heavily in large-scale production capacity. Between 1968 and 1976 the number of breweries in operation fell from 211 to 147, while average output per brewery increased from 146,000 to 268,000 bulk barrels.[3] It might reasonably be expected, therefore, that this investment would by now have brought significant economies of scale which ought to be reflected in the financial performance of the major firms.

The Price Commission sought to show that this was not the case. Firstly it argued that the large firms were considerably *less* efficient than the small and middle-sized firms in the industry. But secondly, in order to support this contention, the Commission sought to differentiate between, on the one hand, the return on capital employed in brewing and wholesaling and, on the other, the return on investment in the retail trade. Figures were produced, therefore, to show that in 1976 the large national brewers had a much lower return on brewing and wholesaling (32%) than either the middle-sized, regional brewers (46%) or the small local brewers (53%). Thus, while it was conceded that the return on capital employed in the retail trade (through the ownership of tied houses and the advancement of loans to free trade customers) was consistently low throughout the industry, the differences on the brewing side meant that the small brewers had a significantly higher overall rate of return (15%) than the large firms (10%). The Commission further maintained that the large firms' costs and prices were higher and their profit margins lower than those of either the regional or the small firms. The conclusion, therefore, was that the large firms' much-vaunted investment programme had brought no benefit to either the consumer or the firms themselves [5, p. 35].

If this conclusion is justified, it would amount to a persuasive refutation of the conventional managerial wisdom which has permeated the brewing industry since the late 1950s. This wisdom holds that historically the industry was inefficient because there were too many small, high cost producers selling too many brands through too many tied outlets. Thus, over the past two decades, productive capacity has been concentrated, the number of brands greatly reduced and large numbers of tied houses either closed or

[3] In 1974 brewing and malting ranked eighth in a group of 22 capital-intensive industries in terms of capital expenditure per employee, or more than three times above the average level for all manufacturing industries (Wood [9]).

sold to private entrepreneurs.[4] In recent years, however, there have been signs of a consumer reaction against the large firms, principally in the form of a growing demand for traditional cask-matured beer. This reaction, stimulated in part by the Campaign for Real Ale and noted with approval by the Price Commission, has undoubtedly benefited the small local brewers who resisted the trend towards keg and top-pressure beer set by the large firms in the 1960s. Its significance in the present context lies in the fact that the development of pressurized beer both preceded and greatly facilitated the emergence of the national groups.[5] Does this consumer reaction, coupled with the Commission's conclusions about the inefficiency of the large firms' investment programme, suggest that the logic of horizontal concentration and national coverage is fundamentally unsound?

The answer would at this stage seem to be negative. While the Commission's general argument certainly underlines the need for further research into the conduct and performance of the brewing industry, its empirical base as presented in the report is weak. The distinction between the return on retailing and that on brewing is particularly dubious. In its evidence to the Monopolies Commission, the Brewers' Society argued that the ownership of public houses and loans to the free trade were an integral part of a brewery's production, distribution and selling operations and that the return on capital must therefore be evaluated across the whole enterprise, not merely in one section of it. Although the Monopolies Commission accepted this point, the Price Commission summarily brushed it aside, asserting that it enabled the brewers to present their overall rate of return as modest in comparison with industry generally. Yet why should the brewers have invested in such an apparently unprofitable asset if it were not for the fact that it has long provided them with a reasonably secure market for their products? The Commission seems to have concluded that simply because the brewers do not consider that a calculation of the return on capital employed in the retail trade is meaningful, they are unable to evaluate the profitability of this investment. Correct investment appraisal, however, does not require an arbitrary allocation of profits between one activity and another, but a valuation of expected total income with and without a particular asset.

A further weakness in the Commission's analysis is its overt reliance on the rate of return on capital employed produced by conventional accounting methods as the acid test of inter-firm efficiency. The Commission itself admitted that calculations of earnings on assets based on balance sheet values 'need to be treated with considerable scepticism' [5, p. 17]. Unfortunately it then proceeded to emphasize the significance of comparative rates

[4] The five largest firms in the industry increased their share of net output from 23 to 64% between 1958 and 1968; between 1967 and 1976 the total number of brands produced was cut from 3000 to 1500; the number of brewery-owned on-licensed houses fell from 58,000 in 1970 to 52,000 in 1974.

[5] Keg and 'pressurized' beer has a much longer life than traditional cask beer and is thus more suited to being transported over long distances in relatively small quantities.

of return without even attempting to quantify the amount or direction of bias in the figures being analysed. Two companies carrying out similar activities with equal efficiency will disclose different accounting rates of return if one carries its assets at their original cost whereas the other revalues them in line with current prices. In 1976, for example, the balance sheet of Wolverhampton and Dudley Breweries Ltd., a regional firm included in the Price Commission's sample, showed a rate of return on capital employed of 23·5%, or nearly double the average of the national brewers. However, the firm's accounts disclosed that its properties were worth £16 million in excess of their balance sheet value, and if this surplus had been included the rate of return would have fallen to 13·6%. Other regional firms (such as Vaux, Greenall Whitley and Greene King) who revalued their assets in 1973–75 disclosed rates of return which were not dissimilar from those of the national brewers who also revalued in this period. Many of the small firms, by contrast, still carried their properties at pre-1965 values. Once allowance is made for unrealistic valuations, the differences in rates of return between the national brewers and the small firms become far less significant than the Price Commission claimed. As long as different firms revalue at different times, it will always be dangerous to draw conclusions about comparative rates of efficiency.

III. MARKET POWER: HORIZONTAL OR VERTICAL?

It may, however, be argued that even allowing for unrevalued assets, the relative performance of the large brewers is by no means as impressive as one might have expected, given all the advantages that are supposed to flow from large-scale production and national distribution. This point is not without substance, but it must be remembered that the rate of concentration in the brewing industry since 1958 is attributable almost entirely to merger activity. Empirical studies of the relationship between mergers and profitability in a variety of industries both in Britain and the USA do not suggest that the relationship is in general a positive one in the short and medium term. Indeed, most studies to date suggest that mergers either lead to a *lower* level of profitability or else have a neutral effect.[6] In a recent analysis of the performance of a group of merger-intensive firms in British manufacturing industry relative to that of a control group of other firms, Utton concluded that 'companies heavily dependent on external expansion may, in a subsequent period of largely internal growth, pay the price of lower overall efficiency (to the extent that this is reflected in their rate of return on net assets), than companies whose long term growth is slower but whose internal efficiency can be sustained . . . perhaps for as long as five years after an acquisition or series of acquisitions the full effects of reorganization and

[6] See, for example, Newbould [4]. Singh [7].

adjustment are making themselves felt on profitability' [8]. There is no reason to suppose that the national brewery groups have been any less prone to post-merger re-adjustment problems than the firms in Utton's sample.

This brings us to the most fundamental weakness in the Price Commission's analysis. The Commission was clearly influenced by the belief that vertical integration has placed an excessive degree of market power in the hands of the brewers, especially the national groups, which manifests itself in the lack of price competition. It was this belief which led the Monopolies Commission to recommend a relaxation in the licensing laws so as to allow a more rapid growth of the free trade. In fact, however, since 1969 there has been a significant expansion in the free trade without any formal changes in the licensing system. Between 1970 and 1974, for example, the proportion of the total number of on- and off-licensed premises owned by the brewers as a whole fell from 48·5 to 40·4%, against an overall growth of nearly 6% in retail outlets. In 1968 the six largest brewers owned 56% of all on-licences; by 1974 they owned only 34% [3], [1]. Similarly, over the period 1967–76 beer sales through the free trade rose from 34 to 44% of total consumption.

The reasons for this growth are fairly obvious. Firstly, consumption of beer per head has risen rapidly since the late 1960s, thereby attracting more private entrepreneurs into the retail trade.[7] Secondly, the expansion of the leisure market in general has brought new opportunities for both brewers and private entrepreneurs to offer a more varied 'package' of amenities in which drink has been combined with food and entertainment. Thirdly, the licensing magistrates have adopted an increasingly liberal approach towards the granting of new licences for on or off consumption.[8] Finally, the widespread closure and sale of tied houses by the brewers, especially the large firms, has resulted in a significant number of licensed properties being offered for sale to private entrepreneurs on the open market.[9] For all these reasons, the market power which the brewers have traditionally held through *vertical* integration has declined. Moreover, it is the national brewers who have in general made the greatest efforts to expand their free trade. Most of the small firms are still heavily dependent on sales through their tied houses.[10] Yet,

[7] Between 1965 and 1975 beer consumption per head per year rose from 207 pints to 263 pints; spirits rose from 5 pints to nearly 9 pints, while wine rose from 7 pints to 15 pints (EIU *Retail Business*, No. 225 [1]).

[8] In the period 1962–71 between 500 and 600 new full on-licences were granted every year. Between 85 and 90% of all applications for new licences were successful, with a tendency for the success rate to increase over the period. Between 1970 and 1974 the total number of on-licences increased by slightly over 5000, while off-licences rose by nearly 3000 (EIU, *Retail Business*, various issues [1]; *Report of Departmental Committee* [6, p. 85]).

[9] The procedure for closing redundant public houses established by the Licensing Act of 1904 encouraged breweries to retain unprofitable outlets. Mergers, however, made it possible for firms which had hitherto competed in the same locality to close or sell off unnecessary houses. Between 1968 and 1973 Whitbread alone closed or sold about 300 houses a year.

[10] By 1976 the national brewers were selling roughly half their total output to the free trade. The small brewers in the Price Commission's sample were selling an average of only 20% to this sector of the market (Price Commission [5]).

according to the Commission, it is these firms who have in recent years made the most efficient use of their assets.

This confusion may be explained by the Commission's evident inability to distinguish between the effects of *vertical* and *horizontal* market power. The Commission obviously approached this reference determined to show that the continued ownership of licensed houses by the brewers would be contrary to the public interest. Yet all that its analysis does is underline the importance of horizontal integration in the conduct and performance of the brewing industry. Economists have long accepted that market power, defined as the ability to determine supply terms without competitive encroachment, essentially derives from a firm's position of horizontal dominance of some market level and not from vertical integration as such. Thus if it is thought desirable in the public interest that price competition in its pure form should be strengthened, it would be more sensible to develop a rigorous anti-trust policy which seeks to break down concentrations of market power resulting from horizontal mergers. The Price Commission's analysis of relative efficiency within the brewing industry, unsatisfactory though it is, points in the same direction. If it is indeed the case that horizontal concentration has not brought measurable gains in efficiency—a point which for the reasons noted above has yet to be proved—then the attention of public policy-makers should again be focused on the possibility of radical structural reform.

It must also be remembered, however, that any policy designed to increase the general level of competition in the brewing industry would have social as well as economic implications. From the late Victorian era until quite recently, the conduct of the liquor trade was governed more by social than by economic values. Brewers and retailers alike were expected by the authorities to restrain their competitive instincts in the interests of discouraging the excessive consumption of liquor.[11] The contemporary view, by contrast, tends to minimize the differences between the liquor trade and other manufacturing industries, and consequently regards with disfavour the psychological and institutional restraints on competition which have been inherited from the past.[12] It is still possible to argue, however, that if a greater degree of competition within the industry was thought desirable, whether by abolishing the licensing system or by radical structural change, the social costs might conceivably outweigh the economic benefits. This is not an argument which bodies such as the Price Commission are equipped to evaluate, yet it lies at the heart of the problems outlined in this paper.

UNIVERSITY OF BRADFORD MANAGEMENT CENTRE

[11] It is interesting to note that for many years the licensing magistrates in several industrial cities (notably Birmingham and Liverpool) insisted that the local brewers should put as many of their houses as possible under direct management as distinct from tenancy. They believed, probably correctly, that this would enable the brewers to discourage drunkeness more effectively.

[12] See, for example, *Report of Departmental Committee* [6, p. 257].

REFERENCES

[1] Economist Intelligence Unit, *Retail Business*, various issues.

[2] Hawkins, Kevin, and Radcliffe, Rosemary, 'Competition in the Brewing Industry', *Journal of Industrial Economics*, **20** (1) (November 1971), pp. 20–41.

[3] Monopolies Commission, *Report on the Supply of Beer* (HMSO, London, 1969).

[4] Newbould, G. D., *Management and Merger Activity* (Guthstead, London, 1970).

[5] Price Commission, *Beer Prices and Margins*, Report No. 31 (HMSO, London, 1977).

[6] *Report of the Departmental Committee on Liquor Licensing*, Cmnd. 5154 (HMSO, London, 1972).

[7] Singh, A., Take Overs, University of Cambridge, Department of Applied Economics, Monograph No. 19 (CUP, 1971).

[8] Utton, M. A., 'On Measuring the Effects of Industrial Mergers', *Scottish Journal of Political Economy*, **21** (1) (February 1974), pp. 20–5.

[9] Wood, E. G., *Comparative Performance of British Industries* (Graham and Trotman, London, 1975).

THE JOURNAL OF INDUSTRIAL ECONOMICS
Vol. XXVII March 1979 No. 3

THE PRICE COMMISSION REPORT ON BOOKS—A SHORT CRITIQUE

P. J. Curwen

In the UK the Price Commission has administered various forms of price control since 1973. Up until July 1977 its hands were tied by a largely non-discretionary Price Code. On 1st August 1977 a new Price Commission Act came into operation which embodied a more flexible approach. Although the Commission's *raison d'être* remains that of price restraint it is now permitted to use its own criteria for deciding whether prices are excessive subject to the proviso that 'efficient suppliers of goods and services' should be allowed to make 'adequate profits'.

During its first six months of operation the new Price Commission produced five sector reports under section II of the 1977 Act. In June 1978, after some delay, the Commission published its sixth report on 'prices, costs and margins in the publishing, printing and distribution of books, with particular reference to technical books'. Precisely why it saw fit to investigate the book industry in the first place remains something of a mystery. On the publishing side which the report dwelt upon in greatest detail there are some 1700 firms producing 36,000 distinct products each year; the overall level of concentration is very low; entry into the industry is unusually easy; collusion to control markets inappropriate; and evidence of price leadership entirely lacking. Furthermore the Commission was expressly forbidden to reappraise the Net Book Agreement which some readers may consider a matter of more legitimate concern.

What appears to have happened is that certain academics complained vociferously about unreasonably high prices of technical books, hence the selection of that area of publishing for special scrutiny. However, this immediately raises the difficulty of defining what is meant by a 'technical' book. The Business Monitor series PQ 489 distinguishes a category called 'technical and scientific' which accounts for some 17–18% of total book output, predominantly in hardback form. The Price Commission prefers to define technical books more widely as 'books used in formal education beyond the secondary stage' thereby including 'scientific, technical, academic, reference, medical and professional books' and excluding school textbooks. Unfortunately there is no mention in the report of the proportion of total book output which is accounted for in this definition. Furthermore the Commission were unable to provide this seemingly crucial information when questioned by the author. Publishers do not normally categorize their output in this way so the process of distinguishing between technical and non-technical is necessarily somewhat arbitrary. In the author's own view a figure of 25% would not be too far off the mark, and this estimate is broadly supported by the Publishers' Association.

A second, and related, problem arises by virtue of the manner in which the Commission chose its sample of firms for investigation. In the case of publishers it includes *all* those with a turnover of more than £5 million per annum together with 1 in 40 of smaller publishers. This yields a sample of 72 publishers of whom 64 submitted usable responses. However, in the sections of the report concerned with publishers the Commission divides firms into 'large' (turnover in excess of £2·5 million) and 'small' (turnover less than £2·5 million), 44 firms falling into the former category and 20 into the latter. As there are approximately 30 firms with a turnover of £5 million per annum the sample of large firms must include about a dozen firms with a turnover between £2·5 and £5 million, or some 50% of all firms falling into that category. It is therefore worth bearing in mind that, first, the sample of large publishers is clearly biased towards the very largest firms in the industry whose performance is unlikely to be representative of the industry as a whole, and that, secondly, there are quite a number of firms in the £2·5 to £5 million turnover category whose output includes a significant proportion of technical books some of whom must surely have been omitted from the Commission's sample. This latter conclusion is borne out by the fact that the 29 large firms sampled produced on average only 12% of total book sales in the form of technical books, perhaps half of the average for all publishers using the Commission's definition as suggested above.

The sampling problem is compounded by the fact that the report confuses matters with respect to technical books by introducing tables based upon different firm samples, e.g. tables 4.3 and 4.4—29 companies; table 4.5—28 companies; table 4.6—19 companies, all of which are significantly smaller than the original large-firm sample of 44 firms. Despite this the report then goes on to isolate seven firms selected from the 29 firm sample because they account for 84% of technical book sales recorded by this group, the other 22 firms accounting between them for the residual 16%. In this way the report implies that the technical book field is heavily concentrated in the hands of a very small number of publishing houses, which is clearly a significant overstatement of the situation in practice, given that there are, according to the Publishers' Association, about 90 technical book publishers of whom some 15 are major publishing houses.

This emphasis upon the performance of a few large firms is heightened in the report by the expedient of playing down the role of the 1630 small firms to the point of insignificance. Small publishers merit a mere two brief paragraphs in the report and the associated table is based upon a 'representative' sample of only six firms.

The core of the report is to be found in table 4.3 which shows that during

1976 and 1977 the contribution to overheads and profit made by technical books increased noticeably as compared to that made by other books, and in the associated calculations of return on capital on an historic cost basis for the years 1974–76. These calculations are derived from the replies to extensive questionnaires sent to the firms sampled. It is not possible to identify these firms, nor does one know to what extent the Price Commission's calculations are based upon definitions different from those ordinarily used in published accounts.

What the report shows most clearly is that 1974 and 1975 were difficult years for all types of publisher. But even in 1976 the report concludes that returns across the board were no more than 'adequate', and were only equivalent to those which had been earned in 1973. This latter statement is incidentally open to question because the Commission relied upon published accounts for its 1973 data whereas it made its own estimates for later years. The sting in the tail of the report comes when the rates of return for the seven technical book specialists referred to above are compared to those of the other 21 large firms sampled. According to the report these seven firms showed a rate of return close to the average in 1975, whereas they averaged 29·9% in 1976 compared to 19·2% for the other 21, and this difference was expected to continue through 1978. It is from these figures that the report eventually goes directly to its conclusion that 'publishers could reasonably exercise restraint in raising prices of technical books for a considerable period'.

But a further criticism which can be directed at the seven firm sample used by the Price Commission is that the latter apparently includes three firms concerned exclusively with publishing in a hardback format. This is somewhat odd in that even the Publishers' Association cannot identify any firms fitting that description. More significantly perhaps the report notes (section 4.24) that the eight large firms which concentrated exclusively upon hardbacks fared much better than paperback publishers. This inevitably leads one to wonder to what extent the high returns earned by the seven technical book specialists can be attributed to the fact that three of them are also hardback-only publishers. Unfortunately the report fails to shed any light upon this alternative hypothesis.

Indeed the report really sheds very little light upon the reasons why certain technical book specialists did better than others in 1976 and 1977, and upon why they did better than firms with other specialisms. There are occasional references to the hypotheses that risk is insignificant (section 4.33) and competition less strong than in other specialisms (sections 8.3 to 8.6), but this is less than satisfactory. In the case of technical book publishing the Commission, having allegedly discovered a highly concentrated market associated with high returns, concludes that the former causes the latter. But when one takes into consideration the fact that the technical book market is much less concentrated than is suggested by figures in the report this relationship ceases to hold water. Besides which the report several times remarks upon the fact that the seven specialists increased their sales substantially during 1976 and 1977. It is noted (section 8.5) that such an expansion of sales depends upon successful titles in a strong list. Yet a strong list surely is a mark of efficiency and skill, so the excellent results obtained by the seven specialists in 1976 may be deemed to be their just reward rather than a monopoly profit. Furthermore the export percentage in technical publishing is probably around 60%, rather higher than is the case for other specialisms. Thus the profits of these specialists are closely linked to their ability to sell abroad in competition with e.g. indigenous publishers. Considered in this light the report's conclusions appear to condemn the successful rather than to control the exercise of market power.

It is also interesting that the justification for stigmatising the seven specialists rests upon the fact that they did much better than the average in 1976 and 1977. At no stage does the Commission attempt to relate rates of return in publishing to those earned in other industries. This may perhaps have been just as well because the rates of return were all calculated on an historic cost basis, which is not all that illuminating during a period of rapid inflation. The Publishers' Association asked independent auditors to convert most of the questionnaires submitted to the Commission on to a current cost accounting basis, which had the effect of reducing the average rate of return in 1976 to 7·5%, and the rate of return earned by the seven specialists to 11%. If these calculations are correct then even the specialists did no better than successful firms in other industries, although it must be borne in mind that particular problems arise in publishing because some half of all capital employed is in the form of stocks which are difficult to revalue over time. Given that the report generally tells us little more, other than that profits in general were 'adequate' without explaining what this means, one inevitably feels a certain sympathy for the PA view that in general profits were 'barely sufficient to provide for future investment and to maintain the value of the business'.

I do not propose to discuss the sections in the report on prices despite the mention in the terms of reference because the report itself finds the topic too full of pitfalls to warrant placing much weight upon available statistics. What is worth remarking upon, however, is the absence of any attempt by the Commission to estimate price elasticity of demand for books of various kinds. This is important because, as we have noted above, the only recommendation in the report refers to 'restraint in raising prices'. But how, one wonders, is that to be done? The report is unforthcoming on this point and the Commission has informed the author that, in effect, it is the publishers' responsibility to keep their profitability down to appropriate levels as they see fit. Clearly a publisher can refrain from raising the prices of his backlist, but new books and new editions may pose problems. It is logical to suppose that the report's recommendation will in general be interpreted to imply that conventional mark-ups on cost should be reduced for technical books in order to depress unit profit. However, the lower prices this produces are likely to stimulate sales in excess of those to be expected at the conventional price and it is not inconceivable that profits will decline much more slowly than prices. It may therefore prove more difficult than the Commission imagines for publishers to comply with the report's recommendations.

In conclusion it must be said that the Commission appears to be scratching around in order to find a justification for the time and expense of an investigation which really should never have taken place at all. For reasons explained above the Commission gives a distorted view of the competition faced by firms in the technical book market, and assumes, in my view unreasonably, that the relatively high profits earned by technical book publishers in 1976 and 1977 constitute a monopoly profit. It is also worthy of note that the Commission, despite its exhaustive questionnaires, found printers and booksellers to be operating in a competitive manner and earning low levels of profit. Earlier sector reports have been widely criticized, but I fear that the Commission cannot expect to enhance its reputation with this, its most recent report.

SHEFFIELD CITY POLYTECHNIC

THE JOURNAL OF INDUSTRIAL ECONOMICS

Published first in October 1952, this Journal was founded to develop the analysis of the problems facing modern industry. It is concerned with the individual business and its relation to the economy—e.g. with outputs and prices and their behaviour in the market, and with the business decisions which affect these. It therefore aims to contribute both to economic theory and to practical public and private policies in the industrial field. The journal is naturally meant to interest business men as well as economists.

The Editors welcome contributions covering the fundamental categories in economics (such as prices, costs, investment, finance, location, wages and productivity) as well as the broader 'background' circumstances (such as the changing structure of industry, management policy and public monopoly policy). Preference is given to MSS bearing on these subjects from the standpoint of individual firms or industries. Theoretical discussion is welcome. Abstract theory is not barred, but authors in this case should provide an introduction and conclusion, so that non-specialist readers may see what the article is about. Alongside articles of more normal length, the Editors are willing to publish shorter notes, especially when these give interim results of important research studies. Books are not reviewed, although books received will be listed, sometimes with a short note; but substantial review articles will be considered. No payment is made to authors, but 40 free offprints are provided. Contributors are asked to send an Abstract, not exceeding 100 words, with their article.

Editorial Offices:

Manuscripts from North America should be sent to Professor H. Michael Mann, Department of Economics, Boston College, Chestnut Hill, Massachusetts, 02167, U.S.A.; manuscripts from the European Continent should be sent to Professor Louis Phlips, Center for Operations Research & Econometrics, Université Catholique de Louvain, 34 Voie du Roman Pays, 1348 Louvain-la-Neuve, Belgium; and from the U.K. and other countries to the General Editor, c/o Department of Economics, University of Lancaster, Bailrigg, Lancaster, England.

Subscriptions, advertising, reprint enquiries, etc.

All correspondence other than that dealing with contributions should be addressed to the Publisher, Messrs. Basil Blackwell & Mott Ltd., 108 Cowley Road, Oxford OX4 1LR, England.

The journal is published quarterly, and the annual subscription for Institutions is £11 (U.K.), £13.20 (Overseas), $30 (U.S.A. and Canada) post free; the prices of single issues are £3.50, £4.20 and $9.50 respectively, post free. For individual subscribers the rates are £9.00 (U.K.), £10.80 (Overseas), $24.00 (U.S.A. and Canada) post free. Remittances should be sent to Basil Blackwell & Mott Ltd.

A photographic reprint is now available of Vols. 1–13, 1952–65, bound in cloth or paper; single volumes in paper only.

CONTRIBUTORS TO THIS NUMBER

DENNIS W. CARLTON: Assistant Professor, Department of Economics, University of Chicago.

P. E. HART: Professor of Economics, University of Reading, Consultant N.I.E.S.R., and Editor of this Journal.

MANFRED NEUMANN: Professor of Economics, Universität Erlangen-Nürnberg.

INGO BÖBEL: Assistant, Universität Erlangen-Nürnberg.

ALFRED HAID: Assistant, Universität Erlangen-Nürnberg.

DAVID P. BARON: Professor of Managerial Economics and Decision Sciences, Northwestern University.

RAYMOND R. DE BONDT: Associate Professor, Katholieke Universiteit Leuven.

ROBERT MICHAELS: Professor of Economics, California State University.

KEITH MACMILLAN: Director of Studies Masters' Programme, The Administrative Staff College, Henley, Ex Brunel University.

DAVID H. FARMER: Director, Henley Management Development and Advisory Service, Henley.

KEVIN HAWKINS: Lecturer in Industrial Relations, University of Bradford.

PETER J. CURWEN: Senior Lecturer in Economics, Sheffield City Polytechnic.

The Contents of Volume XXVII, No. 2, December 1978, were:

Some Problems of the British Post Office by Sir Charles Carter, Vice-Chancellor, University of Lancaster.

Growth of Firms, Capital Market Uncertainty, and Managerial Tenure by G. C. Fethke and K. A. Currie, respectively Associate Professor of Business Administration, University of Iowa, and Assistant Professor of Economics, Case Western Reserve University, Cleveland, Ohio.

The Abandonment of Major Mergers in the UK 1965–75 by J. F. Pickering, Professor of Industrial Economics, University of Manchester Institute of Science and Technology.

The Provision of Municipal Sanitation Services by Private Firms: An Empirical Analysis of the Efficiency of Alternative Market Structures and Regulatory Arrangements by Franklin R. Edwards and Barbara J. Stevens, respectively Professor, Graduate School of Business, Columbia University, New York, and President, ECODATA INC.

Market Structure and Externalities: The Case of Water Pollution in England and Wales by D. J. Storey, Principal Scientific Officer, Centre for Environmental Studies, London.

Economies of Scale in Sewage Purification and Disposal by Martin R. J. Knapp, Research Fellow, Personal Social Services Research Unit, University of Kent at Canterbury.

Monopoly-power as a Means for Pollution-control by A. Endres, Wissenschaftlicher Assistant, University of Konstanz.

Printed in Great Britain by Adlard & Son Ltd., Bartholomew Press, Dorking

THE JOURNAL OF INDUSTRIAL ECONOMICS

Volume XXVII JUNE 1979 **No. 4**

T. WILSON
The Price of Oil: A Case of Negative Marginal Revenue.

G. NORMAN
Economies of Scale in the Cement Industry.

GÜNTHER SCHMID
The Impact of Selective Employment Policy: The Case of a Wage–Cost Subsidy Scheme in Germany 1974–75.

ALEXIS P. JACQUEMIN and CHARLES H. BERRY
Entropy Measure of Diversification and Corporate Growth.

TAKEO NAKAO
Profit Rates and Market Shares of Leading Industrial Firms in Japan.

P. STONEMAN
Patenting Activity: A Re-evaluation of the Influence of Demand Pressures.

ANDREW CHESHER
Testing the Law of Proportionate Effect.

ISSN 0022–1821

BASIL BLACKWELL OXFORD ENGLAND

Price: Single Issues: £3.50 (U.K.), £4.20 (Overseas), $9.50 (U.S.A. and Canada)
Annual Subscription for Institutions: £11.00 (U.K.), £13.20 (Overseas), $30.00 (U.S.A. and Canada)
Annual Subscription for Individuals: £9.00 (U.K.), £10.80 (Overseas), $24.00 (U.S.A. and Canada)

THE JOURNAL OF INDUSTRIAL ECONOMICS
Volume XXVII June 1979 No. 4

THE PRICE OF OIL: A CASE OF NEGATIVE MARGINAL REVENUE*

T. Wilson

In what circumstances might a cartel regard a negative net return from its marginal sales as consistent with the objective of maximizing profits? The posing of this question may be taken as evidence of an odd concern with special cases, with the strange byways and dead-ends of economic theory. In fact, however, the question has been prompted by conditions in the world market for oil where—as will be seen below—the members of OPEC appear to have been producing and selling oil for some years with negative marginal revenue. It may be objected that we are still dealing with a rather special case, although it can scarcely be described as an unimportant one. But it is still of interest to see whether a realistic explanation is to be found without abandoning the usual assumption that profit maximization is the objective of policy. If it is accepted for the moment that marginal revenue has been below marginal cost, and has even been negative, then the explanation that suggests itself immediately is that political considerations have been and remain the determining factor in the formulation of OPEC's policy. That this is indeed an important factor can scarcely be in doubt. It would, however, be premature to suppose that a complete explanation has thus been found and that no further investigation is required. On the contrary, it may be more illuminating to retain the usual assumption that the maximizing of profits is the objective and then to search for any special features of the oil market that might make the pursuit of this objective consistent with negative marginal revenue. A wider possibility may then present itself. For it is conceivable that the conditions in the oil industry, if somewhat special, are not unique and some light may thus be thrown on the situation of other profit-maximizing cartels.

In the next section the generally accepted theory of profit-maximization as applied to the production of a natural resource will be briefly reviewed. It will then be shown that the OPEC case does not in fact fit at all well into this pattern. The section that follows will take into account the constraints imposed on a cartel by its competitors, both actual and potential, and will direct attention to interdependence in the demand functions for the cartel's output between different periods of time. This is clearly an essential ingredient

* The author is indebted to Professor D. W. Pearce of the University of Aberdeen and to Dr. Mary Gregory of the University of Glasgow for their helpful comments on an earlier draft.

in any explanation of the way in which cartels may behave when they do not enjoy a complete and permanent monopoly. For that matter it is an essential ingredient in the explanation of how non-cartelized oligopolists can be expected to behave. This approach is illuminating. It does not, however, seem to provide an adequate explanation in the particular case of the oil cartel. Thus in the last section the scope of the analysis is broadened in order to allow for the fact that we are dealing here with a cartel of such importance that its policies have macro-economic effects. Allowance must therefore be made for macro-economic feedback and, with shifting revenue curves, the rules for profit maximization, even in the extended form developed in the preceding section, lose their analytical definiteness and the operational problem of quantification already difficult enough becomes even more daunting in its complexity.

II

In his well-known Ely lecture of 1974, Solow embarked upon a search for the guidance to be derived from the resources of economics in formulating the economics of resources [11]. He summarized the conclusion previously presented many years before by Hotelling [7] and goes on to say: 'Since the value of a deposit is also the present value of the sales from it, after deduction of extraction costs, resource owners must expect the net price of the ore to be increasing exponentially at a rate equal to the rate of interest. If the mining industry is competitive, net price stands for market price minus extraction costs. If the industry operates under constant costs, that is just market price net of unit extraction costs, or the profit margin. If the industry is more or less monopolistic, as is frequently the case in extractive industry, it is marginal revenue less marginal cost—that has to be growing and expected to grow, proportionally like the rate of interest' [11, pp. 2a–3].

What is being said, with reference to asset markets, is that the owner of a natural resource has this choice: he may sell more of this resource and acquire other assets above the ground for it: or he may keep more of his asset under ground by cutting down his sales and thus be able to add less to his holding of other assets. Equilibrium will be reached when the anticipated rate of appreciation of the deposit is just equal to the anticipated rate of return on the assets to be obtained by further extraction and sale [11].

We are dealing with a natural resource of limited amount and we shall suppose that this amount is confidently believed to be Q. This quantity is to be extracted over n periods. Let NMR stand for net marginal revenue. Then NMR should be expected to grow at a rate corresponding to the rate of return on assets other than the natural resource which could be purchased with marginal net revenue. This condition can be related to the proposition that, for profit-maximization, the present value of NMR should be equal for all periods (e.g. Salant, [10]). If NMRe^{-ij} is to be the same for all values of

($j = 1 \ldots n$) then i, the rate of discount, should be equal to the rate of return obtainable on other assets and both should be equal to the rate at which NMR is expected to grow.

Various complications may, of course, be concealed by using the term 'net revenue'. Thus it may be interesting to observe in passing that there may be factors on the cost side that will operate in the opposite direction from the rate of discount. This possibility was explored in Gray's [4] presentation of the theory of natural resources which was even earlier than Hotelling's. Gray supposed that extraction costs would be a positive function of the speed at which extraction took place and net revenue would thus be reduced as the pace of production was quickened. This factor would naturally tend to work in opposition to the rate of time-discounting and he showed, with arithmetical illustrations, how these conflicting considerations had to be balanced in order to maximize profits. This complication can also be set aside, at least for the moment, by continuing to refer to 'net revenue'.

Now it is apparent, on reflection, that the theory propounded above does not seem to apply to the market for oil, in the sense that it does not explain OPEC's pricing and output policies. In 1973–74 the members of OPEC were *not* in a position where they had to chose between one kind of asset and another. On the contrary, by raising the price, their receipts were roughly quintupled and this huge increase did not involve them in parting with more of their oil. By raising the price they raised their holdings of both kinds of asset: they retained a little more of their oil than they would otherwise have done and they also added massively to their external assets. It might appear that, even without the evidence to be derived from econometric analysis,[1] it could be inferred that the elasticity of demand in response to changes in the f.o.b. price was

[1] The inference of low price elasticity, derived indirectly in the preceding paragraphs, is supported at least for earlier years by the available econometric estimates. Thus the Working Group on Energy Elasticities of the Department of Energy puts the gasoline price elasticity at −0·23. In the long run, this elasticity is expected to *decline* to about −0·1 as car ownership reaches saturation point—unless of course, there are new offsetting factors (*Report of the Working Group on Energy Elasticities* [3, p. 10]). The Department's estimate for industrial oil is −0·24 in the short run but this is expected to rise to about −1·5 in the long run. In the same Report estimates for various countries from a number of sources are presented for petrol and industrial oil and these support our inference with regard to the short run and suggest in most cases less than unitary elasticity even in the long run.

THE OECD's estimates, given in *Energy Prospects to 1985* [9], were all well below unity for 1980 and also for 1985; these estimates related to the USA, Canada, Europe and Japan (OECD, 1975, p. 11). Yager and Steinberg [13, p. 248] took a figure of −0·12 for oil in the USA for 1974–77.

Admittedly these last estimates and some of those quoted by the Department of Energy's Working Group were based on earlier statistics that did not reflect, or could not do so adequately, the response to the large price increases in 1973–74.

It can also be pointed out that these estimates relate to the elasticity of demand from all sources, not just from OPEC. This objection, however, may not matter a great deal. The largest producer is the USSR but her production has no significant effect on world markets. The second largest is the USA, but about half of US consumption has to be met from imports. There are, of course, the new sources of supply—North Sea, North Slope, Mexico, etc.; but it cannot seriously be doubted that OPEC is the price leader and can remain so as long as its members wish it to do so.

very far below unity. Two qualifications must, however, be made. First, it must not be supposed that the movements in price and in quantities demanded were along an unchanged demand curve. For the rise in the price of oil has macro-economic consequences which altered the position of the curve—a complication to be further investigated below. But the shift was, of course, to the left, not to the right, and the inference of inelasticity in the original curve would still seem to follow from the relatively small decline in demand.

The second complication is of a different kind. The final consumers of petroleum products were not faced in 1973–74 with anything like a quintupling of the prices they had to pay. Prices c.i.f. rose less than f.o.b. prices; prices for refined products rose less than c.i.f. prices; finally—and most important—product prices including indirect taxes went up very much less. The rise was something closer to 50% than to 400% in a number of important importing countries in 1974 and 1975. In short the division of the tax-take between the governments of the exporting and those of the importing countries was radically altered in favour of the former. It is easy enough to think of several reasons why the governments of the importing countries did not attempt to defend their tax margins by pushing up the post-tax prices to the extent required and thus confronting consumers with huge increases in prices. Of these reasons, one was presumably the belief on the part of these governments that price elasticity would be low at least in the short run. Perhaps, with sufficient ingenuity, a complex function could be formulated which would reflect all the responses of governments as well as of private purchasers—although it would not be easy to make it operational! Such a function would be markedly inelastic. Without going so far, however, the inelasticity of *private* demand can be inferred from the response to the rise in final prices, including tax, which, if far less than the rise in f.o.b. prices, was nevertheless well above the decline in sales. For demand fell by only about a tenth between 1974 and 1975, and even this modest fall was in part a consequence of the recession, not just a reflection of price elasticity.

Enough has been said to suggest that before 1973 OPEC was producing at a position on the demand curve where the elasicity of demand was less than unity and marginal revenue was therefore negative. This may not occasion much surprise for it may be held that until the autumn of 1973 OPEC was too loosely organized, too little aware of the potentialities of the market or simply too lacking in aggressiveness to attempt to maximize its profits. This would lead on to the question whether the subsequent quintupling of the price had brought the cartel to a new position where marginal revenue is at least positive. No doubt demand has become rather more elastic with the passage of time but it is hard to believe that a position of unitary elasticity has been reached. If macro-economic effects could be ignored—that crucial proviso—then it is surely still the case in the late seventies that a further rise in the real price of oil would increase oil revenue and allow the producers to add once more to both kinds of asset—those above ground and that below.

It is true that OPEC, like all cartels, has its internal strains but one must be careful not to go too far in drawing conclusions from them. Discounts may be provided because a particular country hopes to raise its revenue in this way without all the others doing the same. The particular country is then operating on its own demand curve which may well have more than unitary elasticity. But it is going much too far to suppose that such pressures are likely to break co-operation between the producers. Nor should a readiness to shade prices behind the protection of OPEC's price be taken to indicate any desire to see the OPEC price reduced. On the contrry, it has been the oil-exporters most in need of additional revenue that have been pressing over the years for a *higher* OPEC price.

It is only to be expected, of course, that there will be periods when the market appears to be rather weak. With GNP growing at disappointingly slow rates in the importing countries and with time required for adjustments in supply, the cartel price may seem high enough, even perhaps too high. But a modest reduction in output could quickly eliminate any incipient surplus.

III

A highly inelastic demand curve need occasion no surprise in the short run. But, it may be asked, what about the longer run? When sufficient time has elapsed the supply of oil from countries outside the cartel may be increased, and alternative sources of energy may be expanded. The demand for energy may also be reduced in two ways: (a) by the devising of means of producing any given product with a lower energy input per unit and (b) by structural change in favour of products with a relatively smaller energy input per unit. This, of course, is the kind of response that is to be anticipated. There have been some signs of such developments but, of course, the time-lags are bound to be very long—even when governments do not impede market responses. The speed and scale of these responses provide a fascinating topic for speculation but it is one that lies beyond the scope of this paper. The question to be asked is whether, with such developments in mind, OPEC's apparent failure to maximize revenue in the short run can be explained by the concern of its members to keep up revenue in the longer run. Higher prices might bring larger immediate gain but would stimulate further the production of substitutes and the reduction in energy requirements relatively to output. It would imply that the oil producers, like the manufacturers in the normal-cost theory of price, were paying proper regard to potential as well as actual competition and were restricting themselves to a current (real) price level that could be sustained in the future (cf. Andrews [1], Brunner [2], Harrod [5]). On general grounds this explanation is a plausible one. To take just one empirical illustration, a very large quantity of oil could be obtained from shale and tar-sands and its production on a substantial scale might become economic if the OPEC marker price were pushed up to—say—\$25–30 a barrel. Other examples suggest themselves readily enough. It cannot be inferred, however, that the OPEC price in 1978 was close to this danger zone. There may have been scope for a significant rise in real terms at the cost of extending only marginally the field of economic production for competitors. (Macro-economic complications are another matter. To these we shall turn in the final section but for the moment we shall continue to ignore them.)

Restraint in the short period may mean greater profits later on but, in the meantime, there is a sacrifice of revenue and, furthermore, future gains will normally be discounted at a positive rate. As Hicks has stressed [6] there is, therefore, a balancing of considerations to be made and this may be represented as follows for two periods.

Let p_1 stand for profits in the first period and p_2 for profits per unit of time in the second period. We can then introduce a weight for the profit in each period: w_1 and w_2. What is now to be maximized is the present value of $w_1p_1+w_2p_2$. Let q_1 and q_2 stand for output in the two periods respectively, r_1 and r_2 for revenue and c_1 and c_2 for costs per unit. Then the expression to be maximized is:

$$w_1p_1+w_2p_2=w_1(r_1-c_1)+w_2(r_2-c_2)$$

Maximisation will not, however, be achieved if the two periods are treated in isolation. Interdependence must be taken into account and we shall follow Hicks by introducing cross terms in the following equations for the partial derivates relatively to q_1 and q_2 respectively.

$$w_1\left(\frac{\delta r_1}{\delta q_1}-\frac{\delta c_1}{\delta q_1}\right)+w_2\left(\frac{\delta r_2}{\delta q_1}-\frac{\delta c_2}{\delta q_1}\right) \tag{1}$$

$$w_1\left(\frac{\delta r_1}{\delta q_2}-\frac{\delta c_1}{\delta q_2}\right)+w_2\left(\frac{\delta r_2}{\delta q_2}-\frac{\delta c_2}{\delta q_2}\right) \tag{2}$$

This may be regarded as a convenient summary way of presenting some of the principal considerations to be taken into account by a cartel, or indeed by an oligopolist. Admittedly the simplification obtained by confining attention to two periods looks rather artificial and can in fact be misleading, as we shall see, especially if these periods are too simply identified with the long and short periods of traditional theory. Naturally the interpretation of the equations and the regard to be paid to particular variables will be affected by the type of industry—manufacturing, extractive, service. Hicks was apparently concerned with manufacturing industry and within this group a large range of situations can—need one say?—be distinguished. It will be recalled that, in order to sharpen the point he was making, Hicks grouped firms into 'snatchers' (who wanted a quick profit over the Marshallian short period) and 'stickers' (who took a longer view).[2] Our own concern here is with extractive industry and a number of rather interesting points emerge.

To begin with, there is a point of general application. It concerns the question of *weighting*. Hicks has explained that his weights may 'be taken to be governed by such things as the lengths of time for which the close (short) period and the open (long) periods are expected to last, the rate of time preference, and the willingness to bear risk' [6, p. 215]. First it is necessary to add a word about uncertainty. The response to uncertainty cannot be rationalized but it may differ from one set of factors to another and may therefore affect the respective size of w_1 and w_2. We cannot do much more than recognize this fact and leave it at that. Secondly, there is the question of time preference. The private rate of discount may, of course, be higher than the social rate but it is also true that the latter must not be simply identified with the rate adopted by governments. For a government may be influenced by an approaching election and its rate of discount may well be above the social rate—where the latter is taken to be the rate that would be applied by a well-informed, but not omniscient, observer with no bias between generations and no interest in election returns.[3] In the case of OPEC oil, we are dealing with government rates of discount and, as it happens, many of these governments have no need to worry about elections. Absolute governments can take a long view! It is only to be expected, however, that different members of OPEC will want to discount somewhat differently. Countries

[2] Hicks refers to Andrews' work as follows: 'One begins to ask whether it is not the case that the firms which have been interviewed by Mr. Andrews are firms which are (or think themselves to be) Perfect Stickers?' [6, p. 50]. It is true that in his theory of normal cost pricing Andrews was seeking to explain the behaviour of firms that wish to remain in business. There is, however, a difficulty here in relating the theory of Snatchers and Stickers to the Marshallian long and short periods respectively. First there is the starting position. If we are dealing with firms already in existence, then a firm may sometimes try to snatch what it can and resign itself to going out of business later. If, however, we are supposing that the firm is on its planning curve and is about to set up a plant, then it would be surprising if many firms were predominately influenced by the position in which they could expect to find themselves in the subsequent Marshallian short period with little regard to further prospects. One would surely expect most firms at this starting point to be Stickers—and this appears to be the position in which Hicks envisages his firm to be. Secondly, completely flexible prices in order to ensure, if possible, a continuous equation of MR with MC might involve frequent price changes *within* the Marshallian short period and this would involve cost and inconvenience as Andrews stressed. More stability with corresponding changes in inventories is likely to be preferred by manufacturers.

Firms are unlikely therefore to be Perfect Snatchers but, as Hicks rightly observes, this does mean that they are Perfect Stickers. I do not suppose Andrews would really have disagreed although he was stressing the longer view in order to correct what he discerned—also rightly—as a bias in the theory of the firm as it was usually expounded at the time he was writing.

[3] Cf. Solow: 'An only moderately cynical observer will see a problem here: it is far from clear that the political process can be relied on to be more future-oriented than your average corporation. The conventional pay-out period for business is of the same order of magnitude as the time of the next election and transferring a given individual from the industrial to the government bureaucracy does not transform him into a guardian of the far future's interests' [11, p. 12].

with small reserves and a large capacity to import in the immediate future may take a shorter view than Saudi Arabia, Kuwait or the Emirates. It has been the former, it will be recalled, that have pressed most strongly for higher prices now and it has been the latter that have resisted this pressure. For OPEC as a whole, a compromise is necessary; but it is probably true to say that since 1975, the long view has carried a great deal of weight.

Let us now turn to the interdependence of costs and revenues.

The interdependence of costs has always been substantially recognized in the traditional theory. There is, however, a pitfall here. In his presentation Hicks was, in effect, considering the choices before a firm, presumably in manufacturing industry, that was setting up a new plant. He infers that 'since we are making the usual Marshallian assumption that size of plant is determined by long-period output only, short-period output will have no effect upon long-period cost' [6, p. 46]. It would then follow that cross marginal cost in equation (1) was zero, i.e. $\delta c_2/\delta q_1 = 0$. But this will not do. The purpose of this line of analysis is to allow for the respective requirements of the two periods and it is begging the question to suppose that on the cost side, long-period considerations predominate while assuming that, on the revenue side, short-run considerations may significantly affect a firm's behaviour. The two periods of this simplified presentation must not be identified with the Marshallian long and short periods respectively. In order to reduce this danger it might be better to sacrifice simplicity by presenting the analysis in terms of more than two periods. This would at least help to bring out the point that what we are discussing is really a tilting of the determining factors in one time-direction or another. This point could be brought out by presenting not just two but a larger number of equations with, of course, more arguments contained in each case. I have refrained from doing so partly in order to keep the exposition simple. There is, however, another reason apart from simplicity of exposition. We are engaged here in a search for the considerations that may have determined policy decisions in practice and too much refinement would merely produce criteria that were quite beyond the scope of what is operational.

Our concern here is with extractive industry rather than manufacturing. If costs are rising, then variations in q_1 will affect c_2, and this may be taken into account in determining q_1. But this consideration, if deemed to be valid, would be an argument in favour of restricting output and raising price in the near future. It does not help at all to explain why marginal revenue should be left at a negative value.

It is the recognition of the fact that *revenue curves are not independent* that represents the more important break with the traditional textbook exposition. Admittedly it is hard to know how to assess the effect of q_2 on r_1, as shown in the second equation; but the possible effect of q_1 on r_2 is a crucial part of the theory of normal-cost pricing from Andrews' work onwards with its stress on the need to fend off potential competition. A reduction in q_1 in order to bring marginal revenue into equality with marginal revenue in period 1 may cause the revenue curve to assume a position in period 2 well to the left of where it would be if a more moderate policy were to be adopted for the immediate future. Profits may thus be increased over the two periods combined by leaving marginal revenue below marginal cost in the first period. For normal-cost pricing does not mean that profit-maximization has ceased to be an objective but rather that its pursuit leads along paths more complicated than those of simple textbook theory. It is conceivable that a cartel, or an oligopolist, should be prepared to accept *negative* marginal revenue, at least for a time, if the longer-term gain appeared likely to be on a sufficiently large scale. Discounting will, of course, reduce the present value of this gain, but need not eliminate it. Moreover, in the particular case of oil, reasons have also been advanced above for supposing that some, at least, of the producers may be inclined to take a very long view and therefore, in effect, to discount at a low rate.

It will now be apparent that, when interdependence over time is taken into account, it is necessary to modify the rule for profit-optimizing in the case of natural resources which was summarized above in section II. For prospective profits will no longer be maximized by adjusting planned output so that net marginal revenue is equal, after discounting, in each period. The cross arguments in the equation must also be taken into account: cross-marginal revenue and cross-marginal cost.

Behind this reasoning lies some assumption about the expectations of the future price of the commodity held by the potential producers of substitutes. We need not assume that these expectations will be naively extrapolative. These rival producers may allow for the fact that the cartel could shatter any such naive expectations by adjusting its own price at a later stage and thus making at least some of the production of substitutes uneconomic. But it is also necessary to allow for the possibility that substitutes might be protected by the governments of the countries concerned. Suppose, for example, that additional coal-fired or nuclear plants had been set up. These plants would then be used whether or not black oil had again become cheaper in terms of *total* cost. The price of energy from new or expanded sources of supply might, of course, be forced down to the level of running costs according to the traditional formula; but there might be no need to go nearly so far because it would be easy to ensure that a high proportion of secondary energy was derived from the primary sources favoured by the authorities and sold to largely captive final consumers. Apart from keeping up, in this way, the return on previous investments, governments might well wish to use their power in order to prevent a reinstatement of oil for reasons of security, both financial and political. Thus, over at least some of its important uses, oil could be forced into a residual role in the market for energy and this is something that should be take into account by a cartel in determining its price.

The special situation in an extractive industry requires, in turn, a further modification of the theory as worked out for manufacturing industry. In the latter case it is reasonable to assume that, as a general rule, output is physically capable of being expanded to whatever amount is required to bring about the equation of marginal revenue with marginal cost. With the cross item appropriately taken into account, profit maximization should be achieved when both equations, (1) and (2) above, are zero. It is a different matter when output is physically limited. The available supply of a natural resource may not then permit this to occur. Of course there is bound to be doubt about the size of the reserves; but what matters, in interpreting the behaviour of the decision-makers, is that some physical limit to output is regarded as probable at the time when decisions are being taken even if at a later stage it may be necessary to amend the forecast. In short, with Q put equal to unity, $q_2 = (1 - q_1)$. It is therefore subject to this constraint that profits are to be maximized. Maximization will be achieved when Q_1 is divided between q_1 and q_2 in such a manner that the two equations above are equal, not to zero, but to the same positive figure λ (the Legrange multiplier for the resource constraint), the opportunity cost of the use of the scarce resource in one period in terms of its non-availability in the alternative period. Or, to revert to the previous terminology, discounted net marginal revenue, with the cross arguments included, should be the same in both periods, and each equal to opportunity cost.

Without attempting to refine the analysis further, let us now ask whether this line of reasoning would appear to offer, at least in formal abstract terms, a plausible explanation of OPEC's pricing policy. This analysis can indeed explain why it would be unwise to try to maximize short-run revenue in isolation with no regard to long-run effects. As we have seen, there is a zone where substitutes could begin to become strongly competitive—substitutes in the form of oil from other sources or of other kinds of energy. The incentive to economize in the use of energy could also be sharpened by a further sharp rise in its price. But it is by no means clear from the analysis so far that the OPEC price is already so high that any further rise (in real terms) would reduce profits in the long run. What is more to the point, there is no reason to suppose that it is these price-elasticity considerations of the longer term that have been the only economic factor restraining OPEC from making further increases in price. It is true that the oil shortage previously predicted for the 1980s (e.g. WAES [12]) began to look less menacing as viewed from 1978. But the explanation is to be found largely in more pessimistic forecasts for GNP in the main consuming countries which, given a high income-elasticity of demand, have pulled down the forecasts for oil. Even so, it seems probable that the real price at which demand will be equated to supply in the late eighties will be well above the level of the late seventies—and this might be so even if OPEC were to collapse. Whatever happens in the event, it seems clear enough that OPEC is not being held back by fears of stimulating such a consequential rise in competitive supplies of energy or energy-saving techniques. Indeed there is another remarkable fact that must now be mentioned. This is the way in which some leading members of OPEC—notably Saudi Arabia—have been pleading with their own consumers both to economize in the use of oil and to speed up the production of substitutes. One wonders whether there have been any other cases in history where the most important member of a cartel—a country that could be a price leader even without a cartel—has tried to impress upon its consumers the desirability of taking steps that would reduce their demand for its own product.

No doubt political considerations have come into play, but it would be premature to suppose that the OPEC countries in general, or Saudi Arabia in particular, have abandoned profit-maximization as their objective. The effect of the oil price on real income in the consuming countries must now be taken into account. With an income elasticity of demand generally taken to be close to unity this is obviously an important factor determining the demand for oil.

IV

To recapitulate, production at negative marginal revenue is so contrary to basic theory as to imply irrationality; but there may be other explanations. These explanations may be found by recording and then modifying the assumptions on which the traditional theory is based:

(i) That the position of the revenue curves in later periods will not be affected by price and output decisions in earlier periods.

(ii) That any income effects caused by a rise in price will not be such as to affect significantly the position of the demand curve.

(iii) That the value of any external assets held by the seller will not be adversely affected by a rise in the price of its products.

We have already dealt with one. Although the need for substantial modification has been recognized we have not been able to find in this way an adequate explanation of OPEC policy. It is time to turn to the income effects.

Dearer oil can affect the real income of the importing countries in two ways, as was seen after the increases of price in 1973–74. First, their terms of trade are worsened. This is the income effect of micro-theory which is already reflected in the (non-Marshallian) demand curves. Normally one may be tempted to regard this as a minor complication, but in the case of oil, the micro-income effect was by no means a small one. For example, the fall in Britain's terms of trade was equivalent to about 3% of GNP between 1973 and 1975. Japan experienced a similar loss. Secondly, oil is so important a commodity that a rise in its real price can have massive macro-economic effects and it is with these that we shall now be concerned. It may indeed be held that these effects were avoidable on the ground that a rise in the price of a commodity in money terms could be accommodated by a fall in other prices with no cost-inflationary or demand deflationary effects. We need not, however, enter into this aspect of the monetarist controversy. For the decisive consideration is that the world economy has not been run in that way and, even if it were possible in principle to banish the macro-economic effects, this is not in the least likely to happen in practice. It may be taken for granted that those responsible for OPEC's price policy will start from this realistic premise.

The position in the short run can then be illustrated by means of a simple diagram. The simplification will now be carried to the extent of ignoring marginal cost as though it were zero at least over the period under consideration. Production is assumed to be at OM which implies negative marginal revenue of MH. Total revenue is OMPQ. If the traditional price theory is deemed to be directly applicable then profit is not being maximized in the short run. There may, as we saw in the last section, be long-run considerations which make it sensible not to do so; but these will now be assumed to be

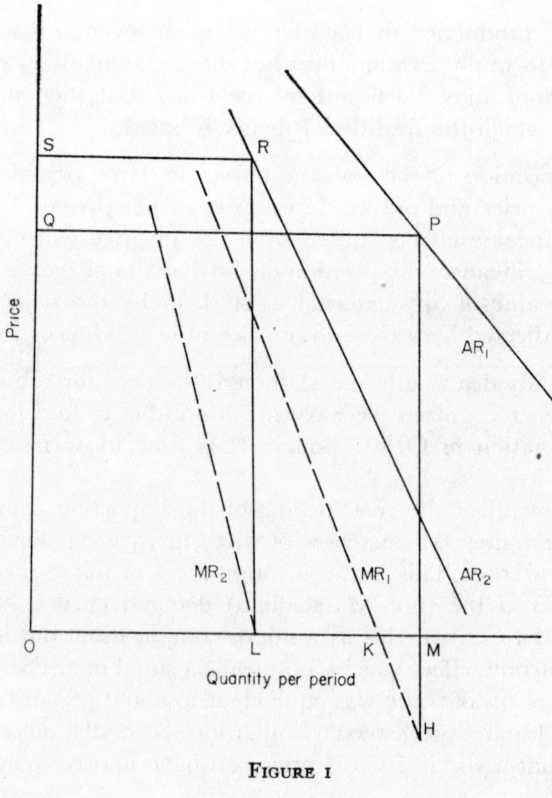

FIGURE 1

unimportant in order to focus attention on the macro-economic effects. Suppose that OPEC now sets out to maximize its short-run profit. It is decided to raise the price of oil with an appropriate restriction of output with the intention of reaching a position where marginal revenue is no longer negative but zero—and therefore equal to marginal cost. Naturally this action will make sense only on the assumption that a position of at least unitary elasticity could be found at once without the elapse of time for the production of substitutes; but this point need not really be debated because there would in any case be no question of moving to successive positions on an unchanged demand curve. The optimum output of static theory—OK—is simply irrelevant because it is unattainable, for macro-economic pressures will shift the demand curve to the left. We shall suppose for the sake of illustration that a position could ultimately be reached on a leftward-lying demand curve where marginal revenue would no longer be zero. At this position the output of oil would be OL and its price, RL. Total revenue will then be OLRS. The question then is whether some *increase* in revenue will have been obtained by moving to this position where MR_2 is zero (i.e. equal to marginal cost which is assumed to be zero). If AR_2 were parallel to AR_1 then the leftward shift would increase elasticity at any given price and would do so, *a fortiori*, at a higher price. If, however, the curve becomes more steep, then dq/dp will decrease and exert an offsetting effect. It is hard to see how, on a purely analytical basis, one can predict that there must be some position which satisfies both conditions: (i) a rise in total revenue and (ii) unitary elasticity. That the first condition may be satisfied is clear enough—and it was shown to be feasible in practice in 1973–74. To combine this with the usual condition for profit-maximization at zero marginal cost—i.e. condition (ii)—is another matter.

The macro-economic implications of dearer oil also help to explain why some of the more far-sighted oil producers have urged their customers to speed up the production of substitutes for oil. Various forecasts have been made of an energy crisis in the late eighties. These forecasts may, of course, prove to be right or wrong, but what concerns us here is not the ultimate accuracy of such forecasts but rather the assumptions on which policy is currently based. We may suppose then that some of the main oil producers anticipate such a crisis—whether in the late eighties or the late nineties. It might perhaps be expected that they would sit back quietly and wait with happy anticipation for a time when oil would be desperately scarce and therefore desperately dear. But such a crisis could have disastrous effects on the world economy with bad longer-term consequences for the oil producers themselves. Some of the more important oil producers are also likely to be deeply concerned by the political repercussions that might follow from such economic disruption.

Finally we must take into account the fact that some of the main oil producers now possess substantial external assets in addition to their oil. If a sharp rise in the real price of oil were to have bad macro-economic consequences, the effect on the oil-producing countries would not be confined to the demand for oil but would also reduce the capital value of these external assets and also the income available from them. This consideration is, of course, much more important for some of the oil producing countries than for others which provides a further explanation of differences of opinion about the most appropriate policy for the price of oil.

V

Even without resorting to econometric analysis, it can be inferred, as we have seen, from general price theory that, before the rise in the oil price in 1973–74, marginal revenue was negative. The resources of economics, of which Solow speaks, are at least sufficient to permit that conclusion to be drawn! Moreover it seems probable that, even in 1978, the price elasticity was below unity. If this factual assumption is made, then the now familiar analysis of the rules for profit maximization from the sale of a natural resource will not do. It will not do partly because no allowance is made for the interdependence between revenue functions over different periods of time. When interdependence is taken into account, it is possible to develop a much more convincing explanation of how cartels—or oligopolists—can be expected to behave. At a later date if the price of oil has then been moved farther up towards the zone where substitutes are economic, this explanation of price strategy will become still more convincing but, in the late seventies, uncertainty about these possibilities and macro-economic considerations—always important in the case of oil—must be taken fully into account in attempting to understand the policy of the cartel.

The operational implications are discouraging. It is hard enough—need one say?—to attach plausible quantities to the arguments in the equations especially when some allowance is made for interdependence on the micro-level. Macro-economic feed-back presents new difficulties. Reasonable estimates can be made of income elasticities in different countries but the forecasting of the probable shifts in income to which these elasticities must be related is another matter, especially when the policy reactions of the importing countries cannot be forecast with confidence nor their quantitative consequences confidently assessed.

UNIVERSITY OF GLASGOW

REFERENCES

[1] ANDREWS, P. W. S., *Manufacturing Business* (Macmillan, London, 1949).
[2] BRUNNER, ELIZABETH, 'Competition and the Theory of the Firm', *Economia Internationale*, **5** (4), (November 1952), pp. 3–40.
[3] *Energy Elasticities, Report of the Working Group on*, Energy Paper Number 17 (Department of Energy, 1977).

[4] GRAY, L. C., 'Rent under the Assumption of Exhaustibility', *Q.J.E.* (1913–14), pp. 466–89.

[5] HARROD, R. F., 'Theory of Imperfect Competition Revisited', *Economic Essays* (Macmillan, London, 1952).

[6] HICKS J. R., 'The Process of Imperfect Competition', *Oxford Economic Papers*, **6** (1) (1954), pp. 41–54.

[7] HOTELLING, H. 'The Economics of Exhaustible Resources', *J. Polit. Econ.*, **39** (April 1931), pp. 137–75.

[8] OECD, *Energy Prospects to 1985* (Paris, 1975).

[9] OECD, *World Energy Outlook* (Paris, 1977).

[10] SALANT, W., 'Exhaustible Resources and Industrial Structure: a Nash–Cournot approach to the World Oil Market', *J. Polit. Econ.*, **84** (5) (April 1976), pp. 1079–93.

[11] SOLOW, R. W., 'The Economics of Resources and the Resources of Economics', *American Economic Review*, **LXIV** (2) (May 1974), Papers and Proceedings, pp. 1–14.

[12] WAES, *Energy: Global Prospects 1985–2000*, Workshop on Alternative Energy Sources (McGraw Hill, 1977).

[13] YAGER, JOSEPH A. and STEINBERG, ELEANOR B., 'Trends in the International Oil Market', in *Higher Oil Prices and the World Economy*, Edward R. Fried and Charles Shultze (ed.) (Brookings Institution, Washington, 1975).

THE JOURNAL OF INDUSTRIAL ECONOMICS
Volume XXVII June 1979 No. 4

ECONOMIES OF SCALE IN THE CEMENT INDUSTRY*

G. Norman

SECTION A

A.1: Introduction

The existence, nature and measurement of economies of scale have been the subjects of debate at least since the times of Adam Smith. The existence debate has long been resolved, but there remains an ongoing discussion regarding the nature of economies of scale and how they are best measured.

Any empirical or theoretical contribution to this discussion must first pose the question: what is meant by the phrase 'economies of scale'? The important points of definition raised by this question are taken up in the remainder of section A. In the light of this discussion we present in sections B and C a brief outline of the cement production process and estimates of the extent to which economies of scale are available to this process. The estimates relate generally to the period 1970–71.

In section D we compare our estimates with those of other researchers. The major conclusions which emerge, at least with respect to cement production, are:

(i) the cement production process is characterized by substantial economies of scale to capital and labour,
(ii) the major items of capital equipment satisfy the classic condition that capacity is closely related to volume (they are generally variants on a tubular shape), but there is no support for the 'two-thirds' rule as a working approximation to the importance of economies of scale to the cement plant,
(iii) any estimates of the elasticity of production costs (including depreciation) with respect to scale must be treated with caution; there is no reason to suppose that this elasticity is invariant with scale.

A.2: Definition of the Production Unit

Any study of economies of scale must first define the production unit with respect to the scale of which economies of scale are to be estimated. In other words we have to indicate whether we are considering economies of scale with respect to the plant, the establishment (which may be made up of a group of contiguous plants), the firm (which can be regarded in the majority of cases as an organizational unit containing a number of establish-

* The author is grateful to Peter Hart and Mark Casson for comments on an earlier draft of this paper. Any remaining errors are completely the author's.

ments), or the enterprise (which will on occasions be made up of a number of firms).

Although the source of economies of scale and their absolute and relative importance will vary with the choice of production unit, there should be no presumption that any one choice of production unit is 'better' or 'more relevant' than another. What should be recognized, however, is that no matter whether it is a plant, establishment, firm or enterprise, the production unit will generally consist of a number of separate production activities which are more or less integrated. The degree of integration and its direction (vertical or horizontal) are important. For example, we should ask whether the pattern of horizontal or vertical integration is fixed. Is there any economic reason why all plants at a particular stage of the production process should contain the same activities in the same relationship to each other? Do firms in an industry organize plants at the various stages of production along the same lines? Clearly, the more variable is the possible intra-plant or intra-firm organization in an industry the more ambiguous will be any empirical investigation of economies of scale for that industry for any choice of production unit other than the individual production activity.

Finally we must define what we mean by the 'scale' of the production unit. Silberston [12] has indicated that scale is a multi-dimensional concept; it refers not only to the rate of output per unit period, but also to the total quantity produced over the life of the production unit, the range of goods produced, etc. Obviously the more complex the choice of production unit the more difficult it will be to find an unambiguous measure of scale, e.g. in any industry the scale of a plant will be easier to define than the scale of a firm or enterprise.

No attempt will be made at this stage to answer the various questions raised above, for the simple reason that they do not admit of general answers. They can only be resolved in the light of knowledge of the particular industry under investigation.

A.3: Definition of Economies of Scale

We propose the following series of assumptions on the basis of which a definition of economies of scale can be formulated for a particular choice of production unit:

Assumption 1: We can identify an unambiguous measure of the scale of the production unit.

Sufficient conditions for this assumption to be satisfied are either that the production unit produces a single output, or that joint products are produced in fixed proportions.

Assumption 2: Inputs and outputs are homogeneous.

Assumption 3: The production unit is utilized for a constant proportion of each week or year.

Assumption 4: Production is in a steady state and the sole determinant of scale is the rate of output per unit period.

The first part of assumption 4 implies that there is no stockbuilding. A sufficient condition for the second part would be that deposits of non-replaceable inputs do not impose any constraints upon the scale of the production unit. A necessary condition is that the expected life of the production unit is independent of its rate of output per unit period.

We shall concentrate on a static definition of economies of scale and so add the further assumption:

Assumption 5: There is a given state of technical knowledge and managerial skill.

We now define economies of scale for a production unit in terms of the elasticity of the cost or production function for that unit. The elasticity of a function f with respect to some decision variable x is defined as:

$$e_x^f = \frac{\text{proportionate change in } f}{\text{proportionate change in } x} \qquad (1)$$

The function f is easily defined for our purposes as being the cost or production function, but the elasticity of f cannot be defined without first defining 'x', the variable with respect to which the elasticity is to be measured. The various alternatives are perhaps best illustrated by reference to the following classificatory scheme:

TABLE I

CLASSIFICATION OF ELASTICITIES

		Elasticity of	
		Production function	Cost function
Elasticity with respect to	Single input	I	II
	All inputs	III	IV

Elasticities I and II will vary depending upon the assumptions we make regarding the behaviour of the other inputs. On the one hand we might assume that the other inputs are fixed. The elasticity of $f(x_1, x_2, \ldots, x_n)$ with respect to x_i is then:

$$e_{x_i}^{\prime f} = \frac{\partial f}{\partial x_i} \cdot \frac{x_i}{f} \qquad (2)$$

Alternatively we might assume that other inputs are adjusted to maintain an optimal input mix, in which case the elasticity of f with respect to x_i is:

(3) $$e''f = \frac{df}{dx_i} \cdot \frac{x_i}{f} = \frac{\sum_j (\partial f/\partial x_j)\, dx_j}{dx_i} \cdot \frac{x_i}{f}$$

We rule out of consideration elasticities (2). Such elasticities relate to the returns to a variable factor used in combination with other factors which are indivisible in the short run, and have no direct relevance to estimates of economies of scale for the production unit.

There are then two main types of elasticity:

(i) *Physical Scale Elasticity:* For each relative factor price regime we can identify the optimum input mix required to produce a given output. Hence we can derive the elasticity of output[1] with respect to each input:

(4) $$e_{x_i}^{''P} = \frac{d \log [P(x^*)]}{d \log (x_i^*)} \qquad (i=1 \ldots n)$$

where: $P(\;)$ = production function,
x^* = optimum input mix for a particular factor price regime.

These elasticities are allocated to I in Table I.

If the production function is homogeneous then there exists a linear expansion path for each relative factor price regime and the elasticity of output with respect to *all* inputs is the degree of homogeneity of the production function. Otherwise III should perhaps contain the elasticity of output with respect to expenditure on all inputs.

(ii) *Cost Scale Elasticity:* For each relative factor price regime we can determine the cost minimizing expenditure on each input required to produce a given output. We then allocate to II the elasticity of expenditure on each input with respect to scale given by:

(5) $$e_q^{''C_i} = \frac{d \log [C_i^*(q)]}{d \log (q)} \qquad (i=1 \ldots n)$$

where: $C_i^*(q)$ = cost minimizing expenditure on factor i under the particular factor price regime,
q = output (scale).

The total cost function is given by:

(6) $$TC^*(q) = \sum_i C_i^*(q)$$

[1] If assumptions 2–4 and the sufficient condition for assumption 1 are satisfied, 'output' and 'scale' or 'capacity' are synonymous.

and we allocate to IV the elasticity:

$$(7) \qquad e_q^{\prime\prime TC} = \frac{\mathrm{d}\log[TC(q)]}{\mathrm{d}\log(q)}$$

It should be emphasized that the elasticities I–IV are defined with respect to a particular set of relative factor prices.[2] In other words we might expect different relative factor price regimes to give rise to different elasticities. One corollary of this is that, no matter which elasticity is considered, this elasticity will not in general be independent of location of the production unit.

It should also be noted that for each relative factor price regime the elasticities I and III are the inverses of the elasticities II and IV respectively. Elasticity IV is in fact the 'scale factor' referred to by Silberston [12] and is the inverse of the degree of homogeneity of the production function.

We can now define what we mean by economies of scale with respect to our choice of production unit. Economies of scale are said to exist with respect to a particular input, or to all inputs, when the appropriate elasticity of the cost (production) function evaluated at constant relative factor prices and incorporating a given technology is less (greater) than unity over some or all of the range of attainable scales.[3]

This definition makes no presumption that the elasticity of the cost (or production) function will be constant with scale. Indeed the work of Griliches and Ringstad [4] would lead us to expect some variation in elasticity, i.e. in the degree of economies of scale available to some or all inputs.

The definition is static since a date has been put on the cost and production functions. Extensions of this definition to include economies of scale deriving from those factors which work to change the position or form of the function should be obvious but will not be considered in this paper.

A.4: The Sources of Economies of Scale

This subsection is of necessity brief, and no attempt will be made to survey the large body of literature which exists. A number of the more important and seminal references are given in footnote 4.

[2] For a non-homogeneous production function the suggested definition of elasticity III also implies constant absolute factor prices.

[3] It should be noted that for scale ranges over which elasticities II and IV are less than unity the appropriate average cost curve will be downward sloping.

[4] The theoretical and empirical literature on this subject is vast. Undoubtedly, however, one of the most important studies is Robinson [10]. Of the more recent work on economies of scale exhibited by production functions, Walters [14] and Diwan [3] are interesting examples of particular sectors, while Griliches and Ringstad [4] provide a wider coverage. Economies of scale exhibited by cost functions were analysed by Haldi and Witcomb [5]. The most important recent work in this field, however, has been produced by Cockerill [1], [2], Pratten and Dean [9] and Pratten [8].

We can identify four major sources of economies of scale within our static definition:

(i) The topological properties of production. For example capacity may be related to volume (oil tankers, rotary kilns, etc.) while materials used (and so cost) may be related to surface area.

(ii) Indivisibilities. It may be necessary to employ certain factors in indivisible 'lumps' independent of the scale of the production unit for at least some ranges of scale.

(iii) Organizational economies. Unit costs may be reduced by changing the degree of vertical or horizontal integration, e.g. by internalizing an imperfect intermediate product market, by reducing the uncertainty of information flows, etc.

(iv) Financial economies: Expansion of the production unit may lead to some internalization of the short-term capital market, give rise to monopsony powers in the factor markets, etc.

As has been indicated, the relative importance of these four sources will vary with the choice of production unit. Thus (i) and (ii) are liable to be the dominant sources for the individual production activity, while (iii) may accrue to the plant or establishment and (iv) to the firm or enterprise.

SECTION B

B.1: The Cement Production Process

There are three distinct operations in cement manufacture. The first process involves assembling, preparing, grinding and amalgamating the raw materials (clay and limestone or chalk) in the appropriate proportions. In the second process the mixture produced by the first process is roasted at high temperature to form cement clinker: this is accomplished using rotary kilns fired usually by oil or pulverized coal. The hot clinker is then conveyed to rotary or stationary coolers prior to the third process in which the clinker together with a small amount of retarding agent (gypsum) is ground to the fine powder known as cement.

It is clear from this summary that the cement production process is capital intensive in the sense of employing several large units of capital equipment. We would expect to find significant economies to capital costs as scale increases since capacity of many of the units will probably be related to volume while cost will be more closely related to surface area. In addition there should be labour economies since labour performs a basically supervisory role.

B.2: The Production Unit

The production process consists of three distinct activities, which must be performed in strict temporal sequence. Further, while there is no reason in principle for these activities to be performed at the same location (i.e.

for each plant to contain all three activities) there is a fairly strong presumption that this will in fact be the case. There are a few examples of plants which merely grind clinker imported from other plants but these are very much the exception to the general rule that quarrying, rotary kilns, and clinker grinders are located within the same plant. We therefore choose the establishment as our production unit.

We are then concerned with estimating the economies which result from varying the scale of the production unit while maintaining its vertically integrated structure. The data on which these estimates are based are described in section C.1. They are such that we follow the cost scale elasticity approach for individual inputs, i.e. we derive estimates of elasticities II in Table I.

Before these estimates are presented however, we should check that our assumptions 1–5 above do not represent too great a departure from 'reality'. The cement industry produces a homogeneous product (Portland cement) which has to satisfy rigorous chemical standards. Some other specialist cements are produced, but in the UK for example these account for no more than 10% of total output by weight. We feel justified therefore in ignoring complications which might arise as a result of changes in the product mix. Materials inputs consist of fuel, chalk or limestone, and clay or shale, each of which can be taken to be individually homogeneous, i.e. we assume that there are no significant variations in the quality of each material.

Secondly, the rotary kiln technology has been in existence since the early 1900s. The technology has advanced in that alterations have been made to the basic shape of the kiln, e.g. with the introduction of 'dumb-bell' kilns, and the maximum feasible capacity of kiln has been increased over the years. But there have been no fundamental changes in the technology.

The data sources used to derive the estimates in section C measure 'scale' in tonnes per annum, assuming a 24 hour day, 330 days per annum. In other words, assumption 3 is implicitly contained in the data. Finally, our discussions with the industry indicated that expected plant life was felt to be invariant with annual plant capacity.

SECTION C

C.1: Data Sources

The data for our estimates relate to the cement industries in West Germany and the United States. There are three data series, denoted A, B and C below. Series A was reported by a United Nations study team [13] and is summarized in Appendix A. This series is

> based primarily on data from a case history study of eighteen new plants constructed during the period 1956–60 and experts' opinions . . . (Capital costs) were adjusted to prices in 1960 (United Nations [13]).

Series B was obtained from the *World Cement Directory* [15]. This directory lists all cement plants in operation at the end of 1970 and for many of these plants reports annual capacity, clinker production, and total number of persons employed. For the United States employment data were reported for 83 of the 176 plants in operation.

Series C was made available to us by a firm which designs cement plants. These data are engineering estimates of the relationship between annual plant capacity and 1971 capital costs for cement plants designed and constructed in West Germany. They are detailed in Appendix B.

As can be seen, the data are drawn from a mixture of actual and hypothetical plants. Any attempt to compare the various series is therefore based on two assumptions about efficiency:

(i) that the estimates derived from observations of actual plants are estimates of the most efficient use of factors of production, and
(ii) that manufacturers in choosing from hypothetical plants will only choose efficient techniques.

These efficiency assumptions are such, in particular, that we can treat each data series as cross-section data thus reducing any problems which might arise from changes in relative factor prices.

Given these assumptions we may ask why it should be efficient to build plants of different scales which apparently do not fully exploit the available economies of scale. The point here is that production conditions are not independent of location or time. Consider for example a monopolist considering how best to serve demand in some small region R. If R contains the basic minerals required for cement production and is sufficiently remote from other feasible production sites it may well be efficient to operate a small-scale plant in R.[5] Alternatively, if demand in some market S is growing slowly (relative to minimum efficient plant scale) an efficient production strategy in S may well involve the sacrifice of production cost economies in order to avoid the costs of carrying spare capacity or incurring additional transport or storage costs.[6]

C.2: Materials and Energy Inputs

Series A indicates that the materials input per tonne of cement is invariant with scale. This result is to be expected given that Portland cement has to satisfy fairly rigorous standards with respect to its chemical composition. Perhaps more surprising is the indication that there are no economies of scale to the energy inputs. The United Nations study team did report however that the consumption of fuel and energy was linearly proportional

[5] This point is in fact central to Norman [7].

[6] This is discussed more fully in Norman [7, Chapter 7], in which it is indicated that plant capacities of less than 200 thousand tonnes p.a. may be perfectly efficient choices in a multi-period situation.

to scale:

> In the view of a number of experts in this field, there appears to be no significant variation in unit fuel requirements with changes in scale of operation ([13, p. 9]).

and

> There appears to be little change in electric power consumption with changes in the scale of operations ([13, p. 10]).

The constancy of unit materials and energy inputs with scale might be expected to offset to some extent economies of scale exhibited by other inputs. Our choice of production unit is such, however, that labour and capital costs incurred in extracting the minerals are included in the estimates of labour and capital costs. Since these latter costs are the only direct costs to be met by the cement companies in mining the minerals, and since we shall find that they exhibit economies of scale, it is not the case that unit materials *costs* are invariant with scale.

Thus only energy costs can be expected to show any constancy with scale.

C.3: Labour Costs

The estimates in this section are derived from the data reported in the *World Cement Directory* (Series B referred to above).

Our hypothesis is that employment is determined by plant capacity. The functional relationship between capacity and employment can take a number of forms and two basic forms were considered. Firstly, we might hypothesize that the labour input consists of a fixed element (probably made up predominantly of managerial and technical staff) plus an element linear in plant capacity. This implies an equation of the form:

(8) $$E = \alpha_1 + \beta_1 C + \epsilon$$

where: E = employment (no.).
C = capacity (thousand tonnes p.a.).
ϵ = error term.

If there are economies of scale to labour and (8) is the appropriate specification, then we would expect:

(9) $$\alpha_1 > 0$$

Alternatively, we might hypothesize that the labour input increases 'smoothly' with capacity, i.e. that the functional form is:

(10) $$E = \alpha_2 C \beta_2 \epsilon_2$$

In this case economies of scale to labour require:

(11) $$\beta_2 < 1$$

The scatter diagram of employment against capacity is illustrated in Figure 1. It should perhaps be noted that the United Nations observations reported in Appendix A exhibit quite a high degree of agreement with those illustrated in Figure 1.

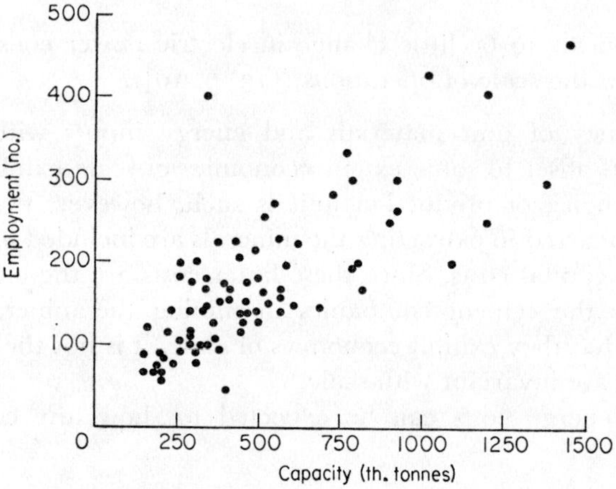

FIGURE 1

It would appear from this scatter diagram that equation (8) is inappropriate. The distribution of plant capacities is positively skewed and there is some indication of heteroscedasticity in the data. We decided therefore to estimate equation (10), and obtained the estimate:[7]

$$\ln(E) = 0{\cdot}8200 + 0{\cdot}6969 \ln(C) \quad (R^2 = 0{\cdot}57;\ 81 \text{ d.f.}) \tag{12}$$
$$(0{\cdot}4089) \quad (0{\cdot}0675)$$

Equation (12) can be rewritten:

$$E = 2{\cdot}2705\, C^{0{\cdot}6969} \tag{13}$$

All coefficients are significant at the 5% level.

Equation (13) supports the hypothesis that there are significant economies of scale to labour in cement production over the range of plants for which we have observations: an index of labour requirements is given in Table II.

C.4: Capital Costs

Series C was used to indicate the relationship between plant scale and capital costs: the data are presented in Appendix B. As was indicated in section C.1, these data are engineering estimates of the relationship between

[7] Standard errors are given in brackets.

TABLE II

LABOUR INPUT PER UNIT OF CEMENT CAPACITY: UNITED STATES CEMENT MANUFACTURE

Capacity (th. tonnes p.a.)	*Unit labour requirement (index)*	*Elasticity of labour requirement with respect to capacity*[a]
100	100·0	
500	61·4	0·6969
1000	49·8	
1500	44·0	

[a] With a constant wage rate this is also the elasticity of labour costs with respect to scale.
Source: See text.

plant scale and 1971 capital costs for plants designed and constructed in West Germany.

Fitting a functional form to the data in Appendix B is somewhat awkward. Both a simple linear and log-linear relationship were estimated, but both were felt to be inappropriate in view of the pattern of residuals they generated.

It would appear that the appropriate functional form is rather more complex than either linear or log-linear. Rather than attempt to describe what that form should be however, Figures 2–5 have been constructed by linear interpolation between adjacent observations in Appendix B.[8] We feel that the characteristics of the data are better seen from the figures.

Figures 2 and 3 illustrate the relationship between total and average capital costs and capacity. Despite the convexity of total capital costs

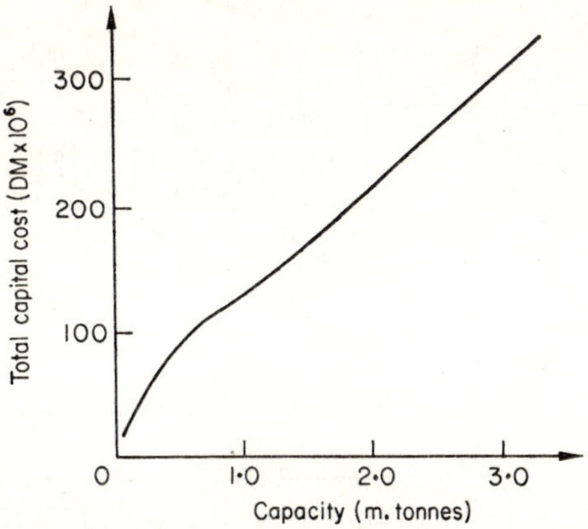

FIGURE 2. Total Capital Costs Related to Capacity

[8] This is felt to be legitimate in that the engineering estimates are probably taken from some composite functional form rather than from observations of actual plants.

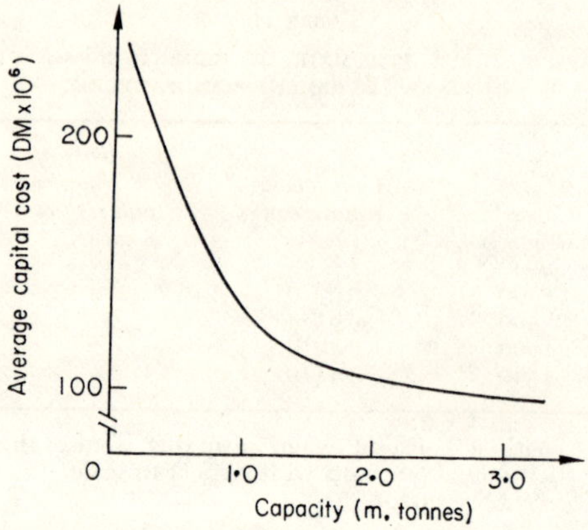

FIGURE 3. Average Capital Costs Related to Capacity

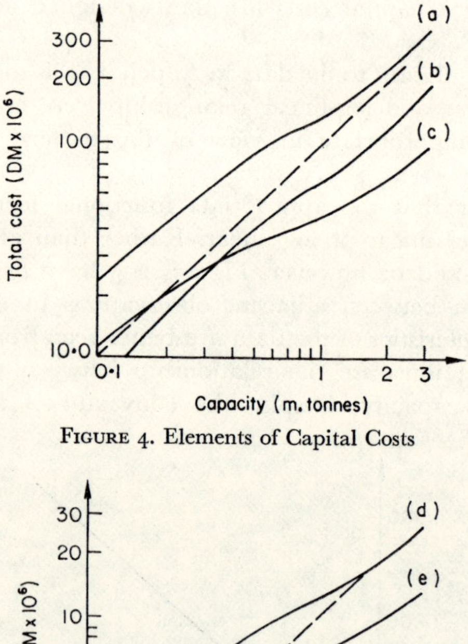

FIGURE 4. Elements of Capital Costs

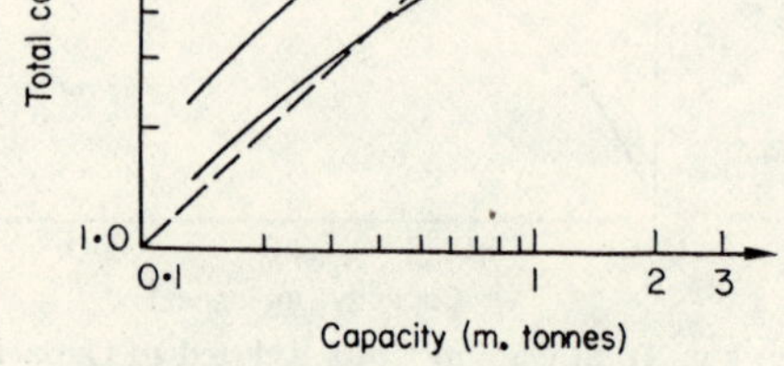

FIGURE 5. Elements of Capital Costs

Notes: (a) total capital costs; (b) mechanical and electrical costs; (c) civil engineering costs; (d) machine erection costs; (e) quarry equipment costs.

for plant capacities in excess of approximately 1·0 million tonnes p.a., Figure 3 indicates that unit capital costs are monotonic decreasing, i.e. there are economies of scale to capital costs throughout the range of plant capacities. While there is a sharp fall in unit capital costs up to plant capacities of about 1·0 million tonnes p.a., however, the reduction in unit capital costs for greater plant capacities is much less pronounced; there is a less than 6% reduction in unit capital costs when capacity is increased from 2·0 to 3·3 million tonnes p.a.

It is perhaps useful to examine the breakdown of capital costs to see whether the various components behave differently. Again a diagrammatic exposition is clearest and we use Figures 4 and 5. These diagrams are drawn on log–log axes to illustrate the extent to which economies of scale are present. With this type of graph any curve with a slope less (greater) than the 45° line exhibits economies (diseconomies) of scale to the particular cost component. The slope of the cost curve at any point is the elasticity of the appropriate cost component with respect to scale; the lower the elasticity the greater the degree of scale economies to that cost component.

Taking total capital costs first, the cost elasticity of scale decreases quite sharply for plant capacities in excess of 250 thousand tonnes p.a. and continues to decrease up to plant capacities of about 1·0 million tonnes p.a. The elasticity then increases gradually but remains less than unity, i.e. unit capital costs continue to fall but at a slower rate for plant capacities in excess of 1·0 million tonnes p.a.

Mechanical and electrical costs form the greater part of total capital costs. It is not surprising therefore that the two series exhibit roughly the same pattern. What is perhaps surprising is that economies of scale to mechanical and electrical costs are not more pronounced at lower plant scales. The basic items of machinery to which these costs refer are rotary kilns, crushers, grinders, etc. On *a priori* grounds we might expect the 'two-thirds rule' to apply, at least approximately, with capacity being related to volume and cost to surface area. On the other hand, while kilns, etc., are basically tubes the capacities of which are related to their volumes, they must be supported and driven. At low scales the costs of peripheral equipment can be expected to form quite a significant proportion of mechanical and electrical costs and might be expected to increase in direct proportion with scale. In addition as scale increases advantage can be taken of various refinements of the basic technology, such as changing the shape of the rotary kiln, which increase the output obtainable from a kiln of a given volume. Beyond some scale, however, the costs of supporting and driving ever larger kilns may well increase more than in proportion to the increase in kiln capacity so offsetting any savings in the materials used to make the kiln. The gauge of metal used in constructing the kiln will also have to increase to maintain its strength so introducing a 'volume' element to mechanical and electrical costs.

Somewhat the same pattern emerges with respect to the other components of total capital costs. It should be noted that there are quite sharp economies of scale to civil engineering costs (site clearance, foundations, etc.) and to the costs of quarry equipment. These iterms form a small proportion of total capital costs with the result that they have little effect on the overall shape of the latter. They do however, give rise to some degree of economies of scale at low plant capacities despite the near constancy of mechanical and electrical costs.

Comparison of the United States capital costs in Appendix A with the West German data in Appendix B would indicate on first sight that the elasticity of capital costs with respect to scale was lower in the US (in the period 1956–60) than in West Germany (in 1970) for plant capacities in the range 0·1–1·0 million tonnes p.a. Table III indicates the respective elasticities.

TABLE III

ELASTICITY OF CAPITAL COSTS: US AND WEST GERMANY

Capacity			*Elasticity of capital costs*[a]				
United States		*West Germany*					
Million tons p.a.	*Million tonnes p.a.*	*Million tonnes p.a.*	*US* (1)		*WG* (2)		*US*[b] (3)
0·120	0·107	0·099	0·76		0·84		0·85
0·510	0·455	0·4125		0·69		0·77	
1·000	0·893	0·9075	0·53		0·60		0·59

[a] Estimated from a relationship $Y = aX^n$ where n = elasticity of Y with respect to X.
[b] See text below.

One possible explanation of the apparent difference is that the data in Appendix A exhibit a consistent bias in capital costs. These data are taken from Appendix I of the United Nations report and represent a sample of seven observations from a total of eighteen. The study team report in the main text that on the basis of all eighteen observations the elasticity of capital costs over the range 0·1–1·0 million tons p.a. was 0·77. Applying the ratio 0·77/0·69 to the estimated elasticities in coulmn (1) of Table III above gives the elasticities in column (3) which are much more in line with the West German estimates.

It would appear therefore that while the maximum feasible capacity of kiln may have increased over the period 1956–71, the elasticity of capital costs with respect to scale has change little, at least for plant capacities up to 1·0 million tonnes p.a.

C.5: Total Costs

The discussion in sections C.2–C.5 indicates that economies of scale are available in particular to the labour and capital inputs to cement production. Data limitations are such that we have had to confine our attention to elasticities II in Table I. It would be informative, however, if some estimate could be made of elasticity IV: the elasticity of the cost function with respect to all inputs.

Any attempt to estimate elasticity IV requires that individual cost components be combined, but this can only be done on the basis of assumptions which are at least heroic. Such an attempt was made (for other reasons) in Norman [7] and the results are given in Table IV.

TABLE IV

TOTAL PRODUCTION COSTS: UK CEMENT MANUFACTURE 1963

Capacity (thousand tonnes p.a.)	*Total cost* (£m)	*Average cost* (£)	*Elasticity of total costs*[a]
82·5	0·546	6·62	
99·0	0·631	6·37	0·79
132·0	0·797	6·04	0·81
166·0	0·963	5·80	0·83
247·5	1·357	5·48	0·86
330·0	1·727	5·23	0·84
412·5	2·073	5·03	0·82
495·0	2·409	4·87	0·82
577·5	2·715	4·70	0·78
660·0	3·009	4·56	0·77
742·5	3·283	4·42	0·74
825·0	3·560	4·32	0·77
907·5	3·820	4·21	0·74
990·0	4·078	4·12	0·75
1155·0	4·616	4·00	0·80
1320·0	5·155	3·91	0·83
1485·0	5·708	3·84	0·87
1650·0	6·288	3·81	0·92
1980·0	7·434	3·75	0·92
2310·0	8·577	3·71	0·93
2640·0	9·718	3·68	0·94
2970·0	10·880	3·66	0·96
3300·0	11·988	3·63	0·92

[a] Elasticity is the arc elasticity in each capacity interval.
Source: Norman [7].

Using Pratten's definition (Pratten [8, p. 26]) of minimum efficient scale (m.e.s.), the estimates in Table IV would imply m.e.s. for the production unit of approximately 1·6 million tonnes p.a.

The estimates refer to a base date of 1963, but costs of production have changed significantly since that time. We should ask therefore how the estimated elasticities in Table IV will change with changes in absolute cost levels.

Total costs have been estimated from a cost function of the form:

$$TC(q) = K(q) + L(q) + V(q) \tag{14}$$

where: $K(q)$ = capital costs
$L(q)$ = labour costs
$V(q)$ = materials and energy costs $= V_m \cdot q$

Hence:

$$TC(q) = K(q) + L(q) + V_m \cdot q \tag{15}$$

and elasticity IV is:

$$e_q^{''TC} = \frac{[K'(q) + L'(q) + V_m] \cdot q}{[K(q) + L(q) + V_m \cdot q]} \tag{16}$$

The behaviour of $e_q^{''TC}$ with respect to each of the cost components is summarized in Table V. Note that a decrease (increase) in $e_q^{''TC}$ indicates stronger (weaker) economies of scale.

The overall effect on cost elasticity of scale in cement production of the inflation in costs since 1963 cannot be estimated without estimates of inflation of each of the individual cost components, but it is unlikely that this will significantly affect the estimated m.e.s. of 1·6 million tonnes p.a.

TABLE V

EFFECT OF COST CHANGES ON COST ELASTICITY OF SCALE

Cost component	*Qualitative change in* $e_q^{''TC}$
Capital costs	Decrease
Labour costs	Decrease
Other variable costs	Increase if $e_q^{''TC} < 1$; decrease if $e_q^{''TC} > 1$

SECTION D

D.1: Comparison with Other Research

There has been a number of studies of economies of scale in the cement industry. Of these the most important are those by Pratten [8], Griliches and Ringstad [4] and Scherer *et al.* [11].[9] Comparison of our estimates with these other studies can be made in a number of ways: we can compare estimates of m.e.s., elasticity, or the behaviour of average costs.

Table VI compares estimates of m.e.s. and indicates the date to which each of the estimates relates.

It would appear that Scherer has underestimated the economies available to the industry. On the other hand, Pratten's estimate takes insufficient account of increasing cost elasticity of scale for plant capacities in excess of 1·0 million tonnes p.a.

[9] Other estimates, e.g. Manne [6], are based on sources also used by one or other of these studies.

TABLE VI

MINIMUM EFFICIENT SCALE

Source	*m.e.s.* (*million tonnes p.a.*)
Norman	1·6 (1963–72)
Pratten	2·0 (1970)
Scherer	1·0 (1965)

Source: See text.

Estimates of the elasticity of capital costs with respect to scale are given in Table VII and of total costs in Table VIII.

Our estimates, when compared with other work, indicate weaker economies of scale at very small plant scales (recall the discussion of capital costs) but somewhat stronger economies to plants in the scale range 0·5–1·0 million tonnes p.a.

TABLE VII

ELASTICITY OF CAPITAL COSTS

Norman	Capacity (million tonnes p.a.)	0·099		0·33		0·66		1·32
	Capital cost (DM × 10^6)	23·3		65·7		105·6		154·4
	Elasticity		0·86		0·68		0·55	
Pratten	Capacity (million tonnes p.a.)	0·1		0·3		0·6		1·2
	Capital cost (£m.)	3·0		7·5		12·5		22·0
	Elasticity		0·83		0·74		0·82	

Source: See text.

TABLE VIII

TOTAL COST ELASTICITY OF SCALE

Norman	Capacity (million tonnes p.a.)	0·099		0·2475		0·495		0·99		1·98
	Average cost (index)	100		86		76		65		59
	Elasticity		0·84		0·82		0·77		0·86	
Pratten	Capacity (million tonnes p.a.)	0·10		0·20		0·50		1·00		2·00
	Average cost (index)	100		85		77		69		62
	Elasticity		0·77		0·89		0·84		0·85	
Scherer	Capacity (million tonnes p.a.)		0·33						1·90	
	Elasticity					0·79				
Griliches and Ringstad	Capacity (million tonnes p.a.)					Undefined				
	Elasticity[a]					0·88–0·94				

[a] Inverse of the degree of homogeneity of the estimated production function.
Source: See text.

D.2: Concluding Remarks

Our estimates indicate that economies of scale are available to both labour and capital inputs to cement production. What has also been indicated, however, is that economies of scale eventually decrease in importance as scale increases.

One implication of these estimates therefore is that a cost function of the form:

$$Y = aX^{b} \tag{14}$$

where: Y = total cost
X = capacity

can only be used to give a local approximation to the degree of economies of scale in cement production. Secondly, the assumption of a concave total cost function must be rejected.

More significantly, the cement production process employs a technology based primarily on the use of tubes (kilns, grinders, etc.). The capacity of these tubes is related to volume and cost might be expected to be related to surface area. This has not been found to be the case however. As a result, the qualitative aspects of our findings can be expected to apply *a fortiori* to other industrial situations.

Two concluding remarks should be made. Firstly, we noted in section C.1 that when the industry is put in a spatial or temporal context the concept of 'minimum efficient scale' is of limited usefulness. In an industry such as cement production where inputs are widely available, demand is dispersed, and overall demand is growing slowly, an optimal production strategy may well involve the sacrifice of production cost economies if total costs are to be minimized, i.e. there can be no presumption that the existence of small-scale plants is evidence of an inefficient production strategy.

Secondly, the estimates presented in this paper refer in general to plants with single kilns. If demand exhibits seasonal fluctuations, however, the establishment may well operate more efficiently if it contains multiple kilns. Such a strategy will weaken the degree of economies of scale available to the establishment, and may well lead once more to a situation in which 'small-scale' plants are an efficient response to prevailing market conditions.

UNIVERSITY OF READING

APPENDIX A

SUMMARY OF UNITED NATIONS (1963) STUDY DATA

TABLE A.1

CAPACITY, CAPITAL COSTS, LABOUR REQUIREMENTS

Capacity (*thousand tonnes p.a.*)	*Capital costs* ($'000)	*Labour requirements*	
		Direct (*no.*)	*Indirect* (*no.*)
100	6,500	75	—
120	7,000	75	12
200	10,800	96	—
210	11,250	95	17
260	13,200	105	19
340	16,000	130	21
400	18,000	128	—
430	19,000	145	21
500	21,500	150	—
510	21,000	150	21
1000	30,000	150	21

TABLE A.2

PHYSICAL INPUTS PER TON OF CEMENT OUTPUT RELATED TO CAPACITY

Capacity (thousand tons p.a.)	120	210	260	340	430	510	1000
Limestone (in tons)	1·6	1·6	1·6	1·6	1·6	1·6	1·6
Clay (in tons)	0·3	0·3	0·3	0·3	0·3	0·3	0·3
Power (in kWh)	115	115	115	115	115	115	115
Fuel (in million Btu)	5·85	5·85	5·85	5·85	5·85	5·85	5·85
Gypsum (in percentage kg of weight)	40	40	40	40	40	40	40

APPENDIX B

TABLE B. 1

RELATIONSHIP BETWEEN PLANT CAPACITY AND CAPITAL COSTS: WEST GERMAN CEMENT INDUSTRY 1971

Capacity (thousand tonnes p.a.)	*Total capital costs*[a] (*DM* × 10⁶)	*Average capital costs* (*DM/tonne*)	*Mechanical and electrical costs* (*DM* × 10⁶)	*Civil engineering costs* (*DM* × 10⁶)	*Machine erection costs* (*DM* × 10⁶)	*Quarry equipment costs* (*DM* × 10⁶)
82·5	19·8	240	6·5	9·9	1·6	1·0
99·0	23·3	235	8·0	11·4	2·0	1·1
132·0	30·1	228	10·5	14·5	2·4	1·5
166·0	36·6	222	13·1	17·2	3·0	1·8
247·5	52·1	210	20·0	22·9	4·5	2·5
330·0	65·7	199	26·4	27·6	5·8	3·2
412·5	77·6	188	33·2	30·3	7·0	3·8
495·0	88·6	179	38·8	33·7	8·0	4·4
577·5	97·6	169	43·8	36·1	8·9	4·8
660·0	105·6	160	48·5	38·0	9·5	5·2
742·5	112·1	151	52·6	39·2	10·1	5·5
825·0	118·8	144	56·8	40·4	10·7	5·9
907·5	124·3	137	61·1	41·0	11·4	6·2
990·0	129·7	131	63·6	42·8	11·6	6·3
1155·0	142·0	123	70·1	46·9	12·3	6·9
1320·0	154·4	117	77·8	49·4	13·4	7·5
1485·0	167·8	113	85·2	53·7	14·3	7·9
1650·0	183·2	111	94·8	56·8	15·5	8·6
1980·0	213·0	108	111·7	66·3	17·6	9·6
2310·0	242·6	105	129·7	72·7	19·8	10·7
2640·0	272·0	103	146·4	81·6	21·7	11·4
1970·0	303·0	102	167·0	87·9	24·1	12·0
3300·0	330·0	100	185·6	92·4	26·0	13·0

[a] Includes an allowance for spares not separately detailed.
Source: A designer in the industry.

REFERENCES

[1] COCKERILL, A., *Economies of Scale in the Brewing Industry* (unpublished dissertation for the degree of M.Phil. of Leeds University, 1971).

[2] ——, *The Steel Industry: International Comparisons of Structure and Performance* (Cambridge University Press, Cambridge, 1974).

[3] DIWAN, R. K., 'Alternative Specifications of Economies of Scale', *Economica* (*New Series*), **33** (November 1966), pp. 442–53.

[4] GRILICHES, Z. and RINGSTAD, V., *Economies of Scale and the Form of the Production Function* (North-Holland, Amsterdam, 1971).

[5] HALDI, J. and WITCOMB, D., 'Economies of Scale in Industrial Plants', *Journal of Political Economy*, **75** (August 1967), pp. 373–85.

[6] MANNE, A. S., *Investments for Capacity Expansion: Size, Location and Time-Phasing* (George Allen and Unwin, London, 1967).

[7] NORMAN, G., *Economies of Scale, Transport Costs, and Location: a Case Study* (unpublished dissertation for the degree of Ph.D. of the University of Cambridge, 1977).

[8] PRATTEN, C. F., *Economies of Scale in Manufacturing Industry* (Cambridge University Press, Cambridge, 1971).

[9] PRATTEN, C. F. and DEAN, R. M. (in collaboration with SILBERSTON, A.), *The Economies of Large-scale Production in British Industry: an Introductory Study* (Cambridge University Press, Cambridge, 1965).

[10] ROBINSON, E. A. G., *The Structure of Competitive Industry* (Cambridge Economic Handbooks, Cambridge University Press, Cambridge, 1931).

[11] SCHERER, F. M. *et al.*, *The Economics of Multi-plant Operation: an International Comparisons Study* (Harvard University Press, Cambridge, Mass., 1975).

[12] SILBERSTON, A., 'Economies of Scale in Theory and Practice', *Economic Journal*, **82** (March 1972, Supplement), pp. 369–91.

[13] UNITED NATIONS, *Studies in the Economics of Industry*, *1* (United Nations, New York, 1963).

[14] WALTERS, A. A., 'Production and Cost Functions: an Econometric Survey', *Econometrica*, **31** (January/April 1963), pp. 1–66.

[15] WORLD CEMENT DIRECTORY (CEMBUREAU, European Cement Association, Paris, 1972).

THE JOURNAL OF INDUSTRIAL ECONOMICS
Volume XXVII June 1979 No. 4

THE IMPACT OF SELECTIVE EMPLOYMENT POLICY: THE CASE OF A WAGE-COST SUBSIDY SCHEME IN GERMANY 1974-75

GÜNTHER SCHMID*

I. INTRODUCTION

DURING the present decade, especially during the last recession, the successful management of the economy via fiscal and monetary measures began to be challenged. What is known as the Phillips curve, the relationship between inflation and unemployment, worsened or became unstable, and made the combined fight against inflation and unemployment more and more difficult. On the other hand, the success of this fight is to a very great extent a question of avoiding social warfare. The extreme alternative to solve conflicts was either to give most people an illusion of income improvement by increasing nominal wage rates, or to let a disadvantaged minority be exposed to insecurity and instability with respect to employment. Beside the fact that both 'solutions' are detrimental to nearly all groups in society, both strategies seem no longer workable.

Governments and other policy makers have to work at other ways to utilize the positive possibilities implied in the existence of unused human and material resources without inducing further inflation. Traditional alternatives to overall demand or supply management, such as training and retraining, mobility-promoting measures, or improving information in order to reduce the mis-match between demand and supply, have shown limited capacities to alleviate the dilemma between unemployment and inflation. Thus, new forms of selective employment policies come into discussion and experience.

Direct job creation through public and selective wage subsidies are such policies designed to alter the mix of employment in favour of workers who experience high rates of unemployment, and/or in favour of regions that are hit by structural unemployment. These measures are also intended to mitigate the conflict between society's goals for unemployment and inflation. The hope is to 'cheat the Phillips curve'. For the short run, this means diminishing the inflationary consequences of higher rates of employment. For the long run, it means diminishing the minimal non-accelerating inflation of unemployment. The basic strategy, as Bailey and Tobin [1] describe it, is simple: shift labour demand to types of workers who are—because of high unemployment, weak bargaining power, rigid wages, or other characteristics—on relatively flat Phillips curves. Let the government hire, or induce

* Thanks go to my colleagues Franz Josef Bade, Bernd Reissert and Dieter Freiburghaus for helpful comments. The study was sponsored by the OECD.

other employers to hire, workers whose unemployment does little or nothing to restrain the advance of wage costs in the aggregate. This idea is indeed appealing: to target employment policy to the most hit groups and/or regions in order to reduce the overall level of unemployment *and* to receive a more equal distribution of welfare *without* worsening *and even* improving the unemployment/inflation dilemma.

Little in the way of quantitative evaluations of programme impacts has apparently been undertaken, especially of Western European programmes. As Haveman and Christainsen [5] suggest, different approaches to do this could be imagined: estimates of aggregate parameters,[1] evaluation of programme efficiency in terms of social benefits and social costs,[2] evaluation of specific aspects. One approach to evaluate certain aspects is to test the net effect of job creation with control group or multiple regression analysis. The effort here is to estimate the employment in target regions (or target firms) with and without the programme, or to explain the variation of the take-up of the scheme by context variables of the respective regions, *and* to assess the impact of the take-up on employment or unemployment by controlling for other independent variables. It is this last approach we applied in evaluating the wage-cost subsidy scheme in Germany during 1974 and 1975.

II. POLICY DESIGN OF THE WAGE-SUBSIDY SCHEME

1. *Circumstances in Which the Scheme was Introduced*

The last quarter of 1974 showed a dramatic increase of unemployment in Germany. From September to December unemployment nearly doubled from about 557,000 to 946,000, and the number of short-time workers (i.e. part-time unemployment) increased from about 165,000 to 703,000. Inflation at the same time reached a peak of about 7%. Under these circumstances the government decided to introduce the first counter-cyclical programme (Konjunkturprogramm). The wage-cost subsidy scheme was part of this larger programme, as well as part of a programme of 'Special Labour Market Measures to Sustain Employment'. The greater part of the counter-cyclical programme went into investment allowances—Investitionszulagen—(amounting to approximately 4000 million DM), into a federal investment programme (1130 million DM), and finally into special Labour Market Measures (600 million DM) composed of wage-cost subsidies, mobility incentives and job creation (Arbeitsbeschaffung).

2. *Objectives and Philosophy of the Scheme*

The scheme was developed with the purpose of reducing unemployment in areas of the country with above average unemployment (0·5 percentage

[1] For examples in this direction see Layard and Nickell [7], Kesselman *et al.* [6] and Bishop and Lerman [3].

[2] As an example related to Sweden see Dahlberg [3].

points above the federal average rate during the months September, October and November 1974). Eligible were those workers who had been out of work for three months or more and registered with the local employment office. The jobs had to be permanent ones which would not have been created in the absence of the subsidy, and there had to be a net increase in employment above a base figure (i.e. the level of employment on December 10th, 1974). Public enterprises, except those of a profit-making character, were excluded from the scheme.

The programme was developed withing the Federal Ministry of Labour, in the subdivision for labour market policies. The basic philosophy behind the programme was to accelerate the effect of the expected upswing on employment, especially in problem regions (high unemployment) and for problem groups (long-term unemployed). It was well known that there is an increasing gap between economic growth and the employment effect, that there are increasing marginal costs when hiring additional workers and that problem groups were mainly affected by this disparity. At that time the perception among officials in government, parties, and political institutions was still widespread that one was dealing only with a normal cyclical phenomenon. Most people did not believe in large-scale structural problems. There was almost certainty about the coming upswing, which—as we know today—came later and was quite modest in relation to expectations. The programme, therefore, should be regarded in the context of these expectations and the whole policy package.

3. *Period of Validity, Form and Amount of Subsidy*

The measure was introduced for a five-month period starting in December 1974. The subsidy paid to employers amounted to a proportion of the prevailing wage for the job, i.e. 60%. In special circumstances the amount could be raised to 100%, as for instance in the case of the placement of a disabled person. The subsidy was calculated for a six-month period and paid as a lump sum. The costs of the scheme were carried by the Federal Budget.

4. *Conditions for Obtaining Subsiay*

The employer, to obtain the wage-cost subsidy, had to:

Offer a permanent and not a temporary job in an area of above-average unemployment to a worker unemployed for at least three months.

Certify that without the subsidy he would not have hired the worker.

Make the offer so that work could start before May 1st, 1975.

Show that there had been a net increase in employment in his firm compared with December 10th, 1974.

Confirm that he would pay back the subsidy

(a) if the subsidy were paid on the basis of incorrect statements in the application,
(b) if another worker were dismissed within a period of six months after hiring of the subsidized worker, unless important reasons were given.

5. *Methods of Operation*

The wage-cost subsidy was paid by the local employment office (Arbeitsamt). This meant contacting the employment office in the area where the firm was located. Claims had to be made no later than one month after the date of engagement.

The day from which the base figure of employment was taken ('Stichtag' December 10th) was set before the official announcement of the programme! The government informed the public some days *after* the 'Stichtag' about the policy package. In principle, therefore, firms could not deliberately reduce employment in order to get the subsidy later on. Rules, however, with regard to the establishment of new firms seem to have provided some possibilities for evading the 'Stichtag'. Such problems need checking in a qualitative follow-up study. Evidence of administrative practice speak at first glance against large scale abuse or fraudulent claims. A check in Southern Bavaria, where most of this suspicion originated, provided information in favour of careful control: 900 contradictions and 80 suits by firms against administrative decisions have been counted.

III. FIRST-ROUND ESTIMATES OF IMPACT

1. *Expenditure and Number of Persons Affected*

The initial budget provision was 600 million DM for both the wage-cost subsidy and a mobility allowance. Expenditure actually came to 408.2 million DM altogether, 382.4 million DM were spent for wage-cost subsidies. This expenditure was 64% of the whole budget provision, 4% for the mobility allowance. Because the whole amount allocated to the Special Labour Market Measures was not used, the other 32% was transferred to job creation measures (ABM).

The number of persons affected by the wage-cost subsidy scheme was 78,940. Average expenditure per head was therefore 4890 DM. Assuming an average monthly income of 1542 DM for an unemployed person, and assuming those taking up the wage-cost subsidy were representative of the unemployed as a whole, an average wage-cost subsidy expenditure of 5551 DM should have been expected.

There was a slow response to the scheme. Payments were high in March, April, and reached a peak in May (see Fig. 1), i.e. after the expiry date for making hirings which qualified for the subsidy. This specific timing of the take-up hints at the potential importance of the seasonal factor. The analytical part of the study below will consider this circumstance explicitly.

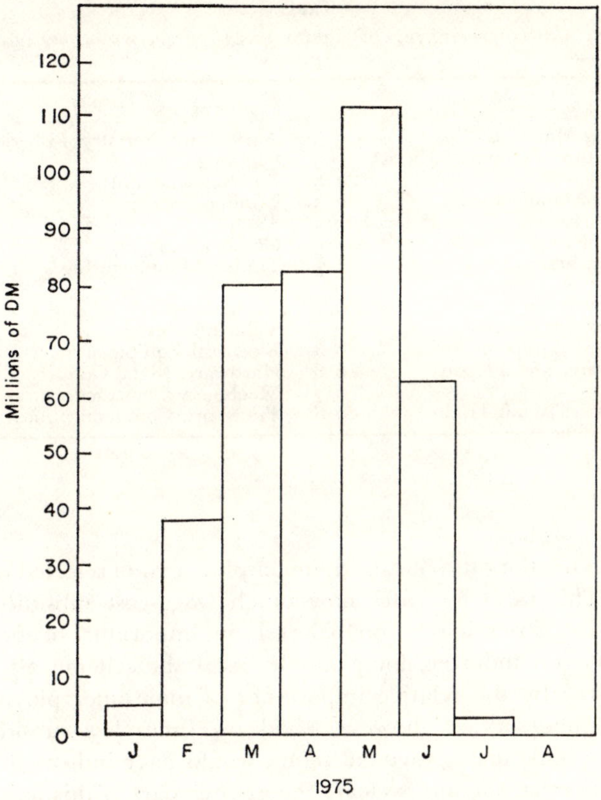

FIGURE 1. Take-up of Wage-cost Subsidies in Germany

2. *Impact of the Scheme in Different Industries*

The construction industry in the wider sense was by far the most important user of the wage-cost subsidy. If affected 39·5% of persons within the construction industry itself. Within manufacturing, the non-metallic building materials industry (Industrie der Stein und Erden) profited the most (6·4% of persons). This industry branch comprises the production of cement, bricks and tiles as well as other building materials. The next important industry affected was timber manufacturing which is also dependent on the construction industry. These three industries together constituted half of all subsidy cases, but only 20% of unemployed people in May 1975. This fact is partially in line with observation that construction, in particular housing construction, was the first and the most severely hit branch of the German economy in the recession. The particularly high ratio of subsidy cases in terms of unemployment, however, needs further explanation.

TABLE I

HIGHEST AND LOWEST RATIOS OF SUBSIDY CASES/UNEMPLOYMENT BY INDUSTRIES AND SEX

Males		*Females*	
Building Materials	5·2	Agriculture, Forestry, Fisheries	2·0
Agriculture, Forestry, Fisheries	3·9	Clothing	1·2
Construction	2·5	Building Materials	1·0
Timber Manufacturing	2·3	Mining, Energy	1·0
Mining, Energy	2·2	Textile	0·9
Clothing	1·5	Construction	0·7
Leather, Shoes	1·3	Timber Manufacturing	0·6
Public Services	0·1	Public Services	0·0
Banking, Insurance	0·3	Vehicle Industry	0·1
Electrical Equipment	0·4	Electrical Equipment	0·1
Hardware, Metal Goods	0·6	Hardware, Metal Goods	0·2
Textile	0·7	Machinery Construction	0·2
Wholesale, Retail Trade	0·8	Transport, Communications	0·2

Table I shows the ratio of subsidy/unemployment of selected rank-ordered industries. This ratio indicates how much wage-cost subsidies have been used within industries, in relation to the relative importance of unemployment. The construction industry, for example, used the scheme 2·5 times more than suggested by the relative importance of male unemployment of that industry; public services, however, had 0·1 times less subsidy cases than their relative male unemployment figure would have indicated. The reason for the public service figure is clear: the greater part of this industry branch was explicitly excluded by programme regulations.

3. *Impact of the Scheme by Regions* (*Länder*)

The regional breakdown (Länder) shows a particularly strong use of subsidies in Südbayern, followed in rank-order by Nordbayern, Schleswig-Holstein-Hamburg, Niedersachsen-Bremen, Rheinland-Pfalz-Saarland. Particularly weak was the take-up in Nordrhein-Westfalen and Hessen. No employment agency within Baden-Württemberg qualified for the scheme; the same holds for Berlin (see Table II).

The finer break-down of the scheme's take-up shows an even more varying distribution. Just three out of 44 eligible agencies account for nearly a quarter of all subsidies; all three agencies belong to Bayern. The impact index (IWCS), i.e. the number of persons affected by the scheme as a percentage of all eligible persons, varies between 0·75 (Deggendorf) and 0·03 (Offenbach). As the tests prove, the reasons for this fact are not to be seen only in the structure of the economy or employment. It seems necessary to explain the particular high take-up of the scheme by contextual variables such as attitude of agencies' staff, firm–agencies relationships, and others.

4. *Impact of the Scheme by Demographic Characteristics*

Men were affected much more than women by the scheme. Men accounted for 83·6% of all subsidies, women for 16·4%. This coincides with the industrial analysis, showing that industries in which women constitute only a small part of employment (such as construction) received a major part of the subsidies. The take-up of the scheme by women was only of some importance in clothing, wholesale and retail trade, and in 'other private services' which accounted for 58% of all subsidies given to women. In relative terms (i.e. compared with the importance of female unemployment by industry), agriculture/forestry/fisheries, clothing, building materials as well as mining and energy played some role in women's take-up of the scheme.

TABLE II

IMPACT INDEX OF THE WAGE-COST SUBSIDY PROGRAMME BY REGIONS (LÄNDER)

Regions (Länder)	*Numbers unemployed at start of programme (unemployment rates in brackets)* 1	*Number of persons eligible for subsidies*[b] 2	*Number of persons affected during period in qualifying regions* 3	*Impact Index of programme (IWCS)* 4=3/2
Schleswig-Holstein Hamburg	13,806 (5·0)[a]	16,700	4,374	0·26
Niedersachsen-Bremen	48,842 (5·4)	60,947	14,050	0·23
Nordrhein-Westfalen	123,858 (4·6)	141,125	20,876	0·15
Hessen	31,122 (4·4)	36,080	3,793	0·11
Rheinland-Pfalz Saarland	40,101 (5·3)	48,378	12,146	0·25
Nordbayern	8,400 (7·0)	12,440	4,795	0·39
Südbayern	17,301 (7·0)	24,432	14,748	0.60

[a] The unemployment rates in column 1 are unweighted averages in the employment agencies within the region which qualified for the scheme.

[b] Estimate of unemployed within the qualified employment agencies, or within the region who were potentially eligible for the scheme, according to the criterion of three month duration of unemployment. For details of the estimate see Schmid [9].

Not much use was made of the provision that the subsidy could be paid for a person taken on for training (1368 persons affected, i.e. 1·7%). Foreigners were only slightly involved in the scheme (1939 cases, i.e. 2·5%).

Young people, however, have the highest impact index if we look at age groups: young people under 20 were affected by the scheme to double the extent than could have been expected by the respective number of unemployed (see Table III). The impact index decreases as we move into older age groups. This unexpected result should be kept in mind in the final assessment of the scheme.

TABLE III

PERSONS AFFECTED BY AGE GROUPS

Age group	*Persons affected by WCS* 1	*As percentage* 2	*Persons unemployed May 1975*[a] 3	*As percentage* 4	*Impact index (2/4)* 5
−20	11,234	14·26	40,851	6·74	2·11
20–25	13,909	17·62	88,406	14·49	1·21
25–45	38,113	48·28	295,162	48·70	0·99
45–60	12,514	15·85	136,603	22·54	0·70
60+	3,170	4·02	42,018	6.93	0·53
Total	78,940	100·00	603,040	100·00	—

[a] Three months and more.

IV. IMPACT ANALYSIS OF WAGE-COST SUBSIDIES

1. *Factors Explaining Take-up Variance*

We are now in the state of second-round estimates about the effect of the wage-cost subsidies, i.e. estimates which are not obvious from the data themselves. All the following results are based on multivariate and cross-section analysis on the basis of employment agencies. We first tried to answer some questions related to the astonishingly big variance of the scheme's take-up.

A stepwise multiple regression with 18 independent variables[3] produced the following results (see Table IV):

1. Labour intensity, skill intensity and size of enterprises did not have an influence on take-up.
2. The under-utilization of the existing work force, measured by the size of unemployment at the start of the programme, explains 10% of the take-up variance. As one could expect: the higher the unemployment rate at the beginning of the scheme, the higher the final take-up.
3. The seasonal factor (fluctuation of manpower utilization) plays the most important role. This result was already expected, but not so high: this factor alone explains 60% of the total variance. This fact needs more interpretation in the next paragraph.
4. The general economic climate, measured as vacancies as a percentage of the existing work force, did not have a significant influence on take-up. One could have expected a positive influence, because of the beginning of the upswing in April/May 1975.
5. Monostructure was expected to have a negative influence on take-up, but this was neither confirmed nor disproved. The same was expected with respect to the factor 'growth potentiality', measured here as the percentage of employment in shrinking industries. Employment agencies with a

[3] See for a much more detailed description and analysis Schmid [9]. Detailed description of the method for estimating the number of eligible persons for wage-cost subsidies is also shown in this original version.

TABLE IV

STEPWISE MULTIPLE REGRESSION FOR SELECTING FACTORS EXPLAINING TAKE-UP VARIANCE OF WCS[a]

Dependent variable: WCSPC = Persons affected by WCS as percentage of labour force

	Summary table					
Variable	*Multiple R*	*R square*	*RSQ change*	*Simple R*	*B*	*Beta*
TVB = Seasonal factor	0·77394	0·59898	0·59898	0·77394	0·71987	0·80719*
TVA = Unemployment rate	0·83781	0·70193	0·10294	0·73326	0·52245	0·45091*
TV06 = Service industry	0·84715	0·71767	0·01574	−0·16549	0·17114	0·49990
TV05 = Construction	0·85921	0·73824	0·02058	0·43231	−0·16374	−0·15103*
TV29 = Wage indicator	0·87167	0·75981	0·02157	0·62683	0·11112	0·26121
TV12 = Growth potentiality	0·87755	0·77010	0·01028	−0·01449	−0·04506	−0·19124
TV09 = Size of enterprises (> 1000)	0·88218	0·77825	0·00815	−0·34033	−0·01835	−0·14577
TV01 = Employment in agriculture	0·88597	0·78494	0·00669	0·55396	−0·13205	−0·50439
TVC = Economic climate	0·88954	0·79129	0·00635	−0·04355	−0·80015	−0·14881
TV11 = Monostructure	0·89186	0·79542	0·00413	−0·11516	0·04067	0·13617
TV44 = Placement activity	0·89341	0·79818	0·00276	−0·10023	−0·73999	−0·13039
TV07 = Size of enterprises (< 50)	0·89427	0·79972	0·00155	0·42603	0·01878	0·08369
TV02 = Manufacturing	0·89550	0·80192	0·00220	0·02498	0·02811	0·12289
TV18 = Unskilled, semiskilled	0·89689	0·80441	0·00249	0·26888	−0·09990	−0·18393
TV16 = White-collar workers	0·89813	0·80664	0·00223	−0·50860	−0·07341	−0·20593
TVD = Foreign workers	0·89878	0·80781	0·00117	−0·45923	0·03721	0·07191
TV17 = Skilled workers	0·89883	0·80789	0·00008	−0·13643	0·01535	0·02032
TV13 = Labour intensity	0·89888	0·80799	0·00010	0·13739	0·00242	0·01367
(Constant)					−4·69536	

[a] Number of cases = 56; i.e. 44 eligible agencies + 12 agencies that took up a few subsidies for other reasons.
* Significant at the 1% level.
B = Unstandardized regression coefficient.
Beta = Standardized regression coefficient.

high proportion of shrinking industries for structural reasons are at a natural disadvantage with regard to policy regulations rewarding marginal or additional employment. This expected association is slightly confirmed, but explains only 1% of the variance.

One could have expected the following association: employment agencies with a high proportion of foreign workers replace foreign workers with German workers. The net employment effect would then be zero, and unemployment would be exported. The model shows no significant regression coefficient, although the correlation coefficient is strongly negative (which would disprove the hypothesis).

We know from the description above that the construction industry accounted for most persons affected by the subsidy scheme. Therefore a positive regression coefficient was expected. The model shows, however, that the sign becomes negative in taking into account the seasonal factor, which is of course associated with the construction industry. The conclusion is that eliminating its seasonal characteristic, the construction industry as such (with its production structure and wage structure) influences the take-up of wage-cost subsidies negatively. This fact, together with the high explanatory power of the seasonal factor, confirms doubts as to whether any of the subsidized jobs in the construction industry created real additional employment.

Service industries play a positive role, but explain only a very small proportion of the take-up variance. Employment in manufacturing explains none of the variance. The wage level, in this study represented by the proportion of unemployed people in low-wage categories, affects some of the take-up: employment agencies with a high proportion of unemployed people in low-wage categories show a high take-up. As we know from the inter-correlation matrix, this result reflects more or less the 'rural factor', or the presence of structurally 'depressed areas', which suggests that the scheme is supporting obsolete structures. This association, however, explains such a small proportion that one should not draw further conclusions from it.

Placement activities as a performance indicator of employment agencies did not affect take-up. As we know that placement activities are a quite incomplete performance indicator, not telling us much more about the 'quality' of an agency, one can almost ignore this relationship. As shown in other studies, high placement activity is correlated with unstable employment within industries, e.g. transport and services; placement there is more an indicator for the structure of employment than for the performance quality of an agency.

2. *Effect of Wage-cost Subsidies on Unemployment*

We know from the official statistics that about 80,000 unemployed persons were affected by the scheme. If no displacement occurred, unemployment would have decreased by the same amount, other things being equal. Unfortunately, several reasons speak for a high probability of internal displacement, which could take different forms:

(a) Short-term unemployed who would otherwise have been hired, are subject to a longer spell of unemployment because unemployed, who fulfil the subsidy criteria, are now being preferred; to the same category belongs the case where an employer hires ten unskilled and long-term unemployed instead of five skilled and short-term unemployed;

(b) People of non-subsidized firms have to be dismissed because of the comparative disadvantage and a lasting lack of general demand.

As far as we can see, there is no way of direct estimation of such displacement processes. One indirect possibility, which we used, is to 'explain' the change of unemployment in *all* employment agencies during the respective period with the raw impact of wage-cost subsidies (IWCS) by controlling the potential influence of other variables on unemployment change. Table V describes the results of this exercise.

The unemployment rate in September 1974 explains most of the unemployment increase during the following months. The unemployment rate September 1974 could be considered as an indicator of 'structural unemployment', because a high unemployment rate at a still relatively low level of unemployment (national U-rate September 1974=2·4%) reflects structural problems rather than demand deficiency. As we stated at the beginning, the recession reached its peak in the time between September and December 1974. It is therefore quite natural that employment agencies with low unemployment rates were relatively the worst hit by the demand deficiency crisis. In addition, the increase of unemployment is positively related to employment in agriculture and 'labour intensity' both reflecting structural factors. Holding constant these and other variables (manufacturing, shrinking industries, etc.), IWCS yields the expected negative regression coefficient, which means: wage-cost subsidies had some effect in lowering unemployment, but this effect 'explains' only 1% of the variance. The whole model, however, explains only 59% of the total variance, 41% remaining unexplained. We are therefore not able to estimate exactly the effect of the subsidies on unemployment.

3. *Effect of Wage-cost Subsidies on Employment*

The objective of the subsidy was to create permanent jobs for unemployed by subsidizing additional employment. During the period when the scheme was effective, employment decreased for reasons of the overall recession. Other things being equal, the programme should have 'caused' a smaller decrease of employment in regions which qualified for the scheme and which used WCS extensively. A simple regression analysis within the group of qualified regions and a comparison of the control-group statistics produces the following results:

TABLE V

EFFECT OF WAGE-COST SUBSIDIES ON UNEMPLOYMENT

Dependent variable: ALAEND = Unemployment May 1975 minus unemployment September 1974 in percentage 1974

Variable	*Summary table*					
	Multiple R	*R square*	*RSQ change*	*Simple R*	*B*	*Beta*
UR74 = U-rate September 1974	0·68994	0·47602	0·47602	−0·68994	−20·75679	−0·60049*
TV01 = Employment in agriculture	0·74266	0·55154	0·07552	0·20545	1·71068	0·30191*
TV13 = Labour intensity	0·75562	0·57096	0·01942	0·23969	0·37784	0·11266*
JWCS = Impact index of WCS (IWCS)	0·76356	0·58303	0·01206	−0·44042	−0·40557	−0·13778*
TV02 = Manufacturing	0·76647	0·58748	0·00446	0·24767	0·21591	0·04970
TVD = Foreign workers	0·76673	0·58788	0·00040	0·33682	0·22925	0·02714
TV14 = Raw material intensive	0·76681	0·58800	0·00012	−0·23533	−0·07094	−0·02039
TV12 = Shrinking industries	0·76694	0·58820	0·00020	−0·13745	0·11480	0·01569
TV11 = Monostructure	0·76699	0·58827	0·00007	0·02788	0·07608	0·01030
(Constant)					118·37469	

* Significant at the 1% level.
Number of cases = 142 (all employment agencies).
Average IWCS (referred to all cases) = 6·99.
B = Unstandardized regression coefficient.
Beta = Standardized regression coefficient.

$$ANAEND = -4{\cdot}89 + 0{\cdot}07\ IWCS$$

$R^2 = 0{\cdot}35$ (44 cases)

$F = 22{\cdot}30$ (significant at the 0·1% level)

	Mean	S.d.	Cases
ANAEND	−3·32	1·88	44
IWCS	22·57	15·95	44
ANAEND°	−3·42	1·28	98

ANAEND = employment September 1975 minus employment September 1974 as percentage of September 1974 within qualified regions.

ANAEND° = ditto within non-qualified regions.

IWCS = impact of wage-cost subsidies, i.e. affected persons as percentage of all eligible persons.

The regression function suggests that without wage-cost subsidies employment would have declined by 4·89% instead of actually 3·32. The mean change of employment within the control group, which is only 0·10% higher, indicates that other factors have to be included in order to explain the real effect of IWCS on employment. Although the following model explains only 37% of the total variance, it reflects the plausible size of IWCS's real effect (see Table VI): the reduction of employment between September 1974 and September 1975 is partially explained by the 'foreign worker' factor which reflects the displacement of foreign workers into their home country. The rural factor (indicator: employment in agriculture) plays a positive role, which means, in this context, keeping employment relatively high in contrast to the manufacturing factor which explains some of the reduction of employment. This was expected because the origin of the recession has to be seen in structural problems of several branches of manufacturing; the foreign worker factor confirms this hypothesis. Small, but still significant, rates of the variation are 'explained' by the unemployment rate May 1975 (as indicator for the severity of recession), and by the participation rate, both in the expected direction, i.e. explaining the decrease of employment. The impact index of wage-cost subsidies has the expected positive beta coefficient which means: wage-cost subsidies 'caused' employment not to be reduced so rapidly as otherwise would have been the case. This positive coefficient is significant at the 1% level, although the association 'explains' only 1·7% of the total variance.

The total regression model explains only 37% of the variance. This is indeed a weak basis for the important conclusions we aim to draw out of the

TABLE VI

EFFECT OF WAGE-COST SUBSIDY ON EMPLOYMENT

Dependent variable: ANAEND = Change of employment September 1974–September 1975 in percentage

Variable	Summary table					
	Muliple R	*R square*	*RSQ change*	*Simple R*	*B*	*Beta*
TVD = Foreign workers	0·40335	0·16269	0·16269	−0·40335	−0·05120	−0·16451*
TV01 = Employment in agriculture	0·46993	0·22084	0·05814	0·39283	0·08832	0·42303*
TV02 = Employment in manufacturing	0·52677	0·27749	0·05665	−0·37190	−0·03093	−0·19319*
U–75 = U-rate May 1975	0.54999	0.30949	0.02501	0.09436	−0.28727	−0.29493*
TV 19 = Participation rate	0.58325	0.34018	0.03769	−0.22735	−0.97311	−0.18920*
IWCS = Impact of wage-cost subsidy	0·59723	0·35668	0·01650	0·28887	0·01603	0·14781*
TV24 = Density of local labour market	0·60651	0·37685	0·01117	0·04770	0·00124	0·11712
(Constant)					2·12597	

* Significant at the 1% level.
142 cases, average IWCS for all cases = 6·99.
B = Unstandardized regression coefficient.
Beta = Standardized regression coefficient.

results, i.e. the net effect of the subsidy programme on employment, other things being equal. We tried to improve the model by using other variables such as monostructure, age structure of unemployment, female participation rates (total, within manufacture), vacancies, labour intensity, shrinking industries! None of these variables increased the explained variance significantly. This trial and error, however, produced some confirmation about the partial influence of the subsidy programme on the employment change: the *B*-coefficient remained always constant within the range of 0·015 and 0·021.

V. EFFECT ON EMPLOYMENT AND BUDGET

1. *Estimate of the Net Number of Jobs Created or Preserved*

In order to realize the final step, i.e. the assessment of net cost accruing to the exchequer, we need an estimate of the net number of jobs created or preserved through the wage-cost subsidy scheme. It has frequently been pointed out in the theoretical literature that the total number of subsidized jobs is an inaccurate indication of the success of a subsidy programme. Four possibilities are usually mentioned which have to be carefully considered in estimating the net number of jobs.[4]

$$NJ = GJ - WJ - DJ - FJ + MJ$$

NJ = Net number of jobs
GJ = gross number of jobs, i.e. total number of subsidized jobs
WJ = 'windfalls', i.e. subsidy payments for manpower which would be increased or preserved in any event
DJ = displacement of unsubsidized labour by subsidized labour
FJ = number of subsidized jobs that are in fact fraudulent claims
MJ = multiplier effects, i.e. jobs created as a consequence of newly created subsidized jobs.

There is, as far as we can see, on the basis of existing data no possibility of isolating WJ, DJ, FJ, and MJ quantitatively. Evidence relating to this differentiation might be gleaned from subsidy programme administrators, participating or non-participating firms, employer and employee organizations and other expert observers.

In principle, however, NJ can be derived from the type of regression analysis we developed in the last section. NJ equals the number of unemployed *or* employed who can be referred to the specific contribution of wage-cost subsidies on the change of unemployment *or* on the change of employment.

[4] Different pieces of work by Gösta Rehn, Layard and Nickell (Centre for Labour Economics at London School of Economics), John Burton (Kingston Polytechnic), Haveman and and Christainsen (University of Wisconsin); for the German wage-cost subsidy scheme see also Hackmann and Keiter [4].

On the basis of the multiple regression equations in Tables V and VI, we can now write:

$$\left.\begin{aligned} NJ_u &= b*IWCS_{ALAEND} \\ NJ_E &= b*IWCS_{ANAEND} \end{aligned}\right\} \text{other things being equal}$$

This conclusion, of course, can only be drawn with some simplifying assumptions: first of all, the assumption that the model is true. As we know from the analysis above, both regressions 'explain' only parts of the total variance, and even with an explanation of 100%, we are never sure if the model is valid in 'causal' terms. Secondly, we assume that all displacement and all multiplier effects are expressed in our unemployment and employment figures which, in fact, is not necessarily the case. For example, older workers or women displaced from full-time jobs to part-time jobs count neither as unemployed nor non-employed. Displacement taking place in other countries because of changing conditions of competition is also not taken into account. We think, however, that we obtained plausible estimates despite these simplifications and despite the weakness of the regression models. Most of the ineffectiveness can be referred to 'windfall' effects, which are partly a consequence of the unfortunate timing of the programme (seasonal factor), to some extent possibly a consequence of failure in administrative control (still to be checked), partly unavoidable for reasons of natural turnover (closure of firms, establishment of new firms) as well as other 'upward dispersion causes' (e.g. as consequence of uneven economic development).

Starting from the effect of the scheme on unemployment (see Table V), we get the following equation (*other things being equal*):

$$NJ_u = ALAEND*AL\ (\text{September } 1974)/100 = b*IWCS*AL\ (\text{September } 1974)/100$$

$$NJ_u = -0{\cdot}406*6{\cdot}99*556{,}981/100$$
$$NJ_u = -15{,}807$$

which means: on average, wage-cost subsidies reduced the (otherwise) increasing unemployment by 15,807 persons. The result in connection with the effect on employment looks a little different (but not too different, see Table VII):

$$NJ_E = ANAEND*AN\ (\text{September } 1974)/100 = b*IWCS*AN\ (\text{September } 1974)$$
$$NJ_E = 0{\cdot}016*6{\cdot}99*20{,}942{,}900/100$$
$$NJ_E = 23{,}423$$

which means: on average, wage-cost subsidies increased the (otherwise) decreasing employment by 23,423 persons. The employment effect appears to be higher than the unemployment effect.

We decided to take simply the mean of both estimates in order to calculate the net number of jobs created or preserved which is: $\overline{NJ} = 19{,}615$. In other words: 19,615 out of 78,940 subsidized jobs (i.e. about 25%) were newly created jobs or jobs which otherwise would not have been preserved. 75% of subsidized jobs would have been increased or preserved in any event, or they displaced non-subsidized jobs.

2. *Cost Balance Sheet for the Exchequer*

In order to estimate the net costs of the subsidy scheme, we need two additional sets of information: (1) the average duration of unemployment for those who were already more than three months unemployed, and (2) expenditure and loss of receipts by the public purse for each unemployed person, i.e. the opportunity costs for subsidy expenditures.

The expected duration of unemployment for those who were already unemployed three months and more is, for males in the age group 25–45, 8·6 months. We applied this figure because the bulk of subsidies went to unemployed men in the age group 25–45, and because the upper and lower deviations of age groups (relatively more young people with lower duration expectation; relatively few old people with higher duration expectation) seem to compensate each other. The estimate of the opportunity costs is shown in Table VII.

If we now assume that every unemployed person affected by the net impact of wage-cost subsidies would otherwise have been unemployed for a further 8·6 months on average, we can write the following equation.

$$NC = OC - RC$$

NC = net costs of the exchequer ('parafisci' included)

OC = opportunity costs

$$OC = NJ * \frac{16{,}453 * 8{\cdot}6}{12} \text{DM}$$

$$= NJ * 11{,}791 \text{ DM}$$

NJ = net number of jobs created or preserved

RC = real costs of wage-cost subsidies

= 382·4 million DM

$$\underline{NC = NJ \ * 11{,}791 - 382{,}400{,}000 \text{ DM}}$$

Our estimate of the programmes' net effect was about 25%. The net costs for the exchequer were therefore negative, i.e. a deficit of about 150 million DM according to Table VIII. The net costs, however, would have been smaller if the programme had a larger acceleration effect with regard to the business cycle, i.e. if employers hired manpower earlier in the expectance of a recovery in order to receive the subsidy. Although Phlips convincingly argued that such an acceleration effect was very unlikely in view of the size

TABLE VII

EXPENDITURE AND LOSS OF RECEIPTS BY THE PUBLIC PURSE FOR EACH UNEMPLOYED PERSON (REFERRED TO THE 'AVERAGE' PERSON AFFECTED BY THE SUBSIDY SCHEME)

Expenditure per year for one person	DM
(a) Unemployment benefit[a] (assumed per month 960 DM)[b]	8,280
(b) Health insurance contribution (assumed ratio 0·2744) or 14% of gross wage	2,272
Total expenditure (a)+(b)	10,552
Loss of receipts per person in case of occupation and at the same wage level per year	
(c) Loss of contribution to the Federal Institute for Labour (at the time 2% of wage, today 3% of wage)	326
(d) Loss of direct taxation (assumed to be 12·2%)	1,989
(e) Loss of indirect taxation (assumed to be 4%)	625
(f) Loss of pension insurance contributions (18%)	2,934
Total loss of receipts (c)+(d)+(e)+(f)	5,901
Total expenditure and loss of receipts (opportunity costs) per year	16,453

[a] In our estimate the average wage amounts to 16,300 DM, because the average expenditure of WCS was 4890 DM which is by definition 60% of the average wage. The estimate is therefore a little lower than shown in the calculation of the Institute for Labour Market and Occupational Research of the Federal Institute for Labour (IAB).

[b] Weekly 158·70 DM=average married/unmarried.

[c] Ratio taken from IAB calculation.

[d] Taking into account the consumption difference between the state of unemployment and employment.

TABLE VIII

ALTERNATIVE NET COSTS FOR THE EXCHEQUER

NEWCS (%)	*NJ*	*OC* 1000 DM	*RC* 1000 *DM*	*NC* 1000 *DM*
1	2	3	4	5=3−4
10	7,894	93,078	382,400	−289,322
25	19,735	232,695	382,400	−149,705
40	31,576	372,313	382,400	−10,087
50	39,470	465,391	382,400	82,991
60	47,364	558,469	382,400	176,089
75	69,205	698,086	382,400	315,686
100	78,940	930,782	382,400	548,382

NEWCS=assumed net effect of wage-cost subsidies in percentage.

and design of the programme,[5] there is one reason, which speaks for some 'take-in-advance effect'. If the time of recovery lies outside the take-up period, employers reasonably will wait until the end of the take-up period to take the subsidy, expecting in a few weeks or months an upswing, i.e. increasing demand.

[5] This argument is developed from a mathematical and theoretical point of view by Phlips [8]. Phlips' rather sceptical view on wage subsidies of the kind discussed in this paper relates heavily on his focus on the acceleration function of such schemes. The empirical results of the analysis presented in this paper do not contradict the results of Phlips' theoretical analysis, if we take into account that the positive net impact of the wage-cost subsidy scheme on employment seems to a great deal due to its effect on the composition of employment.

Very much depends on the size of the subsidy *and* the strength of employers' expectations. The relative size of the subsidy was indeed small; it covered 3·6 months-costs of marginal wage (0·6 times six months). On the other hand, the boom in the automobile industry signalled in April and May 1975 a serious recovery, which was not realized but certainly induced at that time some employers to believe in an overall upswing and to hire some employees earlier in order to receive the subsidy. The subsidy being paid as a lump-sum was probably an additional incentive to hire in advance.

In view of the large negative balance, we may finally argue that the German wage-cost subsidy programme was, in terms of costs, not a success. On the other hand, in view of the fact that other opportunity costs (like psychic or social costs of unemployment, or other economic gains like useful production or preservation of human capital) are not included in our balance sheet, we may also conclude that the programme was not as bad as is sometimes argued. Another argument that speaks for the programme is the obvious impact on the composition of employment accompanied by a redistribution of earned income in favour of low income earners, and in favour of depressed areas.

If programming and implementation could be improved, for instance by targeting the programme better in terms of time, sectors and longer duration, selective subsidy measures like this German wage-cost subsidy programme might prove useful in the policy mix of an active labour market policy.[6] According to the cost alternatives in Table VIII, such a programme up to a net effect of about 42% produces a positive cost balance for the exchequer. A net effect of 50% for example, would bring a gain of 83 million DM.

INTERNATIONAL INSTITUTE OF MANAGEMENT, BERLIN

REFERENCES

[1] BAILY, M. and TOBIN, J., 'Macroeconomic Effects of Selective Public Employment and Wage Subsidies', *Brookings Papers on Economic Activity*, No. 2 (1977). pp. 511–44.

[2] BISHOP, J. and LERMAN, R., 'Wage Subsidies for Income Maintenance and Job Creation', in Taggart, R. (ed.), *Job Creation: What Works?*, pp. 39–74 (Olympus Publishing Company, 1977).

[3] DAHLBERG, A., 'Economic and Social Effects of Stimuli to Geographic Mobility: An Empirical Study', in Schmid, G. and Freiburghaus, D. (eds.), *Active Labour Market Policy in Selected Countries—Conference Proceedings*, Preprint Series of the International Institute of Management I/75–67, pp. 180–99 (Berlin 1975).

[4] HACKMANN, J. and KEITER, H., 'Lohnkostenzuschüsse nach dem "Programm zur Förderung von Beschäftigung und Wachstum bei Stabilität" vom 12. Dezember 1974 in theoretischer Sicht', *Finanzarchiv*, No. 1 (1976), pp. 329–38.

[6] For further proposals to improve the design and implementation of wage subsidy schemes see Schmid [10].

[5] HAVEMAN, R. and CHRISTAINSEN, G., 'Public Employment and Wage Subsidies in Western Europe and the U.S.: What We're Doing and What we Know', Paper prepared for *Conference on Recent European Manpower Policies* organized by the National Commission for Manpower Policy, July 19th–21st, 1978. To be publsihed in the Report Series of the National Commission for Manpower Policy, Washington.

[6] KESSELMAN, J., WILLIAMSON, S. and BERNDT, E., 'Tax Credits for Employment Rather than Investment', *American Economic Review* (June 1977), pp. 339–49.

[7] LAYARD, R. and NICKELL, S., 'The Case for Subsidizing Extra Jobs', mimeo (London School of Economics, London, 1977).

[8] PHLIPS, L., 'Selective Manpower Policies in Germany, with Special Reference to Wage-cost Subsidies', Paper prepared for the *Conference on Recent European Manpower Policies* organized by the National Commission for Manpower Policy, July 19th–21st, 1978; to be published in the Report Series of the National Commission for Manpower Policy, Washington.

[9] SCHMID, G. 'Wage-cost Subsidy Programme in Germany 1974/75. Some Circumstantial Evidence of its Impact and Effect. A Quantitative Study', Discussion paper series of the *International Institute of Management—Wissenschafts-zentrum* (Berlin, December 1977) (Platz der Luftbrücke 1–3, 1000 Berlin).

[10] SCHMID, G. 'Selective Employment Policy in West Germany. Some Evidence of its Development and Impact', paper prepared for the *Conference on Recent European Manpower Policy* organized by the National Commision for Manpower Policy, July 19th–21st, 1978; to be published in the Report Series of the National Commission for Manpower Policy, Washington.

THE JOURNAL OF INDUSTRIAL ECONOMICS
Volume XXVII June 1979 No. 4

ENTROPY MEASURE OF DIVERSIFICATION AND CORPORATE GROWTH

ALEXIS P. JACQUEMIN AND CHARLES H. BERRY*

I. INTRODUCTION

During the past decade or more, a number of authors have proposed (and applied) a number of measures of corporate diversification. These have ranged from simple counts of the number of products to measures which assign various weights to the relative importance of each product within the corporation's total product mix.[1]

For the most part, these measures have direct counterparts in familiar measures of industrial structure. For example, Michael Gort [5] defined, as one measure of corporate diversification, the ratio of the firm's sales within the firm's primary industry to the firm's total sales. This is the equivalent (within the firm) of the primary product specialization ratio reported for 4-digit industries by the Bureau of the Census. A variation of Orris Herfindahl's index of industrial concentration—the sum of the squared shares of each product's contribution to the firm's total output—has been used by one of the authors of this paper [1], [2]. Others have suggested the application to corporate diversification of what has come to be called the entropy measure of industrial concentration.[2] There is no axiomatic analysis or general model of diversification which suggests the advantage of any single index; at this stage it is therefore appropriate to ask which particular index performs best empirically.

This note outlines a theme common to all these measures, identifies a major advantage of the entropy measure in the *analysis* of corporate diversification, and provides some comparative applications of the entropy measure and of the Herfindahl index to 460 of the largest US manufacturing corporations.

II. MEASURES OF CORPORATE CONCENTRATION AND DIVERSIFICATION

Most measures both of industrial concentration and of corporate diversification take the form:

$$I = \sum_{i=1}^{n} P_i w_i$$

* The first author was visiting at Princeton University, with the support of the Collège Interuniversitaire en Management (C.I.M.). They are grateful to L. Phlips for helpful, comments.

[1] Illustrations may be found, for example, in Micharl Gort [5], Paul K. Gorecki [4], Stephen A. Rhodes [12], as well as in A. Jacquemin [8] and Charles H. Berry [1].

[2] See, for example, I. Horowitz [7].

where P_i is the share of either the ith firm (in the case of industry concentration) or the ith industry (in the case of industry diversification within the firm), w_i is an assigned weight, and n the number of firms or products.[3] For the standard four firm concentration ratio, weights of unity are assigned to the share of the four largest firms, with the share of all other firms within the industry receiving a weight of zero. Herfindahl's contribution was the suggestion that the share of each firm be weighted by itself, e.g.

$$H = \sum_{i=1}^{n} P_i P_i$$

The entropy (inverse) measure of industry concentration weights each P_i by the logarithm of $1/P_i$, e.g.

$$E = \sum_{i=1}^{n} P_i \ln 1/P_i$$ [4]

There are lots of additional measures with alternative weights, but these three are the most commonly used—the first (the concentration ratio) because of its historical availability from the Bureau of the Census, the second because of its bounded properties, ease of understanding and intuitive appeal, and the third, entropy, because of the logic of its development and application within the physical sciences. The entropy measure is also more sensitive than the Herfindahl index to very small firms, a difference which led George Stigler [13, p. 33] to give the edge to the Herfindahl index as the more meaningful of the two as a measure of industrial concentration.

As a measure of corporate diversification, however, the advantage runs the other way, and it is more substantial. The degree of diversification for a given corporation obviously depends on the level of product aggregation over which the measure is calculated.[5] For example—and redefining here and subsequently the Herfindahl index as

$$H = \left(1 - \sum_{i=1}^{n} P_i^2\right)$$

to make it *increase* with increasing diversification—the average value in 1960 of the Herfindahl index across *2-digit* industry groups for 460 large manufacturing firms was 0·379.[6] The average value of the index across

[3] For additional discussion and a variety of illustrative applications, see A. Jacquemin and H. deJong [9, esp. pp. 42—50].

[4] A corresponding direct measure may be written as $\Pi_i P_i^{P_i}$ or simply the reciprocal of the antilogarithm of E as defined above. See C. Marfels [11].

[5] This, of course, is also true of industrial concentration. Concentration will generally be lower the more aggregated the industry definitions on which the measure is based.

[6] See Charles H. Berry [1, p. 65]. The 460 large manufacturing firms are the 500 largest industrial corporations in 1960, as identified by *Fortune*, less 36 disappearing because of mergers between 1960 and 1965, three others with no domestic manufacturing facilities, and the Hearst Corporation.

4-digit industries, for these same firms in the same year, was much larger: 0·645 [1, p. 65]. The point is simply that some corporate diversification at the 4-digit level is a consequence of diversification at the 2-digit level. Indeed, interest attaches to just how much diversification at the more detailed (4-digit) level of product classification *is* a consequence of diversification across those broader product groups. It is here that the Herfindahl measure fails. Specifically, the Herfindahl index cannot be decomposed as directly as entropy[7] into additive elements which define the contribution of diversification at each level of product aggregation to the total.

III. ENTROPY AS A MEASURE OF CORPORATE DIVERSIFICATION

Consider a firm active in n 4-digit industries. Those n 4-digit industries in turn aggregate to s 2-digit industry groups ($n \geqslant s$). For a given 2-digit industry group (s), the proportion of the firm's total sales or production within that 2-digit industry is given by:

$$P_s = \sum_{i \in s} P_i$$

and 4-digit diversification (entropy) *within* this 2-digit industry group is:

$$E_W = \sum_{i \in s} \frac{P_i}{P_s} \ln \frac{P_s}{P_i}.$$

Diversification at the 2-digit level—*across* 2-digit industry groups—may be written as:

$$E_A = \sum_{s=1}^{s} P_s \ln \frac{1}{P_s}$$

and the entropy measure of total diversification at the 4-digit level is of course:

$$E_T = \sum_{i=1}^{n} P_i \ln 1/P_i$$

To derive the preceding expressions from this general formula, E_T may be rewritten as:

$$\begin{aligned} E_T &= \sum_{s=1}^{s} \sum_{i \in s} P_i \ln 1/P_i \\ &= \sum_{s=1}^{s} \left[\sum_{i \in s} \frac{P_s}{P_s} P_i \left(\ln \frac{P_s}{P_i} + \ln 1/P_s \right) \right] \\ &= \sum_{s=1}^{s} \left(\sum_{i \in s} \frac{P_s}{P_s} P_i \ln \frac{P_s}{P_i} + \sum_{i \in s} \frac{P_s}{P_s} P_i \ln 1/P_s \right) \end{aligned}$$

[7] For a general statement see H. Theil [14], appendix to Chapter 8] and for an application to the measurement of concentration see A. Jacquemin and A. M. Kumps [10].

which reduces to:

$$E_T = \sum_{s=1}^{s} P_s \left(\sum_{i \in s} \frac{P_i}{P_s} \ln \frac{P_s}{P_i} \right) + \left(\sum_{s=1}^{s} P_s \ln 1/P_s \right)$$

or simply:

$$E_T = \sum_{s=1}^{s} P_s (E_w) + E_A$$

The first term of this last expression is a weighted average of the firm's 4-digit diversification *within* each sector (2-digit industry group in this example) with each sector weighted by its relative importance (P_s). The second term is the diversification of the firm *across* 2-digit industry groups. Thus, by the entropy measure, total diversification is a weighted average of the firm's diversification within sectors plus the firm's diversification across those sectors. Knowing the entropy index of diversification for a firm at the 4-digit level, and also at the 2-digit level, a weighted average diversification at the 4-digit level within those 2-digit industries is therefore correspondingly defined.

IV. SOME EMPIRICAL COMPARISONS

This section, and the one which follows, are based on data for 460 US large industrial corporations which have been analyzed and described elsewhere.[8]

For illustrative purposes, Table I contains values of the Herfindahl and entropy measures for a series of hypothetical distributions of corporate activity across 2- and 4-digit industries, and contrasts differential weighting

TABLE I

ILLUSTRATIVE VALUES OF THE HERFINDAHL AND ENTROPY INDICES

Percentage of firm's sales 2-digit industry					*Index of corporate diversification*			
I 4-digit industry		*II 4-digit industry*			*Herfindahl*	*Entropy*		
(*I-1*)	(*I-2*)	(*II-1*)	(*II-2*)	(*II-3*)	*4-digit*	*4-digit* (E_T)	*2-digit* (E_A)	*'Within' 2-digit* $\sum_{s=1} (P_s E_w)$
95	5	—	—	—	0·10	0·20	0	0·20
90	10	—	—	—	0·18	0·32	0	0·32
80	10	10	—	—	0·34	0·64	0·32	0·32
70	20	10	—	—	0·46	0·80	0·32	0·48
60	40	—	—	—	0·48	0·67	0	0·67
60	10	10	10	10	0·60	1·23	0·61	0·62
50	20	20	10	—	0·66	1·22	0·61	0·61
40	20	20	10	10	0·74	1·47	0·67	0·80
30	20	20	20	10	0·78	1·56	0·69	0·86
20	20	20	20	20	0·80	1·61	0·67	0·94

[8] For a detailed discussion of these data and their limitations see Charles H. Berry [1, pp. 52–8].

of 'market' shares by the two indices.[9] Those weights *decrease* with P_i in the case of the entropy measure and, obviously, increase with P_i for the Herfindahl index. Very small product shares are therefore largely ignored by the Herfindahl index. Conversely, small differences in large product shares make little difference to the value of the entropy measure while the Herfindahl responds more substantially. The Herfindahl index is 0·18 for a firm with 90% of its sales in one industry and 10% in another; it would increase only slightly—to 0·189—if the 10% share were distributed equally among ten different industries. In contrast, the entropy measure would increase by 70% under those same circumstances—from 0·141 to 0·241. There are reversals in the rankings of Table I which reflect this differential weighting.

TABLE II

HERFINDAHL AND ENTROPY INDICES OF CORPORATION DIVERSIFICATION, 460 LARGE INDUSTRIAL CORPORATIONS, 1960 AND 1965

	Year	
Index	*1960*	*1965*
Herfindahl		
4-digit	0·627	0·661
2-digit	0·361	0·396
Entropy		
4-digit	1·455	1·601
2-digit	0·693	0·783
'Within' 2-digit	0·762	0·818

Table II contains actual average values of the Herfindahl and entropy measures for the 460 largest industrial corporations in 1960 and 1965. Both indices are calculated at both the 2- and at the 4-digit level, and both measures show *increasing diversification over time*. The entropy measure also shows a *greater degree of diversification within rather than across 2-digit industry groups* in each of the two years.

Table III shows averages for these same indices expressed as percentages of the maximum values of those indices given the number of products produced. For the Herfindahl index (as that index is defined here), the maximum value is $[1-1/n]$, where n is the number of products. For a firm active in five 4-digit industries, the maximum possible value of the index is therefore 0·8. If, for a particular firm active in five 4-digit industries, the actual value of the Herfindahl index were 0·7, that firm by this measure would be 7/8 as diversified as it could be without increasing the *number*

[9] Note again that the Herfindahl index is defined as

$$\left(1-\sum_{i=1}^{n} P_i^2\right)$$

so that the index *increases* with increasing diversification.

TABLE III

RATIOS OF HERFINDAHL AND ENTROPY INDICES OF DIVERSIFICATION TO CORRESPONDING MAXIMUM VALUES, 460 LARGE INDUSTRIAL CORPORATIONS, 1960 AND 1965

Index	*Year* 1960	1965
Herfindahl		
4-digit	0·744	0·766
2-digit	0·496	0·526
Entropy		
4-digit	0·697	0·709
2-digit	0·498	0·519

of products it produced. By the entropy measure, the corresponding maximum value is ln n, and as with the Herfindahl index, the ratio of the actual value of the index to this maximum value provides a convenient summary statistic of the distribution of the firm's sales among its various products.

Table III contains averages of such ratios for the 460 large manufacturers in 1960 and in 1965. The Herfindahl and entropy measures are consistent. Each shows corporate diversification at the 2-digit level to be only about half that possible given the number of 2-digit industry groups represented. At the 4-digit level, the percentage is higher—about two-thirds of that possible. And although the table does not show it, the implication is that *production or sales across 4-digit industries within 2-digit industries was, for these firms, relatively evenly distributed in comparison with the corresponding distribution across 2-digit industry groups.*[10]

V. GROWTH, PROFITABILITY AND DIVERSIFICATION

It can be expected that growing firms faced with constraints imposed by the growth rates of their industries will face an inducement to diversify in order to avoid those constraints. According to the 'product life cycle

[10] Table III does not contain 'relative entropy'—as these ratios are termed—for the 'within' 2-digit category. This measure is not readily calculated since the maximum diversification possible at the 4-digit level depends in a non-trivial way on existing diversification at the 2-digit level. For example, consider a firm producing equally in two 2-digit industry groups, but with one 4-digit product in one 2-digit industry and three 4-digit products in the other. The maximum degree of 4-digit diversification for this firm, given its actual 2-digit diversification and the number of 2- and 4-digit industries in which it is active, is not ln 4, but $1/2 \ln 2 + 3 \ln 6$. In other words, maximum 'within' 2-digit category diversification, given the number of 4- and 2-digit products produced, is neither the difference between maximum 2- and 4-digit diversification nor the difference between the maximum 4-digit diversification (given the number of 4-digit products) and actual 2-digit diversification. It is the difference between the actual 2-digit diversification and the maximum 4-digit diversification given the 2-digit diversification and the number *and distribution* of 4-digit products across 2-digit industry groups. Even so, however, the lower relative entropy ratios of Table III at the 2-digit level suggest some *tendency for product diversification by these large firms to be relatively greater within areas of the firm's general specialization.* The result is not surprising, and similar results are obtained for the United Kingdom by P. K. Gorecki [3]. See also M. A. Utton [15] and J. Hassid [6].

theory', a slow-growing but profitable oligopoly in which internally generated funds are substantially more than those required to maintain the position in the areas of specialization will tend to expand towards promising industries manufacturing products which are in the first stages of the product cycle. Such diversification, however, can have quite different implications for market behavior depending upon the degree of independence of the markets represented in the product mix of the diversifying firms. In an earlier analysis of the changing diversification of these 460 large industrial corporations, one author concluded:

> . . . The evidence, such as it is, appears to indicate consistently that the 4-digit inter-industry activity that has been most conducive to corporate growth has been *within* rather than *among* 2-digit industry groups. At least one possible interpretation of this finding is that the diversification that has led to relatively rapid rates of corporate growth (or has accompanied it) has not in general been to markets where the entering firm is a new and potentially competitive force. Rather, that 'diversification' has been to markets that are related to—and potentially if not actively competitive with—those in which the entering firm will frequently share whatever market power already exists. That kind of diversification is only one small step removed from the consolidation of market power through horizontal acquisition [2, p. 74].

The analysis underlying this tentative conclusion used Herfindahl indices of diversification to test the sensitivity of relative growth within the group of large industrials to diversification within, rather than across, 2-digit industry groups.

TABLE IV

PERCENTAGE INCREASE IN TOTAL ASSETS ON SELECTED INDEPENDENT VARIABLES, 460 LARGE INDUSTRIAL CORPORATIONS, 1960–65

Independent variable	*Regression (1)*	*Independent variable*	*Regression (2)*
ln total assets, 1960	−6·98 (−3·31)	ln total assets, 1960	−7·73 (3·81)
Earnings, 1960	1·29 (2·61)	Earnings, 1960	1·42 (2·42)
Projected growth	0·375 (3·31)	Projected growth	0·366 (3·18)
Percentage change, 4-digit diversification (Herfindahl)	0·334 (4·02)	Percentage change in entropy *within* 2-digit groups	0·522 (6·48)
Percentage change, 2-digit diversification (Herfindahl)	−0·095 (−0·89)	Percentage change in entropy *across* 2-digit groups	0·347 (5·02)
R^2	0·10	R^2	0·17

t-ratios are shown in parentheses.

Table IV regression (1) presents the corresponding results. The unit of analysis is the firm. Total assets are taken as the reported book value of total assets. Earnings are net profits after tax on a percentage of total assets. Projected growth is defined as

$$\sum_{i=1}^{n} W_i G_i$$

where W_i is the proportion of the firm's activity in the *n*th 4-digit industry, and G_i is the 1958–63 percentage increase on the value of shipments of that industry. Percentage change in diversification is based on Herfindahl indices of diversification for the firm in 1960 and 1965.

First, it is clear that initial size (total assets in 1960) has a negative and significant impact upon the rate of growth, while initial profitability (rate of earnings in 1960) as well as projected growth have a positive and significant effect. Second, only 'narrow spectrum' diversification is related to the rate of growth: the coefficients on changing 4-digit diversification are positive and significant while those on changing diversification at the 2-digit level are negative and not significant. This seems to confirm that only increasing investment in secondary areas closely related to the firm's primary activity and technical expertise is rewarding in terms of growth.

However it is also obvious that changes in 4-digit diversification are not independent of changes in 2-digit diversification.

It is this collinearity which is avoided with the entropy measure. Table IV regression (2) shows corresponding results obtained when diversification is decomposed to its within and across 2-digit industry components. In terms of fit, the entropy measure performs better. More interesting is the sign reversal and significance of the coefficient on 2-digit diversification. Although the coefficient of the 'broad spectrum' diversification is slightly lower than the coefficient of the narrow spectrum component, it appears that not only diversification into closely related industries but also diversification far remote from the original technological base favours the firm's growth.

The origin of the sign reversal can be determined.

Define GRO as the dependent variable, CHE4 as change in total (4-digit) entropy, CHE2 as change in 2-digit entropy, and CHE4W2 as change in 4-digit entropy within 2-digit groups. Regression (2) of Table IV is of the form (though it employs the alternative index) of

$$\begin{aligned} \text{GRO} &= \ldots 0{\cdot}522\ \text{CHE4W2} + 0{\cdot}347\ \text{CHE2} \ldots \\ &= \ldots 0{\cdot}522\ [\text{CHE4} - \text{CHE2}] + 0{\cdot}347\ \text{CHE2} \ldots \\ &= \ldots 0{\cdot}522\ [\text{CHE4}] + [0{\cdot}347 - 0{\cdot}522]\ \text{CHE2} \ldots \\ &= \ldots 0{\cdot}522\ \text{CHE4} - 0{\cdot}175\ \text{CHE2} \ldots \end{aligned}$$

This means that if diversification within and across 2-digit industry groups are positively related to corporate growth, with coefficients α_1 and α_2

TABLE V

PERCENTAGE CHANGE IN TOTAL ASSETS ON SELECTED INDEPENDENT VARIABLES, 460 LARGE INDUSTRIAL CORPORATIONS, 1960–65

Independent variable	*Regressions* (1)	(2)	(3)
ln total assets, 1960	−7·08 (−3·36)	−7·90 (−3·89)	−7·73 (−3·81)
Earnings, 1960	1·31 (2·66)	1·19 (2·51)	1·14 (2·42)
Projected growth	0·367 (3·06)	0·356 (3·08)	0·366 (3·18)
Percentage change *within* 'old' 2-digit groups (Herfindahl)	0·261 (3·96)		
Percentage change to 'new' 2-digit groups (Herfindahl)	0·425 (3·18)		
Percentage change 'within' 'old' 2-digit groups (entropy)		0·414 (6·51)	
Percentage change to 'new' 2-digit groups (entropy)		0·435 (3·89)	
Percentage change in entropy *within* 2-digit groups			0·522 (6·48)
Percentage change in entropy *across* 2-digit groups			0·347 (5·02)
R^2	0·10	0·17	0·17

t-ratios are shown within parentheses.

respectively, and if $\alpha_1 > \alpha_2$, the introduction directly of 2- and 4-digit diversification will, by definition, produce a negative coefficient on the 2-digit measure. This is what is reflected in Table IV. The great advantage of the entropy measure and the primary limitation of the Herfindhal index is that the decomposition can be analytically and very simply derived and the empirical comparisons presented here suggest that this decomposition indeed captures the distinction which is intended.

Table V contains results obtained when the 4-digit Herfindahl index is redefined to measure the percentage change in the index between 1960 and 1965 if activities in 2-digit industry groups entered by the firm during that period are ignored. This is defined as the percentage change in 4-digit diversification within 'old' (or 1960) 2-digit industry groups. The difference between this measure and the total percentage change in 4-digit diversification is defined as *4-digit diversification to 'new' 2-digit industry groups*. For comparative purposes, the entropy measure is also recalculated on this basis—first calculating the change in the index for firms ignoring any activity in 2-digit industry groups entered between 1960 and 1965, and then deducting that change from the total observed change in the 4-digit index—to obtain an alternative measure of diversification to new 2-digit industry groups. Regression (3) in Table V, included for comparison, is regression (2) of Table IV.

These three measures attempt to decompose changing 4-digit diversification into within and across 2-digit components in very different ways.

Given those differences, the results are surprisingly robust. They confirm that *both forms of diversification, viz.* diversification to new 2-digit categories as well as diversification within old 2-digit categories, *have been positively related to the growth rate of these firms*. Furthermore, the coefficients on diversification to new 2-digit categories are similar or exceed those on diversification to 2-digit industry groups within which the firms were previously active.

To conclude, this paper has developed an entropy measure of corporate diversification. The measure is shown to be additive in its application at different levels of product or industry aggregation. This feature of the measure is illustrated at the 2-digit and 4-digit industry levels for 460 large US manufacturing corporations. Preliminary empirical results relating the growth of large corporations to the pattern of diversification appear to confirm the advantage of the entropy measure and suggest a range of analytic applications.

UNIVERSITY OF LOUVAIN AND
PRINCETON UNIVERSITY

REFERENCES

[1] BERRY, CHARLES H., *Corporate Growth and Diversification* (Princeton University Press, Princeton, 1975).

[2] BERRY, CHARLES H., 'Corporate Growth and Industrial Diversification', *Journal of Law and Economics*, **XIV** (October 1971), pp. 371–83.

[3] GORECKI, P. K., 'An Inter-industry Analysis of Diversification in the U.K. Manufacturing Sector', *Journal of Industrial Economics*, **XXIV** (December 1975), pp. 131–46.

[4] GORECKI, PAUL K., 'The Measurement of Enterprise Diversification', *Review of Economics and Statistics*, **LVI** (August 1974), pp. 399–401.

[5] GORT, MICHAEL, *Diversification and Integration in American Industry* (Princeton University Press, Princeton, 1962).

[6] HASSID, J., 'Diversification and the Firm's Rate of Growth', *Manchester School of Economics and Social Studies*, **XLV** (March 1977), pp. 16–28.

[7] HOROWITZ, I., 'Employment Concentration in the Common Market: An Entropy Approach', *Journal of the Royal Statistical Society*, **133**, Series A (1970), pp. 463–79.

[8] JACQUEMIN, A., 'Une Mesure Entropique de la Diversification', *Revue Economique*, **XXVI** (September 1975), pp. 834–8.

[9] JACQUEMIN, A. and DE JONG, H., *European Industrial Organisation* (Macmillan and Wiley, London and New York, 1977).

[10] JACQUEMIN, A. and KUMPS, A. M., 'Changes in the Size Structure of the Largest European Firms: An Entropy Measure', *Journal of Industrial Economics*, **XX** (November 1971), pp. 59–68.

[11] MARFELS, C., 'Absolute and Relative Measures of Concentration Reconsidered', *Kyklos*, No. 4 (1971), pp. 753–66.

[12] RHODES, STEPHEN A., 'A Further Evaluation of the Effect of Diversification on Industry Profit Performance', *Review of Economics and Statistics*, **LVI** (November 1974), pp. 557–9.

[13] STIGLER, GEORGE J., *The Organisation of Industry* (Richard D. Irwin, Homewood, 1968).

[14] THEIL, H., *Economics and Information Theory* (North-Holland, Amsterdam, 1967).

[15] UTTON, M., 'Large Firm Diversification in British Manufacturing Industry', *Economic Journal*, **87** (March 1977), pp. 96–113.

THE JOURNAL OF INDUSTRIAL ECONOMICS
Volume XXVII June 1979 No. 4

PROFIT RATES AND MARKET SHARES OF LEADING INDUSTRIAL FIRMS IN JAPAN

TAKEO NAKAO

I. INTRODUCTION

THE relationship of the top firm's profit rate to its market share, its stock of goodwill and other elements of the market structure was investigated using data on Japanese industrial firms. Traditional microeconomic theory suggests that firms in oligopolistic industries restrict output, raise prices and earn higher profits than do firms in competitive industries, and therefore there will be an important misallocation of resources. To test the validity of this hypothesis there have been a rather large number of studies, beginning with a study by Bain [1], which investigated the relationship between profitability and market structure. Most of these quantitative tests of the structure–performance relationship have been based on data from the United States. Thus, it is of particular interest to see whether similar conclusions concerning the structure–performance relationship can be reached in a fast-growing economy such as that of Japan. This is one justification for adding to the already voluminous literature on this subject.

The second justification for our work is that we have collected data only for top firms—firms whose sales are the largest in their respective industries—and have investigated the relationship of each top firm's profit rate to its market share, its stock of goodwill and other elements of the market structure, which has not been examined previously and which is of some interest. It should be emphasized that the behaviours of non-top firms are likely to differ from that of a top firm, i.e. top firms often behave as leaders, while the remaining firms tend to behave as followers.[1] Therefore, in order to improve the fitness of the structure–performance model, we restrict the sample to top firms.

The third justification for our work is the use of the concept of the stock of goodwill, instead of the advertising/sales ratio. Previous empirical studies have consistently found a strong positive relationship between profit rates and advertising/sales ratios. The advertising/sales ratio has been generally believed to work as a proxy for the height of the product differentiation barrier to entry. Because there is no strong theoretical justification for using the advertising/sales ratio as an independent variable, empirical results based

[1] Market shares of the top firms, and of the largest three firms are given in Appendix B.

on the advertising/sales ratio–profitability relationship are open to Schmalensee's criticism ([15], [16]). Since the theory shows that it is the cumulative effect of advertising that creates a barrier to entry, the stock of goodwill, which is posited as representing the height of the advertising barrier to entry, is used as an independent variable in this study. However, in order to compute the value of the stock of goodwill, we must estimate the rate of depreciation of goodwill, and this requires the use of non-linear multiple regression analysis.

We find that the top firms' profit rates are significantly correlated with the four elements of market structure: market share, demand growth, the stock of goodwill and product differentiation in the narrow sense and that these four elements account for about three-quarters of the variance in the top firms' profit rates. Demand growth has a positive and highly significant relationship to the top firms' profitability. In other words, demand growth emerges as the primary element, with market share and the product differentiation barrier to entry in secondary roles. These findings support the views that (1) demand growth plays the major role in determining the firm's profit rate in a fast-growing economy, and that (2) by creating brand loyalty of consumers advertising constitutes a barrier to entry.

II. THE MODEL

A firm's attainable degree of profitability is believed to be affected by its market position as defined by its rank in the industry, its market share, entry barriers, demand growth and other elements of market structure. Thus, by fitting a model, which specifies that profit rates are a function of these elements, we can clarify the effect of each element on profitability.

The effect of the firm's rank in the industry has not been explicitly taken into account in empirical studies of the structure–performance relationship. There might be, however, differences between the behaviours of a top firm and a non-top firm. A top firm is likely to play a leading role in the industry. In contrast, a non-top firm might be forced to behave as a follower. Therefore, it is probable that the non-top firm's profitability is basically governed by the policy of the dominant firm toward rival firms and/or the internal-group structure, e.g. the relative size of a firm, the differences in costs and the financial structure, rather than entry barriers, demand growth and product differentiation.[2] To improve the likelihood of identifying meaningful relationships between profitability and elements of the market structure, it is necessary to select a comparatively homogeneous sample of firms with similar market positions. Therefore, we have confined our analysis to firms whose

[2] Using a similar sample of firms to that used in the present study, we have shown that the difference in profit rates between the top firms and the second top firms was statistically significant at the 1% level (Nakao [11, p. 191]).

sales are the largest in their respective industries. Therefore, as to the effect of concentration on profitability, the hypothesis to be examined empirically is that for given market demand and entry conditions, a higher market share for a leader firm (MS) gives the leader firm higher profitability.

Product differentiation barriers to entry will also affect profit rates. Advertising has been considered a major source of product differentiation barriers. Thus, the relationship of advertising to profitability has become an increasingly important subject of discussion to economists interested in public policy toward competition and monopoly. There have been a large number of statistical studies aimed at determining the effects of advertising on profit rates (Comanor and Wilson [4], Caves and Uekusa [3], Jones *et al.* [7], Miller [10], Vernon and Nourse [18] and Weiss [19]). Hypothesizing that the advertising/sales ratio affects profit rates through the creation of barriers to entry, most of these studies have examined the correlation between profit rates and advertising/sales ratios. However, Schmalensee [15] has argued that profit rates may be associated positively with advertising/sales ratios if firms fulfil the Dorfman–Steiner condition ([5, p. 828]) for maximum profits, which predicts that the price–cost margin will be highly correlated with the optimum advertising/sales ratio. Thus, statistical studies using the advertising/sales ratio as a product differentiation barrier variable appear to be improper for the investigation of the effects of advertising on profitability. To avoid this problem, at least partly, we have used the concept of goodwill instead of the advertising/sales ratio.

Advertising (A) is believed to have a long-lasting impact on sales. To summarize this aspect of the advertising effect, Nerlove and Arrow [13] have introduced the concept of goodwill (G) which is supposed to represent the effects of current and past advertising expenditures on demand and which is defined by:

$$\dot{G}(t) = A(t) - \delta G(t) \tag{1}$$

where δ is the rate of depreciation of goodwill and the dot denotes differentiation with respect to time (t). Edwards [6] has developed the theory of consumer goodwill with an emphasis on its role as an entry barrier. By combining these two studies we posit that cumulative advertising effects affect profit rates through the creation of goodwill barrier to entry.[3]

Equation (1) can be rewritten in the discrete form as

$$G_t = \sum_{i=1}^{+\infty} (1-\delta)^i A_{t-i}. \tag{2}$$

[3] It should be noted that the heights of the goodwill barrier to entry would be different among firms in the same industry, unless the stock of goodwill of these firms were the same. Obviously, the goodwill barrier to entry of a firm will be the higher, the larger the stock of goodwill of the firm.

The difficulty in using the goodwill variable, in place of the advertising/sales ratio, is the estimation of the depreciation rate of goodwill. We could estimate this using regression analysis of the advertising–sales relationship.[4] But in this study, using the non-linear regression method originally developed by Marquardt [9], we have attempted to estimate the rate of depreciation of goodwill simultaneously.

The use of log G rather than G is justified by the hypothesis that the effect of goodwill on demand decreases, on the average, as the stock of goodwill increases.

Since goodwill is based on the brand loyality of consumers, the goodwill barrier to entry does not exist for non-consumer goods. Therefore, the stock of goodwill for firms which sell a great part of their output to other manufacturers is always assumed to be zero.[5]

Another source of product differentiation barriers to entry is the complexity and/or durability of the product which enable producers to make full use of product differentiation in the narrow sense. These characteristics of the product will, on the one hand, enable producers to differentiate their respective products physically, and on the other hand, may make consumers' judgement of the quality of the products difficult. It is safe to say that these characteristics increase the firm's profitability by creating consumers' brand loyalty. Therefore, we will introduce a dummy variable (DU) which is equal to one if a firm produces primarily consumer durable goods, and zero if otherwise. Thus, DU can be considered to represent the barrier to entry created by product differentiation in the narrow sense.

Firm size (SZ) can also be a main source of barriers to entry. Since firms with larger assets will be less hindered by the capital requirements barrier to entry, the net effect of size on profitability may be positive. In short, the variable SZ is expected to represent the absolute capital requirements barrier.

The growth rate of market demand (GR) is also an important factor which affects profit rates, and associates positively with profitability (see Nakao [12, Proposition 2]).

[4] Using an estimate of the depreciation rate of goodwill obtained from the advertising–sales relationship, Nakao [11] has made a linear regression analysis of the structure–performance relationship using similar data on Japanese industrial firms. This estimate, however, was unsatisfactory for several reasons: (1) there is no theoretical justification for assuming that the rate of depreciation of goodwill obtained from the advertising–sales relationship equals that for the advertising–profit relationship, (2) the estimate was computed using the statistically insignificant estimates of the depreciation rate of goodwill for the individual firms, (3) there were several firms whose estimates of the depreciation rate of goodwill were not available, and (4) data on advertising expenditures used in the estimation were not deflated by the price index of advertising. When the results obtained in [11] are compared with those in the present study, the effects of demand growth on profits seem to be underestimated.

[5] Firms which primarily produce non-consumer goods often advertise to inform buyers of their products. But in these cases the buyers are themselves businessmen, i.e. other manufacturers at higher stages of production. Therefore, the amounts of advertising expenditure for these firms are usually very small, and are not generally included in their financial reports published every half-year.

III. DATA

Careful attention was paid to the selection of the sample of firms to be examined. The reliable data on the market shares of the top firms in Japanese manufacturing industries were extremely limited. The latest statistics (1966) on the market shares of the top firms in Japanese manufacturing industries published by Japan Fair Trade Commission included only 171 industries.[6] Moreover, as the argument in the previous section suggests, in order to exclude the effects of inter-firm profit rate differentials in the respective industries, we must confine our sample of firms to top firms. However, most of the top industrial firms in Japan are highly diversified. We had to omit such firms, because we could not obtain the meaningful measure of market share (or the corresponding profit rate) essential for the present study. We have included only those firms, the majority of whose outputs were made up of a single product or a group of similar products. Thus, only a total of 32 top firms out of 171 were chosen. Of these 32 firms, 16 were the consumer goods firms and 16 were the producer goods firms.

There are a few important problems concerning profit rates. Since Bain's study [1], the rate of return on shareholders' equity (PE) has often been used as the dependent variable. But, as shown by Comanor and Wilson [4, p. 110], PE is considered to be more sensitive to the leverage of the firm than is the rate of return on total assets (PT). Thus, following such recent studies as those of Comanor and Wilson [4], Vernon and Nourse [18] and Miller [10], we have adopted PT as well as PE as a dependent variable.

The relevant profit variable is not the firm's total profits, but operational profits, since non-operational profits such as return on investments on other businesses and interests on loans do not generally depend on market structure defined above. If possible, we should substract the appropriate amount of taxes from operational profits. Unfortunately, however, data concerning taxes on operational profits were not available. The only data concerning taxes published by firms were the taxes on total profits which contained non-operational as well as operational profits. Therefore, we have been obliged to use two alternative values as a profit variable: operational profits after taxes on total profits and operational profits before taxes.

Finally, note that when we calculate profit rates, we do not treat advertising expenditures as an investment in capital assets. By adjusting profit rates in this way, Weiss [19] and Bloch [2] have examined the structure–performance relationship. However, it should be noted that while capital assets are productive, cumulative advertising expenditures are not. Therefore, if we are to analyse the structure–performance relationship in terms of resource allocation, we should not treat the stock of goodwill as a capital asset.

[6] Since 1966 Japan Fair Trade Commission has stopped publishing data on top firms' market share.

The basic model, which consists of a non-linear multiple regression of the two profit-rate variables on a set of independent variables, is summarized below:[7]

Dependent Variables

PE(PEA) The top firm's operational profits after interest expense (and taxes), divided by the shareholders' equity, averaged over the years 1964–69.[8]

PT(PTA) The top firm's operational profits (after taxes) divided by the total assets, averaged over the years 1964–69.

Independent Variables

MS The 1966 market share of the top firm.[9]

GR The ratio of the firm's 1964 sales to the firm's 1969 sales.[10]

DU The dummy variable which equals one if the firm's main product is a consumer durable good or zero if otherwise.

SZ The firm's total assets, averaged over the years 1964–69, in ten thousand millions of yen.

G The firm's stock of goodwill in thousand millions of 1954 yen, averaged over the years 1964–69. To calculate this variable, we use semi-annual

[7] The sources of the data are described in Appendix A and detailed data are given in Appendix B.

[8] For the 20 cases out of 32, we could easily find the top firms in the respective industries, since the market shares of the top firms in these industries were significantly larger than those of the second top firms during the observation period. For the remaining 12 industries there were no significant differences in the market shares of the major firms in the respective industries, and the top firms often changed during the observation period. It would, however, make little difference which firms were selected out of these major firms, since there would probably be no significant differences in the profit rates as well as the market shares of these firms. For these cases, the 1966 sales of individual firms were mainly used to rank firms in the respective industries. (For example, in the case of the sugar industry the market shares of the major firms were very unstable and the top firm defined by individual firm's market shares often changed during the observation period, and in the present study the 1966 top firm (Taito Co. Ltd.) was selected. But for the early two years of the observation period Dai-Nippon Sugar Mfg. Co. Ltd. was the largest. The non-linear regression analysis using data on Dai-Nippon Sugar, however, showed little difference in the results.) In the cases of the camera and detergent industries, the 1966 top firms have diversified and did not meet the criterion about the firm's specialization rate. Therefore, the 1966 second largest firms whose specialization rates were larger than 50% (and which were the top firms in the latter part of the observation period) were selected.

[9] Market shares of the Calpis Food Industry Co. Ltd. and the Lion Dentifrice Co. Ltd. for 1966 were not available. Therefore, the 1968 market share for the former and the 1970 market share for the latter have been used.

[10] One might criticize that the variable GR, defined above, includes price increases made by the top firms. But if profits are increased by price increases due to the rapid growth of demand, such extra-normal profits should be attributed to the rapid growth of demand. On the other hand, if monopolistic price increases are not related with demand growth, they would not, by definition, be correlated with demand growth. Therefore, there is no reason to believe that the variable GR is correlated with monopolistic price increases.

data on advertising expenditures from 1954 to 1969,[11] in thousand millions of 1954 yen (deflated by the price index of advertising).

Table I summarizes these variables.

TABLE I

PROPERTIES OF PROFIT RATES AND STRUCTURAL VARIABLES IN LEADING JAPANESE INDUSTRIAL FIRMS, 1964–69

Market share	Number of firms	Mean assets profit rates		Mean equity profit rates	
		Before taxes	After taxes	Before taxes	After taxes
Below 20%	14(13)[a]	7·8	5·8	16·4	7·3
20–50%	11	10·6	7·6	24·6	14·4
50% and above	7	15·3	9·1	37·7	19·8
Growth of demand during the observation period	*Number of firms*	*Mean assest profit rates*		*Mean equity profit rates*	
		Before taxes	*After taxes*	*Before taxes*	*After taxes*
Below 200%	12(11)[a]	8·7	6·4	18·5	10·1
200–300%	16	10·1	6·8	23·0	11·7
300% and above	4	16·7	10·9	39·1	23·5

[a] There was one firm in the sample whose shareholders' equities were negative. Therefore, this firm was omitted when PE or PEA was used as the dependent variable.

IV. EMPIRICAL RESULTS

The statistical results of relating profit rates to the foregoing independent variables using non-linear multiple regression analysis are reported in Table II. Obviously, the rates of return on total assets are better explained than are the rates of return on the shareholders' equity. Moreover, profit rates using the profit variable before taxes on the total profits are better explained than are those using the profit variable after taxes on the total profits. Thus, out of four alternative dependent variables, PT can be explained best: all signs are correctly positive, and all the variables except SZ are statistically significant.[12] Together they account for three-quarters of the variance in PT. Thus, in the following analysis we will examine the effects of elements of the market structure on profit rates using the results for PT.

As expected, the market share as well as the growth of demand is positively related to the profit rates: the leader firm's profit rate will be increased by

[11] Data on advertising expenditures of the Ito Ham Provisions Co. Ltd. and the Bridgestone Tire Co. Ltd. before 1960 were not available, since these two firms were not listed in the stock market before 1960. To evaluate the importance of the cumulative advertising expenditures of these two firms, we have made a regression analysis using a dummy variable which is one for these firms and zero for other firms. But this variable was completely insignificant. Therefore, we can conclude that the cumulative advertising expenditures of these two firms before 1960 were relatively small and can be disregarded in this study. Kikkoman Shoyu Co. Ltd. and Calpis Food Industry Co. Ltd. published only annual data. Therefore, semi-annual data were computed by dividing annual data by two.

[12] Since we used the non-linear estimation method, figures written in parentheses in Table II are standard errors for the large sample. Therefore, in a strict sense we cannot make use of the '*t*'-test.

the increase in the leader firm's market share as well as in the growth rate of demand for the leader firm's product. However, note that in spite of the significance which economic theory ascribes to concentration, its role is relatively small; even at a very high MS value of 50%, the addition to profit rates would be only four points, while the three-fold growth in demand during the observation period was associated with an increase in profit rates of more than ten points higher. This result forms a sharp contrast to the results for the large US industrial firms reported by Shepherd [17, p. 32].

TABLE II

REGRESSION ANALYSIS OF DETERMINANTS OF PROFIT RATES IN LEADING JAPANESE INDUSTRIAL FIRMS, 1964–69[a]

Dependent variable	Independent variables						
	MS	*GR*	*DU*	*SZ*	*G*	$1-\delta$	$\bar{R}^2$
PT	0·0815	3·52	3·37	0·0915	3·11	0·741	0·705
	(0·0278)	(0·90)	(1·61)	(0·8782)	(1·14)	(0·325)	
PT	0·0809	3·51	3·38		3·12	0·746	0·716
	(0·0266)	(0·88)	(1·57)		(1·11)	(0·306)	
PTA	0·0487	2·13	1·32	0·573	1·16	0·774	0·480
	(0·0222)	(0·70)	(1·27)	(0·695)	(0·88)	(0·493)	
PTA	0·0448	2·09	1·44		1·20	0·832	0·487
	(0·0216)	(0·69)	(1·26)		(0·88)	(0·455)	
PE	0·115	12·9	5·28	−4·16	13·9	0·799	0·578
	(0·116)	(3·63)	(6·62)	(3·61)	(4·60)	(0·207)	
PE	0·143	12·8	4·00		12·9	0·806	0·574
	(0·114)	(3·60)	(6·60)		(4·60)	(0·206)	
PEA	0·0883	8·38	1·81	−0·738	6·79	0·865	0·473
	(0·0825)	(2·62)	(4·72)	(2·582)	(3·29)	(0·285)	
PEA	0·0932	8·59	1·62		6·83	0·850	0·493
	(0·0790)	(2·58)	(4·60)		(3·24)	(0·283)	

[a] Figures in parentheses are the large sample standard errors. Values of $\bar{R}^2$ are corrected for the degrees of freedom.

Thus, it is safe to conclude that in a rapidly growing economy such as that of Japan, dynamic industrial conditions, the most important of which is the growth of demand, are more important for determining profit rates than is the static monopolistic power represented by concentration or the market share.

The other three variables, DU, G, and SZ should constitute barriers to entry, and therefore should be associated positively with profitability. As far as the absolute capital requirements are concerned, SZ is never significant in either profit rate with the correct sign. This again is in contrast with some multivariate studies of US manufacturing industries. The difference may be explained by the rapid growth of the Japanese economy as well as by institutional differences in the two countries (for details on this problem, see Caves and Uekusa [3, p. 95]).

Product differentiation in the narrow sense shows up as significant with the correct sign. This would confirm the well-known hypothesis that in the case of consumer durable goods, the good reputation of established firms sustained by the product differentiation in the narrow sense is a major barrier to entry.

The most important finding in our study is the strong relationship between the leader firm's stock of goodwill and its profit rate. It may be still debatable whether this finding supports the goodwill barrier to entry hypothesis. Because if the advertising/sales ratio is highly correlated with the stock of goodwill, the high correlation between profits and the stock of goodwill might be fully explained by the theoretical argument that profitable firms advertise more. However, as to the 16 consumer goods firms in our sample, the correlation coefficient between the stock of goodwill and the advertising/sales ratio is 0·33, which is not significant at the 5% level. Therefore, Schmalensee's criticism that the firm's profitability can be positively related to the firm's advertising for reasons not necessarily related to entry barriers would not be applicable to our results on the goodwill–profit rate relationship. The evidence in this study seems to lend strong support to the hypothesis that by creating the brand loyality of consumers, advertising gives an established firm the ability to use it to erect a barrier to entry.

It should, however, be noted that the goodwill barrier to entry had only a secondary influence, since even at a very high G value of 7500 millions of 1954 yen,[13] profit rates would be only about six points higher than the intercept.

Finally, thanks to the non-linear regression method, the rate of depreciation of goodwill could be simultaneously estimated. Using the estimates of $1-\delta$, we can calculate the annual rate of depreciation by multiplying the two semi-annual percentages. These estimates ranges from 0·45 to 0·25. The estimate of PT case is 0·44. These values are notably in agreement with the decay rate of the advertising effect estimated from the advertising–sales relationships. For example, the estimates in Palda's Koyck model [14, p. 172] centre on 0·36 and those in Lambin's study [8, p. 115] centre on 0·46. This seems to confirm the validity of our analysis, in which the decay rate of the advertising effect has been indirectly estimated using the advertising–profit rate relationship.

V. SUMMARY

This paper develops and tests a model for the structure–performance relationship. Empirical analysis using data on leading Japanese industrial firms during the period 1964–69 lends support to the basic microeconomic hypothesis that the profit rates of dominant firms are positively related to

[13] There is only one firm in our sample whose stock of goodwill averaged over the years 1964–69 is larger than 7500 millions of 1954 yen.

their market shares, the rate of demand growth, and the height of the product differentiation barriers to entry; the last factor being represented by the consumer durable dummy variable and the stock of goodwill. Jointly, the four variables account for about three-quarters of the variance in profit rates. Although the influence of market share appears to be small, the growth of demand appears to play the main role in determining profitability in a fast-growing economy such as that of Japan. Moreover, since the stock of goodwill, instead of the advertising/sales ratio, has been used as an independent variable, we can safely conclude that the evidence presented in this paper supports the hypothesis that advertising creates a barrier to entry.

DOSHISHA UNIVERSITY

APPENDIX A

SOURCES OF DATA AND PRICE INDEX OF ADVERTISING

We selected a sample of 32 firms from those listed in the stock market whose financial reports have been published every half-year. Data on the total assets, operational profits, interest expenses, equity, taxes on total profits, total sales, and advertising expenditures of individual firms in the sample were obtained from Japan, Ministry of Treasury, *Yukashoken-Hokokusho-Soran* [*The Complete Edition of Financial Reports*] (various issues).

All data on market shares of the top firms in the sample were obtained from Japan Fair Trade Commission, *Nippon no Sangyo Shuchu—1963–1966* [*Industrial Concentration in Japan—1963–1966*] (Toyo Keizai Shinposha, Tokyo, 1969) except as follows:

1. For the Calpis Food Industry Co. Ltd. and the Lion Dentifrice Co. Ltd., data from Toyo Keizai Shinposha, *Tokei Geppo* [*Monthly Report of Statistics*] (June 1968 and June 1970, respectively) were used.
2. For the Toyota Motor Co. Ltd. the 1966 market share was computed from *Jidosha Tokei Nenpo* [*Statistical Report of Automobiles*] (Nippon Jidosha Kogyokai [Association of Japanese Automobile Industry], Tokyo, 1967).
3. For the Shiseido Co. Ltd. the 1966 market share was computed from Japan, Ministry of International Trade and Industry, *Census of Manufacturers* (1966) and the 1966 Shiseido's financial reports.
4. In the case of Nippon Gakki Co. Ltd. the 1968 market share of organs was obtained from *Tokei Geppo* (June 1970). (As to pianos, the 1966 market share was obtained *Nippon no Sangyo Schuchu.*) The market share of pianos and organs was computed using Nippon Gakki's sales of pianos and organs as weights.

The price index of advertising (P_A) was constructed as the weighted sum of the price indices of the major categories in advertising expenditures of Japan. The annual weights were calculated using the shares of advertising expenditures for the major categories. The price indices of the categories were computed as the ratios of the advertising expenditures divided by the quantities of advertising (measured, for example, by hours in the case of television). The advertising expenditure categories included television and radio advertising, magazine and newspaper advertising, and direct mail. The source for these data is Dentsu, *Dentsu Kokoku Nenkan* [*Dentsu Advertising Year Book*] (Dentsu, Tokyo, various issues). These price index estimates are given in Table A.I.

TABLE A.I

PRICE INDEX OF ADVERTISING

Year	P_A
1954	1·000
1955	0·985
1956	1·027
1957	1·163
1958	1·196
1959	1·198
1960	1·214
1961	1·305
1962	1·378
1963	1·487
1964	1·565
1965	1·578
1966	1·616
1967	1·742
1968	1·869
1969	2·081

APPENDIX B

DATA USED IN THE NON-LINEAR REGRESSION ANALYSIS

TABLE B.I

PROFIT RATES (%), MARKET SHARE (%), RATE OF GROWTH IN DEMAND (RATIO 1969/1964), DURABLE DUMMY VARIABLE, TOTAL ASSETS (THOUSAND MILLIONS YEN), AND THREE-FIRM CONCENTRATION RATIO (%)

Firms (primary products)	*PT*	*PTA*	*PE*	*PEA*	*MS*	*GR*	*DU*	*SZ*	*Three-firm CR*
Kirin Brewery (beer)	10·2	6·86	24·9	14·6	50·9	1·74	0·0	1·055	96·0
Taito (sugar)	−0·7	−0·75	−20·4	−20·4	10·2	1·14	0·0	0·128	27·2
Toray Industries (synthetic fibres)	11·1	8·67	18·8	13·0	27·1	1·66	0·0	2·233	50·4
Oji Paper (paper)	8·3	6·99	15·8	10·0	15·2	1·88	0·0	0·682	40·7
Lion Fat & Oil (detergents)	11·6	7·98	51·8	30·8	26·9	2·41	0·0	0·139	67·7
Takeda Chemical Industries (medicines)	16·5	10·72	39·2	23·6	9·8	1·68	0·0	1·232	23·6
Kansai Paint (coatings)	8·2	6·13	14·4	8·2	16·3	2.10	0·0	0·180	38·4
Bridgestone Tire (tyres and tubes)	16·0	11·87	35·5	23·7	46·7	1·82	0·0	0·778	77·2
Onoda Cement (cement)	5·6	4·97	1·9	−0·3	15·1	1·50	0·0	0·880	43·6
Shinagawa Fire-Brick (refractory bricks)	9·5	7·20	18·5	7·9	12·1	2·39	0·0	0·155	29·7
Nippon Light Metal (alminium ingots)	8·6	6·40	13·8	7·0	37·4	2·52	0·0	0·664	84·5
Sumitomo Electric Industries (electric wires and cables)	8·8	7·11	19·0	12·7	15·1	2·42	0·0	0·905	39·7

TABLE B.I (*continued*)

Firms (*primary products*)	*PT*	*PTA*	*PE*	*PEA*	*MS*	*GR*	*DU*	*SZ*	Three-firm *CR*
NHK Spring (springs)	7·7	5·94	14·9	7·8	28·4	2·08	0·0	0·133	47·7
Koyo Seiko (bearings)	10·7	8·35	22·8	15·2	28·1	2·43	0·0	0·361	77·1
Japan Storage Battery (storage batteries)	8·0	6·52	13·9	8·5	37·7	2·03	0·0	0·156	77·3
K. Hattori (watches)	14·5	10·18	30·3	17·3	55·9	2·17	1·0	0·275	94·4
Mitsui Mining (coal)	3·7	3·68	—	—	17·0	1·40	0·0	0·742	32·2
Kikkoman Shoyu (soy sauce)	8·7	5·57	21·8	11·8	20·4	1·67	0·0	0·257	28·8
Nippon Formula-Feed Mfg. (mixed feed)	8·9	6·12	25·4	15·8	7·4	1·48	0·0	0·107	18·4
Nisshin Flour Milling (wheat flour)	8·0	5·97	16·3	7·5	29·0	1·48	0·0	0·352	56·9
Meiji Milk Products (milk)	8·8	5·51	24·6	11·3	21·8	1·95	0·0	0·348	51·0
Fuji Photo Film (photographic film)	13·3	9·44	30·2	19·2	78·0	2·28	0·0	0·539	100·0
Sumitomo Light Metal Industries (aluminium rolled products)	6·6	5·71	12·2	8·1	19·0	2·13	0·0	0·376	47·1
Toyota Motor (small passenger motor cars)	17·7	11·28	36·4	22·1	36·7	3·31	1·0	2·259	77·5
Nippon Kogaku (cameras)	14·2	8·81	39·4	21·0	14·6	3·07	1·0	0·147	45·5
Nippon Gakki (pianos and organs)	16·6	9·54	29·2	15·8	59·4	2·01	1·0	0·287	n.a.[a]
Ito Ham Provisions (ham and sausages)	12·1	9·11	31·3	20·3	14·6	4·87	0·0	0·094	39·8
Katakura Industry (silk)	4·5	4·17	−7·0	−9·6	11·6	2·24	0·0	0·170	23·1
Lion Dentifrice (tooth paste)	13·2	6·47	34·9	15·0	61·0	2·23	0·0	0·109	94·0
Calpis Food Industry (fermented milk drink)	22·8	14·59	49·2	30·6	78·4	3·15	0·0	0·105	91·0
Nippon Oil (petroleum products)	3·0	1·89	4·1	−2·0	13·2	2·02	0·0	1.490	36·0
Shiseido (toiletries)	16·5	6·78	65·0	25·9	50·0	2·09	0·0	0·379	n.a.[a]

[a] Not available.

REFERENCES

[1] BAIN, J. S., 'Relation of Profit Rate to Industry Concentration', *Quarterly Journal of Economics*, **65**, (August 1951), pp. 297–304.

[2] BLOCH, HARRY, 'Advertising and Profitability: A Reappraisal', *Journal of Political Economy*, **82** (2) (March/April 1974), pp. 267–86.

[3] CAVES, R. E. and UEKUSA, M., *Industrial Organization in Japan* (The Brookings Institution, Washington, DC, 1976).

[4] COMANOR, W. S. and WILSON, T. A., *Advertising and Market Power* (Harvard University Press, Cambridge, 1974).

[5] DORFMAN, ROBERT and STEINER, P. E., 'Optimal Advertising and Optimal Quality', *American Economic Review*, **44** (December 1954), pp. 826–36.

[6] EDWARDS, H. R., *Competition and Monopoly in the British Soap Industry* (Clarendon Press, Oxford, 1962).

[7] JONES, J. C. H., LAUDADIO, L. and PERCY, M., 'Profitability and Market Structure: A Cross-section Comparison of Canadian and American Manufacturing Industry', *Journal of Industrial Economics*, **25** (3) (March, 1977), pp. 195–211.

[8] LAMBIN, J. J., *Advertising, Competition and Market Conduct in Oligopoly Over Time* (North-Holland, Amsterdam, 1976).

[9] MARQUARDT, D. W., 'An Algorithm for Least-squares Estimation of Non-linear Parameters', *SIAM, Applied Mathematics*, **2** (2), (June 1963), pp. 431–41.

[10] MILLER, R. A., 'Market Structure and Industrial Performance: Relation of Profit Rates to Concentration, Advertising Intensity, and Diversity', *Journal of Industrial Economics*, **17** (April 1969), pp. 104–18.

[11] NAKAO, TAKEO, 'On the Relationship between Profit Rates and Market Structures in Japanese Manufacturing Industries' (in Japanese), *Economic Studies Quarterly*, **27** (3) (December 1976), pp. 189–200.

[12] ——, 'Demand Growth, Profitability and Entry', Discussion Paper No. 5 (Doshisha Economic Research Association, 1978).

[13] NERLOVE, M. and ARROW, K. J., 'Optimal Advertising Policy under Dynamic Conditions', *Economica*, **39** (May 1962), pp. 129–42.

[14] PALDA, K. S., 'The Measurement of Cumulative Advertising Effects', *Journal of Business*, **38** (April 1965), pp. 162–79.

[15] SCHMALENSEE, RICHARD, *The Economics of Advertising* (North-Holland, Amsterdam, 1972).

[16] ——, 'Advertising and Profitability: Further Implications of the Null Hypothesis', *Journal of Industrial Economics*, **25** (1) (September 1976), pp. 45–54.

[17] SHEPHERD, W. G., 'The Elements of Market Structure', *Review of Economics and Statistics*, **54** (4) (February 1972), pp. 25–35.

[18] VERNON, J. M. and NOURSE, R. E. M., 'Profit Rates and Market Structure of Advertising Intensive Firms', *Journal of Industrial Economics*, **22** (1) (September 1973), pp. 1–20.

[19] WEISS, L. W., 'Advertising, Profits, and Corporate Taxes', *Review of Economics and Statistics*, **52** (3) (November 1969), pp. 421–30.

THE JOURNAL OF INDUSTRIAL ECONOMICS
Volume XXVII June 1979 No. 4

PATENTING ACTIVITY: A RE-EVALUATION OF THE INFLUENCE OF DEMAND PRESSURES*

P. Stoneman

I. INTRODUCTION

In his seminal work, Schmookler [15] investigated the role of economic factors in the determination of the rate of technological change. The latter he approximated by patenting activity. The validity of this approximation has merited considerable discussion (see for example Scherer [14]), but for present purposes we will take the objections as read. Schmookler's major result is that, 'capital goods invention tends to be distributed among industries in proportion to the prevailing distribution of investment. The central reason for this evidently is that inventing is heavily influenced by considerations of profitability.' This represented a considerable advance in that it supported empirically an hypothesis that technological change was endogenous to the economic system. The purpose of the present paper is to investigate the validity of Schmookler's results in the UK case. In particular we wish to stress the effects of cost differences on the level of patenting activity. If costs of invention are an important determinant of patenting activity, then this immediately implies that technological opportunity is important in determining the rate of technological advance, and such a finding is in contrast to those of Schmookler (see Rosenberg [12]) although consistent with theoretical suppositions (Nordhaus [11]). Although considerable effort has gone into the investigation of the relationship between patenting activity and market structure and between technological advance and technological opportunity (see Scherer [14]), the main argument of Schmookler that demand pull factors are of prime importance in the inter-industry distribution of invention seems to have merited little further empirical investigation. If one restricts one's view to the UK case this statement is even more relevant.[1] In section II we develop a model for the explanation of patenting activity,

* I would like to thank two referees of this journal, Ken Wallis, Keith Cowling, John Cubbin and other members of the University of Warwick Industrial Economics Workshop for their comments on an earlier draft of this paper. Steve Freeman put in a considerable effort on data collection and manipulation, and the research was supported by funds from the Centre for Industrial Economic and Business Research at the University of Warwick. The author, however, bears sole responsibility for any views expressed and any errors that remain.

[1] The work closest to the analysis presented here is the US study in Scherer's [13] pre-Schmookler paper, which is essentially concerned with firm size and the output of inventions taking into account technological opportunity and market structure. The major difference between Scherer and Schmookler is Scherer's emphasis on the industry. We follow the latter approach.

in section III discuss data availability and in section IV present some estimates of the model. In section V implications and conclusions are drawn.

II. THE MODEL

Consider firm i in industry j ($i=1 \ldots N_j$, $j=1 \ldots M$) that undertakes invention producing activities. Let the number of patents produced by firm i be x_{ij}, and define the revenue from the kth invention as R_{ijk} ($k=1 \ldots x_{ij}$). The determinants of R_{ijk} may be considered in three categories, (a) invention specific, (b) firm specific, and (c) industry specific. It may well be argued that the return to an invention will be determined by the characteristics of the invention itself. However, the whole thrust of Schmookler's argument is that a count of the number of patents is a good indicator of the rate of technological change. This suggests that all patents can be considered as of equal quality. As the only reasonable quality measure is the financial gain to be made from the patent this would suggest that R_{ijk} is independent of k. As for practical purposes this presumption of equal quality must be assumed in our empirical work, given the absence of detailed knowledge of each patent, we will make the heroic assumption that R_{ijk} is independent of k.

A particular firm specific factor may be considered to be the potential captive market represented by the firm's own output. However, given that in principle the patent can be licensed for use by all firms in an industry, the size of the inventing firm's existing output would not seem to be an important factor. In fact we cannot see any good reason why the return to an invention should vary with the identity of the firm producing it and thus we will assume R_{jik} is independent of i as well as k.

Consider, now, the industry specific factors. Schmookler suggests that the level of investment expenditure of the industry which will use the jth industry's patents (with some lag structure) is a good indicator of the expected revenue from an invention. We suggest three prime determinants of expected revenue. (1) The size of the potential market for an invention (which would seem to be best indicated by the output level of the user industry, especially in the case of a process innovation) would appear to be a prime determinant of expected return. Of course the total market ought to be measured by the output of the user industry when the invention is being used, but it would seem that the best indicator we can get for this, without detailed information on the cost characteristics of specific industries, is the current (or lagged) output level of the user industry. (2) In a world with a fixed patent life, the speed with which an invention is adopted is a crucial determinant of the return to the inventor. A slow diffusion means lower returns than fast diffusion. As an indicator of the expected speed of diffusion for a given industry we suggest the use of the ratio of investment to net output, I/Y, with some lag structure yet to be determined. The reasoning is that process innovations and most probably product innovations require positive gross investment. The faster the acceptance rate the higher the level of gross investment. Thus the ratio of gross investment to output would seem a good indicator of diffusion speed and thus expected return. Moreover, if the inventions were such that certain industries were expecting higher returns from their inventions, then we would expect the higher returns to be reflected in faster diffusion and thus to be captured by I/Y. (3) The third factor we consider important is the number of patents, or inventions, being produced for use in a given industry. One would expect that the greater is the flow of inventions the lower will be the return to any one, either because of technological overtaking or pure competitive pressure.

Related to this final factor is the question of the importance of the market structure of the user industry. Arrow [2] argues that the returns that can be expected from selling an invention to a competitive industry are greater than those to be expected from selling to a monopolized industry. Needham [10], however, disputes this, and whether there is a continuum across differing levels of concentration is not clear. Nor is it clear whether in a world where a number of inventions suitable for adoption are produced (as in the current framework) that the Arrow result holds, for the Arrow result is dependent upon the patent owner having monopoly power. If there are a number of competing patents this power does not exist. Given the doubts we have considered that expected return is solely dependent on the three factors detailed above. In fact, if we define

$x_j = \sum_{i=1}^{N_j} x_{ij}$ = the number of inventions produced by industry j

I_j = investment in the industry using the inventions of industry j

Y_j = output in the industry using the inventions of industry j

and

J_j = some constant

then we postulate that[2] (ignoring lag structures for the moment)

$$R_{ijk} = R_j = J_j \cdot \left(\frac{I_j}{Y_j}\right)^{\xi} \cdot Y_j^{\gamma} \cdot x_j^{\eta^j_{RX}} \qquad 0 > \eta^j_{RX} > -1 \tag{1}$$

where η^j_{RX} = elasticity of expected revenue from a patent in industry j with respect to the number of patents produced in industry j.

We will assume that firms are profit maximizers and that their invention producing activites can be separated from their other activities. Defining π_{ijk} as the profit derived by firm i in industry j from its kth invention, and

[2] We could allow ξ and γ in (1) to be industry specific but this would have the effect of further complicating the notation below without providing any noticeable benefit.

C_{ijk} as the total cost to this firm of making invention k, we then assume that the firm maximizes (2).

$$\sum_{k=1}^{x_{ij}} \pi_{ijk} = \pi_{ij} = \sum_{k=1}^{x_{ij}} R_{ijk} - \sum_{k=1}^{x_{ij}} C_{ijk} \tag{2}$$

which using (1), we write as (3)

$$\pi_{ij} = x_{ij}\, R_j - \sum_{k=1}^{x_{ij}} C_{ijk} \tag{3}$$

Just as we have argued that R_{ijk} cannot for practical reasons (among others) be considered as a function of k, we consider that C_{ijk} can be treated as similarly independent of k. We then hypothesize that C_{ij}, as for any normal cost curve, is a function of x_{ij}, i.e. $C_{ij} = C_{ij}(x_{ij})$, enabling us to write (3) as (4)

$$\pi_{ij} = x_{ij}\, R_j - C_{ij}\,(x_{ij}) \tag{4}$$

The first order condition for profit maximization is given by (5) which may be written as (6), where $\eta^{ij}_{RX} = \partial R_j/\partial x_{ij} \cdot \dfrac{x_{ij}}{R_j}$.

$$0 = R_j + x_{ij} \cdot \frac{\partial R_j}{\partial x_{ij}} - \frac{dC_{ij}}{dx_{ij}} \tag{5}$$

$$0 = R_j\,(1 + \eta^{ij}_{RX}) - \frac{dC_{ij}}{dx_{ij}} \tag{6}$$

From (1) we may derive (7)

$$\eta^{ij}_{RX} = \frac{dx_j}{dx_{ij}} \cdot \frac{x_{ij}}{x_j} \cdot \eta^{j}_{RX} \tag{7}$$

where $dx_j/dx_{ij} \cdot x_{ij}/x_j$ represents expectations of conjectural variations by firm i. We will assume that this is a constant Ω_{ij},[3] and thus may write (6) as (8).

$$R_j(1 + \Omega_{ij} \cdot \eta^{j}_{RX}) = \frac{dC_{ij}}{dx_{ij}} \tag{8}$$

Equation (8) is a condition that holds for firm i. We now move to the industry level of aggregation, letting $\Omega_{ij} = \Omega_j$ for all i and $dC_{ij}/dx_{ij} = \bar{C}_j$ for all i (i.e. marginal cost per patent equals average cost for each firm, and average

[3] This is equivalent to assuming that if firm i increases its output by 1% it expects industry output to increase by Ω_{ij}%. Alternatively one can use $dx_j/dx_{ij} = 1 + \lambda$, i.e. conjectural variations on levels rather than market shares. There does not seem any good *a priori* reason to prefer that form over the one used here.

costs are the same for each firm).[4] We may therefore derive (9) and then using (1) generate (10).

$$R_j = \bar{C}_j / (1 + \Omega_j \, \eta^j_{RX}) \tag{9}$$

$$\log x_j = \{\log \bar{C}_j - \log(1 + \Omega_j \eta^j_{RX}) - \xi \log(I_j/Y_j) - \gamma \log Y_j - \log J_j\} / \eta^j_{RX} \tag{10}$$

i.e. as one would expect, the equilibrium output of inventions is a function of both cost and demand parameters (both of which one would expect to vary across industries) and both have to be considered when we come to estimation. Schmookler's indifference to the cost parameters thus becomes more marked.

Consider then the term, $\bar{C}$, cost per patent produced. Given that $\eta^j_{RX} < 0$, we expect higher levels of cost per patent, *ceteris paribus*, to imply lower levels of patenting activity. It would seem logical to argue that an industry with extensive inventive opportunities would reflect lower costs per patent than one with limited opportunities. We can interpret this factor, therefore, as reflecting the supply side of the inventing industry, i.e. the element not considered empirically by Schmookler and for which he has been criticized by, among others, Rosenberg [12]. We are thus interpreting $\bar{C}_j$ as reflecting technological opportunity. Where attempts have been made before to measure this concept, qualitative measures have been used (see Scherer [14] or Wilson [17]), but these are always subject to personal judgement. We prefer the use of this cost per patent measure. There is however one major problem with this that derives from the work of Dasgupta and Stiglitz [4]. They argue that for a given return a competitively structured 'inventing-industry' will spend more in the search for an invention than will a non-competitive 'inventing-industry'. The basis for this is that with a patent system only the patentee will make any return from an invention, it is thus necessary for a firm to be first in the race to invent in order to gain any return. Thus they argue, in a competitive 'inventing-industry' the inventive process will be undertaken at such a speed that costs of invention are forced up to equal the revenue from inventions. In a non-competitive industry this will not occur. It is feasible therefore that $\bar{C}_j$ will reflect different market structures rather than technological opportunities. We should note however, that the most common market structure is oligopolistic and it is not obvious that this relationship between expenditure and market structure is different for different degrees of oligopoly. We therefore argue that $\bar{C}_j$ will still reflect technological opportunity. Thus although a theoretical possibility, the

[4] We considered a number of aggregation procedures. There seems to be little practical alternative to allowing $\Omega_{ij} = \Omega_j$ without generating large data requirements we cannot satisfy. To assume that marginal and average costs are the same for each firm yields considerable benefits of interpretation below. This leaves the final assumption that all firms have the same average costs $\bar{C}_j$. This, however, would by implied by (6) anyway given the other two assumptions. The main penalty we have imposed is that this aggregation procedure implies that x_{ij} is the same for all i in a given industry. One might argue that all we have done is to assume constant costs and then use the device of the representative firm.

market structure may be much less of an influence than might initially be expected. In many ways the point is related to that of Fisher and Temin [8], who argue that expenditure on inventive activity as a measure of the effectiveness of the inventive process may be biased because of differences in efficiency levels. It would be advantageous, however, if we could purge our estimates of this possible market structure effect to generate an influence solely reflecting technological opportunity. In practice this is not possible. A large part of inventive effort takes place within firms the major function of which is to produce output, i.e. we cannot define a separate 'inventing-industry', and it is the market structure of such an industry that we require to measure. What information we have on market structure relates to market shares for output and not to the level of inventive activity. We must proceed therefore holding the major point in mind, without explicitly correcting for it, and so take care in the interpretation of any results.

The next problem is to find a measure for $\bar{C}$ to use in the empirical work. The proxy we have chosen as the one available and apparently closest to the required concept is R & D expenditure per patent. The patent data we have attribute process patents to their using industry and product patents to the product producing industry. We do not have a breakdown of their source industries. It would seem reasonable however to argue that by far the largest proportion of patents would be generated in the using industry (especially given that most of our industries are defined at the SIC order level). Thus we use R & D expenditure per patent in the tabulated using industry to reflect $\bar{C}$. To the extent that patents are generated outside of this (and even any other) industry this figure will be an underestimate of the true level of resources devoted to invention. However, an opposite effect, which we feel will override this, is that not all R & D expenditure is devoted to producing patented output. Essentially this is a return to the question of whether patenting activity is a good measure of technological advance. If one considers that R & D expenditure on basic and applied research leads to inventions which are patented and then the development expenditure is used in conjunction with the knowledge represented by the patents to produce unpatented commercial products, the share of basic and applied research in total research expenditure should give a rough measure of the overestimation of $\bar{C}$ provided by R & D per patent. In fact about 35% of R & D is devoted to basic and applied research. This suggests that R & D per patent will overestimate the required measure by approximately a factor of 3. We in fact will allow $\bar{C}$ to be represented by $(\mathrm{R\ \&\ D}/x)^{\delta}$ where $\delta \leqslant 1$ may be different for each industry.[5]

These problems with finding a good measure of cost per 'technological advance', are not surprising. With care in interpretation however we can read something into the estimates of the coefficient on the proxy we have chosen.

[5] Scherer [13] suggests a similar variable, R & D employment per patent.

Turn now to the demand side of our relationship. We have stated that our patent data have been distributed across user industries and we have already argued that we equate the patent producing industries with the tabulated patent-using industries. To the extent that patents are employed in a number of industries, to use the characteristics of the attributed industries as a reflection of demand pressures may be misleading, but this is how we must proceed. Moreover, the patent data we have refer to product and process innovations. Schmookler was concerned primarily with capital good inventions (although when data on these were not available he used the combined data). There seems no reason, however, why our model should be so restricted. We thus represent the demand variables by the characteristics of the tabulated user industries of the patents, consider patents of all types, and allow that the patent producing and using industries are the same. We also consider that as I/Y and Y are being used to indicate expected return they ought to enter with some lag. We discuss this lag structure below. Our procedure therefore is to estimate a modified form of (10), equation (11), with lags indicated by the $t-n$ subscript, using data discussed below.

$$(11) \quad \log x_{jt} = \alpha_j + \beta_{1j} \log\left(\frac{\text{R \& D}}{x}\right) jt + \beta_{2j} \log \frac{I}{Y}\, j,t-n + \beta_{3j} \log Y_{j,t-n} + U_{jt}$$

$$\alpha_j = -[\log(1+\Omega_j \eta^j_{RX}) + \log J_j]/\eta^j_{RX} \gtrless 0$$

$$\beta_{1j} = \delta_j/\eta^j_{RX} < 0; \qquad \beta_{2j} = -\xi/\eta^j_{RX} > 0; \qquad \beta_{3j} = -\gamma/\eta^j_{RX} > 0.$$

III. DATA

The patent data are taken from Boehm [3], to whom the reader is referred for details of deficiencies, allocation methods, etc.[6] As stated above, the data refer to all patents issued in a given year and are allocated across industries of application. The data are available for the period 1931–60, although for reasons detailed below we cannot utilize the whole data set. The industry breakdown is by 1958 SIC, Orders I–XVIII.

Data on investment for the pre-war period was obtained from Feinstein [6] at current prices. For the post-war period current price data were taken from *Census of Production* (various) and *National Income and Expenditure* (1955, 1958 and 1962). The output data is derived from Feinstein's [7] series on industrial production and from *National Income and Expenditure* (various), using Feinstein's [7] price series for the generation of real or nominal values where necessary. The investment data were reduced to real terms using Feinstein's [7] price series on plant and machinery. All real variables were expressed in 1963 prices.

[6] One must note initially that his data show that in 1958 total patents were approximately half of the 1957 and 1959 figures. There is no apparent explanation for this. We have thus taken from the Reports of the Comptroller-General that patents in 1958 totalled 26,489 and scaled up all Boehm's figures in proportion for that year.

Data on research and development expenditure always represent something of a problem, especially for these early years. We have managed to construct two observations on R & D expenditure by industry covering 1956 and 1959. From DSIR [5] we have data on industrial R & D expenditure for 1958–59 in almost the same order breakdown as the patent data. From the Advisory Council on Scientific Policy [1] we have data on the employment of scientists and engineers in R & D for 1956 and 1959, with a finer industrial classification. We use the latter to first bring the 1959 data into the same classification as the patent data, and then by using the ratio of R & D expenditure per scientist and engineer in 1959 generate a series of R & D expenditure in 1956 by multiplying by the number of scientists and engineers employed in 1956.

We have managed in fact to collect post-war data on the full data set for 14 industries, the main omissions being Mining; Gas, Electricity and Water; and Agriculture for which we have no R & D data. For the whole time period we have a full data set for 10 of the 14 industries (Food, Drink and Tobacco; Chemicals; Metal Manufacture; Shipbuilding and Marine; Engineering and Electrical; Vehicles; Textiles; Clothing; Paper and Printing), although for the three industries on which there is no R & D data we have an otherwise full data set.

IV. ESTIMATION

Schmookler's empirical work covered both times series and cross-section data sets. Our analysis summarized in equation (11) suggests that the coefficients of the estimating equation will be different for each industry which makes cross-section regression a problem. In another paper, Stoneman and Leech [16], we have used random coefficient regression methods to overcome this difficulty in the analysis of R & D and market structure, but the methods used there are particularly intricate and unwieldy in the present case. The interpretation of any cross-section OLS estimates is thus very difficult. For similar reasons one has to essentially assume the constancy of coefficients over time to proceed with the time series regression. However, as Schmookler presents both cross-section and time series estimates it would seem incumbent upon us to provide some cross-section estimates for comparison. Moreover, we shall below require some extraneous coefficient esimates to use in the time series regression and we can only obtain these from the cross-section estimates. Thus although we do not consider our estimates to be very reliable we have estimated cross-sectional regressions.

The Schmookler hypothesis is represented as in equation (12)

$$\log x_{jt} = \alpha_{js} + \beta_{js} \log I_{jt-n} + U_j \tag{12}$$

where n is the lag on investment expenditure. The actual lag structure to use is also something of a problem. We have experimented with different values for n in the estimates of both equations (11) and (12) and have also used Koyck transformations. However, in each case the results derived from using a simple one period lag indicate the flavour of all the results generated,[7] thus we only present these.

(a) *Cross-section estimates*

In Table I we present our OLS cross-section estimate of equation (11). As we only have two sets of observations on R & D/x, one for 1959 and another for 1956, we have generated two sets of results, one using the latter, one the former. As they differ little we present only those using the latter. Of course the ideal would be to use data for the same year as the patent data, but this was not possible. As these were all the data available on R & D we have only estimated these regressions for post-war years, for this gives us a reasonable set of results without stretching assumptions on the constancy of R & D/x over time too far. The investment and output variables are measured in current prices. The sample is the 14 industries on which we have observations of R & D/x.

Consider then the results in Table I. Our cost term R & D/x is significant at the 5% level in each year, the diffusion speed and market size terms being significant at the 10% level in at least half the years. The main point however is that costs have an important role to play here, and this is of prime importance in our approach. The F statistics are generally significant at the 1% probability level, and the R^2 are satisfactory. The results imply that a 1% increase in R & D/x leads to a 0·5% fall in the number of patents issued. A 1% increase in diffusion speed as measured by I/Y leads to a 0·75% increase in patents issued, and a 1% change in market size (with I/Y constant) means a 0·6% increase in patents issued. If Y changes without a compensating change in I to leave I/Y constant then the net effect is given by $\beta_3 - \beta_2$ which is negative and to take an example, for 1951 equal to $-0{\cdot}348$.

It was felt that the results achieved might differ from Schmookler's because of our respecification of the demand variable. Thus we allowed demand to be represented by Schmookler's proxy, the level of investment expenditure (again lagged one period) and re-estimated the equations. If anything this respecification improved the performance of the cost variable and the overall performance of the regressions. Although we have not presented the results, both demand and cost variables were significant (at least at the 10% probability level) for each year. It would seem that our concern with the cost variable is thus further justified.

In generating these results we have used Ordinary Least Squares estimation methods. It may be argued that because the dependent variable is

[7] Schmookler [15, pp. 144–6] regresses log $(x_{j1948}+x_{j1949}+x_{j1950})$ on log I_{j1947}, i.e. log $(x_{jt}+x_{jt+1}+x_{jt+2})$ on log I_{jt-1}. This must imply that log $(x_{jt+1}+x_{jt+2}+x_{jt+3})$ is dependent on log I_{jt}, and therefore that x_{jt+1} is not independent of I_{jt} and similarly x_{jt+2} is not independent of I_{jt+1}. This would seem to imply that log $(x_{jt}+x_{jt+1}+x_{jt+2})$ is a function of log $I_{jt-1}+$ log $I_{jt}+$ log I_{jt+1} and therefore that Schmookler's estimates suffer from omitted variable bias.

TABLE I

REGRESSION RESULTS, CROSS-SECTION

$\log x_{jt} = \alpha_j + \beta_{1j} \log (\text{R \& D}/x)\, j,\, 56 + \beta_2 j \log (I/Y)\, j,\, t-1 + \beta_{3j} \log Y_{j,\, t-1}$

(Ordinary Least Squares Estimates)

Year	*Constant*	$\log\left(\frac{\text{R \& D}}{x}\right)56$	$\log\frac{I}{Y}\, t-1$	$\log Y_{t-1}$	R^2	N	F
1949	−1·267	−0·506**	0·452	0·524	0·661	14	6·65**
	(−0·457)	(−2·679)	(1·017)	(1·297)			
1950	−1·752	−0·511**	0·615	0·643*	0·721	14	8·62**
	(−0·749)	(−2·915)	(1·471)	(1·817)			
1951	0·267	−0·455**	0·842**	0·494**	0·793	14	12·80**
	(0·124)	(−2·976)	(3·108)	(3·107)			
1952	−0·169	−0·485**	0·816**	0·525	0·774	14	11·51**
	(−0·742)	(−2·930)	(2·236)	(1·658)			
1953	−0·709	−0·489**	0·753**	0·545*	0·794	14	12·84**
	(−0·342)	(−3·047)	(2·305)	(1·873)			
1954	0·079	−0·451**	0·793*	0·544	0·783	14	12·06**
	(0·028)	(−2·686)	(1·949)	(1·641)			
1955	−0·702	−0·424**	0·756	0·685*	0·787	14	12·33**
	(−0·277)	(−2·529)	(1·759)	(2·127)			
1956	0·246	−0·469**	1·053**	0·572*	0·848	14	18·66**
	(0·115)	(−3·215)	(2·817)	(2·045)			
1957	0·078	−0·481**	0·837**	0·452	0·788	14	12·39**
	(0·033)	(−2·794)	(2·299)	(1·344)			
1958	−0·767	−0·476**	0·759**	0·408	0·770	14	11·19**
	(−0·345)	(−2·742)	(2·228)	(1·243)			
1959	−0·637	−0·467**	0·598	0·532	0·775	14	11·46**
	(−0·265)	(−2·631)	(1·794)	(1·628)			
1960	−2·524	−0·459**	0·254	0·731**	0·758	14	10·47**
	(−1·177)	(−2·510)	(0·920)	(2·400)			

Notes: t statistics in parentheses; for coefficient estimates * indicates coefficient significantly different from zero at 10% level and ** indicates coefficient significantly different from zero at 5% level.

For the F statistics, ** represents significance at 1% and * significance at the 5% level.

$\log x_{jt}$ and the independent variables include $\log (\text{R \& D}/x)j$, the results with respect to the influence of technological opportunity solely reflect the appearance of x_{jt} on both sides of the equation (a simultaneity problem). We would however argue against this. First, only for 1956 in Table I are the x_j observations on each side of the equation for the same year, thus (unless x_{jt} and x_{jt-r} for all r are closely correlated) in general there should not be a problem. Second, we have assumed that there are constant returns to scale in patent production, implying that R & D/x does not vary with x, and thus we argue there is no simultaneity problem and the use of OLS techniques is appropriate. Some evidence to support this assumption would be encouraging, but as Fisher and Temin [8] show, no studies to date have appropriately tested the returns to scale in R & D hypothesis. Finally, it is possible to rewrite, for example, the 1956 estimating equation in Table I as

$$\log x_{jt} = \frac{\alpha_j}{1+\beta_{1j}} + \frac{\beta_{1j}}{1+\beta_{1j}} \log \text{R \& D}_{56j} + \frac{\beta_{2j}}{1+\beta_{1j}} \log \frac{I}{Y} j,\, t-1 + \frac{\beta_{3j}}{1+\beta_{1j}} \log Y_{j,\, t-1}$$

in which x_{jt} is no longer on the right-hand side, thus seemingly removing the problem. However, to estimate this form raises other considerations, for R & D is a function of x, and we now have simultaneity which we argued that constant returns to scale would effectively remove from our earlier estimating equations. Moreover as we only have 14 observations upon which to estimate this equation, the advantage of consistency provided by simultaneous estimation methods is of little use to us. However, if we hypothesize that R & D expenditure is related to the number of patents produced and total output, suggesting a scale effect in patent production, and then estimate the above form using current output as an instrumental variable for R & D (which is equivalent to a two-stage least squares procedure) we obtain an estimate for $\beta_1 = -0{\cdot}355$. Although we would not wish to read too much into this, the TSLS estimate is sufficiently close to our OLS estimate to suggest that our arguments above are reasonably well founded and that the results obtained are not solely dependent upon our estimation method.

Prior to drawing some preliminary conclusions, there is one further factor to consider. One of the characteristics of our data is that the observation on vehicles (which includes aircraft) has a relatively very high ratio for R & D/x. To investigate whether this was significantly affecting our estimates the regressions were run omitting this observation. The results led to no material changes in the coefficient estimates or their significance, except that on a few occasions the constant became significant. As we see no reason why the model should not cover this industry as well as the others, the results presented above are preferred.

The interpretation of our results therefore is that both cost and demand variables are important, although our separation of the latter between diffusion speed and market size is not very successful. Our cost proxy is consistently significant, despite the poor nature of the variable.[8] However, the major problem with these cross-section regressions is that we have taken no account of the fact that equation (10) implies that the coefficients of the regression equation will be different for each industry. Thus to put any strength in this interpretation would be misleading. We turn then to the more reliable time series results.

(b) *Time Series Analysis*

Because equation (11) involves problems when estimated cross-sectionally a time series analysis is preferable. We can then estimate the particular coefficients for each industry. We start by providing some estimates of the basic Schmookler hypothesis represented by equation (12). In all these time series regressions the sample covers the period 1931–38, 1948–60, and

[8] The possible measurement errors use of R & D/x implies suggest that our estimate of β_1 will be an underestimate of its true value if the error is simple (Johnston [9]). As we have no good *a priori* information on the nature of the measurement error there is little we can do formally to correct for it.

both investment and output are measured in constant 1963 prices. The reasoning behind this is that it is the expected real return which influences patenting activity and this is best indicated by real and not nominal measures of investment and output. In Table II the estimates of equation (12) using a simple one-period lag are presented for each of the sample industries. As can be seen, the demand variable ($\log I_{jt-1}$) is significant in six of the industries although in all but one of the regressions the constant is significant at the 5% level. Measured by the F statistic only in four industries is the regression significant overall. We have modified the lag structure by applying a Koyck transformation but this did not improve the performance of the demand variable. We also introduced a dummy variable to allow for differences pre- and post-war. This made the demand variable perform even worse and was itself, in general, not significant. We may say therefore that the Schmookler hypothesis is not very successful when tested on these data although demand factors do have some role to play in determining patenting activity.

Consider now the hypothesis proposed in this paper, represented by equation (11). The basic problem we face in estimating this is that we do not have time series data on R & D expenditure to generate our cost proxy.

TABLE II

REGRESSION RESULTS, TIME SERIES

$$\log x_{jt} = \alpha_{js} + \beta_{js} \log I_{jt-1}$$

1931–1938, 1948–1960, no. of observations = 20

	Coefficients				
Sector (j)	α_{js}	β_{js}	R^2	D.W.	F
Mining	1·059 (1·343)	0·455** (2·358)	0·326	1·84	0·73
G.E.W.	3·487** (2·239)	0·233 (0·857)	0·039	0·80	0·73
F.D.T.	5·876** (97·310)	0·0139* (1·739)	0·143	1·30	3·02
Chemicals	7·097** (24·280)	0·280** (4·078)	0·480	0·85	16·63**
Metal Manufacture	7·518** (18·456)	−0·773 (−0·914)	0·044	0·83	0·83
Shipbuilding and Marine	5·074** (36·401)	0·096** (2·300)	0·220	1·05	5·37*
Engineering and Electrical	9·309** (103·528)	0·063** (2·640)	0·270	1·48	6·97*
Vehicles	7·873** (46·321)	−0·066 (−1·378)	0·951	1·31	1·90
Textiles	6·527** (13·415)	0·156 (1·240)	0·078	0·69	1·53
Clothing	5·067** (10·770)	0·079 (0·383)	0·008	0·70	0·15
Paper and Printing	5·88** (35·555)	0·177 (0·386)	0·008	0·95	0·15
Construction	6·193** (31·760)	0·063 (1·052)	0·057	0·73	1·10
Agriculture, Forestry, Fishing	4·157** (29·707)	0·659* (1·858)	0·160	2·37	3·45*

To overcome this we hypothesize that (R & D/x)jt varies over time according to (13).[9]

$$\text{(13)} \qquad \log\left(\frac{R \,\&\, D}{x}\right)jt = \log\left(\frac{R \,\&\, D}{x}\right)j0 + \theta_j \log t$$

where t is time (which we measure with 1920=0). Substituting (13) into (11) we obtain (14)

$$\text{(14)} \qquad \log x_{jt} = a_j + \phi_j \log t + \beta_{2j} \log \frac{I}{Y}j,\ t-n + \beta_{3j} \log Y_{j,\ t-n}$$

where

$$\text{(15)} \qquad a_j = \alpha_j + \beta_{1j} \log\left(\frac{R \,\&\, D}{x}\right)j0$$

and

$$\text{(16)} \qquad \phi_j = \beta_{1j}\theta_j$$

Estimating equation (14) for each industry we generated the results in Table III, (where the lag is such that $n=1$). We have experimented with different lag structures without any material changes in the results. We also introduced a dummy variable to reflect the possibility of differences pre- and post-war. This was insignificant in general except for two cases, Textiles and Agriculture, Forestry and Fishing, where the new results generated F statistics that were significant at 1% but in both cases significant coefficient estimates on $\log I/Yj,\ t-1$ and $\log Y_{jt-1}$ were of the wrong sign (i.e. negative). Consider then the results in Table III, in terms of F statistics, in 7 of the 13 industries the regressions explain a significant proportion of the variance in $\log x_{jt}$, with R^2 peaking at 0·69. The two demand variables perform better than in the Schmookler case, the market size variable ($\log Y_{jt-1}$) being significant in seven industries; in each of these seven industries it is of the correct sign. The diffusion speed variable performs much less well, being significant in only one industry (Paper and Printing), although only in Agriculture and Metal Manufacturing is the estimate of the wrong sign (negative). Thus overall we can say that demand has a significant influence on the level of patenting activity. The time variable is significant in six of the industries and the constant, as in the test of the Schmookler hypothesis, is significant in the majority of the industries.

It has been suggested[10] that in Mining; Gas, Electricity and Water; and Agriculture, Forestry and Fishing for most of the period under consideration,

[9] We also tested the model with

$$\log\left(\frac{R \,\&\, D}{x}\right)jt = \log\left(\frac{R \,\&\, D}{x}\right)j0 + \theta_j t$$

but although the results were little different we prefer the above form.

[10] I wish to thank an anonymous referee for this point.

TABLE III

REGRESSION RESULTS, TIME SERIES

$$\log x_{jt} = a_j + \beta_{1j}\theta_j \log t + \beta_{2j} \log \frac{I}{Y}j, t-1 + \beta_{3j} \log Y_{jt-1}$$

1931–38, 1948–60, number of observations = 20

Sector	a_j	$\beta_{1j}\theta_j$	β_{2j}	β_{3j}	R^2	D.W.	$F_{3.16}$	β_{1j}	θ_j
Food, Drink and Tobacco	−8·905* (−1·930)	−1·868** (−3·499)	0·012 (1·714)	3·219** (3·312)	0·535	2·08	6·14**	3·096** (2·400)	−0·603** (−7·150)
Chemicals	3·455** (2·401)	−2·382** (−3·164)	0·161 (1·295)	2·244** (3·462)	0·691	1·26	11·94**	0·970 (1·253)	−2·455* (−2·051)
Metal Manufacturing	6·799** (4·659)	0·0452 (0·114)	−0·042 (−0·444)	0·022 (0·054)	0·103	0·87	0·61	−1·230** (−2·574)	−0·036 (−0·119)
Ship and Marine	5·551** (8·467)	−0·212 (−1·123)	0·060 (1·047)	0·123 (1·076)	0·283	0·93	2·11	−0·794** (−8·514)	0·266 (1·053)
Engineering and Electrical	7·302** (7·076)	−1·034** (−2·39)	0·061 (1·166)	0·836** (2·515)	0·471	2·02	4·75*	−0·660 (−1·443)	1·566 (0·905)
Vehicles	6·760** (8·502)	−1·004** (−3·192)	0·006 (0·055)	0·701** (2·635)	0·461	1·80	4·55*	−0·831* (−1·814)	1·197 (1·174)
Textiles	8·093* (1·980)	0·027 (0·116)	0·150 (0·694)	−0·098 (−0·130)	0·089	0·72	0·52	−1·483* (−1·748)	−0·018 (−0·122)
Clothing	−3·379 (−0·791)	−0·097 (−0·601)	0·062 (0·384)	1·553** (2·211)	0·568	1·59	7·02**	0·416 (0·982)	−0·235 (−0·394)
Paper and Printing	4·421** (2·861)	−0·447** (−4·268)	0·155** (3·572)	0·543* (1·904)	0·578	1·67	7·31**	−0·406 (−1·577)	1·100 (1·224)
Construction	7·432* (2·011)	0·102 (0·514)	0·046 (0·551)	−0·166 (−0·921)	0·073	0·73	0·42	−0·914* (−1·895)	−0·111 (−0·604)
Mining	0·498 (0·040)	0·189 (0·404)	0·317 (0·817)	0·393 (0·224)	0·244	1·81	1·72	n.a.	n.a.
Gas, Electricity, Water	−1·792 (−1·352)	−3·771** (−3·200)	0·465 (0·929)	3·244** (4·256)	0·684	2·36	11·53**	n.a.	n.a.
Agriculture, Forestry, Fishing	4·757 (0·786)	0·450 (1·125)	−0·061 (−0·747)	−0·300 (−0·277)	0·213	1·74	1·44	n.a.	n.a.

(Column group heading: *Coefficients*)

Notes: See Table I.

investment has been influenced by the government for non-economic reasons and will therefore not be a good measure of the profit to be derived from invention. If we do remove these three industries from our sample then the 'success' of our regressions in Table III as measured by the F statistic rises from 7 in 13 to 6 in 10, and the 'success' of the Schmookler hypothesis in Table II changes from 4 in 13 to 3 in 10, but more significantly, the key Schmookler variable (I_{jt-1}) is now only significant in 4 cases out of 10 in Table II. From the results in Table III, it is clear that our hypothesis does not fit these three industries at all well.

The generally more successful performance of our hypothesis leads us to prefer it over the alternative Schmookler hypothesis. However, a key to our approach is that costs as well as demand are important and as our estimates stand at present we cannot isolate the effects of costs on patenting activity. We would suggest however that the following procedure can yield a reasonably reliable estimate of β_{1j} which is our estimate of this effect.

From (15) and (16) we can derive that

$$(17) \qquad \beta_{1j} = (a_j - \alpha_j)/\log\left(\frac{\text{R \& D}}{x}\right)j0$$

However

$$(18) \qquad \log\left(\frac{\text{R \& D}}{x}\right)j0 = \log\left(\frac{\text{R \& D}}{x}\right)jt - \frac{\phi_j}{\beta_{1j}}\log t$$

using (13) and (16). Thus, with $t=0$ for 1920.

$$(19) \qquad \beta_{1j} = (a_j - \alpha_j)/\left\{\log\left(\frac{\text{R \& D}}{x}\right)j, 56 - \frac{\phi_j}{\beta_{1j}}\log(56-20)\right\}$$

$$= (a_j - \alpha_j + \phi_j \log 36)/\log\left(\frac{\text{R \& D}}{x}\right)j, 56$$

Thus given our data on log (R & D/x)j, 56, if we have an estimate of α_j we can obtain an estimate of β_{1j}. We suggest that we can take the cross-section estimate of the constant as an extraneous estimate of α_j. As this estimate was never significantly different from zero (except when the vehicles observations were excluded) we set $\alpha_j=0$ for all industries. Given our cross-section results this seems the least contentious assumption, although the exercise could be performed with different value for α_j. The main cost of assuming $\alpha_j=0$ for all j, is that because α_j includes the conjectural variation term Ω_j, we are removing the possibility of variations in patenting activity brought about by changes in market structure. Given, however, that $\alpha_j=0$ we can generate the estimates of θ_j and β_{1j} presented in the ninth and tenth columns of Table III. We have no data on R & D for the last three (suspect) industries, but as can be seen, in 7 of the remaining 10 industries our estimates of β_{1j} are significantly different from zero. In each of these cases, except Food, Drink and Tobacco it is of the expected sign (negative). Only in two cases is our estimate of θ_j significant, and in both cases a fall in costs over time is indicated.

Although the above procedure depends on our assumption that $\alpha_j = 0$, the results are considered indicative of the influence of costs on the level of patenting activity. Where our estimate of β_{1j} is significant and negative we can say that the elasticity of patenting activity with respect to costs varies between $-0{\cdot}4$ and $-1{\cdot}48$.

The main thrust of our time series results, therefore, is that both demand and cost factors influence the level of patenting activity. We have also found that output performs as a better demand indicator than investment (this difference between our results and those of Schmookler may be due to the patent data including not only process but also product innovation), but the diffusion speed variable never performs well as a demand indicator. There are also considerable inter-industry differences in the performance of our hypothesis which indicates that there may well be a number of other factors that are important which are not picked up by what is essentially a study at a higher level aggregation than would be preferred if alternative data were available. Moreover, although the cross-section results are suspect, the importance of the cost factor is also reflected there.

V. CONCLUSION AND IMPLICATIONS

Rosenberg [12] argues that the central weakness of Schmookler's approach is his neglect of the supply responsiveness of technology and invention. In this paper we have constructed a simple model to incorporate this factor into a Schmookler type investigation of the level of patenting activity in the UK. Despite rather severe data problems we have shown that the cost of producing an invention as measured by R & D expenditure per patent, significantly influences the level of patenting activity. We may say therefore that we must modify Schmookler's view to one in which both demand and technological opportunity determine the level of patenting activity. In addition we have argued that a preferred measure of the demand effect ought to consider both market size and diffusion speed. Thus although our results confirm Schmookler's hypothesis that the speed of technological change is endogenous, factors other than those considered by Schmookler must also be considered relevant determinants.

UNIVERSITY OF WARWICK

REFERENCES

[1] Advisory Council on Scientific Policy, Committee on Scientific Manpower, *Scientific and Engineering Manpower in G.B. 1959* (HMSO, London, 1959).

[2] Arrow, K. J., 'Economic Welfare and Allocation of Resources to Invention', in NBER, *Rate and Direction of Inventive Activity*, (Princeton University Press, Princeton, 1962).

[3] BOEHM, K., *The British Patent System*, Vol. I, *Administration* (Cambridge University Press, 1967).
[4] DASGUPTA, P. and STIGLITZ, J., *Market Structure and the Nature of Innovative Activity*, paper presented to the World Congress of IEA on Economic Growth and Resources (1977).
[5] Department of Scientific and Industrial Research, *Industrial R & D Expenditure*, (HMSO, London, 1960).
[6] FEINSTEIN, C. H., *Domestic Capital Formation in the U.K. 1920–1938* (Cambridge University Press, 1965).
[7] ——, *National Income Expenditure and Output of the U.K., 1855–1965* (Cambridge University Press, 1972).
[8] FISHER, F. M. and TEMIN, P., 'Returns to Scale in Research and Development', *Journal of Political Economy*, **81**, (1) (Jan/Feb 1973), pp. 56–70.
[9] JOHNSTON, J., *Econometric Methods* (McGraw-Hill, London, 1963).
[10] NEEDHAM, D., 'Market Structure and Firms' R & D Behaviour', *Journal of Industrial Economics*, **33** (4) (June 1975), pp. 241–55.
[11] NORDHAUS, W. D., *Invention, Growth and Welfare* (M.I.T. Press, Cambridge, Massachusetts, 1969).
[12] ROSENBERG, N., 'Science, Invention and Economic Growth', *Economic Journal*, **84** (333) (March 1974), pp. 90–108.
[13] SCHERER, F. M., 'Firm Size, Market Structure, Opportunity and the Output of Patented Inventions', *American Economic Review*, **55** (5) (December, 1965), pp. 1097–125.
[14] ——, *Industrial Market Structure and Economic Performance* (Rand McNally, Chicago, 1973).
[15] SCHMOOKLER, J., *Invention and Economic Growth* (Harvard University Press, 1966).
[16] STONEMAN, P. and LEECH, D., 'An Interindustry Approach to the R & D/ Market Structure Relationship', mimeo (University of Warwick, 1977).
[17] WILSON, R. W., 'The Effect of Technological Environment and Product Rivalry on R & D Effort and Licensing of Inventions', *Review of Economics and Statistics*, **59** (2) (May 1977), pp. 171–8.

THE JOURNAL OF INDUSTRIAL ECONOMICS
Volume XXVII June 1979 No. 4

TESTING THE LAW OF PROPORTIONATE EFFECT

ANDREW CHESHER*

I. INTRODUCTION

IT IS well known that the distribution of companies by size is approximately log–normal. This form arises under certain conditions as the limiting distribution of the product of positive random variates as the number of terms in the product tends to infinity. The current size of a company may be decomposed into the product of past proportionate growth rates and an initial size and sufficiently strong conditions[1] on these growth rates ensure that the distribution of the variate 'company size' becomes log–normal as the time elapsed from the start of the growth process tends to infinity.

The 'law of proportionate effect'[2] provides such a condition if it is applied to identically distributed proportionate growth rates with finite second moments.

> A variate subject to a process of change is said to obey the law of proportionate effect if the change in the variate at any step of the process is a random proportion of the previous value of the variate.

There have been many attempts to determine whether company sizes obey the law of proportionate effect (see for example Hart and Prais [5], Singh and Whittington [12], Utton [14] and Samuels and Chesher [11], work in this field is reviewed in Prais [10]) and to this end the parameters of equations like (1) below have been estimated using observations on successive cross-sections of companies.

$$z_{t,i} = \beta z_{t-1,i} + \epsilon_{t,i} \tag{1}$$

Here $z_{t,i}$ is the deviation of the logarithm of the size of company i at time t from the mean of the logarithms of the sizes of companies at time t (it is assumed without essential loss of generality that natural logarithms are used), β is a parameter to be estimated and $\epsilon_{t,i}$ is a disturbance. A value

* The author acknowledges the helpful comments made by P. E. Hart, M. A. King, T. Lancaster, P. C. B. Phillips and S. J. Prais on earlier drafts of this paper. Any errors are the responsibility of the author.

1 See Aitchison and Brown [1] for a statement of the relevant limit theorem.

2 Also known as the law of proportionate growth and Gibrat's law. The statement here is that which appears in Aitchison and Brown [1]. If proportionate growth rates are not identically distributed conditions on moments of higher order than the second are also required.

of $\hat{\beta}$ close to unity[3] is taken as evidence that the 'law' is in operation at the time of observation. The reasoning which leads to such a conclusion may be seen if both sides of equation (1) are exponentiated. This yields equation (2). Here $S_{t,i}$ denotes the size of company i at time t,

$$(2) \qquad S_{t,i}-S_{t-1,i}=\{\exp(\epsilon_{t,i})S_{t-1,i}^{\beta-1}-1\}S_{t-1,i}$$
$$=g_{t,i}S_{t-1,i}$$

and $g_{t,i}$ is the proportion referred to in the statement of the law of proportionate effect. It is clear that if β is not equal to unity then $g_{t,i}$ and $S_{t-1,i}$ are not independently distributed and the law is not in operation. However, even if β is unity the law will *not* be in operation if the $\epsilon_{t,i}$ are serially correlated, for then also $g_{t,i}$ and $S_{t-1,i}$ are dependent. The law of proportionate effect is in operation *only* if β is equal to one *and* the disturbances in equation (1), $\epsilon_{t,i}$, are independently distributed over time.

When β is not equal to one company, sizes regress towards or away from their mean in the Galtonian sense. When β is less than one, for example, the larger a company is the less may it be expected to grow. Serial correlation in proportionate growth rates can be ascribed to persistence of chance factors which make a company grow abnormally fast or abnormally slowly. One might say when β is not equal to one that 'size encourages (or discourages) growth' and when there is serial correlation in growth rates that 'growth encourages (or discourages) growth'.

It is shown in section II that serial correlation in the disturbances of equation (1) induces dependence between $z_{t-1,i}$ and $\epsilon_{t,i}$ which may render least-squares estimators of β inconsistent, *even though estimation proceeds using cross-sectional data.* The inconsistency of the standard ordinary least squares estimator of β is derived and its sign determined. The analysis presented here differs in a number of respects from that usually accorded to equations with serially correlated disturbances and regressors which are lagged dependent variables. Attention is restricted to the asymptotic properties of estimators but these are calculated using cross-sectional data and it is their behaviour as the size of the observed cross-section increases which is considered.

These results have implications for previous work in this field. The existence of cross-time dependence in the disturbances of (1) has rarely been considered by workers investigating the law of proportionate effect.[4] Therefore with the exceptions noted in footnote 4 their statements concerning the law's validity are suspect on two grounds. First they have neglected to determine whether these disturbances are cross-time dependent, second their estimators of β in (1) are possibly inconsistent.

A simple alternative procedure for testing the law of proportionate

[3] $\hat{\beta}$ denotes an estimator of a parameter β.
[4] See, however, Chesher [2], Creedy [4] and Hart [6].

effect which allows for possible serial correlation in the $\epsilon_{t,i}$ is described in section III and applied to data pertaining to UK companies in the 1960s. The $\epsilon_{t,i}$ are found to be serially correlated and are apparently generated by a first-order autoregressive process. It is concluded that the law of proportionate effect was not in operation during the period considered even though β was close to unity. Finally a policy implication of these results is discussed.

Though the discussion is throughout cast in terms of company sizes the results noted here have wider applicability; for instance, there are obvious extensions to the study of individual wealth or personal income distributions. The conclusions drawn here apply in many situations where stochastic difference equations are estimated using cross-sectional data.

II. THE INCONSISTENCY OF THE ORDINARY LEAST SQUARES ESTIMATOR

The inconsistency of the ordinary least squares (OLS) estimator of β is derived under the assumption that the process generating company sizes is observed a finite period of time after its commencement and that the parameters of the process remain constant as time passes.

Suppose that for $t \geqslant k > 0$ the deviation of the logarithm of the size of the ith company at time k, from the mean of the logarithms of the sizes of companies at time k, $z_{k,i}$, is generated[5] by (3) and (4) for $i = 1, 2, \ldots, N$.

$$z_{k,i} = \beta z_{k-1,i} + \epsilon_{k,i} \tag{3}$$

$$\epsilon_{k,i} = \rho \epsilon_{k-1,i} + u_{k,i} \tag{4}$$

Assume that the process (3) and (4) started at time $k=0$ with the ϵ_{0i} identically zero and that

(i) $\operatorname{plim} N^{-1} \sum_{i=1}^{N} z_{0i}^2 = \sigma_z^2$,

(ii) $\operatorname{plim} N^{-1} \sum_{i=1}^{N} u_{k,i} u_{j,i} = \sigma_u^2 > 0$, when $k=j$ and is zero otherwise, $k, j = 1, 2, \ldots, t$,

(iii) $\operatorname{plim} N^{-1} \sum_{i=1}^{N} u_{k,i} z_{0,i} = 0$, $k = 1, 2, \ldots, t$.

Here probability limits are taken as N, the size of the cross-section of companies, increases.

[5] Only the implications of first order autocorrelated $\epsilon_{k,i}$ are considered in detail. Empirical evidence presented below suggests such a specification is appropriate.

Under these assumptions the probability limit[6] of $\hat{\beta}$, the OLS estimator of β, is constant and equal[7] to

$$(5) \quad \beta^* = \frac{\beta^{2t-1}\sigma_z^2 + \dfrac{\sigma_u^2}{(\rho-\beta)^2} \sum_{k=1}^{t-1} (\rho^{t-k+1} - \beta^{t-k+1})(\rho^{t-k} - \beta^{t-k})}{\beta^{2(t-1)}\sigma_z^2 + \dfrac{\sigma_u^2}{(\rho-\beta)^2} \sum_{k=1}^{t-1} (\rho^{t-k} - \beta^{t-k})^2} \qquad (\rho \neq \beta)$$

When $\rho = \beta$ different results obtain, see Chesher [10] for details.

When $\rho = 0$ and the $\epsilon_{k,i}$ are temporally serially uncorrelated $\beta^* = \beta$. If $\rho \neq 0$ then $\beta^* \neq \beta$ and the OLS estimator of β is inconsistent. The sign of $(\beta^* - \beta)$, the inconsistency of $\hat{\beta}$, is simple to obtain. $\beta^* - \beta$ can be written as the ratio of Φ, defined below, to the denominator of (5). The latter being the constant probability limit of a mean sum of squares is non-negative and so the sign of $\beta^* - \beta$ is the same as that of Φ.

$$(6) \quad \Phi = \frac{\sigma_u^2}{\beta - \rho} \sum_{k=1}^{t-1} \rho^k(\beta^k - \rho^k) \qquad \beta \neq \rho$$

$$= \frac{\sigma_u^2}{\beta - \rho} \left\{ \frac{\rho\beta\{1 - (\rho\beta)^{t-1}\}}{1 - \rho\beta} - \rho \frac{2(1 - \rho^{2(t-1)})}{1 - \rho^2} \right\}$$

When ρ and β are both positive, Φ is positive and plim $\hat{\beta}$ exceeds β. This result holds whatever the magnitude of ρ and β. β is virtually certain to be positive when the $z_{k,i}$ are company sizes. When β is positive and ρ is negative matters are more complicated. For $\beta < \max(-\rho, -\rho^{-1})$, Φ is negative and β exceeds plim $\hat{\beta}$, otherwise Φ is of indeterminate sign. Since $\max(-\rho, -\rho^{-1}) \geqslant 1$, for $\beta < 1$ Φ is negative if ρ is negative.

The 'large-t' properties of plim $\hat{\beta}$ are easy to obtain.[8] If

$$|\beta|, |\rho| < 1 \quad \lim_{t\to\infty} \ (\operatorname*{plim}_{N\to\infty} \hat{\beta}) = (\beta + \rho)/(1 + \beta\rho)$$

Otherwise

$$\lim_{t\to\infty} \ (\operatorname*{plim}_{N\to\infty} \hat{\beta}) = \beta \text{ if } |\beta| > |\rho|$$

$$= \rho \text{ if } |\rho| > |\beta|$$

As the age of the process generating company sizes increases the inconsistency of the OLS estimator of $\hat{\beta}$ does not approach zero except in the special case $\beta > \max(1, \rho)$.

[6] Asymptotic results may be expected to be useful in this area. Note that probability limits are taken as N tends to infinity where N is the size of the cross-sectional sample from which $\hat{\beta}$ is calculated. In published studies N is rarely smaller than 150 and usually much larger.

[7] See Chesher [3], obtainable from the author on request, for a full derivation of (5).

[8] The first limit here is familiar as the inconsistency of the OLS estimator of β where estimation proceeds using time series data on a single company and probability limits are taken as T, the number of time series observations tends to infinity. See for example Malinvaud [9, p. 360].

Table I, which shows the time path of $\underset{N\to\infty}{\text{plim}}\ \hat{\beta}$ for selected values of β and ρ, demonstrates the movement of β towards these limits.

TABLE I

$\underset{N=\infty}{\text{plim}}\ (\hat{\beta})$ FOR VALUES OF t, β AND ρ

t	$\rho=0{\cdot}2$ $\beta=0{\cdot}8$	0·2 0·98	0·2 1·02	−0·2 0·98	−0·2 1·02
2	1·0000	1·1800	1·2200	0·7800	0·8200
3	0·9200	1·0833	1·1199	0·8750	0·9200
4	0·8911	1·0471	1·0826	0·9023	0·9486
5	0·8782	1·0295	1·0644	0·9192	0·9664
6	0·8715	1·0194	1·0540	0·9295	0·9772
7	0·8678	1·0130	1·0473	0·9366	0·9846
8	0·8656	1·0085	1·0426	0·9417	0·9900
9	0·8643	1·0052	1·0392	0·9456	0·9941
10	0·8634	1·0016	1·0366	0·9487	0·9974
11	0·8629	1·0007	1·0346	0·9512	1·0000
12	0·8626	0·9990	1·0329	0·9532	1·0021
13	0·8624	0·9977	1·0315	0·9549	1·0039
14	0·8623	0·9966	1·0304	0·9564	1·0054
15	0·8622	0·9957	1·0294	0·9576	1·0067
∞	0·8620	0·9866	1·0200	0·9701	1·0200

III. THE ESTIMATION OF β AND ρ

To ascertain whether the law of proportionate effect is in operation both β and ρ must be estimated. Neglecting to allow for non-zero ρ will result in inconsistent estimation of β and it may be inferred that β is closer to unity than it in fact is. Noting that $\epsilon_{t,i}$ may be expressed in terms of $z_{t-1,i}$ and $z_{t-2,i}$, equation (1) may be rewritten as in (7) below.

$$z_{t,i}=\gamma_1 z_{t-1,i}+\gamma_2 z_{t-2,i}+u_{t,i} \qquad (7)$$

Here $\gamma_1=\beta+\rho$, $\gamma_2=-\beta\rho$. The application of OLS to cross-sectional data on $z_{t,i}$, $z_{t-1,i}$ and $z_{t-2,i}$ may be expected to yield consistent estimators of the γ's whence 'estimators' of β and ρ may be obtained as in (8)

$$(\tilde{\beta},\tilde{\rho})=\tfrac{1}{2}\{\hat{\gamma}_1\pm(\hat{\gamma}_1^2+4\hat{\gamma}_2)^{1/2}\} \qquad (8)$$

Sample information alone will not indicate which of the estimates on the right-hand side of (8) is $\tilde{\beta}$ and which is $\tilde{\rho}$. This identification problem will be resolved here by appealing to the literature on the stochastic theory of the firm where it is argued that β is close to unity even if the law of proportionate effect is not in operation. Thus the estimate on the right-hand side of (8) closest to unity will be denoted $\tilde{\beta}$, the other $\tilde{\rho}$.[9]

[9] The square root in (8) may be complex. This problem is not addressed as it did not arise in the empirical work which follows. The identification problem disappears if additional exogenous variables appear in (7). This technique, used in Chesher [2], has also been used by Creedy [4]. It is assumed that β and ρ are constant over time. See Hart [6] for an analysis of the case when β is non-constant.

Whether this identification problem is resolved or not, the null hypothesis that the law of proportionate effect is in operation may be tested against the alternative that $\beta \neq 1$ and/or the disturbances, $\epsilon_{k,i}$, are first order autocorrelated by testing:

$$H_0\colon\ (\gamma_1\ \gamma_2) = (1\ 0)$$

$$\text{vs. } H_1\colon\ (\gamma_1\ \gamma_2) \neq (1\ 0)$$

Assuming that the OLS estimators of γ_1 and γ_2 are asymptotically normally distributed the classical test statistic for simple hypotheses concerning subsets of coefficients in a linear regression model may be constructed.[10] Under H_0 with sufficiently large samples this statistic will be approximately a $\chi^2_{(2)}$ variate.

Equation (7) was estimated for various values of t using ordinary least squares with one year as the unit of time.[11] The results are shown in Table II.

TABLE II

ESTIMATES OF THE γ_j, OF β AND ρ

t	$\hat{\gamma}_1$	$\hat{}_2$	$\tilde{\beta}$	$\tilde{\rho}$	X^2
1969	1·229	−0·219	1·012	0·216	12·8
	(0·064)	(0·065)			
1968	1·325	−0·320	1·007	0·318	21·5
	(0·073)	(0·074)			
1966	1·233	−0·227	1·093	0·139	25·8
	(0·046)	(0·046)			

Figures in parentheses are standard errors of OLS estimates, number of observations is 183. Under H_0: $(\gamma_1\gamma_2) = (1\ 0)$, X^2 is a realization of a random variable which is asymptotically distributed as $\chi^2_{(}$. $P(\chi^2_{(2)} \geqslant 10{\cdot}6) = 0{\cdot}005$.

In each case the null hypothesis $(\gamma_1\gamma_2) = (1\ 0)$ is rejected at better than the 0·5% level. The estimator of β is close to one but the estimator of ρ is positive and quite large. It is concluded that the law of proportionate effect was not in operation during this period.

So far it has been tacitly assumed that a first order autoregressive process generates the $\epsilon_{k,i}$. This assumption is open to question. Suppose instead that the $\epsilon_{k,i}$ follow an rth order autoregressive process. The $z_{t,i}$ are then related not to two lagged values of $z_{t-1,i}$ and $z_{t-2,i}$ as in the case of a first

[10] See for instance Malinvaud [9].

[11] The sample of 183 companies is drawn from the population of UK quoted companies classified as 'Commercial and Industrial' in the *Stock Exchange Official Yearbook* [13]. Only companies in existence in 1960 and in 1969 are included in the population. Further details of the sample may be found in Samuels and Chesher [11]. Results reported here use capital employed as a measure of size.

order process but to the $r+1$ variables $z_{t-1,i}, \ldots, z_{t-r-1,i}$. The data available allowed estimation with a seventh order autoregressive process. For details see Chesher [3].

With $t=1968$, the introduction of the regressors $z_{t-2}, \ldots, z_{t-8}$ reduced the squared length of the OLS residual vector from 4·317 to 4·252. Calculation of a test statistic for the hypothesis H_0: the coefficients on these regressors are all zero yielded a value of 2·60. Under H_0 this is a realization of a variate which is asymptotically a $\chi^2_{(6)}$ variate. The null hypothesis cannot be rejected at any reasonable significance level and it is concluded that a first order autoregressive model *is* appropriate for the $\epsilon_{k,i}$.

IV. ECONOMIC IMPLICATIONS OF THE RESULTS

If ordinary least squares is applied to cross-sectional data where each observation in the cross-section is a pair $(z_{t,i}, z_{t-1,i})$ generated by (3) and (4) of section II; where $\rho \neq 0$ and $\beta \neq 1$, then the estimator of β is inconsistent though under the conditions outlined earlier it does possess a probability limit. When β exceeds unity the inconsistency of the estimator tends to zero as the age of the processes (3), (4) increases. However, when β is less than unity the inconsistency persists.[12] When ρ is positive the appropriate limit is reached from above, when ρ is negative (and relatively small in magnitude) it is reached from below.

If β is equal to unity and the $\epsilon_{t,i}$ are serially uncorrelated then the law of proportionate effect is in operation. However, for the reasons noted above, the validity of the law cannot be established by applying OLS to (3) though historically this is the procedure that has been generally adopted.

The possibility that the $\epsilon_{t,i}$ are first order autoregressive may be examined[13] by introducing $z_{t-2,i}$ as an extra regressor in (3). When such an equation is estimated using data pertaining to UK companies in the 1960s estimates of the coefficients on $z_{t-1,i}$ and $z_{t-2,i}$ indicate that the $\epsilon_{t,i}$ *are* first order autoregressive. It appears that β is close to unity. If it is and the processes (3), (4) are sufficiently old then estimation of (3) *may* produce a consistent estimator of β; however, as noted earlier this will *not* constitute verification of the law of proportionate effect. These results are at variance with those presented to uphold the 'higgledy-piggledy growth' hypothesis put forward in Little [7] and Little and Raynor [8],

[12] $|\rho| < |\beta|$ is assumed here. This seems reasonable.

[13] A problem which may arise when applying OLS to (3) or its extension with $z_{t-2,i}$ as an extra regressor is that $\epsilon_{t,i}$ and $\epsilon_{t,j}$ may not be independently distributed. For example if companies i and j are in the same industry they may be expected to have a common component in their disturbance term. The resulting dependence will not affect the consistency of the OLS estimator though it will render our statements as to their accuracy incorrect. It is assumed that any dependence which is present is weak and that its effect is negligible.

but agree to a certain extent with those presented in Singh and Whittington [12] which suggest that there is 'persistence of growth'.

How can serial correlation amongst the $\epsilon_{t,i}$ be interpreted? The growth rate of a company, $S_{t,i}/S_{t-1,i}$ is from (2) equal to exp $\{(\beta-1) \log S_{t-1,i}\}$ exp $(\epsilon_{t,i})$. The first exponent in this expression may be regarded as the growth rate which company i may expect to achieve given its initial size, $S_{t-1,i}$, and the second exponent may be regarded as 'windfall' growth. If the $\epsilon_{t,i}$ are serially correlated and for at least small s, $E(\epsilon_{t,i}\epsilon_{t-s,i})>0$, then some large companies are large because they have experienced persistent positive 'windfall' growth while some companies are small because they have experienced persistent negative 'windfall' growth. This apparently is the case for UK quoted companies in the 1960s. Unless appropriate procedures are used disparity in observed growth rates will be attributed to the 'systematic' part of the relationship (3) and β will be inferred to be larger than it in fact is. Is this of any consequence? Suppose the government wishes to alter the rate of change of industrial concentration. Identifying the variance of z_t as a measure of industrial concentration[14] and defining the change in concentration between $(t-1)$ and t, ΔC_t, as the difference between the variance of z at times $(t-1)$ and t, equation (10) is obtained.

$$\Delta C_t = \beta^{2(t-1)}\left\{\sigma_z^2(\beta^2-1) + \sigma_u^2\left[\frac{(\rho/\beta)^t-1}{(\rho/\beta)-1}\right]^2\right\} \tag{10}$$

The government may change ΔC_t by altering β or ρ (or σ_u^2 though here this option is not considered). If ρ is incorrectly assumed to be zero then ΔC_t will not react as expected to changes in β for $\mathrm{d}\Delta C_t/\mathrm{d}\beta$ clearly depends on ρ. In fact greater flexibility of action may be obtained if it is realized that both β and ρ may be influenced. For instance ρ may be lowered by government action which allows small companies easier access to finance and separately β may be brought closer to zero by the introduction of progressive corporation taxes.

UNIVERSITY OF BIRMINGHAM

REFERENCES

[1] AITCHISON, J. and BROWN, J. A. C., *The Log–Normal Distribution* (Cambridge University Press, Cambridge, 1969).

[2] CHESHER, A. D., *The Observation of the Law of Proportionate Growth*, University of Birmingham Discussion Paper, Series A, No. 157 (1973).

[3] ——, *Appropriate Tests of the Law of Proportionate Effect*, University of Birmingham Discussion Paper, Series A, No. 201 (1978).

[4] CREEDY, J., 'Income Changes over The Life Cycle', *Oxford Economic Papers*, **26** (3) (November 1974), pp. 405–23.

[14] Hart and Prais [5] provide a justification for the choice of this measure.

[5] HART, P. E. and PRAIS, S. J., 'The Analysis of Business Concentration: A Statistical Approach', *Journal of the Royal Statistical Society*, Series A, **119** (2), pp. 150–81.

[6] HART, P. E., 'The Dynamics of Earnings', *Economic Journal*, **86** (September 1976), pp. 551–65.

[7] LITTLE, I. M. D., 'Higgledy-piggledy Growth', *Bulletin of the Oxford University Institute of Statistics*, **24** (4) (1962), pp. 387–412.

[8] LITTLE, I. M. D. and RAYNOR, A. C., '*Higgledy-piggledy Growth Again*' (Blackwell, Oxford, 1966).

[9] MALINVAUD, E., *Statistical Methods of Econometrics* (North-Holland, Amsterdam, 1966).

[10] PRAIS, S. J., *The Evolution of Giant Firms in Britain* (Cambridge University Press, Cambridge, 1976).

[11] SAMUELS, J. M. and CHESHER, A. D., 'Company Growth, Survival and Size', *Market Structure and Corporate Behaviour*, K. Cowling (ed.) (Gray Mills, London, 1972).

[12] SINGH, A. and WHITTINGTON, G., *Growth, Profitability and Valuation* (Cambridge University Press, Cambridge, 1968).

[13] *The Stock Exchange Official Yearbook*, 1960.

[14] UTTON, M. A., 'The Effect of Mergers on Concentration: U.K. Manufacturing Industry 1954–65', *Journal of Industrial Economics*, **20** (1) (November 1971), pp. 42–58.

THE JOURNAL OF INDUSTRIAL ECONOMICS

Published first in October 1952, this Journal was founded to develop the analysis of the problems facing modern industry. It is concerned with the individual business and its relation to the economy—e.g. with outputs and prices and their behaviour in the market, and with the business decisions which affect these. It therefore aims to contribute both to economic theory and to practical public and private policies in the industrial field. The journal is naturally meant to interest business men as well as economists.

The Editors welcome contributions covering the fundamental categories in economics (such as prices, costs, investment, finance, location, wages and productivity) as well as the broader 'background' circumstances (such as the changing structure of industry, management policy and public monopoly policy). Preference is given to MSS bearing on these subjects from the standpoint of individual firms or industries. Theoretical discussion is welcome. Abstract theory is not barred, but authors in this case should provide an introduction and conclusion, so that non-specialist readers may see what the article is about. Alongside articles of more normal length, the Editors are willing to publish shorter notes, especially when these give interim results of important research studies. Books are not reviewed, although books received will be listed, sometimes with a short note; but substantial review articles will be considered. No payment is made to authors, but 40 free offprints are provided. Contributors are asked to send an Abstract, not exceeding 100 words, with their article.

Editorial Offices:

Manuscripts from North America should be sent to Professor H. Michael Mann, Department of Economics, Boston College, Chestnut Hill, Massachusetts, 02167, U.S.A.; manuscripts from the European Continent should be sent to Professor Louis Phlips, Center for Operations Research & Econometrics, Université Catholique de Louvain, 34 Voie du Roman Pays, 1348 Louvain-la-Neuve, Belgium; and from the U.K. and other countries to the General Editor, c/o Department of Economics, University of Lancaster, Bailrigg, Lancaster, England.

Subscriptions, advertising, reprint enquiries, etc.

All correspondence other than that dealing with contributions should be addressed to the Publisher, Messrs. Basil Blackwell & Mott Ltd., 108 Cowley Road, Oxford OX4 1LR, England.

The journal is published quarterly, and the annual subscription for Institutions is £11 (U.K.), £13.20 (Overseas), $30 (U.S.A. and Canada) post free; the prices of single issues are £3.50, £4.20 and $9.50 respectively, post free. For individual subscribers the rates are £9.00 (U.K.), £10.80 (Overseas), $24.00 (U.S.A. and Canada) post free. Remittances should be sent to Basil Blackwell & Mott Ltd.

A photographic reprint is now available of Vols. 1–13, 1952–65, bound in cloth or paper; single volumes in paper only.

CONTRIBUTORS TO THIS NUMBER

T. WILSON: Adam Smith Professor of Political Economy, University of Glasgow, and Editor of this Journal.

GEORGE NORMAN: Lecturer in Economics, University of Reading.

GÜNTHER SCHMID: Research Fellow, International Institute of Management of the Science Center, Berlin.

ALEXIS P. JACQUEMIN: Professor of Economics, University of Louvain (Belgium), and Associate Editor of this Journal.

CHARLES BERRY: Professor of Economics and Public Affairs, Princeton University.

TAKEO NAKAO: Associate Professor of Economics, Doshisha University, Kyoto, Japan.

PAUL L. STONEMAN: Lecturer in Economics, University of Warwick.

ANDREW D. CHESHER: Lecturer in Economics, University of Birmingham.

The Contents of Volume XXVII, No. 3, March 1979, were:

Vertical Integration in Competitive Markets Under Uncertainty by Dennis W. Carlton, Assistant Professor, Department of Economics, University of Chicago.

On Bias and Concentration by P. E. Hart, Professor of Economics, University of Reading, Consultant N.I.E.S.R., and Editor of this Journal.

Profitability, Risk and Market Structure in West German Industries by Manfred Neumann, Ingo Böbel and Alfred Haid, respectively Professor of Economics, and Assistants, Universität Erlangen-Nürnberg.

Fuel Adjustment Mechanisms and Economic Efficiency by David P. Baron and Raymond R. De Bondt, respectively Professor of Managerial Economics and Decision Sciences, Northwestern University, and Associate Professor, Katholieke Universiteit Leuven.

Hedonic Prices and the Structure of the Digital Computer Industry by Robert Michaels Professor of Economics, California State University.

Redefining the Boundaries of the Firm by Keith MacMillan and David Farmer, respectively Director of Studies Masters' Programme, The Administrative Staff College Henley, ex Brunel University, and Director, Henley Management Development and Advisory Service, Henley.

The Price Commission and the Brewing Industry: A Critical Note by Kevin Hawkins, Lecturer in Industrial Relations, University of Bradford.

The Price Commission Report on Books – A Short Critique by P. J. Curwen, Senior Lecturer in Economics, Sheffield City Polytechnic.

Printed in Great Britain by Adlard & Son Ltd., Bartholomew Press, Dorking